ECONOMICS AND THE BUSINESS ENVIRONMENT

Visit the *Economics and the Business Environment*, Third Edition, Companion Website with Grade Tracker at **www.pearsoned.co.uk/sloman** to find valuable **student** learning material including:

- Online workbook and study guide with interactive exercises, diagrams and videos
- Multiple choice questions with Grade Tracker function to test your learning and monitor your progress
- Business issues for each chapter
- Up-to-date case studies with questions for self study
- Topical economic issues relating directly to material in the book
- Economics news articles with features on topical stories, with analysis and links to the book
- Hotlinks to over 200 relevant sites on the web
- Answers to all in-chapter 'Pause for Thought' questions and to odd-numbered end-of-chapter questions
- An online glossary to explain key terms
- eText, a complete online version of the textbook that you can annotate, highlight and search

Companion Website with Grade Tracker looks and performs just like a regular Companion Website. However, the student will need the access code shrink-wrapped with every copy of the book to register and gain access to the website. As the student completes the assessment questions, the scores are automatically entered into the student's personal gradebook, which is accessible through the 'Grade Tracker' link.

Lecturers must also register for access to the Companion Website with Grade Tracker to be able to create a class for students to join. **Lecturers** who choose to participate in providing a class gain access to a class gradebook in which they can track student grades and download their results for integration into other systems.

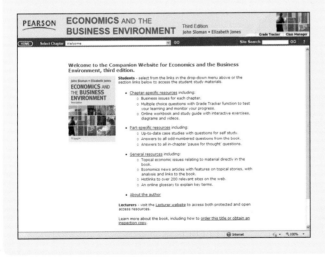

PEARSON

We work with leading authors to develop the
strongest educational materials in economics,
bringing cutting-edge thinking and best learning
practice to a global market.

Under a range of well-known imprints, including
Financial Times Prentice Hall, we craft high-quality
print and electronic publications which help readers
to understand and apply their content, whether
studying or at work.

To find out more about the complete range of our
publishing, please visit us on the World Wide Web at:
www.pearsoned.co.uk.

ECONOMICS AND THE BUSINESS ENVIRONMENT

Third edition

John Sloman and Elizabeth Jones

Financial Times Prentice Hall is an imprint of

Harlow, England • London • New York • Boston • San Francisco • Toronto
Sydney • Tokyo • Singapore • Hong Kong • Seoul • Taipei • New Delhi
Cape Town • Madrid • Mexico City • Amsterdam • Munich • Paris • Milan

Pearson Education Limited
Edinburgh Gate
Harlow
Essex CM20 2JE
England
and Associated Companies throughout the world

Visit us on the World Wide Web at:
www.pearsoned.co.uk

First published 2005
Second edition 2008
Third edition 2011

ISBN: 978-0-273-73480-2

British Library Cataloguing-in-Publication Data
A catalogue record for this book is available from the British Library

Library of Congress Cataloging-in-Publication Data
Sloman, John, 1947-
   Economics and the business environment / John Sloman and Elizabeth Jones. -- 3rd ed.
      p. cm.
   ISBN 978-0-273-73480-2 (pbk.)
   1. Managerial economics. 2. Economics. 3. Business. 4. Industrial management. I.
Jones, Elizabeth, 1984- II. Title.
   HD30.22.S58 2011
   330--dc22
                                                                2010039728

10 9 8 7 6 5 4 3 2 1
14   13   12   11

Typeset in 9/12.5pt Stone Serif by 35
Printed and bound by Graficas Estella, Navarra, Spain

Brief contents

Part D   THE MACROECONOMIC ENVIRONMENT OF BUSINESS

Contents

Part C THE MICROECONOMIC ENVIRONMENT OF BUSINESS

Supporting resources

Visit **www.pearsoned.co.uk/sloman** to find valuable online resources.

Companion Website with Grade Tracker for students

- Online workbook and study guide with interactive exercises, diagrams and videos
- Multiple choice questions with Grade Tracker function to test your learning and monitor your progress
- Business issues for each chapter
- Up-to-date case studies with questions for self study
- Topical economic issues relating directly to material in the book
- Economics news articles with features on topical stories, with analysis and links to the book
- Hotlinks to over 200 relevant sites on the web
- Answers to all in-chapter 'Pause for Thought' questions and to odd-numbered end-of-chapter questions
- An online glossary to explain key terms
- eText, a complete online version of the textbook that you can annotate, highlight and search

Also: The regularly maintained Companion Website with Grade Tracker provides the following features:

- Search tool to help locate specific items of content
- Online help and support to assist with website usage and troubleshooting

For lecturers

- By registering in our Companion Website with Grade Tracker as an instructor you can create a class and allow students to enrol to track individual and class progress
- TestGen testbank of customisable questions for formative or summative assessment
- Customisable lecture plans in PowerPoint with animated figures. One version contains multiple choice questions that can be used for lectures with an electronic audience response system
- Downloadable PowerPoint slides of all figures and most tables from the book
- A range of teaching and learning case studies
- Thirteen workshops in Word for use in class or assessed work
- Answers to all box questions and end-of-chapter questions, and to questions in workshops, and Web Case Studies

These lecturer resources are also available on a memory stick from your Pearson Education sales representative.

For more information please contact your local Pearson Education sales representative or visit
www.pearsoned.co.uk/sloman

Guided tour

The book is divided into four **parts**. Each part contains an introduction to the material covered.

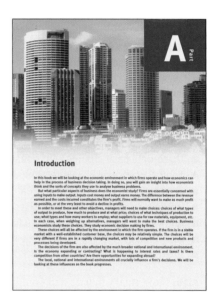

Business issues and **chapter maps,** located at the start of each chapter, highlight and give an overview of the specific topics covered in each chapter.

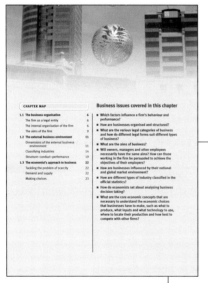

AIDING YOUR UNDERSTANDING

Key terms are highlighted in the text where they first appear and are accompanied by paired **definitions** in the margin. This is very useful for revision and allows you to see the terms used in context. A full **glossary** also appears at the back of the book and online in the Companion Website (**www.pearsoned.co.uk/sloman**).

A total of 29 **key ideas** are highlighted and numbered in the text where they first appear. Key ideas are fundamental to being able 'think like an economist' and help you to see how the subject ties together. They also help you to develop a toolkit of concepts that can be used in a whole host of different contexts. Whenever key ideas re-occur later in the book, a numbered icon appears in the margin.

Pause for thought questions help you to reflect on what you have just read and show how the various ideas and theories relate to different issues. Answers to these questions are given on the book's Companion Website.

Throughout the text you will find **Recap boxes** at the end of each major section as well as consolidated at the end of chapters. Recap boxes allow you to check on your understanding of the material at frequent intervals and function as an important revision tool.

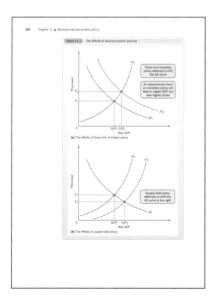

A **full-colour design** allows a consistent use of colour in the **figures**, letting you see at a glance how the figure or diagram is constructed and, additionally, the before and after positions when the diagram is used to illustrate the effects of a change in circumstance.

PRACTISING AND TESTING YOUR LEARNING

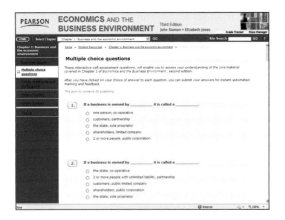

Multiple choice questions on the Companion Website provide a quick method for you to test and assess your progress.

The **Questions** section at the end of each chapter can be used for self testing, class exercises or class debate.

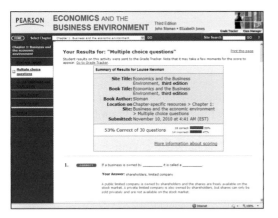

Results graph for MCQs on the Companion Website gives you instant feedback.

APPLYING ECONOMICS TO THE REAL WORLD

There are 88 boxed **Case studies** and **Applications** for this edition. Applied material makes learning much more interesting and helps to bring the subject alive. This is particularly important to enable you to relate economic theory to your other subjects and to the world of business generally. All boxes include questions so as to relate the material back to the chapter in which the box is located.

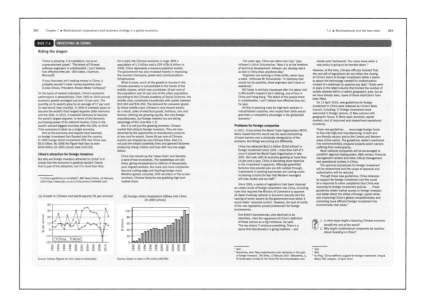

Topical issues, news articles and **hotlinks** on the Companion Website (**www.pearsoned.co.uk/sloman**) provide further context for economic theory. Topical issues provide discussion of some of the key economic issues over the past sixth months related to passages in the book. Economics news articles are updated monthly and provide hotlinks to recent articles.

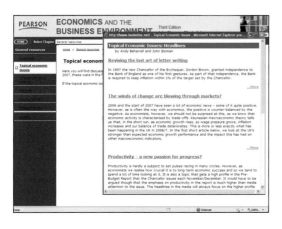

Web material at the end of each part lists additional case studies appearing on the book's Companion Website and references to various other useful websites.

Preface

Welcome to the third edition of this introduction to economics and the business environment. If you are a student on a business or management degree or diploma course and taking a module which includes economics, then this book is written for you. Such modules may go under the title of Business Environment or Business Context, or they may simply be called Introduction to Economics or Introduction to Business Economics. Alternatively, you may be studying on an MBA and need a grounding in basic economic concepts and how they apply to the business environment.

The book covers the core economics that you will need as a business student, but it also covers various business-related topics not typically covered in an introductory economics textbook. These topics include elements of business organisation and business strategy.

As well as making considerable use of business examples throughout the text, we have included many case studies in boxes (88 in all). These illustrate how economics can be used to understand particular business problems or aspects of the business environment. Many of these case studies cover issues that you are likely to read about in the newspapers. Some cover general business issues; others look at specific companies. There are also many additional case studies on the book's website (www.pearsoned.co.uk/sloman). These, along with references to various useful websites, are listed at the end of each of the four parts of the book.

We hope that, in using this book, you will share our fascination for economics. It is a subject that is highly relevant to the world in which we live. And it is a world where many of our needs are served by business – whether as employers or as producers of the goods and services we buy. After graduating, you will probably take up employment in business. A grounding in economic principles and how they relate to the world of business should prove invaluable in the business decisions you may well have to make.

The aim throughout the book is to make this intriguing subject clear for you to understand and as relevant as possible to you as a student of business.

The written style is direct and straightforward, with short paragraphs to aid rapid comprehension. Definitions of all key terms are given in the margin, with defined terms appearing in bold. We have highlighted 29 Key Ideas, which are fundamental to 'thinking like an economist'. We refer back to these every time they recur throughout the book. This helps you to see how the subject ties together, and also helps you to develop a toolkit of concepts that can be used in a whole host of different contexts.

Summaries are given at the end of each section of each chapter. These should help you in reviewing the material you have just covered and in revising for exams. Each chapter finishes with a series of questions. These can be used to check your understanding of the chapter and help you to see how its material can be applied to various business problems.

There are also questions interspersed throughout the text in 'Pause for Thought' panels. These encourage you to reflect on what you are learning and to see how the various ideas and theories relate to different issues. Answers to these questions are given on the book's website.

We hope you enjoy the book and come to appreciate the crucial role that economics plays in all our lives, and in particular in the practice of business.

Good luck and enjoy. Perhaps this will be just the beginning of a life-long interest in economic issues and how they apply to the world of business – and in your own personal life too!

TO THE TUTOR

The aim of this book is to provide a short course in economic principles as they apply to the business environment. It is designed to be used by first-year undergraduates on business studies degrees and diplomas where economics is taught from the business perspective, either as a separate one-semester module or as part of a business environment module. It is also suitable for students studying economics on MBA, CMS, DMS and various professional courses.

In addition to covering core economic principles, various specialist business topics are also covered that do not appear in conventional introductory economics textbooks. The following are some examples of these additional topics:

- Business organisations
- Industrial structure
- STEEPLE analysis (as an extension of PEST analysis)
- The structure–conduct–performance paradigm and its limitations
- The multinational corporation
- Globalisation and business
- Marketing the product
- Strategic analysis and choice
- Principal–agent analysis and the problem of asymmetric information as applied to various business situations
- The problems of adverse selection and moral hazard
- Application of game theory to business situations
- Porter's five forces model
- Growth strategy
- Business strategy in a recession (new to this edition)
- Transactions cost analysis

- Alternative aims of firms
- Pricing in practice
- Price flexibility
- The product life cycle
- The small-firm sector
- Flexible labour markets and firms
- The economics of entrepreneurship
- Business ethics and corporate social responsibility
- Government and the firm, including competition policy and regulation
- The macroeconomic environment of business, including the impact of macroeconomic policy on business
- The competitive advantage of nations
- Trading blocs including the effect of the single European market on business
- Monetary union
- The implications of exchange rate movements and international capital flows for business.

The text is split into four parts containing a total of 13 chapters. Each chapter could be covered in a week, giving enough material for a semester. Each chapter is divided into discrete sections, each with its own summary, providing an ideal coverage for a single study session for a student. Chapters finish with review questions, which can be used for seminars or discussion sessions.

The first nine chapters cover microeconomics and its relation to business. The final four cover the macroeconomic environment of business, both national and international. This higher weighting for microeconomics reflects the structure of many economics for business or business environment modules.

SPECIAL FEATURES

The book contains the following special features:

- *A direct and straightforward written style*, with short paragraphs to aid rapid comprehension. The aim all the time is to provide maximum clarity.
- *Attractive full-colour design*. The careful and consistent use of colour and shading makes the text more attractive to students and easier to use by giving clear signals as to the book's structure.

- *Figures with captions* (new to this edition). Most diagrams have captions to explain their properties and to highlight key features.
- *Key Ideas* highlighted and explained where they first appear. There are 29 of these ideas, which are fundamental to the study of economics on business courses. Students can see them recurring throughout the book, and an icon appears in the

margin to refer back to the page where the idea first appears. Showing how ideas can be used in a variety of contexts helps students to 'think like an economist' and to relate the different parts of the subject together. All 29 Key Ideas are defined in a special section at the very end of the book.

- *Pause for Thought* questions integrated throughout the text. These encourage students to reflect on what they have just read and make the learning process a more active one. Answers to these questions appear in the student section of the book's website. This new edition contains additional Pause for Thought questions.

- *Part opening sections* for each of the four parts of the book, setting the scene and introducing the material to be covered.

- *Chapter opening sections* that identify key business issues to be covered in that chapter.

- *Chapter maps* at the beginning of each chapter to show the topics to be covered and on what pages.

- *All technical terms are highlighted and clearly defined in the margin* on the page they appear. This feature is especially useful for students when revising.

- *A comprehensive index*, including reference to all defined terms. This enables students to look up a definition as required and to see it used in context.

- *Many boxes with additional applied material.* All boxes include questions so as to relate the material back to the chapter in which the box is located. The extensive use of applied material makes learning much more interesting for students and helps to bring the subject alive. This is particularly important for business students who need to relate economic theory to their other subjects and to the world of business generally. There are some new and updated boxes in this edition to provide additional case study material.

- *Additional case studies appearing on the book's website* are referred to at the end of each part.

- *Detailed summaries appear at the end of each section.* These allow students not only to check their comprehension of a section's contents, but also to get a clear overview of the material they have been studying.

- *Review questions at the end of each chapter.* These are designed to test students' understanding of the chapter's salient points. These questions can be used for seminars or as set work to be completed in the students' own time.

- *A list of relevant websites given at the end of each part.* Details of these websites can be found in the Web Appendix at the end of the book. You can easily access any of these sites from the book's own website (at **www.pearsoned.co.uk/sloman**). When you enter the site, click on Hotlinks. You will find all the sites from the Web Appendix listed. Click on the one you want and the 'hotlink' will take you straight to it.

SUPPLEMENTS

WinEcon

The widely acclaimed, award-winning WinEcon software, produced and authored by a consortium of economists drawn from several UK universities and designed to support introductory economics, is now web-enabled and adapted by John Sloman in a special version designed for *Economics and the Business Environment* (third edition), for both institutions and students. There is a separate chapter in this Sloman version of WinEcon to correspond to the relevant chapter in the book. The software includes graphical interactive tutorials, relevant theory, self-assessment questions, economic databases and an economic glossary providing a comprehensive attractive and highly interactive resource. For more information on downloading this software, please go to **www.winecon.com/sloman**.

Website

Visit the book's Companion Website at **www.pearsoned.co.uk/sloman**. This has an extensive range of materials for students and tutors.

For students

- *Study material* designed to help you improve your results. This includes an online workbook and study guide, with interactive exercises, diagrams that you can manipulate, videos and links to articles and other material.

- *Economics news articles*, updated monthly: some 15 to 20 news items per month, with links to one or more newspaper articles per item. There are questions on each item and references to the relevant chapter(s) of the book.
- *Topical economic issues*, with analysis and links to key concepts and pages in the book.
- *Hotlinks* to over 200 useful websites listed in the book's Web Appendix and referenced at the end of each part of the text.
- *Case studies* (88 in total) with questions for self-study. These are the case studies referred to at the end of each part of the text.
- *Answers to all Pause for Thought and odd-numbered end-of-chapter questions* to allow you to check your understanding as you progress.
- Self-test questions, organised chapter by chapter. You get a computer-generated answer to any test you take.

For tutors

- A range of *teaching and learning case studies*, with the focus on improving student learning outcomes.
- All *figures and tables* from the book in PowerPoint®, in two versions, each animated and in full colour.

- Customisable full-colour *lecture plans* in PowerPoint, with integrated animated diagrams and tables. These can also be used for handouts. There are five versions of these, including three with additional multiple-choice questions that can be used in lectures; two of these can be used with an electronic voting system – one for PRS® and one for TurningPoint®.
- Full-colour OHTs of all *figures and tables* and all *lecture plans* with and without figures, tables and questions. These are all on a clear background and are suitable for both colour and black and white printing onto acetate. They can also be used for hand-outs.
- Thirteen workshops in Word, one per chapter. These are suitable for use in class or for homework. Answers are given to each workshop in separate Word files.
- *Answers* to all even-numbered end-of-chapter questions, boxes and web case studies in a secure password protected area of the site.

These website materials are also available on a tutor's memory stick.

ACKNOWLEDGEMENTS

First, many thanks to Elizabeth for coming on board for this new edition and for adding lots of new content. Many thanks too to all the reviewers of the text, who, as with the previous edition, have given me valuable advice for improvements. Thanks also to the team at Pearson, and especially Kate Brewin, Elizabeth Wright, Astrid deRidder and Mary Lince.

Finally, thanks to all my family and especially, as always, to my wife Alison and for her continued patience, love and support.

John Sloman

I am extremely grateful for the continued love and support of my family, in particular my parents, without whom this would not have been possible. In addition, my thanks go to both the team at Pearson and of course to John Sloman, for giving me this wonderful opportunity.

Elizabeth Jones

Custom publishing

Custom publishing allows academics to pick and choose content from one or more textbooks for their course and combine it into a definitive course text.

Here are some common examples of custom solutions which have helped over 500 courses across Europe:

- different chapters from across our publishing imprints combined into one book;
- lecturer's own material combined together with textbook chapters or published in a separate booklet;
- third-party cases and articles that you are keen for your students to read as part of the course;
- any combination of the above.

The Pearson Education custom text published for your course is professionally produced and bound – just as you would expect from a normal Pearson Education text. You can even choose your own cover design and add your university logo. Since many of our titles have online resources accompanying them we can even build a Custom website that matches your course text.

Whatever your choice, our dedicated Editorial and Production teams will work with you throughout the process, right up until you receive a copy of your Custom text.

Some adopters of previous editions of Sloman's *Economics and the Business Environment* have found that the flexibility of custom publishing has allowed them to include additional material on certain aspects of the business environment subject area.

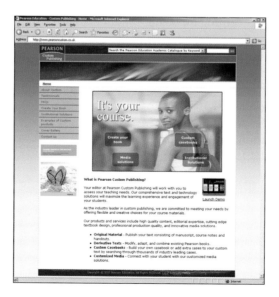

To give you an idea of which texts have proved popular, here is a list of titles covering particular subject areas that could provide extra chapters to match the emphasis of your course:

- **Economics** – Sloman and Wride, *Economics*, Seventh Edition and Sloman and Garratt, *Essentials of Economics*, Fifth Edition
- **Business Economics** – Sloman, Hinde and Garratt, *Economics for Business*, Fifth Edition
- **Legal environment** – Adams, *Law for Business Students*, Sixth Edition
- **Ethics** – Lovell and Fisher, *Business Ethics and Values*, Third Edition
- **Marketing** – Brassington, *Principles of Marketing*, Fourth Edition
- **International marketing** – Hollensen, *Global Marketing*, Fifth Edition
- **International business environment** – Brooks, Weatherston and Wilkinson, *The International Business Environment*, First Edition
- **Business environment** – Worthington and Britton, *The Business Environment*, Sixth Edition

Examples of custom published texts containing material taken from the above list of textbooks:

For more details on any of these books or to browse other material from our entire portfolio, please visit: **www.pearsoned.co.uk**.

If, once you have had time to review this title, you feel that Custom publishing might benefit you and your course, please do get in contact. However minor or major the change, we can help you out.

You can contact us at: **www.pearsoncustom.co.uk** or via your local representative at: **www.pearsoned.co.uk/replocator**.

Publisher's acknowledgements

We are grateful to the following for permission to reproduce copyright material:

Figures

Figure 1.4 after Labour Market Trends and Economic and Labour Market Review (Office for National Statistics), Crown Copyright material is reproduced with permission under the terms of the Click-Use License; Figure 1.5 adapted from *Industrial Market Structure and Economic Performance*, Third ed, New York: Houghton Mifflin (Scherer, F. M. and Ross, D. 1990) Houghton Mifflin, From SCHERER. SPB – SCHERER IND MKT STR&ECON PERF, 3E. © South-Western, a part of Cengage Learning, Inc. Reproduced by permission. www.cengage.com/permissions; Figure on page 101 from Business clusters in the UK – a first assessment, Figure 2, p. 7 (http://www.dti.gov.uk/files/file17396.pdf) (Department of Trade and Industry), Crown Copyright material is reproduced with permission under the terms of the Click-Use License; Figure 6.1 from *Competitive Strategy: Techniques for Analyzing Industries and Competitor* New York: The Free Press (Porter, M. E. 1980) The Free Press, a division of Simon & Schuster Adult Publishing Group, With the permission of The Free Press, a Division of Simon & Schuster, Inc., from Competitive Strategy: Techniques for Analyzing Industries and Competitors by Michael E. Porter. Copyright © 1980, 1998 by The Free Press. All rights reserved; Figure 6.5 after Global Entrepreneurship Monitor 2009 (Global Enterprise Research Association, 2010), Permission to reproduce a figure from the GEM 2009 Global Report, which appears here, has been kindly granted by the copyright holders. The GEM is an international consortium and this report was produced from data collected in, and received from, 54 countries in 2009. Our thanks go to the authors, national teams, researchers, funding bodies and other contributors who have made this possible; Figure on page 197 from Mergers & Acquisitions Note, April 2007 (European Commission, DG ECFIN, 2007), Source: http://europe.eu, © European Communities, 1995–2009; Figure on page 248 from Stern Review on the Economics of Climate Change, Executive Summary, Figure 1 (H. M. Treasury, 2006). (Prepared by Stern Review, from data drawn from World Resources Institute Climate Analysis Indicators Tool (CAIT) on-line database version 3.0.), Crown Copyright material is reproduced with permission under the terms of the Click-Use License; Figure on page 282 from European Economy, Statistical Annex (European Commission, 2009), Source: http://europe.eu, © European Communities, 1995–2009; Figure on page 283 from Business and Consumer Surveys (European Commission, 2009), Source: http://europe.eu, © European Communities, 1995–2009; Figure on page 327 from Pre-Budget Report 2008, Box 3.1, Chart (b) (H. M. Treasury, 2008), Crown Copyright material is reproduced with permission under the terms of the Click-Use License; Figure 11.2 from Budget 2009, Chart 2.3 (H. M. Treasury, 2009), Crown Copyright material is reproduced with permission under the terms of the Click-Use License; Figure 11.4 from Inflation Report, May (Bank of England, 2009); Figure 12.3 from *The Competitive Advantage of Nations*, New York: The Free Press (Porter, M. E. 1998) p. 127 The Free Press, With the permission of The Free Press, a Division of Simon & Schuster, Inc., from The Competitive Advantage of Nations by Michael E. Porter. Copyright © 1990, 1998 by Michael E. Porter. All rights reserved.

Tables

Tables 1.1, 1.2 after Standard Industrial Classification 2007 (Office for National Statistics), Crown Copyright material is reproduced with permission under the terms of the Click-Use License; Table 01.3 after UK Economic

Accounts and Economic and Labour Market Review (Office for National Statistics), Crown Copyright material is reproduced with permission under the terms of the Click-Use License; Table on page 103 from A survey of the economies of scale, *Research on the 'Costs of Non-Europe'*, Volume 2 (Pratten, C. F. 1988), Luxembourg: Office for Official Publications of the European Communities, © European Communities, 1995–2009; Table on page 103 from Economies of scale, *The Single Market Review*, Subseries V, Volume 4 (European Commission/ Economists Advisory Group Ltd 1997), Luxembourg: Office for Official Publications of the European Communities, © European Communities, 1995–2009; Table on page 120 after United Kingdom Input-Output Analyses Table 8.31 (Office of National Statistics), Crown Copyright material is reproduced with permission under the terms of the Click-Use License; Table 11.2 after European Economy Statistical Annex (European Commission, 2010), Source: http://europe.eu, © European Communities, 1995–2009; Table 13.1 from Financial Statistics (Office for National Statistics), Crown Copyright material is reproduced with permission under the terms of the Click-Use License.

Text

Extract on page 300 from Deflation turns into biggest economic risk, *The Sunday Times*, 11/05/2003, NI Syndication Limited, © The Times/The Sun/nisyndication.com

In some instances we have been unable to trace the owners of copyright material, and we would appreciate any information that would enable us to do so.

Introduction

In this book we will be looking at the economic environment in which firms operate and how economics can help in the process of business decision taking. In doing so, you will gain an insight into how economists think and the sorts of concepts they use to analyse business problems.

But what particular aspects of business does the economist study? Firms are essentially concerned with using inputs to make output. Inputs cost money and output earns money. The difference between the revenue earned and the costs incurred constitutes the firm's profit. Firms will normally want to make as much profit as possible, or at the very least to avoid a decline in profits.

In order to meet these and other objectives, managers will need to make choices: choices of what types of output to produce, how much to produce and at what price; choices of what techniques of production to use; what types and how many workers to employ; what suppliers to use for raw materials, equipment, etc. In each case, when weighing up alternatives, managers will want to make the best choices. Business economists study these choices. They study economic decision making by firms.

These choices will all be affected by the environment in which the firm operates. If the firm is in a stable market with a well-established customer base, the choices may be relatively simple. The choices will be very different if firms are in a rapidly changing market, with lots of competition and new products and processes being developed.

The decisions of the firm are also affected by the much broader national and international environment. Is the economy expanding or contracting? What is happening to interest rates and taxes? Is there competition from other countries? Are there opportunities for expanding abroad?

The local, national and international environments all crucially influence a firm's decisions. We will be looking at these influences as the book progresses.

Business issues covered in this chapter

- Which factors influence a firm's behaviour and performance?
- How are businesses organised and structured?
- What are the various legal categories of business and how do different legal forms suit different types of business?
- What are the aims of business?
- Will owners, managers and other employees necessarily have the same aims? How can those working in the firm be persuaded to achieve the objectives of their employers?
- How are businesses influenced by their national and global market environment?
- How are different types of industry classified in the official statistics?
- How do economists set about analysing business decision taking?
- What are the core economic concepts that are necessary to understand the economic choices that businesses have to make, such as what to produce, what inputs and what technology to use, where to locate their production and how best to compete with other firms?

Chapter 1

Business and the economic environment

The world economy has undergone many changes in recent decades, and these changes have had profound effects on businesses across the world. For a start, most countries have increasingly embraced the 'market' as the means of boosting prosperity. You can see this in the abandonment of state planning in former communist countries, the privatisation of state industries around the world, the dismantling of barriers to international trade, the development of global financial markets, the use of government policies to promote competition and reductions in government regulation of business in order to attract inward investment. A consequence has been the growth of multinational businesses seeking the best market opportunities and the cheapest sources of supply. This has also contributed towards increasing interdependence between nations.

Other important influences on businesses around the world have included the development of computers and IT, improvements in transport and communications and, more recently, a rapid growth in the use of the Internet. Firms have had to adapt to these technological advances to maintain their competitiveness, but these advances have also allowed businesses to take advantage of growing market opportunities.

Today, for many firms the world is their market. Their business environment is global. This is obviously the case with large multinational companies, such as McDonald's, Sony, VW, HSBC, Nestlé and Shell. But many small and medium-sized enterprises (SMEs) also have global reach, selling their products in various countries and buying their supplies from wherever in the world they get the best deal.

For other firms, however, their market is much more local. Take a restaurant or firm of heating engineers – in fact, look in the Yellow Pages and you will see a host of companies serving a market whose radius is no more than a few miles. But these firms also often face competition from global companies. A local shop is likely to face competition from a supermarket, such as Tesco or Wal-Mart, both of which have shops around the world and source their supplies from across the globe.

In this chapter, we take an overview of the types of environment in which firms operate and of the role of the economist in business decision taking. We start by looking at the internal environment of the firm – the organisation and aims of the business. We then look at the external environment in which the firm operates – the nature of competition it faces, the type of industry in which it operates, the prices of its inputs, the general state of the economy (e.g. whether growing or in recession), the actions of the government and other authorities that might affect the firm (e.g. changes in taxes or interest rates or changes in competition legislation) and the global environment (e.g. the extent to which the company operates internationally and how it is influenced by global market opportunities and the state of the world economy). Finally we look at the approach of the economist to analysing the business environment and business decision taking.

Box 1.1 introduces many of the topics that you will be covering in this book by taking the case of Gap and seeing how it is affected by its environment.

BOX 1.1   MINDING THE GAP

Making the best of your business environment

Gap Inc. was founded in 1969 with the opening of a single shop in San Francisco. Today it has some 3095 stores, trading under The Gap, babyGap, Gap Kids, Banana Republic and Old Navy brands. With total sales of $14.1 billion in 2009, Gap Inc. has large markets in the USA, Canada, the UK, France, Ireland and Japan and is America's largest clothing chain and one of the world's biggest fashion retailers. It employs 134 000 people worldwide and has begun expanding into other countries, such as Mexico, Saudi Arabia and Jordan and under a franchise deal will be soon be opening up 10 to 15 stores in Australia.[1]

What makes it a global company is not just its stores in several countries, but the fact that it produces its clothes in many locations, mainly in the developing world, where wages are much lower than in industrialised countries.

But has it continued to be successful? Have mistakes been made? What lessons are there for other businesses? How has its performance been affected by its business environment – by consumer tastes, by the actions of its rivals, by the state of the national and world economies and by government policy?

In particular, how would an economist analyse Gap's performance so as to advise it on its best strategy for the future? This is the sort of thing that business economists do and the sort of thing we will be doing throughout this book. We will also look at the impact of the behaviour of businesses on their customers, on employees, on competitors and on society in general.

So let's have a look at some of the issues facing Gap and how they relate to business in general and to the topics covered in this book.

The market environment

To be a successful business, it is important for Gap to get its product right. This means understanding its market and how consumer demand responds to changes in price. We look at how markets work in general in Chapter 2 and then look specifically at consumer demand in Chapter 3.

To stay successful, Gap must both respond to changes in fashion and, to some extent, set fashion. To quote from the Gap website, 'We create emotional connections with customers around the world through inspiring product design, unique store experiences and compelling marketing.'[2]

But Gap hasn't always got things right. In 2000, it reported falling sales and profits and its share price plummeted. According to analyst Mike Goldman, from Verdict Research:

There's a lack of innovation. Go into a store and the styles and ranges haven't changed significantly . . . The one-style-suits-all ethos of Gap may also have lost favour with consumers. Gap may have to embrace 'glocalisation', where they have the reach of a global company but are able to take local tastes into account.[3]

With an attempt to revitalise its brands, the Gap saw some turnaround in its fortunes between 2002 and 2004, with both sales and profits rising. But both fell again in 2005 and 2006. Part of the problem was a lack of responsiveness to fashion trends.

The group's supply chain works with traditional lead times of around nine months, while competitors such as H&M, Charlotte Russe and Forever 21 have adopted 'fast-fashion' lead times of less than three months, enabling them to respond far more quickly to fashion developments.[4]

We look at strategies to estimate, respond to and influence demand in Chapter 3.

Success in selling is not just about the design of the product. It's also about getting the price right, and that depends a lot on what rival companies are doing. Gap's prices must be competitive with those of Next, H&M, Top Shop, etc. Chapter 5 focuses on pricing decisions.

Over the longer term, Gap has to make decisions about which markets to target. In 1986 it launched GapKids and in 1994 GapScents. In 1997 it opened its online store, which has been extremely successful, with revenue passing the $1 billion mark in 2009. Should it expand to furnishing fabrics or to a greater range of fashion accessories? Should it expand to new countries, such as Australia or Malaysia? Should it attempt to take over rivals?

After repeatedly promising investors that a turnround was on the way, Gap has announced a brand strategy review at Old Navy and Gap, and has called in Goldman Sachs to advise it on possible next moves. This raises the possibility that some, or all, of the group might be sold to private investors or others.[5]

Strategic decisions such as growth by expansion in the domestic and global economy are examined in Chapters 6 and 7, respectively.

Production and employment

Being a profitable business depends not just on being able to sell a product, but on how efficiently the product can

---

[1] www.gapinc.com/public/Media/Press_Releases/med_pr_
FranchiseMexico09192008.shtml
[2] www.gapinc.com

[3] http://news.bbc.co.uk/1/hi/uk/875926.stm
[4] 'Size matters in challenge to turn round Gap's fortunes', *Financial Times*, 10 January 2007
[5] *Ibid.*

be produced. This means choosing the most appropriate technology and deploying the labour force in the best way. We explore production and costs in Chapter 4 and the employment of labour in Chapter 8.

Gap is a vertically integrated company. This means that it is involved not only in retailing, but also in the production of the clothes it sells. To quote the Gap website again: 'Located around the globe, employees in Gap Inc.'s Sourcing and Logistics group, along with our buying agents, draw up production schedules and place orders with approved third-party factories in the more than 50 countries where our products are made.'

Gap, as with other companies, must decide on how many workers to employ, what wage rates to pay and what the conditions of employment should be. Such questions are explored in Chapter 8.

Most of Gap's garments are made in low-wage developing countries, where the garments can be made at a fraction of the cost in America or Western Europe. One result is that Gap has come in for fierce criticism from the 'anti-globalisation' protestors about the employment conditions in its factories. According to the international human rights organisation, Global Exchange:

> In Russia we were notified that Gap pays factory workers just 11 cents per hour and keeps them in slave-like conditions. Workers from Macao contacted the Asia Monitor Resource Centre in Hong Kong complaining of abusive treatment by factory managers, who forced them to work excessive overtime and cheated them out of their pay. A delegation from the National Labor Committee in June 1999 reported that Honduran Gap factory workers are subjected to forced pregnancy tests, forced overtime, exceedingly high production goals, locked bathrooms, and wages of $4 per day, which only meet 1/3 of their basic needs.[6]

This raises questions of business ethics and what is known as 'corporate social responsibility'. We examine these broader social issues in Chapter 9, along with government policies to encourage, persuade or force firms to behave in the public interest.

Clearly Gap was worried about the adverse press it was receiving. It was particularly concerned by the campaign by the American labour union UNITE, which highlighted conditions in factories producing clothes for Gap and other US retailers. Gap was thus at pains to be seen to be addressing the problem. In April 2004, the *Corporate Social Responsibility Newswire Service* reported that:

UNITE and speciality apparel retailer Gap Inc. announced that they are supporting an effort by displaced garment workers in El Salvador to open that country's first independent and fully unionised apparel export factory. UNITE and Gap Inc. also said they plan to regularly discuss ways to co-operatively address garment factory issues that are of mutual concern to both organisations.

> 'My daughter asked me if it was OK to shop at Gap now, and when I said "yes," it instantly cost me $80,' said Bruce Raynor, president of UNITE.[7]

However, since these problems, significant steps have been taken, and Gap Inc. has been recognised as one of the world's most ethical companies for the fourth year in a row in 2010. Alex Brigham, Executive Director of the Ethisphere Institute said:

> Gap Inc.'s promotion of a sound ethical environment shines within its industry and shows a clear understanding that operating under the highest standards for business behavior goes beyond goodwill and 'lip-service' and is linked to performance and profitability.[8]

The economy

So do the fortunes of Gap and other companies depend solely on their policies and those of their competitors? The answer is no. One important element of a company's business environment is largely beyond its control: the state of the national economy and, for internationally trading companies, of the global economy. If the world economy is booming, then sales and profits are likely to grow without too much effort by the company. However, when the global economy declines, as happened in the recession of 2008/9, trading conditions become much tougher. Gap Inc.'s sales fell by 8 per cent between the 2007 and 2008 fiscal years, from $15.8 billion to $14.5 billion, and then fell further to $14.1 billion in 2009.[9]

We examine the national and international business environment in Part D. We also examine the impact on business of government policies to affect the economy – policies such as changes in taxation, interest rates, exchange rates and customs duties.

 Choose a well-known company that trades globally and do a Web search to find out how well it has performed in recent years and how it has been influenced by various aspects of its business environment.

---

[6] www.globalexchange.org/campaigns/sweatshops/gap/background.html.pf

[7] www.csrwire.com/print.cgi?sfArticleId=2654
[8] www.earthtimes.org/articles/show/gap-inc-recognized-as-one,1215193.shtml
[9] www.gapinc.com

1.1   THE BUSINESS ORGANISATION

There are many factors that affect the behaviour of firms, and here we focus on three key things:

■ the legal status of the business;
■ the way in which the firm is organised – whether as a simple top-down organisation or as a more complex multi-department or multi-division organisation;
■ the aims of the firm – does the firm simply aim to maximise profits, or are there other aims?

The firm as a legal entity

In a small firm, the owner or owners are likely to play a major part in running the business. Such businesses will normally be one of two types.

The sole proprietor. This is where the business is owned by just one person. Owners of small shops, builders and farmers are typical examples. Such businesses are easy to set up and may require only a relatively small initial capital investment. However, they suffer two main disadvantages

■ *Limited scope for expansion.* Finance is limited to what the owner can raise personally. Also there is a limit to the size of an organisation that one person can effectively control.
■ *Unlimited liability.* The owner is personally liable for any losses that the business might make. This could result in the owner's house, car and other assets being seized to pay off any outstanding debts.

The partnership. This is where two or more people own the business. In most partnerships there is a legal limit of 20 partners. Partnerships are common in the professions: solicitors, accountants, surveyors, etc. Whilst partnerships do mean a loss of control, as decision making is now shared, with more owners there is more scope for expansion, due to the possibility of raising extra finance and as partners can specialise in different areas of the business.

Since 2001 limited liability partnerships have been possible, however many firms still retain unlimited liability. This problem could be very serious, as the mistakes of one partner could jeopardise the personal assets of all the other partners.

Where large amounts of capital are required and/or when the risks of business failure are relatively high, partnerships are not generally an appropriate form of organisation. In such cases it is best to form a company (or **joint-stock company**, to give it its full title).

Companies

A company is legally separate from its owners. This means that it can enter into contracts and own property. Any debts are its debts, not the owners'.

The owners are the shareholders. Each shareholder receives his or her share of the company's distributed profit. The payments to shareholders are called 'dividends'. The owners have only **limited liability**. This means that, if the company goes bankrupt, the owners will lose the amount of money they have invested in the company, but no more. This has the advantage of encouraging people to become shareholders, thereby providing more finance to businesses.

Definitions

Joint-stock company
A company where ownership is distributed between shareholders.

Limited liability
Where the liability of the owners for the debts of a company is limited to the amount they have invested in it.

Shareholders often take no part in the running of the firm. They may elect a board of directors which decides broad issues of company policy. The board of directors in turn appoints managers who make the day-to-day decisions.

There are two types of company: public and private.

Public limited companies (plc). These are companies that can offer new shares publicly: by issuing a prospectus, they can invite the public to subscribe to a new share issue. In addition, many public limited companies are quoted on the Stock Exchange (see section 6.4), where existing shares can be bought and sold. A public limited company must hold an annual shareholders' meeting. Examples of well-known UK public limited companies are Marks & Spencer, BP, Barclays, BSkyB and Tesco.

Private limited companies (ltd). Private limited companies cannot offer their shares publicly. Shares have to be sold privately. This makes it more difficult for private limited companies to raise finance, and consequently they tend to be smaller than public companies. However, they are easier to set up than public companies. One of the most famous examples of a private limited company is Manchester United football club, which, until it was bought out by the Glazer family in 2005, was a public limited company.

Cooperatives

There are also two types of cooperatives

Consumer cooperatives. These are officially owned by the consumers, although they play no part in running the business.

Producer cooperatives. These are owned by the firm's workers, who share in the firm's profits. John Lewis is a prime example of such an organisation.

The internal organisation of the firm

The internal operating structures of firms are frequently governed by their size. Small firms tend to be centrally managed, with decision making operating through a clear managerial hierarchy. In large firms, however, the organisational structure tends to be more complex, although technological change is forcing many organisations to reassess the most suitable organisational structure for their business.

U form

In small to medium-sized firms, the managers of the various departments – marketing, finance, production, etc. – are normally directly responsible to a chief executive, whose function is to coordinate their activities: relaying the firm's overall strategy to them and being responsible for interdepartmental communication. We call this type of structure U (**unitary**) **form** (see Figure 1.1).

When firms expand beyond a certain size, a U-form structure is likely to become inefficient. This inefficiency arises from difficulties in communication, coordination and control. It becomes too difficult to manage the whole organisation from the centre.

M form

To overcome these organisational problems, the firm can adopt an M (**multi-divisional**) **form** of managerial structure (see Figure 1.2).

> **Definitions**
>
> **U-form business organisation**
> One in which the central organisation of the firm (the chief executive or a managerial team) is responsible both for the firm's day-to-day administration and for formulating its business strategy.
>
> **M-form business organisation**
> One in which the business is organised into separate departments, such that responsibility for the day-to-day management of the enterprise is separated from the formulation of the business's strategic plan.

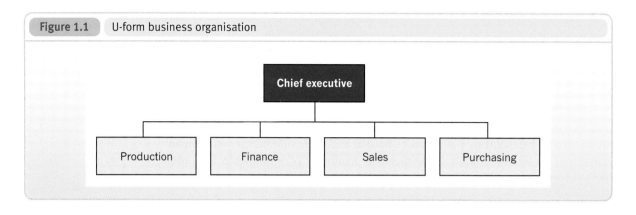

Figure 1.1   U-form business organisation

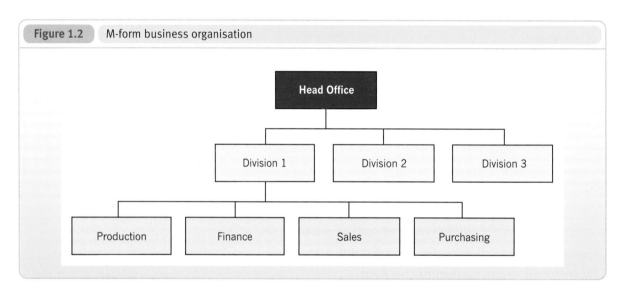

Figure 1.2   M-form business organisation

This suits larger firms. The firm is divided into a number of 'divisions'. Each division could be responsible for a particular stage of production, a particular product or group of products, or a particular market (e.g. a specific country). The day-to-day running and even certain long-term decisions of each division would be the responsibility of the divisional manager(s). This leads to the following benefits:

■ reduced length of information flows;
■ the chief executive being able to concentrate on overall strategic planning;
■ an enhanced level of control, with each division being run as a mini 'firm', competing with other divisions for the limited amount of company resources available.

The flat organisation

One of the major problems with M-form organisations is that they can become very bureaucratic with many layers of management. Recent technological innovations, however, especially in respect to computer systems such as e-mail and management information systems, have enabled senior managers to communicate easily and directly with those lower in the organisational structure. As a result, some companies have moved back towards simpler structures. These **flat organisations**, as they are called, dispense with various layers of middle management.

The holding company

As many businesses have expanded their operations, often on a global scale, more complex forms of business organisation have evolved. One such organisation is the **H-form** or **holding company**. A holding company (or parent company) is one that owns a controlling interest in other subsidiary companies. These subsidiaries, in turn, may also have controlling interests in other companies. There may thus be a complex web of interlocking holdings. While the parent company has ultimate control over its various subsidiaries, it is likely that both tactical and strategic decision making is left to the individual companies within the organisation. A good example of such an organisation would be the Walt Disney Company.

> **Definition**
>
> **Holding company**
> A business organisation in which the parent company holds interests in a number of other companies or subsidiaries.

The aims of the firm

Economists have traditionally assumed that firms want to maximise profits. The 'traditional theory of the firm', as it is called, shows how much output firms should produce and at what price in order to make as much profit as possible. But do firms necessarily want to maximise profits?

Whilst it is reasonable to assume that the *owners* of firms will want to maximise profits, it is not always clear over what time period they will want to do this. For example, if a business adopts a strategy of growth, more will need to be spent on investment in machinery and advertising to increase both production and sales. These large expenditures will reduce the profit available for distribution to shareholders in the short run, but profits in the long run may be maximised. In this case, what is inconsistent with short-run profit maximisation may be wholly consistent with long-run profit maximisation.

A more fundamental criticism of the assumption of profit maximisation, however, is that in large companies it is not the owners that make the decisions about how much to produce and at what price. In such cases other objectives may be pursued.

The divorce of ownership from control

In public limited companies the shareholders elect directors. Directors in turn employ professional managers who are often given considerable discretion in making decisions. There is therefore a *separation between the ownership and control* of a firm.

The owners may want to maximise profits, but what are the objectives of the managers who make the decisions? Managers may be assumed to want to maximise their *own* interests. This may well involve pursuits that conflict with profit maximisation. As the manager of a firm, what are you interested in? A higher salary, greater power or prestige, greater sales, better working conditions or greater popularity with your subordinates? Different managers in the same firm may well pursue different aims.

> **Pause for thought**
>
> *Make a list of four possible aims that a manager of a McDonald's restaurant might have. Which of these might conflict with the interests of McDonald's shareholders?*

Managers will still have to ensure that *sufficient* profits are made to keep shareholders happy, but that may be very different from *maximising* profits. Alternative theories of the firm to those of profit maximisation, therefore, tend to assume that large firms are profit 'satisficers'. That is, managers strive hard for a minimum target level of profit, but are less interested in profits above this level.

The principal–agent relationship

Can the owners of a firm ever be sure that their managers will pursue the business strategy most appropriate to achieving the owners' goals (i.e. profit maximisation)?

Definitions

Principal–agent problem

One where people (principals), as a result of lack of knowledge, cannot ensure that their best interests are served by their agents.

Asymmetric information

A situation in which one party in an economic relationship knows more than another.

This is an example of the **principal–agent problem**. One of the features of a complex modern economy is that people (principals) have to employ others (agents) to carry out their wishes. If you want to go on holiday, it is easier to go to a travel agent to sort out the arrangements than to do it all yourself. Likewise, if you want to sell a house, it is more convenient to go to an estate agent.

The crucial advantage that agents have over their principals is specialist knowledge and information. This is usually why we employ agents. For example, owners employ managers for their specialist knowledge of a market or their understanding of business practice. But this situation of **asymmetric information** – that one party (the agent) knows more than the other (the principal) – means that it will be very difficult for the principal to judge in whose interest the agent is operating. Are the managers pursuing their own goals, rather than the goals of the owner? It is the same in other walks of life. The estate agent may try to convince you that it is necessary to accept a lower price, while the real reason may be to save the agent time, effort and expense.

 KEY IDEA 1   The principal–agent problem. Where people (principals), as a result of a lack of knowledge (asymmetric information), cannot ensure that their best interests are served by their agents. Agents may take advantage of this situation to the disadvantage of the principals.

Principals may attempt to reconcile the fact that they have imperfect information, and are thus in an inherently weak position, in the following ways.

■ *Monitoring* the performance of the agent. Shareholders could monitor the performance of their senior managers through attending annual general meetings. The managers could be questioned by shareholders and ultimately replaced if their performance is unsatisfactory.

■ Establishing a series of *incentives* to ensure that agents act in the principals' best interest. For example, managerial pay could be closely linked to business performance.

Within any firm there will exist a complex chain of principal–agent relationships – between workers and managers, between junior managers and senior managers, between senior managers and directors, and between directors and shareholders. All groups will hold some specialist knowledge which they may use to further their own distinct goals. Predictably, the development of effective monitoring and evaluation programmes and the creation of performance-related pay schemes have been two central themes in the development of business practices in recent years – a sign that the principal is looking to fight back!

Pause for thought

Identify a situation where you, as a consumer, are in a principal–agent relationship with a supplier. How can you minimise the problem of asymmetric information in this relationship?

Staying in business

Aiming for profits, sales, salaries, power, etc. will be useless if the firm does not survive! Trying to *maximise* any of the various objectives may be risky. For example, if a firm tries to maximise its market share by aggressive advertising or price cutting, it might invoke a strong response from its rivals. The resulting war may drive it out of business. Concern with survival, therefore, may make firms cautious.

However, being cautious does not guarantee survival and could even lead to the demise of a business, as market share may be lost to more aggressive competitors.

Ultimately, if a firm is concerned with survival, it must be careful to balance caution against keeping up with competitors, ensuring that the customer is sufficiently satisfied and that costs are kept sufficiently low by efficient management and the introduction of new technology.

Recap

1. There are several types of legal organisation of firms: the sole proprietorship, the partnership, the private limited company, the public limited company and cooperatives. In the first two cases, the owners have unlimited liability. With companies, however, shareholders' liability is limited to the amount they have invested. This reduced risk encourages people to invest in companies.

2. As firms grow, so they tend to move from a U-form to an M-form structure. In recent years, however, with the advance of information technology, many firms have adopted a flat organisation – a return to U-form structure. Multinational companies often adopt relatively complex forms of organisation. Many multinationals adopt a holding company (H-form) structure.

3. Typically, owners of firms will seek to maximise profits. With large companies, however, there is a divorce of ownership from control. Control is by managers, who might pursue goals other than profit.

4. The problem of managers not pursuing the same goals as the owners is an example of the *principal–agent problem*. Agents (in this case the managers) may not always carry out the wishes of their principals (in this case the owners). Because of asymmetric information, managers can pursue their own aims, as long as they produce results that satisfy the owners. The solution for owners is for there to be a better means of monitoring the performance of managers, and incentives for the managers to behave in the owners' interests.

THE EXTERNAL BUSINESS ENVIRONMENT   1.2

The decisions and performance of a firm are affected not just by its internal organisation and aims; they are also affected by the external environment in which the firm operates.

Dimensions of the external business environment

It is normal to identify various dimensions to the external business environment. These include political, economic, social/cultural and technological factors.

Political factors. Firms are directly affected by the actions of government and other political events. These might be major events affecting the whole of the business community, such as the collapse of communism, the Iraq War or a change of government. Alternatively, they may be actions affecting just one part of the economy. For example, the ban on smoking in pubs and restaurants affects the tobacco industry.

Economic factors. Businesses are affected by a whole range of economic factors, such as a rise in the cost of raw materials, or a price cut by a rival firm, or new taxes, or movements in interest rates or exchange rates. A firm must constantly take such factors into account when devising and implementing its business strategy.

It is normal to divide the economic environment in which the firm operates into two levels:

∎ *The microeconomic environment.* This includes all the economic factors that are *specific* to a particular firm operating in its own particular market. Thus one firm may be operating in a highly competitive market, whereas another may not; one firm may be faced by rapidly changing consumer tastes (e.g. a designer clothing manufacturer), while another may be faced with a virtually constant consumer demand (e.g. a potato merchant); one firm may face rapidly rising costs, while another may find that costs are constant or falling.

■ *The macroeconomic environment.* This is the *national* and *international* economic situation in which a business as a whole operates. Business in general will fare much better if the economy is growing than if it is in recession. In examining the macroeconomic environment, we will also be looking at the policies that governments adopt in their attempt to steer the economy, since these policies, by affecting things such as taxation, interest rates and exchange rates, will have a major impact on firms.

Social/cultural factors. This aspect of the business environment concerns social attitudes and values. These include attitudes towards working conditions and the length of the working day, equal opportunities for different groups of people (whether by ethnicity, gender, physical attributes, etc.), the nature and purity of products, the use and abuse of animals, and images portrayed in advertising. The social/cultural environment also includes social trends, such as an increase in the average age of the population, or changes in attitudes towards seeking paid employment while bringing up small children. In recent times, various ethical issues, especially concerning the protection of the environment, have had a big impact on the actions of business and the image that many firms seek to present.

Technological factors. Over the past 25 years, there has been rapid technological change. This has had a huge impact not only on how firms produce products, but also on how their business is organised. The use of robots and other forms of computer-controlled production has changed the nature of work for many workers. It has also created a wide range of new opportunities for businesses, many of which have yet to be realised. The information-technology revolution is also enabling much more rapid communication and making it possible for many workers to do their job from home, while travelling, or from another country.

Definition
PEST (or STEEPLE) analysis Where the political, economic, social and technological factors shaping a business environment are assessed by a business so as to devise future business strategy. STEEPLE analysis would also take into account ethical, legal and environmental factors.

The division of the factors affecting a firm into political, economic, social and technological is commonly known as a **PEST analysis**. More recently, three more elements of the business environment have been added to give what is known as **STEEPLE analysis**. The extra elements are:

Environmental (ecological) factors. The environment has become an increasingly important issue in politics and business. The government has adopted a policy of 'naming and shaming' large polluters. Firms are therefore taking a greener approach to their activities and trying to find ways of minimising adverse effects on the environment, whether through cleaner technologies, or better waste management and recycling, or through greener products. This might create extra costs for firms, but a greener image can also help to drive sales as consumers have become more environmentally aware. It can also provide more finance for firms from the government and those investors seeking to improve their image. Business attitudes towards the environment are examined in section 9.4.

Legal factors. Businesses are affected by the legal framework in which they operate. Examples include industrial relations legislation, product safety standards, regulations governing pricing in the privatised industries and laws preventing collusion between firms to keep prices up. We examine some of these laws in sections 9.3–9.6.

Ethical factors. Firms are increasingly under pressure to adopt a more socially responsible attitude towards business. Corporate responsibility is a major concern for many firms, whether in terms of working conditions, the safety and quality of their products, truthful advertising, their attitudes towards the environment, concern for local residents and the general avoidance of what might be seen as 'suspect' business practices. Business ethics and corporate responsibility are examined in section 9.2.

The PEST or STEEPLE framework is widely used by organisations to audit their business environment and to help them establish a strategic approach to their business activities. It is nevertheless important to recognise that there is a great overlap and interaction among these sets of factors. Laws and government policies reflect social attitudes; technological factors determine economic ones, such as costs and productivity; technological progress often reflects the desire of researchers to meet social or environmental needs; and so on.

To be successful, a business needs to adapt to changes in its business environment and, wherever possible, take advantage of them. Ultimately, the better business managers understand the environment in which they operate, the more likely they are to be successful, either in exploiting ever-changing opportunities or in avoiding potential disasters.

KEY IDEA 2

The behaviour and performance of firms is affected by the business environment. The business environment includes social/cultural (S), technological (T), economic (E), ethical (E), political (P), legal (L) and environmental (E) factors. The mnemonic STEEPLE can be used to remember these.

Although we will be primarily concentrating on the economic environment, we will also look at the other dimensions in PEST and STEEPLE analysis at various points in the book, especially where they impact on the economic environment. Examples include competition legislation, the effect of social factors on consumer demand, changing business attitudes towards pollution and social responsibility, and the effects of technology on costs.

> **Pause for thought**
>
> 1. *Under which heading of a STEEPLE analysis would you locate training and education?*
> 2. *Identify at least one factor under each of the STEEPLE headings facing an electricity generating company.*

Globalisation and the changing business environment

The external business environment of many firms is increasingly becoming a global one. International trade has grown much faster than countries' output, and so too has cross-border investment grown much faster than investment by companies within their home market. Many companies now see the world as their market and source their supplies from wherever in the world they can buy most cheaply. For some this simply means importing their inputs and exporting their products. Increasingly, however, companies set up their own factories or branches abroad.

The world economy is becoming much more integrated and interdependent. This process of **globalisation**, as it is called, has been hastened by various social/cultural, technological, economic, environmental, political and ethical factors (STEEPLE).

- Social/cultural factors include the growing influence of Western consumerist culture as companies such as Nike, Levi, McDonald's and Disney sell their products around the world.
- Technological factors include the communications revolution which, through the Internet, e-mails and computer linking, has allowed companies to communicate

> **Definition**
>
> **Globalisation**
> The process whereby the economies of the world are becoming increasingly integrated.

with their customers, suppliers and subsidiaries as easily halfway round the world as in the next town. Another key technological advance has been the reduction in size or weight of many products. The use of plastics rather than metals and the use of ever smaller and more powerful computer chips are just two examples of why it has become cheaper to transport goods long distances.

■ Economic factors include the globalisation of markets and production, as firms' activities spread across the globe. Markets around the world have tended to become more competitive as domestic firms increasingly face competition from abroad. Then at a macroeconomic level there is increasing convergence of economies, as interest rates, inflation rates and tax rates become more similar from one country to another.

■ Environmental and ethical factors include growing concerns worldwide over the burning of fossil fuels, the depletion of fish stocks, the pollution of land, sea and air, the cutting down of rainforests and the decline in biodiversity. Increasingly these are seen as global rather than national problems. Another example is the growing worldwide concern for human rights and decent employment conditions.

■ Political and legal factors include the development of trading blocs such as the EU and the North America Free Trade Association (NAFTA) (consisting of the USA, Canada and Mexico), international agreements to dismantle barriers to trade and the international movement of finance, the growing influence of international bodies such as the World Trade Organisation, the political power of the USA to influence global events, and meetings of the Group of Eight (G8) major industrialised countries – Canada, France, Germany, Italy, Japan, Russia, the UK and the USA – to agree on means of harmonising their policies.

> **Pause for thought**
>
> *Using the STEEPLE categories, in what ways has the USA influenced the business environment in countries outside the USA?*

We explore the microeconomic effects of globalisation in detail in Chapter 7 and the macroeconomic effects in Chapters 12 and 13.

Classifying industries

One of the most important elements of the economic environment of a firm is the nature of the industry in which it operates and the amount of competition it faces. Knowledge of the structure of an industry is therefore crucial if we are to understand business behaviour and its likely outcomes.

In this section we will consider how the production of different types of goods and services are classified and how firms are located into different industrial groups.

Classifying production

When analysing production it is common to distinguish three broad categories.

> **Definitions**
>
> **Primary production**
> The production and extraction of natural resources, plus agriculture.
>
> **Secondary production**
> The production from manufacturing and construction sectors of the economy.
>
> **Tertiary production**
> The production from the service sector of the economy.

■ **Primary production.** This refers to the production and extraction of natural resources such as minerals and sources of energy. It also includes output from agriculture.

■ **Secondary production.** This refers to the output of the manufacturing and construction sectors of the economy.

■ **Tertiary production.** This refers to the production of services, and includes a wide range of sectors such as finance, the leisure industry, retailing, tourism and transport.

Figures 1.3 and 1.4 show the share of output (or **gross domestic product (GDP)**) and employment of these three sectors in 1974 and 2008. They illustrate how the tertiary sector has expanded rapidly. In 2008, it contributed 76.8 per cent to total output (up from 54.9 per cent in 1974) and employed 80.8 per cent of all workers (up from 54.7 per cent). By contrast, the share of output and employment of the secondary sector has declined. In 2008, it accounted for only 20.1 per cent of output (down from 42.3 per cent in 1974) and 17.0 per cent of employment (down from 41.9 per cent).

Definition

Gross Domestic Product (GDP)
The value of output produced within the country over a 12-month period.

Figure 1.3 Output of industrial sectors (as % of GDP)

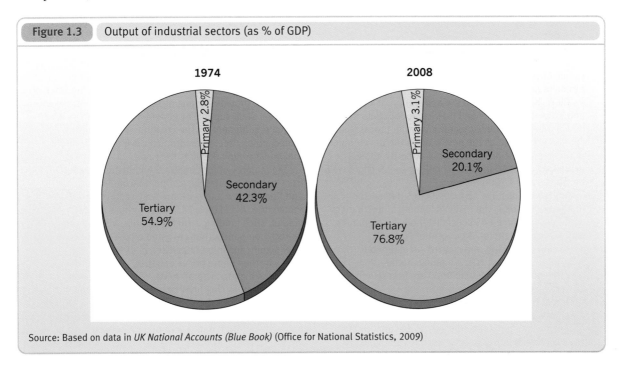

Source: Based on data in *UK National Accounts (Blue Book)* (Office for National Statistics, 2009)

Figure 1.4 Employment by industrial sector (% of total employees)

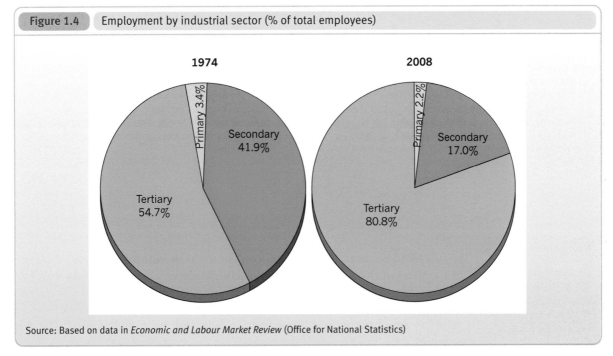

Source: Based on data in *Economic and Labour Market Review* (Office for National Statistics)

BOX 1.2   THE BIOTECHNOLOGY INDUSTRY

Its business environment

There are few areas of business that cause such controversy as biotechnology. It has generated new medicines, created pest-resistant crops, developed eco-friendly industrial processes and, through genetic mapping, is providing incalculable advances in gene therapy. These developments, however, have raised profound ethical issues. Many areas of biotechnology are uncontentious, but genetic modification and cloning have met with considerable public hostility, colouring many people's views of biotechnology in general.

Biotechnology refers to the application of knowledge about living organisms and their components to make new products and develop new industrial processes. For many it is seen as the next wave in the development of the knowledge-based economy. According to EU estimates, by 2010 the biotechnology sector could well be worth some €2000 billion.

In global terms, the USA dominates this sector. In Europe, the UK is the region's leading biotechnology centre. It has some 445 specialist biotech companies, which is equivalent to 23 per cent of Europe's biotechnology sector, and is worth an estimated €5100 million in revenue. It employs some 22 400 staff, of which some 9600 are in research and development.

The industry is dominated by small and medium-sized businesses. In the EU some 51 per cent of these are in human healthcare, 35 per cent in service biotechnology (bioprocessing, chemicals, bioinformatics and genomics), and 14 per cent in agriculture, industrial and environmental products. As in the USA, biotech firms are geographically clustered, forming industry networks around key universities and research institutes. In the UK, clusters can be found in Cambridge, Oxford and London. The link with universities and research institutes taps into the UK's strong science base.

In addition to such clustering, the biotech industry is well supported by the UK government and other charitable organisations such as the Wellcome Trust. Such support helps to fund what is a highly research-intensive sector. The UK government not

only provides finance, but encourages firms to form collaborative agreements, and through such collaboration hopes to encourage better management and use of the results that research generates. It also offers help for biotechnology business start-ups, and guidance on identifying and gaining financial support.

The EU too provides a range of resources to support business within the biotech sector. The EUREKA programme attempts to help create pan-EU partnerships, and the EU Seventh Framework Programme for research (2007–13) provides financing for such collaborative ventures. Such support by governments is seen as a crucial requirement for the creation of a successful biotechnology sector, as product development within the industry can take up to 12 years.

The majority of funding for the industry comes from 'venture capital' (investment by individuals and firms in new and possibly risky sectors). Even though the UK is Europe's largest venture capital market, such funding is highly volatile. Many of the biotech companies that are listed on the stock market, after significant share price rises in 1999 and 2000 then saw their share prices collapse, along with those of various high-tech companies. With a depressed stock market, raising finance becomes much more difficult.

Since 2000 there has been a period of consolidation in the sector. Both public and private biotech companies in Europe have shown an increase in merger and acquisition activity, with 350 mergers between 2000 and 2006. Most of these mergers have been between European firms (49 per cent), though there has also been a significant number of purchases of European companies by US firms (27 per cent).

 From the brief outline above, identify the social/cultural, technological, economic, ethical, political, legal and environmental dimensions shaping the biotechnology industry's business environment.

This trend is symptomatic of a process known as **deindustrialisation** – a decline in the share of the secondary sector in GDP. Many commentators argue that this process of deindustrialisation is inevitable and that the existence of a large and growing tertiary sector in the UK economy reflects its maturity. As people become richer, so a growing proportion of their consumption is of services such as leisure activities.

The classification of production into primary, secondary and tertiary allows us to consider broad changes in the economy. However, if we require a more comprehensive analysis of the structure of industry and its changes over time, then such a general classification is of little value. What we need to do is to classify firms into particular industries.

Pause for thought

Into which of the three sectors would you put (a) the fertiliser industry; (b) a marketing agency serving the electronics industry?

Classifying firms into industries

An **industry** refers to a group of firms that produce a particular category of product. Thus we could refer to the electrical goods industry, the tourism industry, the aircraft industry or the insurance industry. Industries can then be grouped together into broad **industrial sectors**, such as manufacturing industry, or mining and quarrying, or construction, or transport.

Classifying firms into industrial groupings and subgroupings has a number of purposes. It helps us to analyse various trends in the economy and to identify areas of growth and areas of decline. It helps to identify parts of the economy with specific needs, such as training or transport infrastructure. Perhaps most importantly, it helps economists and businesspeople to understand and predict the behaviour of firms that are in direct competition with each other. In such cases, however, it may be necessary to draw the boundaries of an industry quite narrowly.

To illustrate this, take the case of the vehicle industry. The vehicle industry produces cars, lorries, vans and coaches. The common characteristic of these vehicles is that they are self-propelled road transport vehicles. In other words, we could draw the boundaries of an industry in terms of the broad physical or technical characteristics of the products it produces. However, the problem with this type of categorisation is that these products may not be substitutes in an *economic* sense. If you need to buy a new vehicle to replace your car, you're hardly likely to consider buying a coach or a lorry! Lorries are not in competition with cars. If we are to group together products which are genuine competitors for each other, we will want to divide industries into more narrow categories. For example, we could classify cars into several groups according to size, price, function, engine capacity, etc.: e.g. luxury, saloon (of various size categories), estate (again of various size categories), seven seater and sports.

On the other hand, if we draw the boundaries of an industry too narrowly, we may end up ignoring the effects of competition from another closely related industry. For example, if we are to understand the pricing strategies of electricity supply companies in the household market, it might be better to focus on the whole domestic fuel industry.

Thus how narrowly or broadly we draw the boundaries of an industry depends on the purposes of our analysis. If the issue is one of *consumer demand* we might want to focus on the market and group goods together that are in direct competition with each other (e.g. particular types of car). If, however, the issue is one of *supply* – of *production* and *costs* – we might want to group products that are produced in the same companies (e.g. vehicle manufacturers).

Standard Industrial Classification

The formal system under which firms are grouped into industries is known as the **Standard Industrial Classification (SIC)**. The most recent revision in 2007 brings the UK and EU systems of industry classification largely into alignment with each other and this is a crucial part of monitoring business within the internal market. SIC

Definitions

Industry
A group of firms producing a particular product or service.

Industrial sector
A grouping of industries producing similar products or services.

Standard Industrial Classification (SIC)
The name given to the formal classification of firms into industries used by the government in order to collect data on business and industry trends.

Table 1.1	Standard Industrial Classification, 2007

Section

A	Agriculture, forestry and fishing
B	Mining and quarrying
C	Manufacturing
D	Electricity, gas, steam and air conditioning supply
E	Water supply, sewerage, waste management
F	Construction
G	Wholesale and retail trade, repair of motor vehicles
H	Transport and storage
I	Accommodation and food service activities
J	Information and communication
K	Financial and insurance activities
L	Real estate activities
M	Professional, scientific and technical activities
N	Administrative and support service activities
O	Public administration and defence; compulsory social security
P	Education
Q	Human health and social work activities
R	Arts, entertainment and recreation
S	Other service activities
T	Activities of households as employers, and producers of goods and services for own use
U	Extra-territorial organisations and bodies

Source: Based on *Standard Industrial Classification 2007* (Office for National Statistics)

Table 1.2	The classification of the manufacture of a tufted carpet

Section D	**Manufacturing (comprising divisions 10 to 33)**
Division 13	Manufacture of textiles
Group 13.9	Manufacture of other textiles
Class 13.93	Manufacture of carpets and rugs
Subclass 13.93/1	Manufacture of woven or tufted carpets and rugs

Source: Based on *Standard Industrial Classification 2007* (Office for National Statistics)

(2007) is divided into 21 sections (A–U), each representing a production classification (see Table 1.1). One of the sections (C) is in turn divided into divisions; divisions are divided into groups; groups are divided into classes; and some classes are further divided into subclasses. Table 1.2 gives an example of how a manufacturer of a tufted carpet would be classified according to this system.

In total, SIC (2007) has 21 sections, 88 divisions, 272 groups, 618 classes and 191 subclasses.

Changes in the structure of the UK economy

Given such a classification, how has UK industry changed over time? Table 1.3 shows the changes in output and employment of the various sectors identified by the SIC from 1980 to 2008.

You can see from the table that the biggest increases in output have been in the service industries (sectors G to S). If we examine the subsections and divisions within the SIC, we can get a more detailed picture of how the structure of industry has

Table 1.3	UK output and employment by industry in 2008 as a percentage of 1980	
Industry	**Output in 2008 as % of 1980**	**Employment in 2008 as % of 1980**
A	128	72
B	84	23
C	122	40
D, E	170	47
F	177	95
G, I	208	133
H, J	283	103
K–S	206	171

Source: Based on *UK Economic Accounts* and *Economic and Labour Market Review* (Office for National Statistics)

changed. For example, we find that the process of deindustrialisation has not been experienced by all manufacturing industries. Certain divisions, such as instrument and electrical engineering, are in fact among the fastest growing in the whole UK economy. It is the more traditional manufacturing industries, such as metal manufacturing, that have experienced a substantial decline.

In respect to employment, there are again substantial variations between divisions. Thus whereas the financial services sector has seen a rapid growth in employment, there has been a decline in employment in parts of the retail banking sector as a result of technological advances (fewer counter staff are required in high street banks, given the growth in cash machines, direct debits, debit cards, etc.). And whereas there has been a decline in employment in primary industries (such as agriculture and mining) and in traditional manufacturing industries (such as shipbuilding and metal manufacturing), there has been a growth in employment in some of the more 'high-tech' industries.

Structure–conduct–performance

As we shall see throughout the book, business performance is strongly influenced by the market structure within which the firm operates. This is known as the *structure–conduct–performance paradigm* and is illustrated in Figure 1.5.

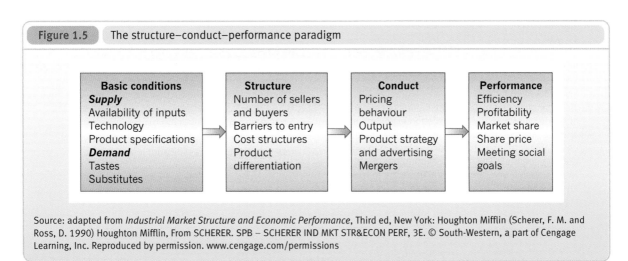

Figure 1.5   The structure–conduct–performance paradigm

Source: adapted from *Industrial Market Structure and Economic Performance*, Third ed, New York: Houghton Mifflin (Scherer, F. M. and Ross, D. 1990) Houghton Mifflin, From SCHERER. SPB – SCHERER IND MKT STR&ECON PERF, 3E. © South-Western, a part of Cengage Learning, Inc. Reproduced by permission. www.cengage.com/permissions

The structure of an industry depends on a number of basic conditions – some concerning production (supply) and some concerning consumer demand. For example, the availability of inputs and technology will influence whether it is more efficient to produce on a large scale or on a small scale. The nature of consumer tastes and whether there are close alternative products ('substitutes') available will influence the range of products produced and whether these should be highly differentiated from one producer to another or very similar across the industry. Such conditions will influence whether the market structure is highly competitive or dominated by just a few producers who are able to erect various barriers to the entry of competitors into the market.

A business operating in a highly competitive market structure will conduct its activities differently from a business in a market with relatively few competitors. For example, the more competitive the market, the more aggressive the business may have to be in order to sell its product and remain competitive. The less competitive the market structure, the greater the chance that collusion between producers might be the preferred strategy, as this reduces the excesses and uncertainties that outright competition might produce.

Such conduct will in turn influence how well businesses perform. Performance can be measured by several different indicators, such as efficiency in terms of cost per unit of output, current or long-term profitability market share or growth in market share, changes in share prices or share prices relative to those of other firms in the industry or to other firms in general, to name some of the most commonly used.

Throughout the book, we shall see how market structure affects business conduct, and how business conduct affects business performance. It would be wrong, however, to argue that business performance is totally shaped by external factors such as market structure. In fact, the internal aims, organisation and strategy of business may be very influential in determining success. We examine business strategy and the factors determining business competitiveness in Chapter 6.

> ## Pause for thought
>
> *Why is a firm facing little competition from rivals likely to have higher profits, but also higher costs, than a firm facing intense competition?*

Recap

1. The external business environment is commonly divided into four dimensions: political, economic, social and technological (PEST analysis); or into seven dimensions, where the additional three are environmental, legal and ethical (STEEPLE analysis).

2. The economic dimension of the business environment is divided into two: the microeconomic environment and the macroeconomic environment. The micro environment refers to the particular market in which the firm operates. The macro environment refers to the national and international economy in which all firms operate.

3. The process of globalisation has meant that for many companies their external environment has an important international dimension.

4. Production is divided into primary, secondary or tertiary sectors. The contribution to output of these different sectors of production has changed over time. Over the years the tertiary sector has grown and the secondary sector contracted.

5. Firms are classified into industries and industries into sectors. Such classification enables us to chart changes in industrial structure over time and to assess changing patterns of industrial concentration.

BOX 1.3   THE CHANGING NATURE OF BUSINESS

Knowledge rules

In the knowledge-driven economy, innovation has become central to achievement in the business world. With this growth in importance, organisations large and small have begun to re-evaluate their products, their services, even their corporate culture in the attempt to maintain their competitiveness in the global markets of today. The more forward-thinking companies have recognised that only through such root and branch reform can they hope to survive in the face of increasing competition.[1]

Knowledge is fundamental to economic success in many industries and, for most firms, key knowledge resides in skilled members of the workforce. The result is a market in knowledge, with those having the knowledge being able to command high salaries and often being 'head hunted'. The 'knowledge economy' is fundamentally changing the nature, organisation and practice of business.

The traditional limited company was based around five fundamental principles:

■ Individual workers needed the business and the income it provided more than the business needed them. After all, employers could always find alternative workers. If a worker loses his job, the opportunity cost to that worker is much bigger than the opportunity cost to the firm. As such, the company was the dominant partner in the employment relationship.

■ Employees tended to be full time and depended upon this work as their sole source of income.

■ The company was integrated, with a single management structure overseeing all the various stages of production. This was seen as the most efficient way to organise productive activity.

■ Suppliers, and especially manufacturers, had considerable power over the customer by controlling information about their product or service.

■ Technology relevant to an industry was often developed within the industry.

In more recent times, with the advent of the knowledge economy, the principles above have all but been turned on their heads.

■ The key resource in a knowledge economy is knowledge itself, and the workers that hold such knowledge. Without such workers, the company is unlikely to succeed. As such, the balance of power between the business and the specialist worker in today's economy is far more equal.

■ Even though the vast majority of employees still work full time, the development of the flexible firm, which has created more diversity in employment contracts, such as part-time and short-term contracts and consultancy, means that full-time work is not the only option. (We examine this in section 8.5.) The result is an increasing number of workers offering their services to business in non-conventional ways: e.g. as consultants.

■ As companies are increasingly supplying their products to a complex global marketplace, so many find they do not have the necessary expertise to do everything themselves – from production through all its stages, research and development, adapting their products to specific markets, to marketing and sales. With communication costs that have become insignificant, businesses are likely to be more efficient and flexible if they outsource and deintegrate. Not only are businesses outsourcing various stages of production, but many are employing specialist companies to provide key areas of management, such as HRM (human resource management) – hiring, firing, training, benefits, etc.

■ Whereas in the past businesses controlled information to their customers, today access to information via sources such as the Internet means that power is shifting towards the consumer.

■ Today, unlike in previous decades, technological developments are less specific to industries. Knowledge developments are diffused and cut across industry boundaries. What this means for businesses, in a knowledge-driven economy, is that they must look beyond their own industry if they are to develop and grow. We frequently see partnerships and joint ventures between businesses that cut across industry types and technology.

What is clear from the above is that the dynamics of the knowledge economy require a quite fundamental change in the nature of business. Organisationally it needs to be more flexible, helping it to respond to the ever-changing market conditions it faces. Successful companies draw upon their core competencies to achieve market advantage, and thus ultimately specialise in what they do best. For other parts of their business, companies must learn to work with others, either through outsourcing specialist tasks, or through more formal strategic partnerships.

Within this new business model the key assets are the specialist people in the organisation – its 'knowledge workers'.

 How is the development of the knowledge economy likely to affect the distribution of income in the economy? Will it become more equal or less equal? (Clue: think about the effects of specialist knowledge on the wage rates of specialists.)

[1] *Innovation Management and the Knowledge-driven Economy* European Commission, Directorate-general for Enterprise (ECSC-EC-EAEC Brussels-Luxembourg, 2004)

1.3 THE ECONOMIST'S APPROACH TO BUSINESS

Tackling the problem of scarcity

We have looked at various aspects of the business environment and the influences on firms. We have also looked at some of the economic problems that businesses face. But what contribution can economists make to the analysis of these problems and to recommending solutions?

To answer this question we need to go back one stage and ask what it is that economists study in general. What is it that makes a problem an *economic* problem? The answer is that there is one central problem faced by all individuals and all societies. This is the problem of *scarcity*.

We define **scarcity** as 'the excess of human wants over what can actually be produced'.

Of course, we do not all face the problem of scarcity to the same degree. A poor person unable to afford enough to eat or a decent place to live will hardly see it as a 'problem' that a rich person cannot afford a second Ferrari. But economists do not claim that we all face an *equal* problem of scarcity. The point is that people, both rich and poor, want more than they can have and this will cause them to behave in certain ways. Economics studies that behaviour.

Two of the key elements in satisfying wants are **consumption** and **production**. As far as consumption is concerned, economics studies how much the population spends; what the pattern of consumption is in the economy; and how much people buy of particular items. The business economist, in particular, studies consumer behaviour; how sensitive consumer demand is to changes in prices, advertising, fashion and other factors; and how the firm can seek to persuade the consumer to buy its products.

As far as production is concerned, economics studies how much the economy produces in total; what influences the rate of growth of production; and why the production of some goods increases and that of others falls. In order to produce, inputs (or 'factors of production') are required and we can identify three main types: human resources (labour); natural resources (land and raw materials); manufactured resources (capital). The business economist tends to focus on the role of the firm in the production process: what determines the output of individual businesses, the range of products they produce, the techniques and inputs they use and why, the amount they invest and how many workers they employ.

Demand and supply

We said that economics is concerned with consumption and production. Another way of looking at this is in terms of *demand* and *supply*. It is quite likely that you already knew that economics had something to do with demand and supply. In fact, demand and supply and the relationship between them lie at the very centre of economics. But what do we mean by the terms, and what is their relationship with the problem of scarcity?

Demand is related to wants. If goods and services were free, people would simply demand whatever they wanted. Such wants are virtually boundless: perhaps only limited by people's imagination. *Supply*, on the other hand, is limited. It is related to resources. The amount that firms can supply depends on the resources and technology available.

Definitions

Scarcity
The excess of human wants over what can actually be produced to fulfil these wants.

Consumption
The act of using goods and services to satisfy wants. This will normally involve purchasing the goods and services.

Production
The transformation of inputs into outputs by firms in order to earn profit (or meet some other objective).

Given the problem of scarcity, and that human wants exceed what can actually be produced, *potential* demands will exceed *potential* supplies. Society therefore has to find some way of dealing with this problem. Somehow it has to try to match demand and supply. This applies at the level of the economy overall: *aggregate* demand will need to be balanced against *aggregate* supply. In other words, total spending in the economy must balance total production. It also applies at the level of individual goods and services. The demand and supply of cabbages must balance, and so must the demand and supply of DVD recorders, books, cars and houses.

But if potential demand exceeds potential supply, how are *actual* demand and supply to be made equal? Either demand has to be curtailed, or supply has to be increased, or a combination of the two. Economics studies this process. It studies how demand adjusts to available supplies, and how supply adjusts to consumer demands.

The business economist studies the role of firms in this process: how they respond to demand, or, indeed, try to create demand for their products; how they combine their inputs to achieve output in the most efficient way; how they decide the amount to produce and the price to charge their customers; and how they make their investment decisions. In this, firms are affected by the economic environment in which they operate. In section 1.2, we saw how we can divide the economic environment into microeconomics and macro-economics. At a *microeconomic* level, firms are affected by their competitors, by technology and by changing consumer tastes. At a *macroeconomic* level they are affected by the state of the economy, by government macroeconomic policies and by the global economy.

> **Pause for thought**
>
> *When you go into a supermarket, the shelves are normally well stocked. Does this mean that the problem of scarcity has been solved?*

Making choices

Because resources are scarce, choices have to be made. There are three main categories of choice that must be made in any society.

■ *What* goods and services are going to be produced and in what quantities, given that there are not enough resources to produce all the things that people desire? How many cars, how much wheat, how much insurance, how many pop concerts, etc. will be produced?

■ *How* are things going to be produced, given that there is normally more than one way of producing things? Which resources will be used and in what quantities? What techniques of production are going to be adopted? Will cars be produced by robots or by assembly-line workers? Will electricity be produced from coal, oil, gas, nuclear fission, renewable resources or a mixture of these?

■ *For whom* are things going to be produced? In other words, how is the nation's income going to be distributed? After all, the higher your income, the more you can consume of the nation's output. What will be the wages of farm workers, printers, cleaners and accountants? How much will pensioners receive? How much profit will owners of private companies receive or state-owned industries make?

All societies have to make these choices, whether they are made by individuals, by business or by the government.

Choice and opportunity cost

Choice involves sacrifice. The more food you choose to buy, the less money you will have to spend on other goods. The more food a nation produces, the fewer resources there will be for producing other goods. In other words, the production or consumption of one thing involves the sacrifice of alternatives. This sacrifice of alternatives in the production (or consumption) of a good is known as its opportunity cost.

Definitions

Opportunity cost
The cost of any activity measured in terms of the best alternative foregone.

Rational choices
Choices that involve weighing up the benefit of any activity against its opportunity cost.

 KEY IDEA 3

Opportunity cost. The opportunity cost of something is what you give up to get it/do it. In other words, it is cost measured in terms of the best alternative foregone.

If a tailor can produce either 100 jackets or 200 pairs of trousers, then the opportunity cost of producing one jacket is the two pairs of trousers foregone. The opportunity cost of you buying this textbook is the new pair of jeans you also wanted that you have had to go without! The opportunity cost of working overtime is the leisure you sacrifice.

Rational choices

Economists often refer to **rational choices**. This simply means the weighing up of the *costs* and *benefits* of any activity, whether it be firms choosing what and how much to produce, workers choosing whether to take a particular job or to work extra hours, or consumers choosing what to buy.

Imagine you are doing your shopping in a supermarket and you want to buy some baked beans. Do you buy expensive Heinz baked beans or do you buy the cheap alternatives, such as the supermarket's own 'value' brand? To make a rational (i.e. sensible) decision, you will need to weigh up the costs and benefits of each alternative. Heinz baked beans may taste better and thus will give you a lot of enjoyment, but they have a high opportunity cost: because they are expensive, you will need to sacrifice quite a lot of consumption of other goods if you decide to buy them. If you buy the cheaper alternatives, although you may not enjoy them as much, you will have more money left over to buy other things: they have a lower opportunity cost.

Thus rational decision making, as far as consumers are concerned, involves choosing those items that give you the best value for money, i.e. the *greatest benefit relative to cost*. One person's choice of which product to buy may not be the same as another's, yet both decisions could still be rational.

The same principles apply to firms when deciding what to produce. For example, should a car firm open up another production line? A rational decision will again involve weighing up the benefits and costs. The benefits are the revenues that the firm will earn from selling the extra cars. The costs will include the extra labour costs, raw material costs, costs of component parts, etc. It will be profitable to open up the new production line only if the revenues earned exceed the costs entailed: in other words, if it earns a profit.

In the more complex situation of deciding which model of a mobile phone to produce, or how many of each model, the firm must weigh up the relative benefits and costs of each: i.e. it will want to produce the most profitable product mix.

Marginal costs and benefits

In economics we argue that rational choices involve weighing up **marginal costs** and **marginal benefits**. These are the costs and benefits of doing a little bit more or a little bit less of a given activity. They can be contrasted with the *total* costs and benefits of the activity. For example, the mobile phone manufacturer we were considering just now will weigh up the marginal costs and benefits of producing mobiles – in other words, it will compare the costs and revenue of producing *additional* mobile phones. If additional phones add more to the firm's revenue than to its costs, it will be profitable to produce them.

 KEY IDEA 4 Rational decision making involves weighing up the marginal benefit and marginal cost of any activity. If the marginal benefit exceeds the marginal cost, it is rational to do the activity (or to do more of it). If the marginal cost exceeds the marginal benefit, it is rational not to do it (or to do less of it).

Choices and the firm

All economic decisions made by firms involve choices. The business economist studies these choices and their results.

We will look at the choices of how much to produce, what price to charge the customer, how many inputs to use and in what combination, whether to expand the scale of the firm's operations, whether to merge with or take over another company, whether to diversify into other markets or whether to export. The right choices (in terms of best meeting the firm's objectives) will vary according to the type of market in which the firm operates, its predictions about future demand, its degree of market power, the actions and reactions of competitors, the degree and type of government intervention, the current tax regime, the availability of finance, and so on. In short, we will be studying the whole range of economic choices made by firms and in a number of different scenarios.

In all these cases, the owners of firms will want the best possible choices to be made, i.e. those choices that best meet the objectives of the firm. As we have seen, making the best choices will involve weighing up the marginal benefits against the marginal opportunity costs of each decision.

Pause for thought

1. *Assume that you have an assignment to write. How would you make a rational choice about whether to work on it today or whether to do something else?*
2. *Assume that you are looking for a job and are offered two. One is more pleasant to do, but pays less. How would you make a rational choice between the two jobs?*

Definitions

Marginal costs
The additional cost of doing a little bit more (or *1 unit* more if a unit can be measured) of an activity.

Marginal benefits
The additional benefits of doing a little bit more (or *1 unit* more if a unit can be measured) of an activity.

Recap

1. The central economic problem is that of scarcity. We have endless wants, but there is a limited supply of resources. As such, it is impossible to provide everybody with everything they want. Potential demands exceed potential supplies.

2. Because resources are scarce, people have to make choices. Society has to choose by some means or other *what* goods and services to produce, *how* to produce them and *for whom* to produce them. Microeconomics studies these choices.

3. Rational choices involve weighing up the marginal benefits of each activity against its marginal opportunity costs. If the marginal benefit exceeds the marginal cost, it is rational to choose to do more of that activity.

4. Businesses are constantly faced with choices: how much to produce, what inputs to use, what price to charge, how much to invest, etc. We will study these choices.

QUESTIONS

1. Compare and contrast the relative strengths and weaknesses of unlimited liability partnerships with public limited companies.

2. Explain why the business objectives of owners and managers are likely to diverge. How might owners attempt to ensure that managers act in their interests and not in the managers' own interests?

3. Assume you are a UK car manufacturer and are seeking to devise an appropriate business strategy. Conduct a STEEPLE analysis of the UK car industry and evaluate the various strategies that the business might pursue.

4. What is the Standard Industrial Classification (SIC)? In what ways might such a classification system be useful? Can you think of any limitations or problems such a system might have over time?

5. Outline the main determinants of business performance. Distinguish whether these are micro- or macroeconomic.

6. Virtually every good is scarce in the sense we have defined it. There are, however, a few exceptions. Under *certain circumstances*, water and air are not scarce. When and where might this be true for (a) water and (b) air? Why is it important to define

water and air very carefully before deciding whether they are scarce or abundant? Under circumstances where they are *not* scarce, would it be possible to charge for them?

7. Which of the following are macroeconomic issues, which are microeconomic ones and which could be either depending on the context?

   (a) Inflation.
   (b) Low wages in certain service industries.
   (c) The rate of exchange between the pound and the euro.
   (d) Why the price of cabbages fluctuates more than that of cars.
   (e) The rate of economic growth this year compared with last year.
   (f) The decline of traditional manufacturing industries.

8. Make a list of three things you did yesterday. What was the opportunity cost of each?

9. How would you use the principle of weighing up marginal costs and marginal benefits when deciding whether to (a) buy a new car; (b) work overtime? How would a firm use the same principle when deciding whether to (a) purchase a new machine; (b) offer overtime to existing workers?

Additional Part A case studies on the *Economics and the Business Environment* website (www.pearsoned.co.uk/sloman)

A.1 **The UK defence industry.** A PEST analysis of the changes in the defence industry in recent years.

A.2 **Downsizing and business reorganisation.** Many companies in recent years have 'downsized' their operations and focused on their core competences. This looks particularly at the case of IBM.

A.3 **Scarcity and abundance.** If scarcity is the central economic problem, is anything truly abundant?

A.4 **Global economics.** This examines how macroeconomics and microeconomics apply at the global level and identifies some key issues.

A.5 **The opportunity cost of studying at university.** An examination of the costs of being a student, using the concept of opportunity cost.

Websites relevant to Part A

Numbers and sections refer to websites listed in the Web Appendix and hotlinked from this book's website at **www.pearsoned.co.uk/sloman/**

■ For a tutorial on finding the best economics websites see site C8 (Internet for Economics).

■ For news articles relevant to Part A, see the Economics News Articles link from the book's website.

■ For general economics news sources see websites in section A of the Web Appendix at the end of the book, and particularly A1–9, 24, 35, 36, 41. See also A38, 39, 43 and 44 for links to newspapers worldwide.

■ For business news items, again see websites in section A of the Web Appendix at the end of the book, and particularly A1–3, 20–26, 35, 36.

■ For sources of economic and business data, see sites in section B and particularly B1–5, 27, 33, 34, 35 and 39.

■ For general sites for students of economics for business, see sites in section C and particularly C1–7.

■ For sites giving links to relevant economics and business websites, organised by topic, see sites I4, 7, 8, 11, 12, 17, 18.

■ For details on companies, see sites B2 and A3.

Markets, demand and supply

One of the key determinants of a business's profitability is the price of its product. In most cases, firms have the option of changing their prices in order to increase their profits. Sometimes, a cut in price might be in order, if the firm anticipates that this will generate a lot more sales. At other times, a firm may prefer to raise its prices, believing there will be little effect on sales – perhaps it believes that its competitors will follow suit; or, perhaps, there are no close competitors, making it easy for the firm to get away with raising prices.

For some firms, however, the prices of the products they sell are determined not by them, but by the market. The 'market' is what we call the coming together of buyers and sellers – whether it be a street market, a shop, an auction, a mail-order system, the Internet or whatever. Thus we talk about the market for apples, the market for oil, for cars, for houses, for televisions and so on. As we shall see, market prices are determined by the interaction of demand (buyers) and supply (sellers).

When the price is determined by the market, the firm is called a *price taker*. It has to accept the market price as given. If the firm attempts to raise the price above the market price, it will simply be unable to sell its product; it will lose all its sales to its competitors. Take the case of farmers selling wheat. They have to accept the price as dictated by the market. If individually they try to sell above the market price, no one will buy from them.

So how does a competitive market work? How are prices determined in such markets? We examine this question in Chapter 2.

In Chapter 3 we look more closely at demand and at firms' attempt to understand demand and the behaviour of consumers. Then in Chapter 4 we look at supply and ask how much a profit maximising firm will produce at the market price.

Business issues covered in this chapter

- How do markets operate?
- How are market prices determined and when are they likely to rise or fall?
- Under what circumstances do firms have to accept a price given by the market rather than being able to set the price themselves?
- What are the influences on consumer demand?
- How responsive is consumer demand to changes in the market price? How responsive is it to changes in consumer incomes and to the prices of competitor products?
- How is a firm's sales revenue affected by a change in price?
- What factors determine the amount of supply coming onto the market?
- How responsive is business output to changes in price?

The working of competitive markets

2 Chapter

BUSINESS IN A PERFECTLY COMPETITIVE MARKET 　　2.1

The price mechanism under perfect competition

In a **free market** individuals can make their own economic decisions. Consumers are free to decide what to buy with their incomes: free to make demand decisions. Firms are free to choose what to sell and what production methods to use: free to make supply decisions.

For simplicity we will examine the case of a **perfectly competitive market**. This is where both producers and consumers are too numerous to have any control over prices whatsoever: a situation where everyone is a **price taker**. In such markets, the demand and supply decisions of consumers and firms are transmitted to each other through their effect on *prices*: through the **price mechanism**. The prices that result are the prices that firms have to accept.

The working of the price mechanism

The price mechanism works as follows. Prices respond to *shortages* and *surpluses*. Shortages result in prices rising. Surpluses result in prices falling. Let us take each of these in turn.

If consumers decide they want more of a good at the current price (or if producers decide to cut back supply), demand will exceed supply. The resulting *shortage* will encourage sellers to *raise* the price of the good. This will act as an incentive for producers to supply more, since production of each unit will now be more profitable. On the other hand, it will discourage consumers from buying so much. *The price will continue rising until the shortage has thereby been eliminated.*

If, on the other hand, consumers decide they want less of a good at the current price (or if producers decide to produce more), supply will exceed demand. The resulting *surplus* will cause sellers to *reduce* the price of the good. This will act as a disincentive to producers, who will supply less, since production of each unit will now be less profitable. At the same time, it will encourage consumers to buy more. *The price will continue falling until the surplus has thereby been eliminated.*

This price, where demand equals supply, is called the **equilibrium price**. By **equilibrium** we mean a point of balance or a point of rest, i.e. a point towards which there is a tendency to move.

The same analysis can be applied to labour (and other input) markets, except that here the demand and supply roles are reversed. Firms are the demanders of labour. Individuals are the suppliers. If the demand for a particular type of labour exceeds its supply, the resulting shortage will drive up the wage rate (i.e. the price of labour) as employers compete with each other for labour. The rise in the wage

Definitions

Free market
One in which there is an absence of government intervention. Individual producers and consumers are free to make their own economic decisions.

Perfectly competitive market
A market in which all producers and consumers of the product are price takers. (There are other features of a perfectly competitive market; these are examined in Chapter 4.)

Price taker
A person or firm with no power to be able to influence the market price.

Price mechanism
The system in a market economy whereby changes in price, in response to changes in demand and supply, have the effect of making demand equal to supply.

Equilibrium price
The price where the quantity demanded equals the quantity supplied; the price where there is no shortage or surplus.

rate will have the effect of curbing firms' demand for that type of labour and encouraging more workers to take up that type of job. Wages will continue rising until demand equals supply, until the shortage is eliminated.

Likewise, if there is a surplus of a particular type of labour, the wage will fall until demand equals supply. As with price, the wage rate where the demand for labour equals the supply is known as the *equilibrium* wage rate.

The response of demand and supply to changes in price illustrates a very important feature of how economies work:

People respond to incentives, such as changes in prices or wages. It is important, therefore, that incentives are appropriate and have the desired effect.

The effect of changes in demand and supply

How will the price mechanism respond to changes in consumer demand or producer supply? After all, the pattern of consumer demand changes over time. For example, people may decide they want more holidays abroad and fewer at home. Likewise the pattern of supply also changes. For example, changes in technology may allow the mass production of microchips at lower cost, while the production of hand-built furniture becomes relatively expensive.

A change in demand

A rise in demand causes a shortage and hence a rise in price. This then acts as an *incentive* for businesses to supply more: it is profitable for them to do so. They divert resources from products with lower prices relative to costs (and hence lower profits) to the product that has gone up in price and hence is now more profitable.

A fall in demand causes a surplus and hence a fall in price. This then acts as an incentive for businesses to supply less. These goods are now less profitable to produce.

A change in supply

A rise in supply (e.g. as a result of improved technology) causes a surplus and hence a fall in price. This then acts as an incentive for consumers to buy more. A fall in supply causes a rise in price. This then acts as an incentive for consumers to buy less.

Changes in demand or supply cause markets to adjust. Whenever such changes occur, the resulting 'disequilibrium' will bring an automatic change in prices, thereby restoring 'equilibrium' (i.e. a balance of demand and supply).

Let us now turn to examine each side of the market – demand and supply – in more detail.

Recap

1. A firm is greatly affected by its market environment. The more competitive the market, the less discretion the firm has in determining its price. In the extreme case of a perfect market, the price is entirely outside the firm's control. The price is determined by demand and supply in the market, and the firm has to accept this price: the firm is a price taker.

2. In a perfect market, price changes act as the mechanism whereby demand and supply are balanced.

3. If there is a shortage, price will rise until the shortage is eliminated. If there is a surplus, price will fall until that is eliminated.

DEMAND   2.2

The relationship between demand and price

The headlines announce, 'Major crop failures in Brazil and East Africa: coffee prices soar.' Shortly afterwards you find that coffee prices have doubled in the shops. What do you do? Presumably you will cut back on the amount of coffee you drink. Perhaps you will reduce it from, say, six cups per day to two. Perhaps you will give up drinking coffee altogether.

This is simply an illustration of the general relationship between price and consumption: *when the price of a good rises, the quantity demanded will fall.* This relationship is known as the **law of demand** and there are two reasons behind it:

- People will feel poorer. They will not be able to afford to buy so much of the good with their money. The purchasing power of their income (their *real income*) has fallen. This is called the **income effect** of a price rise.
- The good is now dearer relative to other goods. People will thus switch to alternative or 'substitute' goods. This is called the **substitution effect** of a price rise.

Have you ever walked into a shop, seen the price of a good and said, 'I can't afford that; I'll buy something else'? This phrase perfectly captures the above effects of a change in price on the quantity demanded.

Similarly, when the price of a good falls, the quantity demanded will rise. People can afford to buy more (the income effect), and they will switch away from consuming alternative goods (the substitution effect).

Therefore, returning to our example of the increase in the price of coffee, we will not be able to afford to buy as much as before (the income effect), and we will probably drink more tea, cocoa, fruit juices or even water instead (the substitution effect).

A word of warning: be careful about the meaning of the words **quantity demanded**. They refer to the amount consumers are willing and able to purchase at a given price over a given time period (e.g. a week, or a month, or a year). They do *not* refer to what people would simply *like* to consume. You might like to own a luxury yacht, but your demand for luxury yachts will almost certainly be zero at current prices!

The demand curve

Consider the hypothetical data in Table 2.1. The table shows how many kilos of potatoes per month would be purchased at various prices.

Definitions

Law of demand
The quantity of a good demanded per period of time will fall as the price rises and rise as the price falls, other things being equal (*ceteris paribus*).

Income effect
The effect of a change in price on quantity demanded arising from the consumer becoming better or worse off as a result of the price change.

Substitution effect
The effect of a change in price on quantity demanded arising from the consumer switching to or from alternative (substitute) products.

Quantity demanded
The amount of a good that a consumer is willing and able to buy at a given price over a given period of time.

Definitions

Demand schedule for an individual

A table showing the different quantities of a good that a person is willing and able to buy at various prices over a given period of time.

Market demand schedule

A table showing the different total quantities of a good that consumers are willing and able to buy at various prices over a given period of time.

Demand curve

A graph showing the relationship between the price of a good and the quantity of the good demanded over a given time period. Price is measured on the vertical axis; quantity demanded is measured on the horizontal axis. A demand curve can be for an individual consumer or a group of consumers, or more usually for the whole market.

Table 2.1   The demand for potatoes (monthly)

	Price (pence per kg) (1)	Tracey's demand (kg) (2)	Darren's demand (kg) (3)	Total market demand (tonnes: 000s) (4)
A	20	28	16	700
B	40	15	11	500
C	60	5	9	350
D	80	1	7	200
E	100	0	6	100

Columns (2) and (3) show the **demand schedules** for two individuals, Tracey and Darren. Column (4), by contrast, shows the total **market demand schedule**. This is the total demand by all consumers. To obtain the market demand schedule for potatoes, we simply add up the quantities demanded at each price by *all* consumers, i.e. Tracey, Darren and everyone else who demands potatoes. Notice that we are talking about demand *over a period of time* (not at a *point* in time). Thus we would talk about daily demand or weekly demand or annual demand or whatever.

The demand schedule can be represented graphically as a **demand curve**. Figure 2.1 shows the market demand curve for potatoes corresponding to the schedule in Table 2.1. The price of potatoes is plotted on the vertical axis. The quantity demanded is plotted on the horizontal axis.

Point *E* shows that at a price of 100p per kilo, 100 000 tonnes of potatoes are demanded each month. When the price falls to 80p we move down the curve to point *D*. This shows that the quantity demanded has now risen to 200 000 tonnes per month. Similarly, if price falls to 60p, we move down the curve again to point *C*: 350 000 tonnes are now demanded. The five points on the graph (*A–E*) correspond

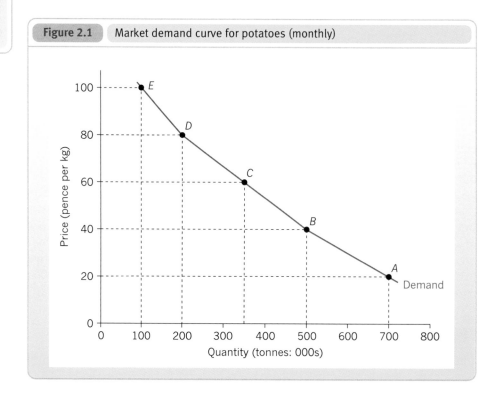

Figure 2.1   Market demand curve for potatoes (monthly)

to the figures in columns (1) and (4) of Table 2.1. The graph also enables us to read off the likely quantities demanded at prices other than those in the table.

A demand curve could also be drawn for an individual consumer. As with market demand curves, individuals' demand curves generally slope downward from left to right: the lower the price of the product, the more a person is likely to buy.

Two points should be noted at this stage:

- In textbooks, demand curves (and other curves too) are only occasionally used to plot specific data. More frequently they are used to illustrate general theoretical arguments. In such cases the axes will simply be price and quantity, with the units unspecified.
- The term 'curve' is used even when the graph is a straight line! In fact, when using demand curves to illustrate arguments we frequently draw them as straight lines – it's easier.

Other determinants of demand

Price is not the only factor that determines how much of a good people will buy. Demand is also affected by the following:

Tastes. The more desirable people find the good, the more they will demand. Tastes are affected by advertising, by fashion, by observing other consumers, by considerations of health and by the experiences from consuming the good on previous occasions.

The number and price of substitute goods (i.e. competitive goods). The higher the price of **substitute goods**, the higher will be the demand for this good as people switch from the substitutes. For example, the demand for coffee will depend on the price of tea. If tea goes up in price, the demand for coffee will rise.

The number and price of complementary goods. **Complementary goods** are those that are consumed together: coffee and milk, cars and petrol, shoes and polish. The higher the price of complementary goods, the fewer of them will be bought and hence the less the demand for this good. For example, the demand for electricity depends on the price of electrical goods. If the price of electrical goods goes up, so that fewer are bought, the demand for electricity will fall.

Income. As people's incomes rise, their demand for most goods will rise. Such goods are called **normal goods**. There are exceptions to this general rule, however. As people get richer, they spend less on **inferior goods**, such as cheap margarine, and switch to better quality goods.

Expectations of future price changes. If people think that prices are going to rise in the future, they are likely to buy more now before the price does go up and so demand will increase. Think about the housing market. If people expect the price of houses to increase, they try to buy now before that happens.

> ### Pause for thought
>
> *Referring to Figure 2.1, what tonnage of potatoes would be purchased per month if the price were 70p per kg?*

> ### Definitions
>
> **Substitute goods**
> A pair of goods which are considered by consumers to be alternatives to each other. As the price of one goes up, the demand for the other rises.
>
> **Complementary goods**
> A pair of goods consumed together. As the price of one goes up, the demand for both goods will fall.
>
> **Normal goods**
> Goods whose demand rises as people's incomes rise. They have a positive income elasticity of demand. Luxury goods will have a higher income elasticity of demand than more basic goods.
>
> **Inferior goods**
> Goods whose demand falls as people's incomes rise. Such goods have a negative income elasticity of demand.

 KEY IDEA 7 **People's actions are influenced by their expectations.** People respond not just to what is happening now (such as a change in price), but to what they anticipate will happen in the future.

Movements along and shifts in the demand curve

A demand curve is constructed on the assumption that 'other things remain equal' (*ceteris paribus*). In other words, it is assumed that none of the determinants of demand, other than price, change. The effect of a change in price is then simply illustrated by a movement along the demand curve, e.g. from point *B* to point *D* in Figure 2.1 when price rises from 40p to 80p per kilo.

> **KEY IDEA 8**
>
> **Partial analysis: other things remaining equal (ceteris paribus).** In economics it is common to look at just one determinant of a variable such as demand or supply and see what happens when the determinant changes. For example, if price is taken as the determinant of demand, we can see what happens to quantity demanded as price changes. In the meantime, we have to assume that other determinants remain unchanged. This is known as the 'other things being equal' assumption (or, using the Latin, the '*ceteris paribus*' assumption). Once we have seen how our chosen determinant affects our variable, we can then see what happens when another determinant changes, and then another, and so on.

Definitions

Change in demand
The term used for a shift in the demand curve. It occurs when a determinant of demand *other* than price changes.

Change in the quantity demanded
The term used for a movement along the demand curve to a new point. It occurs when there is a change in price.

What happens, then, when one of these other determinants changes? The answer is that we have to construct a whole new demand curve; the curve shifts. If a change in one of the other determinants causes demand to rise – say, income rises – the whole curve will shift to the right, assuming we have a normal good. This shows that at each price more will be demanded than before. Thus in Figure 2.2 at a price of P, a quantity of Q_0 was originally demanded. But now, after the increase in demand, Q_1 is demanded. (Note that D_1 is not necessarily parallel to D_0.)

If a change in a determinant other than price causes demand to fall, the whole curve will shift to the left. Less will be demanded at each price than before.

To distinguish between shifts in and movements along demand curves, it is usual to distinguish between a change in *demand* and a change in the *quantity demanded*. A shift in demand is referred to as a **change in demand**, whereas a movement along the demand curve, as a result of a change in price, is referred to as a **change in the quantity demanded**.

Pause for thought

The price of cinema tickets rises and yet it is observed that cinema attendance increases. Does this mean that the demand for cinema tickets is upward sloping?

Recap

1. When the price of a good rises, the quantity demanded per period of time will fall. This is known as the 'law of demand'. It applies both to individuals' demand and to the whole market demand.

2. The law of demand is explained by the income and substitution effects of a price change.

3. The relationship between price and quantity demanded per period of time can be shown in a table (or 'schedule') or as a graph. On the graph, price is plotted on the vertical axis and quantity demanded per period of time on the horizontal axis. The resulting demand curve is downward sloping (negatively sloped).

4. Other determinants of demand include tastes, the number and price of substitute or complementary goods, income and expectations of future price changes. You are a consumer, so anything that influences the goods you buy and how much of them, will be a determinant of demand.

5. If price changes, the effect is shown by a movement along the demand curve. We call this effect 'a change in the quantity demanded'.

6. If any other determinant of demand changes, the whole curve will shift. We call this effect 'a change in demand'. A rightward shift represents an increase in demand; a leftward shift represents a decrease in demand.

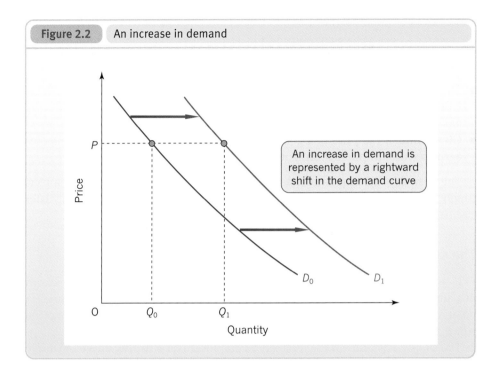

Figure 2.2   An increase in demand

An increase in demand is represented by a rightward shift in the demand curve

SUPPLY   2.3

Supply and price

Imagine you are a farmer deciding what to do with your land. Part of your land is in a fertile valley. Part is on a hillside where the soil is poor. Perhaps, then, you will consider growing vegetables in the valley and keeping sheep on the hillside.

Your decision will depend to a large extent on the price that various vegetables will fetch in the market, and likewise the price you can expect to get from sheep and wool. As far as the valley is concerned, you will plant the vegetables that give the best return. If, for example, the price of potatoes is high, you will probably use a lot of the valley for growing potatoes. If the price gets higher, you may well use the whole of the valley, perhaps being prepared to run the risk of potato disease. If the price is very high indeed, you may even consider growing potatoes on the hillside, even though the yield per hectare is much lower there. In other words, the higher the price of a particular crop, the more you are likely to grow in preference to other crops.

This illustrates the general relationship between supply and price: *when the price of a good rises, the quantity supplied will also rise*. There are three reasons for this.

■ As firms supply more, they are likely to find that, beyond a certain level of output, costs rise more and more rapidly. Only if price rises will it be worth producing more and incurring these higher costs.

In the case of the farm we have just considered, once potatoes have to be grown on the hillside, the costs of producing them will increase. Also if the land has to be used more intensively, say by the use of more and more fertilisers, again the cost of producing extra potatoes is likely to rise quite rapidly. It is the same for manufacturers. Beyond a certain level of output, costs are likely to rise rapidly as workers have to be paid overtime and as machines approach their full capacity. If higher output involves higher costs of production, producers will need to get a higher price if they are to be persuaded to produce extra output.

■ The higher the price of the good, the more profitable it becomes to produce. Firms will thus be encouraged to produce more of it by switching from producing less profitable goods.

■ Given time, if the price of a good remains high, new producers will be encouraged to set up in production. Total market supply thus rises.

The first two determinants affect supply in the short run. The third affects supply in the long run. We distinguish between short-run and long-run supply later (see page 58).

The supply curve

The amount that producers would like to supply at various prices can be shown in a **supply schedule**. Table 2.2 shows a hypothetical monthly supply schedule for potatoes, both for an individual farmer (farmer X) and for all farmers together (the whole market).

The supply schedule can be represented graphically as a **supply curve**. A supply curve may be an individual firm's supply curve or a market supply curve (i.e. that of the whole industry).

Figure 2.3 shows the *market* supply curve of potatoes. As with demand curves, price is plotted on the vertical axis and quantity on the horizontal axis. Each of the points *a–e* corresponds to a figure in Table 2.2. Thus for example, a price rise from 60p per kilogram to 80p per kilogram causes a movement along the supply curve from point *c* to point *d*: total market supply rises from 350 000 tonnes per month to 530 000 tonnes per month.

Not all supply curves are upward sloping (positively sloped). Sometimes they are vertical, or horizontal, or even downward sloping. This depends largely on the time period over which the response of firms to price changes is considered. (This question is examined on page 58.)

Other determinants of supply

As with demand, supply is not determined simply by price. The other determinants of supply are as follows.

Table 2.2	The supply of potatoes (monthly)		
	Price of potatoes (pence per kg)	Farmer X's supply (tonnes)	Total market supply (tonnes: 000s)
a	20	50	100
b	40	70	200
c	60	100	350
d	80	120	530
e	100	130	700

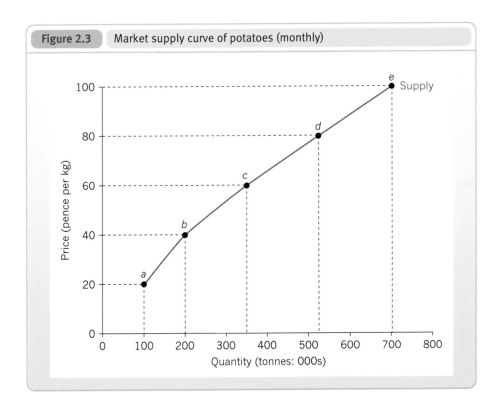

Figure 2.3   Market supply curve of potatoes (monthly)

The costs of production. The higher the costs of production, the less profit will be made at any price. As costs rise, firms will cut back on production, probably switching to alternative products whose costs have not risen so much. As such, less will be supplied at any price. Costs could change as a result of changing input prices, changes in technology, organisational changes within the firm, changes in taxation, etc.

The profitability of alternative products (substitutes in supply). If some alternative product (a **substitute in supply**) becomes more profitable to supply than before, producers are likely to switch from the first good to this alternative. Supply of the first good falls. Substitutes in supply are likely to become more profitable if their price rises or their cost of production falls. For example, if the price of carrots goes up, or the cost of producing carrots comes down, farmers may decide to cut down potato production in order to produce more carrots. The supply of potatoes is there-fore likely to fall.

The profitability of goods in joint supply. Sometimes when one good is produced, another good is also produced at the same time. These are said to be **goods in joint supply.** An example is the refining of crude oil to produce petrol. Other grade fuels will be produced as well, such as diesel and paraffin. If more petrol is produced, due to a rise in demand, then the supply of these other fuels will rise too.

Nature, 'random shocks' and other unpredictable events. In this category we would include the weather and diseases affecting farm output, wars affecting the supply of imported raw materials, the breakdown of machinery, industrial disputes, earthquakes, floods, fire, and so on.

The aims of producers. A profit-maximising firm will supply a different quantity from a firm that has a different aim, such as maximising sales. We considered the aims of the firm in section 1.1.

Definitions

Substitutes in supply
These are two goods where an increased production of one means diverting resources away from producing the other.

Goods in joint supply
These are two goods where the production of more of one leads to the production of more of the other.

Expectations of future price changes. If price is expected to rise, producers may temporarily reduce the amount they sell. Instead they are likely to build up their stocks and only release them on to the market when the price does rise. At the same time they may plan to produce more, by installing new machines, or taking on more labour, so that they can be ready to supply more when the price has risen. Consider the housing market again. If you are thinking of selling your house, but expect that house prices will soon be higher, it would be rational to wait and put your house on the market only when prices have risen.

Movements along and shifts in the supply curve

The principle here is the same as with demand curves. The effect of a change in price is illustrated by a movement along the supply curve: e.g. from point *d* to point *e* in Figure 2.3 when price rises from 80p to 100p. Quantity supplied rises from 530 000 to 700 000 tonnes.

If any other determinant of supply changes, the whole supply curve will shift. A rightward shift illustrates an increase in supply. More will be supplied at any given price. A leftward shift illustrates a decrease in supply. A movement along a supply curve is often referred to as a **change in the quantity supplied**, whereas a shift in the supply curve is simply referred to as a **change in supply**.

Recap

1. When the price of a good rises, the quantity supplied per period of time will usually also rise. This applies both to individual producers' supply and to the whole market supply.

2. There are two reasons in the short run why a higher price encourages producers to supply more: (a) they are now willing to incur the higher costs per unit associated with producing more; (b) they will switch to producing this product and away from now less profitable ones. In the long run there is a third reason: new producers will be attracted into the market.

3. The relationship between price and quantity supplied per period of time can be shown in a table (or schedule) or as a graph. As with a demand curve, price is plotted on the vertical axis and quantity per period

of time on the horizontal axis. The resulting supply curve is upward sloping (positively sloped).

4. Other determinants of supply include the costs of production, the profitability of alternative products, the profitability of goods in joint supply, random shocks and expectations of future price changes.

5. If price changes, the effect is shown by a movement along the supply curve. We call this effect 'a change in the quantity supplied'.

6. If any determinant *other* than price changes, the effect is shown by a shift in the whole supply curve. We call this effect 'a change in supply'. A rightward shift represents an increase in supply; a leftward shift represents a decrease in supply.

2.4 PRICE AND OUTPUT DETERMINATION

Equilibrium price and output

We can now combine our analysis of demand and supply. This will show how the actual price of a product and the actual quantity bought and sold are determined in a free and competitive market.

Let us return to the example of the market demand and market supply of potatoes, and use the data from Tables 2.1 and 2.2. These figures are given again in Table 2.3.

Table 2.3	The market demand and supply of potatoes (monthly)	
Price of potatoes (pence per kg)	Total market demand (tonnes: 000s)	Total market supply (tonnes: 000s)
20	700 (A)	100 (a)
40	500 (B)	200 (b)
60	350 (C)	350 (c)
80	200 (D)	530 (d)
100	100 (E)	700 (e)

What will be the price and output that actually prevail? If the price started at 20p per kilogram, demand would exceed supply by 600 000 tonnes (A – a). Consumers would be unable to obtain all they wanted and would thus be willing to pay a higher price. Producers, unable or unwilling to supply enough to meet the demand, will be only too happy to accept a higher price. The effect of the shortage, then, will be to drive up the price. The same would happen at a price of 40p per kilogram. There would still be a shortage; price would still rise. But as the price rises, the quantity demanded falls and the quantity supplied rises. The shortage is progressively eliminated.

What would happen if the price started at a much higher level: say at 100p per kilogram? In this case supply would exceed demand by 600 000 tonnes (e – E). The effect of this surplus would be to drive down the price as farmers competed against each other to sell their excess supplies. The same would happen at a price of 80p per kilogram. There would still be a surplus; price would still fall.

In fact, only one price is sustainable. This is the price where demand equals supply: namely 60p per kilogram, where both demand and supply are 350 000 tonnes. When supply matches demand the market is said to **clear**. There is no shortage and no surplus.

As we saw on page 31 (the first page of Chapter 2), the price where demand equals supply is called the *equilibrium price*. In Table 2.3, if the price starts at other than 60p per kilogram, there will be a tendency for it to move towards 60p. The equilibrium price is the only price at which producers' and consumers' wishes are mutually reconciled, where the producers' plans to supply exactly match the consumers' plans to buy.

KEY IDEA 9 Equilibrium is the point where conflicting interests are balanced. Only at this point is the amount that demanders are willing to purchase the same as the amount that suppliers are willing to supply. It is a point which will be automatically reached in a free market through the operation of the price mechanism.

Demand and supply curves

The determination of equilibrium price and output can be shown using demand and supply curves. Equilibrium is where the two curves intersect.

Figure 2.4 shows the demand and supply curves of potatoes corresponding to the data in Table 2.3. Equilibrium price is P_e (60p) and equilibrium quantity is Q_e (350 000 tonnes).

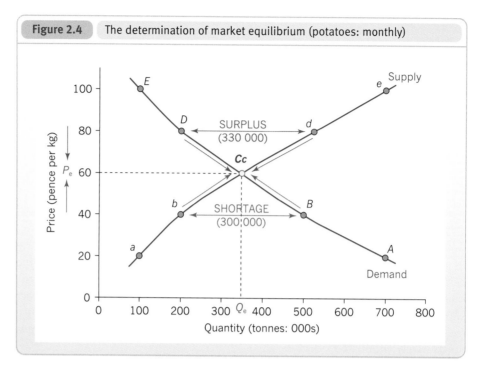

Figure 2.4   The determination of market equilibrium (potatoes: monthly)

At any price above 60p, there would be a surplus. Thus at 80p there is a surplus of 330 000 tonnes ($d - D$). More is supplied than consumers are willing and able to purchase at that price. Thus a price of 80p fails to clear the market. Price will fall to the equilibrium price of 60p. As it does so, there will be a movement along the demand curve from point D to point C, and a movement along the supply curve from point d to point c.

At any price below 60p, there would be a shortage. Thus at 40p there is a shortage of 300 000 tonnes ($B - b$). Price will rise to 60p. This will cause a movement along the supply curve from point b to point c and along the demand curve from point B to point C.

Point Cc is the equilibrium: where demand equals supply.

Movement to a new equilibrium

The equilibrium price will remain unchanged only so long as the demand and supply curves remain unchanged. If either of the curves shifts, a new equilibrium will be formed.

A change in demand

If one of the determinants of demand changes (other than price), the whole demand curve will shift. This will lead to a movement *along* the *supply* curve to the new intersection point.

For example, in Figure 2.5(a), if a rise in consumer incomes led to the demand curve shifting to D_2, there would be a shortage of $h - g$ at the original price P_{e1}. This would cause price to rise to the new equilibrium P_{e2}. As it did so there would be a movement along the supply curve from point g to point i, and along the new demand curve (D_2) from point h to point i. Equilibrium quantity would rise from Q_{e1} to Q_{e2}.

> **Pause for thought**
>
> *What would happen to price and quantity if the demand curve shifted to the left? Draw a diagram to illustrate your answer.*

| **Figure 2.5** | The effect of a shift in the demand or supply curve: (a) effect of a shift in the demand curve; (b) effect of a shift in the supply curve |

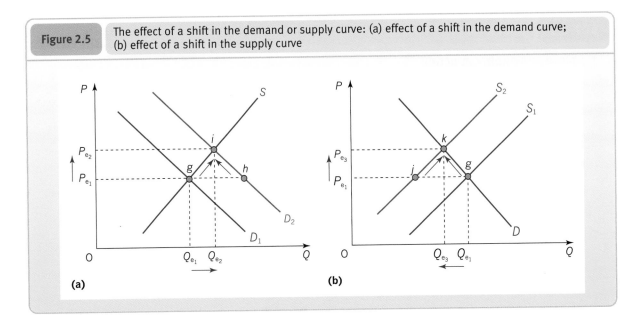

(a)

(b)

The effect of the shift in demand, therefore, has been a movement *along* the supply curve from the old equilibrium to the new: from point *g* to point *i*.

A change in supply

Likewise, if one of the determinants of supply changes (other than price), the whole supply curve will shift. This will lead to a movement *along* the *demand* curve to the new intersection point.

For example, in Figure 2.5(b), if costs of production rose, the supply curve would shift to the left: to S_2. There would be a shortage of $g - j$ at the old price of P_{e1}. Price would rise from P_{e1} to P_{e3}. Quantity would fall from Q_{e1} to Q_{e3}. In other words, there would be a movement along the demand curve from point *g* to point *k*, and along the new supply curve (S_2) from point *j* to point *k*. To summarise: a shift in one curve leads to a movement along the other curve to the new inter-section point.

Sometimes a number of determinants might change. This may lead to a shift in *both* curves. When this happens, equilibrium simply moves from the point where the old curves intersected to the point where the new ones intersect. If this is the case, it is a good idea to consider each effect separately, rather than immediately trying to find the new equilibrium.

> **Pause for thought**
>
> *Referring to Figure 2.4 and Table 2.3, what would happen to the equilibrium price of potatoes if there were a good harvest and the monthly supply of potatoes rose by 300 000 tonnes at all prices?*

Recap

1. If the demand for a good exceeds the supply, there will be a shortage. This will result in a rise in the price of the good.

2. If the supply of a good exceeds the demand, there will be a surplus. This will result in a fall in the price.

3. Price will settle at the equilibrium. The equilibrium price is the one that clears the market, the price where demand equals supply. This is shown in a demand and supply diagram by the point where the two curves intersect.

4. If the demand or supply curves shift, this will lead either to a shortage or to a surplus. Price will therefore either rise or fall until a new equilibrium is reached at the position where the supply and demand curves *now* intersect.

BOX 2.1   STOCK MARKET PRICES

Demand and supply in action

Firms that are quoted on the stock market (see pages 176–7) can raise money by issuing shares. These are sold on the 'primary stock market'. People who own the shares receive a 'dividend' on them, normally paid six-monthly. The amount varies with the profitability of the company.

People or institutions that buy these shares, however, may not wish to hold on to them forever. This is where the 'secondary stock market' comes in. It is where existing shares are bought and sold. There are stock markets, primary and secondary, in all the major countries of the world.

There are more than 3000 companies whose shares and other securities are listed on the London Stock Exchange and trading in them takes place each Monday to Friday (excluding Bank Holidays). The prices of shares depend on demand and supply. For example, if the demand for Tesco shares at any one time exceeds the supply on offer, the price will rise until demand and supply are equal. Share prices fluctuate throughout the trading day and sometimes price changes can be substantial.

To give an overall impression of share price movements, stock exchanges publish share price indices. The best known one in the UK is the FTSE 100, which stands for the 'Financial Times Stock Exchange' index of the 100 largest companies' shares. The index represents an average price of these 100 shares. The chart shows movements in the FTSE 100 from 1995 to 2010. The index was first calculated on 3 January 1984 with a base level of 1000 points. It reached a peak of 6930 points on 30 December 1999 and fell to 3287 on 12 March 2003. It then rose again, reaching a high of 6730 on 12 October 2007, but fell to 3781 on 21 November 2008.

But what causes share prices to change? Why were they so high in 1999, but only just over half that value just three years later? Why did they almost double in value from 2003 to 2007, but then plummet in 2008, only to rise sharply in 2009/10? The answer lies in the determinants of the demand and supply of shares.

Demand

There are five main factors that affect the demand for shares.

The dividend yield. This is the dividend on a share as a percentage of its price. The higher the dividend yields on shares the more attractive they are as a form of saving.

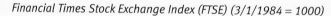

Financial Times Stock Exchange Index (FTSE) (3/1/1984 = 1000)

One of the main explanations of rising stock market prices from 2003 to 2007 was high profits and resulting high dividends.

The price of and/or return on substitutes. The main substitutes for shares in specific companies are other shares. Thus if, in comparison with other shares, Tesco shares are expected to pay high dividends relative to the share price, people will buy Tesco shares. As far as shares in general are concerned, the main substitutes are other forms of saving. Thus if the interest rate on savings accounts in banks and building societies fell, people with such accounts would be tempted to take their money out and buy shares instead.

Another major substitute is property. If house prices rise rapidly, as they did from the late 1990s to 2007, this will reduce the demand for shares as many people switch to buying property in anticipation of even higher prices. If house prices level off, as they did in 2005/6, this makes shares relatively more attractive as an investment and can boost the demand for them.

Incomes. If the economy is growing rapidly and people's incomes are thus rising rapidly, they are likely to buy more shares. Thus in the mid to late 1990s, when UK incomes were rising at an average annual rate of over 3 per cent, share prices rose rapidly (see chart). As growth rates fell in the early 2000s, so share prices fell. But as growth rates then picked up, from 2003 to 2007, so share prices rose again. The trend was then reversed again with the onset of the recession in 2008/9, but they began to rise once more as the economy started to recover.

Wealth. 'Wealth' is people's accumulated savings and property. Wealth rose in the 1990s and many people used their increased wealth to buy shares. It was a similar picture in the mid 2000s. Much of the wealth worldwide was in relatively 'liquid' form – i.e. in a form that can easily be turned into cash (and hence used to buy shares).

Expectations. From 2003 to 2007, people expected share prices to go on rising. They were optimistic about continued growth in the economy and that certain sectors, such as leisure and high-tech industries, would grow particularly strongly. But as people bought shares, this pushed their prices up even more, thereby fuelling further speculation that they would go on rising and encouraging further share buying.

By contrast, in the recession of 2008/9 following the banking crisis of 2007/8, confidence was shaken.

The problem was a global one with output falling around the world. This caused share prices to plummet. As people anticipated further price falls, so they held back from buying, thereby pushing prices even lower. Conversely, as share prices began rising again from 2009, so this boosted the demand for shares, thereby fuelling the surge in share prices.

Supply

The factors affecting supply are largely the same as those affecting demand, but in the opposite direction.

If the return on alternative forms of saving falls, people with shares are likely to hold on to them, as they represent a better form of saving. The supply of shares to the market will fall. If incomes or wealth rises, people again are likely to want to hold on to their shares.

As far as expectations are concerned, if people believe that share prices will rise, they will hold on to the shares they have. Supply to the market will fall, thereby pushing up prices. If, however, they believe that prices will fall, as they did in 2008, they will sell their shares now before prices do fall. Supply will increase, driving down the price.

Share prices and business

Companies are crucially affected by their share price. If a company's share price falls, this is taken as a sign that 'the market' is losing confidence in the company. This will make it more difficult to raise finance, not only by issuing additional shares in the primary market, but also from banks. It will also make the company more vulnerable to a takeover bid. This is where one company seeks to buy out another by offering to buy all its shares. A takeover will succeed if the owners of more than half of the company's shares vote to accept the offered price. Shareholders are more likely to agree to the takeover if the company's shares have not been doing very well recently.

1. *If the rate of economic growth in the economy is 3 per cent in a particular year, why are share prices likely to rise by more than 3 per cent that year?*
2. *Find out what has happened to the FTSE 100 index over the past 12 months and explain why.*

BOX 2.2   UK HOUSE PRICES

The ups and downs of the housing market

If you are thinking of buying a house sometime in the future, then you may well follow the fortunes of the housing market with some trepidation. The chart shows what has happened to annual house price inflation since 1983. In the late 1980s there was a housing price explosion in the UK; in fact, between 1984 and 1989 house prices *doubled*. After several years of falling or gently rising house prices in the early and mid 1990s, there was another boom from 1996 to 2007, with house prices rising by 26 per cent per year at the peak (in the 12 months to January 2003). For many, owning a home of their own was becoming a mere dream. Then, with the banking crisis of 2007 and the subsequent recession, house prices fell sharply in 2008 and the first part of 2009, only then to start slowly rising once more.

House prices are determined by demand and supply. If demand rises (i.e. shifts to the right) or if supply falls (i.e. shifts to the left), the equilibrium price of houses will rise. Similarly, if demand falls or supply rises, the equilibrium price will fall.

So why did house prices rise so rapidly in the 1980s and again in the late 1990s and 2000s, but fall in the early 1990s and late 2000s? The answer lies primarily in changes in the *demand* for housing. Let us examine the various factors that affected the demand for houses.

Incomes (actual and anticipated). The second half of the 1980s and from 1996 to 2007 were periods of rapidly rising incomes. The economy was experiencing an economic 'boom'. Many people wanted to spend their extra incomes on housing, either buying a house for the first time, or moving to a better one. What is more, many people thought that their incomes would continue to grow, and were thus prepared to stretch themselves financially in the short term by buying an expensive house, confident that their mortgage payments would become more and more affordable over time.

The early 1990s and late 2000s, by contrast, were periods of recession, with rising unemployment and much more slowly growing incomes. People had much less confidence about their ability to afford large mortgages.

The cost of mortgages. Most people have to borrow money to buy a house by taking out a mortgage. If mortgages become more affordable, people will tend to borrow more and this will fuel the demand for houses and hence drive up house prices. Mortgages will become more affordable if either the rate of interest falls or people are given longer to pay back the loan.

During the second half of the 1980s, mortgage interest rates were generally falling. Although they were still high compared with rates today, in *real* terms they were negative! In other words, house price inflation was greater than the rate of interest. Even if you paid back none of the mortgage and simply accumulated the interest owed, your house would be rising faster in price than your debt; your 'equity' in the house (i.e. the value of the house minus what you owe on it) would be rising.

In 1989, however, this trend was reversed. Mortgage interest rates were now rising. Many people found it difficult to maintain existing payments, let alone to take on a larger mortgage. From 1990 to 1995, house prices fell by 12.2 per cent. As a result of this, many people found themselves in a position of *negative equity*. This is the situation where the size of their mortgage is greater than the value of their house. In other words, if they sold their house, they would end up still owing money! For this reason many people found that they could not move house.

From 1996 to 2003 mortgage rates were generally reduced again, once more fuelling the demand for houses. Even with gently rising interest rates from 2003 to 2007, mortgages were still relatively affordable.

The availability of mortgages. In the late 1980s and early and mid 2000s, mortgages were readily available. Banks and building societies were prepared to grant mortgages of several times a person's annual income and to accept relatively small deposits on houses. Indeed, in the mid 2000s, some mortgage lenders were willing to lend more than 100 per cent of the value of the property. By contrast, in the early 1990s and late 2000s banks and building societies were much more cautious about granting mortgages. They were aware that with the banking crisis and a global recession contributing to rising unemployment, as well as falling house prices and hence a growing problem of negative equity, there was a growing danger that borrowers would default on payments.

Speculation. In the 1980s and from 1997 to 2007, people generally believed that house prices would continue rising. This encouraged people to buy as soon as possible, and to take out the biggest mortgage possible, before prices went up any further. There was also an effect on supply. Those with houses to sell held back until the last possible moment in the hope of getting a higher price. The net effect was for a rightward shift in the demand curve for houses and a leftward shift in the supply curve. The effect of this speculation, therefore, was to help bring about the very effect that people were predicting (see Box 2.4).

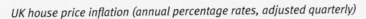

UK house price inflation (annual percentage rates, adjusted quarterly)

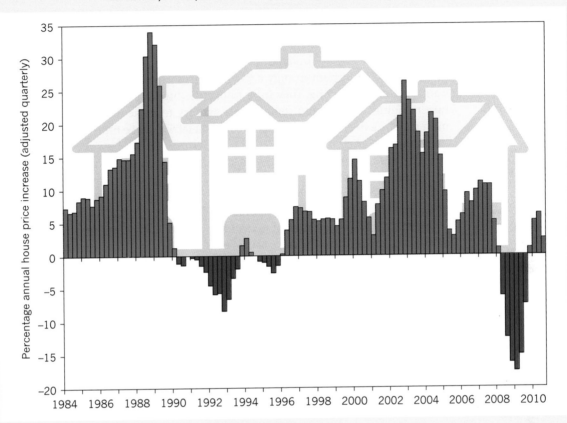

Source: Based on *Halifax House Price Index* (Lloyds Banking Group)

In the early 1990s and late 2000s, the opposite occurred. People thinking of buying houses held back, hoping to buy at a lower price. People with houses to sell tried to sell as quickly as possible before prices fell any further. Again the effect of this speculation was to aggravate the change in prices – this time a fall in prices.

Demographics. The general rise in house prices over the whole period since 1983 has been compounded by demographics: population has grown more rapidly than the housing stock. This has caused demand to grow more rapidly than supply over the long term.

1. Draw supply and demand diagrams to illustrate what was happening to house prices (a) in the second half of the 1980s and from 1997 to 2007; (b) in the early 1990s and 2008–9.
2. Are there any factors on the supply side that contribute to changes in house prices? If so, what are they?
3. Find out what has happened to house prices over the past three years. Attempt an explanation of what has happened.

2.5 ELASTICITY OF DEMAND AND SUPPLY

Price elasticity of demand

When the price of a good rises, the quantity demanded will fall. That much is fairly obvious. But in most cases we will want to know more than this. We will want to know just *how much* the quantity demanded will fall. In other words, we will want to know how *responsive* demand is to a rise in price.

Take the case of two products: petrol and broccoli. In the case of petrol, a rise in price is likely to result in only a slight fall in the quantity demanded. If people want to continue driving, they have to pay the higher prices for fuel. A few may turn to riding bicycles, and some people may try to make fewer journeys, but for most people, a rise in the price of petrol and diesel will make little difference to how much they use their cars.

In the case of broccoli, however, a rise in price may lead to a substantial fall in the quantity demanded. The reason is that there are alternative vegetables that people can buy. Many people, when buying vegetables, are very conscious of their prices and will buy whatever is reasonably priced.

We call the responsiveness of demand to a change in price the **price elasticity of demand**. If we know the price elasticity of demand for a product, we can predict the effect on price and quantity when the *supply* curve for that product shifts.

Definition

Price elasticity of demand

A measure of the responsiveness of quantity demanded to a change in price.

> **KEY IDEA 10**
>
> **Elasticity.** The responsiveness of one variable (e.g. demand) to a change in another (e.g. price). This concept is fundamental to understanding how markets work. The more elastic variables are, the more responsive is the market to changing circumstances.

Figure 2.6 shows the effect of a shift in supply with two quite different demand curves (*D* and *D′*). Curve *D′* is more elastic than curve *D* over any given price

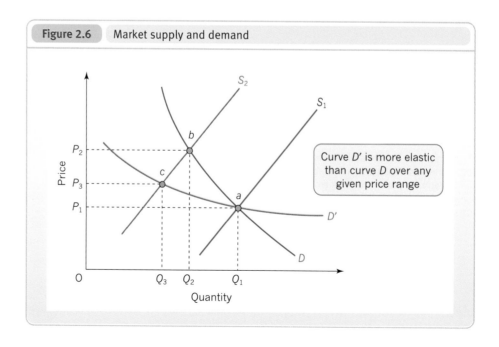

Figure 2.6   Market supply and demand

Curve *D′* is more elastic than curve *D* over any given price range

range. In other words, for any given change in price, there will be a larger change in quantity demanded along curve D' than along curve D.

Assume that initially the supply curve is S_1, and that it intersects with both demand curves at point a, at a price of P_1 and a quantity of Q_1. Now supply shifts to S_2. What will happen to price and quantity? In the case of the less elastic demand curve D, there is a relatively large rise in price (to P_2) and a relatively small fall in quantity (to Q_2): equilibrium is at point b. In the case of the more elastic demand curve D', however, there is only a relatively small rise in price (to P_3) but a relatively large fall in quantity (to Q_3): equilibrium is at point c.

Defining price elasticity of demand

What we want to compare is the size of the change in quantity demanded of a given product with the size of the change in price. Price elasticity of demand does just this. It is defined as follows:

$$P\varepsilon_D = \frac{\text{Proportionate (or percentage) change in quantity demanded}}{\text{Proportionate (or percentage) change in price}}$$

If, for example, a 20 per cent rise in the price of a product causes a 10 per cent fall in the quantity demanded, the price elasticity of demand will be:

$$-10\%/20\% = -0.5$$

Three things should be noted about the figure that is calculated for elasticity.

The use of proportionate or percentage measures. Elasticity is measured in proportionate or percentage terms because this allows comparison of changes in two qualitatively different things, which are thus measured in two different types of unit, i.e. it allows comparison of quantity changes (quantity demanded) with monetary changes (price).

It is also the only sensible way of deciding *how big* a change in price or quantity is. Take a simple example. An item goes up in price by £1. Is this a big increase or a small increase? We can answer this only if we know what the original price was. If a can of beans goes up in price by £1 that is a huge price increase. If, however, the price of a house goes up by £1, that is a tiny price increase. In other words, it is the percentage or proportionate increase in price that we look at in deciding how big a price rise it is.

The sign (positive or negative). If price increases (a positive figure), the quantity demanded will fall (a negative figure). If price falls (a negative figure), the quantity demanded will rise (a positive figure). Thus price elasticity of demand will be negative: a positive figure is being divided by a negative figure (or vice versa).

The value (greater or less than 1). If we now ignore the sign and just concentrate on the value of the figure, this tells us whether demand is *elastic* or *inelastic*.

■ Elastic demand ($\varepsilon > 1$). This is where a change in price causes a proportionately larger change in the quantity demanded. In this case the price elasticity of demand will be greater than 1, since we are dividing a larger figure by a smaller figure.
■ Inelastic demand ($\varepsilon < 1$). This is where a change in price causes a proportionately smaller change in the quantity demanded. In this case the price elasticity of demand will be less than 1, since we are dividing a smaller figure by a larger figure.
■ Unit elastic demand ($\varepsilon = 1$). This is where the quantity demanded changes proportionately the same as price. This will give an elasticity equal to 1, since we are dividing a figure by itself.

Definitions

Elastic demand
If demand is (price) elastic, then any change in price will cause the quantity demanded to change proportionately more. (Ignoring the negative sign) it will have a value greater than 1.

Inelastic demand
If demand is (price) inelastic, then any change will cause the quantity demanded to change by a proportionately smaller amount. (Ignoring the negative sign) it will have a value less than 1.

Unit elasticity
When the price elasticity of demand is unity, this is where quantity demanded changes by the same proportion as the price. Price elasticity is equal to −1.

The determinants of price elasticity of demand

The price elasticity of demand varies enormously from one product to another. But why do some products have a highly elastic demand, whereas others have a highly *in*elastic demand? What determines price elasticity of demand?

The number and closeness of substitute goods. This is the main determinant of price elasticity of demand. The more substitutes there are for a good and the closer they are, the greater will be the price elasticity of demand. The reason is that people will be able to switch to the substitutes when the price of the good rises. The more numerous the substitutes and the closer they are, the more people will switch: in other words, the bigger will be the substitution effect of a price rise.

For example, the price elasticity of demand for a particular brand of a product will probably be fairly high, especially if there are many other, similar brands. If the price of a brand of washing powder goes up, people can simply switch to another brand; there is a large substitution effect. By contrast the demand for a product in general will normally be pretty inelastic. If the price of food in general goes up, demand for food will fall only slightly. People will buy a little less, since they cannot now afford so much; this is the *income* effect of the price rise. But there is no alternative to food that can satisfy our hunger; there is therefore virtually no *substitution* effect.

The proportion of income spent. The higher the proportion of our income we spend on a good, the more we will have to reduce our consumption of it following a rise in price: the more elastic will be the demand. Think about salt – the amount we spend on it accounts for a tiny proportion of our income and so if its price doubles, it makes little difference to our overall expenditure: the income effect of a price rise is very small. However, a car accounts for a much larger proportion of our income and so if the price of cars double, there would be a larger income effect.

The time period. Another important determinant is the *time period*. When price rises, people may take time to adjust their consumption patterns and find alternatives. The longer the time period after a price change, the more elastic is the demand likely to be.

> ### Pause for thought
>
> *Think of two products and estimate which is likely to have the higher price elasticity of demand. Explain your answer.*

Price elasticity of demand and consumer expenditure

One of the most important applications of price elasticity of demand concerns its relationship with the total amount of money consumers spend on a product. **Total consumer expenditure (*TE*)** is simply price multiplied by quantity purchased:

$$TE = P \times Q$$

For example, if consumers buy 3 million units (*Q*) at a price of £2 per unit (*P*), they will spend a total of £6 million (*TE*).

Total consumer expenditure will be the same as the **total revenue (*TR*)** received by firms from the sale of the product (before any taxes or other deductions).

What will happen to consumer expenditure, and hence firms' revenue, if there is a change in price? The answer depends on the price elasticity of demand.

Elastic demand. As price rises, so quantity demanded falls, and vice versa. When demand is elastic, quantity changes proportionately more than price. Thus the change in quantity has a bigger effect on total consumer expenditure than does the change in price. This is summarised in Figure 2.7. In other words, total expenditure and total revenue change in the same direction as *quantity*.

> ### Definitions
>
> **Total consumer expenditure (*TE*) (per period)**
> The price of the product multiplied by the quantity purchased: $TE = P \times Q$.
>
> **Total revenue (*TR*) (per period)**
> The total amount received by firms from the sale of a product, before the deduction of taxes or any other costs. The price multiplied by the quantity sold: $TR = P \times Q$.

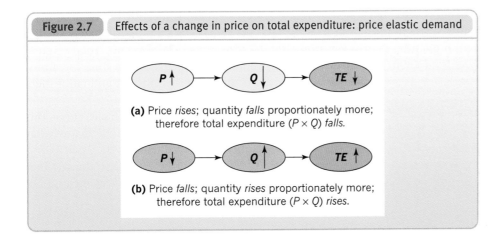

Figure 2.7 Effects of a change in price on total expenditure: price elastic demand

(a) Price *rises*; quantity *falls* proportionately more; therefore total expenditure (P × Q) *falls*.

(b) Price *falls*; quantity *rises* proportionately more; therefore total expenditure (P × Q) *rises*.

This is illustrated in Figure 2.9(a). The areas of the rectangles in the diagram represent total expenditure. Why? The area of a rectangle is its height multiplied by its length. In this case, this is price multiplied by quantity purchased, which is total expenditure. Demand is elastic between points *a* and *b*. A rise in price from £4 to £5 (25 per cent) causes a proportionately larger fall in quantity demanded: from 20m to 10m units (–50 per cent). Total expenditure *falls* from £80m (the shaded area) to £50m (the striped area).

When demand is elastic, then, a rise in price will cause a fall in total expenditure and hence the total revenue earned by the firms selling the product. A reduction in price, however, will result in consumers spending more, and hence firms earning more.

So far we have been looking at the *market* demand curve. If we take the demand curve for a single firm, however, which is also a price taker, its demand curve will be perfectly elastic (i.e. horizontal). The price elasticity of demand is –∞. In other words, being a price taker, it can sell as much as it likes at the given market price. Any increase in its output and sales necessarily results in an increase in its total revenue, since it is selling a higher quantity at the *same* price. (When firms are not price takers, they face a downward-sloping demand curve. We consider such firms in Chapter 5.)

Inelastic demand. When demand is inelastic, price changes proportionately more than quantity. Thus the change in price has a bigger effect on total expenditure than does the change in quantity. This is summarised in Figure 2.8. In other words, total expenditure changes in the same direction as *price*.

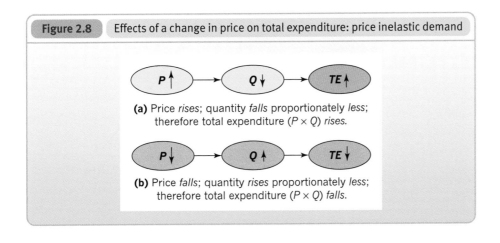

Figure 2.8 Effects of a change in price on total expenditure: price inelastic demand

(a) Price *rises*; quantity *falls* proportionately *less*; therefore total expenditure (P × Q) *rises*.

(b) Price *falls*; quantity *rises* proportionately *less*; therefore total expenditure (P × Q) *falls*.

This effect is illustrated in Figure 2.9(b). Demand is inelastic between points *a* and *c*. A rise in price from £4 to £8 (100 per cent) causes a proportionately smaller fall in quantity demanded: from 20m to 15m units (–25 per cent). Total revenue *rises* from £80m (the shaded area) to £120m (the striped area). In this case, firms' revenue will increase if there is a rise in price, and fall if there is a fall in price.

In the extreme case of a totally inelastic demand curve, this would be represented by a vertical straight line. No matter what happens to price, quantity demanded remains the same and so the price elasticity of demand will be zero. It is obvious that the more the price rises, the bigger will be the level of consumer expenditure.

Pause for thought

If the price of petrol goes up, what will happen to a firm's total revenue? Does your answer change if it is only the price of Esso petrol that increases?

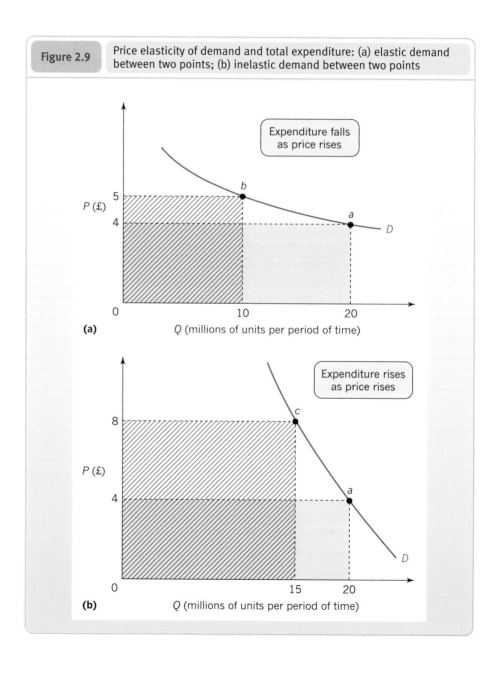

Figure 2.9   Price elasticity of demand and total expenditure: (a) elastic demand between two points; (b) inelastic demand between two points

Other elasticities

Firms are interested to know the responsiveness of demand not just to a change in price; they will also want to know the responsiveness of demand to changes in other determinants, such as consumers' incomes and the prices of substitute or complementary goods to theirs. They will want to know the **income elasticity of demand** – the responsiveness of demand to a change in consumers' incomes (Y) – and the **cross-price elasticity of demand** – the responsiveness of demand for their good to a change in the price of another (whether a substitute or a complement).

Income elasticity of demand ($Y\varepsilon_D$)

We define the income elasticity of demand for a good as follows:

$$Y\varepsilon_D = \frac{\text{Proportionate (or percentage) change in quantity demanded}}{\text{Proportionate (or percentage) change in income}}$$

For example, if a 2 per cent rise in consumer incomes causes an 8 per cent rise in a product's demand, then its income elasticity of demand will be:

8%/2% = 4

Note that in the case of a normal good, the figure for income elasticity will be positive: a *rise* in income leads to a *rise* in demand (a positive figure divided by a positive figure gives a positive answer).

The major determinant of income elasticity of demand is the degree of 'necessity' of the good. Typically, the demand for luxury goods expands rapidly as people's incomes rise, whereas the demand for more basic goods such as bread will only rise

> ### Definitions
>
> **Income elasticity of demand**
> The responsiveness of demand to a change in consumer incomes: the proportionate change in demand divided by the proportionate change in income.
>
> **Cross-price elasticity of demand**
> The responsiveness of demand for one good to a change in the price of another: the proportionate change in demand for one good divided by the proportionate change in price of the other.

BOX 2.3   SHALL WE PUT UP OUR PRICE?

Competition, price and revenue

When you buy a can of drink on a train, or an ice-cream in the cinema, or a bottle of wine in a restaurant, you may well be horrified by its price. How can they get away with it?

The answer is that these firms are *not* price takers. They can choose what price to charge. We will be examining the behaviour of such firms in Chapter 5, but here it is useful to see how price elasticity of demand can help to explain their behaviour.

Take the case of the can of drink on the train. If you are thirsty, and if you haven't brought a drink with you, then you will have to get one from the train's bar, or go without. There is no substitute. What we are saying here is that the demand for drinks on the train is inelastic at the normal shop price. This means that the train operator can put up the price of its drinks, and food too, and earn *more* revenue.

Generally, the less competition a firm faces, the lower will be the elasticity of demand for its products, since there will be fewer substitutes (competitors) to which consumers can turn. The lower the price elasticity of demand, the higher is likely to be the price that the firm charges.

When there is plenty of competition, it is quite a different story. Petrol stations in the same area may compete fiercely in terms of price. One station may hope that by reducing its price by 1p or even 0.1p per litre below that of its competitors, it can attract customers away from them. With a highly elastic demand, a small reduction in price may lead to a substantial increase in their revenue. The problem is, of course, that when they *all* reduce prices, no firm wins. No one attracts customers away from the others! In this case it is the customer who wins.

1. *Why might a restaurant charge very high prices for wine and bottled water and yet quite reasonable prices for food?*
2. *Why are clothes with designer labels so much more expensive than similar 'own brand' clothes from a chain store, even though they may cost a similar amount to produce?*

a little. If your income rises, you are unlikely to buy a lot more bread or milk, but you may buy more DVDs or foreign holidays. Thus items such as foreign holidays or cars have a high income elasticity of demand, whereas items such as potatoes and bus journeys have a low income elasticity of demand.

The demand for some goods actually decreases as income rises. These are inferior goods such as many of the 'value' products in supermarkets. As people earn more, they switch to the supermarket's superior lines or to branded products and hence the demand for the 'value' product falls. Unlike **normal goods**, which have a positive income elasticity of demand, **inferior goods** have a negative income elasticity of demand: a *rise* in income leads to a *fall* in demand (a negative figure divided by a positive figure gives a negative answer).

Income elasticity of demand is an important concept to firms considering the future size of the market for their product. If the product has a high income elasticity of demand, sales are likely to expand rapidly as national income rises, but may also fall significantly if the economy moves into recession.

Firms may also find that some parts of their market have a higher income elasticity of demand than others, and may thus choose to target their marketing campaigns on this group. For example, middle income groups may have a higher income elasticity of demand for high-tech products than lower income groups (who are unlikely to be able to afford such products even if their incomes rise somewhat) or higher income groups (who can probably afford them anyway, and thus would not buy much more if their incomes rose).

Cross-price elasticity of demand ($C\varepsilon_{Dab}$)

This is often known by its less cumbersome title of *cross elasticity of demand*. It is a measure of the responsiveness of demand for one product to a change in the price of another (either a substitute or a complement). It enables us to predict how much the demand curve for the first product will shift when the price of the second product changes. For example, knowledge of the cross elasticity of demand for Coca-Cola with respect to the price of Pepsi would allow Coca-Cola to predict the effect on its own sales if the price of Pepsi were to change.

We define cross-price elasticity as follows:

$$C\varepsilon_D = \frac{\text{Proportionate (or percentage) change in quantity demand for good a}}{\text{Proportionate (or percentage) change in price of good b}}$$

If good B is a *substitute* for good A, A's demand will *rise* as B's price rises. For example, the demand for bicycles will rise as the price of public transport rises. In this case, cross elasticity will be a positive figure. If B is *complementary* to A, however, A's demand will *fall* as B's price rises and thus as the quantity of B demanded falls. For example, the demand for petrol falls as the price of cars rises. In this case, cross elasticity will be a negative figure.

The major determinant of cross elasticity of demand is the closeness of the substitute or complement. The closer it is, the bigger will be the effect on the first good of a change in the price of the substitute or complement, and hence the greater will be the cross elasticity – either positive or negative.

Firms will wish to know the cross elasticity of demand for their product when considering the effect on the demand for their product of a change in the price of a rival's product (a substitute).

If firm B cuts its price, will this make significant inroads into the sales of firm A? If so, firm A may feel forced to cut its prices too; if not, then firm A may keep its price unchanged. The cross-price elasticities of demand between a firm's product and those of each of its rivals are thus vital pieces of information for a firm when making its production, pricing and marketing plans.

Similarly, a firm will wish to know the cross-price elasticity of demand for its product with any complementary good. Car producers will wish to know the effect of petrol price increases on the sales of their cars.

Other elasticities of demand

We could look at the responsiveness of demand to any other determinant. For example, a business is likely to be very interested in how much demand will increase in response to expenditure on a particular advertising campaign or other forms of promotion. It will try to obtain evidence from advertising agencies on the success of their promotions elsewhere in order to estimate whether the likely increase in sales and revenue are worth the expenditure on the advertising. Of course, as with many aspects of business, the figures will only be an estimate, and may be a fairly rough one at that if the campaign is very different from any previous one.

Price elasticity of supply ($P\varepsilon_s$)

Just as we can measure the responsiveness of demand to a change in a determinant of demand, we can also measure the responsiveness of supply to a change in a determinant of supply. The **price elasticity of supply** refers to the responsiveness of supply to a change in price. We define it as follows:

$$P\varepsilon_s = \frac{\text{Proportionate (or Percentage) change in quantity supplied}}{\text{Proportionate (or Percentage) change in price}}$$

Thus if a 15 per cent rise in the price of a product causes a 30 per cent rise in the quantity supplied, the price elasticity of supply will be:

30%/15% = 2

In Figure 2.10 curve S_2 is more elastic between any two prices than curve S_1. Thus, when price rises from P_0 to P_1 there is a larger increase in quantity supplied with S_2 (namely, Q_0 to Q_2) than there is with S_1 (namely, Q_0 to Q_1).

There are two main determinants of the price elasticity of supply.

> **Definition**
>
> **Price elasticity of supply**
> The responsiveness of quantity supplied to a change in price: the proportionate change in quantity supplied divided by the proportionate change in price.

Figure 2.10   Supply curves with different price elasticity of supply

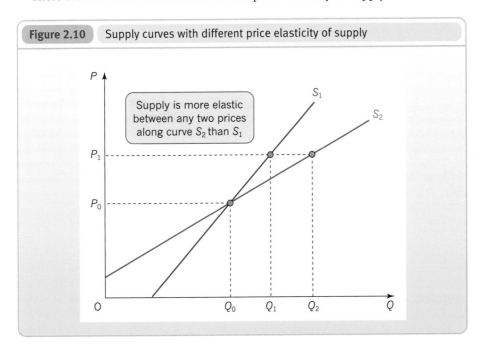

Supply is more elastic between any two prices along curve S_2 than S_1

BOX 2.4   SPECULATION

Taking a gamble on the future

In a world of shifting demand and supply curves, prices do not stay the same. Sometimes they go up; sometimes they come down.

If prices are likely to change in the foreseeable future, this will affect the behaviour of buyers and sellers *now*. If, for example, it is now December and you are thinking of buying a new winter coat, you might decide to wait until the January sales, and in the meantime make do with your old coat. If, on the other hand, when January comes you see a new summer jacket in the sales, you might well buy it now and not wait until the summer for fear that the price will have gone up by then. Thus a belief that prices will go up will cause people to buy now; a belief that prices will come down will cause them to wait.

The reverse applies to sellers. If you are thinking of selling your house and prices are falling, you will want to sell it as quickly as possible. If, on the other hand, prices are rising sharply, you will wait as long as possible so as to get the highest price. Thus a belief that prices will come down will cause people to sell now; a belief that prices will go up will cause them to wait.

This behaviour of looking into the future and making buying and selling decisions based on your predictions is called **speculation**. Speculation is often based on current trends in price behaviour. If prices are currently rising, people may try to decide whether they are about to peak and go back down again, or whether they are likely to go on rising. Having made their prediction, they will then act on it. This speculation will thus affect demand and supply, which in turn will affect price. Speculation is commonplace in many markets: the stock exchange (see Box 2.1), the foreign exchange market and the housing market (see Box 2.2) are three examples. Large firms often employ specialist buyers who choose the right time to buy inputs, depending on what they anticipate will happen to their price.

Speculation tends to be **self-fulfilling**. In other words, the actions of speculators tend to bring about the very effect on prices that speculators had anticipated. For example, if speculators believe that the price of BP shares is about to rise, they will buy more of them. The demand curve for BP shares shifts to the right. Those owning BP shares and thinking of selling will wait until the price has risen. In the meantime, the supply curve shifts to the left. The result of these two shifts is that the share price rises. In other words, the prophecy has become self-fulfilling.

Speculation over commodity prices

The prices of two commodities, oil and copper, illustrate the process of speculation and how it can make price

changes larger. Figure (a) shows changes in the prices of these two commodities from 2002 to 2010. As you can see, they rose dramatically from 2002 to 2008, only to fall back significantly. Why did this happen, and what part did speculation play in the process?

Oil prices. Take first the case of oil prices. Between 2002 and 2008 there was a significant increase in the demand for oil. This was partly the result of increased world economic growth after a slowdown in 2001/2 and partly the result of the massive growth in demand from China and India as their economies powered ahead. Their income elasticity of demand for oil is high, reflecting their high income elasticity of demand for manufacturing, transport and power.

There were also growing problems with supply throughout the 2000s. The war in Iraq and disruptions in supply in other parts of the world meant that supply could not match the growth in demand without substantial price increases.

Speculation compounded this process. As oil prices rose, governments and oil companies increased demand so as to build up stocks (or 'inventories') ahead of any further price increases. At the same time, holders of oil stocks released less onto the market, waiting for the price to rise further.

This is illustrated in Figure (b). A rise in demand from D_1 to D_2 caused by the underlying increase in demand for oil, plus a fall in supply from S_1 to S_2 caused by disruptions in supply, would have resulted in a price rise from P_1 to P_2. But speculation compounded this effect. A further rise in demand to D_3 caused by speculative building of stocks, plus a fall in supply to S_3 as a result of the speculative holding back of supplies, meant that price rose to P_3.

(a) Oil and copper prices

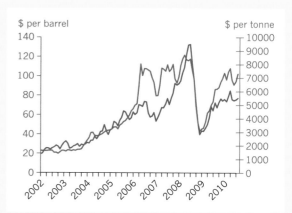

Definition

Speculation

This is where people make buying or selling decisions based on their anticipations of future prices.

(b) Speculation compounding a price increase

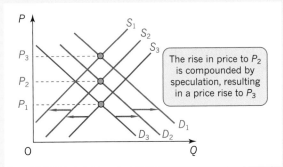

The rise in price to P_2 is compounded by speculation, resulting in a price rise to P_3

Oil prices reached their peak at over $140 per barrel in July 2008. Then things changed dramatically. Investment in new oil wells, stimulated by earlier rises in prices, was beginning to increase supply. At the same time, stocks were near maximum and hence this reduced the demand for further stock building.

The resulting fall in prices put speculation into reverse. Oil stocks were reduced as more oil was released onto the market before prices fell any further. Meanwhile, with growing concerns about the world banking system and fears of a credit shortage, it became clear that the world was heading for recession. This reduced the demand for oil and put further downward pressure on the oil price. By the end of December 2008, oil was trading at around $34 per barrel, a fall in price of 76% in just over five months.

This is illustrated in Figure (c). A fall in demand from D_1 to D_2, plus a rise in supply from S_1 to S_2, would have caused price to fall from P_1 to P_2. But again, speculation compounded this effect, resulting in a further fall in demand to D_3 and a rise in supply to S_3. Price fell to P_3.

(c) Speculation compounding a price fall

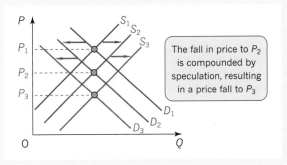

The fall in price to P_2 is compounded by speculation, resulting in a price fall to P_3

Speculation can be extremely volatile. For example, a cold spell in the USA in late January 2007, plus a strike threat in Nigeria led to a 14 per cent increase in the price of oil in less than two weeks.

Copper prices. A similar picture of underlying changes in demand and supply, amplified by speculation, can be seen in the case of copper (see Figure (a)). Surging demand from China and India, with supply unable to keep pace, pushed up prices from 2004. This trend was exaggerated by speculation, as stocks were built in anticipation of further rises.

The trend was temporarily reversed in late 2006. Increased mining output, prompted by the earlier price increases, coupled with slowing worldwide demand and the perception that copper stocks were unnecessarily large, saw copper prices fall by some 35 per cent between June 2006 and February 2007. But then the continuing growth in the world economy caused the copper price to rise again.

With the onset of the credit crunch in mid 2008, however, and then the global recession, so copper prices plummeted – from $8.5 per tonne in July 2008 to $2.9 in December. Once the fall had begun, it was compounded by speculation that it would fall further. Then throughout 2009 and into 2010 the price steadily rose, first because speculators believed that the price had fallen too low to reflect underlying supply and demand, and later as the recovery began to gather pace and speculators anticipated resulting further rises in raw material prices.

These speculative trends in both oil and copper prices were exaggerated by another factor. Financial investors, such as investment banks and insurance companies, have increasingly held commodities in addition to shares, bonds and other assets.[1] They have done so as a means of 'diversifying their portfolios' (their asset holdings) and thereby spreading their risks. This has increased the amount of speculative buying or selling of copper, oil, gold, etc.

1. Under what circumstances are people engaging in speculation likely to (a) gain, (b) lose from doing so?
2. Find out what has happened to the price of (a) oil and (b) copper over the past 12 months and give an explanation. To what extent have the price changes been influenced by speculation?

---

[1] Note that if you buy copper, say, in this way, you don't physically take ownership of the copper, but acquire a paper or electronic asset denoting your ownership

Definition

Self-fulfilling speculation
The actions of speculators tend to cause the very effect that they had anticipated.

The amount that costs rise as output rises. The less the additional costs of producing additional output, the more firms will be encouraged to produce for a given price rise; the more elastic will supply be.

Supply is thus likely to be elastic if firms have plenty of spare capacity, if they can readily get extra supplies of raw materials, if they can easily switch away from producing alternative products and if they can avoid having to introduce overtime working (at higher rates of pay). If all these conditions hold, costs will be little affected by a rise in output and supply will be relatively elastic. The less these conditions apply, the less elastic will supply be.

Time period.

- Immediate time period. Firms are unlikely to be able to increase supply by much immediately. Think about a market stall selling fresh vegetables: supply is virtually fixed, or can vary only according to available stocks. Supply is highly inelastic.
- Short run. If a slightly longer time period is considered, some inputs can be increased (e.g. raw materials), while others will remain fixed (e.g. heavy machinery). Supply can increase somewhat and so is more elastic.
- Long run. In the long run, there will be sufficient time for all inputs to be increased and for new firms to enter the industry. Supply, therefore, is likely to be highly elastic. In some circumstances the supply curve may even slope downwards. (See the section on economies of scale in Chapter 4, pages 95–7.)

Recap

1. Price elasticity of demand measures the responsiveness of the quantity demanded to a change in price. It is defined as the proportionate (or percentage) change in quantity demanded divided by the proportionate (or percentage) change in price.

2. Given that demand curves are downward sloping, price elasticity of demand will be negative.

3. If quantity demanded changes proportionately more than price, the figure for elasticity will be greater than 1 (ignoring the sign): it is elastic. If the quantity demanded changes proportionately less than price, the figure for elasticity will be less than 1: it is inelastic. If they change by the same proportion, the elasticity has a value of 1: it is unit elastic.

4. Demand will be more elastic the greater the number and closeness of substitute goods, the greater the proportion of income spent on the good and the longer the time period that elapses after the change in price.

5. When the demand for a firm's product is price elastic, a rise in price will lead to a reduction in consumer expenditure on the good and hence to a reduction in the total revenue of producers.

6. When demand is price inelastic, however, a rise in price will lead to an increase in total expenditure and revenue.

7. Income elasticity of demand measures the responsiveness of demand to a change in income. For normal goods it has a positive value. Demand will be more income elastic the more luxurious the good.

8. Cross-price elasticity of demand measures the responsiveness of demand for one good to a change in the price of another. For substitute goods the value will be positive; for complements it will be negative. The cross-price elasticity will be greater the closer the two goods are as substitutes or complements.

9. Price elasticity of supply measures the responsiveness of supply to a change in price. It has a positive value. Supply will be more elastic the less costs per unit rise as output rises and the longer the time period.

QUESTIONS

1. Referring to Table 2.1, assume that there are 200 consumers in the market. Of these, 100 have schedules like Tracey's and 100 have schedules like Darren's. What would be the total market demand schedule for potatoes now?

2. Refer to the list of determinants of demand (see page 35). For what reasons might the demand for butter fall?

3. Refer to the list of determinants of supply (see pages 39–40). For what reasons might (a) the supply of potatoes fall; (b) the supply of leather rise?

4. This question is concerned with the supply of oil for central heating. In each case consider whether there is a movement along the supply curve (and in which direction) or a shift in it (and whether left or right): (a) new oil fields start up in production; (b) the demand for central heating rises; (c) the price of gas falls; (d) oil companies anticipate an upsurge in the demand for central heating oil; (e) the demand for petrol rises; (f) new technology decreases the costs of oil refining; (g) all oil products become more expensive.

5. The price of cod is much higher today than it was 20 years ago. Using demand and supply diagrams, explain why this should be so.

6. What will happen to the equilibrium price and quantity of butter in each of the following cases? You should state whether demand or supply or both have shifted and in which direction: (a) a rise in the price of margarine; (b) a rise in the demand for yoghurt; (c) a rise in the price of bread; (d) a rise in the demand for bread; (e) an expected increase in the price of butter in the near future; (f) a tax on butter production; (g) the invention of a new, but expensive, process of removing all cholesterol from butter, plus the passing of a law which states that butter producers must use this process. In each case assume that other things remain the same.

7. Why does price elasticity of demand have a negative value, whereas price elasticity of supply has a positive value?

8. Rank the following in ascending order of elasticity: jeans, black Levi jeans, black jeans, black Levi 501 jeans, trousers, outer garments, clothes.

9. Will a general item of expenditure like food or clothing have a price elastic or inelastic demand? Explain.

10. Explain which of these two pairs are likely to have the highest cross-price elasticity of demand: two brands of coffee, or coffee and tea?

11. Why are both the price elasticity of demand and the price elasticity of supply likely to be greater in the long run?

Business issues covered in this chapter

- What determines the amount of a product that consumers wish to buy at each price?

- How are purchasing patterns dependent on human psychology?

- Why are purchasing decisions sometimes risky for consumers and how can insurance help to reduce or remove the level of risk?

- How do businesses set about gathering information on consumer attitudes and behaviour, and what methods can they use to forecast the demand for their products?

- In what ways can firms differentiate their products from those of their rivals?

- What strategies can firms adopt for gaining market share, developing their products and marketing them?

- What are the effects of advertising and what makes a successful advertising campaign?

- How has the growth of the Internet affected businesses' approach to advertising?

Demand and the consumer

If a business is to be successful, it must be able to predict the strength of demand for its products and be able to respond to any changes in consumer tastes. It will also want to know how its customers are likely to react to changes in its price or its competitors' prices, or to changes in income. In other words, it will want to know the price, cross-price and income elasticities of demand for its product. The better the firm's knowledge of its market, the better will it be able to plan its output to meet demand, and the more able it will be to choose its optimum price, product design, marketing campaigns, etc.

3.1 DEMAND AND THE FIRM

In Chapter 2 we examined how prices are determined in perfectly competitive markets: by the interaction of market demand and market supply. In such markets, although the *market* demand curve is downward sloping, the demand curve faced by the individual firm will be horizontal. This is illustrated in Figure 3.1.

The market price is P_m. The individual firm can sell as much as it likes at this market price, but it is too small to have any influence on the market – it is a price taker. It will not force the price down by producing more because, in terms of the total market, this

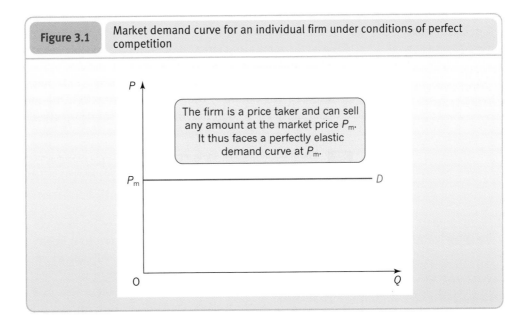

| Figure 3.1 | Market demand curve for an individual firm under conditions of perfect competition |

The firm is a price taker and can sell any amount at the market price P_m. It thus faces a perfectly elastic demand curve at P_m.

extra output would be an infinitesimally small amount. If a farmer doubled the output of wheat sent to the market, it would be too small an increase to affect the world price of wheat!

In practice, however, most firms are not price takers; they have some discretion in choosing their price. Such firms face a downward-sloping demand curve. If they raise their price, they will sell less; if they lower their price, they will sell more. But firms will want to know more than this. They will want to know just *how much* the quantity demanded will change. In other words, they will want to know the price elasticity of demand for their product, as we considered in the previous chapter.

In general, the less price elastic the demand, the better it will be for firms, because this will give them more power over prices. In fact, where the price elasticity of demand for the firm's product is less than one, a rise in price will lead to an *increase* in the firm's revenue (see Figure 2.9(b) on page 52) despite the fall in sales.

It is clearly in firms' interests to try to make the demand for their product less elastic. Firms will generally try to do this by attempting to differentiate their product from those of their rivals. If they can produce a product that consumers feel does not have a close substitute, then demand will be relatively inelastic. Success here will depend partly on designing and producing a product that is clearly different, and partly on achieving an effective marketing and advertising programme.

3.2 UNDERSTANDING CONSUMER BEHAVIOUR

In this section we examine the nature of consumer behaviour and in particular relate consumer demand to the amount of satisfaction that consumers get from products.

Marginal utility

When you buy something, it is normally because you want it. You want it because you expect to get pleasure, satisfaction or some other sort of benefit from it. This applies to everything from chocolate bars, to bus journeys, to CDs, to jeans, to insurance. Economists use the term 'utility' to refer to the benefit or satisfaction we get from consumption.

Clearly, the nature and amount of utility that people get varies from one product to another, and from one person to another. But there is a simple rule that applies to virtually all people and all products: the principle of diminishing marginal utility (Key idea 11). For example, the second cup of tea in the morning gives you less additional satisfaction than the first cup. The third cup gives less still.

KEY IDEA 11 — **The principle of diminishing marginal utility.** As you consume more of a product, and thus become more satisfied, so your desire for additional units of it will decline.

> **Definition**
>
> **Marginal utility (*MU*)**
> The extra satisfaction gained from consuming one extra unit of a good within a given time period.

> **Pause for thought**
>
> *Are there any goods or services where consumers do not experience diminishing marginal utility? If so, give some examples. If not, then explain why.*

The additional utility you get from consuming an extra unit of a product is called the **marginal utility (*MU*)**. The rule states that the marginal utility will fall as we consume more of a product over a given period of time.

However, there is a problem with the concept of marginal utility. How can we measure utility? After all, we cannot get inside each other's heads to find out just how much pleasure we are getting from consuming a product!

One way round the problem is to measure marginal utility in money terms, i.e. the amount that a person would be prepared to pay for one more unit of a product. Thus if you were prepared to pay 50p for an extra packet of crisps per week, then we would say that your marginal utility from consuming it is 50p. As long as you are prepared to pay more or the same as the actual price, you will buy an extra packet. If you are not prepared to pay that price, you will not.

Consumer surplus

The demand curve shows how much consumers are prepared to pay for a given quantity of a good. Yet, quite often, we do not have to pay that full amount. For example, a DVD is priced at £6, but when you walked into the shop, you were willing to pay £10 for it. Obviously, you don't offer the sales assistant £10, but pay the £6 to buy the DVD and benefit from having £4 left in your pocket! The difference between what you were willing to pay for the DVD (£10) and the price you actually paid (£6) is known as the consumer surplus (£4).

> **Definition**
>
> **Consumer surplus**
> The difference between how much a consumer is willing to pay for a good and how much they actually pay for it.

Marginal utility and the demand curve for a good

We can now see how marginal utility relates to a downward-sloping demand curve. As the price of a good falls, it will be worth buying extra units. You will buy more because the price will now be below the amount you are prepared to pay, i.e. price is less than your marginal utility. But as you buy more, your marginal utility from consuming each extra unit will get less and less. How many extra units do you buy? You will stop when the marginal utility has fallen to the new lower price of the good: when $MU = P$. Beyond that point it is not worth buying any more. This represents the optimal consumption point, as rational consumers will aim to maximise their consumer surplus.

An individual's demand curve

Individual people's demand curves for any good are the same as their marginal utility curves for that good, measured in money.

This is demonstrated in Figure 3.2, which shows the marginal utility curve for a particular person and a particular good. The downward-sloping nature of the curve illustrates diminishing marginal utility.

If the price of the good were P_1, the person would consume Q_1: where $MU = P$. Thus point a would be one point on that person's demand curve. If the price fell to P_2, consumption would rise to Q_2, since this is where $MU = P_2$. Thus point b is a second point on the demand curve. Likewise if price fell to P_3, Q_3 would be consumed. Point c is a third point on the demand curve.

Thus as long as individuals aim to maximise consumer surplus and so consume where $P = MU$, their demand curve will be along the same line as their marginal utility curve.

The firm's demand curve

The firm's demand curve will simply be the (horizontal) sum of all individuals' demand curves for its product.

The shape of the demand curve. The price elasticity of demand will reflect the rate at which MU diminishes. If there are close substitutes for a good, it is likely to have

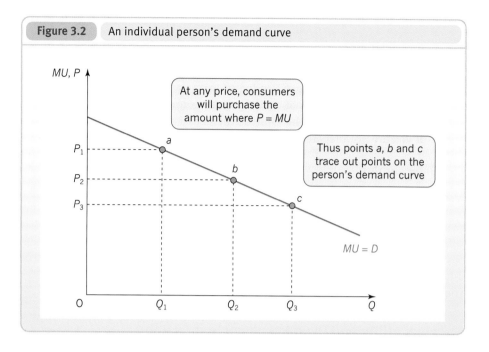

Figure 3.2 An individual person's demand curve

At any price, consumers will purchase the amount where $P = MU$

Thus points a, b and c trace out points on the person's demand curve

an elastic demand, and its MU will diminish slowly as consumption increases. The reason is that increased consumption of this product will be accompanied by *decreased* consumption of the alternative product(s). Since total consumption of this product *plus* the alternatives has increased only slightly (if at all), the marginal utility will fall only slowly.

For example, the demand for a given brand of petrol is likely to have a fairly high price elasticity, since other brands are substitutes. If there is a cut in the price of Esso petrol (assuming the prices of other brands stay constant), consumption of Esso will increase a lot. The MU of Esso petrol will fall slowly, since people consume less of other brands. Petrol consumption *in total* may be only slightly greater and hence the MU of petrol only slightly lower.

Shifts in the demand curve. How do *shifts* in demand relate to marginal utility? For example, how would the marginal utility of (and hence demand for) margarine be affected by a rise in the price of butter? The higher price of butter would cause less butter to be consumed. This would increase the marginal utility of margarine, since if people are using less butter, their desire for margarine is higher. The MU curve (and hence the demand curve) for margarine thus shifts to the right.

The problem of imperfect information

So far we have assumed that when people buy goods and services, they know exactly what price they will pay and how much utility they will gain. In many cases this is a reasonable assumption. When you buy a bar of chocolate, you clearly do know how much you are paying for it and have a very good idea how much you will like it. But what about a DVD recorder, or a car, or a washing machine, or any other **consumer durable**? In each of these cases you are buying something that will last you a long time, that you only buy occasionally; and the further into the future you look, the less certain you will be of its costs and benefits to you.

Take the case of a washing machine costing you £400. If you pay cash, your immediate outlay involves no uncertainty: it is £400. But washing machines can

Definition

Consumer durable
A consumer good that lasts a period of time, during which the consumer can continue gaining utility from it.

break down. In two years' time you could find yourself with a repair bill of £100. This cannot be predicted and yet it is a price you will have to pay, just like the original £400. In other words, when you buy the washing machine, you are uncertain as to the full 'price' it will entail over its lifetime.

If the costs of the washing machine are uncertain, so too are the benefits. You might have been attracted to buy it in the first place by the manufacturer's glossy brochure, or by the look of it, or by adverts on TV, in magazines, etc. When you have used it for a while, however, you will probably discover things you had not anticipated. The spin dryer does not get your clothes as dry as you had hoped; it is noisy; it leaks; the door sticks; and so on.

Buying consumer durables thus involves uncertainty. So too does the purchase of assets, whether a physical asset such as a house or financial assets such as shares. In the case of assets, the uncertainty is over their future *price*. If you buy shares in a currently profitable company, what will happen to their price in the future? Will they shoot up in price, thus enabling you to sell them at a large profit, or will they fall? You cannot know for certain. A lot depends on the company's future performance and what other people think that performance is likely to be.

At this point it is useful to distinguish between uncertainty and risk. **Risk** is where an outcome may or may not occur, but where the *probability* of it occurring is known. **Uncertainty** is where the probability is not known.

Insurance: a way of removing risks

Insurance is a means of eliminating, or at least reducing, uncertainty for people. If, for example, you could lose your job if you are injured, you can remove the risk of loss of income by taking out an appropriate insurance policy.

But why is it that the insurance companies are prepared to shoulder the risks that their customers were not? Do they simply love risk? Definitely not! The answer is that the insurance company is able to **spread its risks**.

The spreading of risks

If there is a one in ten thousand chance of your house burning down each year, although it is only a small chance it would be so disastrous that you are simply not prepared to take the risk. You thus take out house insurance and are prepared to pay a premium of *more than* 0.01 per cent (one in ten thousand).

The insurance company, however, is not just insuring you. It is insuring many others at the same time. If your house burns down, there will be approximately 9999 others that do not. The premiums the insurance company has collected will be more than enough to cover its payments. The more houses it insures, the smaller will be the variation in the proportion that actually burn down each year.

This is an application of the **law of large numbers**. What is unpredictable for an individual becomes highly predictable in the mass. The more people the insurance company insures, the more predictable is the total outcome.

What is more, the insurance company will be in a position to estimate just what the risks are. It can thus work out what premiums it must charge in order to make a profit. With individuals, however, the precise risk is rarely known. Do you know your chances of living to 70? Almost certainly you do not. But a life assurance company will know precisely the chances of a person of your age, sex and occupation living to 70! It will have the statistical data to show this. In other words, an insurance company will be able to convert your *uncertainty* into their *risk*.

Definitions

Risk
This is when an outcome may or may not occur, but where the probability of its occurring is known.

Uncertainty
This is when an outcome may or may not occur and where the probability of its occurring is not known.

Spreading risks (for an insurance company)
The more policies an insurance company issues and the more independent the risks of claims from these policies are, the more predictable will be the number of claims.

Law of large numbers
The larger the number of events of a particular type, the more predictable will be their average outcome.

BOX 3.1   ROGUE TRADERS

Buyer beware!

Markets are usually an efficient way of letting buyers and sellers exchange goods and services. However, this does not stop consumers making complaints about the quality of the goods or services they receive.

It is impossible to get a true measure of customer dissatisfaction because aggrieved consumers do not always complain and data are collected by a number of separate agencies. Particular sectors though seem to be more vulnerable to 'rogue traders' than others. The largest proportion of consumer complaints received by the UK Office of Fair Trading are about builders, plumbers, electricians and decorators in relation to home maintenance, repairs and improvements, including the sale and installation of double glazing. The sale of second-hand motor vehicles and vehicle repairs as well as doorstep selling of gas and electricity contracts are also areas where many complaints are received.

Consumer complaints are also of concern to cross-border sales as the growth of buying over the Internet has blossomed in recent times (see Box 4.6). The figure below reports data from 21 countries on complaints against e-commerce transactions. The largest proportion of complaints relate to internet shopping, online lotteries and internet auction sites such as eBay and Yahoo.

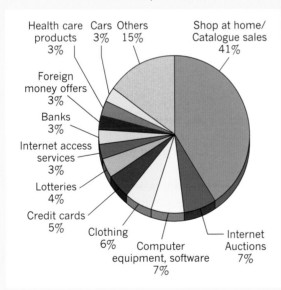

E-consumer complaints, 2009

Source: www.econsumer.gov

Adverse selection and moral hazard

But why does a market, which you would think would respond to consumer wishes, give rise to consumer complaints? Why is it that rogue traders can continue in business? The answer can be found in the concepts of adverse selection and moral hazard. In both cases, the problem is essentially one of 'information asymmetries' and is an example of the 'principal–agent problem' (see pages 9–10). The buyer (the 'principal') has poorer information about the product than the agent (the 'seller').

Information asymmetries. Complaints by consumers are likely to be few if the product is fairly simple and information about the exchange process is publicly available. For example, if I buy apples from a market trader but subsequently return them because some are damaged, they are likely to exchange the apples, or offer a full refund, because failure to do so would lead to the trader's sales falling as information gets out that they sell poor-quality fruit. Here information asymmetries are minimal.

However, where the product is more complex, perhaps with consumers making large outlays, and information is more private, the situation can be very different. The greater the information 'gap' between sellers and consumers, the greater the scope for deception and fraud and the more likely are rogue traders to thrive. In these situations the number of consumer complaints increases.

Consider the sale of a conservatory, a large extension to a house usually comprising a number of various building products, including double-glazed windows and doors. A product such as this involves an expensive outlay for consumers, but they may have very limited information about the price of materials and labour, as well as the method of building a conservatory.

Assume that there is a standard-sized conservatory and that a high-quality seller would be prepared to supply this product at a price of £10 000. Such a price would reflect the quality of their work and would keep them in the business of selling high-quality products. On the other hand, assume that a poor-quality supplier, a 'rogue trader', could provide this conservatory at £5000.

Given information asymmetry, let us assume that consumers are not aware of who is a high-quality or low-quality seller. As a result, rogue traders offer to supply a standard conservatory for, say, £9000.

Adverse selection. This price of £9000, however, is not enough to cover the costs of high-quality sellers, and so they will not want to offer their services to build high-quality conservatories. On the other hand, 'rogue traders' will find this price very profitable and it will attract a higher than normal number of such sellers into the market. Of course, if consumers know that the only sellers in the market are likely to be 'rogue traders', they will not buy conservatories and the market will collapse.

Definition

Adverse selection
Where information is imperfect, high-risk/poor-quality groups will be attracted to profitable market opportunities to the disadvantage of the average buyer (or seller).

The problem just described is an example of **adverse selection**. In this case a group of sellers ('rogue traders') have been attracted to the market by prices considerably greater than their costs even before any transactions have taken place.

 KEY IDEA 12

Adverse selection. Where information is imperfect, high-risk/poor-quality groups will be attracted to profitable market opportunities to the disadvantage of the average buyer (or seller).

Although information is imperfect, things aren't as bad as the above suggests. Consumers do try to find out about sellers before they buy and most consumers get a good product. However, 'rogue traders' also make sales. The poorer the information on the part of consumers, the more adverse will be their selection: the worse the likely quality of the products they buy.

Moral hazard. Once a contract has been signed, the problem of **moral hazard** occurs. In our example, the rogue trader might initially agree to supply and install the conservatory to meet particular high standards of quality for a particular price. However, unless the buyer has full information about the construction of conservatories or can keep a constant watch over the work, defective materials or poor-quality workmanship may be supplied. But the buyer will not know this until a later date when problems start to appear with the conservatory!

Moral hazard results because the seller has acted inappropriately (immorally) and to the detriment of the buyer. The 'hazard' arises because of imperfect information on the part of the consumer. Rogue traders are tempted to supply an inferior product, believing that they can get away with it.

 KEY IDEA 13

Moral hazard. Following a deal, if there are information asymmetries (see pages 9–10), it is likely that one party will engage in problematic (immoral and/or hazardous) behaviour to the detriment of the other. In other words, lack of information by one party to the deal may result in the deal not being honoured by the other party.

Usually, the process of law would work in favour of the buyer because a contract had been established, but in many cases involving rogue traders the business has been declared bankrupt or the costs to buyers of pursuing a legal case are too great.

Solutions

So how can sellers signal to buyers that they offer high-quality products? And how can consumers trust this information? A number of methods exist.

Establishing a reputation. A single firm can establish a reputation for selling high-quality goods, usually over a number of years, or perhaps it has created a valued brand name through advertising. Alternatively, firms can offer guarantees and warranties on their products, such as Kia's new seven-year guarantee. Although this guarantee or a ten-year guarantee on the building work associated with a conservatory is of no use if the firm has gone bankrupt!

Trade associations and other third parties. Firms can also band together collectively and establish a trade association. Examples include the Federation of Master Builders or the Association of British Travel Agents (ABTA). Firms that belong to a trade association have benefits that can extend beyond that of acting alone. For example, if one firm provides a poor-quality product, then consumers may get compensation via the association. ABTA, for example, guarantees to make sure customers will complete their holiday, or obtain a refund, if they have purchased it from a member that has gone bankrupt.

Trade associations are a means by which firms can demonstrate that they regulate themselves rather than have governments impose rules on them.

Sometimes third parties can help firms to signal high quality. The online auction site eBay, for example, provides a feedback system for buyers and sellers so they can register their happiness or otherwise with sales. Likewise, the Office of Fair Trading, under the auspices of the Enterprise Act (2002), has created an Approved Codes of Practice scheme whereby trade associations and their members will guarantee that customers will receive high quality service. Successful associations can display an OFT Approved Codes logo.

Government intervention. On the whole, government does not like to intervene in particular industries, preferring a sector to regulate itself. However, in the case of the financial services industry, the government has directly intervened because the impact of the industry on consumers in recent times has been widespread and financially devastating. Following a number of financial scandals, including the mis-selling of pensions and mortgages, the government replaced ineffective self-regulation in 2000 with the Financial Services Authority, an independent industry regulator with statutory powers, whose Board is appointed by and accountable to the Treasury. In this instance the level of product complexity and information asymmetry between buyer and seller was viewed to be too great for the industry to control itself.

 What are the disadvantages of trade associations?

Definition

Moral hazard

Following a deal, if there are information asymmetries (see page 66), it is likely that one party will engage in problematic (immoral and/or hazardous) behaviour to the detriment of the other. In other words, lack of information by one party to the deal may result in the deal not being honoured by the other party.

BOX 3.2   PROBLEMS FOR UNWARY INSURANCE COMPANIES

'Adverse selection' and 'moral hazard'

In Box 3.1, we saw how consumers may suffer from adverse selection and from moral hazard on the part of suppliers. Adverse selection and moral hazard can also apply the other way round. Insurance companies may incur higher costs from adverse selection and moral hazard on the part of certain policyholders. These higher costs are then likely to be passed on to other policyholders.

Adverse selection

This occurs where the people taking out insurance are those who have the highest risk.

For example, suppose that a company offers medical insurance. It surveys the population and works out that the average person requires £200 of treatment per year. The company thus sets the premium at £250 (the extra £50 to cover its costs and provide a profit). But it is likely that the people most likely to take out the insurance are those most likely to fall sick: those who have been ill before, those whose families have a history of illness, those in jobs that are hazardous to health, etc. These people on average may require £500 of treatment per year, but the insurance company doesn't know this. The insurance company would soon make a loss.

But cannot the company then simply raise premiums to £550 or £600? It can, but the problem is that it will thereby be depriving the person of *average* health of reasonably priced insurance.

The answer is for the company to discriminate more carefully between people. You may have to fill out a questionnaire so that the company can assess your own particular risk and set an appropriate premium. There may need to be legal penalties for people caught lying!

 What details does an insurance company require to know before it will insure a person to drive a car?

Moral hazard

This occurs where having insurance makes you less careful and thus increases your risk to the insurance company. For example, if your bicycle is insured against theft, you may be less concerned to go through the hassle of chaining it up each time you leave it.

Again, if insurance companies work out risks by looking at the *total* number of bicycle thefts, these figures will understate the risks to the company because they will include thefts from *uninsured* people who are likely to be more careful.

 How will the following reduce moral hazard?

(a) A no-claims bonus.
(b) Your having to pay the first so much of any claim.
(c) Offering lower premiums to those less likely to claim (e.g. lower house contents premiums for those with burglar alarms).

The problem of moral hazard occurs in many other walks of life. A good example is that of debt. If someone else is willing to pay your debts (e.g. your parents) it is likely to make you less careful in your spending! This argument has been used by some rich countries for not cancelling the debts of poor countries.

Definitions

Independent risks
Where two risky events are unconnected. The occurrence of one will not affect the likelihood of the occurrence of the other.

Diversification
Where a firm expands into new types of business.

The spreading of risks does not just require that there should be a large number of policies. It also requires that the risks should be **independent**. If any insurance company insured 1000 houses *all in the same neighbourhood*, and then there was a major fire in the area, the claims would be enormous. The risks of fire were not independent. The company would, in fact, have been taking a gamble on a single event. If, however, it provides fire insurance for houses scattered all over the country, the risks *are* independent.

The issue of independent risks was experienced in the UK with the flooding in Cockermouth in 2009. House insurance premiums increased to cover the rapidly rising costs of flooding and some insurance companies were simply not willing to insure homeowners in certain areas. The risks of flood damage are dependent: if one household in Cockermouth claims for flood damage, the probability of all other houses in that area also claiming is pretty high, if not certain.

Insurance companies also tend to offer a diverse range of insurance (houses, cars, travel, health, life) and this **diversification** allows the company to spread their risk: this time across many products. The more types of insurance a company offers, the greater is likely to be the independence of the risks.

Recap

1. Economists call consumer satisfaction 'utility'. Marginal utility diminishes as consumption increases.

2. People will consume more of a good as long as its marginal utility to them (measured in terms of the price they are prepared to pay for it) exceeds its price. They will stop buying additional amounts once *MU* has fallen to equal the price. The difference between what they are willing to pay for a product and what they actually pay for it is called the consumer surplus.

3. An individual's demand curve lies along the same line as the individual's marginal utility curve, when a consumer maximises consumer surplus. The market demand curve is the sum of all individuals' marginal utility curves.

4. When people buy consumer durables they may be uncertain of their benefits and any additional repair and maintenance costs. When they buy financial assets they may be uncertain of what will happen to their price in the future. Buying under these conditions of imperfect knowledge is therefore a form of gambling. When we take such gambles, if we know the odds we are said to be operating under conditions of *risk*. If we do not know the odds we are said to be operating under conditions of *uncertainty*.

5. Insurance is a way of eliminating risks for policyholders. In order to avoid risks, people are prepared to pay premiums in order to obtain insurance. Insurance companies, on the other hand, are prepared to take on these risks because they can spread them over a large number of policies. According to the law of large numbers, what is unpredictable for a single policyholder becomes highly predictable for a large number of them provided that their risks are independent of each other.

ESTIMATING AND PREDICTING DEMAND   3.3

If a business is to be successful, it must have a good understanding of its market. How might a business set about discovering the wants of consumers and hence the intensity of demand? The more effectively a business can identify such wants, the more likely it is to increase its sales and be successful. The clearer idea it can gain of the rate at which the typical consumer's utility will decline as consumption increases, the better estimate it can make of the product's price elasticity. Also the more it can assess the relative utility to the consumer of its product compared with those of its rivals, the more effectively it will be able to compete by differentiating its product from theirs.

In this section we first examine methods for gathering data on consumer behaviour and then see how firms set about forecasting changes in demand over time.

Methods of collecting data on consumer behaviour

There are three general approaches to gathering information about consumers. These are: **observations of market behaviour**, **market surveys** and **market experiments**.

Market observations

The firm can gather data on how demand for its product has changed over time. Virtually all firms will have detailed information on their sales broken down by week, and/or month, and/or year. They will also tend to have information on how sales have varied from one part of the market to another.

In addition, the firm will need to obtain data on how the various determinants of demand (such as price, advertising and the price of competitors' products) have themselves changed over time. Firms are likely to have much of this information already, e.g. the amount spent on advertising and the prices of competitors' products.

Definitions

Observations of market behaviour
Information gathered about consumers from the day-to-day activities of the business within the market.

Market surveys
Information gathered about consumers, usually via a questionnaire, that attempts to enhance the business's understanding of consumer behaviour.

Market experiments
Information gathered about consumers under artificial or simulated conditions. A method used widely in assessing the effects of advertising on consumers.

Other information might be relatively easy to obtain by paying an agency to do the research.

Having obtained this information, the firm can then use it to estimate how changes in the various determinants have affected demand in the past, and hence what effect they will be likely to have in the future.

Even the most sophisticated analysis based on market observations, however, will suffer from one major drawback. Relationships that held in the past will not necessarily hold in the future. Consumers are human, and humans change their minds. Their perceptions of products change (something that the advertising industry relies on!), tastes change and technology changes. It is for this reason that many firms turn to market surveys or market experiments to gain more information about the future.

Market surveys

It is not uncommon to be stopped in a city centre, or to have a knock at the door, and be asked whether you would kindly answer the questions of some market researcher. If the research interviewer misses you, then a postal questionnaire may well seek out the same type of information. A vast quantity of information can be collected in this way. It is a relatively quick and cheap method of data collection. Questions concerning all aspects of consumer behaviour might be asked, such as those relating to present and future patterns of expenditure, or how people might respond to changing product specifications or price, both of the firm in question and of its rivals.

A key feature of the market survey is that it can be targeted at distinct consumer groups, thereby reflecting the specific information requirements of a business. For example, businesses selling luxury goods will be interested only in consumers falling within higher income brackets. Other samples might be drawn from a particular age group or gender, or from those with a particular lifestyle, such as eating habits.

The major drawback with this technique concerns the accuracy of the information acquired. Accurate information requires various conditions to be met.

A random sample. If the sample is not randomly selected, it may fail to represent a cross-section of the population being surveyed.

Clarity of the questions. It is important for the questions to be phrased in an unambiguous way, so as not to mislead the respondent.

Avoidance of leading questions. It is very easy for the respondent to be led into giving the answer the firm wants to hear. For example, when asking whether the person would buy a new product that the firm is thinking of launching, the questionnaire might make the product sound really desirable. The respondents might, as a result, say that they would buy the product, but later, when they see the product in the shops, decide they do not want it.

Truthful response. It is very tempting for respondents who are 'keen to please' to give the answer that they think the questioner wants, or for other somewhat reluctant respondents to give 'mischievous' answers. In other words, people may lie!

Stability of demand. By the time the product is launched, or the changes to an existing product are made, time will have elapsed. The information may then be out of date. Consumer demand may have changed, as tastes and fashions have shifted, or as a result of the actions of competitors.

Market experiments

Rather than asking consumers questions and getting them to *imagine* how they *would* behave, the market experiment involves observing consumer *behaviour* under simulated conditions. It can be used to observe consumer reactions to a new product or to changes in an existing product and, as such, this method is particularly useful when information is scarce.

A simple experiment might involve consumers being asked to conduct a blind taste test for a new brand of toothpaste. The experimenter will ensure that the same amount of paste is applied to the brush, and that the subjects swill their mouths prior to tasting a further brand. Once the experiment is over, the 'consumers' are quizzed about their perceptions of the product.

More sophisticated experiments could be conducted. For example, a *laboratory shop* might be set up to simulate a real shopping experience. People could be given a certain amount of money to spend in the 'shop' and their reactions to changes in prices, packaging, display, etc. could be monitored.

The major drawback with such 'laboratories' is that consumers might behave differently because they are being observed. For example, they might spend more time comparing prices than they would otherwise, simply because they think that this is what a *good*, rational consumer should do. With real shopping, however, it might simply be habit, or something 'irrational' such as the colour of the packaging, that determines which product they select. If you are in a rush, you may simply grab the first brand of orange juice you find, irrespective of its price (see Box 3.3).

> **Pause for thought**
>
> *Identify some other drawbacks in using market experiments to gather data on consumer behaviour.*

BOX 3.3   TAKING ACCOUNT OF EMOTION

The shopping experience

Traditional 'neoclassical' economics assumes that consumers are rational, that they weigh up the marginal utility that they expect to gain from purchasing a product against the price they must pay. But is this how we behave when we go shopping. Are you a 'rational' shopper? Or do your emotions sometimes take over?

In many cases, the experience of the emotion of desire when contemplating buying something, such as a bar of chocolate, is merely an aid to rational behaviour. You imagine the pleasure you will receive, something that is borne out when you do actually eat the chocolate. Similarly, the emotion of displeasure at the thought of paying for the product helps you to be cautious and think of the opportunity cost of buying the product: what will you have to sacrifice?

Sometimes, however, the emotion is misplaced. People may be lured by the packaging and the pleasure they imagine they will gain, rather than the pleasure they actually will gain. Advertisers know this well! To them, perceived pleasure at the time of purchase is more important than actual pleasure at the time of consumption.

In another departure from rationality, people may downplay the costs of a purchase. Research into the brain activity of consumers by George Loewenstein, an economist at Carnegie Mellon University in Pittsburgh suggests that 'rather than weighing the present good against future alternatives, as orthodox economics suggests happens, people actually balance the immediate pleasure of the prospective possession of a product with the immediate pain of paying for it'.[1]

This has profound implications for buying on credit. The abstract nature of credit cards and the fact that payment is deferred until some later date means that many people downplay the costs of the items they buy. No wonder many shops like to offer credit. Not only does it encourage people to buy things now rather than waiting, it may encourage them to buy things they would never otherwise have bought – either now or later!

1. Is it ever 'rational' to buy on credit? Explain.
2. In what other ways might consumer behaviour be regarded as irrational in the traditional sense? How might businesses take advantage of this 'irrationality'?

---

[1] 'The triumph of unreason?', *The Economist*, 11 January 2007

Another type of market experiment involves confining a marketing campaign to a particular town or region. The campaign could involve advertising, or giving out free samples, or discounting the price, or introducing an improved version of the product, but each confined to that particular locality. Sales in that area are then compared with sales in other areas in order to assess the effectiveness of the various campaigns.

Forecasting demand

Businesses are interested not just in knowing the current strength of demand for their products and how demand is likely to be affected by changes in factors such as product specifications and the price of competitors' products. They are also interested in trying to predict *future* demand. After all, if demand is going to increase, they may well want to invest *now* so that they have the extra capacity to meet the extra demand. But it will be a costly mistake to invest in extra capacity if demand is not going to increase.

We now, therefore, turn to examine some of the forecasting techniques used by business.

Simple time-series analysis

Simple time-series analysis involves directly projecting from past sales data into the future. Thus if it is observed that sales of a firm's product have been growing steadily by 3 per cent per annum for the past few years, the firm can use this to predict that sales will continue to grow at approximately the same rate in the future. Similarly, if it is observed that there are clear seasonal fluctuations in demand, as in the case of the demand for holidays, ice cream or winter coats, then again it can be assumed that fluctuations of a similar magnitude will continue into the future.

Using simple time-series analysis assumes that demand in the future will continue to behave in the same way as in the past. The problem is that it may not. Just because demand has followed a clear pattern in the past, it does not inexorably follow that it will continue to exhibit the same pattern in the future. After all, the determinants of demand may well have changed: consumers do change their minds! Successful forecasting, therefore, will usually involve a more sophisticated analysis of trends.

The decomposition of time paths

One way in which the analysis of past data can be made more sophisticated is to identify different elements in the time path of sales. Figure 3.3 illustrates one such time path, the (imaginary) sales of woollen jumpers by firm X. It is shown by the continuous green line, labelled 'Actual sales'. Four different sets of factors normally determine the shape of a time path like this.

Trends. These are increases or decreases in demand over a number of years. In our example, there is a long-term decrease in demand for this firm's woollen jumpers up to year seven and then a recovery in demand thereafter.

Trends may reflect factors such as changes in population structure, or technological innovation or longer-term changes in fashion. Thus if wool were to become more expensive over time compared with other fibres, or if there were a gradual shift in tastes away from woollen jumpers and towards acrylic or cotton jumpers, or towards sweatshirts, this could explain the long-term decline in demand up to year seven. A gradual shift in tastes back towards natural fibres, and to wool in particular, or a gradual reduction in the price of wool, could then explain the subsequent recovery in demand.

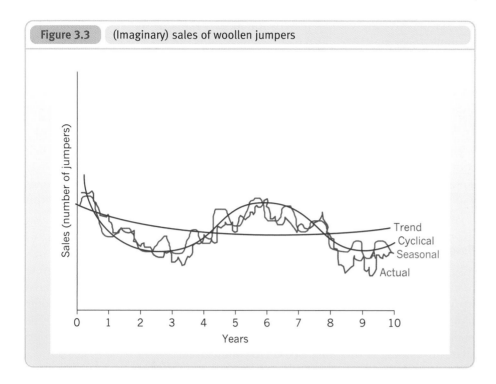

Figure 3.3 (Imaginary) sales of woollen jumpers

Alternatively, trends may reflect changes over time in the structure of an industry. For example, an industry might become more and more competitive, with new firms joining. This would tend to reduce sales for existing firms (unless the market were expanding very rapidly).

Cyclical fluctuations. In practice, the level of actual sales will not follow the trend line precisely. One reason for this is the cyclical upswings and downswings in business activity in the economy as a whole. In some years incomes are rising rapidly and thus demand is buoyant. In other years, the economy will be in recession, with incomes falling. In these years, demand may well also fall. In our example, in boom years people may spend much more on clothes (including woollen jumpers), whereas in a recession, people may make do with their old clothes. The cyclical variations line is thus above the trend line in boom years and falls below the trend line during a recession.

Seasonal fluctuations. The demand for many products also depends on the time of year. In the case of woollen jumpers, the peak demand is likely to be as winter approaches or just before Christmas. Thus the seasonal variations line is above the cyclical variations line in winter and below it in summer.

Short-term shifts in demand or supply. Finally, the actual sales line will also reflect various short-term shifts in demand or supply, causing it to diverge from the smooth seasonal variations line.

There are many reasons why the demand curve might shift. A competitor might increase its price, or there may be a sudden change in fashion, caused, say, by a pop group deciding to wear woollen jumpers for their new video: what was once seen as unfashionable by many people now suddenly becomes fashionable! Alternatively, there may be an unusually cold or hot, or wet or dry spell of weather. This was the case in January 2010, where UK shoppers were prompted to buy scarves, boots and coats as a result of the extremely cold weather.

Likewise there are various reasons for sudden shifts in supply conditions. For example, there may be a sheep disease which ruins the wool of infected sheep. As a result, the price of wool goes up, and sales of woollen jumpers fall.

These sudden shifts in demand or supply conditions are often referred to as 'random shocks' because they are usually unpredictable and temporarily move sales away from the trend. (Note that *long-term* shifts in demand and supply will be shown by a change in the trend line itself.)

Even with sophisticated time-series analysis, which breaks time paths into their constituent elements, there is still one major weakness: time-series analysis is merely a projection of the *past*. Most businesses will want to anticipate *changes* to sales trends – to forecast any deviations from the current time path. One method for doing this is *barometric forecasting*.

Barometric forecasting

Assume that you are a manager of a furniture business and are wondering whether to invest in new capital equipment. You would only want to do this if the demand for your product was likely to rise. You will probably, therefore, look for some indication of this. A good barometer of future demand for furniture would be the number of new houses being built. People will tend to buy new furniture some months after the building of their new house has commenced.

Barometric forecasting involves the use of **leading indicators**, such as housing starts, when attempting to predict the future. In fact some leading indicators, such as increased activity in the construction industry, rises in Stock Exchange prices, a rise in the rate of exchange and a rise in industrial confidence, are good indicators of a general upturn in the economy. In other words, firms use these indicators to predict what is likely to happen to their own demand.

Barometric forecasting suffers from two major weaknesses. The first is that it only allows forecasting a few months ahead – as far ahead as is the time lag between the change in the leading indicator and the variable being forecasted. The second is that it can give only a general indication of changes in demand. It is simply another form of time-series analysis. Just because a relationship existed in the past between a leading indicator and the variable being forecasted, it cannot be assumed that exactly the same relationship will exist in the future.

Normally, then, firms use barometric forecasting merely to give them a rough guide as to likely changes in demand for their product, i.e. whether it is likely to expand or contract, and by 'a lot' or by 'a little'. Nevertheless, information on leading indicators is readily available in government or trade statistics.

Definitions

Barometric forecasting
A technique used to predict future economic trends based upon analysing patterns of time-series data.

Leading indicators
Indicators that help predict future trends in the economy.

Pause for thought

What might be a good leading indicator of the demand for a particular brand of printer ink?

Recap

1. Businesses seek information on consumer behaviour so as to predict market trends and improve strategic decision making.

2. One source of data is the firm's own information on how its sales have varied in the past with changes in the various determinants of demand, such as consumer incomes and the prices of competitors' products.

3. Another source of data is market surveys. These can generate a large quantity of cheap information. Care should be taken, however, to ensure that the sample of consumers investigated reflects the target consumer group.

4. Market experiments involve investigating consumer behaviour within a controlled environment. This

method is particularly useful when considering new products where information is scarce.

5. It is not enough to know what will happen to demand if a determinant changes. Businesses will want to forecast what will actually happen to demand.

6. Time-series analysis bases future trends on past events. Time-series data can be decomposed into different elements: trends, seasonal fluctuations, cyclical fluctuations and random shocks.

7. Barometric forecasting involves making predictions based upon changes in key leading indicators.

STIMULATING DEMAND   3.4

For most firms, selling their product is not simply a question of estimating demand and then choosing an appropriate price and level of production. In other words, they do not simply take their market as given. Instead they will seek to *increase* demand. They will do this by developing their product and differentiating it from those of their rivals, and then marketing it by advertising and other forms of product promotion. This will make their product more price inelastic.

What firms are engaging in here is **non-price competition**. In such situations the job of the manager can be quite complex, involving strategic decisions about product design and quality, product promotion and the provision of various forms of after-sales service.

Product differentiation

Central to non-price competition is **product differentiation**. Most firms' products differ in various ways from those of their rivals. Take the case of washing machines. Although all washing machines wash clothes, and as such are close substitutes for each other, there are many differences between brands. They differ not only in price, but also in their capacity, their styling, their range of programmes, their economy in the use of electricity, hot water and detergent, their reliability, their noise, their after-sales service, etc.

Firms will attempt to design their product so that they can stress its advantages (real or imaginary) over the competitor brands. By doing this, a firm is advertising its product's unique selling point (USP): what it is that makes their product different from its competitors' products. Just think of the specific features of particular models of car, hi-fi equipment or brands of cosmetic, and then consider the ways in which these features are stressed by advertisements. In fact, think of virtually any advertisement and consider how it stresses the features of that particular brand. It doesn't even have to be a high-tech product: look at men's razors. This is a product that undergoes constant innovation, whereby each competitor aims to advertise any new feature that differentiates their product from those of its rivals.

Features of a product

A product has many dimensions, and a strategy to differentiate a product may focus on one or more of these. Dimensions include:

■ *Technical standards.* These relate to the product's level of technical sophistication: how advanced it is in relation to the current state of technology. This would be a very important product dimension if, for example, you were purchasing a PC.

Definitions

Non-price competition
Competition in terms of product promotion (advertising, packaging, etc.) or product development.

Product differentiation
Where a firm's product is in some way distinct from its rivals' products. In the context of growth strategies, this is where a business upgrades existing products or services so as to make them different from those of rival firms.

■ *Quality standards.* These relate to aspects such as the quality of the materials used in the product's construction and the care taken in assembly. These will affect the product's durability and reliability. The purchase of consumer durables, such as televisions, furniture and toys, will be strongly influenced by quality standards.

■ *Design characteristics.* These relate to the product's direct appeal to the consumer in terms of appearance or operating features. Examples of design characteristics are colour, style and even packaging. The demand for fashion products such as clothing will be strongly influenced by design characteristics.

■ *Service characteristics.* This aspect is not directly concerned with the product itself, but with the support and back-up given to the customer after the product has been sold. Servicing, product maintenance and guarantees would be included under this heading. When purchasing a new car, the quality of after-sales service might strongly influence the choice you make.

Market segmentation

Different features of a product will appeal to different consumers. Where features are quite distinct, and where particular features or groups of features can be seen to appeal to a particular category of consumers, it might be useful for producers to divide the market into segments. Taking the example of cars again, the market could be divided into luxury cars, large, medium and small family cars, sports cars, multi-terrain vehicles, seven-seater people carriers, etc. Each type of car occupies a distinct market segment.

When consumer tastes change over time, or where existing models do not cater for every taste, a firm may be able to identify a new segment of the market – a **market niche**. Having identified the appropriate market niche for its product, the marketing division within the firm will then set about targeting the relevant consumer group(s) and developing an appropriate strategy for promoting the product.

> **Definitions**
>
> **Market niche**
> A part of a market (or new market) that has not been filled by an existing brand or business.
>
> **Growth vector matrix**
> A means by which a business might assess its product/market strategy.

Marketing the product

There is no universally accepted definition of marketing, but it is generally agreed that it covers the following activities: establishing the strength of consumer demand in existing parts of the market, and potential demand in new niches; developing an attractive and distinct image for the product; informing potential consumers of various features of the product; fostering a desire by consumers for the product; and, in the light of all these, persuading consumers to buy the product.

Product/market strategy

Once the nature and strength of consumer demand (both current and potential) have been identified, the business will set about meeting and influencing this demand. In most cases it will be hoping to achieve a growth in sales. To do this, one of the first things the firm must decide is its *product/market strategy*. This will involve addressing two major questions:

■ Should it focus on promoting its existing product, or should it develop new products?

■ Should it focus on gaining a bigger share of its existing market, or should it seek to break into new markets?

These choices can be shown in a **growth vector matrix**. This is illustrated in Figure 3.4. The four cells show the possible combinations of answers to the above questions: cell A – *market penetration* (current product, current market); cell B – *product development* (new product, current market); cell C – *market development* (current product, new market); cell D – *diversification* (new product, new market).

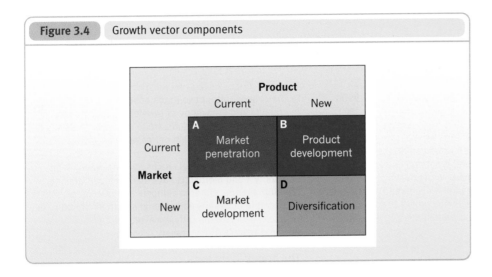

Figure 3.4   Growth vector components

Market penetration. In the market penetration strategy, the business will seek not only to retain existing customers, but to expand its customer base with current products in current markets. Of the four strategies, this is generally the least risky: the business will be able to play to its product's strengths and draw on its knowledge of the market. The business's marketing strategy will tend to focus upon aggressive product promotion and distribution. Such a strategy, however, is likely to lead to fierce competition from existing business rivals, especially if the overall market is not expanding and if the firm can therefore gain an increase in sales only by taking market share from its rivals.

Product development. Product development strategies will involve introducing new models and designs in current markets. It could include the introduction of an upgrade or a completely new model.

Market development. With a market development strategy the business will seek increased sales of current products by expanding into new markets. These may be in a different geographical location (e.g. overseas), or new market segments. Alternatively, the strategy may involve finding new uses and applications for the product.

> **Pause for thought**
>
> *What unknown factors is the business likely to face following a diversification strategy?*

Diversification. A diversification strategy will involve the business expanding into new markets with new products. Of all the strategies, this is the most risky given the unknown factors that the business is likely to face.

Once the product/market strategy has been decided upon, the business will then attempt to devise a suitable *marketing strategy*. This will involve looking at the marketing mix.

The marketing mix

In order to differentiate the firm's product from those of its rivals, there are four variables that can be adjusted. These are as follows:

- product;
- price;
- place (distribution);
- promotion.

BOX 3.4   BRANDS AND OWN BRANDS

What's in a name?

The rise of supermarket own brands in the early 1990s was phenomenal. Their market penetration in the UK became so great that, by 1995, 54.5 per cent of all sales in the major supermarket chains were of own-branded products. In 1992, just three years earlier, the figure had been a mere 27 per cent. What makes this rise even more striking is that it followed a period when branded products dominated the market and seemed to be growing in strength. During the 1980s, the profits of companies such as Kellogg's and Heinz were increasing by as much as 15 per cent a year.

However, towards the end of the 1980s, things started to go horribly wrong for branded products:

■ The economic boom of the time came to an end, and the UK, along with many other countries, went into recession, with the result that consumers became more price conscious.
■ Supermarkets began to develop a more extensive range of own-label products.

As Alan Mitchell argued in *Marketing Week* (6 December 1996):

New technologies [were] allowing own-label manufacturers to produce smaller batch runs at lower costs: so the benefits of economies of scale [declined].

Own-label products also lay claim to cost advantages, both on marketing and distribution – a few dedicated trucks from factory to retailer regional distribution centre are nothing compared with the cost of a fleet serving every retailer, wholesaler, and convenience shop.

This means all the paraphernalia of advertising, distribution, and new product development that made the brand manufacturing model so powerful decades ago is unravelling, and becoming an enormous cost burden instead – a burden that adds up to 50 per cent on to the final consumer price and allows retailers to undercut brands while creaming off higher margins. The virtuous cycle goes into reverse, and becomes a vicious circle.

Such were the cost advantages of the own-label alternative that, for many products, the price discrepancy between brands and own brands had become staggering, forcing brand manufacturers to make substantial price cuts. For example, the dairy producer Kraft was forced to slash prices on many of its cheese products, which in several cases were some 45 per cent more expensive than own-label alternatives.

The position of branded products was further undermined. Technology not only pushed down costs, but also raised the *quality* of products, making it easier for own-label producers to copy established brands, and in many cases to innovate themselves. According to *The Grocer*,[1] about two-thirds of shoppers believe the quality and innovation of own-label products are on a par with branded goods, while over two-thirds say that own-label products are better value for money than branded goods.

The major supermarket chains such as Tesco, Asda, Sainsbury's and Morrisons have all developed their own premium brands, either to compete in particular segments, for example in healthy eating ranges such as 'Be Good to Yourself' or 'Taste the Difference' or, more generally, for example Tesco's 'Finest' range.

The brands fight back

What are brand manufacturers to do? One alternative is to extend a brand to new products and use the brand image to promote them. Not only will this help raise revenue but it will also reduce the producer's reliance on a single product. Take the case of Virgin. The brand no longer applies just to record stores. It now embraces airlines, trains, finance, soft drinks, mobile phones, holidays, bridal wear, cinemas, radio, virtual car showrooms, online books, an online wine store, an Internet service provider, cosmetics, health clubs, balloon rides, gift 'experiences' and stem cell banks. With the launching of Virgin Galactic in 2004 and orders for five 'spaceliners', it now even includes space tourism! This is a prime example of diversification. Other examples include Branston baked beans and Google Base (to rival eBay) and Google Chrome (to rival Internet Explorer).

Another approach is to focus on the perceived high quality of branded products. Part of the reason for a decline in market share of own brands from the early 1990s to 2007 was a period of prolonged economic growth. The rise in disposable income leads to increased conspicuous consumption, and many branded goods are associated with affluence and increased quality of lifestyle. An example is the preference of many consumers for designer-label clothing rather than the supermarket's own clothing ranges, despite considerable differences in prices.

By the mid-2000s, with a rapidly growing economy and a recovery in the demand for branded products, sales of own-label supermarket brands had fallen back from over 50 per cent to about one-third of all sales in supermarket chains. However, with the onset of recession and with falling disposable incomes in 2008/9, supermarkets took advantage of price sensitive consumers with value-for-money own-label products. Branded products did not follow this strategy.

---

[1] *The Grocer*, 1 April 2006

A mixed picture

Although there have been overall movements in the share of branded and own-label products, there are big differences in own-label penetration from one product to another. As the table illustrates, in some product segments the penetration of supermarkets' own brands is considerable, e.g. cheese, bottled water, cakes and cake bars, and frozen burgers. In others, however, branded products dominate, e.g. carbonates, crisps and coffee.

Market penetration of own-label brands in selected markets, 2007

Market segment	Market share (%)	Key brand competitors[a]
Cheese[b]	60.6	Kraft (6.9% – Dairylea), Dairy Crest (5.3% – Cathedral City)
Cakes and cake bars	51	Premier Foods (Mr Kipling, 12%), United Biscuits (McVities, 5%)
Frozen burgers	39	Birds Eye (50%), Dalepak (6%)
Bottled water	35	Volvic (16%), Evian (14%)
Carbonates	25	Coca-Cola (45%), Pepsi (11%), Fanta (7%)
Take-home ice cream	24	Unilever (39% – includes Walls), Masterfoods (5% – includes Mars)
Bread[b]	20	Warburtons (22%), Hovis (21%), Kingsmill (14%)
Breakfast cereals	20	Kelloggs (42% – includes Cornflakes, Rice Krispies, etc.), Cereal Partners (18% – includes all Nestlé products)
Coffee	17	Nescafé (42%), Kraft (19%)
Yellow fats (e.g. butter, margarine)	14.5	Unilever (29.4% – includes Flora, 19.6%), Arlefood (26.8% – includes Lurpak, 18.3%)
Crisps	10.8	Walkers Snack Foods (69% – includes Walkers Crisps, Walkers Sensations), KP (16.8% – includes McCoys)

[a] Market shares by value for key competitors in brackets where available (except Bottled water which is based on volume)
[b] Figures for 2006

Source: Based on various Mintel Reports (2007 and 2008)

Where products are viewed as fairly homogenous, at least in the eyes of the consumer (e.g. cheese, water and frozen burgers), product differentiation by brand is difficult to achieve. There are no real cost advantages and prices are more competitive.

On the other hand, where products are more differentiated, consumers may identify their particular product by branding. Examples include products targeted at a particular group (defined by gender, age or socioeconomic status), products that reflect a certain style of living (e.g. healthy eating), products that embody high quality or innovative characteristics, or have a long history.

1. How has the improvement in the quality of own brands affected the price elasticity of demand for branded products? What implications does this have for the pricing strategy of brand manufacturers?
2. Do the brand manufacturers have any actual or potential cost advantages over own-brand manufacturers?

Definition

Marketing mix
The mix of product, price, place (distribution) and promotion that will determine a business' marketing strategy.

The particular combination of these variables, known as 'the four Ps', represents the business's **marketing mix**, and it is around a manipulation of them that the business will devise its marketing strategy.

Product considerations. These involve issues such as quality and reliability, as well as branding, packaging and after-sales service.

Pricing considerations. These involve not only the product's basic price in relation to those of competitors' products, but also opportunities for practising price discrimination (the practice of charging different prices in different parts of the market; see section 5.6), offering discounts to particular customers, and adjusting the terms of payment for the product.

Place considerations. These focus on the product's distribution network, and involve issues such as where the business's retail outlets should be located, what warehouse facilities the business might require, and how the product should be transported to the market.

Promotion considerations. These focus primarily upon the amount and type of advertising the business should use. In addition, promotion issues might also include selling techniques, special offers, trial discounts and various other public relations 'gimmicks'.

Every product is likely to have a distinct marketing *mix* of these four variables. Thus we cannot talk about an ideal value for one (e.g. the best price), without considering the other three. What is more, the most appropriate mix will vary from product to product and from market to market.

Pause for thought

Give an example of how changing one of the four Ps might conflict with another of them.

What the firm must seek to do is to estimate how sensitive demand is to the various aspects of marketing. The greater the sensitivity (elasticity) in each case, the more the firms should focus on that particular aspect. It is important for a firm to make sure that the four Ps do not come into conflict with each other, which is possible when one element of the marketing mix is adjusted.

Advertising

One of the most important aspects of marketing is advertising. The major aim of advertising is to sell more products, and business spends a vast quantity of money on advertising to achieve this goal. Through advertising, the business is not only making consumers aware of the product, but is purposefully trying to persuade the consumer to buy the good.

In fact, there is a bit more to it than this. Advertisers are trying to do two things:

■ Shift the product's demand curve to the right.
■ Make it less price elastic.

This is illustrated in Figure 3.5. D_1 shows the original demand curve with price at P_1 and sales at Q_1. D_2 shows the curve after an advertising campaign. The rightward shift allows an increased quantity (Q_2) to be sold at the original price. If, at the same time, the demand is made less elastic, the firm can also raise its price and still experience an increase in sales. Thus in the diagram, price can be raised to P_2 and sales will be Q_3 – still substantially above Q_1. The total gain in revenue is shown by the shaded area.

How can advertising bring about this new demand curve?

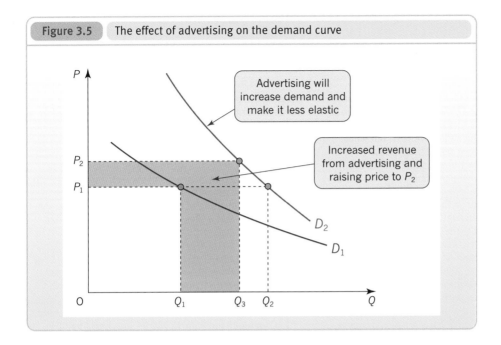

Figure 3.5   The effect of advertising on the demand curve

Shifting the demand curve to the right. This will occur if the advertising brings the product to more people's attention and if it increases people's desire for the product.

Making the demand curve less elastic. This will occur if the advertising creates greater brand loyalty. People must be led to believe (rightly or wrongly) that competitors' brands are inferior. This will allow the firm to raise its price above that of its rivals with no significant fall in sales. There will be only a small substitution effect of this price rise because consumers have been led to believe that there are no close substitutes.

The more successful an advertising campaign is, the more it will shift the demand curve to the right and the more it will reduce the price elasticity of demand.

Advertising and the state of the economy

One final thing to consider is the impact of booms and recessions on marketing and advertising. Take the case of a recession, such as that of 2008/9. Marketing expenditure is a huge expense for a firm, and so cutting back on advertising could significantly reduce a firm's costs and the data suggests that this is what has happened. According to the Advertising Association, advertising expenditure fell from the start of 2008 to the beginning of 2010. Eventually, in mid 2010, advertising picked up as the recovery gathered pace. However, is cutting back on marketing in a recession the right thing to do?

Maintaining or even increasing expenditure on marketing during a recession might enable a firm to take advantage of weaker competitors. Increasing market share during a downturn may mean higher profits when demand recovers. Indeed, Domino's UK saw excellent sales and profits growth, despite the recession. It used advertising to increase its market share.

Pause for thought

Assume that the government runs an advertising campaign to encourage people to stop smoking. How will this affect the position of the demand curve and the price elasticity of demand for cigarettes?

BOX 3.5 **ADVERTISING AND THE LONG RUN**

Promoting quality

It is relatively straightforward to measure the short-term impact of an advertising campaign; a simple before and after assessment of sales will normally give a good indication of the advertising's effectiveness. But what about the medium and longer-term effects of an advertising campaign? How will sales and profits be affected over, say, a five-year period?

The typical impact of advertising on a product's sales is shown in Figure (a). Assume that there is an advertising campaign for the product between time t_1 and t_2. There is a direct effect on sales while the advertising lasts and shortly afterwards. Sales rise from S_1 to S_2. After a while (beyond time t_3), the direct effect of the advertising begins to wear off, and wears off completely by time t_4. This is illustrated by the dashed line. But the higher level of sales declines much more slowly, given that many of the new customers continue to buy the product out of habit. Sales will eventually level off (at point t_5). It is likely, however, that sales will not return to the original level of S_1; there will be some new customers who will stick with the product over the long term. This long-term effect is shown by the increase in sales from S_1 to S_3.

But just what is this long-term effect? One way to explore the impact of advertising over the long run is to evaluate how advertising and profitability in general are linked. Figure (b) shows how advertising shapes the

image of the product and its perceived quality, which the customer then compares with price to determine the product's value. The more that advertising can enhance the perceived quality of a product, the more it will increase the product's profitability.

How this benefits the business over the longer term can be illustrated by the cases of VW Golf and the Famous Grouse whisky, winners of the 2006 Gold and Silver awards of the Institute of Practitioners in Advertising, the UK trade body and professional institute. To quote from the IPA site:

Thirty years ago, a small car called Golf was born. . . . Communications helped create, nourish and nurture the genuinely loved and financially valuable brand Golf is today. The story includes some of the UK's most famous ads – from 'Casino' and 'Changes' in the 1980s, to 'Singing in the Rain' in 2005 – but this is not just about them. It's about how Golf communications have become increasingly sophisticated, based on new thinking about the car buying process, and about the role of communications within it. Golf is now not just a much loved and enduring icon, it has also become the third biggest selling car in UK history.

The Famous Grouse was stuck in the middle of the whisky market in the UK; with its sector

(a) Advertising and the long run

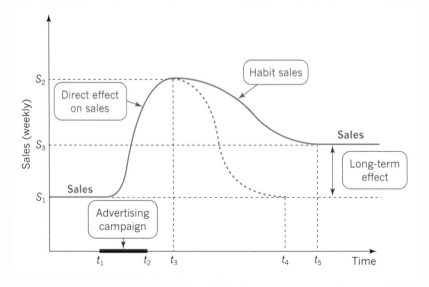

(b) Advertising, profit margins and company growth

```
┌──────────────────────────────────────────────────┐
│   Advertising expenditure relative to competitors  │
└──────────────────────────────────────────────────┘
            │                              │
            ▼                              │
┌──────────────────────┐                  │
│  Product image and    │                  │
│  company reputation   │                  │
└──────────────────────┘                  │
            │                              │
            ▼                              ▼
┌──────────────────────┐        ┌──────────────────────┐
│ Relative quality of   │◄─────►│   Relative price      │
│ offering              │        └──────────────────────┘
└──────────────────────┘                  │
            │                              │
            ▼                              ▼
        ┌──────────────────────────────────┐
        │   (Relative) customer value       │
        └──────────────────────────────────┘
            │                              │
            ▼                              ▼
┌──────────────────────┐        ┌──────────────────────┐
│  Real market growth   │        │   Market share        │
└──────────────────────┘        └──────────────────────┘
            │                              │        │
            ▼                              ▼        ▼
┌──────────────────────┐        ┌──────────────────────┐
│       Growth          │◄───────│   Profit margins      │
└──────────────────────┘        └──────────────────────┘
```

(Blended Scotch) declining while single malts and own-label brands experienced strong growth. It was a small Perthshire company with global ambitions, but without the scale of its global competitors. With the help of AMV BBDO, they overcame this and built a brand-centric advertising platform – one that engaged the consumer, made them love the brand and helped The Famous Grouse stand out from the crowd. They invested in their brand equity in the UK while other brands retreated, and developed a campaign that more than returned their investment, producing a retail sales value in excess of over £513m in the UK.[1]

PG Tips, launched in 1930, is another brand that leads its respective market. The UK tea market has been dominated by PG Tips since 1958, when it became market leader, a position it still holds today, with some 35 per cent of the 'traditional' tea market. The 'chimp' adverts, the Aardman T-Birds and more recently Monkey, have established a clear brand image, enabling PG Tips to hold its ground in a highly competitive market and charge a price premium. (Blind tests have revealed that consumers cannot distinguish between any of the leading tea brands!) Market analysis shows that PG Tips has a price elasticity of demand of −0.4 compared with its nearest rival, Tetley, which has an elasticity of −1.4. It is estimated that between 1980 and 2000 advertising the PG Tips brand cost £100 million but generated in the region of £2 billion in extra sales. Not a bad return!

The message is that advertising should seek to promote a product's quality. This is the key to long-term sales and profits. What is also apparent is that successful brands have advertising campaigns which have been consistent over time. A brand image of quality is not created overnight, but once it is established it can endure and yield profits over the longer term.

[1] www.ipaeffectivenessawards.co.uk/text/2006/shortlist06_text.html#link13

1. *How are long-run profits and advertising linked?*
2. *Why does quality 'win out' in the end?*
3. *How would you advise the owner of the PG Tips brand (Unilever) on a pricing strategy?*

Recap

1. When firms seek to differentiate their products from those of their competitors, they can adjust one or more of four dimensions of the product: its technical standards, its quality, its design characteristics, and the level of customer service.

2. Marketing involves developing a product image and then persuading consumers to purchase it.

3. A business must choose an appropriate product/market strategy. Four such strategies can be identified: market penetration (focusing on existing product and market); product development (new product in existing market); market development (existing product in new markets); diversification (new products in new markets).

4. The marketing strategy of a product involves the manipulation of four key variables: product, price, place and promotion. Every product has a distinct marketing mix.

5. The aims of advertising are to increase demand and make the product less price elastic.

QUESTIONS

1. How would marginal utility and market demand be affected by a rise in the price of (a) a substitute good, (b) a complementary good?

2. How can marginal utility be used to explain the price elasticity of demand for a particular brand of a product?

3. Why are insurance companies unwilling to provide insurance against losses arising from war or 'civil insurrection'? Name some other events where it would be impossible to obtain insurance.

4. What are the relative strengths and weaknesses of using (a) market observations, (b) market surveys and (c) market experiments as means of gathering evidence on consumer demand?

5. You are working for a record company which is thinking of signing up some new bands. What market observations, market surveys and market experiments could you conduct to help you decide which bands to sign?

6. You are about to launch a new range of cosmetics, but you are still to decide upon the content and structure of your advertising campaign. Consider how market surveys and market experiments might be used to help you assess consumer perceptions of the product. What limitations might each of the research methods have in helping you gather data?

7. Imagine that you are an airline attempting to forecast demand for seats over the next two or three years. What do you think could be used as leading indicators?

8. How might we account for the growth in non-price competition within the modern developed economy?

9. Consider how the selection of the product/market strategy (market penetration, market development, product development and diversification) will influence the business's marketing mix. Choose a particular product and identify which elements in the marketing mix would be most significant in developing a successful marketing strategy for it.

10. Think of some advertisements that deliberately seek to make demand less price elastic.

11. Imagine that 'Sunshine' sunflower margarine, a well-known brand, is advertised with the slogan, 'It helps you live longer' (the implication being that butter and margarines high in saturates shorten your life). What do you think would happen to the demand curve for a supermarket's *own* brand of sunflower margarine? Consider both the direction of shift and the effect on elasticity. Will the elasticity differ markedly at different prices? How will this affect the pricing policy and sales of the supermarket's own brand? Could the supermarket respond other than by adjusting the price of its margarine?

Business issues covered in this chapter

- What do profits consist of?
- What is the relationship between inputs and outputs in both the short and long run?
- How do costs vary with output and just what do we mean by 'costs'?
- What are meant by 'economies of scale' and 'diseconomies of scale' and what are the reasons for each?
- What are 'transactions costs' and how do these vary with the degree of vertical integration of the firm?
- How does a business's sales revenue vary with output?
- What do we mean by a price-taking firm?
- How do we measure profits?
- At what output will a firm maximise its profits?
- Why do conditions of perfect competition make being in business a constant battle for survival?

Supply decisions in a perfectly competitive market

In this chapter we turn to supply. In other words, we focus on the amount that firms produce at different prices. In Part C we shall see how the supply decision is affected by the microeconomic environment in which a firm operates, and in particular by the amount of competition it faces. However, in this chapter, we assume that the firm is a price taker. This means that it has to accept the price as given by the market. We also assume that the firm seeks to maximise profits.

Profit is made by firms earning more from the sale of goods than the goods cost to produce. A firm's total profit ($T\Pi$) is thus the difference between its total sales revenue (TR) and its total costs of production (TC).

In order, then, to discover how a firm can maximise its profit, or even make a profit at all, we must first consider what determines costs and revenue. Sections 4.1 and 4.2 examine costs. Section 4.3 considers revenue, and then section 4.4 puts costs and revenue together to examine profit.

4.1 PRODUCTION AND COSTS: SHORT RUN

Production in the short run

The cost of producing any level of output depends on the amount and mix of inputs used and the price that the firm must pay for them. Let us first focus on the quantity and mix of inputs used.

Short-run and long-run changes in production

If a firm wants to increase production, it will take time to acquire a greater quantity of certain inputs. For example, a manufacturer can use more electricity by turning on switches, but it might take a long time to obtain and install more machines, and longer still to build a second or third factory.

If, then, the firm wants to increase output in a hurry, it will only be able to increase the quantity of certain inputs and so the input mix will be adjusted. It can use more raw materials, more fuel, more tools and possibly more labour (by hiring extra workers or offering overtime to its existing workforce). But it will have to make do with its existing buildings and most of its machinery.

The distinction we are making here is between **fixed inputs** and **variable inputs**. A *fixed* input is an input that cannot be increased within a given time period (e.g. buildings). A *variable* input is one that can.

The distinction between fixed and variable inputs allows us to distinguish between the short run and the long run.

The short run. The **short run** is a time period during which at least one input is fixed. In the short run, then, output can be increased only by using more variable inputs. For example, if a shipping line wanted to carry more passengers in response to a rise in demand, it could accommodate more passengers on existing sailings if there was space. It could increase the number of sailings with its existing fleet, by hiring more crew and using more fuel. But in the short run it could not buy more ships; there would not be time for them to be built.

The long run. The **long run** is a time period long enough for all inputs to be varied. Given long enough, the shipping company can have a new ship built.

The short run and long run are not set periods of time and they will be different from firm to firm. Thus if it takes a farmer a year to obtain new land, buildings and equipment, the short run is any time period up to a year and the long run is any time period longer than a year. But if it takes a shipping company three years to obtain an extra ship, the short run is any period up to three years and the long run is any period longer than three years.

For this section we will concentrate on *short-run* production and costs. We will look at the long run in section 4.2.

> **Pause for thought**
>
> How will the length of the short run for the shipping company depend on the state of the shipbuilding industry?

Definitions

Short run

The period of time over which at least one input is fixed.

Long run

The period of time long enough for all inputs to be varied.

Law of diminishing (marginal) returns

When one or more inputs are held fixed, there will come a point beyond which the extra output from additional units of the variable input will diminish.

Production in the short run: the law of diminishing returns

Production in the short run is subject to *diminishing returns*. You may well have heard of 'the law of diminishing returns', it is one of the most famous of all 'laws' of economics. To illustrate how this law underlies short-run production, let us take the simplest possible case where there are just two inputs: one fixed and one variable.

Take the case of a farm. Assume the fixed input is land and the variable input is labour. Since the land is fixed in supply, output per period of time can be increased only by employing extra workers. But imagine what would happen as more and more workers crowded on to a fixed area of land. Workers will begin to get in each other's way and the land simply cannot go on yielding more and more output indefinitely. After a point the additions to total output from each extra worker will begin to diminish.

We can now state the **law of diminishing (marginal) returns**.

 KEY IDEA 14   **The law of diminishing marginal returns.** When increasing amounts of a variable input are used with a given amount of a fixed input, there will come a point when each extra unit of the variable input will produce less extra output than the previous unit.

Opportunity cost

When measuring costs, economists always use the concept of *opportunity cost*. As we saw in section 1.3, opportunity cost is the cost of any activity measured in terms of the sacrifice made in doing it, i.e. the cost measured in terms of the opportunities forgone. If a car manufacturer can produce 10 small saloon cars with the same amount of inputs as it takes to produce 6 large saloon cars, then the opportunity cost of producing 1 small car is 0.6 of a large car. If a taxi and car hire firm chooses to use all of its cars as taxis, then the opportunity cost includes not only the cost of employing taxi drivers and buying fuel, but also the sacrifice of rental income from hiring its vehicles out.

BOX 4.1   DIMINISHING RETURNS AND BUSINESS

What can managers do?

Everywhere you look in business you can see diminishing returns. It applies to both giant multinational corporations and the corner shop; to manufacturing, farming, mining and services. Let us take some examples.

A car manufacturer. In the short run, a company such as Toyota or Ford will have a particular number of factories. If it wants to increase output, there will not be enough time to build a new one. So what does it do? The answer is that it will have to use its existing plants more intensively. For example, it could increase the length of shifts. But as it does so, output per worker is likely to fall as workers become more tired or fed up. It could use its machines more intensively. But as it does so, breakdowns or maintenance problems are likely to increase and at some point the machine will simply not be able to produce any more.

Eventually, no matter how many extra people are employed, the factory will reach full capacity. At this point any additional workers would produce no extra output whatsoever. Returns from additional labour have diminished to zero.

The convenience store. Go into a shop and see what fixed inputs you can see. There will be the shelving, the tills, the warehouse space at the back and, of course, the floor space itself. At busy times the shop may take on more workers, but will each additional worker be able to serve the same number of customers? Probably not. Assume, for example, that there are two tills. Once they are fully in use, taking on more workers will not allow more customers to be served. True, additional workers can make sure the shelves are stocked, collect the trolleys, and so on; but diminishing returns to labour are obvious. Each additional worker is permitting fewer and fewer *extra* customers to be served.

The problem applies similarly to supermarkets. At busy times, queues at the tills get longer and crowding in the shop slows down your progress around it.

The arable farm. In the short run, farmers have a fixed amount of land. They can increase crop yields by applying more fertiliser. However, beyond a certain quantity of fertiliser per hectare, diminishing returns to fertiliser will set in. Additional bags will yield less and less additional output. Case B.13 on the book's website looks at some evidence on diminishing returns to the application of nitrogen fertiliser on farmland.

The firm of solicitors. In the case of professional practices such as this, the number of partners will be fixed in the short run, along with the premises and much of the equipment. It might be possible to hire additional secretarial support or other office staff at short notice, but not another partner. But partners are only human. They get tired and less efficient as the work expands. Each additional hour they work beyond a certain level is likely to result in lower productivity.

The student. Which brings us to you! You have no doubt experienced diminishing returns to study time. Working that extra hour late at night may result in little if any extra learning!

1. *Give some other examples of diminishing returns to inputs other than labour (such as the fertiliser example above).*
2. *If all inputs were variable (as they are in the long run), would expanding output result in diminishing marginal returns? (We examine this question later when we consider the long run.)*

Measuring a firm's opportunity costs

Just how do we measure a firm's opportunity cost? First we must discover what inputs it has used. Then we must measure the sacrifice involved in using them. To do this it is necessary to put inputs into two categories.

Inputs not owned by the firm: explicit costs. The opportunity cost of those inputs not already owned by the firm is simply the price that the firm has to pay for them. Thus if the firm uses £100 worth of electricity, the opportunity cost is £100. The firm has sacrificed £100 which could have been spent on something else.

These costs are called **explicit costs** because they involve direct payment of money by firms.

Inputs already owned by the firm: implicit costs. When the firm already owns inputs (e.g. machinery) it does not as a rule have to pay out money to use them. Their opportunity costs are thus **implicit costs**. They are equal to what the inputs could earn for the firm in some alternative use, either within the firm or hired out to some other firm.

Definitions

Explicit costs
The payments to outside suppliers of inputs.

Implicit costs
Costs which do not involve a direct payment of money to a third party, but which nevertheless involve a sacrifice of some alternative.

Here are some examples of implicit costs:

- Say you own a house. The opportunity cost of living in your house is the rental income you could have earned had you chosen to rent it out to a tenant.
- A firm draws £100 000 from the bank out of its savings in order to invest in a new plant and equipment. The opportunity cost of this investment is not just the £100 000 (an explicit cost), but also the interest it thereby forgoes (an implicit cost).
- The owner of the firm could have earned £30 000 per annum by working for someone else. This £30 000 is the opportunity cost of the owner's time.

If there is no alternative use for an input, as in the case of a machine designed to produce a specific product, and if it has no scrap value, the opportunity cost of using it is *zero*. In such a case, if the output from the machine is worth more than the cost of all the *other* inputs involved, the firm might as well use the machine rather than let it stand idle.

What the firm paid for the machine – its **historic cost** – is irrelevant. Not using the machine will not bring that money back. It has been spent. These are sometimes referred to as 'sunk costs'.

 Sunk costs and the bygones principle. The principle states that sunk (fixed) costs should be ignored when deciding whether to produce or sell more or less of a product. Only variable costs should be taken into account.

Likewise, the **replacement cost** is irrelevant. That should be taken into account only when the firm is considering replacing the machine.

Costs and inputs

A firm's costs of production will depend on the inputs it uses. The more inputs it uses, the greater will its costs be. More precisely, this relationship depends on two elements:

- The productivity of the inputs. The greater their physical productivity, the smaller will be the quantity of them that is needed to produce a given level of output, and hence the lower will be the cost of that output.
- The price of the inputs. The higher their price, the higher will be the costs of production.

In the short run, some inputs are fixed in supply. Their total costs (*TC*), therefore, are fixed, in the sense that they do not vary with output. Rent on land is a **fixed cost**. It is the same whether the firm produces a lot or a little.

The cost of variable inputs, however, does vary with output. The cost of raw materials is a **variable cost**. The more that is produced, the more raw materials are used and therefore the higher is their total cost. **Total cost** is thus total fixed cost (*TFC*) plus total variable cost (*TVC*).

Average and marginal cost

In addition to the total cost of production (fixed and variable) there are two other measures of cost which are particularly important for our analysis of profits. These are average and marginal cost.

Average cost (*AC*) is cost per unit of production:

$$AC = TC/Q$$

Thus if it costs a firm £2000 to produce 100 units of a product, the average cost would be £20 for each unit (£2000/100).

As with total cost, average cost can be divided into the two components, fixed and variable. In other words, average cost equals **average fixed cost** (*AFC = TFC/Q*) plus **average variable cost** (*AVC = TVC/Q*):

$$AC = AFC + AVC$$

Marginal cost (*MC*) is the *extra* cost of producing *one more unit*, i.e. the rise in total cost per one unit rise in output:

$$MC = \frac{\Delta TC}{\Delta Q}$$

where Δ means 'a change in'.

For example, assume that a firm is currently producing 1 000 000 boxes of matches a month. It now increases output by 1000 boxes (another batch): $\Delta Q = 1000$. Assume that as a result its total costs rise by £30: $\Delta TC = £30$. What is the cost of producing *one* more box of matches? It is:

$$MC = \frac{\Delta TC}{\Delta Q} = \frac{£30}{1000} = 3p$$

(Note that all marginal costs are variable, since, by definition, there can be no extra fixed costs as output rises.)

Table 4.1 shows costs for an imaginary firm, firm X, over a given period of time (e.g. a week). The table shows how average and marginal costs can be derived from total costs. It is assumed that total fixed costs are £12 000 (column 2) and that total variable costs are as shown in column 3.

The figures for *TVC* have been chosen to illustrate the law of diminishing returns. Initially, *before* diminishing returns set in, *TVC* rises less and less rapidly as more

Definitions

Average (total) cost (AC)
Total cost (fixed plus variable) per unit of output:
$AC = TC/Q = AFC + AVC$.

Average fixed cost (AFC)
Total fixed cost per unit of output: $AFC = TFC/Q$.

Average variable cost (AVC)
Total variable cost per unit of output: $AVC = TVC/Q$.

Marginal cost (MC)
The cost of producing one more unit of output: $MC = \Delta TC/\Delta Q$.

Table 4.1 Costs for firm X

Output (Q) (1)	TFC (£000) (2)	TVC (£000) (3)	TC (TFC + TVC) (£000) (4)	AFC (TFC/Q) (£000) (5)	AVC (TVC/Q) (£000) (6)	AC (TC/Q) (£000) (7)	MC (ΔTC/ΔQ) (£000) (8)
0	12	0	12	–	–	–	
							10
1	12	10	22	12	10	22	
							6
2	12	16	28	6	8	14	
							5
3	12	21	33	4	7	11	
							7
4	12	28	40	3	7	10	
							12
5	12	40	52	2.4	8	10.4	
							20
6	12	60	72	2	10	12	
							31
7	12	91	103	1.7	13	14.7	

variable factors are added. For example, in the case of a factory with a fixed supply of machinery, initially as more workers are taken on, the workers can do increasingly specialist tasks and make a fuller use of the capital equipment. Extra workers are producing more and more extra output. However, above a certain output (3 units in Table 4.1), diminishing returns set in. Given that extra workers (the extra variable factors) are producing less and less extra output, the extra units of output they do produce will be costing more and more in terms of wage costs. Thus *TVC* rises more and more rapidly. You can see this by examining column 3.

The figures in the remaining columns in Table 4.1 are derived from columns 1 to 3. Look at the figures in each of the columns and check how the figures are derived. Note the figures for marginal cost are plotted between the lines to illustrate that marginal cost represents the increase in costs as output increases from one unit to the next.

We can use the data in Table 4.1 to draw *MC*, *AFC*, *AVC* and *AC* curves (see Figure 4.1 on page 94).

> **Pause for thought**
>
> *Use the figures in the first three columns of Table 4.1 to plot TFC, TVC and TC curves (where costs are plotted on the vertical axis and quantity on the horizontal axis). Mark the point on each of the TVC and TC curves where diminishing returns set in. What do you notice about the slope of the two curves at this output?*

Marginal cost (MC). The shape of the *MC* curve follows directly from the law of diminishing returns. Initially, in Figure 4.1, as more of the variable input is used, extra units of output cost less than previous units. *MC* falls.

Beyond a certain level of output, however, diminishing returns set in. This is shown as point *x*. Thereafter *MC* rises. Additional units of output cost more and more to produce, since they require ever-increasing amounts of the variable input.

Average fixed cost (AFC). This falls continuously as output rises, since total fixed costs are being spread over a greater and greater output. If a firm finds that its fixed costs represent a large proportion of its total costs, expanding output can be a good strategy to adopt, as average fixed costs will begin to fall.

Average (total) cost (AC). This is the vertical sum of the average fixed cost and the average variable cost curves. As you can see from Figure 4.1, as *AFC* falls, the gap between *AVC* and *AC* decreases.

The relationship between average cost and marginal cost. The shape of the *AC* curve depends on the shape of the *MC* curve. As long as new units of output cost less than the average, their production must pull the average cost down. That is, if *MC* is less than *AC*, *AC* must be falling. Likewise, if new units cost more than the average, their production must pull the average up. That is, if *MC* is greater than *AC*, *AC* must be rising. Therefore, the *MC* curve crosses the *AC* curve at its minimum point (point *z* in Figure 4.1). If you find this concept difficult, then try inserting some data for *AC*, *MC* and *TC* at different levels of output.

For example, say 4 units of output cost £5 each to produce. Total cost = £20 (4 × 5) and average cost = £5 (20/4). If output is increased by 1 unit and this unit costs an extra £5 to produce, (the same as the average cost) then the average cost simply remains at £5 (Average cost = $TC/Q = 25/5$ = £5). However, now assume that the marginal cost of this fifth unit is £6 (*MC > AC*). Total costs for 6 units are now £26 and the average cost is: $AC = TC/Q = 26/5 = £5.20$. The average cost has been pulled up by the higher marginal cost. The opposite will happen if marginal cost is lower than average cost.

> **Pause for thought**
>
> *Before you read on can you explain why the marginal cost curve will always cut the average cost curve at its lowest point?*

Average variable cost (AVC). Since $AVC = AC - AFC$, the AVC curve is simply the vertical difference between the AC and the AFC curves. Again, note that as AFC gets less, the gap between AVC and AC narrows. Since all marginal costs are variable (by definition, there are no marginal fixed costs), the same relationship holds between MC and AVC as it did between MC and AC. That is, if MC is less than AVC, AVC must be falling, and if MC is greater than AVC, AVC must be rising. Therefore, as with the AC curve, the MC curve crosses the AVC curve at its minimum point (point y in Figure 4.1).

Figure 4.1	Average and marginal costs

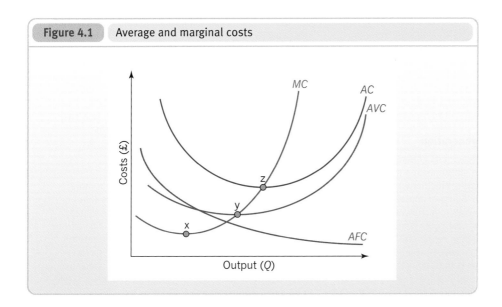

Recap

1. Production in the short run is subject to diminishing returns. As greater quantities of the variable input(s) are used, so each additional unit of the variable input will add less to output than previous units, i.e. output will rise less and less rapidly.

2. When measuring costs of production, we should be careful to use the concept of opportunity cost. In the case of inputs not owned by the firm, the opportunity cost is simply the explicit cost of purchasing or hiring them: it is the price paid for them. In the case of inputs already owned by the firm, it is the implicit cost of what the factor could have earned for the firm in its best alternative use.

3. As some factors are fixed in supply in the short run, their total costs are fixed with respect to output.

In the case of variable factors, their total cost increases as more output is produced and hence as more of them are used. Total cost can be divided into total fixed and total variable cost.

4. Marginal cost is the cost of producing one more unit of output. It will probably fall at first but will start to rise as soon as diminishing returns set in.

5. Average cost, like total cost, can be divided into fixed and variable costs. Average fixed cost will decline as more output is produced. The reason is that the total fixed cost is being spread over a greater and greater number of units of output. Average variable cost will tend to decline at first, but once the marginal cost has risen above it, it must then rise. The same applies to average cost.

BOX 4.2   MAKING USE OF YOUR FIXED INPUTS

Business practices to reduce average fixed costs

The distinction between fixed and variable costs has profound implications for the behaviour of any business. In the short run, if a firm increases its output, total variable costs will increase; total fixed costs will not. Put another way, average variable costs may well rise, but average fixed costs will fall (as Figure 4.1 illustrates).

So why is this so important for business? The answer is that no firm will want to have its fixed inputs underused, except for short periods of time. After all, using more of them incurs no extra fixed costs – by definition. The larger the proportion of fixed costs to variable costs, the more important this becomes. It becomes especially important when a business has more than one production plant and where the ratio of fixed and variable costs vary between them.

The case of electricity generation

Let's take the example of electricity generation and compare a gas-fired power station with a nuclear one. The average cost of generating electricity from these two types of power station is approximately the same: around 2.5 pence per kilowatt hour. However, the proportion of fixed and variable costs is very different.

A nuclear power station has very high fixed costs: average fixed cost at full capacity is around 82 per cent of average cost. The reason is that nuclear power stations are very expensive to build and maintain, and then to decommission at the end of their life. On the other hand, variable costs (mainly fuel) are very low compared with other forms of generation.

Gas-fired power stations, however, are relatively cheap to build. Average fixed cost at normal capacity account for only just over 30 per cent of average cost. Fuel costs, by contrast, are some four times as much per kilowatt as nuclear power.

So what are the implications of these differences? The answer is to keep nuclear power stations working to full capacity so as to spread their high total fixed costs over as much output as possible. In other words, because average fixed costs fall as more is produced, and because

fixed costs account for such a large proportion of the total costs of nuclear generation, average costs fall substantially as output is increased. Put another way, the marginal cost of electricity generation from nuclear plants is low and so they should be used to full capacity.

With gas-fired power stations, the picture is very different. Because the demand for electricity fluctuates with the time of day and the weather, and because there must always be the capacity to meet demand (since electricity cannot be stored), there must always be some spare capacity to enable the system to respond to a surge in demand. Gas-fired power stations can fill this role, since they have low fixed costs. Cutting back production will not significantly increase average fixed cost.

Thus the output of nuclear power stations is virtually constant, while the output of gas-fired stations fluctuates with demand.

Lessons for business in general

Many businesses have more than one plant or more than one production line. For example, a firm could have a relatively new production line using the latest technology and an older one using a previous technology. It is quite likely that the new line will be more capital intensive, with high capital (fixed) costs, but using less labour, and possibly less raw materials too, and thus with lower variable costs. The older technology is likely to be more labour intensive and thus have higher average variable costs and high marginal costs.

If demand for the firm's product fluctuates, it is likely to keep the automated production line working at full capacity (marginal cost is low) and vary output from the older line, since that has the higher marginal cost.

 On a diagram similar to Figure 4.1, sketch the AFC, AVC, AC *and* MC *curves for (a) a nuclear power station and (b) a gas-fired power station. For simplicity assume that both stations would produce the same amount of electricity at full capacity.*

4.2   PRODUCTION AND COSTS: LONG RUN

In the long run *all* inputs are variable. There is time for the firm to build a new factory (maybe in a different part of the country), to install new machines, to use different techniques of production, and in general to combine its inputs in whatever proportion and in whatever quantities it chooses.

In the long run, then, a firm will have to make a number of decisions about the scale of its operations and the techniques of production it will use. These decisions will affect the costs of production. It is important, therefore, to get them right, as many of them will be costly to reverse or could even be totally irreversible.

Table 4.2	Short-run and long-run increases in output					
	Short run			**Long run**		
Input 1	**Input 2**	**Output**	**Input 1**	**Input 2**	**Output**	
3	1	25	1	1	15	
3	2	45	2	2	35	
3	3	60	3	3	60	
3	4	70	4	4	90	
3	5	75	5	5	125	

The scale of production

If a firm were to double all of its inputs – something it could do in the long run – would it double its output? Or would output more than double or less than double? We can distinguish three possible situations.

Constant returns to scale. This is where a given percentage increase in inputs will lead to the same percenage increase in output.

Increasing returns to scale. This is where a given percentage increase in inputs will lead to a larger percentage increase in output.

Decreasing returns to scale. This is where a given percentage increase in inputs will lead to a smaller percentage increase in output.

Notice the terminology here. The words 'to scale' mean that *all* inputs increase by the same proportion. Decreasing returns to *scale* are therefore quite different from *diminishing* marginal returns (where only the *variable* input increases). The differences between marginal returns to a variable input and returns to scale are illustrated in Table 4.2.

In the short run, input 1 is assumed to be fixed in supply (at 3 units). Output can be increased only by using more of the variable input (input 2). In the long run, however, both input 1 and input 2 are variable.

In the short-run situation, diminishing returns can be seen from the fact that as input 2 is increased, output increases at a decreasing rate (25 to 45 to 60 to 70 to 75). In the long-run situation, the table illustrates increasing returns to scale. As both inputs are increased, output increases at an *increasing* rate (15 to 35 to 60 to 90 to 125).

Economies of scale

The concept of increasing returns to scale is closely linked to that of **economies of scale**. A firm experiences economies of scale if costs per unit of output fall as the scale of production increases. Clearly, if a firm is getting increasing returns to scale from its inputs, then as it produces more, it will be using smaller and smaller amounts of inputs per unit of output. Other things being equal, this means that it will be producing at a lower unit cost.

There are a number of reasons why firms are likely to experience economies of scale. Some are due to increasing returns to scale, some are not:

Specialisation and division of labour. In large-scale plants, workers can do more simple repetitive jobs. With this **specialisation and division of labour**, less training is

Definitions

Economies of scale
When increasing the scale of production leads to a lower cost per unit of output.

Specialisation and division of labour
Where production is broken down into a number of simpler, more specialised tasks, thus allowing workers to acquire a high degree of efficiency.

needed; workers can become highly efficient in their particular job, especially with long production runs; there is less time lost in workers switching from one operation to another; each worker only needs one set of tools; supervision is easier. Workers and managers who have specific skills in specific areas can be employed and this may improve productivity.

Indivisibilities. Some inputs are of a minimum size. They are indivisible. The most obvious example is machinery. Take the case of a combine harvester. A small-scale farmer could not make full use of one. They only become economical to use, therefore, on farms above a certain size. The problem of **indivisibilities** is made worse when different machines, each of which is part of the production process, are of a different size. For example, if there are two types of machine, one producing 6 units a day, the other packaging 4 units a day, a minimum of 12 units per day will have to be produced, involving two production machines and three packaging machines, if all machines are to be fully utilised.

The 'container principle'. Any capital equipment that contains things (blast furnaces, oil tankers, pipes, vats, etc.) will tend to cost less per unit of output the larger its size. The reason has to do with the relationship between a container's volume and its surface area. A container's cost will depend largely on the materials used to build it and hence roughly on its *surface area*. Its output will depend largely on its *volume*. Large containers have a bigger volume relative to surface area than do small containers. For example, a container with a bottom, top and four sides, with each side measuring 1 metre, has a volume of 1 cubic metre and a surface area of 6 square metres (6 surfaces of 1 square metre each). If each side were now to be doubled in length to 2 metres, the volume would be 8 cubic metres and the surface area 24 square metres (6 surfaces of 4 square metres each). Thus an eightfold increase in capacity has been gained at only a fourfold increase in the container's surface area, and hence an approximate fourfold increase in cost.

Greater efficiency of large machines. Large machines may be more efficient, in the sense that more output can be gained for a given amount of inputs. For example, only one worker may be required to operate a machine whether it be large or small. Also, a large machine may make a more efficient use of raw materials.

By-products. With production on a large scale, there may be sufficient waste products to enable them to make some by-product, thereby spreading costs over more units of output.

Multi-stage production. A large factory may be able to take a product through several stages in its manufacture. This saves time and cost moving the semi-finished product from one firm or factory to another. For example, a large cardboard-manufacturing firm may be able to convert trees or waste paper into cardboard and then into cardboard boxes in a continuous sequence.

All the above are examples of **plant economies of scale**. They are due to an individual factory or workplace or machine being large. There are other economies of scale that are associated with the business itself being large – perhaps with many factories.

Organisational. With a large business, individual plants can specialise in particular functions. There can also be centralised administration of the plants. Often, after a merger between two firms, savings can be made by **rationalising** their activities in this way.

Spreading overheads. Some expenditures are economic only when the *business* is large, such as research and development; only a large business can afford to set up a research laboratory. This is another example of indivisibilities, only this time at the level of the whole business rather than the plant. The greater the business's output, the more these **overhead costs** are spread.

Financial economies. Large businesses may be able to obtain finance at lower interest rates than small ones. They may be able to obtain certain inputs cheaper by buying in bulk. This relates to the concept of opportunity cost. The larger is a business's order of raw materials, the more likely it is that the supplier will offer a discount, as the opportunity cost of losing the business is relatively high.

Economies of scope. Often a business is large because it produces a range of products. This can result in each individual product being produced more cheaply than if it was produced in a single-product firm. The reason for these **economies of scope** is that various overhead costs and financial and organisational economies can be shared between the products. For example, a firm that produces a whole range of CD players, receivers, amplifiers and tuners can benefit from shared marketing and distribution costs and the bulk purchase of electronic components. Producing a range of products also allows a business to spread its risks and hence insulate itself against a fall in demand for one of its products.

Diseconomies of scale

When businesses get beyond a certain size, costs per unit of output may start to increase. There are several reasons for such **diseconomies of scale**:

- Management problems of coordination may increase as the business becomes larger and more complex, and as lines of communication get longer. There may be a lack of personal involvement by management.
- Workers may feel 'alienated' if their jobs are boring and repetitive, and if they feel an insignificantly small part of a large organisation. Poor motivation may lead to shoddy work.
- Industrial relations may deteriorate as a result of these factors and also as a result of the more complex interrelationships between different categories of worker.
- Production line processes and the complex interdependencies of mass production can lead to great disruption if there are hold-ups in any one part of the business.

Whether businesses experience economies or diseconomies of scale will depend on the conditions applying in each individual business.

The size of the whole industry

As an *industry* grows in size, this can lead to **external economies of scale** for its member firms. This is where a firm, whatever its own individual size, benefits from the *whole industry* being large. For example, the firm may benefit from having access to specialist raw material or component suppliers, labour with specific skills, firms that specialise in marketing the finished product, sharing research and development, and banks and other financial institutions with experience of the industry's requirements. What we are referring to here is the **industry's infrastructure**: the facilities, support services, skills and experience that can be shared by its members.

Definitions

Overheads
Costs arising from the general running of an organisation, and only indirectly related to the level of output.

Economies of scope
When increasing the range of products produced by a firm reduces the cost of producing each one.

Diseconomies of scale
Where costs per unit of output increase as the scale of production increases.

External economies of scale
Where a firm's costs per unit of output decrease as the size of the whole industry grows.

Industry's infrastructure
The network of supply agents, communications, skills, training facilities, distribution channels, specialised financial services, etc. that support a particular industry.

Pause for thought

Which of the economies of scale we have considered are due to increasing returns to scale and which are due to other factors?

Pause for thought

Would you expect external economies of scale to be associated with the concentration of an industry in a particular region? Explain.

When industries form a cluster in an area, external economies are likely to be experienced. We examine such industrial clusters in Box 4.3.

The member firms of a particular industry might, however, experience **external diseconomies of scale**. For example, as an industry grows larger, this may create a growing shortage of specific raw materials or skilled labour. This will push up their prices, and hence the firms' costs. If the industry grows larger in a particular region, the price of land could increase and there may be increased pollution and congestion in the surrounding area.

Definitions

External diseconomies of scale

Where a firm's costs per unit of output increase as the size of the whole industry increases.

Long-run average cost curve

A curve that shows how average cost varies with output on the assumption that all factors are variable.

Long-run average cost

We turn now to *long-run* cost curves. Since there are no fixed inputs in the long run, there are no long-run fixed costs. For example, a firm may rent more land in order to expand its operations. Its rent bill therefore goes up as it expands its output. All costs, then, in the long run are variable costs.

Although it is possible to draw long-run total, marginal and average cost curves, we will concentrate on **long-run average cost (*LRAC*) curves**. These can take various shapes, but a typical one is shown in Figure 4.2.

It is often assumed that as a firm expands, it will initially experience economies of scale and thus face a downward-sloping *LRAC* curve. After a point, however, all such economies will have been achieved and thus the curve will flatten out. Then (possibly after a period of constant *LRAC*), the firm will get so large that it will start experiencing diseconomies of scale and thus a rising *LRAC*. At this stage, production and financial economies begin to be offset by the managerial problems of running a giant organisation. There is evidence to show that this is the case within growing businesses, but there is less evidence to indicate that technical diseconomies of scale exist.

Figure 4.2   A typical long-run average cost curve

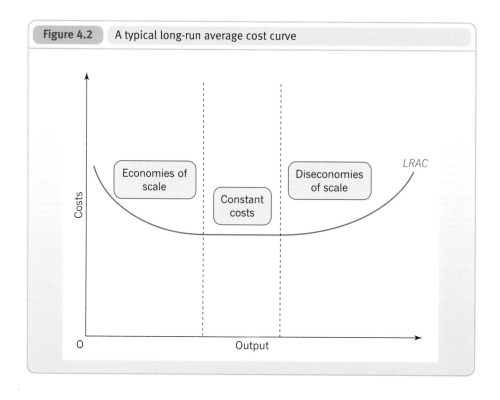

Assumptions behind the long-run average cost curve

We make three key assumptions when constructing long-run average cost curves:

Input prices are given. At each output, a firm will face a given set of input prices. If input prices *change*, therefore, both short- and long-run cost curves will shift. Thus an increase in wages would shift the curves upwards.

However, input prices might be different at *different* levels of output. For example, one of the economies of scale that many firms enjoy is the ability to obtain bulk discount on raw materials and other supplies. In such cases the curve does *not* shift. The different input prices are merely experienced at different points along the curve, and are reflected in the shape of the curve. Input prices are still given for any particular level of output.

The state of technology and input quality are given. These are assumed to change only in the *very* long run. If a firm gains economies of scale, it is because it is able to exploit *existing* technologies and make better use of the existing availability of inputs.

Firms operate efficiently. The assumption here is that firms operate efficiently: that they choose the cheapest possible way of producing any level of output. If the firm did not operate efficiently, it would be producing at a point above the *LRAC* curve.

Transactions costs

So far we have concentrated largely on production costs: the cost of the inputs used in the production process. There is another category of costs, however, that businesses will need to take into account when considering the scale and scope of their organisation. These are **transactions costs**: costs associated with the process of buying or selling. There are four main categories of transactions costs:

Search costs. The firm will incur costs in searching out the best supplier in terms of price and/or quality. The problem here is that the firm starts with imperfect information and it takes time and money to obtain that information. It may employ a **logistics** company to seek out the best sources of supply, but obviously the logistics company will charge for its services. What is more, the firm may well run into the principal–agent problem unless it can monitor the behaviour of the logistics company – i.e. its agent (see pages 9–10).

Contract costs. When a supplier is found, then time and effort may be incurred in bargaining over price and quality. If the supplier is to continue supplying over a period of time, then a contract will probably be negotiated. There will be costs in drawing up such contracts, including legal costs and the time of specialists to ensure that specifications are correct.

Monitoring and enforcement costs. When a contract has been drawn up, it is unlikely to cover every eventuality. To use the jargon, it is 'incomplete'. For example, if a logistics company is contracted to provide transportation of a manufacturing firm's products, the contract may specify maximum times for delivery. The manufacturing firm is then likely to incur costs in ensuring that the logistics firm sticks to the contract – and in taking action if it does not. What is more, there is a moral hazard involved (see page 67). If the logistics firm *could* deliver items more quickly than specified in the contract, it will have no incentive to do so, even though it would have been in the manufacturer's interests.

Definitions

Transactions costs
The costs associated with exchanging products. For buyers it is the costs over and above the price of the product. For sellers it is the costs over and above the costs of production.

Logistics
The business of managing and handling inputs to and outputs from a firm.

Pause for thought

What transactions costs do you incur when (a) going to the supermarket to do a regular shop; (b) buying a new laptop?

BOX 4.3   INDUSTRIAL CLUSTERS AND COMPETITIVENESS

External economies of scale in practice

In May 2003, the Department of Trade and Industry published a report by Michael Porter and Christian Ketels of Harvard Business School on the UK's competitiveness and how it might be improved.[1] The authors declared that since 1980 the UK had done remarkably well in halting its economic decline in world markets, and had in fact matched and even bettered its main rivals in many industrial sectors. Other sectors, however, were faring less well.

According to Porter and Ketels, a key part in any country's success is the development of successful industrial clusters, such as IT in California's Silicon Valley and financial services in the City of London. Such clusters can bring substantial external economies of scale, with individual firms benefiting from being part of a cluster.

> Clusters are geographically proximate groups of interconnected companies, suppliers, service providers, and associated institutions in a particular field, linked by commonalties and complementarities.[2]

Porter suggests that clusters are vital for competitiveness in three crucial respects:

- Clusters improve productivity. The close proximity of suppliers and other service providers enhances flexibility.
- Clusters aid innovation. Interaction among business within a cluster stimulates new ideas and aids their dissemination.
- Clusters contribute to new business formation. Clusters are self-reinforcing, in so far as specialist factors such as dedicated venture capital, and labour skills, help reduce costs and lower the risks of new business start-up.

The UK's industrial clusters were seen by Porter and Ketels as being relatively weak. In fact, many traditional clusters, such as steel and car manufacturing, had thinned to the point where they now lacked critical mass and failed to benefit from the clustering effect.

The UK mainly had strengths in the services sector, such as financial services, media, defence, products for personal use, health care and telecommunications. Lesser clusters were identified in entertainment, semiconductors and computers, transportation and office products.

In 2001, the DTI produced a cluster map for the UK (see opposite). This showed that 'there were clusters throughout the UK: aerospace in the North West, textiles in the East Midlands, and IT around the M4 to name but three'.[3]

Porter and Ketels conclude that, to improve its competitiveness, the UK must not only support what clusters it has, but endeavour to upgrade and contribute to their development.

> The UK needs to mount a sustained programme of cluster development to create a more conducive environment for productivity growth and innovation through the collective action of companies and other institutions . . . It will be essential to mobilise businesses and business institutions that are willing and able to engage in the upgrading of their clusters.[4]

But, according to Porter and Ketels, the onus should not just be on government: businesses themselves need to take a more active role in developing clusters.

> Business leaders must take a more prominent role in cluster development and other efforts to upgrade UK and regional competitiveness. Without improvements in their business environments, companies' investments will otherwise be less profitable and effective.[5]

Also, more research needs to be conducted to understand the process of development of clusters and how best to exploit them.

Cluster development and upgrading needs to be based on a more rigorous understanding of emerging or established clusters in the UK. Past efforts have been incomplete and rigorous data to support cluster development is not yet available. The UK needs to mount a new, more comprehensive statistical effort on clusters at the national and regional level. New data requirements for companies may be needed to support the new economy.[6]

What policies or initiatives might a 'programme of cluster development' involve? Distinguish between policies that government and business might initiate.

---

[1] Porter, Michael E. and Ketels, Christian H. M. 'UK competitiveness: moving to the next stage' (DTI and ESRC, May 2003)
[2] *Ibid.* p. 27
[3] Ecotec Research & Consulting 'A practical guide to cluster development' (DTI, April 2004)
[4] Porter and Ketels, 'UK competitiveness', p. 46
[5] *Ibid.* p. 46
[6] *Ibid.* p. 47

UK cluster map

Source: *Business clusters in the UK – a first assessment*, Figure 2, p. 7 (http://www.dti.gov.uk/files/file17396.pdf)
(Department of Trade and Industry). Reproduced under the terms of the click-use licence

BOX 4.4   MINIMUM EFFICIENT SCALE

The extent of economies of scale in practice

Two of the most important studies of economies of scale have been those made by C. F. Pratten[1] in the late 1980s and by a group advising the European Commission[2] in 1997. Both studies found strong evidence that many firms, especially in manufacturing, experienced substantial economies of scale.

In a few cases, long-run average costs fell continuously as output increased. For most firms, however, they fell up to a certain level of output and then remained constant.

The extent of economies of scale can be measured by looking at a firm's *minimum efficient scale* (*MES*). The *MES* is the size beyond which no significant additional economies of scale can be achieved; in other words, the point where the *LRAC* curve flattens off. In Pratten's studies he defined this level as the minimum scale above which any possible doubling in scale would reduce average costs by less than 5 per cent (i.e. virtually the bottom of the *LRAC* curve). In the diagram *MES* is shown at point *a*.

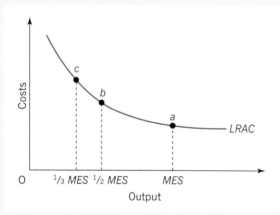

The *MES* can be expressed in terms either of an individual factory or of the whole firm. Where it refers to the minimum efficient scale of an individual factory, the *MES* is known as the *minimum efficient plant size* (*MEPS*).

The *MES* can then be expressed as a percentage of the total size of the market or of total domestic production. Table (a), based on the Pratten study, shows *MES* for plants and firms in various industries. The first column shows *MES* as a percentage of total UK production. The second column shows *MES* as a percentage of total EU production. Table (b), based on the 1997 study, shows *MES* for various plants as a percentage of total EU production.

Expressing *MES* as a percentage of total output gives an indication of how competitive the industry could be. In some industries (such as footwear and carpets), economies of scale were exhausted (i.e. *MES* was reached) with plants or firms that were still small relative to total UK production and even smaller relative to total EU production. In such industries there would be room for many firms and thus scope for considerable competition.

In other industries, however, even if a single plant or firm were large enough to produce the whole output of the industry in the UK, it would still not be large enough to experience the full potential economies of scale; the *MES* is greater than 100 per cent. Examples from Table (a) include factories producing cellulose fibres, and car manufacturers. In such industries there is no possibility of competition. In fact, as long as the *MES* exceeds 50 per cent there will not be room for more than one firm large enough to gain full economies of scale. In this case the industry is said to be a *natural monopoly*. As we shall see in the next few chapters, when competition is lacking consumers may suffer by firms charging prices considerably above costs.

A second way of measuring the extent of economies of scale is to see how much costs would increase if production were reduced to a certain fraction of *MES*. The normal fractions used are $^1/_2$ or $^1/_3$ *MES*. This is illustrated in the diagram. Point *b* corresponds to $^1/_2$ *MES*; point *c* to $^1/_3$ *MES*. The greater the percentage by which *LRAC* at point *b* or *c* is higher than at point *a*, the greater will be the economies of scale to be gained by producing at *MES* rather than at $^1/_2$ *MES* or $^1/_3$ *MES*. For example, in the table there are greater economies of scale to be gained from moving from $^1/_2$ *MES* to *MES* in the production of electric motors than in cigarettes.

---

[1] Pratten, C. F. 'A survey of the economies of scale', in *Research on the 'Costs of Non-Europe'*, Volume 2 (Luxembourg: Office for Official Publications of the European Communities, 1988). Copyright © 1988 European Communities

[2] European Commission/Economists Advisory Group Ltd, 'Economies of scale', in *The Single Market Review*, Subseries V, Volume 4 (Luxembourg: Office for Official Publications of the European Communities, 1997). Copyright © 1997 European Communities

Table (a)

Product	MES as % of production		% additional cost at half MES
	UK	EU	
Individual plants			
Cellulose fibres	125	16	3
Rolled aluminium semi-manufactures	114	15	15
Refrigerators	85	11	4
Steel	72	10	6
Electric motors	60	6	15
TV sets	40	9	9
Cigarettes	24	6	1.4
Ball-bearings	20	2	6
Beer	12	3	7
Nylon	4	1	12
Bricks	1	0.2	25
Tufted carpets	0.3	0.04	10
Shoes	0.3	0.03	1
Firms			
Cars	200	20	9
Lorries	104	21	7.5
Mainframe computers	>100	n.a.	5
Aircraft	100	n.a.	5
Tractors	98	19	6

Sources: see footnote 1 opposite

Table (b)

Plants	MES as % of total EU production
Aerospace	12.19
Tractors and agricultural machinery	6.57
Electric lighting	3.76
Steel tubes	2.42
Shipbuilding	1.63
Rubber	1.06
Radio and TV	0.69
Footwear	0.08
Carpets	0.03

Source: see footnote 2 opposite

The main purpose of the studies was to determine whether a single EU market is big enough to allow both economies of scale and competition. The tables suggest that in all cases, other things being equal, the EU market is large enough for firms to gain the full economies of scale *and* for there to be enough firms for the market to be competitive.

The second study also found that 47 of the 53 manufacturing sectors analysed had scope for further exploitation of economies of scale.

1. *Why might a firm operating with one plant achieve MEPS and yet not be large enough to achieve MES? (Clue: are all economies of scale achieved at plant level?)*
2. *Why might a firm producing bricks have an MES which is only 0.2 per cent of total EU production and yet face little effective competition from other EU countries?*

Definitions

Vertically integrated firm
A firm that produces at more than one stage in the production and distribution of a product.

Supply chain
The flow of inputs into a finished product, from the raw materials stage, through manufacturing and distribution, right through to the sale to the final consumer.

Backward integration
Where a firm expands backwards down the supply chain to earlier stages of production.

Forward integration
Where a firm expands forward up the supply chain towards the sale of the finished product.

Transport and handling costs. The more firms rely on buying components from other firms, rather than making them in-house, the greater will be the costs of transporting and handling these materials.

 Transactions costs. The costs associated with exchanging products. For buyers it is the costs over and above the price of the product. For sellers it is the costs over and above the costs of production. Transactions costs include search costs, contract costs, monitoring and enforcement costs, and transport and handling costs.

Transactions costs and the scale and scope of the firm

One way of reducing transactions costs is for the firm to produce more *within* the firm rather than buying inputs from other firms or supplying to other firms. What we are describing here is a **vertically integrated firm**. This is where a firm is involved in several stages of the production of a good, such as component production, assembly and wholesale and retail distribution.

Firms may expand their operations vertically by integrating backwards down the **supply chain** or forwards up it. **Backward integration** is where a firm itself produces the inputs it needs. Thus a car manufacturer may itself produce components such as body panels, engines and trimmings. **Forward integration** is where a firm itself moves into producing stages closer to the end consumer. Thus a manufacturer of building materials may move into construction or become a builder's merchant.

The costs of vertical integration. Whilst vertical integration sounds like a good idea and a business will save on transactions costs, it is likely to incur other costs. A large vertically integrated organisation could be more bureaucratic, with the increased complexity involving more complex management tasks. Although the firm is saving on the costs of monitoring contracts with other firms, managers still have to monitor the behaviour of their own internal divisions and employees and so there is a potential for diseconomies of scale. Managers may set targets for the various divisions, but unless these are both carefully specified and comprehensive, the problem of moral hazard is likely to occur. Employees may meet the targets but may underperform in areas which are not specifically targeted. One response to this problem is to create more and more specific targets. This, however, is likely to remove flexibility and the opportunity for junior managers to take initiative.

Another problem is that, by producing components in-house, the firm will not then be able to source them from elsewhere if cheaper suppliers become available (see Box 4.5 on page 111). Similarly, if a manufacturer buys its components from outside, it could possibly change supplier if the first supplier lets it down. If it produces the components itself, however, switching to an outside supplier may prove more difficult if internal hold-ups occur. Thus in-house production can prove more risky.

Finally production costs may be higher. Despite the fact that a vertically integrated firm may be large, the *individual* parts of the company may be too small to gain full economies of scale. For example, if a car company produces its own carpets, this carpet production will be on a much smaller scale than if a specialist car carpet manufacturer were to supply *several* car companies.

In deciding its optimum degree of vertical integration, therefore, a firm must weigh up the transactions costs of not integrating against the internal costs of integrating.

Recap

1. In the long run, a firm is able to vary the quantity of all its inputs. There are no fixed inputs and hence there are no fixed costs.

2. If it increases all inputs by the same proportion, it may experience constant, increasing or decreasing returns to scale.

3. Economies of scale occur when costs per unit of output fall as the scale of production increases. This can be due to a number of factors, some of which are directly caused by increasing (physical) returns to scale. These include the benefits of specialisation and division of labour, the use of larger and more efficient machines, and the ability to have a more integrated system of production. Other economies of scale arise from the financial and administrative benefits of large-scale organisations.

4. Typically, *LRAC* curves are drawn as L-shaped or as saucer-shaped. As output expands, initially there are economies of scale. When these are exhausted, the curve will become flat. When the firm becomes very large, it may begin to experience diseconomies of scale. If this happens, the *LRAC* curve will begin to slope upwards again.

5. Transactions costs are the costs associated with exchanging products. They include search costs, the costs of drawing up and monitoring contracts and transport and handling costs. The more firms rely on other firms as suppliers or buyers, the larger these costs are likely to be. Vertical integration can reduce transactions costs, but is likely to incur other costs instead.

REVENUE   4.3

Remember that we defined a firm's total profit as its total revenue minus its total costs of production. In the last two sections we have examined costs. We now turn to revenue.

As with costs, we distinguish between three revenue concepts: total revenue (*TR*), average revenue (*AR*) and marginal revenue (*MR*).

Total, average and marginal revenue

Total revenue (TR)

Total revenue is the firm's total earnings per period of time from the sale of a particular amount of output (Q).

For example, if a firm sells 1000 units (Q) per month at a price of £5 each (P), then its monthly total revenue will be £5000: in other words, £5 × 1000 ($P \times Q$). Thus:

$$TR = P \times Q$$

Average revenue (AR)

Average revenue is the amount the firm earns per unit sold. Thus:

$$AR = TR/Q$$

So if the firm earns £5000 (*TR*) from selling 1000 units (Q), it will earn £5 per unit. But this is simply the price! Thus:

$$AR = P$$

Marginal revenue (MR)

Marginal revenue is the extra total revenue gained by selling one more unit (per time period). So if a firm sells an extra 20 units this month compared with what it

Definitions

Total revenue (*TR*) (per period)
The total amount received by firms from the sale of a product, before the deduction of taxes or any other costs. The price multiplied by the quantity sold: $TR = P \times Q$.

Average revenue (*AR*)
Total revenue per unit of output. When all output is sold at the same price, average revenue will be the same as price: $AR = TR/Q = P$.

Marginal revenue (*MR*)
The extra revenue gained by selling one or more units per time period: $MR = \Delta TR/\Delta Q$.

expected to sell, and in the process earns an extra £100, then it is getting an extra £5 for each extra unit sold: $MR = £5$. Thus:

$$MR = \Delta TR/\Delta Q$$

We now need to see how revenue varies with output. We concentrate on average and marginal revenue. We can show this relationship graphically in the same way as we did with costs.

The relationship will depend on the market conditions under which a firm operates. The revenue curves we look at in this section are for a price-taking firm: a firm that faces a horizontal demand curve (see section 3.1). When firms face a downward-sloping demand curve and are thus able to choose their price, they will face different revenue curves. We look at such curves in the next chapter.

Average and marginal revenue curves

Average revenue. We are assuming in this chapter that the firm is a price taker. That is, it has to accept the price given by the intersection of demand and supply in the whole market. But, being so small, it can sell as much as it is capable of producing at that price. This is illustrated in Figure 4.3.

Figure 4.3(a) shows market demand and supply. Equilibrium price is £5. Figure 4.3(b) looks at the demand for an individual firm which is tiny relative to the whole market. (Look at the difference in the scale of the horizontal axes in the two diagrams.)

Being so small, any change in the firm's output will be too insignificant to affect the market price. The firm thus faces a horizontal demand 'curve' at this price. It can sell 200 units, 600 units, 1200 units or whatever without affecting this £5 price.

Average revenue is thus constant at £5. The firm's average revenue curve must therefore lie along exactly the same line as its demand curve.

Marginal revenue. In the case of a horizontal demand curve, the marginal revenue curve will be the same as the average revenue curve, since selling one more unit at a constant price (AR) merely adds that amount to total revenue. If an extra unit is sold at a constant price of £5, an extra £5 is earned.

Figure 4.3	Deriving a firm's *AR* and *MR*: price-taking firm

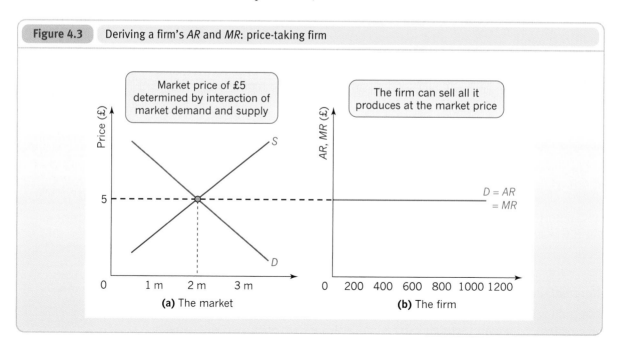

(a) The market   **(b)** The firm

Recap

1. Total revenue (*TR*) is the total amount a firm earns from its sales in a given time period. It is simply price multiplied by quantity: $TR = P \times Q$.

2. Average revenue (*AR*) is total revenue per unit: $AR = TR/Q$. In other words, $AR = P$.

3. Marginal revenue is the extra revenue earned from the sale of one more unit per time period: $MR = \Delta TR/DQ$.

4. The *AR* curve will be the same as the demand curve for the firm's product. In the case of a price taker, the demand curve and hence the *AR* curve will be a horizontal straight line and will also be the same as the *MR* curve.

PROFIT MAXIMISATION   4.4

We are now in a position to put costs and revenue together to find the output at which profit is maximised, and also to find out how much that profit will be. First we need to look a little more precisely at what we mean by the term 'profit'.

The meaning of 'profit'

One element of cost is the opportunity cost to the owners of the firm incurred by being in business. This is the minimum return that the owners must make on their capital in order to prevent them from eventually deciding to close down and perhaps move into some alternative business. It is a *cost* since, just as with wages, rent, etc., it has to be covered if the firm is to continue producing. This opportunity cost to the owners is sometimes known as **normal profit**, and is included in the cost curves.

What determines this normal rate of profit? It has two components. First, someone setting up in business invests capital in it. There is thus an opportunity cost. This is the interest that could have been earned by lending it in some riskless form (e.g. by putting it in a savings account in a bank). Nobody would set up a business unless they expected to earn at least this rate of profit. Running a business is far from riskless, however, and hence a second element is a return to compensate for risk. Thus:

Normal profit (%) = rate of interest on a riskless loan + a risk premium

The risk premium varies according to the line of business. In those with fairly predictable patterns, such as food retailing, it is relatively low. Where outcomes are very uncertain, such as mineral exploration or the manufacture of fashion garments, it is relatively high. Thus if owners of a business earn normal profit, they will (just) be content to remain in that industry.

Any excess of profit over normal profit is known as **supernormal profit**. If firms earn supernormal profit, they will clearly prefer to stay in this business. Such profit will also tend to attract new firms into the industry, since it will give them a better return on capital than elsewhere. If firms earn *less* than normal profit, however, then after a time they will consider leaving and using their capital for some other purpose.

Short-run profit maximising

In the **short run under perfect competition**, we assume that the number of firms in an industry cannot be increased: there is simply not time for new firms to enter the market.

Definitions

Normal profit
The opportunity cost of being in business. It consists of the interest that could be earned on a riskless asset, plus a return for risk taking in this particular industry. It is counted as a cost of production.

Supernormal profit
The excess of total profit above normal profit.

Short run under perfect competition
The period during which there is too little time for new firms to enter the industry.

| Figure 4.4 | Short-run equilibrium of industry and firm under perfect competition |

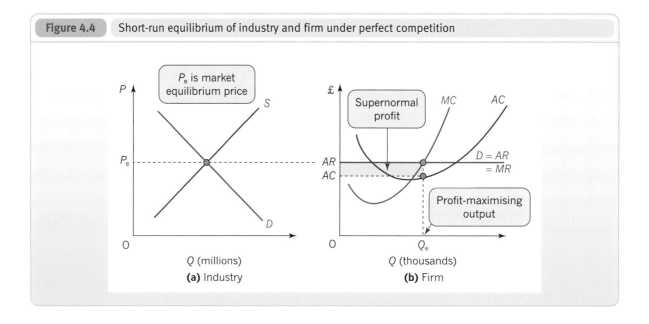

(a) Industry   **(b)** Firm

Figure 4.4 shows a short-run equilibrium for an industry and the profit-maximising position for a firm under perfect competition. Both parts of the diagram have the same scale for the vertical axis. The horizontal axes have totally different scales, however. For example, if the horizontal axis for the firm were measured in, say, thousands of units, the horizontal axis for the whole industry might be measured in millions or tens of millions of units, depending on the number of firms in the industry.

Let us examine the determination of price, output and profit in turn.

Price. The price is determined in the industry by the intersection of demand and supply. The firm faces a horizontal demand (or average revenue) 'curve' at this price. It can sell all it can produce at the market price (P_e), but nothing at a price above P_e.

Output. The firm will maximise profit where marginal cost equals marginal revenue ($MR = MC$), at an output of Q_e. In fact this **profit-maximising rule** will apply to firms in all types of market, so it is very important to understand.

But why are profits maximised when $MR = MC$? The simplest way of answering this is to see what the position would be if MR did not equal MC.

Referring to Figure 4.4, at a level of output below Q_e, MR exceeds MC. This means that by producing more units there will be a bigger addition to revenue (MR) than to cost (MC). Total profit will *increase*. As long as MR exceeds MC, *profit can be increased by increasing production*.

At a level of output above Q_e, MC exceeds MR. All levels of output above Q_e thus add more to cost than to revenue and hence *reduce* profit. As long as MC exceeds MR, *profit can be increased by cutting back on production*.

Profits are thus maximised where $MC = MR$: at an output of Q_e.

Students worry sometimes about the argument that profits are maximised when $MR = MC$. Surely, they say, if the last unit is making no profit, how can profit be at a *maximum*? The answer is very simple. If you cannot add anything more to a total, the total must be at the maximum. Take the simple analogy of going up a hill. When you cannot go any higher, you must be at the top.

Definition

Profit-maximising rule
Profit is maximised where marginal revenue equals marginal cost.

Profit. Once the profit-maximising output has been discovered, we now use the average curves to measure the *amount* of profit at the maximum. Remember that normal profit is included in the AC curve. If, therefore, $AC = AR$, just normal profit will be made. For example, if the price (AR) were £8 and AC were also £8, then the firm would be earning enough revenue to cover all its costs and still earn normal profit, but no supernormal profit.

If the firm's average cost (AC) curve dips below the average revenue (AR) 'curve', as in Figure 4.4, the firm will earn supernormal profit. Supernormal profit per unit at Q_e is the vertical difference between AR and AC at Q_e. So if AR (= P) were £10 and AC were £8, then supernormal profit per unit would be £2.

Total supernormal profit at Q_e is found by multiplying super-normal profit per unit ($AR - AC$) by the total number of units sold (Q_e). This is given by the area of the shaded rectangle in Figure 4.4. The reason is that the area of a rectangle is found by multiplying its height ($AR - AC$) by its width (Q_e).

Loss minimising. Sometimes there is no output at which the firm can make even normal profit. Such a situation is illustrated in Figure 4.5. With the average revenue 'curve' given by AR_1, the AC curve is above the AR curve at all levels of output.

In this case, the output where $MR = MC$ will be the loss-minimising output. The amount of loss at the point where $MR = MC$ is shown by the shaded area in Figure 4.5.

Whether or not to produce. If a firm is making a loss, however, should it shut down? To answer this we need to return to our distinction between fixed and variable costs. Fixed costs have to be paid even if the firm is producing nothing at all. Rent has to be paid, business rates have to be paid, and so forth. Providing, therefore, that the firm is more than covering its *variable* costs, it can go some way to paying off these fixed costs and therefore will continue to produce.

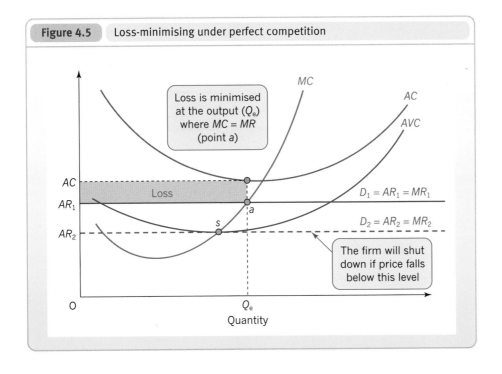

Figure 4.5 Loss-minimising under perfect competition

It will shut down if it cannot cover its variable costs, i.e. if the price (*AR*) is below AR_2 in Figure 4.5. This situation is known as the **short-run shut-down point** and is shown by point *S*.

The long-run equilibrium of the firm

Under perfect competition, we assume that there are no barriers to entry for new firms and in the **long run** we assume that there is time for firms to enter the industry. This will occur if typical firms are making supernormal profits. Likewise, if existing firms can make supernormal profits by increasing the scale of their operations, they will do so, since all inputs are variable in the long run.

The effect of the entry of new firms and/or the expansion of existing firms is to increase industry supply. This is illustrated in Figure 4.6.

The industry supply curve shifts to the right. This in turn leads to a fall in price. Supply will go on increasing, and price falling, until firms are making just normal profits. This will be when price has fallen to the point where the demand 'curve' for the firm just touches the bottom of its long-run average cost curve. This is shown as curve D_L. Q_L is thus the long-run equilibrium output of the firm, with P_L the long-run equilibrium market price. If the firm is unable to cover its long-run average costs, it will shut down.

Does the firm benefit from operating under perfect competition?

Under perfect competition the firm faces a constant battle for survival. If it becomes less efficient than other firms, it will make less than normal profits and be driven out of business. If it becomes more efficient, it will earn supernormal profits. But these supernormal profits will not last for long. Soon other firms, in order to survive themselves, will be forced to copy the more efficient methods of the new firm.

It is the same with the development of new products. If a firm is able to produce a new product that is popular with consumers, it will be able to gain a temporary

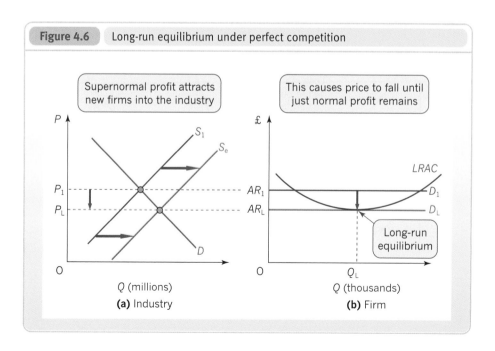

Figure 4.6   Long-run equilibrium under perfect competition

BOX 4.5 THE LOGIC OF LOGISTICS

Driving up profits

One key to a company's success is the logistics of its operations. As we have seen, logistics refers to the management of the inflow of resources to a company and the outflow of goods from it: in other words, to 'supply-chain management'. It includes the purchasing of supplies, transporting them, production sequencing, stock control, delivery to customers, and so on.

Modern developments in logistics have transformed the operation of many industries.

Driving down costs

With the widespread use of containerisation and the development of giant distribution companies, such as FedEx, UPS and DHL, transporting materials and goods around the world has become much faster and much cheaper. Instead of having to make parts and materials in-house, companies can now use the logistics industry to obtain them at lower cost elsewhere, often from the other side of the world.

With deliveries becoming more and more reliable, firms no longer need to keep large stocks of parts. They simply buy them as they need them. This is the idea of just-in-time (JIT) production.

The globalisation of logistics, with increasing use of the Internet, has resulted in a hugely complex logistics industry. Companies that were once solely concerned with delivery are now being employed to manage companies' supply chains and achieve large cost savings for them.

Driving up revenue

Efficient logistics has not just resulted in lower costs. The flexibility it gives firms has allowed many to increase their sales.

Carrying small stocks and switching from supplier to supplier, with the process often being managed by a logistics company, can allow companies to change their products more rapidly. They can be more responsive to consumer demand. Fashion goods can get to the shops ahead of the competition. Perishable goods can arrive fresher.

 What dangers are there in keeping stocks to a minimum and relying on complex supply chains?

---

advantage over its rivals. But again, any supernormal profits will last only as long as it takes other firms to respond. Soon the increase in supply of the new product will drive the price down and eliminate these supernormal profits. Similarly, the firm must be quick to copy new products developed by its rivals. If it does not, it will soon make a loss and be driven out of the market.

Thus being in perfect competition is a constant battle for survival. It might benefit the consumer, but most firms in such an environment would love to be able to gain some market power: power to be able to restrict competition and to retain supernormal profits into the long run. Market power is the subject of the next chapter.

> **Pause for thought**
>
> *Why is it highly unlikely that an industry where firms can gain substantial economies of scale can also be perfectly competitive?*

Recap

1. Normal profit is the minimum profit that must be made to persuade a firm to stay in business in the long run. It is counted as part of the firm's costs. Supernormal profit is any profit over and above normal profit.

2. The maximum profit output is where marginal revenue equals marginal cost. Having found this output, the level of maximum (supernormal) profit can be found by finding the average (supernormal) profit ($AR - AC$) and then multiplying it by the level of output.

3. For a firm that cannot make a profit at any level of output, the point where $MR = MC$ represents the loss-minimising output. In the short run, a firm will close down if it cannot cover its variable costs. In the long run, it will close down if it cannot make normal profits.

4. In the short run, there is not time for new firms to enter the market, and thus supernormal profits can persist. In the long run, however, any supernormal profits will be competed away by the entry of new firms.

BOX 4.6   E-COMMERCE

A modern form of perfect competition?

The relentless drive towards big business in recent decades has seen markets become more concentrated and increasingly dominated by large producers. And yet forces are at work that are undermining this dominance, and bringing more competition to markets. One of these forces is *e-commerce*.

In this case study, we shall first review the model of perfect competition and then consider how e-commerce is returning 'power to the people'.

A perfectly competitive market

As we have seen, under perfect competition firms are price takers: they have to accept the price as given by the market. Firms are faced with a constant battle for survival. The effect is to drive down costs. With firms freely entering the industry, only normal profits will be made in the long run. So only the fittest will survive, and the fittest will be in a constant struggle to produce at a lower cost.

So what conditions are necessary for the market for a particular good to be perfectly competitive and thus for firms to be price takers? In addition to freedom of entry to the market for new firms, consumers must have knowledge of the quality, availability and price of the good. There must also be a large number of firms in the market. Only that way will competition be sufficient to ensure that no firm has any power over prices, and thus faces a perfectly elastic demand curve.

E-commerce and competition

How does e-commerce make markets more competitive and even, in some cases, become virtually perfectly competitive?

Consumer knowledge. There are various ways in which e-commerce is adding to the consumer's knowledge. There is greater price transparency, with consumers able to compare prices online. Online shopping agents such as Kelkoo, DealTime and Froogle can quickly locate a list of alternative suppliers. There is greater information on product availability and quality. Virtual shopping malls, full of e-retailers, place the high street retailer under intense competitive pressure.

The pressure is even greater in the market for intermediate products. Many firms are constantly searching for cheaper sources of supply, and the Internet provides a cheap and easy means of conducting such searches.

Large number of firms. The growth of e-commerce has led to many new firms starting up in business. It's not just large firms like Amazon that are providing increased competition for established firms, but the thousands of small online companies that are being established every day. Many of these firms are selling directly to us as consumers. This is known as 'B2C' e-commerce (business-to-consumers). But many more are selling to other firms ('B2B'). More and more companies, from the biggest to the smallest, are transferring their purchasing to the Web and are keen to get value for money.

The reach of the Web is global. This means that firms, whether conventional or web-based, have to keep an eye on the prices and products of competitors in the rest of the world, not just in the local neighbourhood. Firms' demand curves are thus becoming very price elastic. This is especially so for goods that are cheap to transport, or for services such as travel agents, insurance and banking.

Freedom of entry. Internet companies often have lower start-up costs than their conventional rivals. Their premises are generally much smaller, with no 'shop-front' costs and lower levels of stock holding. Marketing costs can also be relatively low, especially given the ease with which companies can be located with search engines. Internet companies are often smaller and more specialist, relying on Internet 'outsourcing' (buying parts, equipment and other supplies through the Internet), rather than making everything themselves. They are also more likely to use delivery firms rather than having their own transport fleet.

All this makes it relatively cheap for new firms to set up and begin trading over the Internet.

In fact, the distinction between firms and consumers is becoming increasingly blurred. With the rise of eBay, more and more people are finding going into business incredibly easy. Suddenly people are finding a market for all the junk they've collected over the years! As the eBay TV advertisement says, 'someone wants everything'. There are some 200 million registered eBay users worldwide, and hundreds of thousands of people make a full-time living from buying and selling on eBay. Annual sales on eBay are worth over £30 billion.

Not only do all the above factors make markets more price competitive, they also bring other benefits. Costs are driven down, as firms economise on stock holding, rely more on outsourcing and develop more efficient relationships with suppliers. 'Procurement hubs', on-line exchanges and trading communities are now well established in many industries. The competition also encourages innovation, which improves quality and the range of products.

The limits to e-commerce

In 20 years, will we be doing all our shopping on the net? Will the only shopping malls be virtual ones? Although e-commerce is revolutionising some markets, it is unlikely that things will go anything like that far.

The benefits of 'shop shopping' are that you get to see the good, touch it and use it. You can buy the good there and then, and take instant possession of it; you don't have to wait. Shopping is also an enjoyable experience. Many people like wandering round the shops, meeting friends, seeing what takes their fancy, trying on clothes, browsing through CDs and so on. 'Retail therapy' for many is an important means of 'de-stressing' and hence it gives consumers utility.

Online shopping is limited by the screen; Internet access may be slow and frustrating; 'surfing' may instead become 'wading'; you have to wait for goods to be delivered; and what if deliveries are late or fail completely?

Also, costs might not be as low as expected. How efficient is it to have many small deliveries of goods? How significant are the lost cost savings from economies of scale that larger producers or retailers are likely to generate?

Nevertheless, e-commerce has made many markets, both retail and B2B, more competitive. This is especially so for services and for goods whose quality is easy to identify online. Many firms are being forced to face up to having their prices determined by the market.

1. *Why may the Internet work better for replacement buys than for new purchases?*
2. *Give three examples of products that are particularly suitable for selling over the Internet and three that are not. Explain your answer.*

1. Are all explicit costs variable costs? Are all variable costs explicit costs?

2. Up to roughly how long is the short run in the following cases?

   (a) A mobile disco firm;
   (b) Electricity power generation;
   (c) A small grocery retailing business;
   (d) 'Superstore Hypermarkets plc'.
   In each case, specify your assumptions.

3. The following are some costs incurred by a shoe manufacturer. Decide whether each one is a fixed cost or a variable cost or has some element of both.

   (a) The cost of leather;
   (b) The fee paid to an advertising agency;
   (c) Wear and tear on machinery;
   (d) Business rates on the factory;
   (e) Electricity for heating and lighting;
   (f) Electricity for running the machines;
   (g) Basic minimum wages agreed with the union;
   (h) Overtime pay;
   (i) Depreciation of machines as a result purely of their age (irrespective of their condition).

4. Why does the marginal cost curve pass through the bottom of the average cost curve?

5. Does the marginal value of a variable (such as cost, revenue or profit) determine the average value of the variable, or does the average value of the variable determine the marginal value? Explain your answer.

6. What economies of scale is a large department store likely to experience?

7. Why are many firms likely to experience economies of scale up to a certain size and then diseconomies of scale after some point beyond that?

8. Normal profits are regarded as a cost (and are included in the cost curves). Explain why.

9. What determines the size of normal profit? Will it vary with the general state of the economy?

10. A firm will continue producing in the short run even if it is making a loss, providing it can cover its variable costs. Explain why. Just how long will it be willing to continue making such a loss?

11. Would it ever be worthwhile for a firm to try to continue in production if it could not cover its *long-run* average (total) costs?

12. The price of pocket calculators and digital watches fell significantly in the years after they were first introduced and at the same time demand for them increased substantially. Use cost and revenue diagrams to illustrate these events. Explain the reasoning behind the diagram(s) you have drawn.

13. Illustrate on a diagram similar to Figure 4.6 what would happen in the long run if price were initially below P_L.

Additional Part B case studies on the *Economics and the Business Environment* website (www.pearsoned.co.uk/sloman)

B.1 **Coffee prices.** An examination of the coffee market and the implications of fluctuations in the coffee harvest for growers and coffee drinkers.

B.2 **The measurement of elasticity.** This examines how to work out the value for elasticity using the 'mid-point' method.

B.3 **Any more fares?** Pricing on the buses: an illustration of the relationship between price and total revenue.

B.4 **Elasticities of demand for various foodstuffs.** An examination of the evidence about price and income elasticities of demand for food in the UK.

B.5 **Adjusting to oil price shocks.** A case study showing how demand and supply analysis can be used to examine the price changes in the oil market since 1973.

B.6 **The role of the speculator.** This assesses whether the activities of speculators are beneficial or harmful to the rest of society.

B.7 **The demand for butter.** An examination of a real-world demand function.

B.8 **Markets where prices are controlled.** This examines what happens if price is set either above or below the equilibrium.

B.9 **Agriculture and minimum prices.** This shows how setting (high) minimum prices is likely to lead to surpluses.

B.10 **Diminishing returns in the bread shop.** An illustration of the law of diminishing returns.

B.11 **Dealing in futures markets.** How buying and selling in futures markets can reduce uncertainty.

B.12 **Short-run production.** An analysis of how output varies with increases in the quantity of variable inputs used.

B.13 **Diminishing returns to nitrogen fertiliser.** This case study provided a good illustration of diminishing returns in practice by showing the effects on grass yields of the application of increasing accounts of nitrogen fertiliser.

B.14 **The fallacy of using historic costs.** A demonstration of how it is important to use opportunity costs and not historic costs when working out prices and output.

B.15 **The relationship between averages and marginals.** An examination of the rules showing how an average curve relates to a marginal curve.

B.16 **Short-run cost curves in practice.** Why *AVC* and *MC* curves may have a flat bottom.

B.17 **The characteristics approach.** An approach to analying consumer behaviour and how consumers choose between products.

Websites relevant to Part B

Numbers and sections refer to websites listed in the Web Appendix and hotlinked from this book's website at **www.pearsoned.co.uk/sloman/**

- For new articles relevant to Part B, see the Economics News Articles link from the book's website.

- For general news on markets, demand and supply see websites in section A of the Web Appendix, and particularly A2, 3, 4, 5, 8, 9, 11, 12, 18, 20–26, 35, 36. See also sites A41, 43, 44 for links to economics news articles from newspapers worldwide.

- For links to sites on markets, see the relevant sections of I4, 7, 11, 13, 17.

- For data, information and sites on products and marketing, see sites B2, 10; I7, 11, 13, 17.

- For data on advertising, see sites E37.

- For links to sites on various aspects of advertising and marketing, see section Industry and Commerce > Consumer Protection > Advertising in site I7.

- For links to sites on various aspects of production and costs, see section Microeconomics > Production in site I7.

- For a case study examining costs, see site D2.

- For student resources relevant to Part B, see sites C1–7, 9, 10, 14, 19, 20, 24; D3, 5, 14, 17, 19.

- For sites favouring the free market, see C17 and E34.

The microeconomic environment of business

Whatever the aims of firms, if they are to be successful in pursuing them, they must take account of the environment in which they operate. In Part C we look at the microeconomic environment of firms, i.e. the market conditions that firms face in their particular industry.

Most firms are not price takers; they can choose the prices they charge. But in doing so they must take account of the reactions of their rivals. We look at pricing and output decisions in Chapter 5 and see how firms' aims affect these decisions.

However, it is not just in terms of pricing and output decisions that firms must take account of rivals. They must also do so in planning out their longer-term strategy – in making decisions about developing and launching new products, how quickly and how much to expand, the methods of production to use, their supply chain, the balance of what should be produced in-house and what should be 'outsourced' (i.e. bought in from other firms), their sources of finance, and whether to target international markets or to confine themselves to producing and selling domestically. These strategic decisions are the subject of Chapters 6 and 7.

In Chapter 8, we turn to the labour market environment of business. What power does the firm have in setting wages; what is the role of trade unions; how flexibly can the firm use labour? These issues all affect the profitability of business, its organisation and its choice of techniques.

Finally, in Chapter 9 we look at the impact of government policy towards business and how this in turn impacts on firms' decision making. How much does government legislation constrain business activity? How much can government force firms to behave in the society's interests and how much will firms choose to take a socially responsible attitude towards things such as ethical trading, the environment, product standards and conditions for their workforce?

Business issues covered in this chapter

- What determines the degree of market power of a firm?
- How do firms become monopolies and retain such market power?
- At what price and output will a monopolist maximise profits and how much profit will it make?
- How well or badly do monopolies serve the consumer?
- How are firms likely to behave when there are just a few of them competing ('oligopolies')? Will they engage in all-out competition or will they collude with each other?
- What strategic games are oligopolists likely to play in their attempt to outdo their rivals?
- Does oligopoly serve the consumer's interests?
- Why may managers pursue goals other than maximising profit? What other goals might they pursue and what will be the effect on price and output?
- How are prices determined in practice?
- Why do firms sometimes charge different prices to different customers for the same product (e.g. seats on a plane)?

Pricing and output decisions in imperfectly competitive markets

5 Chapter

In the previous chapter we looked at price-taking firms, which face a perfectly elastic demand curve. In this chapter we examine firms that face a downward-sloping demand curve. Such firms are said to have 'market power'. In other words, they have the power to raise their price. Of course, if they do so, their sales will fall, and clearly they will have to trade off the benefit of higher prices against the cost of lower sales.

The degree of a firm's market power depends on the price elasticity of demand for its product. The less elastic the demand, the less will sales fall for any given rise in price, and the greater, therefore, is the firm's market power.

> **KEY IDEA 17**
>
> **Market power benefits the powerful at the expense of others.** When firms have market power over prices, they can use this to raise prices and profits above the perfectly competitive level. Other things being equal, the firm will gain at the expense of the consumer. Similarly, if consumers or workers have market power they can use this to their own benefit.

The most extreme case of market power is **monopoly**. This is where there is just one firm in the industry, and hence no competition from *within* the industry. Normally the monopoly will have effective means of keeping other firms out of the industry. We look at monopoly in section 5.2.

When firms face a downward-sloping demand curve but are not monopolies, we call this situation **imperfect competition**. The vast majority of firms in the real world operate under imperfect competition.

Imperfect competition is normally divided into two types. The more competitive of the two is **monopolistic competition** (not to be confused with monopoly). This involves quite a lot of firms competing and there is freedom for new firms to enter the industry. As a result, if existing firms are making supernormal profits, new firms will enter the industry (given time). Thus, as under perfect competition, this will have the effect of driving down profits to the normal level.

Examples of monopolistic competition can be found by flicking through the *Yellow Pages*. Taxi companies, restaurants, small retailers, small builders, plumbers, electrical contractors, etc. all normally operate under monopolistic competition. As a result, their profits are kept down by the intense competition in the industry. However, competition is not perfect, as the firms are all trying to differentiate their product or service from their rivals'. They have *some* power over prices: their demand curve, whilst relatively elastic, is not horizontal.

Definitions

Monopoly
A market structure where there is only one firm in the industry.

Imperfect competition
The collective name for monopolistic competition and oligopoly.

Monopolistic competition
A market structure where, like perfect competition, there are many firms and freedom of entry into the industry, but where each firm produces a differentiated product and thus has some control over its price.

BOX 5.1 | **CONCENTRATION RATIOS**

Measuring the degree of competition

5-firm and 15-firm concentration ratios for various industries (by output)

Industry	5-firm ratio	15-firm ratio	Industry	5-firm ratio	15-firm ratio
Sugar	99	99	Alcoholic beverages	50	78
Tobacco products	99	99	Soap and toiletries	40	64
Oils and fats	88	95	Accountancy services	36	47
Confectionary	81	91	Motor vehicles	34	54
Gas distribution	82	87	Glass and glass products	26	49
Soft drinks, mineral water	75	93	Fishing	16	19
Postal/courier services	65	75	Advertising	10	20
Telecommunications	61	75	Wholesale distribution	6	11
Inorganic chemicals	57	80	Furniture	5	13
Pharmaceuticals	57	74	Construction	5	9

Source: Based on data in *United Kingdom Input-Output Analyses*, Table 8.31 (Office of National Statistics). Reproduced under terms of the click-use licence

We can get some indication of how competitive a market is by observing the number of firms; the more the firms, the more competitive the market would seem to be. However, this does not tell us anything about how *concentrated* the market might be. There may be *many* firms (suggesting a situation of perfect competition or monopolistic competition), but the largest two firms might produce 95 per cent of total output. This would make these two firms more like oligopolists.

Thus even though a large number of producers may make the market *seem* highly competitive, this could be deceiving. Another approach, therefore, to measuring the degree of competition is to focus on the level of concentration of firms.

The simplest measure of industrial concentration involves adding together the market share of the largest so many firms: e.g. the largest 3, 5 or 15. This would give what is known as the '3-firm', '5-firm' or '15-firm concentration ratio'. There are different ways of estimating market share: by revenue, by output, by profit, etc.

The table shows the 5-firm and 15-firm concentration ratios of selected industries in the UK by output. As you can see, there is an enormous variation in the degree of concentration from one industry to another.

One of the main reasons for this is differences in the percentage of total industry output at which economies

of scale are exhausted (see Box 4.4 on page 102). If this occurs at a low level of output, there will be room for several firms in the industry which are all benefiting from the maximum economies of scale.

The degree of concentration will also depend on the barriers to entry of other firms into the industry (see pages 122–3) and on various factors such as transport costs and historical accident. It will also depend on how varied the products are within any one industrial category. For example, in categories as large as furniture and construction there is room for many firms, each producing a specialised range of products.

So is the degree of concentration a good guide to the degree of competitiveness of the industry? The answer is that it is *some* guide, but on its own it can be misleading. In particular it ignores the degree of competition from abroad, and from other industries within the country.

1. *What are the advantages and disadvantages of using a 5-firm concentration ratio rather than a 15-firm, 3-firm or even a 1-firm ratio?*
2. *Why are some industries like bread baking and brewing relatively concentrated, in that a few firms produce a large proportion of total output (see web cases C.4 and C.5), and yet there are also many small producers?*

The other type of imperfect competition is known as **oligopoly**. This literally means 'few sellers'. As under monopoly, the entry of new firms is restricted. We examine oligopoly in section 5.3.

Table 5.1 summarises the features of the four different types of market structure.

Definition

Oligopoly
A market structure where there are few enough firms to enable barriers to be erected against the entry of new firms.

Pause for thought

Give one more example in each of the four market categories in Table 5.1.

Table 5.1	Features of the four market structures			
Type of market	**Number of firms**	**Freedom of entry**	**Examples of product**	**Implication for demand curve for firm's product**
Perfect competition	Very many	Unrestricted	Fresh fruit, and vegetables, shares	Horizontal. The firm is a price taker
Monopolistic competition	Many/several	Unrestricted	Builders, restaurants	Downward sloping, but relatively elastic. The firm has some control over price
Oligopoly	Few	Restricted	Cars, electrical appliances	Downward sloping, relatively inelastic, but depends on reactions of rivals to a price change
Monopoly	One	Restricted or completely blocked	Local water company, many prescription drugs	Downward sloping; more inelastic than oligopoly. Firm has considerable control over price

Market structure and the conduct and performance of firms

The market structure under which a firm operates will determine its behaviour. firms under perfect competition behave quite differently from firms that are monopolists, which behave differently again from firms under oligopoly or monopolistic competition.

This behaviour (or 'conduct') will in turn affect the firm's performance: its prices, profits, efficiency, etc. In many cases it will also affect other firms' performance: *their* prices, profits, efficiency, etc. The collective conduct of all the firms in the industry will affect the whole industry's performance.

Some economists thus see a causal chain running from market structure to the performance of that industry. This paradigm was first considered in section 1.2:

Structure → Conduct → Performance

MONOPOLY   5.2

What is a monopoly?

This may seem a strange question because the answer seems obvious. A monopoly exists when there is only one firm in the industry.

But whether an industry can be classed as a monopoly is not always clear. It depends on how narrowly the industry is defined. For example, a textile company may have a monopoly on certain types of fabric, but it does not have a monopoly on fabrics in general. The consumer can buy fabrics other than those supplied by the company. A rail company may have a monopoly over rail services between two cities, but it does not have a monopoly over public transport between these two cities. People can travel by coach or air. They could also use private transport. When you went to an adventure playground as a child, your parents may have refused to buy you an ice cream, because they were too expensive. The ice cream seller had a local monopoly, but it was obviously not the only seller of ice creams in the UK!

To some extent, the boundaries of an industry are arbitrary. What is more important for a firm is the amount of monopoly *power* it has, and that depends on the closeness of substitutes produced by rival industries. The Post Office in the UK, before 2006, had a monopoly over the delivery of letters, but it faces competition in communications from telephone, faxes and e-mail.

Barriers to entry

For a firm to maintain its monopoly position, there must be barriers to the entry of new firms. Barriers also exist under oligopoly, but in the case of monopoly they must be high enough to block the entry of new firms. Barriers can take various forms:

> **Definition**
>
> **Natural monopoly**
> A situation where long-run average costs would be lower if an industry were under monopoly than if it were shared between two or more competitors.

Economies of scale. If the monopolist's costs go on falling significantly up to the output that satisfies the whole market, the industry may not be able to support more than one producer. This case is known as **natural monopoly**. It is particularly likely if the market is small. For example, two bus companies might find it unprofitable to serve the same routes, each running with perhaps only half-full buses, whereas one company with a monopoly of the routes could make a profit. Electricity transmission via a national grid is another example of a natural monopoly.

Even if a market could support more than one firm, a new entrant is unlikely to be able to start up on a very large scale. Thus the monopolist, which is already experiencing economies of scale, can charge a price below the cost of the new entrant and drive it out of business. If, however, the new entrant is a firm already established in another industry, it may be able to survive this competition.

Economies of scope. A firm that produces a range of products is also likely to experience a lower average cost of production. For example, a large pharmaceutical company producing a range of drugs and toiletries can use shared research, marketing, storage and transport facilities across its range of products. These lower costs make it difficult for a new single-product entrant to the market, since the large firm will be able to undercut its price and drive it out of the market.

Product differentiation and brand loyalty. If a firm produces a clearly differentiated product, where the consumer associates the product with the brand, it will be very difficult for a new firm to break into that market. Rank Xerox invented, and patented, the plain paper photocopier. After this legal monopoly (see below) ran out, people still associated photocopiers with Rank Xerox. It was not unusual to hear someone say that they are going to 'Xerox the article' or, for that matter, 'Hoover their carpet'. Other examples of strong brand image include Guinness, Kellogg's Cornflakes, Coca-Cola, Nescafé and Sellotape.

Lower costs for an established firm. An established monopoly is likely to have developed specialised production and marketing skills. It is more likely to be aware of the most efficient techniques and the most reliable and/or cheapest suppliers. It is likely to have access to cheaper finance and is thus operating on a lower cost curve. New firms would therefore find it hard to compete and would be likely to lose any price war.

Ownership of, or control over, key inputs or outlets. If a firm governs the supply of vital inputs (say by owning the sole supplier of some component part, through 'backward vertical integration'), it can deny access to these inputs to potential rivals. On a world scale, the de Beers company has a monopoly in fine diamonds because all diamond producers market their diamonds through de Beers.

Similarly, if a firm controls the outlets through which the product must be sold, (through 'forward vertical integration'), it can prevent potential rivals from gaining access to consumers. For example, Birds Eye Wall's used to supply freezers free to shops on the condition that they stocked only Wall's ice cream in them.

Legal protection. The firm's monopoly position may be protected by patents on essential processes, by copyright, by various forms of licensing (allowing, say, only one firm to operate in a particular area) and by tariffs (i.e. customs duties) and other trade restrictions to keep out foreign competitors. Examples of monopolies protected by patents include most new medicines developed by pharmaceutical companies (e.g. anti-AIDS drugs), Microsoft's Windows operating systems and agro-chemical companies, such as Monsanto, with various genetically modified plant varieties and pesticides.

Mergers and takeovers. The monopolist can put in a takeover bid for any new entrant. The sheer threat of takeovers may discourage new entrants.

Retained profits. An established firm is likely to have some retained profits behind it. If a new firm enters the market, the established firm could reduce prices and thus start a price war, or start a massive advertising campaign, knowing that it could sustain losses until the new entrant leaves the market. The threat of this can act as a barrier to entry. Alternatively, a firm could begin aggressive advertising.

Profit maximising under monopoly

The rule for profit maximising under monopoly is the same as for a firm under perfect competition. It should produce the output where marginal cost equals marginal revenue. The costs curves for a monopolist will look similar to those for a firm under perfect competition. The revenue curves, however, will look different, as the firm is no longer a price taker.

Average and marginal revenue

Compared with other market structures, demand under monopoly will be relatively inelastic at each price. The monopolist can raise its price and consumers have no alternative supplier to turn to within the industry. They either pay the higher price, or go without the good altogether.

Because the firm faces a downward-sloping demand curve, its average and marginal revenue curves will also be downward sloping. This is illustrated in Figure 5.1, which is based on Table 5.2.

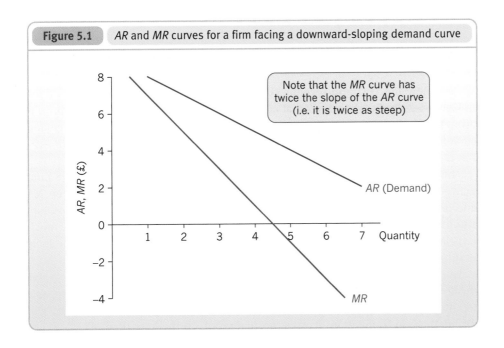

Figure 5.1   *AR* and *MR* curves for a firm facing a downward-sloping demand curve

Note that the *MR* curve has twice the slope of the *AR* curve (i.e. it is twice as steep)

Table 5.2	Revenue for a monopolist		
Q (units)	P = AR (£)	TR (£)	MR (£)
1	8	8	8
2	7	14	6
3	6	18	4
4	5	20	2
5	4	20	0
6	3	18	−2
7	2	14	−4

Note that, as in the case of a price-taking firm, the demand curve and the *AR* curve lie along exactly the same line. The reason for this is simple: *AR* = *P*, and thus the curve relating price to quantity (the demand curve) must be the same as that relating average revenue to quantity (the *AR* curve).

When a firm faces a downward-sloping demand curve, marginal revenue will be less than average revenue, and may even be negative. But why?

Whilst a monopolist can set its price, it is still constrained by its (and hence the industry) demand curve. If a firm is to sell more per time period, it must lower its price (assuming it does not advertise). This will mean lowering the price not just for the extra units it hopes to sell, but also for those units it would have sold had it not lowered the price.

Thus the marginal revenue is the price at which it sells the last unit, *minus* the loss in revenue it has incurred by reducing the price on those units it could otherwise have sold at the higher price. This can be illustrated with Table 5.2.

Assume that price is currently £7. Two units are thus sold. The firm now wishes to sell an extra unit and so it must lower the price to £6. It thus gains £6 from the sale of the third unit, but loses £2 by having to reduce the price by £1 on the two units it could otherwise have sold at £7. Its net gain is therefore £6 − £2 = £4. This is the marginal revenue: it is the extra revenue gained by the firm from selling one more unit.

Profit-maximising output and price

We can now put cost and revenue curves together on one diagram. This is done in Figure 5.2. Profit is maximised at an output of Q_m, where *MC* = *MR*. The price is given by the demand curve. Thus at Q_m the price is *AR* = *P* (point *a* on the demand curve). Average cost (*AC*) is found at point *b*. Supernormal profit per unit is *AR* − *AC* (i.e. *a* − *b*). Total supernormal profit is shown by the shaded area.

These profits will tend to be larger the less elastic is the demand curve (and hence the steeper is the *MR* curve), and thus the bigger is the gap between *MR* and price (*AR*). The actual elasticity will depend on whether reasonably close substitutes are available in *other* industries. The demand for a rail service will be much less elastic (and the potential for profit greater) if there is no bus service to the same destination.

Under both monopolistic and perfect competition, any supernormal profits made in the short run will be competed away in the long run, as new firms are able to enter the industry. Significant barriers to entry under monopoly, however, will enable the firm to maintain its supernormal profits in the long run.

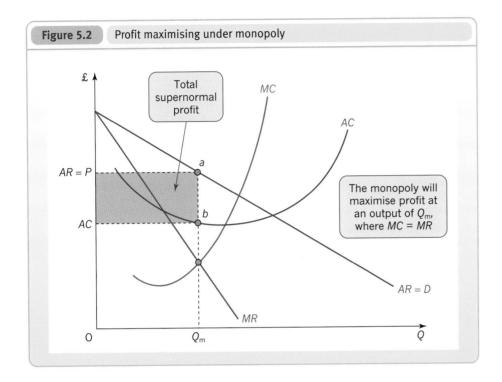

Figure 5.2   Profit maximising under monopoly

Comparing monopoly with perfect competition

Because it faces a different type of market environment, the monopolist will produce a quite different output and at a quite different price from a perfectly competitive industry. Typically a monopolist will charge a price above the market price of an equivalent industry under perfect competition. There are three main reasons for this:

- Under perfect competition price equals marginal cost (see Figure 4.4 on page 108). Under monopoly, however, price is above marginal cost (see Figure 5.2). The less elastic the demand curve, the higher will price be above marginal cost.
- As we have just discussed, since there are barriers to the entry of new firms, a monopolist's supernormal profits will not be competed away in the long run. There is no competition to drive down the price. The monopolist is not forced to operate at the bottom of the *LRAC* curve. Thus, other things being equal, long-run prices will tend to be higher, and hence output lower, under monopoly.
- The monopolist's cost curves may be higher. The sheer survival of a firm in the long run under perfect competition requires that it uses the most efficient known technique, and develops new techniques wherever possible. The monopolist, however, sheltered by barriers to entry, can still make large profits even if it is not using the most efficient technique. It has less incentive, therefore, to be efficient.

> **Pause for thought**
>
> *If the shares in a monopoly (such as a water company) were very widely distributed among the population, would the shareholders necessarily want the firm to use its monopoly power to make larger profits?*

It is possible, however, that a monopolist will operate with *lower* costs than an equivalent industry under perfect competition. The monopoly may be able to achieve substantial economies of scale due to larger plant, centralised administration and the avoidance of unnecessary duplication (e.g. a monopoly water company would eliminate the need for several sets of rival water mains under each street). If this

BOX 5.2   WINDOWS CLEANING

Microsoft, the Internet and the US Justice Department

On 18 May 1998, the US government initiated its biggest competition case for 20 years: it sued Microsoft, the world's largest software company. It accused Microsoft of abusing its market power and seeking to crush its rivals. By controlling the *Windows* operating software, Microsoft could force its own Internet browser, *Internet Explorer*, on to consumers and computer manufacturers. The US Justice Department alleged that Microsoft had committed the following anti-competitive actions:

■ Back in May 1995, Microsoft attempted to collude with Netscape Communications to divide the Internet browser market. Netscape Communications refused.
■ Microsoft had forced personal computer manufacturers to install Internet Explorer in order to obtain a *Windows* operating licence.
■ Microsoft insisted that PC manufacturers conformed to a Microsoft front screen for Windows. This included specified icons, one of which was Microsoft's *Internet Explorer*.
■ It had set up reciprocal advertising arrangements with America's largest Internet service providers, such as America Online (AOL). Here Microsoft would promote AOL via Windows. In return, AOL would not promote Netscape's browsers.

Network effects

The key issue in respect to Microsoft, then, was not so much the browser war, but far more fundamentally to do with the operating system, and how Microsoft used its ownership of this system to extend its leverage into other related high-technology markets.

> An operating system attracts software developed around that operating system, thereby discouraging new competition since any alternative faces not only the challenge of creating a better operating system but competing against a whole array of already existing software applications . . . These so-called 'network effects' give an incredible anti-competitive edge to companies like Microsoft that control so many different parts of the network.[1]

Network effects arise when consumers of a product benefit from it being used by other consumers. In the case of Microsoft's products, firms benefit from being able to communicate more easily with one another. They also benefit from lower training costs because individuals who have learnt to use Microsoft products elsewhere can be readily absorbed into the firm. Individuals benefit too because they do not have to learn to use new software when they move to another organisation and the learning costs are fairly low as a new version of the software is introduced.

The negative aspect of developing strong networks is that users can get 'locked in' to using the software and they become reluctant to switch to alternative systems. This results in the establishment of a monopoly or near monopoly with high barriers to entry.

US court findings

A verdict was reached on 7 June 2000. Microsoft was ordered to be split in two to prevent it operating as a monopoly. One company would produce and market the *Windows* operating system; the other would produce and market the applications software, such as *Microsoft Office* and the Web browser, *Internet Explorer*.

This was overturned on appeal in June 2001 and Microsoft agreed to provide technical information about *Windows* to other companies so that potential rivals could compete with Microsoft's own software. Also, Microsoft would not be allowed to retaliate against computer manufacturers that installed rival products or removed icons for Microsoft applications.

European Commission findings

Legal action against Microsoft was not confined to the USA. In March 2004, the European Commission fined Microsoft a record €497 million for abusing its monopoly position. It found that Microsoft had harmed competition in the media player market by bundling Windows Media Player with its operating system. Further, Microsoft had refused to supply information about its secret software code to suppliers of alternative network software at reasonable rates. Without it, firms who had purchased Windows Network servers would be solely tied in to Microsoft server software. This, in turn, would discourage the development of application software products by Microsoft's rivals.

In April 2006, Microsoft launched an appeal against the judgment, claiming that the EU's ruling violated international law by forcing the company to share information with rivals. However, the Court of First Instance found in the Commission's favour. Microsoft complied with the first ruling and un-bundled Windows Media Player

---

[1] N. Newman, from 'MS Word to MS world: how microsoft is building a global monopoly', www.netaction.org/msoft/world (1997)

from its operating systems. However, until October 2007 Microsoft continued to charge high royalty rates and fees for interoperability information that would allow competitors to access the secret source code on the Windows Network System. As a result, in February 2008 the Commission penalised Microsoft a further €899 million for non-compliance with its 2004 decision and Microsoft became the first company in 50 years of EU competition policy to be fined for non-compliance with a Commission decision.

Then, in June 2009, the Commission ordered Microsoft to un-bundle Internet Explorer from its new operating system, Windows 7, thereby allowing consumers to choose between Internet browsers.

Following an agreement reached in December 2009 between Microsoft and the European Commission, in March 2010 Microsoft released a patch to its operating systems that launched a pop-up giving information about alternative browsers. This allowed users to choose one of at least 12 browsers, including Mozilla Firefox, Google Chrome, Apple Safari and Opera.

Microsoft and the public interest

These lawsuits raise an important issue: is Microsoft acting for or against the public interest? Clearly it has monopoly power. However, the competition authorities have never penalised Microsoft simply for possessing monopoly power. It has been fined when it has abused its market power, such as by raising barriers to entry and restricting the opportunities for potential rival firms to offer alternative products to customers.

In its defence, Microsoft has argued that it has continually sought to reinvest its profits in new product development and offered a number of innovative solutions over the past 30 years for individuals and businesses alike. Just think of all the versions of Windows and the 'free updates' there have been!

Further, in an environment where technology is changing rapidly, Microsoft's control over standards gives the user a measure of stability, knowing that any new products and applications will be compatible with existing ones. In other words, new software can be incorporated into existing systems. In this respect Microsoft can be viewed as operating in society's interest. Also Microsoft argues that it has a right to protect its in-house software code from competitors and receive a fair price for it. Indeed, it is a natural response for a firm to protect its intellectual property rights. Failure to do so could lead to the firm's demise.

Challenges to Microsoft monopoly

Microsoft is facing increasing competitive pressure. The recent challenges from competition authorities have opened up the browser market, for example. Microsoft's Internet Explorer is still the dominant browser, but as other browsers become more popular, its market share has fallen. By 2010 its share was 61.6 per cent. This compared with Mozilla Firefox (24.2 per cent), Google Chrome (5.6 per cent), Apple's Safari (4.5 per cent) and Opera (2.4 per cent).

There is also a growing challenge from other Internet firms, such as Google and Facebook. Both Google and Facebook have created enormous networks of users who are then targeted with tailored adverts paid for by firms which want to reach these vast audiences.

This is a very different business model from that of Microsoft and, as part of the desire to create large networks of users, free products are being released that will compete with that of Microsoft. For example, Google's Open Office competes with Microsoft's Office. This, however, still has a very small market share at present.

It remains unclear whether Microsoft's dominance in the operating system market will be challenged in the near future. Apple is the only likely rival to Microsoft for operating systems on standalone computers. However, it has a small market share of the operating system market because it wants to concentrate on particular sorts of user – those who appreciate good design. It has also shifted its business emphasis in recent times by developing iPhone and iTunes technologies.

The open-source operating system, Linux, still has less than 5 per cent of the operating system market and is also no threat to Microsoft at the moment. However, things do change rapidly in the technology sector.

You might want to follow subsequent events as the news unfolds (see section A of the Hotlinks section of this book's website for links to newspaper sites).

1. *In what ways was Microsoft's behaviour (a) against the public interest; (b) in the public interest?*
2. *Being locked in to a product or technology is only a problem if such a product can be clearly shown to be inferior to an alternative. What difficulties might there be in establishing such a case?*

results in an *MC* curve substantially below that of the same industry under perfect competition, the monopoly may even produce a *higher* output at a *lower* price.

Another reason why a monopolist may operate with lower costs is that it can use part of its supernormal profits for research and development and investment. It may not have the same *incentive* to become efficient as the perfectly competitive firm which is fighting for survival, but it may have a much greater *ability* to become efficient than has the small firm with limited funds.

Although a monopoly faces no competition in the goods market, it may face an alternative form of competition in financial markets. A monopoly, with potentially low costs, which is currently run inefficiently, is likely to be subject to a takeover bid from another company. This **competition for corporate control** may thus force the monopoly to be efficient in order to prevent it being taken over.

Finally, the promise of supernormal profits, protected perhaps by patents, may encourage the development of new (monopoly) industries producing new products. It is this chance of making monopoly profits that encourages many people to take the risks of going into business.

Recap

1. There are four alternative market structures under which firms operate. In ascending order of firms' market power, they are: perfect competition, monopolistic competition, oligopoly and monopoly.

2. A monopoly is where there is only one firm in an industry. In practice, it is difficult to determine where a monopoly exists because it depends on how narrowly an industry is defined.

3. Barriers to the entry of new firms will normally be necessary to protect a monopoly from competition. Such barriers include economies of scale (making the firm a natural monopoly or at least giving it a cost advantage over new, smaller, competitors), control over supplies of inputs or over outlets, patents or copyright, and tactics to eliminate competition (such as takeovers or aggressive advertising).

4. The demand curve (*AR* curve) for a monopolist is downward sloping. The *MR* curve is below it and steeper.

5. Profits for the monopolist (as for other firms) are maximised where *MC = MR*.

6. If demand and cost curves are the same in a monopoly and a perfectly competitive industry, the monopoly will produce a lower output and at a higher price than the perfectly competitive industry.

7. On the other hand, any economies of scale will in part be passed on to consumers in lower prices, and the monopolist's high profits may be used for research and development and investment, which in turn may lead to better products at possibly lower prices.

5.3 OLIGOPOLY

Oligopoly occurs when just a few firms between them share a large proportion of the industry. Most oligopolists produce differentiated products (e.g. cars, soap powder, soft drinks, electrical appliances). Much of the competition between such oligopolists is in terms of the marketing of their particular brand.

As with monopoly, there are barriers to the entry of new firms (see pages 122–3). The size of the barriers, however, varies from industry to industry. In some cases entry is relatively easy; in others it is virtually impossible.

Interdependence of the firms

Because there are only a few firms under oligopoly, each firm is likely to have a relatively large market share, and so its actions will affect the other firms in the industry. As such, a firm will have to take account of the others. This means that they are mutually dependent: they are **interdependent**. Each firm is affected by its rivals' actions. If a firm changes the price or specification of its product or the amount of its advertising, the sales of its rivals will be affected. The rivals may then respond by changing their price, specification or advertising. No firm can therefore afford to ignore the actions and reactions of other firms in the industry.

 People often think and behave strategically. How you think others will respond to your actions is likely to influence your own behaviour. Firms, for example, when considering a price or product change will often take into account the likely reactions of their rivals.

It is impossible, therefore, to predict the effect on a firm's sales of, say, a change in its price without first making some assumption about the reactions of other firms. Different assumptions will yield different predictions. For this reason there is no single generally accepted theory of oligopoly. Firms may react differently and unpredictably.

Competition and collusion

Oligopolists are pulled in two different directions:

■ The interdependence of firms may make them wish to *collude* with each other. If they can club together and act as if they were a monopoly, they could jointly maximise industry profits.
■ On the other hand, they will be tempted to *compete* with their rivals to gain a bigger share of industry profits for themselves.

These two policies are incompatible. The more fiercely firms compete to gain a bigger share of industry profits, the smaller these industry profits will become! For example, price competition drives down the average industry price, while competition through advertising raises industry costs. Either way, industry profits fall.

Sometimes firms will collude. Sometimes they will not. The following sections examine first **collusive oligopoly** (both open and tacit), and then **non-collusive oligopoly**.

Collusive oligopoly

When firms under oligopoly engage in collusion, they may agree on prices, market share, advertising expenditure, etc. Such collusion reduces the uncertainty they face. It reduces the fear of engaging in competitive price cutting or retaliatory advertising, both of which could reduce total industry profits.

A cartel

A formal collusive agreement is called a **cartel**. The cartel will maximise profits if it acts like a monopoly, if the members behave as if they were a single firm. This is illustrated in Figure 5.3.

The total market demand curve is shown with the corresponding market *MR* curve. The cartel's *MC* curve is the *horizontal* sum of the *MC* curves of its members (since we are adding the *output* of each of the cartel members at each level of marginal cost). Profit for the whole industry is maximised at Q_1 where $MC = MR$. The cartel must therefore set a price of P_1 (at which Q_1 will be demanded).

Definitions

Interdependence (under oligopoly)
One of the two key features of oligopoly. Each firm will be affected by its rivals' decisions. Likewise its decisions will affect its rivals. Firms recognise this interdependence. This recognition will affect their decisions.

Collusive oligopoly
When oligopolists agree (formally or informally) to limit competition between themselves. They may set output quotas, fix prices, limit product promotion or development, or agree not to 'poach' each other's markets.

Non-collusive oligopoly
When oligopolists have no agreement between themselves – formal, informal or tacit.

Cartel
A formal collusive agreement.

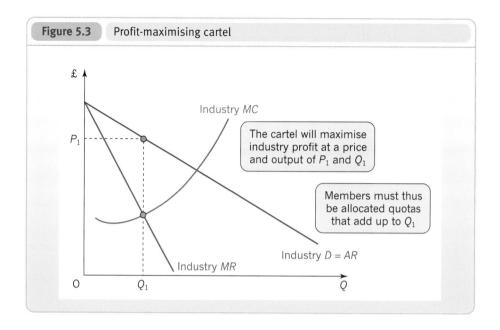

Figure 5.3   Profit-maximising cartel

But, having agreed on price, how is the resulting output (Q_1) divided between the cartel members? The members may simply compete against each other using *non-price competition* to gain as big a share of resulting sales (Q_1) as they can.

Alternatively, the cartel members may somehow agree to divide the market between them. Each member would be given a **quota**. The sum of all the quotas must add up to Q_1. If the quotas exceeded Q_1, either there would be output unsold if price remained fixed at P_1, or the price would fall.

In many countries cartels are illegal, being seen by the government as a means of driving up prices and profits and thereby as being against the public interest. Government policy towards cartels is examined in section 9.5.

Tacit collusion

Where open collusion is illegal, firms may simply break the law, or get round it. Alternatively, firms may stay within the law, but still *tacitly* collude by watching each other's prices and keeping theirs similar. Firms may tacitly 'agree' to avoid price wars or aggressive advertising campaigns.

One form of **tacit collusion** is where firms keep to the price that is set by an established leader. Such **price leadership** is more likely when there is a dominant firm in the industry, normally the largest.

Other forms include having an established set of rules that everyone follows, such as adding a certain percentage on top of average costs for profit. Alternatively, there are certain benchmark prices, which firms follow, such as goods priced at £9.99, rather than at £10.13.

A recent example of price fixing can be found in the petrol industry in Melbourne, Australia, in 2009. The ACCC (Australian Competition and Consumer Commission) studied the pricing decisions of a number of petrol stations in the same area and in 49 of the 53 weeks studied, when one of the big three petrol stations changed their price, the industry followed these movements exactly. Whilst there was no formal collusive agreement in place, this is an example of tacit collusion.

Definitions

Quota (set by a cartel)
The output that a given member of a cartel is allowed to produce (production quota) or sell (sales quota).

Tacit collusion
When oligopolists take care not to engage in price cutting, excessive advertising or other forms of competition. There may be unwritten 'rules' of collusive behaviour such as price leadership.

Price leadership
When firms (the followers) choose the same price as that set by one of the firms in he industry (the leader). The leader will normally be the largest firm.

Factors favouring collusion

Collusion between firms, whether formal or tacit, is more likely when firms can clearly identify with each other or some leader and when they trust each other not to break agreements. It will be easier for firms to collude if the following conditions apply:

■ There are only very few firms, all well known to each other.
■ They are open with each other about costs and production methods.
■ They have similar production methods and average costs, and are thus likely to want to change prices at the same time and by the same percentage.
■ They produce similar products and can thus more easily reach agreements on price.
■ There is a dominant firm.
■ There are significant barriers to entry and thus there is little fear of disruption by new firms.
■ The market is stable. If industry demand or production costs fluctuate wildly, it will be difficult to make agreements, partly due to difficulties in predicting and partly because agreements may frequently have to be amended. There is a particular problem in a declining market where firms may be tempted to undercut each other's price in order to maintain their sales.
■ There are no government measures to curb collusion.

Elements of competition under collusive oligopoly

Even when oligopolists collude over price, they may compete intensively though product development and marketing. As we saw in section 3.4, such 'non-price competition' can make the job of the manager quite complex, involving strategic decisions about product design and quality, product promotion and the provision of various forms of after-sales service.

Although non-price competition assumes that price is given in the short run, price may well be affected over the longer term. Industries with intensive non-price competition are likely to face higher marketing costs, and this can result in a higher collusive price.

Even if there is collusion, for example to fix price, firms will always have an incentive to cheat, by undercutting the cartel price or selling more than their quota. Whilst the firm can gain from this action, there is a danger of retaliation leading to a price war. As long as the firm that undercuts the cartel price is confident of winning any price war, this may be a good strategy to follow. We consider this idea further in section 5.4.

Non-collusive oligopoly

In some oligopolies, there may be only a few (if any) factors favouring collusion. In such cases, the likelihood of price competition is greater.

The kinked demand curve

Even when oligopolists do not collude over price, however, the price is often relatively stable. The reason is that oligopolists may believe that they face a **kinked demand curve**. But why? The firm makes two key assumptions:

■ If it cuts its price, its rivals will feel forced to follow suit and cut theirs, to prevent losing customers to the first firm.
■ If it raises its price, however, its rivals will *not* follow suit since, by keeping their prices the same, they will thereby gain customers from the first firm.

> **Definition**
>
> **Kinked demand theory**
> The theory that oligopolists face a demand curve that is kinked at the current price: demand being significantly more elastic above the current price than below. The effect of this is to create a situation of price stability.

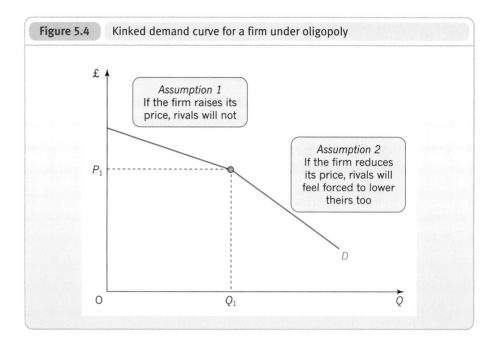

Figure 5.4   Kinked demand curve for a firm under oligopoly

On these assumptions, the oligopolist's perceived demand curve is *kinked* at the current price and output (see Figure 5.4). It believes that if it raises its price (and its rivals do not follow) this will lead to a large fall in its sales as customers switch to the now relatively lower-priced rivals. The firm will thus be reluctant to raise its price. Demand is relatively elastic above the kink. On the other hand, it believes that if it reduces price, this will bring only a modest increase in sales, since rivals will lower their prices too and therefore customers do not switch. The firm will thus also be reluctant to reduce its price. Demand is relatively inelastic below the kink. Thus oligopolists will be reluctant to change prices at all.

Oligopoly and the consumer

When oligopolists act collusively and jointly maximise industry profits, they are in effect acting together as a monopoly. In such cases, prices may be very high. This is clearly not in the best interests of consumers.

Furthermore, in two respects, oligopoly may be more disadvantageous than monopoly:

■ Depending on the size of the individual oligopolists, there may be less scope for economies of scale to mitigate the effects of market power.
■ Oligopolists are likely to engage in much more extensive advertising and marketing than a monopolist. To the extent that this is linked with product development and provides better information about the product's characteristics, there are clearly gains to the consumer. To the extent, however, that the costs of advertising and marketing result in higher prices, the consumer will lose.

These problems will be less severe, however, if oligopolists do not collude, if there is some degree of price competition and if barriers to entry are weak.

Indeed, in some respects, oligopoly may be more beneficial to the consumer than other market structures:

BOX 5.3   SUPERMARKET WARS

Genuine competition or tacit collusion?

Food retailing in the UK is a good example of oligopoly. As the chart shows, the largest four supermarket chains have a combined market share of more than 75 per cent. What is more, for many consumers there are only one or two supermarkets within their area.

In 2007, the Competition Commission (see section 9.5) said that it was 'concerned with whether Tesco, or any other supermarket, can get into such a strong position, either nationally or locally, that no other retailer can compete effectively'.[1] The government's Office of Fair Trading had identified four major areas where the supermarkets might gain from the use (or abuse) of market power: (i) barriers to entry to new competitors, (ii) the relationship between the large supermarket chains and their suppliers, (iii) the lack of effective price competition and (iv) reducing competition in the convenience store sector.

Barriers to entry. The most important barrier to entry is the difficulty in getting planning permission to open a new supermarket. Some of the supermarkets have bought tracts of land in areas where rivals might gain such permission in order to prevent them building rival stores and hence this reduces consumer choice. Also, the large economies of scale and the huge buying power of the established supermarkets would make it virtually impossible for a new player to match their low costs.

Relationships between supermarkets and their suppliers. One of the most contentious issues concerns the major supermarket chains' huge buying and selling power. They have been able to drive costs down by forcing suppliers to offer discounts. Many suppliers, such as growers, have found their profit margins cut to the bone. However, these cost savings have not been passed on from supplier to shopper.

Lack of effective price competition. The supermarket chains have adopted a system of 'shadow pricing', a form of tacit collusion whereby they all observe each other's prices and ensure that they remain at similar levels – often similarly high levels rather than similarly low levels! This has limited the extent of true price competition, and the resulting high prices have seen profits grow as costs have been driven ever downwards.

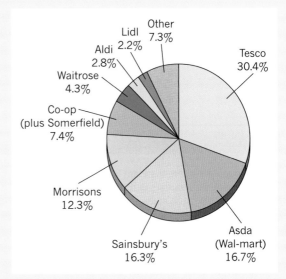

UK supermarket food market share (2010)

Other 7.3%
Lidl 2.2%
Aldi 2.8%
Waitrose 4.3%
Co-op (plus Somerfield) 7.4%
Morrisons 12.3%
Sainsbury's 16.3%
Asda (Wal-mart) 16.7%
Tesco 30.4%

Supermarkets *do* compete on price, and since the £6.4 billion takeover in 1999 of Asda by Wal-Mart, the world's largest retailer, price wars in the supermarket sector have become more cut-throat. Asda has slashed prices on hundreds of products. Tesco in response, striving to extend its position as the UK's number one supermarket retailer, launched its own price-cutting campaign. In the past few years, there have been many TV adverts by the leading supermarkets, with each arguing that they have about a million baskets of goods cheaper than their rivals!

But intense price competition tends to be only over basic items, such as the own-brand 'value' products. To get to the basic items, you normally have to pass the more luxurious ones, which are much more highly priced! Supermarkets rely on shoppers making impulse buys of the more expensive lines: lines that have much higher profit margins.

Reducing competition in the convenience store sector. The opening of convenience stores, such as Tesco Metro, Tesco Express and Sainsbury's Local, has driven many independent retailers from the market. The large companies use their scale to keep prices low while local competition remains, only to raise prices when local competitors have closed down.

---

[1] News Release from Competition Commission, 23 January 2007, 'Grocery enquiry goes local', Peter Freeman, Chairman of the Competition Commission and Inquiry Chairman, www.competition.commission.org.uk/press_rel/2007/jan/pdf/03-07.pdf

1. *In what forms of tacit collusion are supermarket chains likely to engage?*
2. *In what ways can convenience stores compete with supermarkets?*

- Oligopolists, like monopolists, can use part of their supernormal profit for research and development. Unlike monopolists, however, oligopolists will have a considerable *incentive* to do so. If the product design is improved, this may allow the firm to capture a larger share of the market, and it may be some time before rivals can respond with a similarly improved product.
- Non-price competition through product differentiation may result in greater choice for the consumer. Take the case of stereo equipment. Non-price competition has led to a huge range of different products of many different specifications, each meeting the specific requirements of different consumers.

It is difficult to draw any general conclusions, since oligopolies differ so much in their performance.

Recap

1. An oligopoly is where there are just a few firms in the industry with barriers to the entry of new firms. Firms recognise their mutual dependence.

2. Whether oligopolists compete or collude depends on the conditions in the industry. They are more likely to collude if there are few of them; if they are open with each other; if they have similar products and cost structures; if there is a dominant firm; if there are significant entry barriers; if the market is stable; and if there is no government legislation to prevent collusion.

3. A formal collusive agreement is called a 'cartel'. A cartel aims to act as a monopoly. It can set a price and leave the members to compete for market share, or it can assign quotas. There is always a temptation for cartel members to 'cheat' by undercutting the cartel price if they think they can get away with it and not trigger a price war.

4. Tacit collusion can take the form of price leadership, or firms can follow an 'agreed' set of rules.

5. When firms do not collude, prices may still be relatively stable. One reason for this is that firms face a kinked demand curve. They are unwilling to raise prices for fear of losing sales to rivals. They are also unwilling to lower prices for fear of sparking off a price war.

6. Whether consumers benefit from oligopoly depends on the particular oligopoly and how competitive it is; whether the firms engage in extensive advertising and of what type; whether product differentiation results in a wide range of choice for the consumer; and how much of the profits are ploughed back into research and development.

5.4 GAME THEORY

When considering whether to cut prices, and thereby hopefully gain a bigger market share, a firm will ask: (1) 'How much can we get away with without inviting retaliation?' and (2) 'If a price war does result, will we be the winners? Will we succeed in driving some or all of our rivals out of business and yet survive ourselves, and thereby gain greater market power?'

The position of rival firms under oligopoly, therefore, is rather like that of generals of opposing armies or the players in a game. It is a question of choosing the appropriate *strategy*: the strategy that will best succeed in outwitting your opponents. Of course, the strategy that a firm adopts will be concerned not just with price, but also with advertising and product development.

The firm's choice of strategy will depend on (a) how it thinks its rivals will react to any price changes or other changes it makes; (b) its willingness to take a gamble. Economists have developed **game theory**, which examines the best strategy that a firm can adopt for each assumption about its rivals' behaviour.

Definition

Game theory (or the theory of games)

The study of alternative strategies that oligopolists may choose to adopt, depending on their assumptions about their rivals' behaviour.

We examine game theory in this section. In the next chapter we look at other aspects of business strategy, such as whether to expand the business, whether to launch new products or how the business should position itself in the industry relative to its rivals.

Single-move games

The simplest type of 'game' is a **single-move** or **single-period game** (sometimes known as a **normal-form game**). This involves just one 'move' by each firm involved. For example, two or more firms are considering what price to bid for a contract which will be awarded to the lowest bidder. Each makes its bid by considering what its rivals are likely to do. Once the bids have been made and the contract has been awarded to the lowest bidder, the 'game' is over.

Dominant strategy games

Many single-period games have predictable outcomes, no matter what each firm assumes about its rivals' behaviour. Such games are known as **dominant strategy games**.

A simple example is where there are just two firms with identical costs, products and demand. They are both considering which of two alternative prices to charge. Table 5.3 shows typical profits they could each make.

Let us assume that at present both firms (X and Y) are charging a price of £2 and that they are each making a profit of £10 million, giving a total industry profit of £20 million. This is shown in the top left-hand cell (A).

Now assume they are both (independently) considering reducing their price to £1.80. In making this decision, they will need to take into account what their rival might do, and how this will affect them. Let us consider X's position. In our simple example there are just two things that its rival, firm Y, might do. Either Y could cut its price to £1.80, or it could leave its price at £2. What should X do?

One alternative is to go for the *cautious* approach and think of the worst thing that its rival could do. If X kept its price at £2, the worst thing for X would be if its rival Y cut its price. This is shown by cell C: X's profit falls to £5 million. If, however, X cut its price to £1.80, the worst outcome would again be for Y to cut its price, but this time X's profit only falls to £8 million (cell D). In this case, then, if X is cautious, it will *cut its price to £1.80*, as it would much rather have £8 million

Table 5.3 Profits for firms A and B at different prices

		X's price £2.00	X's price £1.80
Y's price	£2.00	A: £10m each	B: £5m for Y, £12m for X
	£1.80	C: £12m for Y, £5m for X	D: £8m each

of profit (from cutting its price) than £5 million (from keeping its price at £2). Note
that Y will argue along similar lines, and if it is cautious, it too will cut its price to
£1.80. The result is that the firms end up in cell D.

An alternative strategy is to go for the *optimistic* approach and assume that your
rivals react in the way most favourable to you. Here the firm will go for the strategy
that yields the highest possible profit. In X's case this will be again to cut price, only
this time on the optimistic assumption that firm Y will leave its price unchanged. If
firm X is correct in its assumption, it will move to cell B and achieve the maximum
possible profit of £12 million. Note that again the same argument applies to Y, which
will also cut its price. Again, the result is that the firms end up in cell D.

This game is a dominant strategy game, since *both* approaches, cautious and
optimistic, lead to the *same* strategy (namely, cutting price). Both firms do what
is best for them, given their assumptions about their rivals' behaviour. The result is
that the firms will end up in cell D, earning a lower profit (£8 million each) than if
they had charged the higher price (£10 million each in cell A).

Nash equilibrium. The equilibrium outcome of a game where there is no collusion
between the players (cell D in the above game) is known as a **Nash equilibrium**,
after John Nash, a US mathematician (and subject of the film *A Beautiful Mind*) who
introduced the concept in 1951.

Nash equilibrium. The position resulting from everyone making their optimal decision
based on their assumptions about their rivals' decisions. Such an outcome, however, is
unlikely to maximise the collective benefit. Nevertheless, without collusion in this 'game',
whether open or tacit, there is no incentive to move from this position.

The prisoners' dilemma. In the game we have just looked at, collusion rather than a
price war would have benefited both firms. Yet even if they did collude both would
still be tempted to cheat and cut prices. This is known as the **prisoners' dilemma**:
the dilemma faced by suspects of a crime who are in custody and wondering
whether to 'shop' their fellow suspects in the hope of getting
a lighter sentence. The police rely on the fact that suspects are
tempted to own up in case their fellow prisoners do so first.
The result is that everyone owns up, even though collusion to
keep quiet would have been in all the suspects' interests. The
prisoners' dilemma is examined in Box 5.4.

More complex games with no dominant strategy

More complex 'games' can be devised with more than two firms, many alternative
prices, differentiated products and various forms of non-price competition (e.g.
advertising). In such cases, the cautious strategy may suggest a different policy (e.g.
do nothing) from the high-risk (optimistic) strategy (e.g. cut prices substantially).

In many situations, firms will have a number of different options open to them
and a number of possible reactions by rivals. In such cases, the choices facing firms
may be many. They may opt for a compromise strategy between the optimistic and
the cautious approaches. This could be a strategy that is more risky than the cautious
one, but with the chance of a higher profit; but not as risky as the optimistic one,
but where the maximum profit possible is not so high.

The better the firm's information about (a) its rivals' costs and demand, (b) the
likely reactions of rivals to its actions and (c) the effects of these reactions on its

own profit, the better the firm's 'move in the game' is likely to be. It is similar to a card game: the more you know about your opponents' cards and how your opponents are likely to react to your moves, and the better you can calculate the effects of their moves on you, the better your moves in the game are likely to be.

Multiple-move games

In many business situations firms will *react* to what their rivals do. Their rivals, in turn, will react to what they do. In other words, the game goes back and forth from one 'player' to the other, rather like chess or a game of cards. Firms will still have to think strategically (as you do in chess), considering the likely responses of rivals to what they do. These multiple-move games are known as **repeated games** or **extensive-form games**.

One of the simplest repeated games is the **tit-for-tat game**. This is where a firm will *only* cut prices (or make some other aggressive move) if the rival does first. To illustrate this in a multiple-move situation, consider the example we looked at in Table 5.3, but this time we will extend it beyond one period.

Assume that firm X is adopting the tit-for-tat strategy. If firm Y cuts its price, firm X then responds in round 2 by cutting its price. The two firms end up in cell D – worse off than if neither had cut price. If, however, firm Y had left its price at £2.00, then firm X would respond by leaving its price unchanged too. Both would remain in cell A with a higher profit than cell D.

As long as firm Y knows that firm X will behave in this way, it has an incentive not to cut its price. To make sure that Y 'understands', X will probably let it be known how it will react. It other words, it will make a threat.

The importance of threats and promises

There are many situations where an oligopolist will make a threat or promise (either openly or implied) that it will act in a certain way. As long as the threat or promise is **credible** (i.e. its competitors believe it), the firm can gain and it will influence its rivals' behaviour.

Take the simple situation where a large oil company, such as Esso, states that it will match the price charged by any competitor within a given radius. Assume that competitors believe this 'price promise' but also that Esso will not try to *undercut* their price. In the simple situation where there is only one other filling station in the area, what price should it charge? Clearly it should charge the price which would maximise its profits, assuming that Esso will charge the *same* price. In the absence of other filling stations in the area, this is likely to be a relatively high price.

Now assume that there are several filling stations in the area. What should the company do now? Its best bet is probably to charge the same price as Esso and hope that no other company charges a lower price and forces Esso to cut its price. Assuming that Esso's threat is credible, other companies are likely to reason in a similar way.

The importance of timing: decision trees

Most decisions by oligopolists are made by one firm at a time rather than simultaneously by all firms. Sometimes a firm will take the initiative. At other times it will respond to decisions taken by other firms.

Definitions

Repeated or **extensive-form games**
Where firms decide in turn, in the light of what their rivals do. Such games thus involve two or more moves.

Tit-for-tat game
Where you will copy whatever your rival does. Thus if your rival cuts price, you will too. If your rival does not, neither will you.

Credible threat (or promise)
One that is believable to rivals because it is in the threatener's interests to carry it out.

Pause for thought

Assume that there are two major oil companies operating filling stations in an area. The first promises to match the other's prices. The other promises to sell at 1p per litre cheaper than the first. Describe the likely sequence of events in this 'game' and the likely eventual outcome. Could the promise of the second company be seen as credible?

BOX 5.4	THE PRISONERS' DILEMMA

When confession may be the best strategy

Game theory is relevant not just to business and economics. A famous non-economic example is the origin of the term 'prisoners' dilemma'. Take the case of Nigel and Amanda who have been arrested for a joint crime of serious fraud. Each is interviewed separately and given the following alternatives:

■ First, if they say nothing, the court has enough evidence to sentence both to a year's imprisonment.

■ Second, if either Nigel or Amanda *alone* confesses, he or she is likely to get only a three-month sentence but the partner could get up to ten years.

■ Third, if both confess, they are likely to get three years each.

Let us consider Nigel's dilemma. Should he confess in order to get the short sentence? This is better than the year he would get for not confessing. There is, however, an even better reason for confessing. Suppose Nigel doesn't confess but, unknown to him, Amanda does confess. Then Nigel ends up with the long sentence. Better than this is to confess and to get no more than three years: this is the safest strategy.

Amanda is in the same dilemma. The result is simple. When both prisoners act in their own self-interest by confessing, they both end up in position D with relatively long prison terms. Only when they collude will they end up in position A with relatively short prison terms, the best combined solution.

Of course the police know this and will do their best to prevent any collusion. They will keep Nigel and Amanda in separate cells and try to persuade each of them that the other is bound to confess.

Thus the choice of strategy depends on:

■ Nigel's and Amanda's risk attitudes, i.e. are they 'risk lovers' or 'risk averse'?

■ Nigel's and Amanda's estimates of how likely the other is to own up.

1. *Devise a box diagram for the above case, similar to that in Table 5.3. Why is this a dominant strategy game?*
2. *How would Nigel's choice of strategy be affected if he had instead been involved in a joint crime with Jeremy, Pauline, Diana and Dave, and they had all been caught?*

Some other examples

Standing at concerts. When people go to some public event, such as a concert or a match, they often stand in order to get a better view. But once people start standing, everyone is likely to do so: after all, if they stayed sitting, they would not see at all. In this Nash equilibrium, most people are worse off, since, except for tall people, their view is likely to be worse and they lose the comfort of sitting down.

Too much advertising. Why do firms spend so much on advertising? If they are aggressive, they probably do so to get ahead of their rivals. If they are cautious, they probably do so for fear of their rivals increasing their advertising. Although in both cases it may be in the individual firm's best interests to increase advertising, the resulting Nash equilibrium is likely to be one of excessive advertising: the total spent on advertising (by all firms) is not recouped in additional sales.

Union membership. The more employees of a business there are who are members of a trade union, the more powerful will the union be and the bigger the pay rise it is likely to gain. But here is the prisoners' dilemma. Workers motivated by self-interest will be tempted *not* to join the union and thus save the membership subscription. But the more workers there are who do this, the smaller the union membership and the less the pay rise is likely to be.

Give one or two other examples (economic or non-economic) of the prisoners' dilemma.

Definition

Decision tree (or game tree)
A diagram showing the sequence of possible decisions by competitor firms and the outcome of each combination of decisions.

Take the case of a new generation of large passenger aircraft which can fly further without refuelling. Assume that there is a market for a 500-seater version of this type of aircraft and a 400-seater version, but that the market for each sized aircraft is not big enough for the two manufacturers, Boeing and Airbus, to share it profitably. Let us also assume that the 400-seater market would give an annual profit of £50 million to a single manufacturer and the 500-seater would give an annual profit of £30 million, but that if both manufacturers produced the same version, they would each make an annual loss of £10 million.

Assume that Boeing announces that it is building the 400-seater plane. What should Airbus do? The choice is illustrated in Figure 5.5. This diagram is called a **decision tree** and shows the sequence of events. The small square at the left of the

Figure 5.5   A decision tree

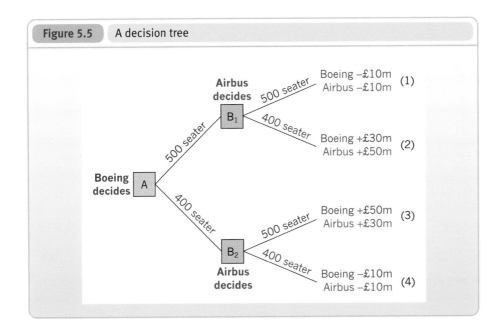

diagram is Boeing's decision point (point A). If it had decided to build the 500-seater plane, we would move up the top branch. Airbus would now have to make a decision (point B_1). If it too built the 500-seater plane, we would move to outcome 1: a loss of £10m for both manufacturers. Clearly, with Boeing building a 500-seater plane, Airbus would choose the 400-seater plane: we would move to outcome 2, with Boeing making a profit of £30m and Airbus a profit £50m. Airbus would be very pleased!

Boeing's best strategy at point A, however, would be to build the 400-seater plane. We would then move to Airbus's decision point B_2. In this case, it is in Airbus's interests to build the 500-seater plane. Its profit would be only £30m (outcome 3), but this is better than a £10m loss if it too built the 400-seater plane (outcome 4). With Boeing deciding first, the Nash equilibrium will thus be outcome 3.

There is clearly a **first-mover advantage** here. Once Boeing has decided to build the more profitable version of the plane, Airbus is forced to build the less profitable one. Naturally, Airbus would like to build the more profitable one and be the first mover. Which company succeeds in going first depends on how advanced they are in their research and development and in their production capacity.

More complex decision trees. The aircraft example is the simplest version of a decision tree, with just two companies and each one making only one key decision. In many business situations, much more complex trees could be constructed. The 'game' would be more like one of chess, with many moves and several options on each move. If there were more than two companies, the decision tree would be more complex still.

> **Pause for thought**
>
> *Give an example of decisions that two firms could make in sequence, each one affecting the other's next decision.*

> **Definition**
>
> **First-mover advantage**
> When a firm gains from being the first to take action.

Recap

1. Game theory examines various strategies that firms can adopt when the outcome of each is not certain.

2. In a single-move game, they must decide what to do on the basis of what they think rivals will do.

3. They can adopt a cautious strategy of choosing the policy that has the least possible worst outcome, or a high-risk optimistic strategy of choosing the policy with the best possible outcome, or some compromise. Either way, a 'Nash' equilibrium is likely to be reached which is not in the best interests of the firms collectively. It will entail a lower level of profit than if they had colluded.

4. In multiple-move games, firms will respond not only to what firms do, but what they say they will do. To this end, a firm's threats or promises must be credible, if they are to influence rivals' decisions.

5. A firm may gain a strategic advantage over its rivals by being the first one to take action (e.g. launch a new product). A decision tree can be constructed to show the possible sequence of moves in a multiple-move game.

5.5 ALTERNATIVE AIMS OF THE FIRM

The traditional profit-maximising theories of the firm have been criticised for being unrealistic. They assume that it is the *owners* of the firm that make price and output decisions. It is reasonable to assume that owners will want to maximise profits: this much most of the critics of the traditional theory accept. But as we saw in Chapter 1, in public limited companies there is generally a separation of ownership and control of companies, which creates a principal–agent problem (see page 10). *Managers*, as agents of the owners (their principals), are the decision makers and may well be motivated by objectives other than maximising profits, such as increasing their own utility by maximising sales or claiming large expenses. Different managers in the same firm may well pursue different aims.

Managers will still have to ensure that *sufficient* profits are made to keep shareholders happy, but that may be very different from *maximising* profits. Alternative theories of the firm to those of profit maximisation, therefore, tend to assume that large firms are **profit satisficers**. That is, managers strive hard for a minimum target level of profit, but are less interested in profits above this level.

Such theories fall into two categories: first, those that assume that firms attempt to maximise some other aim, provided that sufficient profits are achieved; and second, those that assume that firms pursue a number of potentially conflicting aims, of which sufficient profit is merely one. We examine each in turn.

Alternative maximising aims

Sales revenue maximisation

Perhaps the most famous of all alternative theories of the firm is the theory of **sales revenue maximisation**. So why should managers want to maximise their firm's sales revenue? The answer is that the success of managers, and especially sales managers, may be judged according to the level of the firm's sales. Sales figures are an obvious barometer of the firm's health. Managers' salaries, power and prestige may depend directly on sales revenue. The firm's sales representatives may be paid commission on their sales. Thus sales revenue maximisation may be a more dominant aim in the firm than profit maximisation, particularly if it has a dominant sales department.

Definitions

Profit satisficing

Where decision makers in a firm aim for a target level of profit rather than the absolute maximum level.

Sales revenue maximisation

An alternative theory of the firm which assumes that managers aim to maximise the firm's short-run total revenue.

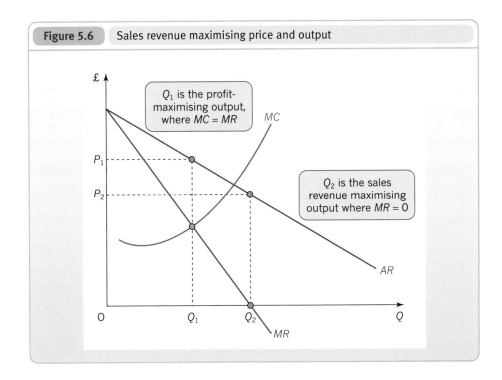

Figure 5.6   Sales revenue maximising price and output

Q_1 is the profit-maximising output, where $MC = MR$

Q_2 is the sales revenue maximising output where $MR = 0$

Total sales revenue (*TR*) will be maximised at a higher output and lower price than will profits. This is illustrated in Figure 5.6. Profits are maximised at output Q_1 and price P_1, where $MC = MR$. Sales revenue, however, is maximised at the higher output Q_2 and lower price P_2, where $MR = 0$. The reason is that if MR equals zero, nothing more can be added to total revenue (*TR*) by producing extra and thus *TR* must be at the maximum. Indeed, by producing above Q_2, MR would be negative and thus *TR* would fall.

Sales revenue maximisation tends to involve more advertising than does profit maximisation. Ideally the profit-maximising firm will advertise up to the point where the marginal revenue of advertising equals the marginal cost of advertising (assuming diminishing returns to advertising). The firm aiming to maximise sales revenue will go beyond this, since further advertising, although costing more than it earns the firm, will still add to total revenue. The firm will continue advertising until surplus profits above the minimum have been used up.

Growth maximisation

Rather than aiming to maximise *short-run* revenue, managers may take a longer-term perspective and aim for **growth maximisation** in the size of the firm. They may gain directly from being part of a rapidly growing 'dynamic' organisation; promotion prospects are greater in an expanding organisation, since new posts tend to be created; large firms may pay higher salaries; managers may obtain greater power in a large firm.

Growth is probably best measured in terms of a growth in sales revenue, since sales revenue (or 'turnover') is the simplest way of measuring the size of a business. An alternative would be to measure the capital value of a firm, but this will depend on the ups and downs of the stock market and is thus a rather unreliable method.

If a firm is to maximise growth, it needs to be clear about the time period over which it is setting itself this objective. For example, maximum growth over the next

Definition

Growth maximisation An alternative theory which assumes that managers seek to maximise the growth in sales revenue (or the capital value of the firm) over time.

two or three years might be obtained by running factories to absolute maximum capacity, cramming in as many machines and workers as possible, and backing this up with massive advertising campaigns and price cuts. Such policies, however, may not be sustainable in the longer run. The firm may simply not be able to finance them. A longer-term perspective (say, 5–10 years) may therefore require the firm to 'pace' itself, and perhaps to direct resources away from current production and sales into the development of new products that have a potentially high and growing long-term demand.

Equilibrium for a growth-maximising firm. What will a growth-maximising firm's price and output be? Unfortunately, there is no simple formula for predicting this.

In the short run, the firm may choose the profit-maximising price and output – so as to provide the greatest funds for investment. On the other hand, it may be prepared to sacrifice some short-term profits in order to mount an advertising campaign. It all depends on the strategy it considers most suitable to achieve growth.

In the long run, prediction is more difficult still. The policies that a firm adopts will depend crucially on the assessments of market opportunities made by managers. But this involves judgement, not fine calculation. Different managers will judge a situation differently.

One prediction can be made. Growth-maximising firms are likely to diversify into different products, especially as they approach the limits to expansion in existing markets. We considered the Growth Vector Matrix in section 3.4 and will go on to analyse alternative growth strategies in Chapter 6.

> **Pause for thought**
>
> *How will competition between growth-maximising firms benefit the consumer?*

Multiple aims

Satisficing and the setting of targets

Large firms are often complex institutions with several departments (sales, production, design, purchasing, personnel, finance, etc.). Each department is likely to have its own specific set of aims and objectives, which may possibly come into conflict with those of other departments. In such cases not all the aims will be able to be maximised. Instead a 'satisficing' approach must be taken (see page 140).

These aims in turn will be constrained by the interests of shareholders, workers, customers and creditors (collectively known as **stakeholders**), who will need to be kept sufficiently happy (see Box 5.5).

A satisficing approach will normally involve setting targets for production, sales, profit, stock holding, etc. If, in practice, target levels are not achieved, a 'search' procedure will be started to find what went wrong and how to rectify it. If the problem cannot be rectified, managers will probably adjust the target downwards. If, on the other hand, targets are easily achieved, managers may adjust them upwards. Thus the targets to which managers aspire depend to a large extent on the success in achieving *previous* targets.

Targets are also influenced by expectations of demand and costs, by the achievements of competitors and by expectations of competitors' future behaviour. For example, if it is expected that the economy is likely to move into recession, sales and profit targets may be adjusted downwards.

If targets conflict, the conflict will be settled by a bargaining process between managers. The outcome of the bargaining, however, will depend on the power and ability of the individual managers concerned. Thus a similar set of conflicting targets may be resolved differently in different firms.

> **Definition**
>
> **Stakeholders (in a company)**
>
> People who are affected by a company's activities and/or performance (customers, employees, owners, creditors, people living in the neighbourhood, etc.). They may or may not be in a position to take decisions, or influence decision taking, in the firm.

BOX 5.5 STAKEHOLDER POWER?

Who governs the firm?

The concept of the 'stakeholder economy' became fashionable in the late 1990s. Rather than the economy being governed by big business, and rather than businesses being governed in the interests of shareholders (many of whom are big institutions, such as insurance companies and pension funds), the economy should serve the interests of everyone. But what does this mean for the governance of firms?

Meeting the interests of various stakeholders

The stakeholders of a firm include customers, employees (from senior managers to the lowest paid workers), shareholders, suppliers, lenders and the local and national communities.

The supporters of a stakeholding economy argue that *all* these interest groups ought to have a say in the decisions of the firm. Trade unions or workers' councils ought to be included in decisions affecting the workforce, or indeed all company decisions. They could be represented on decision-making bodies and perhaps have seats on the board of directors. Alternatively, the workforce might be given the power to elect managers.

Banks or other institutions lending to firms ought to be included in investment decisions. In Germany, where banks finance a large proportion of investment, they are represented on the boards of most large companies.

Local communities ought to have a say in any projects (such as new buildings or the discharge of effluent) that affect the local environment. Customers ought to have more say in the quality of products being produced, for example by being given legal protection against the production of shoddy or unsafe goods.

Where interest groups cannot be directly represented in decision making, then companies ought to be regulated by the government in order to protect the interests of the various groups. For example, if farmers and other suppliers to supermarkets are paid very low prices, then the purchasing behaviour of the supermarkets could be regulated by some government agency.

Of course, the interests of various stakeholders may conflict. Thus a 'satisficing' approach would have to be adopted if businesses were to take them into account.

In other words, satisfactory target levels would have to be set for each of the various objectives, with adjustments made when any targets conflicted with each other.

Are businesses becoming more or less responsive to stakeholders' interests?

But is this vision of a stakeholder economy likely to become reality? Trends in the international economy suggest that the opposite might be occurring. The growth of multinational corporations, with their ability to move finance and production to wherever it is most profitable, has weakened the power of employees, local interest groups and even national governments.

Employees in one part of the multinational may have little in the way of common interests with employees in another. In fact, they may vie with each other, for example over which plant should be expanded or closed down. What is more, many firms are employing a larger and larger proportion of casual, part-time, temporary or agency workers. With these new 'flexible labour markets' such employees have far less say in the company than permanent members of staff: they are 'outsiders' to decision making within the firm (see section 8.5).

Also, the widespread introduction of share incentive schemes for managers (whereby managers are rewarded with shares), has increasingly made profits their driving goal. Finally, the policies of opening up markets and deregulation, policies that were adopted by many governments round the world up to the mid 1990s, have again weakened the power of many stakeholders.

Nevertheless, many companies find themselves under increased pressure to respond to social and environmental concerns and to practise 'corporate social responsibility (CSR)'. An 'irresponsible' firm is likely to attract adverse publicity – which could impact on sales and profit. We examine CSR in section 9.2.

 Are customers' interests best served by profit-maximising firms, answerable primarily to shareholders, or by firms where various stakeholder groups are represented in decision taking?

Organisational slack

Since changing targets often involves search procedures and bargaining processes and is therefore time-consuming, and since many managers prefer to avoid conflict, targets tend to be changed fairly infrequently. Business conditions, however, often change rapidly. To avoid the need to change targets, therefore, managers will tend to be fairly conservative in their aspirations. This leads to the phenomenon known as **organisational slack**.

When the firm does better than planned, it will allow slack to develop. This slack can then be taken up if the firm does worse than planned. For example, if the firm

> **Definition**
>
> **Organisational slack**
> When managers allow spare capacity to exist, thereby enabling them to respond more easily to changed circumstances.

Definitions

Just-in-time methods
Where a firm purchases supplies and produces both components and finished products as they are required. This minimises stock holding and its associated costs.

Average cost or **mark-up pricing**
Where firms set the price by adding a profit mark-up to average costs.

produces more than it planned, it will build up stocks of finished goods and draw on them if production subsequently falls. It would not, in the meantime, increase its sales target or reduce its production target. If it did, and production then fell below target, the production department might not be able to supply the sales department with its full requirement.

Thus keeping targets fairly low and allowing slack to develop allows all targets to be met with minimum conflict.

Organisational slack, however, adds to a firm's costs. If firms are operating in a competitive environment, they may be forced to cut slack in order to survive. In the 1970s, many Japanese firms succeeded in cutting slack by using **just-in-time** methods of production. These involve keeping stocks to a minimum and ensuring that inputs are delivered as required. Clearly, this requires that production is tightly controlled and that suppliers are reliable. Many firms today have successfully cut their warehouse costs by using such methods. These methods are examined in section 8.5.

Recap

1. In large companies, shareholders (the owners) may want maximum profits, but it is the managers who make the decisions, and managers are likely to aim to maximise their own self-interest rather than that of the shareholders. This leads to profit 'satisficing'. This is where managers aim to achieve sufficient profits to keep shareholders happy, but this is a secondary aim to one or more alternative aims.

2. Managers may seek to maximise sales revenue. The output of a sales-revenue-maximising firm will be higher than that of a profit-maximising one. Its level of advertising will also tend to be higher.

3. Many managers aim for maximum growth of their organisation, believing that this will help their salaries, power, prestige, etc. It is difficult, however, to predict the price and output strategies of a growth-maximising firm.

4. In large firms, decisions are taken by, or influenced by, a number of different people, including various managers and other stakeholders. If interests conflict, a satisficing approach will generally be adopted. This involves setting consistent targets, which will be adjusted in the light of experience and may involve a process of bargaining.

5. Life is made easier for managers if conflict can be avoided. This will be possible if slack is allowed to develop in various parts of the firm. If targets are not being met, the slack can then be taken up without requiring adjustments in other targets.

5.6 SETTING PRICE

How are prices determined in practice? Is there actually an equilibrium price? In many cases, probably not. Do firms construct marginal cost and marginal revenue curves (or equations) and find the output where they are equal? Do they then use an average revenue curve (or equation) to work out the price at that output?

The problem is that firms often do not have the information to do so, even if they wanted to. In practice, firms look for rules of pricing that are relatively simple to apply.

Cost-based pricing

One approach is **average cost** or **mark-up pricing**. Here producers work out the price by simply adding a certain percentage (mark-up) for profit on top of average costs (average fixed costs plus average variable costs).

$$P = AFC + AVC + \text{Profit mark-up}$$

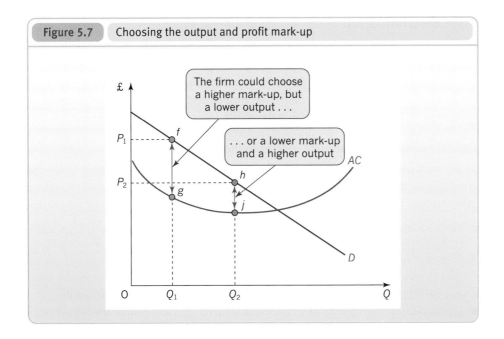

Figure 5.7   Choosing the output and profit mark-up

The firm could choose a higher mark-up, but a lower output . . .

. . . or a lower mark-up and a higher output

Choosing the mark-up

The level of profit mark-up on top of average cost will depend on the firm's aims: whether it is aiming for high or even maximum profits, or merely a target based on previous profit. It will also depend on the likely actions of rivals and their responses to changes in this firm's price and how these responses will affect demand.

If a firm could estimate its demand curve, it could then set its output and profit mark-up at levels to avoid a shortage or surplus. Thus in Figure 5.7 it could choose a lower output (Q_1) with a higher mark-up (*fg*), or a higher output (Q_2) with a lower mark-up (*hj*). If a firm could not estimate its demand curve, then it could adjust its mark-up and output over time by a process of trial and error, according to its success in meeting profit and sales aims.

> **Pause for thought**
>
> *If a firm has a typical-shaped average cost curve and sets prices 10 per cent above average cost, what will its supply curve look like?*

Variations in the mark-up

In most firms, the mark-up is not rigid. In expanding markets, or markets where firms have monopoly/oligopoly power, the size of the mark-up is likely to be greater. In contracting markets, or under conditions of rising costs and constant demand, a firm may well be forced to accept lower profits and thus reduce the mark-up.

The firm is likely to take account of the actions and possible reactions of its competitors, as we saw under the model of oligopoly. It may well be unwilling to change prices when costs or demand change, for fear of the reactions of competitors (see the kinked demand curve theory on pages 131–2). If prices are kept constant and yet costs change, either due to a movement along the *AC* curve in response to a change in demand or due to a shift in the *AC* curve, the firm must necessarily change the size of the mark-up.

All this suggests that, whereas the mark-up may well be based on a target profit, firms are often prepared to change their target and hence their mark-up.

> **Pause for thought**
>
> *If the firm adjusts the size of its mark-up according to changes in demand and the actions of competitors, could its actions approximate to setting price and output where $MC = MR$?*

Price discrimination

Up to now we have assumed that a firm will sell its output at a single price. Sometimes, however, firms may practise **price discrimination**. This is where the firm charges different prices to different customers, where the price differences are *unrelated to costs*. Thus an airline may charge much higher ticket prices to late bookers than to early bookers for identical seats on the same flight (see Box 5.6).

Conditions necessary for price discrimination to operate

As we shall see, a firm will be able to increase its profits if it can engage in price discrimination. But under what circumstances will it be able to charge discriminatory prices? There are three conditions that must be met:

■ The firm must be able to set its price. Thus price discrimination will be impossible under perfect competition, where firms are price takers.
■ The markets must be separate. Consumers in the low-priced market must not be able to resell the product in the high-priced market. For example, children must not be able to resell a half-priced child's cinema ticket for use by an adult.
■ Demand elasticity must differ in each market. The firm will charge the higher price in the market where demand is less elastic, and thus less sensitive to a price rise.

Advantages to the firm

Price discrimination will allow the firm to earn a higher revenue from any given level of sales. This is illustrated in Figure 5.8, which shows a firm's overall demand curve. If it is to sell 200 units without price discrimination, it must charge a price of P_1. The total revenue it earns is shown by the green area. If, however, it can practise price discrimination by selling 150 of those 200 units at the higher price of P_2, it will gain the mauve area in addition to the green area.

Another advantage to the firm of price discrimination is that it may be able to use it to drive competitors out of business. If a firm has a monopoly in one market (e.g. the home market), it may be able to charge a high price due to relatively inelastic demand, and thus make high profits. If it is under oligopoly in another

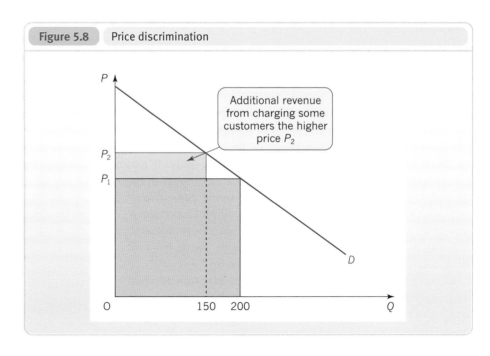

Figure 5.8   Price discrimination

Additional revenue from charging some customers the higher price P_2

BOX 5.6   EASY PRICING

Getting the most revenue from a plane

A good example of price discrimination is the pricing strategy of easyJet. The first few seats on every flight are sold at a very low price (typically from £6.99 to £21.99 depending on the distance). Then as the plane fills up, so the prices rise (typically to around £170 to £200 for the last few seats). With carefully chosen prices, this strategy allows easyJet to maximise the revenue from its passengers. The last-minute business passengers will pay a high price, while those prepared to book a long time in advance for a cheap break, but willing to shop around to get a bargain, will be charged a low price – but probably close to the maximum they would be prepared to pay anyway. We considered this idea when we looked at consumer surplus in Chapter 3 (see page 63).

This strategy can be illustrated with the demand curve shown in the diagram. Assume that the plane has 150 seats and that the pricing strategy manages to fill the plane. Assume also that the first 20 seats are sold at a price of £19.99. Seat prices then rise in bands with the final 20 seats being priced at £199.99.

What the demand curve shows is that there are 20 people who would be prepared to pay at least £199.99, but that to sell all 150 seats, at least one must be offered at a price as low as £19.99. Of course, in practice, it's not quite as simple as this, as some of the people buying tickets at low prices might have been prepared to pay more.

The other part of easyJet's business model is to keep costs to a minimum. Practices include: no tickets; no seat allocations; direct web booking (including 18 language options); no agents; no free food; cabin crew collecting rubbish; avoiding congested airports; reduced turnaround times; maximum utilisation of planes; and a relatively modern fleet to reduce maintenance and operating costs.

1. *Would you advise easyJet to offer a business class option? Explain why or why not.*
2. *Referring to the above demand curve for an easyJet flight, how could additional revenue be earned from the same demand curve?*

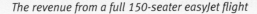

The revenue from a full 150-seater easyJet flight

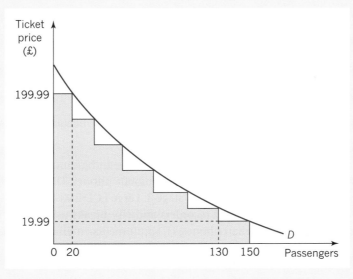

market (e.g. the export market), it may use the high profits in the first market to subsidise a very low price in the oligopolistic market, thus forcing its competitors out of business.

It may also provide the firm with opportunities to enter new markets. Again, if the firm has high profits in its established market, it may not only be able to enter another market, but also use these profits to help it survive a price war, should one emerge in this new market. In this way, price discrimination could actually help to increase competition.

Pause for thought

To what extent do consumers gain or lose from price discrimination?

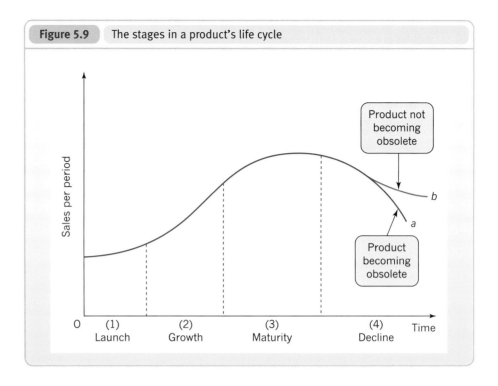

Figure 5.9   The stages in a product's life cycle

Pricing and the product life cycle

New products are launched and then become established. Later they may be replaced by more up-to-date products. Many products go through such a 'life cycle'. Four stages can be identified in a typical life cycle (see Figure 5.9):

1. Being launched.
2. A rapid growth in sales.
3. Maturity: a levelling off in sales.
4. Decline: sales begin to fall as the market becomes saturated, or as the product becomes out of date.

Analogue televisions, audio cassettes and gramophone records have all reached stage 4. Writable CDs, traditional mobile phones, DIY products and automatic washing machines have reached stage 3. Large LCD TVs, speed dating events, herbal teas, induction hobs, DVD recorders and city breaks using budget airlines are probably still in stage 2. Smart phones, HD multimedia entertainment devices and biodiesel are probably still in stage 1, but things do change very quickly, especially with high-tech products!

At each stage, the firm is likely to be faced with quite different market conditions: not only in terms of consumer demand, but also in terms of competition from rivals. What does this mean for pricing strategy?

The launch stage

In this stage the firm will probably have a monopoly (unless there is a simultaneous launch by rivals).

Given the lack of substitutes, the firm may be able to exploit its first-mover advantage (see page 139) and charge very high prices, thereby making large profits. This will be especially true if it is a radically new product – like the ballpoint pen, the home computer, the mobile phone and the iPod were. Such products are likely to have a rapidly expanding and price-inelastic demand.

The danger of a high-price policy is that the resulting high profits may tempt competitors to break into the industry, even if barriers are quite high. As an alternative, then, the firm may go for maximum 'market penetration' (see the Growth Vector Matrix on pages 76–7): keeping the price low to get as many sales and as much brand loyalty as possible, before rivals can become established.

Which policy the firm adopts will depend on its assessment of its current price elasticity of demand and the likelihood of an early entry by rivals.

> **Pause for thought**
>
> *If entry barriers are high, should a firm always charge a high price during this phase?*

The growth stage

Unless entry barriers are very high, the rapid growth in sales will attract new firms. The industry becomes oligopolistic.

Despite the growth in the number of firms, sales are expanding so rapidly that all firms can increase their sales. Some price competition may emerge, but it is unlikely to be intense at this stage. New entrants may choose to compete in terms of minor product differences, while following the price lead set by the original firm.

The maturity stage

Now that the market has grown large, there are many firms competing. New firms – or, more likely, firms diversifying into this market – will be entering to get 'a piece of the action'. At the same time, the growth in sales is slowing down.

Competition is now likely to be more intense and any collusion may well begin to break down. Pricing policy may become more aggressive as businesses attempt to hold on to their market share. Price wars may break out, only to be followed later by a 'truce' and a degree of price collusion.

It is in this stage particularly that firms may invest considerably in product innovation in order to 'breathe new life' into old products, especially if there is competition from new types of product. Thus the upgrading of hi-fi cassette recorders, with additional features such as Dolby S, was one way in which it was hoped to beat off competition from digital cassette recorders and later minidisc recorders and CD burners.

The decline stage

Eventually, as the market becomes saturated, or as new superior alternative products are launched, sales will start to fall. For example, once most households had a fridge, the demand for fridges fell back as people simply bought them to replace worn-out ones, or to obtain a more up-to-date one. Initially in this stage competition is likely to be intense. All sorts of price offers, extended guarantees, better after-sales service, added features, etc., will be introduced as firms seek to maintain their sales. Some firms may be driven out of the market, unable to survive the competition.

After a time, however, the level of sales may stop falling. Provided the product has not become obsolete, people still need replacements. This is illustrated by line *b* in Figure 5.9. The market may thus return to a stable oligopoly with a high degree of tacit price collusion.

Alternatively, the product becomes obsolete (line *a*) and sales dry up. Firms will leave the market. It is pointless trying to compete.

How flexible are prices?

Evidence from the USA[1] and the eurozone[2] suggests that the frequency and magnitude of price changes varies enormously from product to product.

> Generally speaking, the greater the share of raw materials in a product, the more often its price moves: petrol prices change, on average, in five months out of six in both America and Europe; the prices of fresh food are altered far more frequently than those of processed food. The prices of services are stickier than those of goods. This may be because services tend to be more labour-intensive than goods, and because wages are stickier (downwards, anyway) than other prices.[3]

> For most products, prices change relatively infrequently in Europe, with retail prices changing on average just over once per year. In the USA, sales are much more common, especially with clothes, furniture and processed food. The prices of services also change more frequently in the USA. In Europe services are more regulated and wages (a large proportion of the cost of most services) are less flexible.

> How often individual prices move is an important question. Shifts in prices are like the traffic lights of an economy, signalling to people to buy more of this and less of that, to spend or to save, or to find new jobs. If the lights change readily, resources can be redirected smoothly; if they get stuck, so does the economy. In particular, if neither prices nor wages fall easily, the cost in output and jobs of reducing inflation can be high. Sticky prices also mean that an inflationary shock – an increase in oil prices, say – can take a long time to work its way through the system.[4]

> As far as the magnitude of price changes is concerned, in both the USA and Europe, price changes are typically much bigger than the rate of inflation. In Europe, average price increases are 8 per cent and average price reductions 10 per cent.

Pause for thought

Why, do you think, are percentage price changes bigger, both up and down, than the rate of inflation?

Recap

1. Traditional economic theory assumes that businesses will set prices corresponding to the output where the marginal costs of production are equal to marginal revenue. They will do so in pursuit of maximum profits. The difficulties that a business faces in deriving its marginal cost and revenue curves suggest that this is unlikely to be a widely practised pricing strategy.

2. Cost-based pricing involves the business adding a profit mark-up to its average costs of production. The profit mark-up set by the business is likely to alter depending upon market conditions.

3. Many businesses practise price discrimination in an attempt to maximise profits from the sale of a product. For a business to practise price discrimination it must be able to set prices, separate markets so as to prevent resale from the cheap to the expensive market, and identify distinct demand elasticities in each market.

4. Products will be priced differently depending upon where they are in the product's life cycle. New products can be priced cheaply so as to gain market share, or priced expensively to recoup cost. Later on in the product's life cycle, prices will have to reflect the degree of competition, which may become intense as the market stabilises or even declines.

5. Price flexibility varies from product to product. Generally the greater the proportion of raw materials in a product, the more frequently its price changes. In Europe, average price increases are 8 per cent and average price reductions 10 per cent.

[1] Nakamura, Emi and Steinsson, Jón 'Five facts about prices: a reevaluation of menu cost models', *Quarterly Journal of Economics*, Vol. 123, No. 4 (November 2008), pp. 1415–64
[2] Dhyne, Emmanuel et al., 'Price setting in the euro area: some stylized facts from individual consumer price data', *ECB Working Paper Series*, No. 524, (September 2005)
[3] 'Sticky situations', *The Economist* (9 November 2006)
[4] *Ibid.*

QUESTIONS

1. Think of four different products or services and estimate roughly how many firms there are in the market. You will need to decide whether 'the market' is a local one, a national one or an international one. In what ways do the firms compete in each of the cases you have identified?

2. As an illustration of the difficulty in identifying monopolies, try to decide which of the following are monopolies: a train operating company; your local evening newspaper; the village post office; the Royal Mail; Microsoft Office suite of programs; Interflora; the London Underground; ice creams in the cinema; Guinness; food on trains; the board game 'Monopoly'.

3. For what reasons would you expect a monopoly to charge (a) a higher price, and (b) a lower price than if the industry were operating under perfect competition?

4. Will competition between oligopolists always reduce total industry profits?

5. In which of the following industries is collusion likely to occur: bricks, beer, margarine, cement, crisps, washing powder, blank audio or video cassettes, carpets? Explain why.

6. Devise a box diagram like that in Table 5.3, only this time assume that there are three firms, each considering the two strategies of keeping price the same or reducing it by a set amount. Identify the optimistic, cautious and compromise approaches. Is the game still a 'dominant strategy game'?

7. What are the limitations of game theory in predicting oligopoly behaviour?

8. Make a list of six aims that a manager of a high street department store might have. Identify some conflicts that might arise between these aims.

9. When are increased profits in a manager's personal interest?

10. Since advertising increases a firm's costs, will prices necessarily be lower with sales revenue maximisation than with profit maximisation?

11. A frequent complaint of junior and some senior managers is that they are frequently faced with new targets from above, and that this makes their life difficult. If their complaint is true, does this conflict with the hypothesis that managers will try to build in slack?

12. Outline the main factors that might influence the size of the profit mark-up set by a business.

13. If a cinema could sell all its seats to adults in the evenings at the end of the week, but only a few on Mondays and Tuesdays, what price discrimination policy would you recommend to the cinema in order for it to maximise its weekly revenue?

14. How will a business's pricing strategy differ at each stage of its product's life cycle? First assume that the business has a monopoly position at the launch stage; then assume that it faces a high degree of competition right from the outset.

Business issues covered in this chapter

- What are the objectives of strategic management?
- What are the key competitive forces affecting a business?
- What choices of strategy towards competitors are open to a business?
- What internal strategic choices are open to a business and how can it make best use of its core competences when deciding on its internal organisation?
- By what means can a business grow and how can growth be financed?
- Should businesses seek to raise finance through the stock market?
- Under what circumstances might a business want to merge with another?
- What are the advantages and problems of remaining a small business?
- What issues arise in starting up a business?

Business growth and strategy

STRATEGIC ANALYSIS 6.1

For much of the time most managers are concerned with routine day-to-day activities of the business, such as dealing with personnel issues, checking budgets and looking for ways to enhance efficiency. In other words, they are involved in the detailed operational activities of the business.

Some managers, however, especially those high up in the business organisation, such as the managing director, will be busy in a different way, thinking about big, potentially complex issues which affect the whole company. For example, they might be analysing the behaviour of competitors, or evaluating the company's share price or considering ways to expand the business. In other words, these managers are involved in the *strategic* long-term activities of the business. This is known as **strategic management**.

Strategic management involves *analysing* the alternative long-term courses of action for the firm and then *making choices* of what strategy to pursue.

The strategic choices that are made depend on the aims of the firm. Most firms have a 'mission statement' which sets out the broad aims, but as we saw in the last chapter, the aims in practice might be difficult to establish, given the number of different stakeholders in the business. It is thus in the *actual* decisions that are taken that the firm's aims can best be judged. In practice these aims are often complex, with economic objectives, such as profit, market share, product development and growth being mixed with broader social, ethical and environmental objectives.

We look at strategic analysis in this section and strategic choices in section 6.2.

Definitions

Strategic management
The management of the strategic long-term decisions and activities of the business.

Competitive advantage
The various factors, such as lower costs or a better product, that give a firm an advantage over its rivals.

Strategic analysis of the external business environment

In Chapter 1 we considered the various dimensions of the business environment and how they shape and influence business activity. Initially, we divided the business environment into four distinct sets of factors: political, economic, social and technological. Such factors comprise what we call a PEST analysis. We looked, then, at a development of this in STEEPLE analysis, which also includes ethical, legal and environmental factors. In this section we will take our analysis of the business environment forward and consider more closely those factors that are likely to influence the **competitive advantage** of the organisation.

Competitive advantage. The various factors that enable a firm to compete more effectively with its rivals. These can be supply-side factors, such as superior technology, better organisation, or greater power or efficiency in sourcing its supplies – resulting in lower costs; or they could be demand-side ones, such as producing a superior or better-value product in the eyes of consumers, or being more conveniently located – resulting in higher and/or less elastic demand.

The greater the competitive advantage of a firm, whether through lower costs or through less elastic demand for its products, the greater the rate of supernormal profit it will be able to make. In developing their strategy, firms seek to address these two dimensions: costs and demand.

The Five Forces Model of competition

Developed by Professor Michael Porter of Harvard Business School in 1980, the Five Forces Model sets out to identify those factors which are likely to affect an organisation's competitiveness (see Figure 6.1).[1] This then helps a firm choose an appropriate strategy to enhance its competitive opportunities and to protect itself from competitive threats. The five forces that Porter identifies are:

- the bargaining power of suppliers;
- the bargaining power of buyers;
- the threat of potential new entrants;
- the threat of substitute products;
- the extent of competitive rivalry.

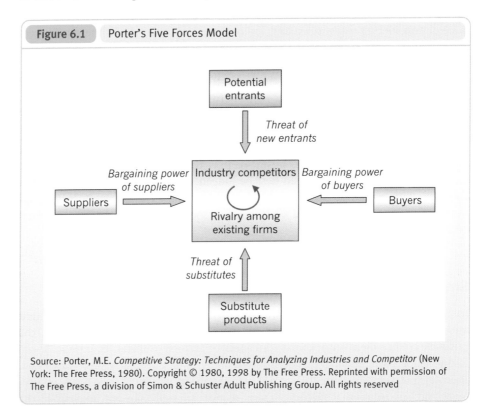

Figure 6.1   Porter's Five Forces Model

Source: Porter, M.E. *Competitive Strategy: Techniques for Analyzing Industries and Competitor* (New York: The Free Press, 1980). Copyright © 1980, 1998 by The Free Press. Reprinted with permission of The Free Press, a division of Simon & Schuster Adult Publishing Group. All rights reserved

---

[1] Porter, Michael E. *Competitive Strategy: Techniques for Analyzing Industries and Competitors* (The Free Press, 1980)

The bargaining power of suppliers. Most business organisations depend upon suppliers to some extent, whether to provide raw materials or simply stationery. Indeed, many businesses have extensive supply or 'value chain' networks (as we shall discuss below). Such suppliers can have a significant and powerful effect on a business when:

■ there are relatively few suppliers in the market, reducing the ability of the business to switch from one supply source to another;
■ there are no alternative supplies that can be used;
■ the cost of the supplies forms a large part of the firm's total costs;
■ a supplier's customers are small and fragmented and as such have little power over the supplying business.

Car dealers often find that car manufacturers can exert considerable pressure over them in terms of pricing, display and after-sales service.

The bargaining power of buyers. The bargaining power of companies that purchase a firm's products will be greater when:

■ these purchasing companies are large and there are relatively few of them;
■ there are many other firms competing for the purchasing companies' custom, and hence a firm that produces an undifferentiated product (such as vegetables) is likely to be more prone to 'buyer power' than one that produces a unique or differentiated product (such as CDs of a particular band);
■ the costs for the purchasing companies of switching to other suppliers are low;
■ purchasing companies could relatively easily produce the good themselves and thereby displace the supplying firm.

As we saw in Box 5.3, the UK grocery retailing sector is dominated by a small number of large supermarket chains such as Tesco, Sainsbury's and Asda/Wal-Mart. These exert massive levels of buyer power over farmers and food processors. Not only do such supermarkets dominate the market, but they can normally find many alternative supply sources, both domestic and international, at relatively little switching cost. As a result, suppliers are forced to reduce their prices and hence their profit margins are cut. Also, all the supermarkets sell own-brand labels, either produced themselves or through agreement with existing manufacturers, and these are often sold at prices considerably below those of equivalent branded products (see Box 3.4 on page 78).

Generally purchasing companies are able to exert greater power over their suppliers when they can source supplies from across the globe. This is increasingly the case with globalisation, which has made communication and transport both easier and cheaper. For example, large manufacturers in the developed world are often able to obtain their supplies from developing countries very cheaply because, by shopping around, they put suppliers in developing countries in competition with each other. This may, however, raise some ethical issues, as we consider in section 9.2.

The threat of potential new entrants. The ability of new firms to enter the market depends largely on the existence and effectiveness of various barriers to entry. These barriers to entry were described in section 5.2 (pages 122–3).

Barriers to entry tend to be very industry, product and market specific. Nevertheless, two useful generalisations can be made. First, companies with products that have a strong brand identity will often attempt to use this form of product differentiation to restrict competition; second, manufacturers will tend to rely on economies of scale and low costs gained from experience as means of retaining a cost advantage over potential rivals.

The threat of substitutes. The availability of substitute products can be a major threat to a business and its profitability, as many close substitutes implies a relatively price elastic demand. Issues that businesses need to consider in relation to the availability of substitute products are:

■ the ability and cost to customers of switching to the substitute;
■ the threat of competitors bringing out a more advanced or up-to-date product;
■ the impact that substitute products are likely to have on pricing policy.

The market for video recorders and videotapes is a good example of one that has been greatly affected by the arrival of a substitute in the form of DVD players and recorders, and writable and rewritable DVDs. As DVD players have fallen in price, the prices of video players and videotapes have plummeted. Early switching costs, such as those of obtaining DVDs, are slowly being overcome as DVD recorders have entered the market. Clearly video recorders and tapes are facing imminent obsolescence.

The extent of competitive rivalry. As we saw in the previous two chapters, the degree of competition a firm faces is a crucial element in shaping its strategic analysis. Competitive rivalry will be enhanced when there is the potential for new firms to enter the market, when there is a real threat from substitute products and when buyers and suppliers have some element of influence over the firm's performance. In addition to this, competitive rivalry is likely to be enhanced in the following circumstances:

■ There are many competitors, each of a similar size. This is a particular issue when firms are competing in a global market.
■ Markets are growing slowly. This makes it difficult to acquire additional sales without taking market share from rivals.
■ Product differentiation is difficult to achieve; hence switching by consumers to competitors' products is a real threat.
■ There are high exit costs. When a business invests in non-transferable fixed assets, such as highly specialist capital equipment, it may be reluctant to leave a market. It may thus compete fiercely to maintain its market position. On the other hand, high exit costs may deter firms from entering a market in the first place and thus reduce the threat of competition.
■ There exists the possibility for merger and acquisition. This competition for corporate control may have considerable influence on the firm's strategy.

Porter's model is designed to identify and analyse the competitive factors influencing the firm. Often, however, success might be achievable not via competition but rather through cooperation and collaboration. For example, a business might set up close links with one of its major buyers; or businesses in an industry might collaborate over research and development, thereby saving on costs. As we saw in sections 5.3 and 5.4, firms have a considerable incentive to collude with their rivals so as to increase their combined profits and avoid damaging competition.

Ideally, in order to plan its strategy, a firm should be able to identify and quantify each of the five forces affecting it. In practice, however, firms often face considerable uncertainty about the market in which they operate. Just how will rivals, suppliers and buyers behave? How will consumer tastes change? What new firms and new products will enter the market?

The actions of complementors. Some economists add a sixth force – that of 'complementors' (a term coined by Andrew Grove of Intel). **Complementors** are firms producing complements. For example, Intel, with its Core 2, Centrino and Pentium processors is a complementor to both Microsoft, with its Windows, and various computer manufacturers, such as Dell and HP. Where firms are complementors, there is an incentive to form strategic alliances (see page 172) so as to benefit from cooperation and a reduction in uncertainty.

Porter himself added an alternative sixth force – that of government. Clearly there are many ways in which government policies impact on business and hence on the strategies that should be adopted. Throughout the recession of 2008/9 and with the 2010 election, this factor was a key influence on business strategy. We examine government policies at a micro level in Chapter 9. Chapter 11 looks at macroeconomic policies.

Pause for thought

1. Given that the stronger the competitive forces the lower the profit potential for firms, describe what five-force characteristics an attractive and unattractive industry might have.
2. Go through each of the five forces and identify to what extent they influence (a) costs and (b) demand elasticity.

Internal strategic analysis: analysing the value chain

It is not enough to analyse the competitive environment the business faces. If it is to develop an advantage over its rivals, a business needs to be organised effectively. Strategic analysis, therefore, also involves managers assessing the internal workings of the business, right from the purchase and delivery of inputs, to the production process, to delivering and marketing the product, to providing after-sales service.

Value-chain analysis, also developed by Michael Porter, is concerned with how each of these various operations adds value to the product and contributes to the competitive position of the business. Ultimately it is these value-creating activities that shape a firm's strategic capabilities. A firm's value chain can be split into two separate sets of activities: primary and support (see Figure 6.2).

Definitions

Complementors
Firms producing complementary goods (products that are used together).

Value chain
The stages or activities that help to create product value.

Figure 6.2	The value chain

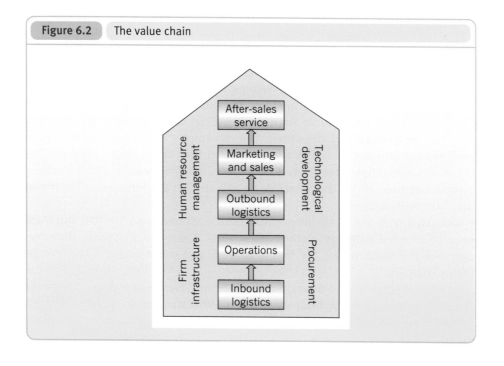

Primary activities

Primary activities cover those that involve the product's physical creation or delivery, its sale and distribution and its after-sales service. Such primary activities can be grouped into five categories:

- *Inbound logistics*. Here we are concerned with the handling of inputs, and the storage and distribution of such inputs throughout the business.
- *Operations*. These activities involve the conversion of inputs into the final product or service. Operations might include manufacturing, packaging and assembly.
- *Outbound logistics*. These are concerned with transferring the final product to the consumer. Such activities would include warehousing and transport.
- *Marketing and sales*. This section of the value chain is concerned with bringing the product to the consumer's attention and would involve product advertising and promotion.
- *Service*. This can include activities such as installation and repair, as well as customer requirements such as training.

A business might attempt to add value to its activities by improving its performance in one or more of the above categories. For example, it might attempt to lower production costs or be more efficient in outbound logistics.

Support activities

Such primary activities are underpinned by support activities. These are activities that do not add value directly to any particular stage within the value chain. They do, however, provide support to such a chain and ensure that its various stages are undertaken effectively. Support activities include:

- *Procurement*. This involves the acquisition of inputs by the firm.
- *Technological development*. This includes activities within the business that support new product and process developments, such as the use of research departments.
- *Human resource management*. Activities in this category include things such as recruitment, training and wage negotiation and determination.
- *Firm infrastructure*. This category includes activities such as financial planning and control systems, quality control and information management.

Pause for thought

Is it possible to add value to the firm by improving any or all of these support activities?

As well as creating value directly themselves, most firms buy in certain value-chain activities, such as employing another firm to do its advertising, or using an external delivery firm to distribute its products. The outsourcing of these activities might prove to be far more beneficial to a business than providing the activities itself. You can employ the best advertisers or the most reliable distributors. It may also be cheaper than doing things in-house. The companies you employ are likely to have economies of scale in their specialist activity (see pages 95–7) and therefore be able to offer the service at a lower cost than you could achieve.

Outsourcing, however, involves transactions costs (see pages 99–104) and these must be weighed against the other cost savings. Value-chain analysis, therefore, concerns any business that the firm deals with and hence a value chain can be highly complex.

With the background to strategic analysis defined, we can now shift our focus to consider strategic choice and implementation. What strategies are potentially open to businesses and how do they choose the right ones and set about implementing them?

Recap

1. Strategic management differs from operational management (the day-to-day running of the business) as it focuses on issues which affect the whole business, usually over the long term.

2. In conducting strategic analysis the business should assess its external and internal environment.

3. The Five Forces Model of the external environment identifies those factors that are most likely to influence the competition faced by a business. The five forces are: the bargaining power of suppliers, the bargaining power of buyers, the threat of potential new entrants, the threat of substitutes, and the extent of competitive rivalry.

4. To these five, some economists add a sixth – the actions of complementors. Porter added an alternative sixth factor – the government.

5. The internal environment can be assessed by value-chain analysis. The value chain can be split into primary and support activities. Primary activities are those that directly create value, such as operations, marketing and sales. Support activities are those that underpin value creation in other areas, such as procurement and human resource management.

STRATEGIC CHOICE   6.2

As with strategic analysis, strategic choices fall into two main categories. The first concerns choices to do with the external business environment, e.g. choices of how to compete and what markets to target. The second concerns choices about the internal organisation of the firm and how to use its resources.

Environment- or market-based strategic choices

As with many other areas in this field, our analysis of market-based choices starts with the observations of Michael Porter. As an extension of his Five Forces Model of competition, Porter argued that there are three fundamental (or 'generic') strategies that a business might adopt:

■ cost leadership – competing through lower costs;
■ differentiation – competing by producing a product different from rivals' products;
■ focus – producing a specialised product for a market niche.

In order to identify which of these was the most appropriate strategy, a business would need to establish two things: (a) the basis of its competitive advantage – whether it lies in lower costs or product differentiation; (b) the nature of the target market – is it broad or a distinct market niche?

Cost leadership

As the title implies, a business that is a low-cost leader is able to manufacture and deliver its product more cheaply than its rivals, thereby gaining competitive advantage. The strategic emphasis here is on driving out inefficiency at every stage of the value chain. 'No-frills' budget airlines, such as easyJet and Ryanair, are classic examples of companies that pursue a cost-leadership strategy.

A strategy based upon cost leadership may require a fundamentally different use of resources or organisational structure if the firm is to stay ahead of its rivals. Wal-Mart's hub and spoke distribution system would be an example in point. Here the company distributes its products to shops from regional depots in order to minimise transport costs.

BOX 6.1   BUSINESS STRATEGY THE SAMSUNG WAY

Staying ahead of the game

Samsung is a major South Korean conglomerate involved in a number of industries, including machinery and heavy engineering, chemicals, financial services and consumer electronics. It has over 164 000 employees globally and is a major international investor and exporter.

This box outlines some of the strategic initiatives that have been taken in recent times by one of its most successful divisions, Samsung Electronics, which is the world's largest producer of colour monitors, LCD TVs, public display monitors, memory chips, flash memory, LCD panels for desktop and laptop computers, CDMA mobile phones and blu-ray players.

Samsung's success over the past few years is quite an achievement, given the massive financial problems it faced following the Asian financial crisis in the late 1990s. Since that time it has managed not only to shake off its debts and post significant improvements in profits, but to reposition itself in the upmarket segment of the consumer electronics industry.

How has Samsung achieved this? What have been the keys to its success?

Strong leadership. This has come from Mr Yoon-Woo Lee, vice-chairman and CEO of Samsung Electronics. He, in turn, is supported by a determined management team. Together they have a clear vision of the future of the sector. They want Samsung to become the leading electronics company in the world, measured by the quantity and quality of the goods that it produces. By 2006, Samsung was already the third largest by sales, after Siemens and Hitachi and by 2008, it had overtaken Hitachi to be ranked as the second largest electronics and electrical equipment firm in the world by revenues.

Reorganisation. There has been a dramatic streamlining of the business and the decision-making structure following poor financial performance in the mid 1990s and an association with low-end brands in televisions and air-conditioning units. Aggressive measures were taken to improve the division's finances by cutting jobs, closing unprofitable factories, reducing inventory levels and selling corporate assets. The company was then 'de-layered', ensuring that managers had to go through fewer layers of bureaucracy, thereby speeding up the approval of new products, budgets and marketing plans.

New products. Samsung Electronics has been investing heavily in research and development (R&D) to increase its product portfolio and reduce the lead time from product conception to product launch. In light of this, the number of employees within R&D has increased substantially and it has engaged in a number of strategic alliances with major players such as Sony, IBM and Hewlett Packard to share R&D costs. It aimed to have 20 number one products in terms of world market share by 2010 (in March 2010 the company had 13 such products). This aggressive innovation strategy, coupled with low inventories and shortening product life cycles, allows Samsung to charge premium prices for state-of-the-art products.

This strategy is important in the rapidly changing world of consumer electronics, where a high-priced new product of today can become a low-priced mass-produced product of tomorrow. Large panel LCD TVs, flash memory chips and mobile phones are all examples. In fact, Samsung saw its profits fall in

---

In addition, firms that base their operations on low costs in order to achieve low prices (although that may not necessarily be the aim of low costs) are unlikely to have a high level of brand loyalty. In other words, if customer choice is going to be driven largely by price, demand is likely to be relatively price elastic. Other virtues of the product that might tie in buyers, such as quality or after-sales service, are largely absent from such firms' strategic goals.

Differentiation

A differentiation strategy aims to emphasise and promote the uniqueness of the firm's product; to make demand less elastic. Therefore, high rather than low prices are often attached to such products. Product characteristics such as quality, design and reliability are the basis of the firm's competitive advantage. Hence a strategy that adds to such differences and creates value for the customer needs to be identified.

Such a strategy might result in higher costs, especially in the short term, as the firm pursues constant product development through innovation, design and research. However, with the ability to charge premium prices, revenues may increase more than costs, i.e. the firm may achieve higher profits. Games console manufacturers, such as Sony with its PlayStation 3, Microsoft with its XBox 360 and Nintendo with

late 2006 and early 2007 as prices of all these three products dropped dramatically. Samsung is now aiming to achieve product growth through investment in mass storage devices, digital TVs and flash memory chips. It 2009, Samsung released the first full HD camcorder and the world's first infrared video phone.

Driving down costs. Samsung invests heavily in modern factories that can cope with large production runs and gain maximum economies of scale. To this end Samsung also supplies components to its competitors as well as making them for its own product range. For example it sells flash memory chips for Apple's iPod, Nokia phones and digital cameras. Further, production systems are flexible enough to allow customisation for individual buyers, ensuring that selling prices are above the industry average. Alongside longer production runs, Samsung is concerned with ensuring that production costs are minimised by making its own business units compete with external rivals. For example, Samsung buys half of its colour filters from Sumitomo Chemical Company of Japan and the other half is sourced from its own factories.

Developing its brand image. Even though it makes most of its profits on semiconductors, investment in less profitable consumer products with a clear brand identity helps to raise the profile of all its products. It spends a great deal on sports sponsorship. For example, it sponsors Chelsea football club, it has invested heavily in successive Olympic games and it sponsors a range of championships in golf, show jumping, running and Taekwondo. In 2009 Business

Week's Interbrand ranked Samsung Electronics 19th in the list of the top 100 global brands, a two place jump from the previous year.

Samsung's brand value was ranked the second highest among consumer electronics makers after Finland's Nokia, which ranked in the top 5 of global brands. Sony, its Japanese rival, was ranked 29th as its brand value tumbled 12 percent to US$11.9 billion.[1]

Lambro Skropidis, Head of Corporate Marketing, Samsung Australia is delighted with the success Samsung is seeing in both the local and international markets. 'We listen to consumers' feedback and work closely with our partners to instil the passion we have for innovation in everything we do. This latest accolade is testament to our hard work and understanding of our markets. We continue to put products and campaigns into place that further build a brand connection with our customers and I look forward to seeing the fruition of these relationships translated into further success next year!'[2]

1. *What dangers do you see with Samsung's recent business strategy?*
2. *What makes Samsung's policies that we have examined in this box 'strategic' as opposed to merely 'operational'?*

---

[1] www.telecomskorea.com/market-7665.html
[2] www.samsung.com/au/news/newsRead.do?news_seq=14796

Wii, are good examples. Even though they are in fierce competition with each other, each manufacturer focuses its strategy on trying to differentiate its product from the rivals'. This differentiation is in terms of features and performance, not price. Processor speed, online capabilities, player control, software support and product image are all characteristics used in the competitive battle.

Differentiation through product features, design and quality can be a costly and risky process, especially in the high-tech market, as technology changes so rapidly. However, the rewards are potentially large.

Focus strategy

Rather than considering a whole market as a potential for sales, a focus strategy involves identifying market niches and designing and promoting products for them. In doing so a business may be able to exploit some advantage over its rivals, whether in terms of costs, or product difference. An example is Häagen-Dazs ice cream (a division of General Mills). The mass low-cost ice cream market is served by other large multinational food manufacturers and processors (such as Unilever, with its Wall's brand), and by supermarkets' own brands, but the existence of niche high-quality ice cream markets offers opportunities for companies like Häagen-Dazs and Ben & Jerry's. By focusing on such consumers they are able to sell and market their product at premium prices.

Niche markets, however profitable, are by their nature small and as such limited in their growth potential. There is also the possibility that niches might shift over time or even disappear. This would require a business to be flexible in setting out its strategic position.

Internal resource-based strategic choices

Resource-based strategy focuses on exploiting a firm's internal organisation and production processes in order to develop its competitive advantage. It is important that the firm does certain things better or more cheaply than its rivals. What the firm will seek to exploit or to develop is one or more 'core competencies'.

Core competencies

> **Definition**
>
> **Core competencies**
> The key skills of a business that underpin its competitive advantage.

Core competencies are those skills, knowledge, technologies and product specifications that underpin the organisation's competitive advantage over its rivals. These competencies are likely to differ from one business to another, reflecting the uniqueness of each individual organisation, and ultimately determining its potential for success. The business should seek to exploit these competencies, whether in the design of the product or in its methods of production.

 KEY IDEA 21 **Core competencies.** The areas of specialised expertise within a business that underpin its competitive advantage over its rivals. These competencies could be in production technologies or organisation, in relationships with suppliers, in the nature and specifications of the product, or in the firm's ability to innovate and develop its products and brand image.

Thus Volvo has a core competence in building cars that are safe and reliable; Coca-Cola has a core competence in developing an image of a product; Tesco has a core competence in sourcing cheap but reliable supplies; Dell has a core competence in online selling of bespoke computers built to the consumer's specifications; Toys R Us, Mothercare and Saga have core competencies in selling a wide variety of products to a very specific group of customers and in developing that customer base; Intel has a core competence in technological research and development that can yield significant continuing advances in the speed and efficiency of memory chips and processor cores; Ikea has a core competence in sourcing low-cost furniture and accessories and selling them at a highly competitive price in low-cost suburban sites where a wide choice is on view and instantly available.

In many cases, however, firms do not have any competencies that give them a distinctive competitive advantage, even though they may still be profitable. In such instances, strategy often focuses either on *developing* such competencies or simply on more effectively using the resources the firm already has.

Can a core competence be sustained?

A core competence (or core resource), if carefully exploited, will give the firm a competitive advantage. If this advantage is to be sustained into the *long run*, however, the competence must satisfy the following four criteria. It must be:

■ *valuable*: a competence that helps the firm deal with threats or contributes to business opportunities;

- *rare*: a competence or resource that is not possessed by competitors;
- *costly to imitate*: a competence or resource that other firms find difficult to develop and copy;
- *non-substitutable*: a competence or resource for which there is no alternative.

Reactions of competitors

The success of a firm's strategic choices depends crucially on the reactions of rival firms. As we saw in the section on game theory (section 5.4), a firm has to be careful that strategic choices, such as developing new product lines or breaking into new markets, do not result in a 'war' with rivals that will end up with all 'players' worse off. The technology to produce a virtually everlasting light bulb has been available for many years, but it has not been in the interests of manufacturers to produce one, as it would force rivals to do the same with a resulting loss of future sales. To avoid this classic prisoners' dilemma (see page 136) there has been tacit collusion between manufacturers not to launch such a product.

Sometimes, it is worth firms taking the risk of stimulating retaliatory action from rivals. If it estimates that its market position or core competencies give it a competitive advantage, then it will take the risk of launching a new product, embarking on a marketing campaign, using a new technology or restructuring its organisation. If rivals do retaliate, its core competencies may enable it to do well in any competitive battle.

Definitions

Internal expansion
Where a business adds to its productive capacity by adding to existing or by building new plants.

External expansion
Where business growth is achieved by merging with or taking over businesses within a market or industry.

Recap

1. Strategic choice often involves a consideration of both external and internal factors.
2. External environment- or market-based strategies are of three types: cost leadership strategy, where competitiveness is achieved by lower costs; differentiation strategy, where the business promotes the uniqueness of its product; focus strategy, where competitiveness is achieved by identifying market niches and tailoring products for different groups of consumers.
3. Internal strategy normally involves identifying core competencies as the key to a business's competitive advantage. To give a business a sustained competitive advantage, core competencies must be valuable, rare, costly to imitate and non-substitutable.
4. When making strategic choices, firms should take into account the likely reactions of competitors.

GROWTH STRATEGY   6.3

Whether or not businesses wish to grow, many are forced to. The dynamic competitive process of the market drives producers to expand in order to remain in the marketplace. If a business fails to grow, this may benefit its more aggressive rivals. They may secure a greater share of the market, leaving the first firm with reduced profits. Thus business growth is often vital if a firm is to survive.

In this section we consider the various growth strategies open to firms and assess their respective advantages and disadvantages. Growth may be achieved by either **internal** or **external expansion**.

Merger

The outcome of a mutual agreement made by two firms to combine their business activities.

Takeover (or acquisition)

Where one business acquires another. A takeover may not necessarily involve mutual agreement between the two parties. In such cases, the takeover might be viewed as 'hostile'.

Strategic alliance

Where two or more firms work together, formally or informally, to achieve a mutually desirable goal.

Internal expansion. This is where a business looks to expand its productive capacity by adding to an existing plant or by building a new plant.

External expansion. This is where a business grows by engaging with another. It may do so in one of two ways:

■ The first is to join with another firm to form a single legal identity, through merger or takeover. A **merger** is a situation in which, as a result of mutual agreement, two firms decide to bring together their business operations as one firm. A merger is distinct from a takeover in so far as a **takeover** involves one firm bidding for another's shares – often against the will of the directors of the target firm. One firm thereby acquires another. For simplicity, we will use the term 'merger' to refer to *both* mergers ('mutual agreements') and takeovers ('acquisitions').

■ The second is to form a **strategic alliance** with one or more firms. This is where firms agree to work together but retain their separate identities.

Whether the business embarks upon internal or external expansion, a number of alternative growth paths are open to it. Figure 6.3 shows these various routes, which are considered in the following pages.

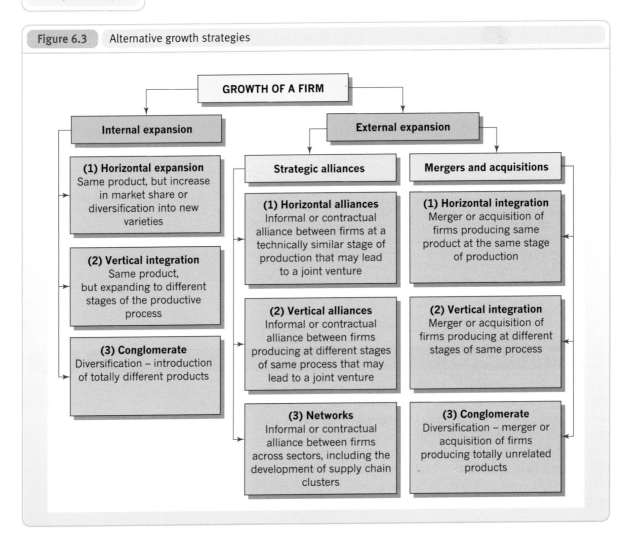

Figure 6.3   Alternative growth strategies

Growth by internal expansion

Financing internal growth

Internal growth requires an increase in sales, which in turn requires an increase in the firm's productive capacity. In order to increase its *sales*, the firm is likely to engage in extensive product promotion and to try to launch new products. In order to increase *productive capacity*, the firm will require new investment. Both product promotion and investment will require finance.

In the short run, the firm can finance growth by borrowing, by retaining profits or by a new issue of shares. What limits the amount of finance that a firm can acquire, and hence the rate at which it can grow?

If the firm *borrows* too much, the interest payments it incurs will make it difficult to maintain the level of dividends to shareholders. Similarly, if the firm *retains* too much *profit*, there will be less available to pay out in dividends. Also, if it attempts to raise capital by a *new issue of shares*, the distributed profits will have to be divided between a larger number of shares. Therefore, whichever way it finances investment, the more it invests, the more the dividends on shares in the short run will probably fall.

This could lead shareholders to sell their shares, unless they are confident that *long-run* profits and hence dividends will rise again, thus causing the share price to remain high in the long run. If shareholders do sell their shares, this will cause share prices to fall. If they fall too far, the firm runs the risk of being taken over and of certain managers losing their jobs. This **takeover constraint** therefore requires that the growth-maximising firm distribute sufficient profits to avoid being taken over. This is the idea of profit 'satisficing': making sufficient profits to keep shareholders happy.

Hence the rate of business growth is influenced by shareholder demands and expectations and by the fear of takeover.

In the long run, a rapidly growing firm may find its profits increasing, especially if it can achieve economies of scale and a bigger share of the market. These profits can then be used to finance further growth.

Clearly there is a crucial link between growth and profitability and it works in two ways. First, growth depends on profitability, as the more profitable the firm is, the more likely it is to be able to raise finance for investment. Second, as we have just seen, growth affects profitability. In the short run, growth may reduce profits, because of necessary expenditure on advertising and investment. However, in the long run growth may lead to expansion and hence can increase profits.

Forms of internal expansion

There are three main ways in which a business can grow through internal expansion (see Figure 6.3):

- It can expand or **differentiate its product** within existing markets, by, for example, updating or restyling its product, or improving its technical characteristics. We examined such strategies in Chapter 3.
- Alternatively, the business might seek to expand via **vertical integration**. This involves the firm expanding within the same product market, but at a different stage of production. For example, a car manufacturer might wish to produce its own components ('backward vertical integration') or distribute and sell its own car models ('forward vertical integration').
- As a third option, the business might seek to expand outside of its current product range, and move into new markets. This is known as a process of **diversification**.

Definitions

Takeover constraint
The effect that the fear of being taken over has on a firm's willingness to undertake projects that reduce distributed profits.

Product differentiation
In the context of growth strategies, this is where a business upgrades existing products or services so as to make them different from those of rival firms.

Vertical integration
A business growth strategy that involves expanding within an existing market, but at a different stage of production. Vertical integration can be 'forward', such as moving into distribution or retail, or 'backward', such as expanding into extracting raw materials or producing components.

Diversification
A business growth strategy in which a business expands into new markets outside of its current interests

Growth through vertical integration

If market conditions make growth through increased sales difficult, then a firm may choose to grow through vertical integration. This has a number of advantages:

Economies of scale. These can occur by the business performing *complementary* stages of production within a single business unit. The classic example of this is the steel manufacturer combining the furnacing and milling stages of production, saving the costs that would have been required to reheat the iron had such operations been undertaken by independent businesses. Clearly, for most firms, performing more than one stage on a single site is likely to reduce transport costs, as semi-finished products no longer have to be moved from one plant to another.

Other benefits to the vertically integrated firm may include more favourable borrowing rates from financial institutions, due to its size; the ability to negotiate better deals with suppliers and the need for less managerial supervision.

Reduced transactions costs. Vertical integration allows the firm to avoid the buying, selling and other costs associated with dealing with other firms, whether as suppliers or purchasers. We examined these costs on pages 99–104.

Consider two firms, one a motor vehicle manufacturer, the other a supplier of car exhausts. Both the car and the exhaust manufacturer will also be involved in frequent transactions between each other. The car manufacturer sells a lot of cars and so will need a lot of exhausts on a regular basis.

In addition, if the economic environment is uncertain and there is information asymmetry in the exchange, there is then the likelihood of a principal–agent problem, giving rise to a potential for moral hazard (see Boxes 3.1 and 3.2 on pages 66–8). One or both of the parties could exploit the situation to their own advantage because they have different sets of information about the markets in which they operate. The exhaust manufacturer could claim that rising steel prices forces it to put up prices. The car manufacturer could argue that poorer than expected sales forces it to reduce the price it can pay for the exhausts. Only if the contract between them is very tightly specified (is 'complete') can situations such as this be avoided.

If there is a binding contract, then this will prevent the car manufacturer from seeking alternative suppliers that could offer the exhausts more cheaply. Renegotiating the contract may be possible, but this too will incur costs. If a firm *is* free to seek alternative suppliers, then this may be risky (see below).

To avoid these transactions costs, then, firms may prefer to integrate vertically through internal expansion or merger.

Reduced uncertainty. A business that is not vertically integrated may find itself subject to various uncertainties in the marketplace. Examples include uncertainty over future price movements, supply reliability or access to markets.

Backward vertical integration will enable the business to control its supply chain. Without such integration the firm may feel very vulnerable, especially if there are only a few suppliers within the market. In such cases the suppliers would be able to exert considerable control over price. Alternatively, suppliers may be unreliable.

Forward vertical integration creates greater certainty in so far as it gives the business guaranteed access to distribution and retailing on its own terms. As with supply, forward markets might be dominated by large buyers, which are able not only to dictate price, but also to threaten market foreclosure (being shut out from a market). Forward vertical integration can remove the possibility of such events occurring.

Barriers to entry. Vertical integration may give the firm greater power in the market by enabling it to erect entry barriers to potential competitors. For example, a firm that undertakes backward vertical integration and acquires a key input resource can effectively close the market to potential new entrants, either by simply refusing to supply a competitor, or by charging a very high price for the input such that new firms face an absolute cost disadvantage.

Pause for thought

See if you can identify two companies that are vertically integrated and what advantages they have from such integration.

The major problem with vertical integration is that it may reduce the firm's ability to respond to changing market demands. A business that integrates, either backward or forward, ties itself to particular supply sources or particular retail outlets. If, by contrast, it were free to choose between suppliers, inputs might be obtained at a lower price than the firm could achieve by supplying itself. In other words, outsourcing, rather than in-house production, while less secure, can *save* costs by allowing the firm to buy from the cheapest and/or best suppliers. Such suppliers are likely to be in competition with each other and this helps to keep their prices down and quality up. Equally, the ability to shift between retail outlets would allow the firm's products to be sold in the best locations. This may not be possible if it is tied to its own retail network.

Many firms are finding that it is better *not* to be vertically integrated but to focus on their core competencies and to outsource their supplies, their marketing and many other functions. That way they put alternative suppliers and distributors in competition with each other.

An alternative is to be *partially* vertically integrated, through a process known as **tapered vertical integration**. To some extent, this enables the firm to receive the benefits of vertical integration without incurring the costs.

Definition

Tapered vertical integration
Where a firm is partially integrated with an earlier stage of production; where it produces some of an input itself and buys some from another firm.

Tapered vertical integration. This involves firms making part of a given input themselves and subcontracting the production of the remainder to one or more other firms. For example, Coca-Cola and Pepsi are large vertically integrated enterprises. They have, as part of their operations, wholly-owned bottling subsidiaries. However, in certain markets they subcontract to independent bottlers both to produce and to market their product.

By making a certain amount of an input itself, the firm is less reliant on suppliers and saves on transactions costs, but does not require as much capital equipment as if it produced all the input itself. A policy of tapered vertical integration suits many multinational companies. In certain countries, they produce the inputs themselves; in others, they rely on local suppliers, drawing on the supplier's competitive advantage in that local market.

Of course, tapered vertical integration may not allow the firm to gain such substantial economies of scale and production may thus be less efficient than under vertical integration. It is, therefore, important to realise that for much of the time firms will face a trade-off.

Growth through diversification

An alternative internal growth strategy to vertical integration is that of diversification. A good example of a highly diversified company is Virgin. As we saw in Box 3.4 (page 78), Virgin's interests include planes, trains, cars, finance, music, mobile phones, holidays, wine, cinemas, radio, cosmetics, publishing, stem cells and even space travel.

If the current market is saturated, stagnant or in decline, diversification might be the only avenue open to the business if it wishes to maintain a high growth performance. In other words, it is not only the level of profits that may be limited in the current market, but also the growth of sales.

Diversification also has the advantage of spreading risks. So long as a business produces a single product in a single market, it is vulnerable to changes in that market's conditions. If a farmer produces nothing but potatoes, and the potato harvest fails, the farmer is ruined. If, however, the farmer produces a whole range of vegetable products, or even diversifies into livestock, then he or she is less subject to the forces of nature and the unpredictability of the market.

In some cases, however, diversification may actually be a risky strategy, as a firm might be developing both a new product and entering a new market. But in most cases, diversification should allow the business to use and adapt existing technology and knowledge to its advantage. The experience, skills and market knowledge of the managers of the business will be crucial to ensure that such a strategy is successful.

Growth through merger

Similar growth paths can be pursued via external expansion. However, in this case the business does not create the productive facilities itself, but purchases existing production. As Figure 6.3 identified, we can distinguish three types of merger: horizontal, vertical and conglomerate.

> **Definitions**
>
> **Horizontal merger**
> Where two firms in the same industry at the same stage of the production process merge.
>
> **Vertical merger**
> Where two firms in the same industry at different stages in the production process merge.
>
> **Conglomerate merger**
> Where two firms in different industries merge.

- A **horizontal merger** is where two firms at the same stage of production within an industry merge. An example of this is the merger in 2008 of Lloyds-TSB and HBOS, two major British banks.
- A **vertical merger** is where businesses at different stages of production within the same industry merge. As such we might identify backward and forward vertical mergers for any given firm involved in the merger. One example of this is where TomTom, the Dutch producer of portable navigation devices (e.g. satnavs in cars), bought TeleAtlas, the Dutch provider of navigable maps in 2008. In Europe there have been several vertical mergers in the electricity industry between generators and distributors, creating vertically integrated companies such as Electricité de France (EDF), and E.ON of Germany.
- A **conglomerate merger** is where firms in totally unrelated industries merge. Many of the big multinational corporations operate in a number of sectors and regularly buy other firms. The purchase of Vivendi by General Electric in 2004 is an example of such a merger.

A further dimension of business growth that we should note at this point is that all of the above-mentioned growth paths can be achieved by the business looking beyond its national markets. In other words, the business might decide to become multinational and invest in expansion overseas. This raises a further set of issues, problems and advantages that a business might face. These will be discussed in Chapter 7 when we consider multinational business.

Why merge?

Why do firms want to merge with or take over others? Is it purely that they want to grow; are mergers simply evidence of the hypothesis that firms are growth maximisers? Or are there other motives that influence the predatory drive?

Merger for growth. Mergers provide a much quicker means to growth than internal expansion. Not only does the firm acquire new capacity, experience and skills, but also it acquires additional consumer demand. Building up this level of consumer demand by internal expansion might have taken a considerable length of time.

Merger for economies of scale. Once the merger has taken place, the constituent parts can be reorganised through a process of 'rationalisation'. The result can be a reduction in costs. For example, only one head office will now be needed. On the marketing side, the two parts of the newly merged company may now share distribution and retail channels, benefiting from each other's knowledge and operation in distinct market segments or geographical locations.

In fact, the evidence on costs suggests that most mergers result in few if any cost savings: either potential economies of scale are not exploited due to a lack of rationalisation, or diseconomies result from the disruptions of reorganisation. New managers installed by the parent company are often seen as unsympathetic, and morale may go down.

Merger for monopoly power. Here the motive is to reduce competition and thereby gain greater market power and larger profits. This applies mainly to horizontal mergers. With less competition, the firm will face a less elastic demand and be able to charge a higher percentage above marginal cost. What is more, the new more powerful company will be in a stronger position to regulate entry into the market by erecting effective entry barriers, thereby enhancing its monopoly position yet further.

Pause for thought

Which of the three types of merger (horizontal, vertical and conglomerate) are most likely to lead to (a) reductions in average costs; (b) increased market power?

Merger for increased market valuation. A merger can benefit shareholders of *both* firms if it leads to an increase in the stock market valuation of the merged firm. If both sets of shareholders believe that they will make a capital gain on their shares then they are more likely to give the go-ahead for the merger.

What is the evidence? In the early stages of a merger boom, such as 2004/5 (see figure in Box 7.2 on page 196), when some good deals may be had, the share price of acquiring firms may rise. However, as the merger boom develops, more marginal firms are acquired. Take the merger boom of the late 1990s. In some 80 per cent of cases there was a significant *fall* in the share value of the acquiring firm.

Merger to reduce uncertainty. Firms face uncertainty at two levels. The first is in their own markets. The behaviour of rivals may be highly unpredictable. Mergers, by reducing the number of rivals, can correspondingly reduce uncertainty. At the same time, they can reduce the *costs* of competition (e.g. reducing the need to advertise).

The second source of uncertainty is the economic environment. In a period of rapid change, such as often accompanies a boom, firms may seek to protect themselves by merging with others.

Other motives. Other motives for mergers include:

■ Getting bigger so as to become less likely to be taken over oneself.
■ Opportunistic. Firms are presented with an unforeseen opportunity. As you can imagine, mergers based on such a motive are virtually impossible to predict.
■ Merging with another firm so as to defend it from an unwanted predator (the 'White Knight' strategy).
■ Asset stripping. This is where a firm takes over another and then breaks it up, selling off the profitable bits and probably closing down the remainder.

BOX 6.2   RECESSIONARY STRATEGIES

A testing time for any business is when demand for its products begins to fall and then remains low. This is what happened to many businesses during the 2008/9 recession, especially as it was not just the UK that was affected, but the global economy. What then is the best strategy for a business to pursue when faced with this situation?

When market demand, and hence revenue, falls, there will be a big effect on profitability and cash flow, especially for a business operating with low profit margins. The natural response is to cut costs, and according to the UK's CEO Survey,[1] 96 per cent of chief executive officers did make cost reductions. These were in areas such as staff, advertising and marketing, service and training.

Staff. The labour force is a key component of any firm, but at the same time, it represents a significant cost. With falling demand, firms had surplus staff, and this led to massive job losses across the UK. Unemployment rose from 5.2 per cent (1.6m) in mid 2008 to 8 per cent (2.5m) by early 2010, and, with large cuts in public expenditure expected, the rate could peak at around 3 million in 2011. In addition, many firms managed to reach agreement with employees for a temporary reduction in hours in an attempt to avoid redundancies.

Whilst cutting back on unneeded staff is a rational and even efficient response for a business, it could mean even lower demand, as a greater percentage of the population see their incomes fall. Such cutbacks, however, may provide a firm with the opportunity to reorganise its business, perhaps through a process of de-layering, to improve the speed and effectiveness of decisions and making a more efficient use of its human resources. Of the 96 per cent of UK firms that reduced costs, some two-thirds of these involved cutting back on staff and aiming to improve efficiency.

Training. Whilst a necessity for all firms, training is costly, and hence during a recession this is another budget that is often cut. However, training is used to increase productivity, so any cuts in this area could actually reduce the efficiency of staff, and so it may cost a firm more than it saves, especially in the long run. There may also be repercussions in terms of product quality or customer service, which should be two key components to a business's strategy during a recession. Crucial to success, therefore, could be to invest in training in any revenue-generating activities.

Training is time-consuming and the opportunity cost of it is lost output in the short run. However, in a recession, demand falls, and so rather than laying off workers, it might be a prime opportunity to invest in training staff to increase their productivity, in preparation for the recovery. In November 2008, the Institute of Directors surveyed its members, and it revealed a strong reluctance to cut training, despite the harsh economic climate.

The campaign (IoD) encourages employers to maintain investment in training during the recession, both in recognition of the fact that skills have never been more important to the UK's competitiveness in general and also that investing in skills in the downturn can help to put individual businesses in a better position to gain competitive advantage in recovery.[2]

One way in which businesses have maintained their investment in training, while containing costs, is to adapt their methods. This includes in-house training, using more experienced staff to train others and sharing training with other companies. This strategy, while viable in a larger company, may not be a suitable strategy for SMEs.

Advertising. As with training, marketing and advertising are extremely costly, hence cutting this budget can be crucial to reducing costs. The Advertising Association confirmed this when it reported that total advertising expenditure in 2009 fell by some 12 per cent and was only just beginning to recover in the first two quarters of 2010.

In 2009, the World Advertising Research Centre recorded six consecutive quarters of falling advertising spending. Newspapers were down by 27.6 per cent, magazines by 33.3 per cent, outdoor advertising fell by 26.1 per cent and cinema and radio were down by 14.7 and 14.4 per cent respectively. The Internet has been claiming a growing share of advertising expenditure for a number of years, and this form of advertising has been more resilient: it was stable in the three months to June 2009.

However, is cutting spending on advertising and marketing the right thing to do? Domino's UK, for example, saw the recession and the subsequent cuts in advertising across other firms as a prime opportunity to increase its share of the pizza market. With lower demand for advertising agencies, the company took advantage of these favourable conditions in the advertising industry. It was able to gain market share from other pizza companies, which had cut back on advertising expenditure and also attracted other customers, who began to order cheaper take-outs rather than pay for expensive meals out. Chief Executive Officer Chris Moore said:

We continue to succeed, even in the current harsh economic conditions, because of our unrelenting focus on the quality of our pizzas, intense devotion to service and by marketing to our customers when and where they want to order.[3]

---

[1] 13th Annual Global CEO Survey, PWC, January 2010

[2] Training in the recession: Winner or loser? Institute of Directors Survey Report, November 2008
[3] Domino's Pizza UK & IRL plc News; 16 February 2010

Thanks to advertising and discounts, the company saw overall sales jump 15.4 per cent to £196.4m in the six months to 28 June.[4]

Surviving a recession might depend on aggressive and comprehensive advertising. This may involve developing a 'unique selling point' (USP) to help a business to stand out from its rivals or even changing marketing tactics.

> The company . . . has taken full advantage of the drop in advertising rates to continue to promote its discounts and deals to a cash-strapped public . . . Our tactical marketing campaigns have played a major role in our success during the period, supported by the firepower of the national advertising fund and the deflationary media market.[5]

Hold on to your customers. Sales may decrease during a recession, but the key thing for a business is to maintain market share, by keeping existing customers. Central to this strategy is maintaining excellent customer service and delivering what the customer wants. Many businesses have focused on this strategy, by adapting products, menus and service to satisfy consumer demands. It may require market research and extra training, both of which are costly, but if it means creating customer loyalty, it is a worthwhile expenditure. This is especially true in the long term, as once the economic recovery starts, a loyal customer base will help a firm grow.

Diversify your product and customer base. In section 3.4, we considered the Growth Vector Matrix, which looks at both of these strategies. If demand in an existing market is stagnant or falling, looking elsewhere for sales may be a crucial strategy for surviving a recession. This could be either through product differentiation, such as a new design/model, or through diversifying the market in which the product is sold. This could involve new geographical locations or simply new market segments. Returning to Domino's, it took the opportunity to differentiate its product in response to the changing climate. As more people began to eat in, and aimed for cheaper lunch options, Domino's (and the coffee industry, as discussed below) tapped further into these markets.

> Over the course of 2009, Domino's introduced some lighter menu options such as pasta, sandwiches and desserts in a bid to gain a greater share of the casual lunch market.[6]

With global trading an increasingly easy option nowadays, one business response to the recession is to expand overseas. This is a risky strategy (as discussed in section 7.3), especially when the recession has hit countries across the world. However, stagnant conditions may provide opportunities for firms, such as employing highly skilled staff at lower wages, as the pool of unemployed workers grows.

The coffee industry is one that has not been significantly affected by the recession. In 2008, research showed that the six main chains actually increased the number of outlets by 47 per cent during the 2007/8 period. Likewise, the number of independent coffee shops increased by 8.5 per cent in major town centres. One explanation for this trend is that coffee shops increasingly have everything that businesspeople need, whether it's comfy seats or access to Wifi. As companies were forced to cut costs, hiring out meeting or conference rooms became an unaffordable luxury, and so coffee shops became a substitute meeting place. Furthermore, coffee shops began to sell cheaper lunch options, as eating out also became an expensive luxury.

It is examples like this which demonstrate the importance of responding to customer needs in order to maintain a successful business.

Careful cash flow management. Putting a business plan in place will go some way to helping a firm manage its organisation in an efficient and successful way. Whatever the state of the global economy, having sufficient working capital is vital. However, in a recession, it becomes even more important to manage cash flow. This could involve more accurate financial reporting, a stricter process of credit checking customers and ensuring that products are paid for on time. The 'DNA of an entrepreneur' study reported that a third of SME bosses cut their own salaries in a bid to cut operating costs and improve cash flow.

Pricing and promotions. As we saw in Chapter 2, prices are central to a consumer's buying decision. Consumers become more price sensitive during recessions and are after value for money. All of the main supermarkets advertise on TV, but from the onset of recession in 2008 these adverts increasingly focused on prices. Discount stores, such as Aldi and Lidl experienced rising demand for their cheap products, and so the supermarket giants responded by cutting prices and increasing promotions. An Asda spokesperson said, 'Times are getting tough and people are feeling the pinch, so we have reduced the price of these 10 staple items over the weekend.'[7] Tesco responded by cutting prices by 50 per cent on thousands of items and Sainsbury's reduced prices on items, such as summer groceries.

Cutting prices and, crucially, offering promotions were strategies that many businesses adopted during the recession in a bid to retain existing customers and increase sales. The effectiveness of such policies, however, depends on the price elasticity of demand for

---

[4] 'Domino's Pizza sees sales surge and expects swine flu fillip', *Guardian*, 20 July 2009

[5] 'Domino's Pizza sees customers rise as recession keeps people at home', *Guardian*, 1 October 2009

[6] 'Domino's Pizza: evolution of business leads to income rise', *Trading Markets*, 2 March 2010

[7] 'Supermarkets battle on prices', BBC News, 27 June 2008

►

the products, and on the prices and promotions being offered by competitors. A restaurant manager said:

> They [consumers] still want to go out. But you have to make it affordable for them. You can price yourself out of the market, and then you're in trouble. So keep your prices reasonable, make a little less profit, but make sure you get people through the door.[8]

An optimal solution?

In a recession, there is no one-size-fits-all solution. The strategy that works for one firm will not necessarily be right for another. Unfortunately, there is no optimal solution. How a business reacts to a recession, with both low and falling demand, will depend on its product, the size of the firm, the actions of competitors, its organisational structure and, to a large extent, on the

culture within the firm. Some businesses will go under, but it is the ones that change their strategy to make it work that will come out of the other side stronger.

> For many organisations the downturn should be looked at as an opportunity – those firms that are able to invest now will grow quicker when the market picks up.[9]

1. Are there any other things a business should focus on to help it get through a recession? What are they and why are they important?
2. Select a business. How has it managed to survive the recession? (Hint: use the Internet to help you research its strategy.)
3. Of the strategies considered in this box, which do you think is the most important?

_____
[8] *Ibid.*

_____
[9] *Ibid.*

■ Empire building. This is where owners or managers favour takeovers because of the power or prestige of owning or controlling several (preferably well-known) companies.

■ Geographical expansion. The motive here is to broaden the geographical base of the company by merging with a firm in a different part of the country or the world.

Mergers, especially horizontal ones, will generally have the effect of increasing the market power of those firms involved. This could lead to less choice and higher prices for the consumer. For this reason, mergers have become the target for government competition policy. Such policy is the subject of section 9.5.

Growth through strategic alliances

One means of achieving growth is through the formation of strategic alliances with other firms: either horizontally or vertically within an industry or as a network of firms across different industries. They are a means of expanding business operations relatively quickly and at relatively low cost, and are a common way in which firms can deepen their involvement in global markets.

A well-known example of strategic alliances is in the airline industry (see Figure 6.4 opposite). Members cooperate over frequent flyer programmes, share business-class airport lounges and code share on various flights.

What forms can strategic alliances take?

Definition
Joint venture Where two or more firms set up and jointly own a new independent firm.

Joint ventures. A **joint venture** is where two or more firms decide to create, and jointly own, a new independent organisation. Joint ventures can be either horizontal or vertical. An example of a horizontal alliance is the decision by Samsung and Sony to cooperate and build LCD screens in Korea; another is the Sony–NEC joint venture to produce hard disk drives. FilmFlex is an example of a vertical strategic alliance, which brings film and TV makers into the retail sector. The service is provided jointly by Walt Disney Television International, Sony Picture television and the pay-TV group, ON Demand.

| Figure 6.4 | Airline strategic alliances, 2009 |

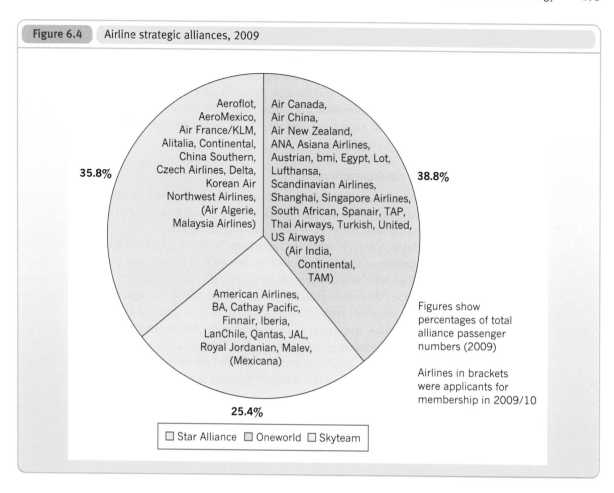

Aeroflot, AeroMexico, Air France/KLM, Alitalia, Continental, China Southern, Czech Airlines, Delta, Korean Air Northwest Airlines, (Air Algerie, Malaysia Airlines)   **35.8%**

Air Canada, Air China, Air New Zealand, ANA, Asiana Airlines, Austrian, bmi, Egypt, Lot, Lufthansa, Scandinavian Airlines, Shanghai, Singapore Airlines, South African, Spanair, TAP, Thai Airways, Turkish, United, US Airways (Air India, Continental, TAM)   **38.8%**

American Airlines, BA, Cathay Pacific, Finnair, Iberia, LanChile, Qantas, JAL, Royal Jordanian, Malev, (Mexicana)   **25.4%**

Figures show percentages of total alliance passenger numbers (2009)

Airlines in brackets were applicants for membership in 2009/10

☐ Star Alliance   ☐ Oneworld   ☐ Skyteam

Consortia. A **consortium** is usually created for very specific projects, such as a large civil engineering work. As such, it has a very focused objective and once the project is completed the consortium is sometimes dissolved. TransManche Link, the Anglo-French company that built the Channel Tunnel, is an example of a defunct consortium. Camelot, by contrast, the company that runs the UK National Lottery, is still on-going. It is owned in equal shares by Cadbury Schweppes (taken over by Kraft in 2010), De La Rue, Fujitsu Services, Royal Mail Enterprises and Thales Electronics, each of which had particular expertise to bring to the consortium.

Franchising and licensing. A less formal strategic alliance is where a business agrees to **franchise** its operations to third parties. McDonald's and Coca-Cola are good examples of businesses that use a franchise network. In such a relationship the franchisee is responsible for manufacturing and/or selling, and the franchiser retains responsibility for branding and marketing. A similar type of arrangement is that of **licensing**. Some lagers and beers sold in the UK, for example, are brewed under licence.

Subcontracting. Like franchising, **subcontracting** is a less formal source of strategic alliance, where companies maintain their independence. When a business subcontracts, it employs an independent business to manufacture or supply some service rather than conduct the activity itself. Car manufacturers are major subcontractors. Given the multitude and complexity of components that are required to manufacture a car, the use of subcontractors to supply specialist items, such as brakes and lights, seems a logical way to organise the business.

Definitions

Consortium
Where two or more firms work together on a specific project and create a separate company to run the project.

Franchise
A formal agreement whereby a company uses another company to produce or sell some or all of its product.

Licensing
Where the owner of a patented product allows another firm to produce it for a fee.

Subcontracting
Where a firm employs another firm to produce part of its output or some of its input(s).

Networks. **Networks** are less formal than any of the above alliances. A network is where two or more businesses work collaboratively but without any formal relationship binding one to the other. Rather than a formal contract regulating the behaviour of the partners to the agreement, their relationship is based upon an understanding of trust and loyalty. Networks are common in the motor vehicle, electronics, pharmaceutical and other high-tech sectors. Networks can be at both the national and local level and give firms access to technology and resources at lower costs.

Why form strategic alliances?

As a business expands, possibly internationally, it may well be advantageous to join with an existing player in the market. Such a business would have local knowledge and an established network of suppliers and distributors.

In addition, strategic alliances allow firms to share risk. The Channel Tunnel and the consortium of firms that built it is one such example. The construction of the Channel Tunnel was a massive undertaking and far too risky for any single firm to embark upon. With the creation of a consortium, risk was spread, and the various consortium members were able to specialise in their areas of expertise.

They also allow firms to pool capital. Projects that might have prohibitively high start-up costs, or running costs, may become feasible if firms cooperate and pool their capital. In addition, an alliance of firms, with their combined assets and credibility, may find it easier to generate finance, whether from investors in the stock market or from the banking sector.

The past 20 years have seen a flourishing of strategic alliances. They have become a key growth strategy for business both domestically and internationally. They are seen as a way of expanding business operations quickly without the difficulties associated with the more aggressive approach of acquisition or the more lengthy process of merger.

Pause for thought

Give two reasons why a firm may prefer to form a strategic alliance with another firm rather than merging with it or taking it over.

Recap

1. A business can expand either internally or externally by merging with other firms or by forming strategic alliances. In each case, there are three potential growth strategies open to business: product differentiation, vertical integration and diversification.

2. Growth by internal expansion may be financed by ploughing back profits, by share issue or by borrowing. Whichever method a firm uses, it will require sufficient profits if it is to avoid becoming vulnerable to a takeover.

3. Vertical integration involves remaining in the same market, but expanding into a different stage of production. Vertical integration can reduce a firm's costs through various economies of scale. It can eliminate the various transactions costs associated with dealing with other firms. It can also help to reduce uncertainty, as the vertically

integrated business can hopefully secure supply routes and/or retail outlets. This strategy can also enhance the business's market power by enabling it to erect various barriers to entry.

4. Diversification offers the business a growth strategy that not only frees it from the limitations of a particular market, but also enables it to spread its risks and seek profit in potentially fast-growing markets.

5. There are three types of merger: horizontal, vertical and conglomerate. There are various possible advantages of mergers, including growth, economies of scale, market power, increased share values or reduction in uncertainty.

6. One means of achieving growth is through the formation of strategic alliances with other firms. They have the advantage of allowing easier access to new markets, risk sharing and capital pooling.

FINANCING GROWTH AND INVESTMENT   6.4

If businesses are to grow, they will need to invest. In this section we consider the sources of finance for investment, and the roles played by various financial institutions.

Sources of business finance

As mentioned in section 6.3 above, the firm can finance growth by borrowing, by retaining profits or by a new issue of shares.

Many companies rely on their own resources to finance investment and growth. Indeed, the largest source of finance for investment in the UK is firms' own internal funds (i.e. ploughed-back profit). In a 2006 survey,[2] 79 per cent of Chief Executive Officers stated that they planned to fund future activities in this way.

Given, however, that business profitability depends in large part on the general state of the economy, internal funds as a source of business finance are likely to show considerable cyclical variation. When profits are squeezed in a recession, as was the case in 2008/9, this source of investment will decline (but so also will the *demand* for investment; after all, what is the point in investing if your market is declining?).

Other sources of finance, which include borrowing and the issue of shares and debentures, are known as 'external funds'. These are then categorised as short-term, medium-term or long-term sources of finance.

- Short-term finance is usually in the form of a short-term bank loan or overdraft facility, and is used by firms as a form of working capital to aid them in their day-to-day business operations.
- Medium-term finance, again provided largely by banks, is usually in the form of a loan with set repayment targets. It is common for such loans to be made at a fixed rate of interest, with repayments being designed to fit in with the business's expected cash flow. Bank lending tends to be the most volatile source of business finance, and has been particularly sensitive to the state of the economy, as we have seen during the credit crunch. While part of the reason is the lower demand for loans during a recession, part of the reason is the caution of banks in granting loans if prospects for the economy are poor.
- Long-term finance, especially in the UK, tends to be acquired through the stock and bond markets. The proportion of business financing from this source clearly depends on the state of the stock market. In the late 1990s, with a buoyant stock market, the proportion of funds obtained through share issue increased. Then with a decline in stock market prices from 2000 to early 2003, this proportion fell, only to rise again as the stock market surged ahead after 2004. However, with fears of a global recession, the stock market began to decline in late 2007. As the global economy sunk into recession and bank lending practically ceased, the stock market plummeted and only really began to recover in 2009.

Despite the traditional reliance on the stock market for long-term sources of finance, there has been a growing involvement of banks in recent years. Banks have become more willing to provide finance for business start-ups and for diversification.

---

[2] *Global CEO Survey 2006*, PricewaterhouseCoopers

Nevertheless, there is a concern that banks are still relatively cautious. This results in a problem of **short-termism**, with bankers often demanding a quick return on their money or charging high interest rates, and being less concerned to finance long-term investment.

Another source of finance is that from outside the country. Part of this is direct investment by externally based companies in the domestic economy. Part is finance from foreign financial institutions. In either case, a major determinant of the amount of finance from this source is the current state of the economy and predictions of its future state. One of the major considerations here is anticipated changes in the exchange rate (see Chapter 13). If the exchange rate is expected to rise, this will increase the value of any given profit in terms of foreign currency. As would be expected, this source of finance is particularly volatile.

The stock market

In this section, we will look at the role of the stock market and consider the advantages and limitations of raising capital through it. We will also consider whether the stock market is efficient.

The role of the Stock Exchange

The London Stock Exchange operates as both a primary and secondary market in capital.

As a **primary market** it is where public limited companies (see page 7) can raise finance by issuing new shares, whether to new shareholders or to existing ones. To raise finance on the Stock Exchange a business must be 'listed'. The Listing Agreement involves directors agreeing to abide by a strict set of rules governing behaviour and levels of reporting to shareholders. A company must have at least three years' trading experience and make at least 25 per cent of its shares available to the public. In March 2010, there were over 1120 UK and 323 international companies on the Official List. During 2009, companies on this list raised £77.4 billion's worth of new capital by selling equity (ordinary shares) and fixed-interest securities on the London Stock Exchange. This is much higher than the figure for 2007, when, with the onset of the credit crunch and the prospects of a consequent recession, only £28.6 billion was raised.

As well as those on the Official List, there are some 1258 companies on what is known as the Alternative Investment Market (AIM). Companies listed here tend to be young but with growth potential, and do not have to meet the strict criteria or pay such high costs as companies on the Official List.

As a **secondary market**, the Stock Exchange operates as a market where investors can sell existing shares to one another. In 2009, on an average day's trading, £44.2 billion of trading in UK equities and debt securities took place.

The advantages and disadvantages of using the stock market to raise capital

As a market for raising capital the stock market has a number of advantages:

■ It brings together those that wish to invest and those that seek investment. It thus represents a way that savings can be mobilised to create output, and does so in a relatively low-cost way.

- Firms that are listed on the Stock Exchange are subject to strict regulations. This is likely to stimulate investor confidence, making it easier for businesses to raise finance.
- The process of merger and acquisition is facilitated by having a share system. It enables a business more effectively to pursue this as a growth strategy.

The main weaknesses of the stock market for raising capital are:

- The cost to a business of getting listed can be immense, not only in a financial sense, but also in being open to public scrutiny. Directors' and senior managers' decisions will often be driven by how the market is likely to react, rather by what they perceive to be in the business's best interests. They always have to think about the reactions of those large shareholders in the City that control a large proportion of their shares.
- It is often claimed that the stock market suffers from *short-termism*. Investors on the Stock Exchange are more concerned with a company's short-term perform-ance and its share value. In responding to this, the business might neglect its long-term performance and potential.

Is the stock market efficient?

One of the arguments made in favour of the stock market is that it acts as an arena within which share values can be accurately or efficiently priced. If new informa-tion comes on to the market concerning a business and its performance, this will be quickly and rationally transferred into the business's share value. This is known as the **efficient market hypothesis**. So for example, if an investment analyst found that, in terms of its actual and expected dividends, a particular share was under-priced and thus represented a 'bargain', the analyst would advise investors to buy. As people then bought the shares, their price would rise, pushing their value up to their full worth. So by attempting to gain from inefficiently priced securities, investors will encourage the market to become more efficient.

 KEY IDEA 22 **Efficient capital markets.** Capital markets are efficient when the prices of shares accurately reflect information about companies' current and expected future performance.

If the market were perfectly efficient in this sense, then no gain could be made from studying a company's performance and prospects, as any such information would *already* be included in the current share price. In selecting shares, you would do just as well by pinning the financial pages of a newspaper on the wall, throwing darts at them, and buying the shares the darts hit!

If the stock market were perfectly efficient, it would only be unanticipated information that would cause share prices to deviate from that which reflected expected average yields. Such information must, by its nature, be random, and as such would cause share prices to deviate randomly from their expected price, or follow what we call a **random walk**. Evidence suggests that share prices do tend to follow random patterns.

Pause for thought

1. *For what reasons is the stock market not perfectly efficient?*
2. *How might some people gain from the lack of efficiency?*

Recap

1. Business finance can come from internal and external sources. Sources external to the firm include borrowing and the issue of shares.

2. The stock market operates as both a primary and secondary market in capital. As a primary market it channels finance to companies as people purchase new shares. It is also a market for existing shares.

3. It helps to stimulate growth and investment by bringing together companies and people who

want to invest in them. By regulating firms and by keeping transaction costs of investment low, it helps to ensure that investment is efficient.

4. It does impose costs on firms, however. It is expensive for firms to be listed and the public exposure may make them too keen to 'please' the market. It can also foster short-termism.

5. The stock market is relatively efficient. It achieves efficiency by allowing share prices to respond quickly and fully to publicly available information.

6.5 STARTING SMALL

How often do you hear of small business making it big? Not very often, and yet many of the world's major corporations began life as small businesses. From acorns have grown oak trees! But small and large businesses are usually organised and run quite differently and face very different problems.

Unfortunately, there is no single agreed definition of a 'small' firm. In fact, a firm considered to be small in one sector of business, such as manufacturing, may be considerably different in size from one in, say, the road haulage business. Nevertheless, the most widely used definition is that adopted by the EU for its statistical data. Three categories of small and medium-sized enterprise (SME) are distinguished. These are shown in Table 6.1.

Of the whole UK economy in 2008, micro businesses (between 0 and 9 employees) accounted for 95.7 per cent of all firms, 21.7 per cent of turnover and provided 33.5 per cent of all employment. All SMEs together (less than 250 employees) accounted for 99.9 per cent of all firms, 50.1 per cent of turnover and 59.4 per cent of employment.

Evidence suggests that a small business stands a significantly higher chance of failure than a large business, and yet many small businesses survive and some grow. What characteristics distinguish a successful small business from one that is likely to fail?

Pause for thought

Before you read on, try to identify what competitive advantages a small business might have over larger rivals.

Table 6.1	EU SME definitions			
Criterion		**Micro**	**Small**	**Medium**
1. Maximum number of employees		9	49	249
2a. Maximum annual turnover		€2m	€10m	€50m
2b. Maximum annual balance sheet total		€2m	€10m	€43m
3. Maximum % owned by other firms which are large enterprise(s)		25%	25%	25%

Note: to qualify as an SME criteria 1 and 3 must be met and either 2a or 2b

Competitive advantage and the small-firm sector

The following have been found to be the key competitive advantages that small firms might hold:

Flexibility. Small firms are better able to respond to changes in market conditions and to meet customer requirements effectively. For example, they may be able to develop or adapt products for specific needs. Small firms may also be able to make decisions quickly, avoiding the bureaucratic and formal decision-making processes that typify many larger companies.

Quality of service. Small firms are more able to deal with customers in a personal manner and offer a more effective after-sales service.

Production efficiency and low overhead costs. Small firms can avoid some of the diseconomies of scale that beset large companies. A small firm can benefit from: management that avoids waste; good labour relations; the employment of a skilled and motivated workforce; lower accommodation costs.

Product development. Many small businesses operate in niche markets, offering specialist goods or services. The distinctiveness of such products gives the small firm a crucial advantage over its larger rivals. A successful small business strategy, therefore, would be to produce products that are clearly differentiated from those of large firms in the market, thereby avoiding head-on competition – competition which the small firm would probably not be able to survive.

Innovation. Small businesses, especially those located in high-technology markets, are frequently product or process innovators. Such businesses, usually through entrepreneurial vision, manage successfully to match such innovations to changing market needs. Many small businesses are, in this respect, path breakers or market leaders.

Small businesses do, however, suffer from a number of significant limitations.

Problems facing small businesses

The following points have been found to hinder the success of small firms.

Selling and marketing. Small firms face many problems in selling and marketing their products, especially overseas. Small firms are perceived by their customers to be less stable and reliable than their larger rivals. This lack of credibility is likely to hinder their ability to trade. This is a particular problem for 'new' small firms which have not had long enough to establish a sound reputation.

Funding R&D. Given the specialist nature of many small firms, their long-run survival may depend upon developing new products and processes in order to keep pace with changing market needs. Such developments may require significant investment in research and development. However, the ability of small firms to attract finance is limited, as many of them have virtually no collateral and they are frequently perceived by banks as a highly risky investment.

Management skills. A crucial element in ensuring that small businesses not only survive but grow is the quality of management. If key management skills, such as being able to market a product effectively, are limited, then this will limit the success of the business.

Economies of scale. Small firms will have fewer opportunities and scope to gain economies of scale, and hence their costs may be somewhat higher than their larger rivals. This will obviously limit their ability to compete on price.

The role of the entrepreneur

Crucial to the success and growth of small businesses are the personality, skills and flair of the owner(s). Fostering their entrepreneurial talents has become a key element in government economic strategy around the world. Indeed, the creation of an entrepreneurial culture within society is often considered a prerequisite for economic prosperity.

But what exactly is an entrepreneur? Entrepreneurs are sources of new ideas and new ways of doing things. That is, they are at the forefront of invention and innovation, providing new products and developing markets.

The *Global Entrepreneurship Monitor* (GEM) provides a framework for analysing entrepreneurship. It suggests that entrepreneurship is a complex phenomenon that can exist at various stages of the development of a business. So someone who is just starting a venture and trying to make it in a highly competitive environment is entrepreneurial. And so too, but in a different way, are established business owners if they are innovative, competitive and growth-minded.

As far as new businesses are concerned, the GEM publishes a total entrepreneurial activity (TEA) index. This shows the proportion of the adult working age population to have established a firm within the past 42 months. Figure 6.5 shows the TEA for various industrial countries. You can see that in 2009 entrepreneurial activity was extremely high in the United Arab Emirates and Iceland. Within the European

Figure 6.5	Entrepreneurial activity: TEA as % of adult population (average 2006–9)

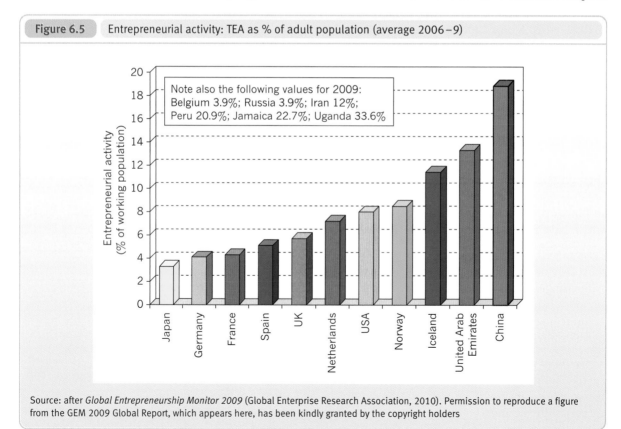

Source: after *Global Entrepreneurship Monitor 2009* (Global Enterprise Research Association, 2010). Permission to reproduce a figure from the GEM 2009 Global Report, which appears here, has been kindly granted by the copyright holders

BOX 6.3   THE DYSON DUAL CYCLONE VACUUM CLEANER

A small business redefining the Hoover

In the 2007 New Years Honours, James Dyson, founder of Dyson Appliances, was knighted. Sir James said that he hoped that the honour would 'encourage other engineers and people who have ideas and inventions to go out and commercialise them and make them international successes'.[1]

The tale of the Dyson Dual Cyclone vacuum cleaner records the successful and dramatic rise of James Dyson. As a budding entrepreneur, in the early 1980s he invented a revolutionary bagless vacuum cleaner, which worked, in effect, by creating a mini cyclone, whereby a high-speed air vortex pushed dust particles to the side of a collector. Without a bag, the suction power of the cleaner would not diminish over time, unlike conventional vacuums. When he initially developed this product (there were 5000 prototypes before a marketable product was finalised), neither Electrolux nor Hoover was interested – largely because of the profits they made from selling bags!

After an early and unsuccessful attempt to launch the project, Dyson managed to secure a deal with a Japanese company to produce and sell the vacuum in Japan. Launched in 1983, the pink-and-lavender 'G-Force' was a hit with Japanese consumers, who fell in love with its revolutionary design and looks. Nevertheless, at the staggering price of £1200, it was unlikely to yield the mass sales Dyson hoped for. Thus Dyson set out to manufacture it himself.

Finding it difficult to raise capital and find backers, Dyson reinvested his profits from the Japanese sales, and in 1993 managed to raise the £4.5 million required to design and patent his product, to establish a network of subcontractor suppliers, and to create an assembly plant near his home in the UK. With his DC01 vacuum cleaner priced at a relatively affordable £200, Dyson hoped to enter the mass market. By the end of the decade the Wiltshire plant was producing some 800 000 machines a year.

Today, Dyson's vacuum cleaner has nearly 50 per cent of the UK market, a third of the US and Western European markets and, with the launch of the compact DC12 vacuum, became the market leader in Japan, where homes are generally smaller.

The Dyson story is a classic example of how a small business with a revolutionary product can have a massive impact on a market, and within a short period of time become established as a market leader. The company now has an annual turnover of around £600 million, 80 per cent of it from exports. In 2005, Dyson's salary was £31.5m – more than twice that of any FTSE 100 chief executive! However, his salary saw significant reductions throughout the recession of the late 2000s, falling to £12.5 million in 2007 and then to £457 000 in 2008. During this period, a cost-cutting process was implemented, in particular a 6 per cent cut in R&D. At the same time, pre-tax profits fell by 4 per cent to £85.3 million.

In recognition of his contribution to innovation, the Trade and Industry Secretary, Patricia Hewitt, in 2003 named James Dyson as her 'innovation tsar' and he has now been crowned as the Conservative's 'technology czar'.

The Dyson story has not, however, been all good news for the UK: in 2002, Dyson shifted production from the UK plant to Malaysia, with the loss of 560 UK jobs. Dyson countered criticisms of the move by arguing that fierce competition from companies which were selling bagless cleaners for half the price of Dysons forced the company to relocate its manufacturing to a country where labour was much cheaper and which was close to suppliers of parts.

Yet things have turned out just as globalisation advocates would have hoped. Three factories in Malaysia now make 4m vacuum cleaners a year, with all the suppliers within a ten-mile radius, at one-third of the cost in Britain. The Wiltshire factory has become a research and design centre; Dyson employs more people than before, and in more highly skilled jobs. A new phase of R&D has produced a miniature digital motor with a power-to-weight ratio five times that of a Formula 1 racing car, which is being used in a tiny new vacuum cleaner and a super-hygienic, energy-efficient hand drier. Innovative firms like Dyson can grow from small beginnings to world-beaters. Global competition is turning many products into commodities, so innovation is essential if companies – and countries – want to stay in business.[2]

Innovative new products include the vacuum that steers on balls instead of wheels (this became Britain's biggest selling vacuum cleaner within a month), a desk fan for greener air-conditioning and the Airblade hand-dryer. Sir James Dyson has said that 'By investing in long-term research and development, we've been able to keep launching new technologies'.[3]

1. What conditions existed to enable James Dyson's small business to do so well in such a short period of time?
2. By 2007, a robotic Dyson vacuum cleaner (the DC06) had been over six years in development, involved several prototypes and cost a considerable amount of money. How would you assess whether the venture should have been scrapped?

---

[1] James Dyson speaking after his knighthood for services to the business world, 30 December 2006

[2] 'Suck it and see', The Economist, 1 February 2007
[3] 'Dyson's pay cut as profits fall', Times Online, 7 November 2009

countries, the UK appeared midway: above France and Germany, but behind Norway and the Netherlands. The UK was also ranked below the USA, while the highest figure for TEA occurred in Uganda.

Attitudes towards entrepreneurship in the UK

Attitudes to entrepreneurship are generally positive in the UK, with many creative and imaginative people starting businesses in niche markets, from organic and green products, to specialist computer services, to fashion products, to extreme sports, to painting and decorating, to financial services. A YouGov poll in 2006 found that a third of the population of working age wanted to run their own business.[3] But, as Figure 6.5 shows, only 5.7 per cent had started a business within the previous $3^1/_2$ years. According to the 2009 GEM, 4 per cent expect to start a business over the next three years and 24 per cent see good business opportunities. Both of these figures are lower than in previous years.

Of the reasons holding back entrepreneurial activity, financial problems are the most cited. In 2008, over 50 per cent perceived that getting finance for their business was the single most important obstacle to their entrepreneurial activity. In the 2009 survey, 'the business not being profitable' was the most reported financial problem. Furthermore, over 50 per cent surveyed said that they felt it was more difficult to start a new business in 2009 than in 2008. The report also found that a significant proportion of the adult population of working age (32 per cent) has a fear of business failure. This compares with 27 per cent in the USA.

However, much of the fear of potential entrepreneurs is misplaced. Less than 20 per cent of loan applications are rejected; it is very easy to set up a business – you just have to inform HM Revenue and Customs; there is considerable support and advice available from various government agencies, such as *Business Link*; the amount of paperwork in running a small business is generally less than people expect; revenue from a new business's first year's trading on average turns out to be about double what the owners had expected.

Nevertheless, there are risks in setting up a business that should not be trivialised. The three-year survival rate for UK businesses that started in 2004 is 65.3 per cent. A dangerous period for a new business is between 12 and 18 months after start-up. It is then that a business often runs short of cash, and revenues are not coming in quickly enough. It is then, too, that initial interest from customers may wane.

Pause for thought

Is business failure necessarily a 'bad thing' for a country?

Recap

1. Small firms survive because they provide or hold distinct advantages over their larger rivals. Such advantages include: greater flexibility, greater quality of service, production efficiency, low overhead costs and product innovation.

2. Small businesses are prone to high rates of failure, however. This is due to problems of credibility, finance and limited management skills.

3. Entrepreneurial activity varies from country to country, but most recognise that is an important ingredient in the health of the economy. Generally, the difficulties and risks of setting up a new business are less than people expect.

---

[3] YouGov Global, http://today.yougov.co.uk

QUESTIONS

1. What do you understand by the term 'business strategy'? Explain why different types of business will see strategic management in different ways. Give examples.

2. Outline the Five Forces Model of competition. Identify the strengths and weaknesses of analysing industry in this manner.

3. Investigate a particular industry and assess its competitive environment using the Five Forces approach.

4. Distinguish between a business's primary and support activities in its value chain. Why might a business be inclined to outsource its support activities? Can you see any weaknesses in doing this?

5. What do you understand by the term 'core competence' when applied to a business? What are the arguments for and against a firm narrowly focusing on its core competencies?

6. Explain the two-way relationship between a business's rate of growth and its profitability.

7. Distinguish between internal and external growth strategy. Identify a range of factors which might determine whether an internal or external strategy is pursued.

8. What is meant by the term 'vertical integration'? Why might a business wish to pursue such a growth strategy?

9. A firm can grow by merging with or taking over another firm. Such mergers or takeovers can be of three types: horizontal, vertical or conglomerate. Which of the following is an example of which type of merger (takeover)?

   (a) A soft drinks manufacturer merges with a pharmaceutical company.
   (b) A car manufacturer merges with a car distribution company.
   (c) A large supermarket chain takes over a number of independent grocers.

   To what extent will consumers gain or lose from the three different types of merger identified above?

10. Assume that an independent film company, which has up to now specialised in producing documentaries for a particular television broadcasting company, wishes to expand. Identify some possible horizontal, vertical and other closely related fields into which it may choose to expand.

11. What are the advantages and disadvantages for a company in using the stock market to raise finance for expansion?

12. In what sense can the stock market be said to be efficient? Why is it unlikely to be perfectly efficient?

13. Compare and contrast the competitive advantages held by both small and big business.

14. How did the recession of 2008/9 affect small businesses? Do you think it is easier or more difficult to set up a business during a recession? Explain your answer.

Business issues covered in this chapter

■ What is the magnitude and pattern of global foreign direct investment?

■ What forms do multinational corporations take?

■ For what reasons do companies become multinational?

■ In what ways do multinationals have a cost advantage over companies based in a single country?

■ What competitive advantages do multinationals have over companies based in a single country?

■ What disadvantages are companies likely to face from having their operations spread over a number of countries?

■ What are the advantages and disadvantages of multinational investment for the host state and how can the multinational use its position to gain the best deal from the host state?

Multinational corporations and business strategy in a global economy

7 Chapter

The world economy has become increasingly interdependent over the past few decades, with improved communications and an increasingly global financial system. This has meant that in many respects a firm's global strategy is simply an extension of its strategy within its own domestic market. However, opening up to global markets can provide an obvious means for a business to expand its markets and spread its risks, especially with the process of globalisation. It also is a means of reducing costs, whether through economies of scale or from accessing cheap sources of supply or low-wage production facilities.

A firm's global growth strategy may involve simply exporting or opening up factories or outlets abroad, or it may involve merging with businesses in other countries or forming strategic alliances. As barriers to trade and the international flow of capital have come down, so more and more businesses have sought to become multinational. The result is that the global business environment has tended to become more and more competitive.

For developing economies, such as India and China, the benefits of this new wave of globalisation are substantial. Foreign companies invest in high value-added, knowledge-rich production, most of which is subsequently exported. Economic growth is stimulated and wages rise. Increased consumption then spreads the benefits more widely throughout the economy. There are, however, costs. Many are left behind by the growth, and inequalities deepen both between and within countries. There are also often significant environmental costs as rapid growth leads to increased pollution, environmental degradation and the depletion of resources.

7.1 MULTINATIONAL CORPORATIONS

There are some 77 000 **multinational corporations** (MNCs) worldwide. Between them they control over 780 000 foreign subsidiaries, which employ some 81.6 million people. In 2008, the global stock of foreign direct investment (FDI) was over $16 trillion. Sales by foreign affiliates accounted for $30.3 trillion in 2008, or almost 50 per cent of world GDP. The largest MNCs have affiliates in an average of 40 foreign countries each.

Definition

Multinational corporations
Businesses that either own or control foreign subsidiaries in more than one country.

But just what is an MNC? At the most basic level it is a business that either owns or controls subsidiaries in more than one country. It is this ownership or control of productive assets in other countries that makes the MNC distinct from an enterprise that does business overseas by simply exporting goods or services. However, merely to define an MNC as a company with overseas subsidiaries fails to reflect the immense diversity of multinationals.

Diversity among MNCs

Size. Many, if not most, of the world's largest firms – Wal-Mart, Shell, General Motors, etc. – are multinationals. Indeed, the turnover of some of them exceeds the national income of many smaller countries (see Table 7.1).

And yet there are also thousands of very small, often specialist multinationals, which are a mere fraction of the size of the giants. What is more, since the mid 1980s many large multinational businesses have been downsizing. They have been shrinking the size of their headquarters, removing layers of bureaucracy to speed up decision making, and reorganising their global operations into smaller autonomous profit centres. Gone is the philosophy that big companies will inevitably do better than small ones.

In fact, it now appears that multinationals are seeking to create a hybrid form of business organisation, which combines the advantages of size (i.e. economies of

Table 7.1	Comparison of the ten largest MNCs (by gross revenue) and selected countries (GDP),[1] 2009	
MNC rank	**Country or company (headquarters)**	**GDP ($bn) or gross revenue ($bn)**
	USA	*14 250.0*
	UK	*2 165.0*
1	Royal Dutch Shell	458.4
	Pakistan	*448.1*
2	Exxon Mobil	442.9
3	Wal-Mart Stores	405.6
	Belgium	*381.4*
	Malaysia	*378.9*
4	BP	367.1
	Greece	*339.2*
	Sweden	*333.2*
5	Chevron	263.2
	Czech Republic	*256.7*
	Bangladesh	*242.2*
6	Total	234.7
	Singapore	*234.5*
	Portugal	*232.2*
7	ConocoPhillips	230.8
8	ING Group	226.6
9	Sinopec	207.8
	Israel	*205.2*
10	Toyota Motor	204.4
	Ireland	*117.3*
	Cyprus	*22.9*
	Somalia	*5.7*

Note: GDP figures corrected by using exchange rates that reflect purchasing power
Sources: Companies: Fortune Global 500 (www.fortune.com/fortune/global500/);
Countries: World Economic Outlook database, IMF

scale) with the responsiveness and market knowledge of smaller firms. The key for the modern multinational is flexibility, and to be at one and the same time both global and local.

The nature of business. MNCs cover the entire spectrum of business activity, from manufacturing to extraction, agricultural production, chemicals, processing, service provision and finance. There is no 'typical' line of activity of a multinational.

Production locations. Some MNCs are truly 'global', with production located in a wide variety of countries and regions. Other MNCs, by contrast, locate in only one other region, or in a very narrow range of countries.

There are, however, several potentially constraining factors on the location of multinational businesses. For example, businesses concerned with the extraction of raw materials will locate as nature dictates! Businesses that provide luxury services will tend to locate in advanced countries, where the demand for such services is high. Others locate according to the resource intensity of the stage of production. Thus a labour-intensive stage might be located in a developing country where wage rates are relatively low. Another stage, which requires a high level of automation, might be located in an industrially advanced country that has the necessary technology and workforce skills.

Ownership patterns. As businesses expand overseas, they are faced with a number of options. They can decide to go it alone and create wholly owned subsidiaries. Alternatively, they might share ownership and hence some of the risk, by establishing a joint venture with a foreign company. In such cases the MNC might have a majority or minority stake in the overseas enterprise. In certain countries, where MNC investment is regulated, many governments insist on owning or controlling a share in the new enterprise. Much of the time, it will depend on the type of business and how important it is to the host country.

The above characteristics of MNCs reveal that they represent a wide and very diverse group of enterprises. Beyond sharing the common link of having production activities in more than one country, MNCs differ widely in the nature and forms of their overseas business, and in the relationship between the parent and its subsidiaries.

> **Pause for thought**
>
> *Given the diverse nature of multinational business, how useful is the definition given on pages 185–6 for describing a multinational corporation?*

Trends in multinational investment

We can estimate the size of multinational investment by looking at figures for foreign direct investment. FDI represents the finance used either to purchase the assets for setting up a new subsidiary (or expanding an existing one), or to acquire an existing business operation through merger or acquisition.

From 2005 to 2007, FDI flows rose by an average of 39.3 per cent per year, to stand at $2.1 trillion in 2007 (see Figure 7.1). This rise was largely the result of an increase in mergers and acquisitions, reflecting growing confidence in the world economy. It was a similar picture in the years 1997 to 2000. By contrast, when world growth is low or negative (as in the early 2000s and the recession of 2008/9), FDI tends to fall as companies become less aggressive. FDI inflows fell to $1.8 trillion in 2008 and to $1.1 trillion in 2009, with a slow recovery expected to cause them to rise to $1.4 and then $1.8 trillion in 2010 and 2011, respectively.

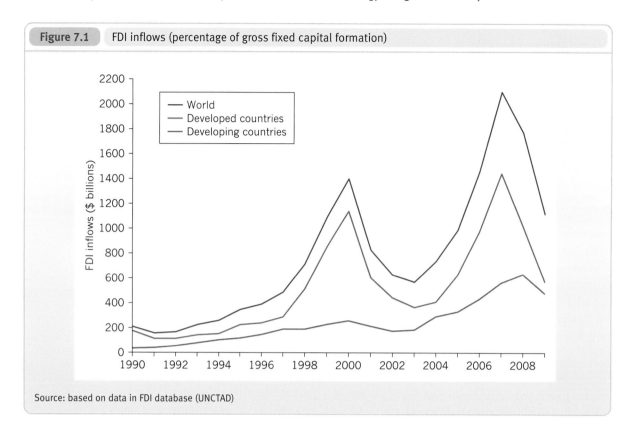

Figure 7.1   FDI inflows (percentage of gross fixed capital formation)

Source: based on data in FDI database (UNCTAD)

FDI is highly concentrated, so much so that in 2008 the world's 40 most heavily indebted developing countries received 4.7 per cent of total FDI to developing countries, and only 1.2 per cent of world FDI. The whole of Africa received only 5.2 per cent. By contrast, the ten largest FDI host countries received 61 per cent of world FDI in 2008. The advanced countries as a whole accounted for around 57 per cent of inward FDI and 81 per cent of outward FDI.

FDI and the UK

In 2008, the UK's share of world FDI was 5.2 per cent for inflows and 8.4 per cent for outflows. However, these figures fell to 4.1 and 1.7 per cent respectively in 2009, as the recession affecting the world hit the UK particularly severely. Figure 7.2 shows FDI flows to and from the UK in billions of US dollars. It also shows FDI inflows as a percentage of both world FDI inflows and the inflows to the 15 countries ('EU15') that were EU members prior to 2004.

Over the years, outward investment from the UK has tended to exceed inward investment. By 2009, the accumulated stock of investment abroad by the UK was $1652 billion, while the stock of foreign investment in the UK was $1125 billion. Investment yields income to the investing company. Because UK investment abroad is normally greater than foreign investment in the UK, inflows of income earned from abroad are generally greater than outflows of income from the UK. In 2008, direct investment income inflows were £69.3 billion, while outflows were only £10.6 billion – a surplus of £58.6 billion.

Countries that have a large foreign multinational sector, such as the UK, are significantly affected by foreign business actions and their decisions about where to locate and invest. MNCs generally have higher rates of productivity than domestic

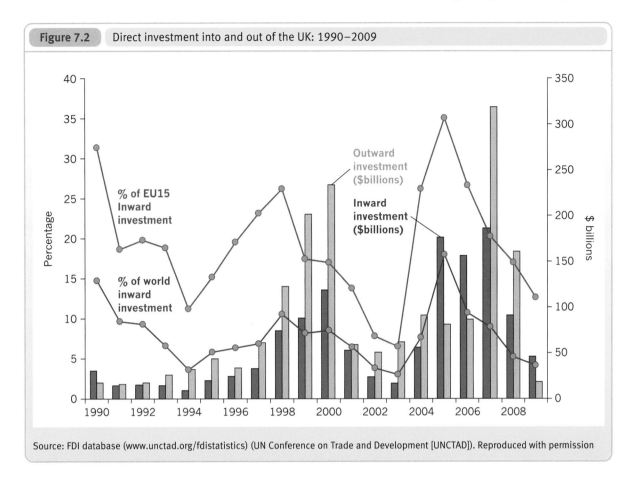

Figure 7.2   Direct investment into and out of the UK: 1990–2009

Source: FDI database (www.unctad.org/fdistatistics) (UN Conference on Trade and Development [UNCTAD]). Reproduced with permission

firms, and this puts competitive pressure on domestic firms to increase their productivity. In the UK, some 45 per cent of R&D expenditure is by foreign affiliates.

Recap

1. There is great diversity among multinationals in respect to size, nature of business, size of overseas operations, location, ownership and organisational structure.

2. Foreign direct investment (FDI) tends to fluctuate with the ups and downs of the world economy. Over the years, however, FDI has accounted for a larger and larger proportion of total investment.

3. The UK is a net investor overseas and hence inflows of income earned from abroad are generally greater than outflows of income from the UK.

BUSINESS STRATEGY IN A GLOBAL ECONOMY   7.2

The global marketplace can provide massive opportunities for firms to expand: access to new markets, new customers, new supply sources, new ideas and skills. At the same time, the growth of multinationals presents major competitive threats to domestic firms, as new market entrants from abroad arrive with lower costs, innovative products and marketing, or some other core competence which the domestic firm finds difficult to match. In this section we explore the strategic implications for business in facing up to the global economic system.

Types of multinational expansion

As we saw in section 6.3, businesses can look to expand in one of two ways: through either internal or external expansion. MNCs are no exception to this rule. They can expand overseas, either by creating a new production facility from scratch (such as Nissan in the north-east of England), or by merging with or taking over existing foreign producers (such as the acquisition of Asda by Wal-Mart or of Jaguar by Ford). They can also engage in an international strategic alliance (for example, the joint venture in 2006 between Finland's Nokia and Japan's Sanyo to produce mobile phones for the North American market).

We need also to distinguish between horizontal, vertical or conglomerate expansion.

> **Definitions**
>
> **Horizontally integrated multinational**
> A multinational that produces the same product in many different countries.
>
> **Vertically integrated multinational**
> A multinational that undertakes the various stages of production for a given product in different countries.
>
> **Conglomerate multinational**
> A multinational that produces different products in different countries.

- A **horizontally integrated multinational**. This type of multinational seeks to produce essentially the same product in different countries (but perhaps with some variations in product specification to suit the needs of the local market). The primary objective of this strategy is to achieve growth by expanding into new markets, as shown by cell C in the Growth Vector Matrix on page 77.

- A **vertically integrated multinational**. In this case, the multinational undertakes the various stages of production in different countries. Thus in some countries it will go backwards into the business's supply chain to the components or raw materials stages, and in others it will go forwards into the product's assembly or distribution. Oil companies such as Shell and Exxon (Esso) are good examples of vertically integrated multinationals, undertaking in a global operation the extraction of crude oil, controlling its transportation, refining it and producing by-products, and controlling the retail sale of petrol and other oil products. The principal motive behind such a growth strategy is to be able to exert greater control over costs and reduce the uncertainty of the business environment.

- A **conglomerate multinational**. Such multinationals produce a range of different products in different countries. By this process of diversification, conglomerate multinationals look to spread risks, and maximise returns through the careful buying of overseas assets. Unilever is a good example of a conglomerate multinational. It employs over 163 000 people in some 360 manufacturing sites in over 100 countries, producing various food, home care and personal care products, which are sold in more than 170 countries. It has around 400 brands (including a leading global position in seven categories) including Wall's, Carte D'Or and Ben & Jerry's ice cream; Birds Eye and Findus frozen foods; Slim-Fast diet foods; Knorr soups; Lawry's spices; Bertorelli pasta sauces; Hellman's mayonnaise; Lipton and PG Tips tea; Flora, Blue Band and Rama margarines; Bovril and Marmite spreads; Colman's mustard; Boursin cheese; Signal toothpaste; Domestos, Cif, Omo, Persil and Comfort; Organics, Timotei and SunSilk shampoos; Vaseline, Dove and Lux soaps; Pond's skin care products; Impulse, Lynx, Sure fragrances and antiperspirants.

As noted at the beginning of the chapter, MNCs are a diverse group of enterprises and we can distinguish between their different motives for going abroad. Some MNCs use their multinational base primarily as a means of reducing costs (vertically integrated multinationals), whereas others use it primarily to achieve growth (horizontal and conglomerate multinationals). Let us now consider how, by going multinational, such goals might be achieved.

Going global to reduce costs

The costs and availability of labour and other resources. Nations, like individuals, are not equally endowed with resources. Some nations are rich in labour, some in capital and some in raw materials. In general, the more plentiful a resource, the lower will be its cost. Multinationals take advantage of this. For example, they might locate labour-intensive activities, such as an assembly plant, in low-wage developing countries, but complex R&D operations in countries with the necessary technology and skilled labour. It is factors such as this which give MNCs a competitive advantage over purely national firms.

> **Pause for thought**
>
> *Before reading on, try to identify ways in which locating production overseas might help to reduce costs.*

Cost differences between countries are ruthlessly exploited by Nike, the American sportswear manufacturer. Nike has organised itself globally such that it can respond rapidly to changing cost conditions in its international subsidiaries. Its product development operations are carried out in the USA, but all of its production operations are subcontracted out to over 40 overseas locations, mostly in South and South-East Asia. If wage rates, and hence costs, rise in one host country, then production is simply transferred to a lower-cost subsidiary. Another example is Gap Inc., which was examined in Box 1.1 (see pages 4–5).

> **Pause for thought**
>
> *Identify some of the potential strengths and weaknesses of businesses having their value chains located in a variety of different countries.*

As businesses relocate many dimensions of their value chain, the structure and organisation of the business takes on a web-like appearance, with its various operations being spread throughout the world.

The quality of inputs. The location of multinational operations does not depend simply on wages and other input *prices*; it also depends on the *quality* of resources. For example, a country might have a highly skilled or highly industrious workforce, and it is this, rather than simple wage rates, that attracts multinational investment. The issue here is still largely one of costs. Highly skilled workers might cost more to employ *per hour*, but if their productivity is higher, they might well cost less to employ *per unit of output*. Take the case of Nike again. Product innovation and research, along with marketing and promotion, are all undertaken in the USA, which has a cost advantage in these areas, not through lower wage rates, but through experience and skills.

If a country has both lower-priced resources and high-quality resources, it will be very attractive to multinational investors. In recent years, the UK government has sought to attract multinational investment through its lower labour costs and more flexible employment conditions than those of its European rivals, while still having a relatively highly trained labour force compared with those in developing countries. However, as the relocation of many call-centre and IT jobs to developing countries shows, such advantages are disappearing fast in many sectors.

Entrepreneurial and managerial skills. Managers in MNCs are often more innovative in the way they do business and organise the value chain than managers of domestic firms. In some cases, this is essential. With the arrival of Japanese multinationals in the UK, it became instantly apparent that Japanese managers conducted business in a very different way from their British counterparts. The most fundamental difference concerned working practices, such as the use of quality circles. Japanese MNCs quickly established themselves as among the most efficient and productive businesses in the UK (see section 8.5 on the flexible firm) and this made it necessary for UK firms to respond.

Cost reductions through 'learning by doing'. This is where skills and productivity improve with experience. Such learning effects apply not only to workers in production, sales, distribution, etc., but also to managers, who learn to develop more efficient forms of organisation. When a firm expands globally, there may be more scope for learning

| BOX 7.1 | THE TRANSNATIONALITY INDEX |

A measure of global significance

As part of the UNCTAD annual World Investment Report, a 'transnationality' index is given for both host countries and multinational businesses. Transnationality refers to the significance of foreign activities in the country or for the business.

The transnationality index (TNI) for host countries

The transnationality index for a country is based on the average of four variables:

▪ FDI inflows as a percentage of gross fixed capital formation (investment);
▪ FDI inward stock as a percentage of GDP;
▪ value added by foreign affiliates as a percentage of GDP;
▪ employment by foreign affiliates as a percentage of total employment.

In 2005 the average transnationality index for the 73 countries for which it was calculated was just over 21.9 per cent. The world's most transnational host economy is Hong Kong (103.7 per cent), followed by Belgium (65.9 per cent), Singapore (65.2 per cent), Luxembourg (64.8 per cent) and Estonia (49.5 per cent) (see chart).

The degree of internationalisation of companies varies significantly from country to country. For example, in 2007, it was above average for the UK and below average for Germany, Japan and the USA.

The transnationality index for business

The transnationality index for multinational business is composed of the average of three ratios:

▪ foreign assets to total assets;
▪ foreign sales to total sales;
▪ foreign employment to total employment.

Between 1993 and 2008 the average transnationality index (TNI) for the world's 100 largest multinational companies rose from under 50 per cent to 62.5 per cent, implying a growing level of transnationality. For the largest 100 MNCs from developing countries the growth in the index has been more dramatic, rising from under 20 per cent to 54.4 per cent between 1993 and 2007. The top 10 global companies ranked by transnationality are given in the table.

Transnationality varies by type of business. Thus companies in the food and beverages, telecommunications and pharmaceuticals industries tend to have a higher TNI than those in the motor vehicles, utilities or oil industries.

1. Looking at the table, can you offer any explanation as to why no Japanese or American owned companies appear on this list?
2. How adequate do you feel such indices are in identifying how open or global an economy or business is? Should other indicators be considered as well? If so what?
3. The leading nations in the transnationality index are all small. Is there a relationship between their size and the fact that they are at the top of the index?

The world's top 10 MNCs in terms of transnationality (2007)

Ranking					
TNI	Foreign assets	Corporation	Home country	Industry	TNI (%)
1	42	Xstrata Plc	UK	Mining & quarrying	94.1
2	63	Linde AG	Germany	Chemicals	89.5
3	11	ArcelorMittal	Luxembourg	Metals & mineral products	89.4
4	77	Pernod Ricard SA	France	Beverages	88.8
5	67	WPP group plc	UK	Business services	88.1
6	2	Vodaphone Group Plc	UK	Telecommunications	87.0
7	28	Nestlé SA	Switzerland	Food and beverages	86.6
8	97	AkzoNobel	Netherlands	Pharmaceuticals	85.2
9	48	Nokia	Finland	Telecommunications	84.2
10	21	Thomson Reuters	Canada	Business services	83.8

Source: based on data in Annex Table A.1.9, pp. 225–7, *World Investment Report 2009* (UNCTAD, 2009)

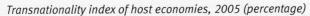

Transnationality index of host economies, 2005 (percentage)

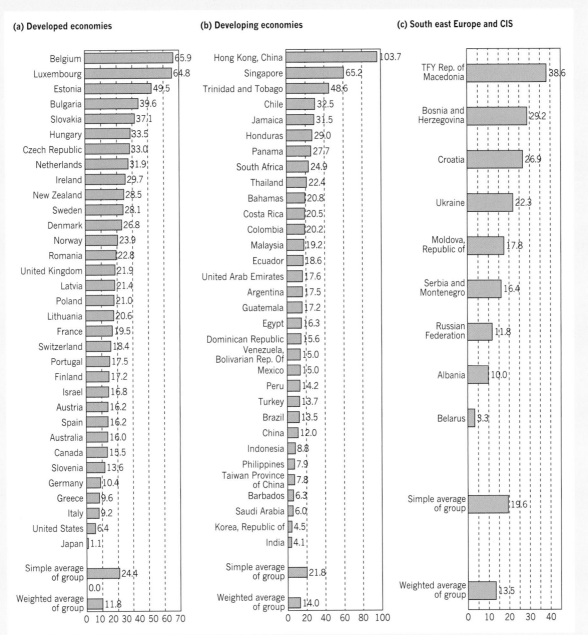

(a) Developed economies

Belgium	65.9
Luxembourg	64.8
Estonia	49.5
Bulgaria	39.6
Slovakia	37.1
Hungary	33.5
Czech Republic	33.0
Netherlands	31.9
Ireland	29.7
New Zealand	28.5
Sweden	28.1
Denmark	26.8
Norway	23.9
Romania	22.8
United Kingdom	21.9
Latvia	21.4
Poland	21.0
Lithuania	20.6
France	19.5
Switzerland	18.4
Portugal	17.5
Finland	17.2
Israel	16.8
Austria	16.2
Spain	16.2
Australia	16.0
Canada	15.5
Slovenia	13.6
Germany	10.4
Greece	9.6
Italy	9.2
United States	6.4
Japan	1.1
Simple average of group	24.4
	0.0
Weighted average of group	11.8

0 10 20 30 40 50 60 70

(b) Developing economies

Hong Kong, China	103.7
Singapore	65.2
Trinidad and Tobago	48.6
Chile	32.5
Jamaica	31.5
Honduras	29.0
Panama	27.7
South Africa	24.9
Thailand	22.4
Bahamas	20.8
Costa Rica	20.5
Colombia	20.2
Malaysia	19.2
Ecuador	18.6
United Arab Emirates	17.6
Argentina	17.5
Guatemala	17.2
Egypt	16.3
Dominican Republic	15.6
Venezuela, Bolivarian Rep. Of	15.0
Mexico	15.0
Peru	14.2
Turkey	13.7
Brazil	13.5
China	12.0
Indonesia	8.8
Philippines	7.9
Taiwan Province of China	7.8
Barbados	6.3
Saudi Arabia	6.0
Korea, Republic of	4.5
India	4.1
Simple average of group	21.8
Weighted average of group	14.0

0 20 40 60 80 100

(c) South east Europe and CIS

TFY Rep. of Macedonia	38.6
Bosnia and Herzegovina	29.2
Croatia	26.9
Ukraine	22.3
Moldova, Republic of	17.8
Serbia and Montenegro	16.4
Russian Federation	11.8
Albania	10.0
Belarus	3.3
Simple average of group	19.6
Weighted average of group	13.5

0 10 20 30 40

Source: *World Investment Report 2008* (UNCTAD, 2009)

by doing. For example, if a firm employs low-cost labour in developing countries, initially the lower cost per worker will, to some extent, be offset by lower productivity. As learning by doing takes place, and productivity increases, so initial small cost advantages may become much more substantial.

Economies of scale. By increasing the scale of its operation, and by each plant in each country specialising in a particular part of the value chain, the multinational may be able to gain substantial economies of scale.

MNCs are likely to invest heavily in R&D in an attempt to maintain their global competitiveness. The global scale of their operations allows them to spread the costs of this R&D over a large output (i.e. the R&D has a low average fixed cost). MNCs, therefore, are often world leaders in process innovation and product development.

Reducing transactions costs. By setting up an overseas subsidiary (as opposed merely to exporting to that country), the MNC can save on the transactions costs of arranging a contract with an overseas import agent or with a firm in the host country to make the product under licence. Many firms go through a sequence from exporting to overseas investment. Nissan, for example, exported its cars to the UK using local motor vehicle retailers to distribute them prior to establishing a greenfield manufacturing site in the North East of England in 1984. Toyota and Honda entered the UK in the same way.

Transport costs. A business locating production overseas would be able to reduce transport costs if those overseas plants served local or regional markets, or used local raw materials.

Government policies. One of the biggest cost advantages concerns the avoidance of tariffs (customs duties). If a country imposes tariffs on imports, then, by locating within that country (i.e. behind the 'tariff wall'), the MNC gains a competitive advantage over its rivals which are attempting to import their products from outside the country, and which are thus having to pay the tariff. MNCs may, therefore, be able to pass their cost savings on to consumers in the form of lower prices, or maintain prices and increase their profit margins. These, in turn, could be used for R&D.

Costs might also be reduced as a result of various government incentives to attract inward investment. Examples include: favourable tax rates, substantial depreciation allowances and the provision of subsidised premises. Such cost-cutting incentives may help to reduce the fixed costs of the investment and hence reduce its risk. A fairly recent case in the UK saw a potential investor offered financial incentives valued at £37 000 per employee to locate production in an area of Wales!

In highly competitive global markets, even small cost savings might mean the difference between success and failure. Thus MNCs will be constantly searching for ways of minimising costs and locating production where the greatest advantage might be gained.

Going global to access new markets

International markets can offer businesses massive new opportunities for growth and expansion. Such markets would be particularly attractive to a business where domestic growth opportunities are limited as a result of either the maturity of the market or shifting consumer tastes. In addition to the simple possibility of extra sales, expanding into new markets offers other advantages:

Spreading risks. One of the main advantages of a larger and more diverse market is to spread risks. The firm is no longer tied to the specific market conditions of one particular country or region. As such, falling sales in one region of the global economy might be effectively offset by increased sales elsewhere.

A large number of German and Japanese businesses have diversified globally in order to reduce their reliance on domestic markets, which in recent years have been growing very slowly and, in the case of Japan, have been suffering from a significant squeeze on prices. For example, Toyota and Honda, the two largest Japanese car manufacturers, both reported record profits for 2002 despite the depressed state of the Japanese economy. They were able to do this by focusing on production in foreign markets – in particular the USA, where three-quarters of the cars sold by Honda and Toyota are also manufactured there.

Exploiting competitive advantages in new markets. The multinational's superior technology, superior-quality products and more effective marketing may allow it to compete particularly effectively in markets that, up until now, have been dominated by domestic producers.

Learning from experience in diverse markets. Successful businesses will learn from their global operations, copying or amending production techniques, organisation, marketing, etc. from one country to another as appropriate. In other words, they can draw lessons from experiences in one country for use in another.

Increasingly it seems that the globalisation of business is like a game of competitive leapfrog, with businesses having to look overseas in order to maintain their competitive position in respect to their rivals. A fiercely competitive global environment, in which small cost differences or design improvements can mean the difference between business success and failure, ensures that strategic thinking within a global context is high on the business agenda.

The product life cycle and the multinational company

By shifting production overseas at a particular point in the product's life cycle, the business is able to reduce costs and maintain competitiveness. The product life cycle hypothesis was discussed in section 5.6 (page 146). However, it is worth reviewing its elements here in order to identify how an MNC, by altering the geographical production of a good, might extend its profitability.

A product's life cycle can be split into four phases: launch, growth, maturity and decline. These were shown in Figure 5.9 (page 148).

The launch phase. This will tend to see the new product produced in the economy where the product is developed. It will be exported to the rest of the world. At this stage of the product's life cycle, the novelty of the product and the monopoly position of the producer enable the business to charge high prices and make high profits.

The growth phase. As the market begins to grow, other producers will seek to copy or imitate the new product. Hence supply increases and prices begin to fall. In order to maintain competitiveness, the business will look to reduce costs, and at this stage might consider shifting production overseas to lower cost production centres.

Maturity. At the early stage of maturity, the business is still looking to sell its product in the markets of the developed economies. Thus it may still be happy to locate

BOX 7.2	MERGER ACTIVITY

An international perspective

What have been the trends, patterns and driving factors in mergers and acquisitions (M&A) around the world in recent years? An overview of cross-border M&A is given in the chart.

The 1990s saw a rapid growth in M&A as the world economy boomed. Then with a slowing down in economic growth after 2000, M&A activity declined, both in value and in the number of deals, but from 2004 to 2007 they rose back dramatically with the rapid growth in the world economy. But then in 2008, there was a global banking crisis followed by the credit crunch and recession. M&A activity fell substantially, as you can see from Chart (a).

The 1990s

The early years of the 1990s saw relatively low M&A activity as the world was in recession, but as world economic growth picked up, so worldwide M&A activity increased. Economic growth was particularly rapid in the USA, which became the major target for acquisitions.

There was also an acceleration in the process of 'globalisation'. With the dismantling of trade barriers around the world and increasing financial deregulation, so international competition increased. Companies felt the need to become bigger in order to compete more effectively.

In Europe, M&A activity was boosted by the development of the Single Market, which came into being in January 1993. Companies took advantage of the abolition of trade barriers in the EU, which made it cheaper and easier for them to operate on an EU-wide basis. As 1999 approached, and with it the arrival of the euro, so European merger activity reached fever pitch, stimulated also by the strong economic growth experienced throughout the EU.

By 2000, annual worldwide M&A activity was some three times the level of the beginning of the 1990s. Around this time there were some very large mergers indeed. These included a $67 billion marriage of pharmaceutical companies Zeneca of the UK and Astra of Sweden in 1998, a $183 billion takeover of telecomms giant Mannesmann of Germany by Vodafone of the UK in 1999 and a $40.3 billion takeover of Orange of the UK by France Telecom in 2000.

Other sectors in which merger activity was rife included financial services and the privatised utilities sector. In the UK in particular, most of the privatised water and electricity companies were taken over, with buyers attracted by the sector's monopoly profits. French and US buyers were prominent.

(a) Cross-border mergers and acquisitions by target: 1990–2009

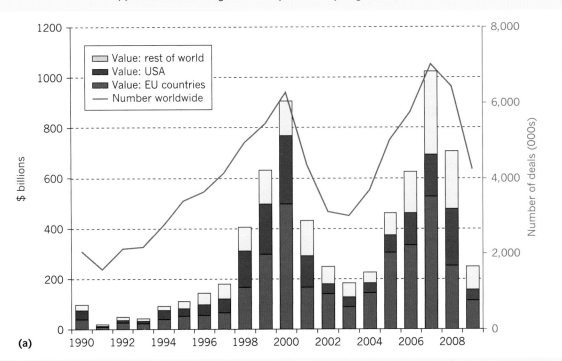

Note: The data cover only those deals that involve an acquisition of an equity of more than 10%

Source: *Cross Border Mergers & Acquisitions* (World Investment Report Annex Tables, UNCTAD, June 2010)

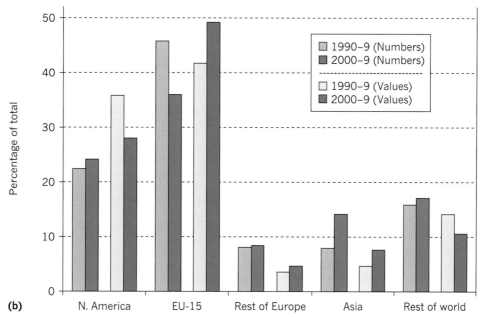

(b) Cross-border mergers and acquisitions by target region (% of total number and value)

Note: The data cover only those deals that involve an acquisition of an equity of more than 10%
Source: *Cross Border Mergers & Acquisitions* (World Investment Report Annex Tables, UNCTAD, June 2010)

The 2000s

The period from 2000 to 2008 saw a change in the worldwide pattern of M&A activity. Whilst this predominantly involved a company in a neighbouring country, or a country that is a traditional trading partner, increasingly both European and US companies have looked to other parts of the world to expand their activities.

Two of the major target regions have been (a) the rest of Europe, especially the 10 countries joining the EU in 2004 plus Russia, and (b) developing countries, especially China, Brazil and India. These new markets have the twin attractions of rapidly growing demand and low costs, including cheap skilled labour and low tax rates.

North America saw a small proportionate growth in its global share of cross-border M&As from 22.4 per cent in the 1990s to 24.2 per cent in the 2000s, although its share measured by value fell from 35.8 per cent to 28.0 per cent. Asian countries have been an increasing target, with the share of global M&A increasing by both number and value (see chart (b)). The EU-15 (i.e. those fifteen countries which were EU members before the accession of ten new counties in 2004 and another two in 2007), whilst seeing a reduction in the number of cross-border M&As, actually saw an increase in their value from 41.8 per cent to 49.2 per cent. In 2007, the biggest completed cross-border M&A was the $98.2 billion purchase of the Dutch Bank ABN-AMRO by RBS Holdings.

M&A activity has become more widespread across industrial sectors. In the 1997–2000 boom, the companies targeted were predominantly in the telecomms and media sectors. The boom of the mid 2000s, by contrast, saw companies involved in M&A from across the range of industries. According to a 2006 survey of Chief Executive Officers around the world,[1] 47 per cent were actively engaged in M&A activity. The figure rises to 61 per cent for CEOs of large companies (those with revenue of more than $10 billion).

> Overwhelmingly, gaining access to new markets and customers is the main purpose given for cross-border M&A, cited by nearly two-thirds of CEOs. However, CEOs do not under-estimate the difficulties faced in cross-border acquisition and integration. Cultural issues and conflicts, differences in regulations and unexpected costs are the main obstacles to cross-border M&A activity cited by CEOs.

---

[1] *Global CEO Survey 2006*, PricewaterhouseCoopers

. . . The global winners of tomorrow are those that can change their outlook from local to global in the true sense, and learn to operate in a world now subject to far more influences from a wider array of sources than ever before.[2]

As previously mentioned, in 2008/9 the global economy sank into recession and both the number and value of completed cross-border M&As fell significantly across the world. Recession creates uncertainty and hence it becomes more difficult to make a deal and to follow it through. According to data from Thomson Reuters, M&As in 2009 totalled $2059 billion, which was down 29 percent from 2008 and down 51 percent from the record high in 2007.[3] Chart (a) shows an even bigger fall in cross-border M&A. With the faltering recovery of 2010, however, there was a small increase in global M&A.

Types of M&A activity

Some 12 per cent of M&A deals are 'hostile' (up from 2 per cent in 2000). In other words, the company being taken over does not want to be. The deals are often concluded after prolonged boardroom battles, with bosses of the acquiring company seeking opportunities to build empires, and bosses of the target company attempting all sorts of manoeuvres to avoid being taken over. This may involve seeking deals with alternative, more 'friendly' companies. Generally companies are increasingly using the services of investment banks to help them in the process of making or warding off deals – this was the case with Cadbury, which hired Goldman Sachs, Morgan Standley and UBS to defend it against takeover (unsuccessfully, as it turned out). In 2010, hostile deals included Kraft's $21.4 billion takeover of Cadbury in February and Astellas Pharma Inc.'s $3.5 billion bid for OSI Pharmaceuticals Inc. in March.

Despite the growing number of horizontal mergers, there has also been a tendency for companies to become more focused, by selling off parts of their business which are not seen as 'core activities'. For example, not long after its takeover of Wellcome, Glaxo decided to concentrate on the production of prescription drugs, and as a consequence to sell its share of Warner Wellcome, which produced non-prescription drugs. Another example was Volvo. After unsuccessfully attempting to merge with Renault in 1993, it subsequently divested itself of several companies that it owned in a variety of industries, ranging from banking and finance to food, matches and pharmaceuticals.

This trend of horizontal mergers and conglomerate and vertical de-mergers has allowed companies to increase their market power in those specific sectors where they have expertise. Consumers may gain from lower costs, but the motives of the companies are largely to gain increased market power – something of dubious benefit to consumers.

[2] 'Global CEOs' business confidence reaches record levels', PricewaterhouseCoopers Press Release, 24 January 2007
[3] *Preliminary Mergers and Acquisitions Review*, Thomson Reuters, 25 June 2010

 Are the motives for merger likely to be different in a recession from in a period of rapid economic growth?

some of its plants in such economies. As the original market becomes increasingly saturated, however, the MNC will seek to expand into markets abroad which are at an earlier stage of development. Part of this expansion will be by the MNC simply exporting to more of these economies, but increasingly it will involve relocating its production there too.

Maturity and decline. By the time the original markets are fully mature and moving into decline, the only way to extend the product's life may be to cut costs and sell the product in the markets of developing countries. The location of production may shift once again, this time to even lower cost countries. By this stage, the country in which the product was developed will almost certainly be a net importer (if there is a market left for the product), but it may well be importing the product from a subsidiary of the same company that produced it within that country in the first place! Thus the product life cycle model explains how firms might first export and then engage in FDI. It explains how firms transfer production to different locations to reduce costs and enable profits to be made from a product that could have become unprofitable if its production had continued from its original production base.

BOX 7.3   GROCERS GO GLOBAL

International expertise plus local knowledge – a winning combination?

In Carrefour's Chinese stores, you will see a fresh snake counter alongside the fish department! Wal-Mart boasts that in its Chinese stores you can find local delicacies such as whole roasted pigs and live frogs. Are fresh snakes and live frogs what's needed to succeed in China? It would seem so. Global companies thinking local, customising themselves to each market, is increasingly seen as the key to success in Asia and elsewhere around the world.

The expansion of European and American supermarkets into countries around the world has been underway for a number of years. Driven by stagnant markets at home with limited growth opportunities, the major players, such as Wal-Mart from the USA, Carrefour and Casino from France, Tesco in the UK, Ahold from Holland and, Metro from Germany, have been looking to expand their overseas operations – but with mixed success.

In recent times, Asia has been the market's growth sector. Tesco entered the Thai market in 1998. Tesco Lotus, the company's regional subsidiary, is now the country's number one retailer. In 2009 it had 476 stores employing 35 269 people. Carrefour and the US-based Wal-Mart have also opened hundreds of new outlets within the region over the past few years.

The advantages that international retailers have over their domestic competitors are expertise in systems, distribution, the range of products and merchandising. However, given the distinctive nature of markets within Asia, businesses must learn to adapt to local conditions. Joint ventures and local knowledge are seen as the key ingredients to success. Even the most closed markets, such as those of Japan, are not immune from the global grocers' onslaught. Wal-Mart acquired a large stake in the ailing 400-store food and clothing chain Seiyu and by 2010 Tesco had opened 128 stores in Japan employing 3604 people.

Facing up to the big boys

With the rapid expansion of hypermarkets throughout Asia, the retail landscape is undergoing revolutionary change. With a wide range of products all under one roof, from groceries to pharmaceuticals to white goods, and at cut-rate prices, local neighbourhood stores stand little chance in the competitive battle. 'Mom and pop operations have no economies of scale.' As well as local retailers, local suppliers are also facing a squeeze on profits, as hypermarkets demand lower prices and use their buying power as leverage.

Such has been the dramatic impact these stores have had upon the retail and grocery sector that a number of Asian economies, such as Malaysia and Thailand, have introduced restrictions on the building of new outlets.

China, one of the toughest markets to enter, had restricted foreign companies to joint venture arrangements until 2004. Tesco's answer to these restrictions had been to go into partnership with Taiwanese food supplier Ting Hsin. In 2009 they employed 17 471 people in 56 Happy Shopper stores in mainland China. These bear none of the hallmarks of Tesco. The colour scheme is orange and there are few brands that the average British shopper would recognise. The staff, up to middle management, are all Chinese. Only the most senior executives are British. In 2006, Tesco increased its stake in Happy Shopper from 50 to 90 per cent.

With the lifting of restrictions, there has been a surge of new stores opened in China by the world's large supermarket chains. At the end of 2009, Carrefour, the biggest international retailer in the Chinese market, had 157 hypermarkets and 320 discount stores. Wal-Mart had 160 outlets. These figures are still dwarfed, however, by the domestic leader, Hualian, which operates some 2000 stores.

With their home markets reaching saturation, it's easy to see why the big-box foreign retailers are flocking to China. The economy of the world's most populous country is growing at more than 9 per cent a year. And with a rapidly expanding middle class, consumer spending is on the rise . . . The grocery market alone accounts for more than half of the total retail market, with sales expected to rise from $482 billion in 2006 to $700 billion within five years, says Paul Roberts, head of global research at Planet M&M, a London-based retail consultancy. 'That's a much faster rate of growth than the home markets of Tesco, Wal-Mart, or Carrefour.'[1]

What are the advantages and disadvantages to developing countries of the expansion of global supermarket chains?

---

[1] 'Tesco ups its stake in China', *Yahoo Finance*, 21 December 2006

Recap

1. Why businesses go multinational depends largely on the nature of their business and their corporate strategy. Two of the major reasons are (a) reducing costs by locating production where inputs are cheaper and/or more productive; (b) accessing markets in other countries in order to achieve growth in sales.

2. MNC investment is often governed by the product life cycle. In this theory, a business will shift production around the world seeking to reduce costs and extend a given product's life. The phases of a product's life will be conducted in different countries. As the product nears maturity and competition grows, reducing costs to maintain competitiveness will force business to locate production in low-cost markets, such as developing economies.

7.3 PROBLEMS FACING MULTINATIONALS

In the vast majority of cases, businesses go multinational for sound business and economic reasons, which we have outlined above. However, multinational corporations may face a number of problems resulting from their geographical expansion:

- *Language barriers*. The problem of working in different languages is a barrier that the MNC must overcome. However, the language barrier is less of a difficulty for (say) UK MNCs in many developed nations than it is in the developing markets of, for example, Africa or Latin America, where local people are less familiar with English. Further, if a UK MNC tends to employ expatriates, communication will be more difficult and local staff may feel alienated and thus be less productive.

- *Selling and marketing in foreign markets*. Strategies that work at home might fail overseas, given wide social and cultural differences. Many US multinationals, such as McDonald's and Coca-Cola, are frequently accused of imposing American values in the design and promotion of their products, irrespective of the country and its culture. This can lead to resentment and hostility in the host country, which may ultimately backfire on the MNC.

- *Attitudes of host governments*. Governments will often try to get the best possible deal for their country from multinationals. This could result in governments insisting on part ownership in the subsidiary (either by themselves or by domestic firms), or tight rules and regulations governing the MNC's behaviour, or harsh tax regimes. In response, the MNC can always threaten to locate elsewhere.

- *Communication and coordination between subsidiaries*. Diseconomies of scale may result from an expanding global business. Lines of communication become longer and more complex, especially when language is an issue. These problems are likely to be greater, the greater is the attempted level of control exerted by the parent company, i.e. the more the parent company attempts to conduct business as though the subsidiaries were regional branches. Multinational organisational structures where international subsidiaries operate largely independently of the parent company will tend to minimise such problems.

Within any global strategy there will be a degree of economic and political risk. However, as MNCs look to invest more in developing economies or emerging markets such as China, this risk will increase, as there are more and more uncertainties. However, it is often within emerging markets that the greatest returns are achieved. It is essentially this trade-off between potential returns and risk that a firm needs to consider in its strategic decisions (see Box 7.4).

A global business will need a strategy for effectively embracing foreign cultures and traditions in its working practices, and for devising an efficient global supply chain. Some businesses may be more suited to deal with such global issues than others.

The global strategy trade-off

A firm's drive to reduce costs and enhance profitability by embracing a global strategy is tempered by one critical consideration – the need to meet the very different demands of customers in foreign markets. To minimise costs, a firm may seek to standardise its product and its operations throughout the world. However, to meet foreign buyers' needs and respond to local market conditions, a firm may be required to differentiate both its product and its operations, such as marketing. In such cases, customisation will *add* to costs and generate a degree of duplication within the business. If a business is required to respond to local market conditions in many different markets, it might be faced with significantly higher costs. But if it fails to take into account the uniqueness of the market in which it wishes to sell, it may lose market share.

The trade-off between the cost reduction and local responsiveness can be a key strategic consideration for a firm to take into account when selling or producing overseas. As a general rule we will tend to find that cost pressures will be greatest in those markets where price is the principal competitive weapon. Where product differentiation is high, and attributes such as quality or some other non-price factor predominates within the competitive process, local responsiveness will tend to shape business thinking. In other words, cost considerations will tend to be secondary.

Recap

1. Although becoming an MNC is largely advantageous to the business, it can experience problems with language barriers, selling and marketing in foreign markets, attitudes of the host state and the communication and coordination of global business activities.

2. An MNC will often find a trade-off between producing a standardised product in order to cut costs and producing a customised product in order to take account of local demand conditions.

MULTINATIONALS AND THE HOST STATE   7.4

FDI is more likely to occur if a nation has buoyant economic growth, large market size, high disposable income, an appropriate demographic mix, low inflation, low taxation, few restrictive regulations on business, a good transport network, an excellent education system, a significant research culture, etc. In highly competitive global markets, such factors may make the difference between success and failure.

Advantages

Host governments are always on the look-out to attract foreign direct investment, and are prepared to put up considerable finance and make significant concessions, such as tax breaks, to attract overseas business. So what benefits do MNCs bring to the economy?

Riding the dragon

'China is amazing. It *is* capitalism, but at an unprecedented speed.' 'The talent of Chinese software engineers is unbelievable. I can't believe how effective they are.' (Bill Gates, Chairman, Microsoft)

'If your business isn't making money in China, it probably wouldn't make money anywhere else.' (Carlos Ghosn, President, Nissan Motor Company)[1]

On the basis of several indicators, China's economic performance is extraordinary. From 1992 to 2010 annual economic growth averaged just over 10 per cent. The quantity as its exports grew by an average of 17 per cent (in real terms) (see chart(a)). In 2004 it overtook Japan to become the world's third largest exporter (after Germany and the USA). In 2010, it overtook Germany to become the world's largest exporter. In terms of the domestic purchasing power of its national income, China is the world's second biggest economy after the USA, or third if the eurozone is taken as a single economy.

And as the economy and exports have boomed, so foreign investment has flooded into the country. In 1990 foreign direct investment (FDI) into China was $3.6 billion. By 2008 the figure had risen to over $100 billion (in 2005 prices) (see chart (b)).

China's attraction for foreign investors

But why are foreign investors attracted to China? Is it simply that the economy is growing rapidly? Clearly that is part of the attraction, but it is more than that.

---

[1] 'Is China a goldmine or minefield?', *BBC News Online*, 19 February 2004 (http://news.bbc.co.uk/1/hi/business/3494069.stm)

For a start, the Chinese economy is huge. With a population of 1.3 billion and a GDP of $4.8 trillion in 2009, China represents a massive potential market. The government has also invested heavily in improving the country's transport, power and communications infrastructure.

What is more, much of the growth in income in the Chinese economy is concentrated in the hands of the middle classes, which now constitutes 20 per cent of the population and 50 per cent of the urban population. According to the Chinese Academy of Social Sciences, the middle class constitutes households with assets between $18 000 and $36 000. The demand for consumer goods by these middle-class Chinese is very income elastic. As a result, sales of electrical goods, furniture, cars and fashion clothing are growing rapidly. Not only foreign manufacturers, but foreign retailers too are taking advantage of this (see Box 7.3).

But it is not just the growing domestic Chinese market that attracts foreign investors. They are also attracted by the opportunity to manufacture products at low cost for export. Some 58 per cent of Chinese exports are shipped by non-Chinese firms. And it is not just the simple assembly lines and garment factories producing cheap clothes and toys with very low-wage labour.

China has moved up the 'value chain' and become a land of two economies. The sweatshops are still there, giving employment to millions of desperately poor migrant workers. But more and more companies become cutting edge and leapfrog foreign rivals. Whether games consoles, DVD recorders or flat-screen monitors, Chinese factories are grabbing high-tech market share.

(a) Growth in Chinese and world exports (% per annum)

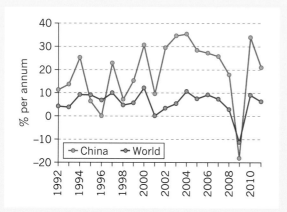

Source: Various (figures for 2011 base on forecasts)

(b) Foreign direct investment inflows into China (in 2005 prices)

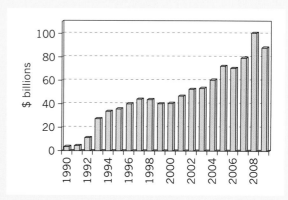

Source: based on data in *FDI online* (UNCTAD)

'Ten years ago, China was about low cost,' says Infineon's Ulrich Schumacher. 'Now it is at the forefront of technical development. Infineon can develop twice as fast in China than anywhere else.'

'Engineers are working in three shifts, seven days a week,' enthuses Mr Schumacher. 'In Germany that would not be possible, there engineers don't work on weekends.'

Bill Gates is similarly impressed after his latest visit to Microsoft's research lab in Beijing, one of four in China and Hong Kong. 'The talent of the people there is unbelievable, I can't believe how effective they are,' he says.

All this is worrying news for high-tech workers in industrialised countries, who hoped their skills would give them a competitive advantage in the globalised economy.[2]

Problems for foreign companies

In 2001, China joined the World Trade Organisation (WTO). Many hoped that this would see the rapid dismantling of trade barriers and a wholesale deregulation of the economy. But things are turning out differently.

China has attracted $622.4 billion (£340 billion) in foreign investment since 1978 – more than half of it since it joined the World Trade Organisation in late 2001. But now, with its economy growing at more than 10 per cent a year, China is becoming more selective in the investment it approves. Although greenfield factories that provide jobs are still nodded through, investments in existing businesses are coming under increasing scrutiny for fear that Western managers will strip assets and cut staff.[3]

Since 2006, a series of regulations had been imposed on certain kinds of foreign investment into China, including rules that required the Ministry of Commerce to approve all deals involving national or economic security and the naming of seven sectors by the government over which it would retain 'absolute control'. However, the lack of clarity of the new legislation proved problematic for foreign businessmen.

One British businessman, who declined to be identified, cited the vagueness of China's definition of these sectors as a big hindrance. He said: 'The two letters IT embrace everything. There is a sense that liberalisation is going nowhere – and

maybe even backwards. You never know when a new policy is going to be handed down.'[4]

However, at the time, Chinese officials insisted 'that the new raft of regulations do not reflect the closing of China's doors to foreign investment rather a desire to attract the technology needed for modernisation instead of a readiness to approve any deal'.[5] Rules were in place in the retail industry that limited the number of outlets allowed within a certain geographic area, but as we have already seen, some of these restrictions have been lifted.

On 13 April 2010, new guidelines for foreign investment in China were released by China's State Council, including: 1) Foreign investment more welcomed in foreign sectors; 2) New policies with geographic focus; 3) More open domestic capital markets; and 4) Improved and streamlined operational incentives.

These new guidelines . . . encourage foreign funds to flow into high-end manufacturing, hi-tech and eco-friendly sectors and to the Central and Western areas of the nation. The guidelines restrict investment into environmentally unsound projects and in sectors suffering from overcapacity.

Multi-national companies will be encouraged to establish regional headquarters, R&D centers, financial management centers and other critical management and operational centers in China.

The approval procedures for foreign investment will be streamlined and the scope of approval and authorisation will be reduced.

Through these new guidelines, China reiterates its support for foreign investment and this could be a response to some complaints that China was reversing its foreign investment policies . . . These guidelines widen market access to foreign investors and better direct the inflow of foreign capital while also improving China's global competitiveness and promoting more efficient foreign investment into economically vital areas.[6]

1. *In what ways might a booming Chinese economy benefit the rest of the world?*
2. *Why might multinational companies be cautious about investing in China?*

[2] *Ibid.*
[3] Macartney, Jane 'New protectionism puts obstacles in the path of foreign investors', *The Times*, 12 February 2007. (Macartney, J.), NI Syndication Limited © The Times/The Sun/nisyndication.com

[4] *Ibid.*
[5] *Ibid.*
[6] Xu Ping, 'China reaffirms support for foreign investment', King & Wood, PRC Lawyers, 19 April 2010

Employment

If MNC investment is in new plant (as opposed to taking over an existing company) this will generate employment. Most countries attempt to entice MNCs to depressed regions where investment is low and unemployment is high. Often these will be regions where a major industry has closed (e.g. the coal mining regions of South Wales). The employment that MNCs create is both direct, in the form of people employed in the new production facility, and indirect, through the impact that the MNC has on the local economy. This might be the consequence of establishing a new supply network, or simply the result of the increase in local incomes and expenditure, and hence the stimulus to local business.

> **Pause for thought**
>
> *Why might the size of these regional 'knock-on effects' of inward investment be difficult to estimate?*

The Welsh Affairs Committee[1] reports that inward investment in Wales over the period 1997 to 2004 created more than 30 000 new jobs and safeguarded 20 000 others in supporting businesses. Total inward FDI over that period was £3 billion.

It is possible, however, that jobs created in one region of a country by a new MNC venture, with its superior technology and working practices, might cause a business to fold elsewhere, thus leading to increased unemployment in that region.

The balance of payments

A country's balance of payments is likely to improve on a number of counts as a result of inward MNC investment (we look at the balance of payments in detail in section 13.1). First, the investment will represent a direct flow of capital into the country. Second, and perhaps more importantly (especially in the long term), MNC investment is likely to result in both **import substitution** and export promotion. Import substitution will occur as products, previously purchased as imports, are now produced domestically. Export promotion will be enhanced as many multinationals use their new production facilities as export platforms. For example, many Japanese MNCs invest in the UK in order to gain access to the European Union.

> **Definitions**
>
> **Import substitution**
> The replacement of imports by domestically produced goods or services.
>
> **Technology transfer**
> Where a host state benefits from the new technology that an MNC brings with its investment.

The beneficial effect on the balance of payments, however, will be offset to the extent that profits earned from the investment are repatriated to the parent country, and to the extent that the exports of the MNC displace the exports of domestic producers.

In the UK it is estimated that around half of all output produced by overseas-owned manufacturers is exported, and that the net effect of inward investment represents a positive contribution to the UK balance of payments of about £1 billion a year.

Technology transfer

Technology transfer refers to the benefits gained by domestic producers from the technology imported by the MNC. Such benefits can occur in a number of ways. The most common is where domestic producers copy the production technology and working practices of the MNC. This is referred to as the 'demonstration effect' and has occurred widely in the UK, as British businesses have attempted to emulate many of the practices brought into the country by Japanese multinationals.

---

[1] 'Manufacturing and trade in Wales and Public Services Ombudsman (Wales) Bill: Government responses to the Committee's second and third reports of session 2004–5 First Special Report of Session 2005–6' House of Commons, Welsh Affairs Committee (TSO, July 2005)

In addition to copying best practice, technology might also be transferred through the training of workers. When workers move jobs from the MNC to other firms in the industry, or to other industrial sectors, they take their newly acquired technical knowledge and skills with them.

Taxation

MNCs, like domestic producers, are required to pay tax and therefore contribute to public finances. Given the highly profitable nature of many MNCs, the level of tax revenue raised from this source could be highly significant.

Disadvantages

Thus far we have focused on the positive effects resulting from multinational investment. However, multinational investment may not always be beneficial in either the short or the long term.

Uncertainty. MNCs are often 'footloose', meaning that they can simply close down their operations in foreign countries and move if opportunities present themselves elsewhere. This is especially likely with older plants which would need updating if the MNC were to remain, or with plants that can be easily sold without too much loss. Also, during the maturity and decline stage of the product life cycle, cost-cutting may be essential and the MNC may move production to even lower cost countries. The ability to close down its business operations and shift production, while being a distinct economic advantage to the MNC, is a prime concern facing the host nation. If a country has a large foreign multinational sector within the economy, it will become very vulnerable to such footloose activity, and face great uncertainty in the long term. It may thus be forced to offer the multinational 'perks' (e.g. grants, special tax relief or specific facilities) in order to persuade it to remain. These perks are clearly costly to the taxpayer.

Control. The fact that an MNC can shift production locations not only gives it economic flexibility, but enables it to exert various controls over the host country. This is particularly so in many developing countries, where MNCs are not only major employers but in many cases the principal wealth creators. Thus attempts by the host state, for example, to improve worker safety or impose pollution controls may be against what the MNC sees as its own best interests. It might thus oppose such measures or even threaten to withdraw from the country if such measures are not modified or dropped. The host nation is in a very weak position.

Transfer pricing. MNCs, like domestic producers, are always attempting to reduce their tax liabilities. One unique way that an MNC can do this is through a process known as **transfer pricing**, which refers to the price a business charges itself for transferring partly finished products from one division of the company to another. By manipulating this internal pricing system, the MNC can reduce its profits in countries with high rates of profit tax, and increase them in countries with low rates of profit tax.

For example, take a vertically integrated MNC where subsidiary A in one country supplies components to subsidiary B in another. The price at which the components are transferred between the two subsidiaries (the 'transfer price') will ultimately determine the costs and hence the levels of profit made in each country. Assume that in the country where subsidiary A is located, the level of corporation tax (the tax on company profits) is half that of the country where subsidiary B is located. If

> **Definition**
>
> **Transfer pricing**
> The pricing system used within a business to transfer intermediate products between its various divisions, often in different countries.

components are transferred from A to B at very high prices, then B's costs will rise and its profitability will fall. Conversely, A's profitability will rise. The MNC clearly benefits as more profit is taxed at the lower rather than the higher rate. Had it been the other way around, with subsidiary B facing the lower rate of tax, then the components would be transferred at a low price. This would increase subsidiary B's profits and reduce A's.

The practice of transfer pricing was most starkly revealed in the *Guardian* newspaper in February 2009. Citing a paper that examined the flows of goods priced from US subsidiaries in Africa back to the USA, it stated that 'the public may be horrified to learn that companies have priced flash bulbs at $321.90 each, pillow cases at $909.29 each and a ton of sand at $1993.67, when the average world trade price was 66 cents, 62 cents and $11.20 respectively'.[2]

> **Pause for thought**
>
> 1. What problems is a developing country likely to experience if it adopts a policy of restricting, or even preventing, access to its markets by multinational business?
> 2. To what extent is the relationship between host state and multinational a principal–agent one? What problems arise specifically from this relationship?

The environment. Many MNCs are accused of simply investing in countries to gain access to natural resources, which are subsequently extracted or used in a way that is not sensitive to the environment. Host nations, especially developing countries that are keen for investment, are frequently prepared to allow MNCs to do this. They often put more store on the short-run gains from the MNC's presence than on the long-run depletion of precious natural resources or damage to the environment. Governments, like many businesses, often have a very short-run focus; they are concerned more with their political survival (whether through the ballot box or through military force) than with the long-term interests of their people.

> **Recap**
>
> 1. Host states find multinational investment advantageous in respect to employment creation, contributions to the balance of payments, the transfer of technology and the contribution to taxation.
> 2. They find it disadvantageous, however, in so far as it creates uncertainty; foreign business can control or manipulate the country or regions within it; tax payments can be avoided by transfer pricing; and MNCs might misuse the environment.

---

[2] 'Shifting profits across borders', *Guardian*, 12 February 2009. Available at www.guardian.co.uk/commentisfree/2009/feb/11/taxavoidance-tax

QUESTIONS

1. Using the UNCTAD FDI database in the statistics section of the UNCTAD website at (www.unctad. org), find out what has happened to FDI flows over the past five years (a) worldwide; (b) to and from developed countries; (c) to and from developing countries; (d) to and from the UK. Explain any patterns that emerge.

2. What are the advantages and disadvantages to an economy, such as the UK, of having a large multinational sector?

3. How might the structure of a multinational differ depending on whether its objective of being multinational is to reduce costs or to grow?

4. Choose a multinational company and then, by using its website, assess its global strategy.

5. How might a business's strategy in the domestic and global economy be affected by the onset of recession?

6. If reducing costs is so important for many multinationals, why is it that they tend to locate production not in low-cost developing economies, but in economies within the developed world?

7. 'Going global, thinking local.' Explain this phrase, and identify the potential conflicts for a business in behaving in this way.

8. Explain the link between the life cycle of a product and multinational business.

9. Assess the advantages and disadvantages facing a host state when receiving MNC investment.

Business issues covered in this chapter

- How has the UK labour market changed over the years?
- How are wage rates determined in a perfect labour market?
- What are the determinants of the demand and supply of labour and their respective elasticities?
- What forms of market power exist in the labour market and what determines the power of employers and labour?
- What effects do powerful employers and trade unions have on wages and employment?
- How has the minimum wage affected business and employment?
- What is meant by a 'flexible' labour market and how has increased flexibility affected working practices, employment and wages?
- How will various incentives affect the motivation and productivity of workers?
- Should senior executives be given large bonuses and stock options?

Labour and employment

In this chapter we consider how labour markets affect business. In particular, we will focus on the determination of wage rates in different types of market: ones where employers are wage takers, ones where they can choose the wage rate, and ones where wage rates are determined by a process of collective bargaining.

We start by examining some of the key trends in the structure of the labour market.

8.1 THE UK LABOUR MARKET

The labour market has undergone great change in recent years. Advances in technology, changes in the pattern of output, a need to be competitive in international markets and various social changes have all contributed to changes in work practices and in the structure and composition of the workforce.

Major changes in the UK include the following:

- *A shift from agricultural and manufacturing to service-sector employment.* Figure 8.1 reveals that employment in agriculture has been falling over a long historical period. The fall in manufacturing employment, however, has been more recent, starting in the 1960s and gathering pace through the 1970s, 1980s and 1990s. By contrast, employment in the service industries has grown steadily since 1946. In fact since 1979, it has expanded by over 7 million jobs.
- *A rise in part-time employment.* In 1971, 17 per cent of those in employment worked part time; by 2010 this had risen to 27 per cent. In the EU as a whole, the figure was 19 per cent. The growth in part-time work reflects the growth in the service sector, where many jobs are part time. Since 1979 part-time employment has risen by over 2.6 million.
- *A rise in female participation rates.* Women now constitute approximately half of the paid labour force. The rise in participation rates is strongly associated with the growth in the service sector, the creation of part-time positions and changes in family structure. Some 43 per cent of females in employment, about 5.8 million, work part time.
- *A rise in the proportion of workers employed on fixed-term contracts, or on a temporary or casual basis.* Many firms nowadays prefer to employ only their core workers/managers on a permanent ('continuing') basis. They feel that it gives them more flexibility to respond to changing market conditions to have the remainder of their workers employed on a short-term basis and, perhaps, to make use of agency staff or to contract out work.
- *Downsizing.* It has become very fashionable in recent years for companies to try to 'trim' the numbers of their employees in order to reduce costs. There is now, however, a growing consensus that the process may have gone too far. The cost of reducing its

Definition

Downsizing
Where a business reorganises and reduces its size, especially in respect to levels of employment, in order to cut costs.

| Figure 8.1 | Employment in different sectors of the UK economy |

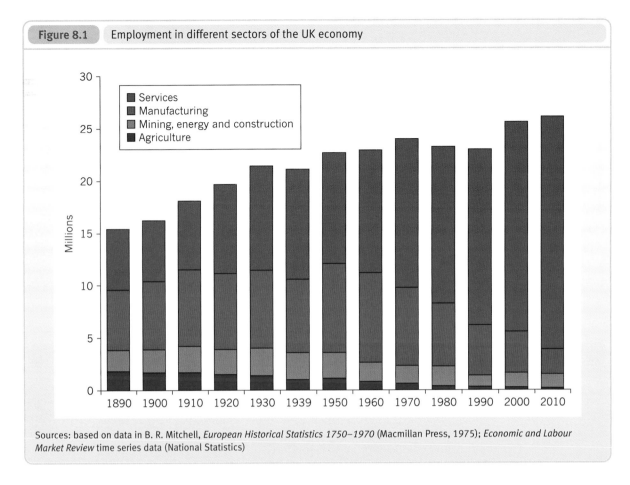

Sources: based on data in B. R. Mitchell, *European Historical Statistics 1750–1970* (Macmillan Press, 1975); *Economic and Labour Market Review* time series data (National Statistics)

workforce may be that a company loses revenue; if it cuts back on people employed to market its products, develop new products or ensure that quality is maintained, then it is likely to lose market share. It might reduce unit costs, but total profits could nevertheless fall, not rise.

8.2 MARKET-DETERMINED WAGE RATES AND EMPLOYMENT

Perfect labour markets

When looking at the market for labour, it is useful to make a similar distinction to that made in the market for goods and services: the distinction between perfect and imperfect markets. Although in practice few labour markets are totally perfect, many do at least approximate to it.

The key assumption of a perfect labour market is that everyone is a **wage taker**. In other words, neither employers nor employees have any economic power to affect wage rates. This situation is not uncommon. Small employers are likely to have to pay the 'going wage rate' to their employees, especially where the employee is of a clear category, such as an electrician, a bar worker, a secretary or a porter. As far as employees are concerned, being a wage taker means not being a member of a union and therefore not being able to use collective bargaining to push up the wage rate.

Definition

Wage taker
The wage rate is determined by market forces.

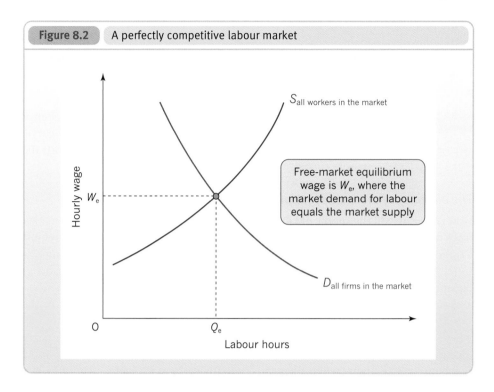

Figure 8.2   A perfectly competitive labour market

$S_{\text{all workers in the market}}$

Free-market equilibrium wage is W_e, where the market demand for labour equals the market supply

W_e

$D_{\text{all firms in the market}}$

Hourly wage

O Q_e

Labour hours

We assume also that there is perfect knowledge on the part of workers and employers and that there are no barriers that prevent the movement of labour. Therefore, workers are aware of available jobs and can move to new jobs and different parts of the country in response to higher wages or better working conditions etc. Finally, it is normally assumed that workers of a given category are identical in terms of productivity.

Wage rates and employment under perfect competition are determined by the interaction of the market demand and supply of labour. This is illustrated in Figure 8.2. The curves show the total number of hours workers would supply and the number of hours of labour firms would demand for each wage rate in a particular labour market. The equilibrium market wage rate is W_e, where demand equals supply. Equilibrium employment in terms of the total number of hours people are employed in the market is Q_e.

Generally it would be expected that the supply and demand curves slope the same way as in goods markets. The higher the wage paid for a certain type of job, the more workers will want to do that job. This gives an upward-sloping supply curve of labour. On the other hand, the higher the wage that employers have to pay, the less labour they will want to employ. Either they will simply produce less output, or they will substitute other factors of production, like machinery, for labour. Thus the demand curve for labour slopes downwards.

We now turn to look at the supply and demand for labour in more detail.

The supply of labour

As we have seen, the supply of labour curve will typically be upward sloping. The *position* of the market supply curve of labour will depend on the number of people willing and able to do the job at each given wage rate. This depends on three things:

- the number of qualified people;
- the non-wage benefits or costs of the job, such as the pleasantness or otherwise of the working environment, job satisfaction or dissatisfaction, status, power, the degree of job security, holidays, perks and other fringe benefits;
- the wages and non-wage benefits in alternative jobs.

> **Pause for thought**
>
> *Which way will the supply curve shift if the wage rates in alternative jobs rise?*

The wage rate is measured on the vertical axis, so a change in this variable will cause a movement along the supply curve. A change in any of these other three determinants will shift the whole curve.

The elasticity of the market supply of labour

How *responsive* will the supply of labour be to a change in the wage rate? If the market wage rate goes up, will a lot more labour become available or only a little? It's not just a question of workers being *willing* to work, but also about them actually being *able* to increase the supply of labour at the higher wage. This responsiveness (elasticity) depends on (a) the difficulties and costs of changing jobs and (b) the time period.

> **Definition**
>
> **Mobility of labour**
> The ease with which labour can either shift between jobs (occupational mobility) or move to other parts of the country in search of work (geographical mobility).

Another way of looking at the elasticity of supply of labour is in terms of the mobility of labour: the willingness and ability of labour to move to another job, whether in a different location (geographical mobility) or in a different industry (occupational mobility). The mobility of labour (and hence the elasticity of supply of labour) will be higher when there are alternative jobs in the same location, when alternative jobs require similar skills and when people have good information about these jobs.

It is also much higher in the long run, when people have the time to acquire new skills and when the education system has had time to adapt to the changing demands of industry.

The demand for labour: the marginal productivity theory

> **Pause for thought**
>
> *What effect has the entry of 10 member states to the EU in 2004 and a further two in 2007, including several from Eastern Europe, had on the position and elasticity of the supply curve of various types of labour?*

The market demand curve for labour will typically be downward sloping. To see why, let us examine the behaviour of a profit-maximising firm.

The profit-maximising approach

How many workers will a profit-maximising firm want to employ? The firm will answer this question by weighing up the costs of employing extra labour against the benefits. It will use exactly the same principles as in deciding how much output to produce.

In the goods market, the firm will maximise profits where the marginal cost of an extra unit of *goods* produced equals the marginal revenue from selling it: $MC = MR$.

In the labour market, the firm will maximise profits where the marginal cost of employing an extra *worker* equals the marginal revenue that the worker's output earns for the firm: MC of labour $= MR$ of labour. To understand this, consider what would happen if they were not equal. If an extra worker adds more to a firm's revenue than to its costs, the firm's profits will increase. It will be worth employing that worker. But as more workers are employed, diminishing returns to labour will set in (see page 88). Each extra worker will produce less than the previous one, and thus earn less revenue for the firm. Eventually the marginal revenue from extra workers will fall to the level of their marginal cost. At that point the firm will stop employing extra workers. There are no additional profits to be gained. Profits are at a maximum.

BOX 8.1 'TELECOMMUTERS'

The electronic cottage

The increasing sophistication of information technology, with direct computer linking, broadband access to the Internet, fax machines and mobile phones, has meant that many people can work at home. The number of these 'telecommuters' has grown steadily since the information technology revolution of the early 1980s. Some 16 per cent of US workers telecommute all or part of the time.

It has been found that where 'telecommuting networks' have been established, gains in productivity levels have been significant when compared with comparable office workers. Most studies indicate rises in productivity of over 35 per cent. With fewer interruptions and less chatting with fellow workers, less working time is lost. Add to this the stress-free environment, free from the strain of commuting, and the individual worker's performance is enhanced.

With further savings in time, in the renting and maintenance of offices (often in high-cost inner city locations) and in heating and lighting costs, the economic arguments in favour of telecommuting seem very persuasive. What is more, concerns that managers lose control over their employees, and that the quality of work falls, appear unfounded. In fact the reverse seems to have occurred: the quality of work in many cases has improved.

These technological developments have been the equivalent of an increase in labour mobility. Work can be taken to the workers rather than the workers coming to the work. The effect is to reduce the premium that needs to be paid to workers in commercial centres, such as the City of London.

Then there are the broader gains to society. Telecommuting opens up the labour market to a wider group of workers who might find it difficult to leave the home – groups such as single parents and the disabled. This not only improves efficiency, as a better use is made of the full labour force, but enhances equity as well. Also there are environmental gains, as fewer journeys to work mean less traffic congestion and less pollution.

But do people working from home feel isolated? For many people, work is an important part of their social environment, providing them with an opportunity to meet others and to work as a team. For those who are unable to leave the home, however, telecommuting may be the *only* means of earning a living: the choice of travelling to work may simply not be open to them.

However, telecommuters can be exploited. The Low Pay Commission has found that many homeworkers are paid well below the minimum wage because employers pay by the amount of work done and underestimate the amount of time it takes to complete work.

International telecommuting

There is no reason, of course, why telecommuters cannot work in different countries. With the creation of transoceanic fibre optical cable networks, international data transmission has become both faster and cheaper. Increasingly, therefore, companies in developed countries are employing relatively low-wage workers in the developing world to do data processing, telesales and various 'back-office' work – work that is often highly skilled. More than 500 multinational companies employ IT workers in Bangalore alone.

Some of the international teleworkers work in call centres; others work from their own homes. Increasingly telecommuters in India are being provided with computers and broadband connection to enable them to do so.

> Call-centres of tomorrow will not be the ones operating from under a single roof. Instead, it will be a network of customer service agents (CSAs) working from their own homes miles away from each other . . . With all the push that the [Indian] government is giving to increase broadband penetration, this concept will trigger a revolution in the way call-centres of today operate.[1]

International telecommuting can be closer to home. Growing numbers of UK workers have moved to France or Spain, where property is much cheaper and, thanks to broadband, they can carry on their UK jobs from there. When they do have to come into the office, cheap travel by budget airline makes that possible.

1. *What effect is telecommuting likely to have on (a) trade union membership; (b) trade union power?*
2. *How are the developments referred to in this box likely to affect relative house prices between capital cities and the regions?*

---

[1] 'Telecommuting: the work-from-home option', DQChannels of India (www.dqchannels.com/content/mirror/105021801.asp)

Measuring the marginal cost and revenue of labour

Marginal cost of labour (MC_L). This is the extra cost of employing one more worker. Under perfect competition the firm is too small to affect the market wage. It faces a horizontal supply curve. In other words, it can employ as many workers as it

Definition

Marginal revenue product of labour

The extra revenue a firm earns from employing one more unit of labour.

chooses at the market wage rate. Thus the additional cost of employing one more person will simply be the wage rate: $MC_L = W$.

Marginal revenue of labour (MRP_L). The marginal revenue that the firm gains from employing one more worker is called the **marginal revenue product of labour** (MRP_L). The MRP_L is found by multiplying two elements – the *marginal physical product* of labour (MPP_L) and the marginal revenue gained by selling one more unit of output (*MR*):

$$MRP_L = MPP_L \times MR$$

The MPP_L is the extra output produced by the last worker. Thus if the last worker produces 100 tonnes of output per week (MPP_L), and if the firm can sell each unit for £2 (*MR*), then the worker's *MRP* is £200. This extra worker is adding £200 to the firm's revenue.

The profit-maximising level of employment for a firm

The MRP_L curve is illustrated in Figure 8.3. As more workers are employed, there will come a point when diminishing returns set in (point *x*). Thereafter the MRP_L curve slopes downwards. The figure also shows the MC_L 'curve' at the current market wage W_e. Every worker is paid an identical wage and so the curve is horizontal, showing that the cost of employing each extra worker (MC_L) is the same, whether it is the 50th or the 500th worker.

Profits are maximised at an employment level of Q_e, where MC_L (i.e. *W*) = MRP_L. Why? At levels of employment below Q_e, MRP_L exceeds MC_L. The firm will increase profits by employing more labour. At levels of employment above Q_e, MC_L exceeds MRP_L. In this case the firm will increase profits by reducing employment.

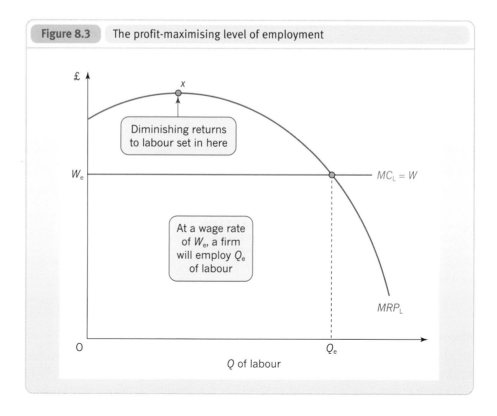

Figure 8.3 The profit-maximising level of employment

Derivation of the firm's demand curve for labour

No matter what the wage rate is, if a firm is a profit-maximising employer of labour, the quantity of labour demanded will be found from the intersection of W (MC_L) and MRP_L (see Figure 8.4). At a wage rate of W_1, Q_1 labour is demanded (point a); at W_2, Q_2 is demanded (point b); at W_3, Q_3 is demanded (point c).

Thus the MRP_L curve shows the quantity of labour employed at each wage rate. But this is just what the demand curve for labour shows. Thus the MRP_L curve is the demand curve for labour.

There are three determinants of the demand for labour:

- *The wage rate*. This determines the position *on* the demand curve. (Strictly speaking, we would refer here to the wage determining the 'quantity demanded' rather than the 'demand'.)
- *The productivity of labour* (MPP_L). This determines the position *of* the demand curve.
- *The demand for the good*. The higher the market demand for the good, the higher will be its market price, and hence the higher will be the MR, and thus the MRP_L. This too determines the position of the demand curve. It shows how the demand for labour (and other factors) is a **derived demand**, i.e. one derived from the demand for the good. For example, the higher the demand for houses, and hence the higher their price, the higher will be the demand for bricklayers.

A change in the wage rate is represented by a movement *along* the demand curve for labour. A change in the productivity of labour or in the demand for the good *shifts* the curve.

Definition

Derived demand
The demand for a factor of production depends on the demand for the good that uses it.

Market demand and its elasticity

For the same reason that the firm's demand for labour is downward sloping, so the whole market demand for labour will be downward sloping. At higher wage rates,

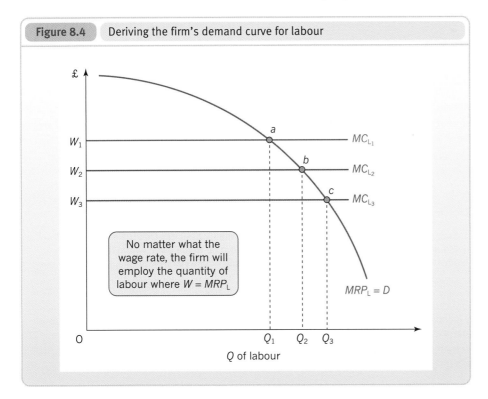

Figure 8.4 Deriving the firm's demand curve for labour

Pause for thought

If the productivity of a group of workers rises by 10 per cent, will the wage rate they are paid also rise by 10 per cent? Explain why or why not.

firms in total will employ less labour. The *elasticity* of this market demand for labour (with respect to changes in the wage rate) depends on various factors. Elasticity will be greater:

The greater the price elasticity of demand for the good. A rise in the wage rate, being a cost of production, will drive up the price of the good. If the market demand for the good is elastic, this rise in price will lead to a lot less being sold and hence a lot fewer people being employed.

The easier it is to substitute labour for other inputs and vice versa. If labour can be readily replaced by other inputs (e.g. machinery), then a rise in the wage rate will lead to a large reduction in labour as workers are replaced by these other inputs.

The greater the wage cost as a proportion of total costs. If wages are a large proportion of total costs and the wage rate rises, total costs will rise significantly; therefore production and sales will fall significantly, and so will the demand for labour.

The longer the time period. Given sufficient time, firms can respond to a rise in wage rates by reorganising their production processes. For example they could introduce robot production lines.

Wages and profits under perfect competition

The wage rate (W) is determined by the interaction of demand and supply in the labour market. This will be equal to the value of the output that the last person produces (MRP_L).

Profits to the individual firm will arise from the fact that the MRP_L curve slopes downward (diminishing returns). Thus the last worker adds less to the revenue of firms than previous workers already employed.

If *all* workers in the firm receive a wage equal to the *MRP* of the *last* worker, everyone but the last worker will receive a wage *less* than their *MRP*. This excess of MRP_L over W of previous workers provides a surplus to the firm over its wages bill (see Figure 8.5). Part of this will be required for paying non-wage costs; part will be the profits for the firm.

Perfect competition between firms will ensure that profits are kept down to *normal* profits. If the surplus over wages is such that *supernormal* profits are made, new firms will enter the industry. As supply rises, the price of the good (and hence MRP_L) will fall, and as these new firms demand more labour, the wage will be bid up, until only normal profits remain.

Recap

1. Wages in a competitive labour market are determined by the interaction of demand and supply. The market supply of labour in any labour market is likely to be upward sloping.

2. The elasticity of labour supply will depend largely upon the geographical and occupational mobility of labour. The more readily labour can transfer between jobs and regions, the more elastic the supply.

3. The demand for labour is traditionally assumed to be based upon labour's productivity. Marginal productivity theory assumes that the employer will demand labour up to the point where the cost of employing one additional worker (MC_L) is equal to the revenue earned from the output of that worker (MRP_L). The firm's demand curve for labour is its MRP_L curve.

4. The elasticity of demand for labour is determined by: the price elasticity of demand for the good that labour produces; the substitutability of labour for other factors; the proportion of wages to total costs; and time.

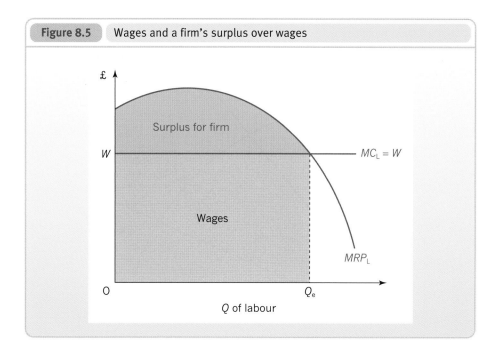

Figure 8.5   Wages and a firm's surplus over wages

POWER IN THE LABOUR MARKET

8.3

Firms with power

In the real world, many firms have the power to influence wage rates: they are not wage takers. This is one of the major types of labour market 'imperfection'.

When a firm is the only employer of a particular type of labour, this situation is called a **monopsony**. The Post Office used to be a monopsony employer of postal workers. Another example is when a factory is the only employer of certain types of labour in that district. It therefore has local monopsony power. When there are just a few employers, this is called **oligopsony**.

Monopsonists (and oligopsonists too) are 'wage setters', not 'wage takers'. Thus a large employer in a small town may have considerable power to resist wage increases or even to force wage rates down.

Such firms face an upward-sloping supply curve of labour. This is illustrated in Figure 8.6. If the firm wants to take on more labour, it will have to pay a higher wage rate to attract workers away from other industries. But conversely, by employing less labour it can get away with paying a lower wage rate.

The supply curve shows the wage that must be paid to attract a given quantity of labour. The wage it pays is the *average cost* to the firm of employing labour (AC_L): i.e. the cost per worker. The supply curve is also therefore the AC_L curve.

The *marginal* cost of employing one more worker (MC_L) will be above the wage (AC_L) (see Figure 8.6). The reason is that the wage rate has to be raised to attract extra workers. The MC_L will thus be the new higher wage paid to the new employee *plus* the small rise in the total wages bill for existing employees: after all, they will be paid the higher wage too.

The profit-maximising employment of labour would be at Q_1, where $MC_L = MRP_L$. The wage (found from the AC_L curve) would thus be W_1.

Definitions

Monopsony
A market with a single buyer or employer.

Oligopsony
A market with just a few buyers or employers.

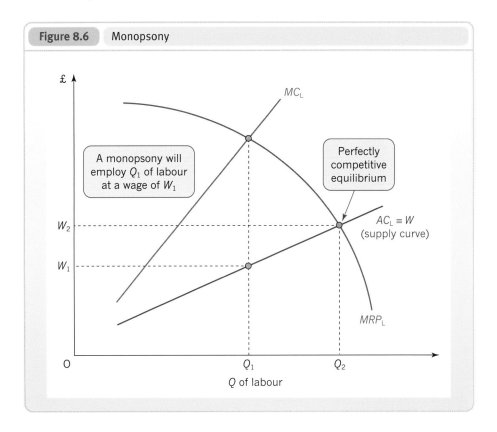

Figure 8.6   Monopsony

A monopsony will employ Q_1 of labour at a wage of W_1

Perfectly competitive equilibrium

$AC_L \equiv W$ (supply curve)

MC_L

MRP_L

O Q_1 Q_2

Q of labour

If this had been a perfectly competitive labour market, employment would have been at the higher level Q_2, with the wage rate at the higher level W_2, where $W = MRP_L$. What in effect the monopsonist is doing, therefore, is forcing the wage rate down by restricting the number of workers employed.

The role of trade unions

How can unions influence the determination of wages, and what might be the consequences of their actions?

The extent to which unions will succeed in pushing up wage rates depends on their power and militancy. It also depends on the power of firms to resist and on their ability to pay higher wages. In particular, the scope for unions to gain a better deal for their members depends on the sort of market in which the employers are producing.

Unions facing competitive employers

If the employers are producing in a highly competitive goods market, unions can raise wages only at the expense of employment. Firms are likely to be earning little more than normal profit. Thus if unions force up wages, the marginal firms will go bankrupt and leave the industry. Fewer workers will be employed. The fall in output will lead to higher prices. This will enable the remaining firms to pay a higher wage rate.

Figure 8.7 illustrates these effects. If unions force the wage rate up from W_1 to W_2, employment will fall from Q_1 to Q_2. There will be a surplus of people ($Q_3 - Q_2$) wishing to work in this industry for whom no jobs are available.

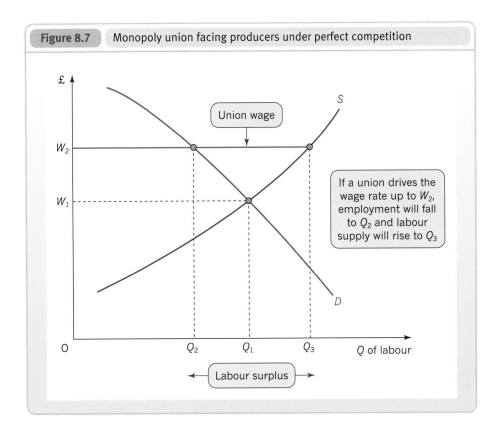

Figure 8.7 Monopoly union facing producers under perfect competition

The union is in a doubly weak position. Not only will jobs be lost as a result of forcing up the wage rate, but also there is a danger that these unemployed people could undercut the union wage, unless the union can prevent firms employing non-unionised labour.

In a competitive market, then, the union is faced with the choice between wages and jobs. Its actions will depend on its objectives.

Wages can be increased without a reduction in the level of employment only if, as part of the bargain, the productivity of labour is increased. This is called a **productivity deal**. The MRP curve, and hence the demand curve in Figure 8.7, shifts to the right.

> **Pause for thought**
>
> *At what wage rate in Figure 8.7 would employment be maximised: (a) W_1; (b) a wage rate above W_1; (c) a wage rate below W_1?*

Bilateral monopoly

What happens when a union monopoly faces a monopsony employer? What will the wage rate be? What will the level of employment be? Unfortunately, economic theory cannot give a precise answer to these questions. There is no 'equilibrium' level as such. Ultimately, the wage rate and level of employment will depend on the relative bargaining strengths and skills of unions and management.

Strange as it may seem, unions may be in a stronger position to make substantial gains for their members when they are facing a powerful employer. There is often considerable scope for them to increase wage rates *without* this leading to a reduction in employment, or even for them to increase both the wage rate *and* employment. The reason is that if firms have power in the *goods* market too, and are making supernormal profit, then there is scope for a powerful union to redistribute some of these profits as wages.

> **Definition**
>
> **Productivity deal**
> Where, in return for a wage increase, a union agrees to changes in working practices that will increase output per worker.

BOX 8.2   THE WINTER OF DISCONTENT

The Sequel?

In 1978/9, the UK economy almost ground to a halt when workers across the country went on strike. Miners, postal workers, binmen, grave diggers, healthcare ancillaries, train and bus drivers, gas and electricity workers, lorry drivers for companies such as BP and Esso and workers at Ford all went on strike; there were even unofficial strikes by ambulance drivers. Although this occurred over 30 years ago, it looked as though lightning was about to strike for the second time in 2009 as the world economy plummeted into a deep recession in the aftermath of the credit crunch.

> There are fears that Britain is entering months of industrial unrest, as bus drivers, binmen and firefighters follow the postal workers' lead and protest at changes to their pay, shift patterns and working conditions. British Airways and London Underground staff are also considering strike action over pay disputes.[1]

In the latter half of 2009 and early 2010, industrial action spread rapidly in the UK (and in other countries across the world). From bins to buses, and trains to planes, there was massive disruption, affecting everyone and reducing output at a time when it was the last thing the country needed.

Postal services

Throughout 2009, members of the Communication Workers Union (CWU) held intermittent one-day strikes, and in October 2009, a national strike went ahead. The confrontation was concerned with pay, working conditions, a pension deficit and the introduction of modern efficient technology, which the CWU expected to lead to job losses and office closures. With undelivered letters and packets rising to over 150 million, increased pressure was put on Royal Mail management to reach an agreement, especially as they faced legal action by the CWU when 30 000 temporary workers were brought in.

So, what were the effects? The most obvious was delayed post, which was particularly concerning with Christmas not far away. Greetings cards companies were worried that it would deter people from sending cards, and significantly affect profitability at their busiest time of year. Households also faced worrying times as bills and payments were delayed.

Other businesses were adversely affected as supplies failed to arrive, orders were delayed and customer service was restricted. Those trading on eBay had to hold back packages, as goods traded across the world were stuck in sorting offices. Businesses were forced to employ other delivery services, raising costs and reducing profits, and inevitably they lost customers, through no fault of their own. Research by the London Chamber of Commerce suggested that the week of postal strikes cost London more than £500 million in lost business. The Chief Executive of the organisation said:

Not being able to rely on a normal postal service forces companies to pay extra for couriers, delays consumer spending, damages client relationships and plays havoc with a firm's cash flow.[2]

But the news was not all bad, at least not for the Royal Mail's competitors, such as TNT, Fedex and DHL. During the first 24 hours of the strike, TNT handled an extra 16 000 items, as companies looked for a substitute delivery service. However, even TNT suffered delays, as many of the bank statements and bills which they sort are still delivered by the Royal Mail, which has a legal monopoly on the delivery of all mail valued under £1. The Chief Executive of TNT Post stated:

> There are regulatory barriers in the postal market which prevent TNT Post from providing a full end-to-end delivery of mail. The strikes show it is high time that these barriers are lifted in order for a real alternative service to Royal Mail's to be introduced.[3]

Airlines

While post failed to get from A to B, so did passengers, as talks with BA cabin crew over pay freezes, working practices and redundancies broke down. Strikes occurred over Christmas and then again in 2010, with those in March estimated to have cost BA £45 million.

The Spanish airline, Iberia, also experienced strikes over the renewal of contracts in 2009, which led it to cancel over 400 flights in two days, leaving thousands of passengers stranded and facing increased costs to get home, because of more expensive plane tickets and rearranged transport plans. Pilots from India's Jet Airways held a five-day strike during September 2009, and Germany's Lufthansa had to cancel thousands of flights in early 2010, when 4000 pilots went on strike. This action derived from fears that the airline would bring in foreign pilots at lower wages to ensure profitability, following Lufthansa's purchase of Austrian Airlines. Estimates suggest this cost the company some £21.9 million per day.

Airlines were severely hit by the recession, as holidays abroad became a luxury for cash-strapped consumers. Whilst many airlines had other problems as well, lower revenues and profits meant that cost savings were needed, and so staff had to be cut. BA lost over £400m in 2008, due to lower passenger numbers, and the resulting strike action imposed further costs.

> The financial impact of the recent strike not only includes lost revenue, but the cost of hiring in planes and crew, as well as buying seats on rival carriers.[4]

---

[1] Doward, Jamie and Wainright, Martin 'Postal strike hangover could hit Christmas' *Guardian*, 25 October 2009

[2] Sands, Tom 'Postal strike costs London £500m', *Pacrl2Go.com*, 26 October 2009

[3] 'How the postal strike might change Britain', *BBC News*, 27 October 2009

[4] BA strike: talks between airline and union resume, *BBC News*, 7 April 2010

The volcanic ash cloud from Iceland that grounded planes across northern Europe in April 2010 was a further blow to the airlines and cost them some £130m per day.

BA's problems were set to increase. A ballot of 12 000 members of the British Airlines Stewards and Stewardesses Association in April 2010 and a recommendation by the union, Unite, to reject BA's latest offer were likely to mean more strikes, further wage losses for the strikers and more disruption for everyone else.

Other problems

Over 800 drivers in Bolton, Bury and Wigan held numerous 24-hour strikes during 2009, because of disputes with First Bus over pay. At the same time, 1.5 million customers were affected when thousands of Underground workers went on strike. Once again, these strikes cost businesses, as staff struggled to get to work, meaning lost hours, and as shoppers had problems getting to London, meaning lost sales. Also, the growing possibility of a national rail strike was threatening to cost the economy a staggering £600m per day, according to the Federation of Small Businesses.

The National Union of Teachers has also threatened strike action over their working week and excessive workload. Head Teachers and Deputy Heads will be balloted as to whether 'Sats' in English and Maths for 11-year-olds should be boycotted. These problems follow strikes in 2008 by nearly half the schools in some areas, such as Waltham Forest, which affected exam preparation for thousands of students.

Fire fighters in Essex voted in favour of strikes in July 2009, in response to proposed job cuts on the frontline and in April 2010, for the first time in its 105-year history, workers at the AA voted for a national strike, over changes to its pension scheme.

A strike by refuse workers in Leeds continued for several weeks, after 92 per cent of workers refused the Council's offer relating to their working week and pay. This led to piles of rubbish lining the streets for months. Whilst there may not have been significant direct costs for businesses, although it is hardly an incentive for shoppers, the main cost was simply the fact that wherever you walked, there was rubbish. A resident commented:

> Why should we pay council tax and have to live like this? The smell is so disgusting you can't open your windows and there are flies and rats. You come out of the house to get to the car and a load of rats run out from under it. It was the same back in the late Seventies, and it does look as if history is repeating itself.[5]

In this case, 'external costs' were imposed on consumers and utility was adversely affected, not least because they were still paying council taxes for a service that was not occurring. We consider external costs in the next chapter.

The sequel?

The Winter of Discontent of 1978/9 saw massive labour stoppages across the country, and whilst the widespread industrial action in late 2009 did disrupt the lives of millions of people, the extent still did not compare with that of the late 1970s. However, with the government pledged to cut the huge public sector deficit, the sequel may still go ahead.

> Trade unions are already mobilising against the inevitable spending curbs. The RMT rail union is organising anti-cuts rallies over the May Day weekend in Belfast, London and the regions.
>
> Bob Crow said: 'Working men and women, and the public services they deliver, should not have to pick up a £50bn bill for the bankers bailout while the City spivs and the bankers are back on board the bonus gravy train. There is no question that there will be widespread industrial action and public resistance to the savage cuts that are being cooked up behind closed doors.
>
> The RMT is threatening a national rail strike after the election, unless agreement is reached in talks at the conciliation service, ACAS. Industrial action is also threatened on the London Underground over job losses.
>
> In the UK, we cannot afford to wait for the politicians to unleash a £50bn slash-and-burn attack on our public services, our jobs and our living standards after 6 May. We have to start the fight-back now and that means concerted action by trade unions to resist the all-out assault that we know is coming.'
>
> The Public and Commercial Services Union is threatening to re-launch strikes which began in March involving 200 000 civil servants after the action was suspended for the election. A spokesman said: 'If the cuts are anything like what is being suggested, industrial action by the unions is not only likely, it's inevitable.'[6]

In recent years, there has been growing recognition that employers and employees can learn from each other and with cooperation everyone can be made better off. However, negotiations across the UK have failed to resolve many issues, and estimates across all affected industries now paint a stark picture of the economic costs incurred by recent industrial action and possible action to come.

1. Are strikes the best course of action for workers? In the cases outlined above, would you have advised any other responses by either side?
2. Which strike do you think was the most costly to (a) consumers, (b) businesses and (c) the economy? Explain.
3. Why might strains on public finances lead to more industrial unrest in the future?

---

[5] Worthington, Debra 'We've bin here before', *The Sun*, 3 November 2009

[6] Grice, Andrew and Brown, Colin 'Bank of England Governor: poll winner will be out of power for a generation', *The Independent*, 30 April 2010

The actual wage rate under bilateral monopoly is usually determined through a process of negotiation or 'collective bargaining'. The outcome of this bargaining will depend on a wide range of factors, which vary substantially from one industry or firm to another.

Collective bargaining

Sometimes when unions and management negotiate, *both* sides can gain from the resulting agreement. For example, the introduction of new technology may allow higher wages, improved working conditions and higher profits. Usually, however, one side's gain is the other's loss. Higher wages mean lower profits. Either way, both sides will want to gain the maximum for themselves.

The outcome of the negotiations will depend on the relative bargaining strengths of both sides. In bargaining there are various threats or promises that either side can make. For these to be effective, of course, the other side must believe that they will be carried out.

Union *threats* might include strike action, **picketing**, **working to rule** or refusing to cooperate with management, for example in the introduction of new technology. Alternatively, in return for higher wages or better working conditions, unions might *offer* no-strike agreements (or an informal promise not to take industrial action), increased productivity, reductions in the workforce or long-term deals over pay.

In turn, employers might threaten employees with plant closure, **lock-outs**, redundancies or the employment of non-union labour. Or they might offer, in return for lower wage increases, various 'perks' such as productivity bonuses, profit-sharing schemes, better working conditions, more overtime, better holidays or security of employment.

Strikes, lock-outs and other forms of industrial action impose costs on both unions and firms. Unions lose pay. Firms lose revenue. This is an example of a 'prisoners' dilemma game' (see page 136). If played out, it will probably result in both sides losing. It is usually in both sides' interests, therefore, to settle by negotiation. Nevertheless, to gain the maximum advantage at the negotiations, each side must persuade the other that it will carry out its threats if pushed.

The approach described so far has essentially been one of confrontation. The alternative is for both sides to concentrate on increasing the total net income of the firm by cooperating on ways to increase efficiency or the quality of the product. This approach is more likely when unions and management have built up an atmosphere of trust over time.

Definitions

Picketing
Where people on strike gather at the entrance to the firm and attempt to dissuade workers or delivery vehicles from entering.

Working to rule
Workers do no more than they are supposed to, as set out in their job descriptions.

Lock-outs
Union members are temporarily laid off until they are prepared to agree to the firm's conditions.

Recap

1. In an imperfect labour market, where a business has monopoly power in employing labour, it is known as a monopsonist. Such a firm will employ workers to the point where $MRP_L = MC_L$. Since the wage is below the MC_L, the monopsonist, other things being equal, will employ fewer workers at a lower wage than would be employed in a perfectly competitive labour market.

2. If a union has monopoly power, its power to raise wages will be limited if the employer operates in a highly competitive goods market. A rise in wage rates will force the employer to cut back on employment, unless there is a corresponding rise in productivity.

3. In a situation of bilateral monopoly (where a monopoly union faces a monopsony employer), the union may have considerable scope to raise wages above the monopsony level, without the employer wishing to reduce the level of employment. There is no unique equilibrium wage. The wage will depend on the outcome of a process of collective bargaining between union and management.

MINIMUM WAGES

Many countries have a statutory minimum wage that businesses must pay, including the UK since 1999. In 2010/11 the UK minimum wage was £5.93 for those aged 21 and over, £4.92 for those between 18 and 20 and £3.64 for those aged 16 and 17. In the same year the 21 and over minimum wage was 52.6 per cent of the median and 40.3 per cent of the mean hourly wage rate. In 1999, the year that the minimum wage was introduced, it was 47.0 and 36.8 per cent of the median and mean respectively. It had peaked in 2007 at 54.0 and 41.3 per cent.

Many businesses argue that having to pay such wages erodes profit and hence leads to a reduction in employment, as they demand fewer workers. Supporters argue that not only does a minimum wage help to reduce poverty among the low paid, but also it has little or no adverse effects on unemployment. Some go further. They argue that it can actually *increase* employment. Let us analyse the effects.

Minimum wages in a competitive labour market

In a competitive labour market, workers will be hired up to the point where the marginal revenue product of labour (MRP_L), i.e. the demand for labour, is equal to the marginal cost of labour (MC_L), which gives the supply curve. Referring back to Figure 8.7 on page 219, the free-market equilibrium wage is W_1 in this particular industry and the level of employment is Q_1. A national minimum wage, set at W_2, will reduce the level of employment to Q_2 and increase the supply of labour to Q_3, thereby creating unemployment of the amount $Q_3 - Q_2$.

The level of unemployment created as a result of the national minimum wage will be determined not only by the level of the minimum wage, but also by the elasticity of labour demand and supply. The more elastic the demand and supply of labour, the bigger the unemployment effect will be. Evidence suggests that the demand for low-skilled workers by any given employer is likely to be relatively wage sensitive. The most likely reason for this is that many of the goods or services produced by low-paid workers are very price sensitive, the firms frequently operating in very competitive markets, where there are many substitutes. If one firm alone raised its prices, to compensate for higher wage rates, it might well lose a considerable number of sales and hence reduce employment.

However, minimum wage legislation applies to *all* firms. If all the firms in an industry or sector put up their prices in response to higher wages, demand for any one firm would fall much less. Here the problem of consumers switching away from a firm's products, and hence of that firm being forced to reduce its workforce, would mainly only occur (a) if there were cheaper competitor products from abroad or (b) if other firms produced the products with more capital-intensive techniques, involving fewer workers to whom the minimum wage legislation applied.

Minimum wages and monopsony employers

In an imperfect labour market where the employer has some influence over rates of pay, the impact of the national minimum wage on levels of employment is even less clear-cut.

The situation is illustrated in Figure 8.8 (which is similar to Figure 8.6 on page 218). With no minimum wage a monopsonistic employer will employ Q_1 workers: where the MC_L is equal to MRP_L. At this point the firm is maximising its return from the labour it employs. Remember that the MC_L curve lies above the supply of labour

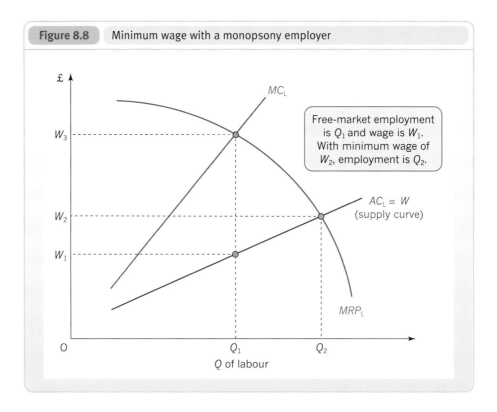

Figure 8.8   Minimum wage with a monopsony employer

Free-market employment is Q_1 and wage is W_1. With minimum wage of W_2, employment is Q_2.

MC_L

W_3

$AC_L \equiv W$ (supply curve)

W_2

W_1

MRP_L

O Q_1 Q_2

Q of labour

£

curve (AC_L), since the additional cost of employing one more unit of labour involves paying all existing employees the new wage. The wage rate paid by the monopsonist will be W_1.

If the minimum wage is set at W_2, the level of employment within the firm is likely to grow! Why should this be so? The reason is that the minimum wage cannot be bid down by the monopsonist cutting back on its workforce. The minimum wage rate is thus both the new AC_L and also the new MC_L; employers will thus choose to employ Q_2 workers, where MRP_L = (the new) MC_L. Thus the imposition of a minimum wage rate has *increased* the level of employment.

Clearly, if the minimum wage rate were very high then, other things being equal, the level of employment would fall. This would occur in Figure 8.8 if the minimum wage rate were above W_3. Employment would be below Q_1. But even this argument is not clear-cut, given that (a) a higher wage rate may increase labour productivity by improving worker motivation and (b) other firms, with which the firm might compete in the product market, will also be faced with paying the higher minimum wage rate. The resulting rise in prices is likely to shift the MRP_L curve to the right.

On the other hand, to the extent that the imposition of a minimum wage rate reduces a firm's profits, this may lead it to cut down on investment, which may threaten long-term employment prospects.

Pause for thought

If a rise in the minimum wage causes employers to substitute machines for workers, will this necessarily lead to higher unemployment?

Evidence on the effect of minimum wages

Evidence from the various countries suggests that modest increases in the minimum wage have had little effect upon employment. Employers have not responded by employing fewer workers. In the UK, after the introduction of the national minimum wage in 1999, unemployment rates actually fell up until about 2005. This, however, can be explained by a buoyant economy and increasing labour market flexibility (see section 8.5). Similarly, rises in unemployment from 2008 can be explained by the onset of recession, rather than rises in the minimum wage. However, many employers have claimed that paying the minimum wage has been problematic, with falling demand and hence falling revenue. Whether there would continue to be little effect if the minimum wage were to rise substantially is another matter! The issue, then, seems to be how *high* can the minimum wage be set before unemployment begins to rise.

Recap

1. Statutory minimum wage rates have been adopted in many countries.

2. In a perfect labour market, where employers are forced to accept the wage as determined by the market, any attempt to impose a minimum wage above this level will create unemployment. Amounts of additional unemployment are likely to be low, however, because the demand and supply of labour are relatively inelastic to changes in wage rates that apply to *all* firms.

3. In an imperfect labour market, where an employer has some monopsonistic power, the impact of a minimum wage is uncertain. The impact will depend largely upon how much workers are currently paid below their *MRP* and whether a higher wage encourages them to work more productively.

THE FLEXIBLE FIRM AND THE MARKET FOR LABOUR   8.5

The past 25 years have seen sweeping changes in the ways that firms organise their workforce. Three world recessions combined with rapid changes in technology have led many firms to question the wisdom of appointing workers on a permanent basis to specific jobs. Instead, they want to have the greatest flexibility possible to respond to new situations. If demand falls, they want to be able to 'shed' labour without facing large redundancy costs. If demand rises, they want rapid access to additional labour supplies. If technology changes, say with the introduction of new computerised processes, they want to have the flexibility to move workers around, or to take on new workers in some areas and lose workers in others.

What many firms seek, therefore, is flexibility in employing and allocating labour. What countries are experiencing is an increasingly flexible labour market, as workers and employment agencies respond to the new 'flexible firm'. More than half of all firms today are using flexible forms of work.

There are three main types of flexibility in the use of labour:

- **Functional flexibility.** This is where an employer is able to transfer labour between different tasks within the production process. It contrasts with traditional forms of organisation where people were employed to do a specific job, and then stuck to it. A functionally flexible labour force will tend to be multi-skilled and relatively highly trained to enable them to move effectively between jobs, as needed.
- **Numerical flexibility.** This is where the firm is able to adjust the size and composition of its workforce according to changing market conditions. To achieve this, the firm is likely to employ a large proportion of its labour on a part-time or casual basis, or even subcontract out specialist requirements, rather than employing such labour skills itself. Also, the changing nature of the family structure has

Definitions

Functional flexibility
Where employers can switch workers from job to job as requirements change.

Numerical flexibility
Where employers can change the size of their workforce as their labour requirements change.

Definitions

Financial flexibility

Where employers can vary their wage costs by changing the composition of their workforce or the terms on which workers are employed.

Flexible firm

A firm that has the flexibility to respond to changing market conditions by changing the composition of its workforce.

Primary labour market

The market for permanent full-time core workers.

Secondary labour market

The market for peripheral workers, usually employed on a temporary or part-time basis, or a less secure 'permanent' basis.

increased the availability of part-time and casual workers, as women's participation in the workforce continues to grow.

■ **Financial flexibility.** This is where the firm has flexibility in its wage costs. In large part it is a result of functional and numerical flexibility. Financial flexibility can be achieved by rewarding individual effort and productivity rather than paying a given rate for a particular job. Such rates of pay are increasingly negotiated at the local level rather than being nationally set. The result is not only a widening of pay differentials between skilled and unskilled workers, but also growing differentials in pay between workers within the same industry but in different parts of the country.

Figure 8.9 shows how these three forms of flexibility are reflected in the organisation of a **flexible firm**, an organisation quite different from that of the traditional firm. The most significant difference is that the labour force is segmented. The core group, drawn from the **primary labour market**, will be composed of *functionally* flexible workers, who have relatively secure employment and are generally on full-time permanent contracts. Such workers will be relatively well paid and receive wages reflecting their scarce skills.

The periphery, drawn from the **secondary labour market**, is more fragmented than the core, and can be subdivided into a first and a second peripheral group. The first peripheral group is composed of workers with a lower level of skill than those in the core, skills that tend to be general rather than firm specific. Thus workers in the first peripheral group can usually be drawn from the external labour market.

Figure 8.9   The flexible firm

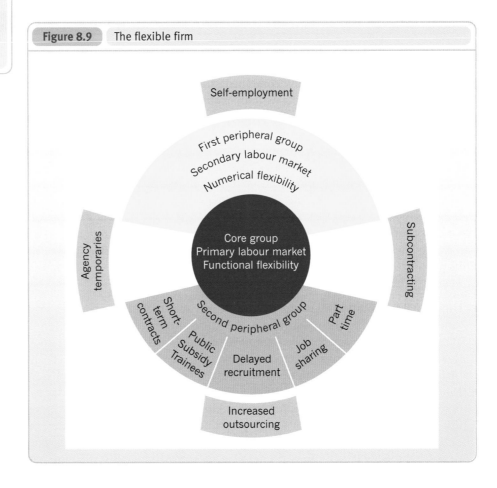

Such workers may be employed on full-time contracts, but they will generally face less secure employment than those workers in the core.

The business gains a greater level of numerical flexibility by drawing labour from the second peripheral group. Here workers are employed on a variety of short-term, part-time contracts, often through a recruitment agency. Some of these workers may be working from home, or online from another country, such as India, where wage rates are much lower. Workers in the second peripheral group have little job security.

As well as supplementing the level of labour in the first peripheral group, the second periphery can also provide high-level specialist skills that supplement the core. In this instance the business can subcontract or hire self-employed labour, minimising its commitment to such workers. The business thereby gains both functional and numerical flexibility simultaneously.

> **Pause for thought**
>
> *How is the advent of flexible firms likely to alter the gender balance of employment and unemployment?*

The Japanese model

The application of new flexible working patterns is becoming more prevalent in businesses in the UK and elsewhere in Europe and North America. In Japan, flexibility has been part of the business way of life for many years and was crucial in shaping the country's economic success in the 1970s and 1980s. In fact we now talk of a Japanese model of business organisation, which many of its competitors seek to emulate.

BOX 8.3   THE INTERNET AND LABOUR MOBILITY

Online flexibility

A firm may wish to be flexible, but is the labour market sufficiently flexible to meet the firm's needs?

It is all well and good a firm looking to expand employment in a prosperous period, but how will it find the individuals it needs, whether they be self-employed, subcontracted or added to the core labour group? This question becomes far more critical the more highly skilled (and hence scarce) are the workers that the firm requires. Generally, it is the core/skilled workers that flexible firms find most difficulty in recruiting.

But the Internet is making the process much easier. There are growing numbers of online recruitment agencies, which are competing with each other, and firms have begun to use social networking sites, such as Facebook, to increase the efficiency of their matching process between employers and job seekers. This development also reduces a firm's recruitment costs.

Employment agencies such as Reed, Manpower and Adecco have revolutionised the way in which people can search for jobs.

Paul Rapacioli is head of Reed Online, the Internet branch of the recruitment agency Reed. He says that '. . . People have been talking about labour market flexibility and mobility for years, but until recently the reality has been that a London-based worker prepared to work in Manchester has had to go up there and scout around.' Now, he says, the Internet can search the pool of jobs on offer across the country, identify suitable matches and automatically e-mail them to job-seekers, or send text messages to their mobile phones.

Economists say the behaviour of the whole labour market could be revolutionised by such developments. Professor Richard Layard, a leading labour market expert and government adviser at the London School of Economics, says the Internet could help bring a long-awaited improvement in the matching process between the unemployed and available jobs.[1]

Use of the Internet is efficient both for workers, as there are more jobs in more industries open to them, and also for employers, as they face a greater choice of individuals and skills.

The result, therefore, of the developments in internet technology has been an increase in labour mobility and the speed with which jobs can be filled. The better the information on the jobs sites and the easier they are to use, the better the matching is likely to be and the more their use is likely to grow.

 Explain how a firm's flexibility can be enhanced by online recruitment. What imperfection in information, for both employer and job seeker, still remains?

---

[1] *Financial Times*, 22 February 2000

The model is based around four principles:

■ *Total quality management (TQM).* This involves all employees working towards continuously improving all aspects of quality, both of the finished product and of methods of production.
■ *Elimination of waste.* According to the 'just-in-time' (JIT) principle, businesses should take delivery of just sufficient quantities of raw materials and parts, at the right time and place. Stocks are kept to a minimum and hence the whole system of production runs with little, if any, slack. For example, supermarkets today have smaller storerooms relative to the total shopping area than they did in the past, and take more frequent deliveries.
■ *A belief in the superiority of teamwork.* Collective effort is a vital element in Japanese working practices. Teamwork is seen not only to enhance individual performance, but also to involve the individual in the running of the business and thus to create a sense of commitment.
■ *Functional and numerical flexibility.* Both are seen as vital components in maintaining high levels of productivity.

The principles of this model are now widely accepted as being important in creating and maintaining a competitive business in a competitive marketplace.

Before the recession of the late 2000s, the UK had been one of the most successful countries in the EU in cutting unemployment and creating jobs. Much of this has been attributed to increased labour market flexibility. As a result, other EU countries, such as Italy and Germany, are seeking to emulate many of the measures the UK has adopted.

Recap

1. Changes in technology have had a massive impact upon the process of production and the experience of work. Labour markets and business organisations have become more flexible as a consequence.

2. There are three major forms of flexibility: functional, numerical and financial. The flexible firm incorporates these different forms of flexibility into its business operations.

3. It organises production around a core workforce, which it supplements with workers and skills drawn from a periphery. Peripheral workers tend to hold general skills rather than firm-specific skills, and are employed on part-time and temporary contracts.

4. The application of the flexible firm model is closely mirrored in the practices of Japanese business. Commitments to improve quality, reduce waste, build teamwork and introduce flexible labour markets are seen as key components in the success of Japanese business organisation.

8.6 THE LABOUR MARKET AND INCENTIVES

Wages are a reward for labour. They are also, from a business perspective, a means of motivating the labour force. For example, the possibility of promotion to a post paying a higher wage can be a key incentive for employees to improve their performance. Another example is piece rates. This is where workers are paid according to the amount they produce. The more they produce, the higher their pay. Similarly a firm may pay commission to its sales force – as an incentive to sell more. Sometimes the firm will pay its senior executives bonuses related to company performance.

Because of the use of pay as a means of encouraging better performance by workers or management, firms will sometimes pay above the market rate. They pay what is known as an **efficiency wage rate**.

Efficiency wages

The **efficiency wage hypothesis** states that the productivity of workers rises as the wage rate rises. As a result, employers are frequently prepared to offer wage rates above the market-clearing level, attempting to balance increased wage costs against gains in productivity. But why may higher wage rates lead to higher productivity? There are three main explanations.

Less 'shirking'. In many jobs it is difficult to monitor the effort that individuals put into their work. In such cases piece rates or commission may be impracticable. Workers may thus get away with shirking or careless behaviour.

The business could attempt to reduce shirking by imposing a series of sanctions, the most serious of which would be dismissal. The greater the wage rate currently received, the greater will be the cost to the individual of dismissal (the opportunity cost in terms of the salary forgone), and the less likely it is that workers will shirk. The business will benefit not only from the additional output, but also from a reduction in the costs of having to monitor workers' performance. As a consequence, the efficiency wage rate for the business will lie above the market-determined wage rate.

Reduced labour turnover. If workers receive on-the-job training or retraining, then to lose a worker once the training has been completed is a significant cost to the business, as it does not receive any of the benefits, yet incurs all of the costs. A few decades ago, workers tended to remain in the same job for much of their lives, but the labour market has changed, and it is now not unusual for workers to change jobs several times throughout their working life. As such, this issue of training has become more problematic. However, labour turnover, and hence its associated costs, can be reduced by paying a wage above the market-clearing rate. By paying such a wage, the business is seeking a degree of loyalty from its employees.

Morale. A simple reason for offering wage rates above the market-clearing level is to motivate the workforce – to create the feeling that the firm is a 'good' employer that cares about its employees. As a consequence, workers might be more industrious and more willing to accept the introduction of new technology (with the reorganisation that it involves).

The paying of efficiency wages above the market-clearing wage will depend upon the type of work involved. Workers who occupy skilled positions, especially where the business has invested time in their training (thus making them costly to replace), are likely to receive efficiency wages considerably above the market wage. By contrast, workers in unskilled positions, where shirking can be easily monitored, little training takes place and workers can be easily replaced, are unlikely to command an 'efficiency wage premium'. In such situations, rather than keeping wage rates high, the business will probably try to pay as little as possible.

Definitions

Efficiency wage rate
The profit-maximising wage rate for the firm after taking into account the effects of wage rates on worker motivation, turnover and recruitment.

Efficiency wage hypothesis
A hypothesis that states that a worker's productivity is linked to the wage he or she receives.

Pause for thought

Give some examples of things an employer could do to increase the morale of the workforce other than raising wages. How would you assess whether they were in the interests of the employer?

Principal–agent relationships in the labour market

The need to pay efficiency wages above the market rate is an example of the principal–agent problem (see pages 9–10). The worker, as an agent of the employer (the principal), is not necessarily going to act in the principal's interest.

At the time when people are interviewed for a job, they will clearly be keen to make a good impression on their potential employer and may promise all sorts of things. Once employed, however, a 'moral hazard' occurs (see pages 67–8) – workers will be tempted to take it easy. The principal (the firm) will therefore attempt to prevent this occurring. One solution, as we have seen, is to pay an efficiency wage. Another is to tighten up on job monitoring by managers. For example, regular performance appraisal could be instituted, with sanctions imposed on workers who underperform. Such sanctions could range from support in the form of additional training to penalties in the form of closer monitoring, lost pay, lost bonuses or even dismissal. Another solution is to offer rewards for good performance in the form of bonuses or promotion.

In general, however, the poorer the information on the part of the principal (the greater the 'information asymmetry'), the more the employee will be able to get away with.

There is also an 'adverse selection' problem for the employer (see pages 67–8). The most able workers are those most likely to leave for a better job elsewhere. The workers who elect to stay are likely to be the least able. To counter this problem, the employer might need to be willing to promote people to more senior posts to encourage them to stay.

> **Pause for thought**
>
> *Does a moral hazard apply to employers as well as workers? If so, how might it affect employers' behaviour?*

Executive pay

There has been much resentment in recent years over the huge pay increases received by top managers and none more so than in 2008/9, with the global financial crisis. Up to the mid 1980s, the median pay of US top executives was some 30 times higher than average wages. By 2000, the figure had soared to 120 times. Although it fell somewhat with the slowdown of the economy in 2001–3, it has risen sharply since.

The picture is very similar in the UK. In 2009, the average remuneration for chief executives in the 10 top paying companies was over £17 million, over 500 times the wage of the average worker in those companies. Pay rises for these top earners have been averaging around 25 per cent per annum. This compares with just 4 per cent for the average worker.

The nature of executive awards

For the top earners, salaries account for a relatively small percentage. Incentives and bonuses often considerably outstrip basic salaries. Incentives are normally related to company performance, such as profit or turnover (revenue). Bonuses, however, are given retrospectively and are often unrelated to performance. They are often given even when the company is underperforming.

In recent years, bankers' bonuses have seen huge news coverage. In February 2010, it was reported that the Chief Executive of Lloyds Banking Group was to be awarded a £2.3m bonus, despite the bank making losses of some £7bn. This bonus was turned down. Royal Bank of Scotland (RBS) is 70 per cent owned by the public, after requiring a bailout by the government. Yet, at the end of 2009, RBS directors threatened to quit if an estimated £1.5bn bonus pool for staff at the investment arm of the bank was blocked by the government. These bonuses would give about 20 000 RBS bankers a salary at least three times greater than the national average.

The banking crisis is a prime example of executives receiving large bonuses, even when the company does badly. The argument is that the bonuses are used as an incentive to ensure that the best talent is attracted and remains at the company. There has, unsurprisingly, been a significant public outcry against what is seen as totally undeserved rewards.[1]

Then there are shares and **share options**. These are normally given as a longer term incentive. In the case of shares, these must be held for a period of time (say three years) before they can be cashed in. In the case of share options, the option is for the executive to buy shares at a price set when the option is granted, even though the current market price might be considerably higher. The argument is that both shares and share options give the executive an incentive to ensure that the company performs well and its share price rises as a result.

In addition to these rewards, top executives often receive generous pensions and large severance pay when they leave.

Incentive effects?

So do these huge increases represent the necessary incentives and rewards for those leading industrial growth and taking risks? Or are they the result of market imperfections, where greedy executives can persuade complicit company boards of directors to give them what they want? Are they a sign of poor governance of industry?

> Extraordinary pay for great performance is fine, it is routinely said. But many executives have been paid a fortune for presiding over mediocrity. The Corporate Library, an American corporate-governance consultancy, last year [2006] identified 11 large and well known but poorly governed companies, including AT&T, Merck and Time Warner, where the chief executive had been paid at least $15m a year for two successive years even as the company's shares had underperformed. Robert Nardelli received a $210m pay-off when he lost his job earlier this month even though the shares of his company, Home Depot, fell slightly during his six years in charge. Carly Fiorina, ejected from Hewlett-Packard almost $180m better off – including a severance payment of $21.6m – after a lacklustre tenure as chief executive, let it be known in her autobiography that money was not important to her. Not everyone believed her.[2]

As far as genuine incentive schemes are concerned, they may indeed encourage risk taking and good performance. High remuneration may be necessary in some cases to attract the right talent and persuade them to stay. Generous bonuses for executives of poorly performing companies, however, clearly have the opposite effect – as do generous severance packages for executives leaving early.

Then there are the incentives for workers. If they feel that their senior managers' pay is unjustified, this can breed resentment and harm industrial relations.

> Ultimately, businesses function with the blessing of workers, shareholders, customers and voters. If business leaders are universally seen as immoral and grasping, cynicism and mistrust will flourish and choke enterprise.[3]

Definition

Share (or **stock**) **options** The right to buy shares in the future at a fixed price set today. When granted to senior executives as a reward they do not involve any outlay by the company. They act as an incentive, however, since the better the company performs, the more the market value of its shares is likely to rise above the option price and the more the executive stands to gain by exercising the option to buy shares at the fixed price and then selling them at the market price.

---

[1] 'Royal Bank of Scotland and bankers' bonuses', *Guardian*, 25 February 2010
[2] 'In the money', *The Economist*, 18 January 2007
[3] *Ibid.*

BOX 8.4 **THE MARKET FOR TALENT**

The price of brainpower

More and more companies are seeing talent as a key to their success.

> Obsession with talent is no longer confined to blue-chip companies such as Goldman Sachs and General Electric. It can be found everywhere in the corporate world, from credit-card companies to hotel chains to the retail trade. Many firms reckon that they have pushed re-engineering and automation as hard as they can. Now they must raise productivity by managing talent better.
>
> . . . When the Corporate Executive Board (CEB), a provider of business research and executive education based in Washington, DC, recently conducted an international poll of senior human-resources managers, three-quarters of them said that 'attracting and retaining' talent was their number one priority. Some 62 per cent worried about company-wide talent shortages. The CEB also surveyed some 4000 hiring managers in more than 30 companies, and was told that the average quality of candidates had declined by 10 per cent since 2004 and the average time to fill a vacancy had increased from 37 days to 51 days.[1]

But while hiring talented staff may be a necessary condition for success, it doesn't guarantee it. One problem is that talented staff may be very ambitious and are likely to be more concerned with their own careers than the long-term interests of their employers. There is a 'moral hazard' here (see page 67). The firm may invest a lot of time and expense in training talented workers, only to see them leave for another job. In other words, employing a person does not guarantee a commitment on their part to stay. Such people are often sought out by other companies, which may use 'head hunting' agencies to find and recruit them.

Then there are the ethics of a number of these employees. There have been some spectacular cases of greed and malpractice in recent years, where accounting fraud has allowed some staff to get rich at the expense of customers and shareholders.

The most famous case in the past few years has been that of Lehman Brothers, the American investment bank, whose collapse in September 2008 was the biggest bankruptcy in US history and triggered the worldwide financial crisis and recession.

According to a report filed in March 2010 by Bankruptcy Examiner Anton Valukas in the federal court of Manhattan, Lehman Bros manipulated its balance sheet and betrayed its shareholders. The report claimed that Richard Fuld, Lehman's former chief executive, was 'grossly negligent' in submitting misleading reports. All sorts of 'accounting gimmicks' had been used to move up to $50 billion of toxic assets from the balance sheet to avoid disclosing them to the government, rating agencies, investors or Lehman's board – and this was despite its accounts being audited by accountants Ernst & Young, which earned $31 million from Lehman Bros in 2007. The report accused Ernst & Young of being 'professionally negligent' for hiding the details.

> Prem Sikka, a professor of accounting at Essex University and a leading critic of the accounting profession, warned that without deep-rooted reform the crisis could repeat itself. 'The report into the collapse of Lehmans is indicative of a deeper malaise,' he said. 'We rely on the discretion of eminent firms of auditors and lawyers that are paid millions of pounds for their efforts, but that discretion is too often abused.'[2]

Charges were likely to be brought against Fuld and other former Lehman directors by the US financial regulator, the Securities and Exchange Commission. Any criminal prosecution, however, would need the government to prove intent to defraud or knowledge that statements were false or misleading.

Managing talent

Talent is a vital ingredient for many companies in the rapidly changing business environment in which they operate. It is something, however, that needs to be tamed and harnessed with the right incentives and careful monitoring. So what can be done to avoid the pitfalls?

One solution is to allow talented people to play to their strengths. This means carefully structuring jobs so that people feel challenged and valued and use their particular talents to the full. Another is to provide training schemes so that people's talents can be further developed. Another is for new recruits to work on projects that are seen as central to the success of the organisation. This helps make the recruits feel like insiders rather than as people merely hired for a particular skill.

Finally, companies should develop opportunities for promotions and transfers within the organisation. This can allow people to further their careers while at the same time developing a greater sense of loyalty to the company.

1. *How would you attempt to measure the marginal productivity of a person hired for a specific talent?*
2. *Why might companies be wise to pay talented people more than the value of their marginal product?*

---

[1] 'The battle for brainpower', *The Economist*, 5 October 2006

[2] 'Auditors face inquiry call after Lehman revelations', *Guardian*, 14 March 2010

Recap

1. The efficiency wage hypothesis states that a business is likely to pay a wage above the market-clearing rate in order to: reduce shirking; reduce labour turnover; and stimulate worker morale.

2. Employment is an example of a principal–agent relationship. Workers (the agents) may underperform as a result of lack of information on their performance by their employer (the principal). To combat this problem, employers may link pay more closely with output or monitor the performance of workers more closely.

3. Executive pay has risen much more rapidly than average pay. In addition to high salaries, many senior managers receive considerable bonuses, shares, share options and other perks. High pay may be necessary to act as an incentive for risk taking and to attract high calibre people. It is also often, however, a reflection of poor governance at the top of industry and in many cases is unrelated to performance.

QUESTIONS

1. If a firm faces a shortage of workers with very specific skills, it may decide to undertake the necessary training itself. If on the other hand it faces a shortage of unskilled workers it may well offer a small wage increase in order to obtain the extra labour. In the first case it is responding to an increase in demand for labour by attempting to shift the supply curve. In the second case it is merely allowing a movement along the supply curve. Use a demand and supply diagram to illustrate each case. Given that elasticity of supply is different in each case, do you think that these are the best policies for the firm to follow?

2. The wage rate a firm has to pay and the output it can produce varies with the number of workers as follows (all figures are hourly):

Number of workers	1	2	3	4	5	6	7	8
Wage rate (AC_L) (£)	3	4	5	6	7	8	9	10
Total output (TPP_L)	10	22	32	40	46	50	52	52

Assume that output sells at £2 per unit.

(a) Copy the table and add additional rows for TC_L, MC_L, TRP_L and MRP_L. Put the figures for MC_L and MRP_L in the spaces between the columns.
(b) How many workers will the firm employ in order to maximise profits?
(c) What will be its hourly wage bill at this level of employment?
(d) How much hourly revenue will it earn at this level of employment?
(e) Assuming that the firm faces other (fixed) costs of £30 per hour, how much hourly profit will it make?
(f) Assume that the workers now form a union and that the firm agrees to pay the negotiated wage rate to all employees. What is the maximum to which the hourly wage rate could rise without causing the firm to try to reduce employment below that in (b) above? (See Figures 8.6 and 8.8.)
(g) What would be the firm's hourly profit now?

3. For what types of reason does the marginal revenue product differ between workers in different jobs?

4. If, unlike a perfectly competitive employer, a monopsonist has to pay a higher wage to attract more workers, why, other things being equal, will a monopsonist pay a lower wage than a perfectly competitive employer?

5. The following are figures for a monopsonist employer:

Number of workers (1)	Wage rate (£) (2)	Total cost of labour (£) (3)	Marginal cost of labour (£) (4)	Marginal revenue product (£) (5)
1	100	100		
2	105	210	110	230
3	110	230	120	240
4	115			240
5	120			230
6	125			210
7	130			190
8	135			170
9	140			150
10	145			130

Fill in the missing figures for columns (3) and (4). How many workers should the firm employ if it wishes to maximise profits?

6. To what extent could a trade union succeed in gaining a pay increase from an employer with no loss in employment?

7. Using some recent examples, consider the extent to which strike action is likely to help trade union members achieve their various aims.

8. Do any of the following contradict the theory that the demand for labour equals the marginal revenue product: wage scales related to length of service (incremental scales), nationally negotiated wage rates, discrimination, firms taking the lead from other firms in determining this year's pay increase?

9. What is the efficiency wage hypothesis? Explain what employers might gain from paying wages above the market-clearing level.

10. 'Statutory minimum wages will cause unemployment.' Is this so?

11. Identify the potential costs and benefits of the flexible firm to (a) employers and (b) employees.

12. How have changes in society, laws and technology affected the UK labour market?

Business issues covered in this chapter

- To what extent does business meet the interests of consumers and society in general?

- In what sense are perfect markets 'socially efficient' and why do most markets fail to achieve social efficiency?

- How do business ethics influence business behaviour?

- In what ways do governments intervene in markets and attempt to influence business behaviour?

- What forms do government environmental policies take, and how do they affect business?

- How does the government attempt to prevent both the abuse of monopoly power and collusion by oligopolists?

- How are privatised industries regulated and how has competition been increased in these industries?

Government, the firm and the market

Despite the fact that most countries today can be classified as 'market economies', governments nevertheless intervene substantially in the activities of business in order to protect the interests of consumers, workers or the environment.

Firms might collude to fix prices, use misleading advertising, create pollution, produce unsafe products, or use unacceptable employment practices. In such cases, government is expected to intervene to correct for the failings of the market system, e.g. by outlawing collusion, by establishing advertising standards, by taxing or otherwise penalising polluting firms, by imposing safety standards on firms' behaviour and products, or by protecting employment rights.

In this chapter we examine the ways in which markets might fail to protect people's interests, whether as consumers or simply as members of society. We also look at the different types of policy the government can adopt to correct these 'market failures'.

9.1 MARKET FAILURES

Definitions

Marginal social benefit (*MSB*)
The additional benefit gained by society of producing or consuming one more unit of a good.

Marginal social cost (*MSC*)
The additional cost incurred by society of producing or consuming one more unit of a good.

Social efficiency
Production and consumption at the point where *MSB* = *MSC*.

Markets and social objectives

One of the key arguments for government intervention in the behaviour of business is that, if left to its own devices, the private enterprise system will fail to achieve 'social efficiency'.

So what is meant by social efficiency? If the extra benefits to society – or **marginal social benefit** (*MSB*) – of producing more of any given good or service exceed the extra costs to society – or **marginal social cost** (*MSC*) – then it is said to be socially efficient to produce more. For example, if people's gains from having additional motorways exceed *all* the additional costs to society (both financial and non-financial) then it is socially efficient to construct more motorways.

If, however, the marginal social cost of producing more of any good or service exceeds the marginal social benefit, then it is socially efficient to produce less.

It follows that if the marginal social benefit of any activity is equal to the marginal social cost, then the current level is the optimum. To summarise, for **social efficiency** in the production of any good or service:

$$MSB > MSC \rightarrow \text{produce more}$$
$$MSC > MSB \rightarrow \text{produce less}$$
$$MSB = MSC \rightarrow \text{keep production at its current level}$$

Similar rules apply to consumption. For example, if the marginal social benefit of consuming more of any good or service exceeds the marginal social cost, then society would benefit from more of the good being consumed.

Social efficiency. This is achieved where no further net social gain can be made by producing more or less of a good. This will occur where marginal social benefit equals marginal social cost.

In the real world, the market rarely leads to social efficiency: the marginal social benefits from the production of most goods and services do not equal the marginal social costs. In this section we examine why the free market fails to lead to social efficiency and what the government can do to rectify the situation.

Types of market failure

Externalities

The market will not lead to social efficiency if the actions of producers or consumers affect people *other than themselves*. These effects on other people are known as **externalities**; they are the side-effects, or 'third-party' effects, of production or consumption. Externalities can be either desirable or undesirable. Whenever other people are affected beneficially, there are said to be **external benefits**. Whenever other people are affected adversely, there are said to be **external costs**.

 Externalities are spillover costs or benefits. Where these exist, even an otherwise perfect market will fail to achieve social efficiency.

Definitions

Externalities

Costs or benefits of production or consumption experienced by society but not by the producers or consumers themselves. Sometimes referred to as 'spillover' or 'third-party' costs or benefits.

External benefits

Benefits from production (or consumption) experienced by people other than the producer (or consumer).

External costs

Costs of production (or consumption) borne by people other than the producer (or consumer).

Social cost

Private cost plus externalities in production.

Social benefit

Private benefit plus externalities in consumption.

Thus the full cost to society (the **social cost**) of the production of any good or service is the private cost faced by firms plus any externalities of production (positive or negative). Likewise the full benefit to society (the **social benefit**) from the consumption of any good is the private benefit enjoyed by consumers plus any externalities of consumption (positive or negative).

External costs produced by business. Let us take the case of a chemical firm that dumps waste in a river or pollutes the air. In such a case, the community bears costs additional to those borne by the firm. The marginal social cost (MSC) of chemical production exceeds the marginal private cost (MC). Diagrammatically, the MSC curve is above the MC curve. This is shown in Figure 9.1, which assumes that the firm in other respects is operating in a perfect market, and is therefore a price taker (i.e. faces a horizontal demand curve).

The firm maximises profits at Q_1: the output where marginal cost equals price (see section 4.4 on page 108). The price is what people buying the good are prepared to pay for one more unit (if it wasn't they wouldn't buy it) and therefore reflects their marginal benefit. We assume no externalities from consumption, and therefore the marginal benefit to consumers is the same as the marginal *social* benefit (MSB).

The socially optimum output would be Q_2, where P (i.e. MSB) = MSC. The firm, however, produces Q_1, as it is only concerned with the costs *it* incurs by producing, such as raw material and labour costs. This output, however, is more than the optimum. Thus external costs lead to *overproduction* from society's point of view.

The problem of external costs arises in a free market economy because no one has legal ownership of the air or rivers and no one, therefore, can prevent or charge for their use as a dump for waste. Such a 'market' is missing. Control must, therefore, be left to the government or local authorities.

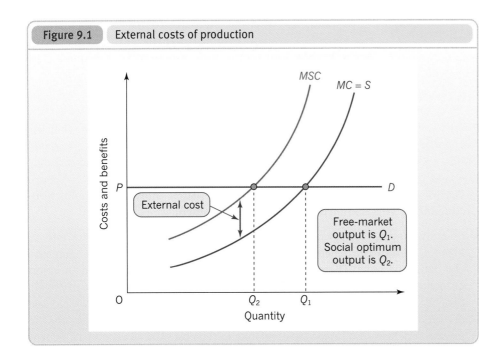

Figure 9.1   External costs of production

Other examples of firms producing external costs include extensive farming that destroys hedgerows and wildlife, acid rain caused by smoke from coal-fired power stations, nuclear waste from nuclear power stations and global warming from carbon emissions. In all of these cases, society bears some of the costs of production.

Other examples of externalities. Sometimes firms' actions *benefit* people other than consumers. An example is research and development. If other firms have access to the results of the research, then clearly the benefits extend beyond the firm that finances it. However, since the firm only receives the private benefits, it will conduct less than the optimal amount of research. What is the point in a firm conducting further research if many of the benefits simply go to other firms? Similarly, a forestry company planting new woodlands will not take into account the beneficial effect on the atmosphere, and hence it will plant less than the socially optimal number of trees.

Externalities occur in consumption too. For example, when people use their cars, other people suffer from their exhaust, the added congestion, the noise, etc. These 'negative externalities' make the marginal social benefit of using cars less than the marginal private benefit (i.e. marginal utility to the car user). Other examples of negative externalities of consumption include noisy radios in public places, the smoke from cigarettes, and litter. Others suffer from people smoking, or from people dropping litter.

Consumption externalities could be positive. For example, when people travel by train rather than by car, other people benefit by there being less congestion and exhaust and fewer accidents on the roads. Thus the marginal social benefit of rail travel is greater than the marginal private benefit (i.e. the marginal utility to the rail passenger). Other examples of positive externalities of consumption include deodorants, vaccinations and attractive gardens in front of people's houses. For example if one person is vaccinated against a disease, it not only benefits them, but also benefits others, who can no longer catch the disease from that person.

To summarise, whenever there are external costs, there will be too much produced or consumed. Whenever there are external benefits, there will be too little produced or consumed. The market will not equate *MSB* and *MSC*.

Public goods

There is a category of goods where the positive externalities are so great that the free market, whether perfect or imperfect, may not produce at all. They are called **public goods**. Examples include lighthouses, pavements, flood control dams, public drainage, public services such as the police and even government itself.

Public goods have two important characteristics: **non-rivalry** and **non-excludability**. This is known as the **free-rider problem**.

- If I consume a bar of chocolate, it cannot then be consumed by someone else. If, however, I enjoy the benefits of street lighting, it does not prevent you or anyone else doing the same. There is thus what we call non-rivalry in the consumption of such goods. These goods tend to have large external benefits relative to private benefits. This makes them socially desirable, but privately unprofitable. No one person on their own would pay to have a pavement built along their street. The private benefit would be too small relative to the cost. And yet the social benefit to all the other people using the pavement may far outweigh the cost.

- If I spend money erecting a flood control dam to protect my house, my neighbours will also be protected by the dam. I cannot prevent them enjoying the benefits of my expenditure. This feature of non-excludability means that they would get the benefits free, and would therefore have no incentive to pay themselves. This is known as the free-rider problem.

 KEY IDEA 25   The free-rider problem. People are often unwilling to pay for things if they can make use of things other people have bought. This problem can lead to people not purchasing things which it would be to their benefit and that of other members of society to have.

When goods have these two features, the free market will simply not provide them. Thus these public goods can only be provided by the government or by the government subsidising private firms. Their provision will be financed through taxation and will significantly increase the utility of society. (Note that not all goods and services produced by the public sector come into the category of public goods and services; thus education and health are publicly provided, but they *can* be, and indeed are, privately provided too.)

We have defined public goods as non-excludable and non-rival, but a common question is what, then, are the characteristics of private goods? It's very simple really. Private goods are excludable and rival! Let us return to the example of the chocolate bar. If I consume it, no one else can, hence it is a rival good. It is also excludable, as a price is charged for it. Hence, if I buy the chocolate bar, other people will be prevented from enjoying it.

Market power

When there are no externalities, a perfect market will result in social efficiency. This can be seen from Figure 9.1. If there are no externalities, then the *MSC* and *MC* curves will be one and the same. Firms will produce where *MC* (= *MSC*) = *P* (= *MSB*):

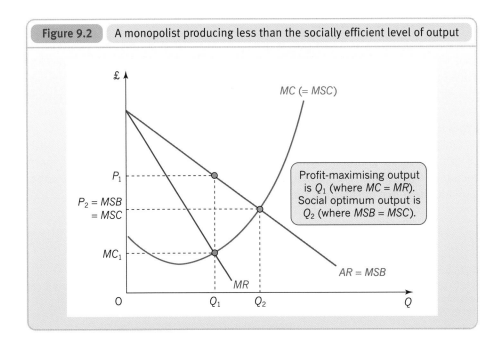

Figure 9.2   A monopolist producing less than the socially efficient level of output

Profit-maximising output is Q_1 (where $MC = MR$). Social optimum output is Q_2 (where $MSB = MSC$).

they will produce the socially optimal level of output. Note that $P = MSB$ since the price is equal to marginal utility (see pages 63–4). Marginal utility is the marginal private benefit that consumers gain, which, in the absence of externalities, will be the same as the MSB.

However, whenever markets are imperfect, whether as pure monopoly or monopsony or as some form of imperfect competition, the market will fail to equate MSB and MSC, even if there are no externalities.

Take the case of monopoly. A monopoly will produce less than the socially efficient output. This is illustrated in Figure 9.2. A monopoly faces a downward-sloping demand curve, and therefore marginal revenue is below average revenue ($= P = MSB$). Profits are maximised at an output of Q_1, where marginal revenue equals marginal cost (see Figure 5.2 on page 125). Assuming no externalities, the socially efficient output would be at the higher level of Q_2, where $MSB = MSC$.

To summarise, firms with market power, if they are trying to maximise (or even increase) profit, will tend to raise prices and thus reduce output below the socially efficient level.

Imperfect information

Markets can only operate efficiently if people have good knowledge of costs and benefits as they affect them. In the real world there is often a great deal of ignorance and uncertainty. Consumers are often ignorant of the properties of goods until they have bought them – by which time it is too late. This is especially relevant for larger consumer 'durables' that are purchased infrequently, such as washing machines or cars. Advertising may contribute to people's ignorance by misleading them as to the benefits of a good.

Firms are often ignorant of market opportunities, prices, costs, the productivity of labour (especially white-collar workers), the activity of rivals, etc.

Many economic decisions are based on expected future conditions. Since the future can never be known for certain, many decisions will be taken that later turn out to be wrong.

Protecting people's interests

The government may feel that people need protecting from poor economic decisions that they make on their own behalf. It may feel that in a free market people will consume too many harmful things. Thus if the government wants to discourage smoking and drinking, it can put taxes on tobacco and alcohol. In more extreme cases it could make various activities illegal, activities such as prostitution, certain types of gambling, and the sale and consumption of drugs.

On the other hand, the government may feel that people consume too little of things that are good for them, things such as education, health care and sports facilities. Such goods are known as **merit goods**. The government could either provide them free or subsidise their production.

Recap

1. Social efficiency is achieved where $MSC = MSB$ for each good and service. In practice, however, markets will fail to achieve social efficiency. This provides a justification for government intervention in the market.

2. Externalities are spillover costs or benefits. Whenever there are external costs, the market will (other things being equal) lead to a level of production and consumption above the socially efficient level. Whenever there are external benefits, the market will (other things being equal) lead to a level of production and consumption below the socially efficient level.

3. Public goods will not be provided by the market. The problem is that they have large external benefits relative to private benefits, and without government intervention it would not be possible to prevent people having a 'free ride', thereby making it unprofitable to supply.

4. Monopoly power will (other things being equal) lead to a level of output below the socially efficient level.

5. Ignorance and uncertainty may prevent people and firms from consuming or producing at the levels they would otherwise choose.

6. In a free market there may be inadequate provision for dependants and an inadequate output of merit goods.

9.2 BUSINESS ETHICS AND CORPORATE SOCIAL RESPONSIBILITY

It is often assumed that firms are simply concerned with maximising profits: that they are not concerned with broader issues of **corporate social responsibility**. In other words, firms tend to be more concerned with the interests of shareholders than they are about the interests of society. Indeed, many forms of market failure can be attributed directly to business practices that could not be classified as 'socially responsible': advertising campaigns that seek to misinform, or in some way deceive the consumer; monopoly producers exploiting their monopoly position through charging excessively high prices; the conscious decision to ignore water and air pollution limits, knowing that the chances of being caught are slim.

Changing business attitudes?

To some extent, however, the role of modern business has changed, and society expects business to adhere to certain moral and social principles. Indeed, social responsibility is a key component in many companies' **business ethics**.

Modern businesses often see themselves as more than economic institutions, as they are actively involved in society's social, political and legal environments. As such, all businesses are responsible not only to their shareholders but to all **stakeholders**. Stakeholders are all those affected by the business's operations, not only shareholders, but workers, customers, suppliers, creditors and people living in the neighbourhood. Given the far-reaching environmental effects of many businesses, stakeholding might extend to the whole of society.

In many top corporations, **environmental scanning** is now an integral part of the planning process. This involves the business surveying changing social and political trends in order to remain in tune with consumer concerns. For example, the general public's growing concern over 'green' issues has significantly influenced many businesses' product development programmes and R&D strategies. The more successful a business is in being able to associate the image of 'environmentally friendly' to a particular product or brand, the more likely it is to enhance its sales or establish a measure of brand loyalty, and thereby to strengthen its competitive position.

Several companies in recent years have made great play of their social responsibility. In 2007, Marks & Spencer launched its 'Plan A':

> Plan A is our five-year, 100-point plan to tackle some of the biggest challenges facing our business and our world. It will see us working with our customers and our suppliers to combat climate change, reduce waste, safeguard natural resources, trade ethically and build a healthier nation. We're doing this because it's what you want us to do. It's also the right thing to do. We're calling it Plan A because we believe it's now the only way to do business.[1]

In the very same week that M&S launched Plan A, Tesco unveiled its plans to cut carbon emissions from existing stores worldwide by at least 50 per cent by 2020 and to make the reduction of its carbon footprint 'a central business driver'. To help achieve this, it was commissioning independent research to map the total carbon footprint of its activities across the world. It would also encourage people to buy environmentally friendly products, with more special offers and more of such products in the value range. It was also introducing a carbon labelling system for all its products to help consumers make greener choices.

> **Definition**
>
> **Environmental scanning**
> Where a business surveys social and political trends in order to take account of changes in its decision-making process.

> **Pause for thought**
>
> *Green taxes (e.g. on carbon emission) are designed to 'internalise' environmental externalities and thereby force firms to take such externalities into account in their decision making. Should such taxes be reduced for firms that adopt a more environmentally responsible approach?*

Social responsibility and profitability

Clearly, M&S, Tesco and the many other companies that are openly committed to sustainability and ethical practices hope that such policies will also improve their profitability. As consumers become more concerned with such issues, so they are likely to favour such companies.

As we saw in Box 1.1 (pages 4–5), Gap received bad press coverage over the poor employment conditions in its factories in developing countries. The company, clearly worried about its image and the effect on sales, was at pains to be seen to be addressing this issue.

A reputation for social responsibility may also help the firm in raising finance and attracting trading partners. Investment in ethically screened investment funds has grown rapidly in recent years. This has been driven not only by the demands of shareholders for ethical funds, but also by a realisation from investors generally that socially responsible business has the potential to be hugely profitable.

Socially responsible companies also may find it easier to recruit and hold on to their employees. In a number of surveys of graduate employment intentions,

---

[1] www2.marksandspencer.com/thecompany/plana/index.shtml

BOX 9.1	THE BODY SHOP

Is it 'worth it'?

The Body Shop shot to fame in the 1980s. It stood for environmental awareness and an ethical approach to business. But its success had as much to do with what it sold as what it stood for. It sold natural cosmetics, Raspberry Ripple Bathing Bubbles and Camomile Shampoo, products that were immensely popular with consumers.

Its profits increased from a little over £1 million in 1985 to nearly £44 million in 2007. Sales, meanwhile, grew even more dramatically, from £4.9 million to £600 million in 2008. By the end of 2008, Body Shop International had 2550 stores worldwide, opening 124 stores in the year.

What makes this success so remarkable is that The Body Shop did virtually no advertising. Its promotion stemmed largely from the activities and environmental campaigning of its founder Anita Roddick, and the company's uncompromising claims that it sold only 'green' products and conducted its business operations with high ethical standards. It actively supported green causes such as saving whales and protecting rainforests, and it refused to allow its products to be tested on animals. Perhaps most surprising in the world of big business was its high-profile initiative 'trade not aid', whereby it claimed to pay 'fair' prices for its ingredients, especially those supplied from people in developing countries, who were open to exploitation by large companies.

The growth strategy of The Body Shop, since its founding in 1976, has focused on developing a distinctive and highly innovative product range, and at the same time identifying such products with major social issues of the day, such as the environment and animal rights.

Its initial expansion was based on a process of franchising:

> . . . franchising. We didn't know what it was, but all these women came to us and said, if you can do this and you can't even read a balance sheet, then we can do it. I had a cabal of female friends all around Brighton, Hove and Chichester, and they started opening little units, all called The Body Shop. I just supplied them with gallons of products – we only had 19 different products, but we made it look like more as we sold them in five different sizes![1]

In 1984 the company went public. In the 1990s, however, sales growth was less rapid and in 1998 Anita Roddick stepped down as Chief Executive, but for a while she and her husband remained as co-chairmen. In 2003 she was awarded a knighthood and became Dame Anita Roddick. Sales began to grow rapidly from 2004 to 2006 from €553 million to €709 million.

Acquisition of The Body Shop by L'Oréal

A dramatic strategic event occurred in 2006 when The Body Shop was sold to the French cosmetics giant L'Oréal, which was 26 per cent owned by Nestlé. The event resulted in the magazine, *Ethical Consumer*, downgrading The Body Shop's ethical rating from 11 out of 20 to a mere 2.5 and calling for a boycott of the company.

There were a number of reasons for this. L'Oréal's animal-testing policies conflict with those of The Body Shop and L'Oréal has been accused of being involved in price fixing with other French perfume houses. L'Oréal's part-owner, Nestlé, has also been subject to various criticisms for ethical misconduct, including promoting formula milk to mothers with babies in poor countries rather than breast milk and using slave labour in cocoa farms in West Africa.

Anita Roddick, however, believed that, by taking over The Body Shop, L'Oréal would develop a more ethical approach to business. L'Oréal has publicly recognised that it would have to develop its ethical policies.

Sadly, Anita Roddick died in 2007 and so has not been able to witness changes. L'Oréal though has begun to address its ethical approach. It adopted a new Code of Business Ethics in 2007 and it is gaining some external accreditation for its approach to sustainability and ethics. Notably, L'Oréal was ranked as one of the world's 100 most ethical companies by Ethisphere in 2007. It has also allowed The Body Shop to continue with its ethical policies.

L'Oréal has, however, looked to inject greater finance into the company aimed at improving the marketing of products. In autumn 2006 a transactional website was launched and there have been greater press marketing campaigns. Profits continued to rise in 2006 and 2007, but fell back quite dramatically from €64 million in 2007 to €36 million in 2008 as recession hit the high streets. They fell by a further 8 per cent in 2009, but growth was expected throughout 2010.

So, it is probably too early to answer the question of 'why did L'Oréal acquire the Body Shop?' with the answer from their own advertising slogan, 'Because they're worth it' – but time will tell.

1. What assumptions has The Body Shop made about the 'rational consumer'?
2. How has The Body Shop's economic performance been affected by its attitudes towards ethical issues? (You could do an Internet search to find further evidence about its performance and the effects of its sale to L'Oréal.)

---

[1] Anita Roddick interview, Startups.co.uk/ 6678842908657825127/anita-roddick.html

students have claimed that they would be prepared to take a lower salary in order to work for a business with high ethical standards and a commitment to socially responsible business practices. An international survey in 2005 showed that 28 per cent of job seekers considered the ethical conduct and values of an employer to be an important factor in deciding whether to apply for work there.[2]

Social responsibility appears not only to bring a range of benefits to business and society, but also to be generally profitable. It is likely to enhance business performance, strengthen brand image, reduce employee turnover and increase access to stock market funds. The Cooperative Bank's annual *Ethical Consumerism Report* showed that the proportion of people who purchased a product at least once a year for ethical reasons rose from 29 per cent in 1999 to 41 per cent in 2008.[3] Box 9.1 gives an example of a company that has built its reputation of being socially and environmentally responsible – The Body Shop.

However, perhaps what is more important is the cost of not being socially responsible. In 2010, the massive oil spill from the Deepwater Horizon rig in the Gulf of Mexico, which killed 11 workers, was blamed on poor safety standards and taking excessive risks with the environment. From the blowout on April 20 to the final capping in August, some 4.9 million barrels of oil leaked into the Gulf of Mexico, causing immense environmental damage and destroying the livelihoods of people in the fishing and tourist industries. It cost the owner, BP, some $3.5 billion in containment and clear-up operations, although the final cost to the company could be many times that amount. Its reputation plummeted in the USA, with motorists boycotting its gas stations. Its share price plummeted from £628 in April to £296 in July.

Despite the concern about cases like this, there are still many firms and consumers that care little about the social or natural environment. There is thus a strong case for government intervention to correct market failures.

Recap

1. Sometimes firms are not aggressive profit maximisers but, instead, take a more socially responsible approach to business.

2. Evidence suggests that economic performance is often enhanced as the corporate responsibility of firms grows.

3. Although there are growing numbers of consumers and businesses that are concerned with ethical and environmental issues, these still represent a niche market.

GOVERNMENT INTERVENTION IN THE MARKET 9.3

Given the various failures of the free market, what forms can government intervention take? There are several policy instruments that the government can use. At one extreme, it can totally replace the market by providing goods and services itself. At the other extreme, it can merely seek to persuade producers, consumers or workers to act differently. Between the two extremes the government has a number of instruments it can use to change the way markets operate. The major ones are taxes, subsidies, laws and regulatory bodies.

[2] *What Makes a Great Employer?* (MORI survey for Manpower, October 2005)
[3] Cooperative Bank, *The Ethical Consumerism Report* (2008). Available at www.goodwithmoney.co.uk

Taxes and subsidies

When there are imperfections in the market, social efficiency will not be achieved. Marginal social benefit (*MSB*) will not equal marginal social cost (*MSC*). A different level of output would be more desirable.

Taxes and subsidies can be used to correct these imperfections. Essentially the approach is to tax those goods or activities where the market produces too much, and subsidise those where the market produces too little.

Let us return to the chemical firm polluting the air as depicted in Figure 9.1 on page 239. The pollution is costly to society, but the firm does not directly incur any of these costs, hence more than the social optimum will be produced. However, by taxing the firm, the government is able to make the firm pay for the pollution it causes. The effect of the tax is to shift the marginal private cost (*MC*) curve upwards and closer to the *MSC* curve. It internalises the externality and so makes the profit-maximising output closer to the socially optimum output.

In section 9.4 we examine how taxes and subsidies can be used to achieve various environmental and social goals.

Legislation and regulation

Laws are frequently used to correct market imperfections. Laws can be of three main types: those that prohibit or regulate behaviour that imposes external costs, those that prevent firms providing false or misleading information, and those that prevent or regulate monopolies and oligopolies.

The advantage of legal restrictions is that they are usually easy to understand and administer. Furthermore, it is often safer to make products illegal rather than merely imposing taxes. However, legal restrictions tend to be a rather blunt weapon. For example, imposing a legal limit on pollution levels leaves little incentive for firms to continue reducing their emissions once the target has been met.

Thus, rather than using the blunt weapon of general legislation to ban or restrict various activities, a more 'subtle' approach can be adopted. This involves the use of various regulatory bodies. Having identified possible cases where action might be required (e.g. potential cases of pollution, misleading information or the abuse of monopoly power), the regulatory body would probably conduct an investigation and then prepare a report containing its findings and recommendations. It might also have the power to enforce its decisions.

In the UK there are regulatory bodies for each of the major privatised utilities (see section 9.6). Another example is the Office of Fair Trading (OFT), which investigates and reports on suspected cases of anti-competitive practices. The OFT can order such firms to cease or modify these practices. Alternatively it can refer them to the Competition Commission (CC), which then conducts an investigation, and makes a ruling (see section 9.5).

Government provision

As we saw with public goods, such as street lights and lighthouses, private firms do not have an incentive to provide them. Therefore, these goods will only be produced if the government intervenes and provides them itself, or subsidises private firms. In some cases, the government will provide goods and services that are not public goods. Neither education nor healthcare are public goods, yet in the UK and many others countries, they are provided by the government. In this way, the government ensures that individuals consume the 'right' amount of the good or service. This is especially important if consumers are unaware of how beneficial the good might be.

Another way in which governments may intervene to correct market failures is through the provision of information. By providing information about the negative effects of smoking or of eating certain foods, the government is trying to reduce the consumption of these goods to their social optimum. Information is also provided about schools, employment and prices to help consumers make more informed decisions.

Recap

1. Governments intervene in markets in a number of ways. One is the use of taxes to curb production or subsidies to increase it.

2. Another is to use legislation or regulation to encourage or force businesses to behave in a more socially desirable way.

3. In some cases, the government or an agency may provide information to correct a market failure. However, if the market failure is so substantial, then the government may choose to intervene and provide the good itself.

ENVIRONMENTAL POLICY   9.4

Growing concerns over global warming, acid rain, the depletion of the ozone layer, industrial and domestic waste, traffic fumes and other forms of pollution have made the protection of the environment a major political and economic issue. So what policy instruments are open to government to tackle the problems?

Green taxes and subsidies

Increasingly countries are introducing 'green' taxes in order to discourage pollution as goods are produced, consumed or disposed of.

Table 9.1 shows the range of green taxes used around the world. Such green taxes are highest in Scandinavia, reflecting the strength of their environmental concerns. In 2007, green tax revenues accounted for 4.6 per cent of GDP in Denmark. Of the

Table 9.1   Types of environmental taxes and charges

Motor fuels	Other goods	Air transport
Leaded/unleaded	Batteries	Noise charges
Diesel (quality differential)	Plastic carrier bags	Aviation fuels
Carbon/energy taxation	Glass containers	
Sulphur tax	Drink cans	**Water**
	Tyres	Water charges
Other energy products	CFCs/halons	Sewage charges
Carbon/energy tax	Disposable razors/cameras	Water effluent charges
Sulphur tax or charge	Lubricant oil charge	Manure charges
NO_2 charge	Oil pollutant charge	
Methane charge	Solvents	**Direct tax provisions**
		Tax relief on green investment
Agricultural inputs		Taxation on free company cars
Fertilisers	**Waste disposal**	Employer-paid commuting
Pesticides	Municipal waste charges	expenses taxable
Manure	Waste-disposal charges	Employer-paid parking
	Hazardous waste charges	expenses taxable
Vehicle-related taxation	Landfill tax or charges	Commuter use of public
Sales tax depends on car size	Duties on waste water	transport tax deductible
Road tax depends on car size		

major industrialised countries, they are lowest in the USA, accounting for just 0.8 per cent of GDP in 2007.

By far the largest green tax revenues come from fuel taxes. Fuel taxes are relatively high in the UK and so, therefore, are green tax revenues, accounting for 2.4 per cent in 2007.

Choosing the tax rate

The rule here is simple: to achieve the socially efficient output of a polluting activity, the government should impose a tax equal to the marginal external cost (or grant a subsidy equal to the marginal external benefit).

| BOX 9.2 | A STERN WARNING |

It's much cheaper to act now on global warming than to wait

The analysis of global warming is not just for climate scientists. Economists have a major part to play in examining its causes and consequences and the possible solutions. And these solutions are likely to have a major impact on business.

Perhaps the most influential study of climate change in recent times has been the Stern Review. This was an independent review, commissioned by the UK Chancellor of the Exchequer, and headed by Sir Nicholas Stern, head of the Government Economic Service and former chief economist of the World Bank. Here was an economist using the methods of economics to analyse perhaps the most serious problem facing the world.

Climate change presents a unique challenge for economics: it is the greatest and widest-ranging market failure ever seen. The economic analysis must therefore be global, deal with long time horizons, have the economics of risk and uncertainty at centre stage, and examine the possibility of major,

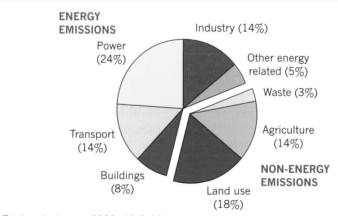

Greenhouse gas emissions in 2000, by source

Total emissions in 2000: 42 GtCO$_2$e.
Energy emissions are mostly CO$_2$ (some non-CO$_2$ in industry and other energy related).
Non-energy emissions are CO$_2$ (land use) and non-CO$_2$ (agriculture and waste).

Assume, for example, that a chemical works emits smoke from a chimney and thus pollutes the atmosphere. This creates external costs for the people who breathe in the smoke. The marginal social cost of producing the chemicals thus exceeds the marginal private cost to the firm: $MSC > MC$.

This is illustrated in Figure 9.3. For simplicity, it is assumed that the firm is a price taker. It produces Q_1 where $P = MC$ (its profit-maximising output), but in doing so takes no account of the external pollution costs it imposes on society. If the government imposes a tax on production equal to the marginal pollution cost, it will effectively 'internalise' the externality. The firm will have to pay an amount equal to the external cost it creates. The firm's MC curve thus shifts upwards to

non-marginal change. To meet these requirements, the Review draws on ideas and techniques from most of the important areas of economics, including many recent advances.[1]

First the bad news . . .

According to the Stern Report, if no action is taken, global temperatures will rise by some 2–3°C within the next 50 years. As a result the world economy will shrink by up to 20 per cent – and that would be just the average. The countries most seriously affected by floods, drought and crop failure could shrink by considerably more. These tend to be the poorest countries, least able to bear the costs of these changes.

Rising sea levels could displace some 200 million people; droughts could create tens or even hundreds of millions of 'climate refugees'. 'Ecosystems will be particularly vulnerable to climate change, with around 15–40 per cent of species potentially facing extinction after only 2°C of warming.' The Stern Report suggested that if CO_2 emissions are not reduced, the environmental impacts could lead to falls in GDP of between 5 and 20 per cent.

. . . Then the good

If action is taken now, these consequences could be averted – and at relatively low cost. According to the Stern Report, a sacrifice of just 1 per cent of global GDP (global income) could, if correctly targeted, be enough to stabilise greenhouse gases to an equivalent of 500–550 ppm of CO_2 – a level generally considered to be sustainable. However, in 2008, Lord Stern adjusted this estimate, saying that CO_2 levels needed to be reduced to 500 ppm and that the cost would be 2 per cent of global GDP per annum.[2] To achieve this, action would need to be taken to cut emissions from their various sources (see the chart). This would involve a mixture of four things:

■ Reducing consumer demand for emissions-intensive goods and services.
■ Increased efficiency, which can save both money and emissions.
■ Action on non-energy emissions, such as avoiding deforestation.
■ Switching to lower-carbon technologies for power, heat and transport.

What policies did Sir Nicholas recommend to achieve these four objectives? Essentially the answer is to alter incentives. This could involve taxing polluting activities; subsidising green alternatives, including the development of green technology; establishing a price for carbon through trading carbon (see the section on tradable permits on pages 251–3) and regulating its production; and encouraging behavioural change through education, better labelling of products, imposing minimum standards for building and encouraging public debate.

We consider some of these alternatives in this section of the chapter.

[1] *Stern Review: Executive Summary* (http://www.hm-treasury.gov.uk/ media/8AC/F7/Executive_Summary)
[2] Cline, W. R. 'Meeting the challenge of global warming', Copenhagen Consensus Challenge Paper, 2004. Available at www.copenhagenconsensus.com/Admin/Public/ DWSWownload.aspx?File=Files%2fFiler%2fCC%2fPapers% 2fClimate_Change_300404.pdf

1. *Would it be in the interests of a business to reduce its carbon emissions if this involved it in increased costs?*
2. *How is the concept of 'opportunity cost' relevant in analysing the impact of business decisions on the environment?*

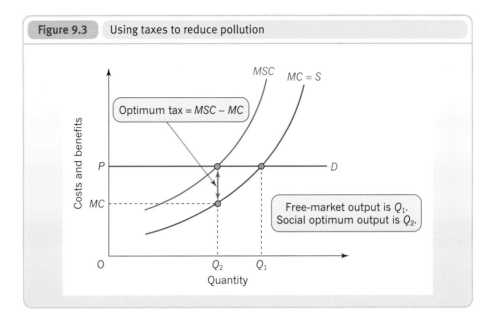

Figure 9.3   Using taxes to reduce pollution

become the same as the *MSC* curve. It will therefore now maximise profits at Q_2, which is the socially optimum output where $MSB = MSC$.

Advantages of taxes and subsidies

Many economists favour the tax/subsidy solution to market imperfections (especially the problem of externalities) because it still allows the market to operate. It forces firms to take on board the full social costs and benefits of their actions. It also has the flexibility of being adjustable according to the magnitude of the problem. For example, the bigger the external costs of a firm's actions, the bigger the tax can be.

What is more, by taxing firms for polluting, they are encouraged to find cleaner ways of producing. The tax thus acts as an incentive over the longer run to reduce pollution: the more a firm can reduce its pollution, the more taxes it can save.

Likewise, when *good* practices are subsidised, firms have the incentive to adopt more good practices.

Disadvantages of taxes and subsidies

Infeasible to use different tax and subsidy rates. Each firm produces different levels and types of externality and operates under different degrees of imperfect competition. It would be expensive and administratively very difficult, if not impossible, to charge every offending firm its own particular tax rate (or grant every relevant firm its own particular rate of subsidy).

Lack of knowledge. Even if a government did decide to charge a tax equal to each offending firm's marginal external costs, it would still have the problem of measuring that cost. The damage from pollution is often extremely difficult to assess. It is also difficult to apportion blame. For example, the damage to lakes and forests from acid rain has been a major concern since the beginning of the 1980s. But just how serious is that damage? What is its current monetary cost? How long lasting is the

Pause for thought

Assume that production by a firm has beneficial spillover effects, i.e. that there are positive externalities which have the effect of positioning the MSC curve below the MC curve. Illustrate this on a diagram similar to Figure 9.3 and show (a) the profit-maximising level of output; (b) the socially efficient level of output; (c) the optimum level of subsidy.

damage? What will be the position in 20 years? Just what and who are to blame? These are questions that cannot be answered precisely. It is thus impossible to fix the 'correct' pollution tax on, say, a particular coal-fired power station.

Despite these problems, it is nevertheless possible to charge firms by the amount of a particular emission. For example, firms could be charged for chimney smoke by so many parts per million of a given pollutant. Although it is difficult to 'fine-tune' such a system so that the charge reflects the precise number of people affected by the pollutant and by how much, it does go some way to internalising the externality.

> **Pause for thought**
>
> *Why is it easier to use taxes and subsidies to tackle the problem of car exhaust pollution than to tackle the problem of peak-time traffic congestion in cities?*

Laws and regulations

The traditional way of tackling pollution has been to set maximum permitted levels of emission or resource use, or minimum acceptable levels of environmental quality, and then to fine firms contravening these limits. Measures of this type are known as **command-and-control (CAC) systems.** Clearly, there have to be inspectors to monitor the amount of pollution, and the fines have to be large enough to deter firms from exceeding the limit.

Virtually all countries have environmental regulations of one sort or another. For example, the EU has over 200 items of legislation covering areas such as air and water pollution, noise, the marketing and use of dangerous chemicals, waste management, the environmental impacts of new projects (such as power stations, roads and quarries), recycling, depletion of the ozone layer and global warming.

Assessing CAC systems. Given the uncertainty over the environmental impacts of pollutants, especially over the longer term, it is often better to play safe and set tough emissions standards. These could always be relaxed at a later stage if the effects turn out to be less damaging, but it might be too late to reverse damage if the effects turn out to be more serious. Taxes may be a more sophisticated means of reaching a socially efficient output, but CAC methods are usually more straightforward to devise, easier to understand by firms and easier to implement.

The weakness of command-and-control systems is that they fail to offer business any incentive to do better than the legally specified level. By contrast, with a pollution tax, the lower the pollution level, the less tax there will be to pay. There is thus a continuing incentive for businesses progressively to cut pollution levels and introduce cleaner technology.

> **Definitions**
>
> **Command-and-control (CAC) systems**
> The use of laws or regulations backed up by inspections and penalties (such as fines) for non-compliance.
>
> **Tradable permits**
> Each firm is given a permit to produce a given level of pollution. If less than the permitted amount is produced, the firm is given a credit. This can then be sold to another firm, allowing it to exceed its original limit. This is known as a 'cap and trade' scheme.

Tradable permits

A policy measure that has grown in popularity in recent years is that of **tradable permits.** This is a combination of command-and-control and market-based systems. A maximum permitted level of emission is set for a given pollutant for a given factory, and the firm is given a permit to emit up to this amount. If it emits less than this amount, it is given a credit for the difference, which it can then use in another of its factories. Another option is to sell the credits to another firm. This firm can then pollute over its permitted level, by an amount equal to the credits. Thus the overall level of emissions is set by CAC methods, whereas their distribution is determined by the market.

Take the example of firms A and B, which are currently producing 12 units of a pollutant each. Now assume that a standard is set permitting them to produce only

10 units each. If firm A managed to reduce the pollutant to 8 units, it would be given a credit for 2 units. It could then sell this to firm B, enabling B to continue emitting 12 units. The effect would still be a total reduction of 4 units between the two firms. However, by allowing them to trade in pollution permits, pollution reduction can be concentrated in the firms where it can be achieved at lowest cost. In our example, if it cost firm B more to reduce its pollution than firm A, then the permits could be sold from A to B at a price that was profitable to both (i.e. at a price above the cost of emission reduction to A, but below the cost of emission reduction to B).

> **Pause for thought**
>
> *To what extent will the introduction of tradable permits lead to a lower level of total pollution (as opposed to its redistribution)?*

BOX 9.3   THE PROBLEM OF URBAN TRAFFIC CONGESTION

Does London have the answer?

Traffic congestion is a classic example of the problem of externalities. When people use their cars, not only do they incur private costs (petrol, wear and tear on the vehicle, tolls, the time taken to travel, etc.), but also they impose costs on other people. These external costs include the following:

Congestion costs: time. When a person uses a car on a congested road, it adds to the congestion. This therefore slows down the traffic even more and increases the journey time of other car users.

Congestion costs: monetary. Congestion increases fuel consumption, and the stopping and starting increases the costs of wear and tear. When a motorist adds to congestion, therefore, there are additional monetary costs imposed on other motorists.

Environmental costs. When motorists use a road they reduce the quality of the environment for others. Cars emit fumes and create noise. This is bad enough for pedestrians and other car users, but can be particularly distressing for people living along the road. Driving can cause accidents, a problem that increases as drivers become more impatient as a result of delays.

Exhaust gases cause long-term environmental damage and are one of the main causes of the greenhouse effect and of the increased acidity of lakes and rivers and the poisoning of forests. They can also cause long-term health problems (e.g. for asthma sufferers).

The socially efficient level of road usage

These externalities mean that road usage will be above the social optimum. This is illustrated in the diagram. Costs and benefits are shown on the vertical axis and are measured in money terms. Thus any non-monetary costs or benefits (such as time costs) must be given a monetary value. The horizontal axis measures road usage in terms of cars per minute passing a specified point on the road.

For simplicity it is assumed that there are no external benefits from car use and that therefore marginal private and marginal social benefits are the same. The *MSB* curve is shown as downward sloping. The reason for this is that different road users put a different value on any given journey. If the marginal (private) cost of making the journey were high, only those for whom the journey had a high marginal benefit would travel along the road. If the marginal cost of making the journey fell, more people would make the journey: people choosing to make the journey as long as the marginal cost of the journey was less than the marginal benefit. Thus the greater the number of cars, the lower the marginal benefit.

The marginal (private) cost curve (*MC*) is likely to be constant up to the level of traffic flow at which congestion begins to occur. This is shown as point *a* in the diagram. Beyond this point, marginal cost is likely to rise as time costs increase (i.e. journey times lengthen) and as fuel consumption rises.

The marginal *social* cost curve (*MSC*) is drawn above the marginal private cost curve. The vertical difference between the two represents the external costs. Up to point *b*, external costs are simply the environmental costs. Beyond point *b*, there are also external congestion costs, since additional road users slow down the journey of *other* road users. These external costs get progressively greater as traffic grinds to a halt.

The actual level of traffic flow will be at Q_1, where marginal private costs and benefits are equal (point *e*).

Actual and optimum road usage

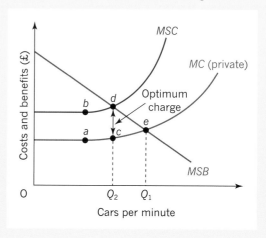

A similar principle can be used for using natural resources. Thus fish quotas could be assigned to fishing boats or fleets or countries. Any parts of these quotas not used could then be sold.

The EU carbon trading system

In the EU, a carbon Emissions Trading Scheme (ETS) has been in place since January 2005 as part of the EU's approach to meeting its targets under the Kyoto Treaty (see Web Case C.17). Under the scheme, some 11 500 industrial plants have been allocated CO_2 emissions allowances, or credits, by their respective governments. Companies that exceed their limits must purchase credits to cover the difference,

The socially efficient level of traffic flow, however, will be at the lower level of Q_2 where marginal social costs and benefits are equal (point *d*). In other words, there will be an excessive level of road usage.

So what can governments do to 'internalise' these externalities? To achieve a reduction in traffic to Q_2 the motorist should be charged an amount equal to *d–c* in the diagram. How can this be achieved? In practice this is difficult, given that congestion and its costs vary with location and the time of day. Also the external cost is hard to measure. One, albeit imperfect, solution is to impose charges on cars entering a 'congestion zone'. This solution is the one adopted in London.

Congestion charging in London

In London, car drivers must pay £8 per day to enter the inner London area (or 'congestion zone') any time between 7.00 and 18.00, Monday to Friday. Payment can be made by various means, including post, Internet, telephone, mobile phone SMS text message and at various shops and petrol stations. Payment can be in advance or up to midnight on the day of travel, or up to midnight on the following charging day for an extra £2. Cars entering the congestion zone have their number plate recorded by camera and a computer check then leads to a fine of £120 being sent to those who have not paid (reduced to £60 for payment within 14 days).

The system was introduced in 2003 and the charging zone was extended in 2007. The initial effect was to reduce traffic in the zone by about 20 per cent and significantly increase the rate of traffic flow. Traffic in the zone has crept back somewhat since, but this is partly the result of a general increase in traffic.

The charge is not a marginal one, however, in the sense that it does not vary with the degree of congestion or the amount of time spent or distance travelled by a motorist within the zone. Nevertheless, its simplicity makes it easy to understand and relatively cheap to operate.

More sophisticated electronic road pricing

More sophisticated schemes attempt to relate directly the price charged to the motorist to the specific level of marginal external cost. In Singapore, for example, cars are fitted with a dashboard device into which you must insert a smart card which contains pre-paid units, much as a photocopying or telephone card. The cards can be recharged. On specified roads, overhead gantries read the device and deduct units from the card. Charges vary with the time of day. If a car does not have sufficient funds on its card, the car's details are relayed to a control centre and a fine is sent to the owner.

The most sophisticated scheme, still under development in parts of the world, would involve equipping all cars with a receiver. Their position is located by satellite tracking. Charges are then imposed according to location, distance travelled, time of day and type of vehicle. The charges can operate either through smart cards in a dashboard device or though central computerised billing.

Proposals to introduce a similar system in the UK have met with stiff opposition. People resent paying more to travel and many see such a scheme as merely a means of raising additional revenue. Many also worry that it would be unfair on people who are forced to travel long distances or through congested areas simply to get to work.

But such taxes can be revenue neutral if other taxes, such as the road fund licence, are cut. Also, they act as an incentive for people to reduce the amount they travel or to avoid peak times. They also put pressure on companies to use more flexible working times and to allow telecommuting (see Box 8.1 on page 213). Clearly congestion imposes large costs on society and tackling it is likely to involve increasing the costs of motoring one way or another. At least road pricing directly relates charging to congestion.

1. Referring to a town or city with which you are familiar, consider what would be the most appropriate mix of policies to deal with its traffic congestion problems.
2. Explain how, by varying the charge to motorists according to the time of day or level of congestion, a socially optimal level of road use can be achieved.

while those that reduce their emissions can sell their surplus credits for a profit. Companies can trade directly with each other or through brokers operating throughout Europe.

As part of the EU 2020 Climate and Energy Package, a more environmentally friendly Directive was agreed in December 2008, to come in force in 2013. A key aim is to have a more ambitious, certain and consistent approach across the EU.

Assessing the system of tradable permits

The main advantage of tradable permits is that they combine the simplicity of CAC methods with the benefits of achieving pollution reduction in the most efficient way. There is also the advantage that firms have a financial incentive to cut pollution. This might then make it easier for governments to impose tougher standards (i.e. impose lower permitted levels of emission).

There are, however, various problems with tradable permits. One is the possibility that trade will lead to pollution being concentrated in certain geographical areas. Another is that it may reduce the pressure on dirtier factories (or countries) to cut their emissions. Finally, the system will lead to significant cuts in pollution only if the permitted levels are low. Once the system is in place, the government might then feel that the pressure is off to *reduce* the permitted levels.

A major criticism of the EU's initial ETS was that the carbon allowances were set far too high. As a result many firms found it easy to produce surplus credits, which pushed their price to a low level, reaching a minuscule €0.02 per tonne by the end of 2007. According to the Stern Report (see Box 9.2), carbon prices of $30 to $50 are necessary to stabilise levels of CO_2. In answer to this, the allowances were somewhat tighter in the second trading period (2008–12). By mid 2008, carbon was trading at around €28 per tonne. With the recession of 2008/9, however, the price fell as firms cut back production.

By mid 2009, the price had risen to about €14. However, following the international summit on climate change in Copenhagen in December 2009, carbon prices dropped to a six-month low of €12.40 in December 2009, as a failure to reach a binding agreement to cut emissions disappointed traders. As global recovery continued through 2010, however, so the carbon price rose again, due to higher energy demand and the expectation of a continuing growth in demand for credits.

Pause for thought

Should all emitters of carbon, including aircraft and agriculture, be included in carbon trading schemes?

Recap

1. There are three main types of environmental policy instrument: taxes and subsidies; command-and-control systems; tradable permits.

2. Taxes and subsidies have the advantages of 'internalising' externalities and of providing incentives to reduce external costs. The problem with using taxes and subsidies is in identifying the appropriate rates, since these will vary according to the environmental impact.

3. Command-and-control systems, such as making certain practices illegal or putting limits on discharges, are a less sophisticated alternative to taxes or subsidies. However, they may be preferable when the environmental costs of certain actions are unknown and it is wise to play safe.

4. Tradable permits are where firms are given permits to emit a certain level of pollution and then these can be traded. A firm that can relatively cheaply reduce its pollution below its permitted level can sell this credit to another firm which finds it more costly to do so.

COMPETITION POLICY AND BUSINESS BEHAVIOUR   9.5

Competition, monopoly and the public interest

Most markets in the real world are imperfect, with firms having varying degrees of market power. But will this power be against the public interest? This question has been addressed by successive governments in framing legislation to deal with monopolies and oligopolies.

It might be thought that market power is always 'a bad thing', certainly as far as the consumer is concerned. After all, it enables firms to make supernormal profit, thereby 'exploiting' the consumer. The less substitute products there are, the greater the firm's power and the higher prices will be relative to the costs of production. This is illustrated in Figure 9.4 (which is similar to Figure 5.2 on page 125).

The firm maximises profits at Q_1, where $MC = MR$. Profits are shown by the shaded area. The greater the firm's market power, the steeper will be the firm's AR curve and also the MR curve. The bigger will be the gap between price (point a) and marginal cost (point b). Remember that under perfect competition, price equals marginal cost (see Figure 4.4 on page 108). This is shown by point c, which is at a lower price and a higher output.

Not only does a lack of competition result in a higher price, it also removes the incentive to become more efficient.

But market power is not necessarily a bad thing. Firms may not fully exploit their position of power – perhaps for fear that very high profits would eventually lead to other firms overcoming entry barriers, or perhaps because they are not aggressive profit maximisers. Even if they do make large supernormal profits, they may still charge a lower price than more competitive sectors of the industry because of their economies of scale. This may lead to them having a lower marginal cost curve than a more competitive firm. Finally, they may use their profits for research and development and for capital investment. The consumer might then benefit from improved products at lower prices, or indeed new products.

Figure 9.4	Profit maximising under monopoly

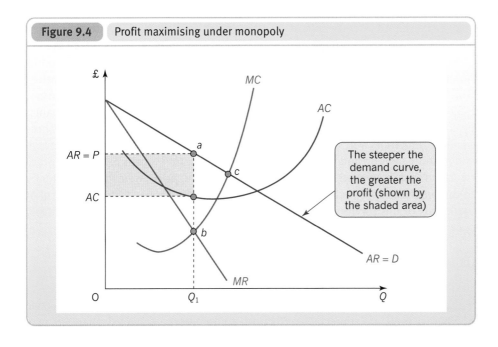

Competition policy could seek to ban various structures or activities. For example, it could ban mergers leading to market share of more than a certain amount, or it could ban price-fixing arrangements between oligopolists. However, most countries prefer to adopt a more flexible approach and examine each case on its merits. Such an approach does not presume that the mere possession of power is against the public interest, but rather that certain uses of that power may be.

UK competition policy

Current UK policy is based on the 1998 Competition Act and the 2002 Enterprise Act. These Acts bring UK policy in line with EU competition policy (which is largely confined to firms trading between EU members).

The Competition Act has two key sets (or 'chapters') of prohibitions. Chapter I prohibits various collusive practices of oligopolies ('restrictive practices') (see pages 129–31). Chapter II prohibits various abuses of monopoly power. The Enterprise Act strengthened the Competition Act and introduced new measures for the control of mergers.

Under the two Acts, the body charged with ensuring that the prohibitions are carried out is the Office of Fair Trading (OFT). The OFT can investigate any firms suspected of engaging in one or more of the prohibited practices. Its officers have the power to enter and search premises, and can require the production and explanation of documents.

Where the OFT decides that an infringement of one of the prohibitions has occurred, it can direct the offending firms to modify their behaviour or cease their practices altogether. Companies in breach of a prohibition are liable to fines of up to 10 per cent of their annual UK turnover. Third parties adversely affected by such breaches can seek compensation through the courts.

The Competition Act also set up a Competition Commission (CC) to which the OFT can refer cases for further investigation. The CC is charged with determining whether the structure of an industry or the practices of firms within it are detrimental to competition.

If a case is referred to the Competition Commission, it will carry out an investigation to establish whether competition is adversely affected. If it finds that it is, it will decide on the appropriate remedies, such as prohibiting various practices.

In January 2010, the local bus sector was referred to the Competition Commission by the Office of Fair Trading, following the publication of their Consultation, which derived from complaints of 'predatory tactics' by companies in the industry. Established firms were accused of acting aggressively towards smaller bus companies by charging prices below average cost on routes where they were competing. These smaller competitors were thus forced out of the market, thereby limiting competition and pushing fares up and the quality of service down. Investigations into the industry found that in areas where competition was limited, prices were 9p higher. Many of the problems appeared to stem from a number of takeovers, which meant that two-thirds of bus services were controlled by only five operators, each effectively controlling particular towns or regions.

UK restrictive practices policy

Under the 2002 Enterprise Act it is a *criminal* offence to engage in cartel agreements (i.e. horizontal, rather than vertical, agreements between firms), irrespective of whether there are appreciable effects on competition. Convicted offenders may receive a prison sentence of up to five years and/or an unlimited fine. Prosecutions may be brought by the Serious Fraud Office or the OFT.

But what practices constitute 'cartel agreements'? These involve one or more of the following agreements by firms: price fixing; limiting supply, perhaps by each firm agreeing to an output quota; sharing out markets by geographical area, type or size of customer or nature of outlet (e.g. bus companies agreeing not to run services in each other's areas); **collusive tendering** for a contract, where two or more firms put in a tender at secretly agreed (high) prices; or agreements between purchasers (e.g. supermarkets) to keep down prices paid to suppliers (e.g. farmers).

In the case of other types of agreement, the OFT has the discretion to decide, on a case-by-case basis, whether or not competition is appreciably restricted, and whether, therefore, they should be terminated or the firms should be exempted. Such cases include the following:

- *Vertical price-fixing agreements*. These are price agreements between purchasing firms and their suppliers. An example of this is resale price maintenance. This is where a manufacturer or distributor sets the price for retailers to charge. It may well distribute a price list to retailers (e.g. a car manufacturer may distribute a price list to car showrooms). **Resale price maintenance** is a way of preventing competition between retailers driving down retail prices and ultimately the price they pay to the manufacturer. Both manufacturers and retailers, therefore, are likely to gain from resale price maintenance.
- *Agreements to exchange information that could have the effect of reducing competition*. For example, if producers exchange information on their price intentions, it is a way of allowing price leadership (see page 130), a form of tacit collusion, to continue.

A problem with any policy to deal with collusion is the difficulty in rooting it out. When firms do all their deals 'behind closed doors' and are careful not to keep records or give clues, then collusion can be very hard to spot.

UK monopoly policy

Under the Chapter II prohibition of the 1998 Competition Act, it is illegal for a dominant firm to exercise its market power in such a way as to reduce competition. Any suspected case is investigated by the OFT, which uses a two-stage process in deciding whether an abuse has taken place.

The first stage is to establish whether a firm has a position of dominance. The firm does not literally have to be a monopoly. Rather 'dominance' normally involves the firm having at least a 40 per cent share of the market (national or local, whichever is appropriate), although this figure will vary from industry to industry. Also dominance depends on the barriers to entry to new competitors. The higher the barriers to the entry of new firms, the less 'contestable' will be the market, and the more dominant a firm is likely to be for any given current market share.

If the firm *is* deemed to be dominant, the second stage involves the OFT deciding whether the firm's practices constitute an abuse of its position. Examples of such practices include:

- *Charging excessively high prices*. These are prices above those that the firm would charge if it faced effective competition. One sign of excessively high prices is abnormally high rates of profit.

> **Pause for thought**
>
> *Are all such agreements necessarily against the interests of consumers?*

> **Definitions**
>
> **Collusive tendering**
> Where two or more firms secretly agree on the prices they will tender for a contract. These prices will be above those which would be put in under a genuinely competitive tendering process.
>
> **Resale price maintenance**
> Where the manufacturer of a product (legally) insists that the product should be sold at a specified retail price.

- *Price discrimination.* This is regarded as an abuse only to the extent that the higher prices are excessive or the lower prices are used to exclude competitors.
- *Predatory pricing.* This is where the price of a product is set at loss-making levels, so as to undercut competitors and drive them out of business. The firm uses profitable parts of its business to subsidise this loss making.
- *Vertical restraints.* This is where a supplying firm imposes conditions on a purchasing firm (or vice versa). For example, a manufacturer may impose rules on retailers about displaying the product or the provision of after-sales service, or it may refuse to supply certain outlets (e.g. perfume manufacturers refusing to supply discount chains, such as Superdrug).

The simple *existence* of any of these practices may not constitute an abuse. The OFT has to decide whether their *effect* is to restrict competition. If the case is not

---

BOX 9.4   A LIFT TO PROFITS?

Record EU fine for operating a lift and escalator cartel

EU competition policy applies to companies operating in two or more EU countries. The UK legislation described in this section of the chapter is very similar to EU legislation, which is largely contained in Articles 81 and 82 of the Treaty of Amsterdam. Article 81 is concerned with restrictive practices and Article 82 with the abuse of market power. The policy is implemented by the European Commission and it has the power to levy substantial fines on companies found to be in breach of the legislation.

In February 2007, the Commission imposed a record fine of €992 million on four lift and escalator manufacturers for operating a price-fixing cartel. According to the EU Commission, the companies – ThyssenKrupp of Germany, Otis of the USA, Kone of Finland and Schindler of Switzerland – sought to freeze market share and fix prices. 'Projects that were rigged included lifts and escalators for hospitals, railway stations, shopping centres and commercial buildings.'[1]

> The Commission last year passed new fining guidelines that will allow Brussels to further increase the financial pain on abusive companies in all new cases. Officials have argued that the new rules will mean that more companies will be hit with the maximum penalty – a fine equivalent to 10 per cent of their annual global turnover.
>
> The lift cartel operated in Germany, the Netherlands, Belgium and Luxembourg between at least 1995 and 2004. According to the Commission, the groups co-ordinated their bids to ensure that a designated group would win specific contracts.
>
> '[To agree on bids] they usually met in bars and restaurants, they travelled to the countryside or even abroad, and they used pre-paid mobile cards to avoid tracking,' the Commission said.[2]

According to Jonathan Todd of the EU, 'the result of this cartel is that taxpayers, public authorities and property developers have been ripped off big time. The companies ensured that, by rigging the bids [i.e. collusive tendering] and sharing the markets, the prices paid for the installation and the maintenance were way above what they would have been if there had been a competitive market.'[3]

Neelie Kroes, the EU Competition Commissioner, said that 'the national management of these companies knew what they were doing was wrong, but they tried to conceal their action and went ahead anyway. The damage caused by this cartel will last for many years because it covered not only the initial supply but also the subsequent maintenance of lifts and escalators.'

Of the four companies, ThyssenKrupp was given the largest fine (€480 million), and the biggest ever for a single company, because it was a 'repeat offender'. It had received a previous fine of €3.2 million in 1998 for fixing stainless steel prices. Under guidelines issued in 2006, repeat offenders face an automatic 50 per cent increase in fines.

 What factors determine the likelihood that firms will collude to fix prices – despite the prospect of facing fines of up to 10 per cent of their annual global turnover?

---

[1] 'Record EU fine for lift cartel', BBC News, 21 February 2007
[2] 'Brussels imposes €992m fine on lift cartel', *Financial Times*, 22 February 2007

[3] Europea, Press Release, Competition: 'Commission fines members of lifts and escalators cartels over €990 million', 21 February 2007, http://europa.en/rapid/ pressReleases Action.do?reference=IP/07/ 209&format=HTML

straightforward, the OFT can refer it to the Competition Commission. The CC will then carry out a detailed investigation to establish whether competition is restricted or distorted. If it is, the CC will rule what actions must be taken to remedy the situation.

BOX 9.5 | **WHAT PRICE FOR PEACE OF MIND?**

Exploiting monopoly power in the sale of extended warranties on electrical goods

If you go into Curry's, Comet, PC World or virtually any other High Street retailer to buy an electrical good, such as a DVD player, a fridge or PC, the sales assistant will probably be very keen to sell you an extended warranty (EW). These EWs are typically for three to five years and sometimes merely extend the product's guarantee against breakdown beyond its normal one- or two-year expiry date. Sometimes they go further and provide cover against other risks, such as accidental damage or theft.

These EWs are highly profitable for the retailer. In 2002 they accounted for approximately 40 per cent of Dixons' profits and 80 per cent of Comet's. It's hardly surprising that retailers are very keen to sell them to you!

In 2002 the Office of Fair Trading published a report on EWs and concluded that 'there is insufficient competition and information to ensure that consumers get good value, and that many electrical retailers may make considerable profits on the sale of EWs'.

Research conducted by the OFT indicates that customers can feel pressurised to rush to a decision to buy an extended warranty when they buy their new appliance. A high percentage of consumers had not thought about buying an extended warranty before they arrive at the store.

Buyers should think whether extended warranties offer them value for money. OFT research found that the average washing machine repair costs between £45 to £65. So if a five year extended warranty costs £150 on a £300 washing machine, it would need to break down four times for a consumer to benefit.

A recent 'Which?' report highlights that modern domestic appliances are generally reliable. It found that 81 per cent of washing machines didn't break down at all in the first six years.

. . . Some sales staff are paid commission on each extended warranty they sell, so may be keen for a customer to sign on the dotted line.[1]

The OFT was concerned that retailers were using their market power at the point of sale and benefiting from consumers' ignorance. It decided, therefore, to refer the case to the Competition Commission, which published its report in December 2003.

The CC report found that there was a 'complex monopoly'[2] in the market, worth £900 million per year,

which was working against the public interest. It concluded that there had been an abuse of monopoly power, stating that:

> Were this market fully competitive such that the top five EW retailers' returns were no greater than their cost of capital,[3] We estimate that EW prices would have been, on average, up to one-third lower.
> . . . Many of the practices that we have identified during the course of our investigation operate or may be expected to operate against the public interest. They result in lack of choice, excessive prices, insufficient information, insufficient competition at point of sale, limited but not insignificant sales pressure, some terms which could be disadvantageous, and lack of information about the scope of protection under service-backed schemes.[4]

Despite these findings, the Competition Commission did not recommend banning shops from bundling warranties with electrical goods at the point of sale, despite many of the EWs being 'unfair and uncompetitive'. Instead, it recommended that retailers should display prices for EWs alongside the price of the goods, both in shops and in advertisements. It also recommended that the shops should provide information about customers' rights and that customers should get a full refund on the EW if they cancelled within 45 days.

The government minister, the Secretary of State for Trade and Industry, Patricia Hewitt, accepted these findings and ruled that they should be implemented – which they were in April 2005.

1. *What features of the market for EWs distort competition?*
2. *To what extent will the ruling by the government make the market for EWs competitive?*

---

[1] OFT News Release, PN 68/02, October 2002
[2] A complex monopoly is where several companies separately (i.e. not collusively) are in a position to exploit a particular market advantage to the detriment of the consumer

[3] A measure of 'normal profit'
[4] Summary to 'Extended warranties on domestic electrical goods: a report on the supply of extended warranties on domestic electrical goods within the UK', Competition Commission, December 2003 (www.competition-commission.org.uk/reprpub/reports/2003/485xwars.htm#summary)

UK merger policy

Merger policy is covered by the 2002 Enterprise Act. It seeks to prevent mergers that are likely to result in a substantial lessening of competition.

A merger or takeover will be investigated by the OFT if the target company has a turnover of £70 million or more, or if the merger results in the new company having a market share of 25 per cent or more. The OFT conducts a preliminary investigation to see whether competition is likely to be threatened. If it is, and if there are unlikely to be any substantial compensating benefits to consumers, the OFT refers the case to the Competition Commission.

If reference is made to the CC, it conducts a detailed investigation to establish whether the merger is likely to lead to a significant reduction in competition. If so, it can prohibit the merger. Alternatively, it can require the merged firm to behave in certain ways in order to protect consumers' interests. In such cases, the OFT then monitors the firm to ensure that it is abiding by the CC's conditions. CC investigations must normally be completed within 24 weeks.

Recap

1. Competition policy in most countries recognises that monopolies, mergers and restrictive practices can bring both costs and benefits to the consumer. Generally, though, restrictive practices tend to be more damaging to consumers' interests than simple monopoly power or mergers.

2. UK legislation is covered by the 1998 Competition Act and 2002 Enterprise Act. The Office of Fair Trading is charged with ensuring that firms abide by the legislation. Where there is doubt, it can refer cases to the Competition Commission for a ruling.

3. Cartel agreements are a criminal offence and certain other types of collusive behaviour can be curtailed by the OFT if they are against the public interest.

4. The abuse of monopoly power by a dominant firm can also be prevented by the OFT. Such abuses include charging excessively high prices.

5. Mergers over a certain size are investigated by the OFT, with possible reference to the Competition Commission for a ruling as to whether they should be permitted.

9.6 THE REGULATION OF BUSINESS

Regulation and the privatised industries

Definitions

Nationalised industries
State-owned industries that produce goods or services that are sold in the market.

Privatisation
Selling nationalised industries to the private sector. This may be through the public issue of shares, by a management buyout or by selling it to a private company.

In the late 1940s and early 1950s the Labour government **nationalised** many of the key transport, communications and power industries, such as the railways, freight transport, airlines, coal, gas, electricity and steel. The Thatcher and Major governments in the 1980s and early 1990s sold these industries to the private sector in a programme of **privatisation**. However, many of these privatised industries had considerable market power and so it was felt necessary to regulate their behaviour.

Regulation in practice

To some extent the behaviour of privatised industries may be governed by general monopoly and restrictive practice legislation. For example, in the UK privatised firms can be investigated by the Office of Fair Trading and if necessary referred to the Competition Commission.

In addition to this, there is a separate regulatory office to oversee the structure and behaviour of each of the privatised utilities. These regulators are as follows: the Office for Gas and Electricity Markets (Ofgem), the Office of Communications

(Ofcom), the Office of the Rail Regulator (ORR) and the Office of Water Services (Ofwat). The regulators set terms under which the industries have to operate. For example, ORR sets the terms under which rail companies have access to the track and stations. The terms set by the regulator can be reviewed by negotiation between the regulator and the industry. If agreement cannot be reached, the Competition Commission acts as an appeal court and its decision is binding.

The regulator for each industry also sets limits to the prices that certain parts of the industry can charge. These parts are those where there is little or no competition, e.g. the charges made to electricity and gas retailers by National Grid Transco, the owner of the electricity grid and major gas pipelines.

The price-setting formulae are essentially of the 'RPI minus X' variety. What this means is that the industries can raise their prices by the rate of increase in the retail price index (i.e. by the rate of inflation) *minus* a certain percentage (X) to take account of expected increases in efficiency. Thus if the rate of inflation were 6 per cent, and if the regulator considered that the industry (or firm) could be expected to reduce its costs by 2 per cent ($X = 2$ per cent), then price rises would be capped at 4 per cent. The $RPI - X$ system is thus an example of **price-cap regulation**. The idea of this system of regulation is that it forces the industry to pass cost savings on to the consumer.

> **Definition**
>
> **Price-cap regulation**
> Where the regulator puts a ceiling on the amount by which a firm can raise its price.

> **Pause for thought**
>
> *If an industry regulator adopts an RPI – X formula for price regulation, is it desirable that the value of X should be adjusted as soon as cost conditions change?*

Assessing the system of regulation in the UK

The system that has evolved in the UK has various advantages:

- It is a discretionary system, with the regulator able to judge individual examples of the behaviour of the industry on their own merits. The regulator has a detailed knowledge of the industry which would not be available to government ministers or other bodies such as the Office of Fair Trading. The regulator could thus be argued to be the best person to decide on whether the industry is acting in the public interest.
- The system is flexible, since it allows for the licence and price formula to be changed as circumstances change.
- The 'RPI minus X' formula provides an incentive for the privatised firms to be as efficient as possible. If they can lower their costs by more than X, they will, in theory, be able to make larger profits and keep them. If on the other hand, they do not succeed in reducing costs sufficiently, they will make a loss. There is thus a continuing pressure on them to cut costs.

There are, however, some inherent problems with the way in which regulation operates in the UK:

- The 'RPI minus X' formula was designed to provide an incentive for the firms to cut costs. But if X is set too low, the firm might make excessive profits. Frequently, regulators have underestimated the scope for cost reductions resulting from new technology and reorganisation, and have thus initially set X too low. As a result, instead of X remaining constant for a number of years, as intended, new higher values for X have been set after only one or two years. Alternatively, one-off price cuts have been ordered, as happened when the water companies were required by Ofwat to cut prices by an average of 10 per cent in 2000. In either case, the incentive for the industry to cut costs is reduced. What is the point of being more efficient if the regulator is merely going to insist on a higher value for X and thus take away the extra profits?

- Regulation is becoming increasingly complex. This makes it difficult for the industries to plan and may lead to a growth of 'short-termism'. One of the claimed advantages of privatisation was to give greater independence to the industries from short-term government interference, and allow them to plan for the longer term. In practice, one type of interference may have been replaced by another.

- As regulation becomes more detailed and complex and as the regulator becomes more and more involved in the detailed running of the industry, so managers and regulators will become increasingly involved in a game of strategy, each trying to outwit the other. Information will become distorted and time and energy will be wasted in playing this game of cat and mouse. This is an example of the principal–agent problem (see pages 9–10), where the agent (the company) is trying to avoid carrying out the wishes of the principal (the regulator).

- There is also the problem that as the regulator becomes more involved in the industry, they may be persuaded to see the managers' point of view and hence they could become less strict. This idea is known as **regulatory capture**.

Definition

Regulatory capture
Where the regulator is persuaded to operate in the industry's interests rather than those of the consumer.

One way in which the dangers of ineffective or over-intrusive regulation can be avoided is to replace regulation with competition wherever this is possible. Indeed, one of the major concerns of the regulators has been to do just this. (See Web Case C.24 for ways in which competition has been increased in the electricity industry.)

Regulation versus competition

Where natural monopoly exists (see page 122), competition is impossible in a free market. Of course, the industry *could* be broken up by the government, with firms prohibited from owning more than a certain percentage of the industry. But this would lead to higher costs of production. Firms would be operating further back up a downward-sloping long-run average cost curve.

However, many parts of the privatised industries are not natural monopolies. Generally it is only the *grid* that is a natural monopoly. In the case of gas and water, it is the pipelines. It would be wasteful to duplicate these. In the case of electricity, it is the power lines: the national grid and the local power lines. In the case of the railways, it is the track.

Other parts of these industries, however, have generally been opened up to competition (with the exception of water). Thus there are now many producers and sellers of electricity and gas. This is possible because they are given access, by law, to the national and local electricity grids and gas pipelines. The telecommunications market too has become more competitive with the growth of mobile phones and lines supplied by cable operators.

As competition has been introduced into these industries, so price-cap regulation has been progressively abandoned. For example, in 2006 Ofcom abandoned price control of BT and other phone companies over line rentals and phone charges. This was in response to the growth in competition from cable operators, mobile phones and free Internet calls from companies such as Skype via VoIP (voice Internet protocol).

Despite attempts to introduce competition into the privatised industries, they are still dominated by giant companies. Even if they are no longer strictly monopolies, they still have considerable market power and the scope for price leadership or other forms of oligopolistic collusion is great. Thus although regulation through the price formula has been progressively abandoned as elements of competition have been introduced, the regulators have retained a role similar to that of the OFT, namely to prevent cases of collusion and the abuse of monopoly power. The companies, however, do have the right of appeal to the Competition Commission.

Recap

1. Regulation in the UK has involved setting up regulatory offices for the major privatised utilities. These generally operate informally, using negotiation and bargaining to persuade the industries to behave in the public interest.

2. As far as prices are concerned, parts of the industries are required to abide by an 'RPI minus X' formula. This forces them to pass potential cost reductions on to the consumer. At the same time they are allowed to retain any additional profits gained from cost reductions

greater than X. This provides them with an incentive to achieve even greater increases in efficiency.

3. Many parts of the privatised industries are not natural monopolies. In these parts, competition may be a more effective means of pursuing the public interest.

4. Various attempts have been made to make the privatised industries more competitive, often at the instigation of the regulator. Nevertheless, considerable market power remains in the hands of many privatised firms, and thus the need for regulation will continue.

QUESTIONS

1. Assume that a firm discharges waste into a river. As a result, the marginal social costs (*MSC*) are greater than the firm's marginal (private) costs (*MC*). The following table shows how *MC*, *MSC*, *AR* and *MR* vary with output.

Output	1	2	3	4	5	6	7	8
MC (£)	23	21	23	25	27	30	35	42
MSC (£)	35	34	38	42	46	52	60	72
TR (£)	60	102	138	168	195	219	238	252
AR (£)	60	51	46	42	39	36.5	34	31.5
MR (£)	60	42	36	30	27	24	19	14

(a) How much will the firm produce if it seeks to maximise profits?

(b) What is the socially efficient level of output (assuming no externalities on the demand side)?

(c) How much is the marginal external cost at this level of output?

(d) What size tax would be necessary for the firm to reduce its output to the socially efficient level?

(e) Why is the tax less than the marginal externality?

(f) Why might it be equitable to impose a lump-sum tax on this firm?

(g) Why will a lump-sum tax not affect the firm's output (assuming that in the long run the firm can still make at least normal profit)?

2. Distinguish between publicly provided goods, public goods and merit goods.

3. Some roads could be regarded as a public good, but some could be provided by the market. Which types of road could be provided by the market? Why? Would it be a good idea?

4. Make a list of pieces of information a firm might want to know and consider whether it could buy

the information and how reliable that information might be.

5. Why might it be better to ban certain activities that cause environmental damage rather than to tax them?

6. How suitable are legal restrictions in the following cases?

(a) Ensuring adequate vehicle safety (e.g. that tyres have sufficient tread or that the vehicle is roadworthy).

(b) Reducing traffic congestion.

(c) Preventing the use of monopoly power.

(d) Ensuring that mergers are in the public interest.

(e) Ensuring that firms charge a price equal to marginal cost.

7. In what ways might business be socially responsible?

8. What economic costs and benefits might a business experience if it decided to adopt a more socially responsible position? How might such costs and benefits change over the longer term?

9. Using a demand and supply diagram, explain why carbon prices fell at the beginning of the

Emissions Trading Scheme (ETS), due to emissions allowances being too generous.

10. What problems are likely to arise in identifying which firms' practices are anti-competitive? Should the OFT take firms' assurances into account when deciding whether to grant an exemption?

11. If anti-monopoly legislation is effective enough, is there ever any need to prevent mergers from going ahead?

12. If two or more firms were charging similar prices, what types of evidence would you look for to

prove that this was collusion rather than mere coincidence?

13. Should governments or regulators always attempt to eliminate the supernormal profits of monopolists/oligopolists?

14. Should regulators of utilities that have been privatised into several separate companies permit (a) horizontal mergers (within the industry); (b) vertical mergers; (c) mergers with firms in other related industries (e.g. gas and electricity suppliers)?

Additional Part C case studies on the *Economics and the Business Environment* website (www.pearsoned.co.uk/sloman)

C.1 B2B electronic marketplaces. This case study examines the growth of firms trading with each other over the Internet (business to business or 'B2B') and considers the effects on competition.

C.2 Measuring monopoly power. This analyses how the degree of monopoly power possessed by a firm can be measured.

C.3 Airline deregulation in the USA and Europe. Whether the deregulation of various routes has led to more competition and lower prices.

C.4 Bakeries: oligopoly or monopolistic competition. A case study on the bread industry, showing that small-scale local bakeries can exist alongside giant national bakeries.

C.5 Oligopoly in the brewing industry. A case study showing how the UK brewing industry is becoming more concentrated.

C.6 OPEC. A case study examining OPEC's influence over oil prices from the early 1970s to the present day.

C.7 Hybrid strategy. Is it good for companies to use a mix of strategies?

C.8 Stakeholder power. An examination of the various stakeholders of a business and their influence on business behaviour.

C.9 Logistics. A case study of the use of the logistics industry by companies seeking to outsource their supply chain.

C.10 Peak-load pricing. An example of price discrimination: charging more when it costs more to produce.

C.11 The rise and decline of the labour movement. A brief history of trade unions in the UK.

C.12 How useful is marginal productivity theory? How accurately does the theory describe employment decisions by firms?

C.13 Should health care provision be left to the market? This identifies the market failures that would occur if health care provision were left to the free market.

C.14 Corporate social responsibility. An examination of social responsibility as a goal of firms and its effect on business performance.

C.15 Technology and economic change. How to get the benefits from technological advance.

C.16 Green taxes. Are they the perfect answer to the problem of pollution?

C.17 Selling the environment. The market-led solution of the Kyoto Protocol.

C.18 Road pricing in Singapore. A case study showing the methods Singapore has used to cut traffic congestion.

C.19 Environmental auditing. Are businesses becoming greener? A growing number of firms are subjecting themselves to an 'environmental audit' to judge just how 'green' they are.

C.20 Cartels set in concrete, steel and cardboard. This examines some of the best-known Europe-wide cartels of recent years.

C.21 Taking your vitamins at a price. A case study showing how vitamin-producing companies were fined for price fixing.

C.22 The right track to reform. Reorganising the railways in the UK.

C.23 Competition in the pipeline. An examination of attempts to introduce competition into the gas industry in the UK.

C.24 Selling power to the people. Attempts to introduce competition into the UK electricity industry.

Websites relevant to Part C

Numbers and sections refer to websites listed in the Web Appendix and hotlinked from this book's website at **www.pearsoned.co.uk/sloman/**

- For news articles relevant to Part C, see the *Economics News Articles* link from the book's website.

- For general news on the microeconomic environment of business see websites in section A of the Web Appendix, and particularly A1–5, 8, 9, 11, 12, 20–26, 35, 36. See also A38, 43 and 44 for links to newspapers worldwide; and A41 for links to economics news articles from newspapers worldwide.

- For student resources relevant to Part C, see sites C1–7, 9, 10, 14, 19; D3.

- For sites that look at competition and market power, see B2; E4, 10, 18; G7, 8. See also links in I7, 11, 14 and 17. In particular see the following links in sites I7: *Microeconomics > Competition and Monopoly*.

- For a site on game theory, see A40 including its home page. See also D4, 5, 13, 14, 18, 19; I17 and 4 (in the EconDirectory section).

- For information on mergers, see sites E4, 10, 18, 20; G1, 8.

- For information on stock markets, see sites F18 and A3, 22, 25, 26; B27.

- Site I7 contains links to *Financial Economics*.

- For data on SMEs, see the SME database in B3 or E10.

- For information on pricing, see site E10 and the sites of the regulators of the privatised industries: E15, 16, 19, 22.

- Site I7 in the Business section contains links to *Business > Management > Organisational Management*.

- For data on labour markets, see links in B1, especially to *Labour Market Trends* on the National Statistics site. Also see B9 and links in B19. Also see the labour topic in B33 and the *resources > statistics* links in H3.

- For information on international labour standards and employment rights, see site H3.

- Site I7 contains links to Labour economics, Labour force and markets and Labour unions in the *Microeconomics* section and to Distribution of income and wealth in the *Macroeconomics* section. Site I4 has links in the Directory section to Labor and labor economics. Site I17 in the Labor economics section has links to various topics, such as Labor unions, Minimum wage, Poverty and work.

- Links to the TUC and Confederation of British Industry sites can be found at E32 and 33.

- Site I7 contains links to Competition and monopoly, Policy and regulation and Transport in the *Microeconomics* section; they also have an Industry and commerce section. Site I4 has links to Environmental and Environmental economics in the EconDirectory section. Site I17 has several sections of links in the Issues in Society section.

- Site I7 also contains links to sites related to corporate social responsibility: see *Industry and commerce > Fair trade > Corporate social responsibility*.

- For information on taxes and subsidies, see E30, 36; G13. For use of green taxes, see H5; G11; E2, 14, 30.

- For information on health and the economics of health care (Web case C.13; see above), see E8; H9. See also links in I8 and 17.

- For sites favouring the free market, see C17; D34. See also C18 for the development of ideas on the market and government intervention.

- For the economics of the environment, see links in I4, 7, 11, 17. For policy on the environment and transport, see E2, 7, 11, 14, 29, 39; G10, 11. See also H11.

- UK and EU departments relevant to competition policy can be found at sites E10; G7, 8.

- UK regulatory bodies can be found at sites E4, 11, 15, 16, 18, 19, 22, 29.

The macroeconomic environment of business

The success of an individual business depends not only on its own particular market and its own particular decisions. It also depends on the whole macroeconomic environment in which it operates.

If the economy is booming, then individual businesses are likely to be more profitable than if the economy is in recession. It is thus important for businesses to understand the forces that affect the whole business climate.

One of these forces is the level of confidence, both of consumers and business. If business confidence is high, then firms are likely to invest. Similarly, if consumer confidence is high, spending in the shops is likely to be high and this will increase business profitability. The result will be economic growth. If, however, people are predicting a recession, firms will hold off investing and consumer spending may well decline. This could tip the economy into recession.

In Chapter 10 we look at the various national forces affecting the performance of the economy.

Another key ingredient of the macroeconomic environment is government policy and the actions of the central bank (the Bank of England in the UK). If the government raises taxes or the central bank raises interest rates this could impact directly on business profitability and on business confidence. We examine domestic macroeconomic policies in Chapter 11.

In the final two chapters we turn to the international macroeconomic environment. In Chapter 12 we look at the role of international trade. We see how countries and firms can gain from trade and why, despite this, governments sometimes choose to restrict trade.

Then in Chapter 13 we examine the flows of finance across international exchanges. We see how exchange rates are determined and how changes in exchange rates affect business. We study the euro and whether having a single currency for many EU countries benefits business. Finally, we look at attempts by governments worldwide to coordinate their macroeconomic policies.

Business issues covered in this chapter

- What are the main macroeconomic objectives and how do they conflict with each other?

- What determines the level of activity in the economy and hence the overall business climate?

- If a stimulus is given to the economy, what will be the effect on business output?

- Why do economies experience periods of boom followed by periods of recession? What determines the length and magnitude of these 'phases' of the business cycle?

- How are interest rates determined and what is the role of the money supply in the process?

- What determines the supply of money in the economy?

- What are the causes of unemployment and how does unemployment relate to the level of business activity?

- What are the causes of inflation and how does inflation relate to the level of business activity?

10

The economy and business activity

THE KEY MACROECONOMIC OBJECTIVES
10.1

There are several macroeconomic variables that governments seek to control. All these elements in the macroeconomic environment influence businesses – their markets, their costs and their potential profitability. We can group them into four key areas.

Economic growth. Governments aim to achieve economic growth over the long term. They will aim for a stable **rate of economic growth**, which avoids both short-term rapid growth that cannot be sustained and periods of recession. However, economies are unstable and growth rates will fluctuate, as is evident by the 2008/9 recession.

Unemployment. Unemployment is obviously costly for the individual, but it also represents a waste of resources, as there are people willing to work that are unable to find a job. Furthermore, it poses a strain on public finances, due to lower tax revenues and higher benefit payments. Reducing unemployment is, therefore, another major macroeconomic objective for government. We take a closer look at unemployment in section 10.6.

Inflation. This refers to a general rise in prices throughout the economy. The **rate of inflation** is the percentage increase in the level of prices over a 12-month period.

Government policy aims to keep inflation low, but also to keep it stable, as this will aid economic decision making. A key factor that affects the business climate is confidence and this, in turn, is affected by uncertainty. If inflation is low and stable, there will be a degree of certainty, which will enable businesses to set prices and wages rates, as well as make investment decisions with much more confidence. If, on the other hand, inflation is high, it tends to be more volatile and hence uncertainty becomes a deterrent to investment.

During the 1990s, inflation rates in many developed countries hit double figures. In 1991, UK inflation reached 11 per cent. (It had been as high as 24 per cent in 1975.) However, in more recent years, we have been used to inflation rates of 2–3 per cent per year, although in early 2010 the inflation rate in the UK rose above 3 per cent. In most developed countries, a policy of inflation targeting has been adopted. In the UK, the target is 2 per cent and it is the Bank of England's job to use interest rates to keep inflation near its target level.

> **Definitions**
>
> **Rate of economic growth**
> The percentage increase in output over a twelve-month period.
>
> **Rate of inflation**
> The percentage increase in prices over a 12-month period.

The balance of payments. Governments aim to provide an environment in which exports can grow without an excessive growth in imports. They also aim to make the economy attractive to inward investment. In other words, they seek to create a climate in which the country's earnings of foreign currency at least match, or preferably exceed, the country's demand for foreign currency: they seek to achieve a favourable **balance of payments**.

The sale of exports and any other receipts earn foreign currency. The purchase of imports or any other payments abroad use up foreign currency. If we start to spend more foreign currency than we earn, one of two things must happen. Both are likely to be a problem:

■ *The balance of payments will go into deficit.* In other words, there will be a shortfall of foreign currencies. The government will therefore have to borrow money from abroad, or draw on its foreign currency reserves to make up the shortfall. This is a problem because, if it goes on too long, overseas debts will mount, along with the interest that must be paid; and/or reserves will begin to run low.

■ *The exchange rate will fall.* The **exchange rate** is the rate at which one currency exchanges for another. For example, the exchange rate of the pound into the dollar might be £1 = $1.50.

If the government does nothing to correct the balance of payments deficit, then the exchange rate must fall. A falling exchange rate is a problem because it pushes up the price of imports and may fuel inflation. Also, if the exchange rate fluctuates, this can cause great uncertainty for traders and can damage international trade and economic growth.

Government macroeconomic policy

From the above four issues we can identify four macroeconomic policy objectives that governments typically pursue:

■ High and stable economic growth.
■ Low unemployment.
■ Low inflation.
■ The avoidance of balance of payments deficits and excessive exchange rate fluctuations.

Unfortunately, these policy objectives may conflict. For example, a policy designed to accelerate the rate of economic growth may result in a higher rate of inflation and a balance of payments deficit. Governments are thus often faced with awkward policy choices. All the choices they make will impact on business.

Recap

1. The government has four key macroeconomic objectives, which it seeks to effect. They are high and stable growth, reducing unemployment, low and stable inflation and avoiding balance of payments and exchange rate problems.

2. Governments also aim to achieve a balanced budget and to enable the redistribution of income.

Furthermore, they are facing increasing pressures to develop policies to prevent environmental damage.

3. The macroeconomic objectives of governments will conflict with each other and so, to some extent, governments will have to prioritise.

BUSINESS ACTIVITY AND THE CIRCULAR FLOW OF INCOME   10.2

We now turn our examination of the macroeconomic environment to the question of what determines the overall level of business activity. One of the most important determinants, at least in the short run, is the level of spending on firms' output. The more consumers spend, the more firms will want to produce in order to meet that consumer demand.

We use the term 'aggregate demand' (AD) to represent the total level of spending on the goods and services produced within the country over a given time period (normally a year). This spending consists of four elements: consumer spending on domestically produced goods and services (C_d), investment expenditure within the country by firms, whether on plant and equipment or on building up stocks (I), government spending on goods and services (such as health, education and transport) (G) and the expenditure by residents abroad on this country's exports (X). Thus:

$$AD = C_d + I + G + X$$

The total annual output of goods and services on which aggregate demand is spent is called GDP, or 'gross domestic product'. As long as there is spare capacity in the economy, a rise in aggregate demand will stimulate firms to produce more. GDP will rise.

A simple way of understanding this process is to use a 'circular flow of income diagram'. This is shown in Figure 10.1.

In the diagram, the economy is divided into two major groups: *firms* and *households*. Each group has two roles. Firms are producers of goods and services; they are also the employers of labour. Households (which is the word we use for individuals) are the consumers of goods and services; they are also the suppliers of labour. In the diagram there is an inner flow and various outer flows of income between these two groups.

The inner flow, withdrawals and injections

The inner flow

Firms pay incomes to households in the form of wages and salaries. Some households also receive incomes from firms in the form of dividends on shares, or interest on loans or rent on property. Thus on the left-hand side of the diagram money flows directly from firms to households as household incomes.

Households, in turn, pay money to domestic firms when they **consume domestically produced goods and services** (C_d). This is shown on the right-hand side of the inner flow. There is thus a circular flow of payments from firms to households to firms and so on.

If households spend *all* their incomes on buying domestic goods and services, and if firms pay out *all* this income they receive to domestic households, and if the speed at which money flows around the system does not change, the flow will continue at the same level indefinitely. The money just goes round and round at the same speed and incomes remain unchanged.

In the real world, of course, it is not as simple as this. Not all income gets passed on round the inner flow; some is *withdrawn*. At the same time, incomes are *injected* into the flow from outside. Let us examine these withdrawals and injections.

Definition

Consumption of domestically produced goods and services (C_d)
The direct flow of money payments from households to firms.

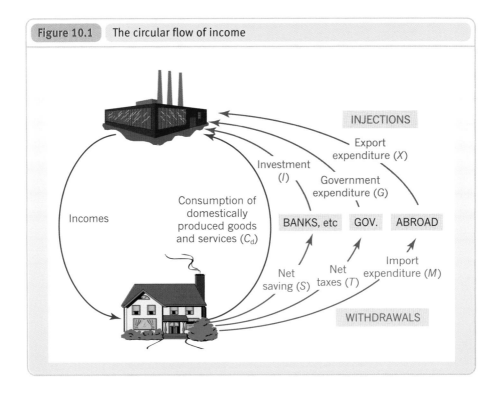

Figure 10.1   The circular flow of income

Withdrawals

When households receive income, not all of it will be spent on domestic goods and services and hence there will be withdrawals from the inner flow. There are three forms of **withdrawals (*W*)** (or **leakages**, as they are sometimes called):

Net saving (S). Saving is income that households choose not to spend but to put aside for the future. Savings are normally deposited in financial institutions such as banks and building societies. This is shown in the bottom right of the diagram. Money flows from households to 'banks, etc.'. What we are seeking to measure here, however, is the net flow from households to the banking sector. We therefore have to subtract from saving any borrowing or drawing on past savings by households in order to get the *net* saving flow. Of course, if household borrowing exceeded saving, the net flow would be in the other direction; it would be negative.

Net taxes (T). When people pay taxes (to either central or local government), this represents a withdrawal of money from the inner flow in much the same way as saving; only in this case people have no choice! Some taxes, such as income tax and employees' national insurance contributions, are paid out of household incomes. Others, such as VAT and excise duties, are paid out of consumer expenditure. Yet others, such as corporation tax, are paid out of firms' incomes before being received by households as dividends on shares. (For simplicity, however, we show taxes being withdrawn at just one point. It does not affect the argument.)

When, however, people receive *benefits* from the government, such as working tax credit, child benefit and pensions, the money flows the other way. Benefits are thus equivalent to a 'negative tax'. These benefits are known as **transfer payments**. They transfer money from one group of people (taxpayers) to others (the recipients).

In the model, 'net taxes' (T) represents the *net* flow to the government from households and firms. It consists of total taxes minus benefits.

Import expenditure (M). Not all consumption is of home-produced goods. Households spend some of their incomes on imported goods and services. Although the money that consumers spend on such goods initially flows to domestic retailers, most of it will eventually find its way abroad when the retailers or wholesalers themselves import them. This expenditure on imports constitutes the third withdrawal from the inner flow. This money flows abroad.

Total withdrawals are simply the sum of net saving, net taxes and the expenditure on imports:

$$W = S + T + M$$

Injections

Only part of the demand for firms' output (aggregate demand) arises from consumers' expenditure. The remainder comes from other sources outside the inner flow. These additional components of spending are known as **injections** (J). There are three types of injection:

Investment (I). This is the flow of money that firms spend which they obtain from various financial institutions – either past savings or loans, or through a new issue of shares. They may invest in plant and equipment or may simply spend the money on building up stocks of inputs, semi-finished or finished goods.

Government expenditure (G). When the government spends money on goods and services produced by firms, this counts as an injection. Examples of such government expenditure are spending on roads, hospitals and schools. (Note that government expenditure in this model does not include state benefits. These transfer payments, as we saw above, are the equivalent of negative taxes and have the effect of reducing the T component of withdrawals.)

Export expenditure (X). Money flows into the circular flow from abroad when residents abroad buy our exports of goods and services.

Total injections are thus the sum of investment, government expenditure and exports:

$$J = I + G + X$$

Aggregate demand, which is the total spending on output, is thus $C_d + J$.

> **Definition**
>
> **Injections (J)**
> Expenditure on the production of domestic firms coming from outside the inner flow of the circular flow of income. Injections equal investment (I) plus government expenditure (G) plus expenditure on exports (X).

The relationship between withdrawals and injections

There are indirect links between saving and investment via financial institutions, between taxation and government expenditure via the government (central and local), and between imports and exports via foreign countries. These links, however, do not guarantee that $S = I$ or $G = T$ or $M = X$.

Take investment and saving. The point here is that the decisions to save and invest are made by *different* people, and thus they plan to save and invest different amounts. Likewise the demand for imports may not equal the demand for exports. As far as the government is concerned, it may choose not to make $T = G$. It may choose not to spend all its tax revenues and thus run a 'budget surplus' ($T > G$); or it may choose to spend more than it receives in taxes and run a 'budget deficit' ($G > T$), by borrowing or printing money to make up the difference. This issue has been of great concern in the UK since the recession of 2008/9. By April 2010, the budget deficit was £163.4 billion, or nearly 12 per cent of GDP.

Thus planned injections (J) may not equal planned withdrawals (W). But if they are not equal, what will be the consequences?

If injections exceed withdrawals, the level of expenditure will rise (the increase in spending from injections is greater than the reduction in spending from withdrawals). The extra spending will generate extra incomes. In other words, GDP will rise; there will be economic growth. This, as we shall see later in the chapter, will tend to reduce unemployment as firms take on more labour to meet the extra demand. It may, however, lead to a rise in inflation as the extra demand drives up the price of goods and services more rapidly than would have been the case.

If planned injections are *less* than planned withdrawals then the opposite of each of the above will occur. GDP will fall (there will be negative economic growth); unemployment will rise and inflation will fall.

> **Pause for thought**
>
> *If injections exceed withdrawals, will GDP go on rising indefinitely, or will a new equilibrium be reached? If so, explain how. (We answer this in the next section.)*

Changes in injections and withdrawals thus have a crucial effect on the whole macroeconomic environment in which businesses operate.

Recap

1. Business activity is affected by the level of aggregate demand. Aggregate demand equals $C_d + I + G + X$.

2. The circular flow of income model depicts the flows of money income and expenditure round the economy. The inner flow shows the direct flows between firms and households. Money flows from firms to households in the form of wages and other incomes, and back again as consumer expenditure on domestically produced goods and services.

3. Not all incomes get passed on directly round the inner flow. Some is withdrawn in the form of saving; some is paid in taxes; and some goes abroad as expenditure on imports.

4. Likewise not all expenditure on domestic firms' products is by domestic consumers. Some is injected from outside the inner flow in the form of investment expenditure, government expenditure and expenditure on the country's exports.

5. Planned injections and withdrawals are unlikely to be the same.

6. If injections exceed withdrawals, GDP will rise. As a result unemployment will tend to fall and inflation will tend to rise. The reverse will happen if withdrawals exceed injections.

10.3 THE DETERMINATION OF BUSINESS ACTIVITY

> **Definition**
>
> **Multiplier effect**
> An initial increase in aggregate demand of £xm leads to an eventual rise in GDP that is greater than £xm.

We have seen that the relationship between planned injections and planned withdrawals determines whether GDP will rise or fall. But *by how much*?

Assume there is a rise in injections – say firms decide to invest more. Aggregate demand ($C_d + J$) will be higher. Firms will use more labour and other resources and thus pay out more incomes to households. Households will respond to this by consuming more and so firms will sell more.

Firms will respond to this by producing more, and thus using still more labour and other resources. Household incomes will rise again. Consumption and hence production will rise again, and so on. There will thus be a *multiplied* rise in GDP and employment. This is known as the **multiplier effect**.

The process, however, does not go on for ever. Each time household incomes rise, households save more, pay more taxes and buy more imports. In other words, withdrawals rise. When withdrawals have risen to match the increase in injections, **equilibrium** will be achieved and GDP and employment will stop rising. The process can be summarised as follows:

$$J > W \rightarrow GDP \uparrow \rightarrow W \uparrow \text{ unit } J = W$$

Similarly, an initial fall in injections (or rise in withdrawals) will lead to a multiplied fall in GDP and employment:

$$J > W \rightarrow GDP \uparrow \rightarrow W \downarrow \text{ unit } J = W$$

Thus equilibrium in the circular flow of income can be at *any* level of GDP and employment.

Identifying the equilibrium level of GDP

Equilibrium can be shown on a 'Keynesian 45° line diagram'. This is named after the great economist, John Maynard Keynes (1883–1946). Keynes argued that GDP is determined by aggregate demand. A rise in aggregate demand will cause GDP to rise; a fall in aggregate demand will cause GDP to fall.

Equilibrium GDP can be at any level of capacity usage. If aggregate demand is buoyant, equilibrium GDP can be where businesses are operating at full capacity with full employment. If aggregate demand is low, however, equilibrium GDP can be at well below full capacity with high unemployment (i.e. a recession, as occurred in 2009). Keynes argued that it is important, therefore, for governments to manage the level of aggregate demand to avoid recessions.

Figure 10.2 plots various elements of the circular flow of income, such as consumption, withdrawals, injections and aggregate demand, against GDP (national

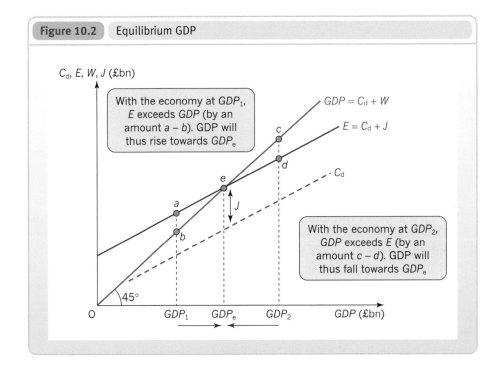

Figure 10.2   Equilibrium GDP

C_d, E, W, J (£bn)

With the economy at GDP_1, E exceeds GDP (by an amount $a - b$). GDP will thus rise towards GDP_e

$GDP = C_d + W$

$E = C_d + J$

C_d

With the economy at GDP_2, GDP exceeds E (by an amount $c - d$). GDP will thus fall towards GDP_e

45°

O GDP_1 GDP_e GDP_2 GDP (£bn)

income). Two continuous lines are shown. The 45° line out from the origin plots $C_d + W$ against GDP. It is a 45° line because by definition GDP = $C_d + W$. To understand this, consider what can happen to the income earned from GDP: either it must be spent on domestically produced goods (C_d) or it must be withdrawn from the circular flow – there is nothing else that can happen to it. Thus if GDP were £100 billion, then $C_d + W$ must also be £100 billion. If you draw a line such that whatever value is plotted on the horizontal axis (GDP) is also plotted on the vertical axis ($C_d + W$), the line will be at 45° (assuming that the axes are drawn to the same scale).

The other continuous line plots aggregate demand. In this diagram it is conventional to call it the 'aggregate expenditure line' (E). It consists of $C_d + J$, i.e. the total spending on domestic firms.

To show how this line is constructed, consider the dashed line. This shows C_d. It is flatter than the 45° line. The reason is that for any given rise in GDP and hence people's incomes, only *part* will be spent on domestic products, while the remainder will be withdrawn, i.e. C_d rises less quickly than GDP. The E line consists of $C_d + J$. But we have assumed that J is constant with respect to changes in GDP. Thus the E line is simply the C_d line shifted upward by the amount of J.

If aggregate expenditure exceeded GDP, at say GDP_1, there would be excess demand in the economy (of $a - b$). In other words, people would be buying more than was currently being produced. Firms would thus find their stocks dwindling and would therefore increase their level of production. In doing so, they would employ more labour and other inputs. GDP would thus rise. As it did so, C_d and hence E would rise. There would be a movement up along the E line.

But because not all the extra incomes earned from the rise in GDP would be consumed (i.e. some would be withdrawn), expenditure would rise less quickly than income: the E line is flatter than the GDP line. As income rises towards GDP_e, the gap between the GDP and E lines gets smaller. Once point e is reached, $GDP = E$. There is then no further tendency for GDP to rise.

If GDP exceeded aggregate expenditure, at say GDP_2, there would be insufficient demand for the goods and services currently being produced ($c - d$). Firms would find their stocks of unsold goods building up. They would thus respond by producing less and employing fewer factors of production. GDP would thus fall and go on falling until GDP_e was reached.

The multiplier

Definition

The multiplier
The number of times a rise in GDP (ΔGDP) is bigger than the initial rise in aggregate expenditure (ΔE) that caused it. Using the letter k to stand for the multiplier, the multiplier is defined as $k = \Delta GDP/\Delta E$.

As we have seen, when aggregate expenditure rises, this will cause a multiplied rise in GDP. The size of the **multiplier** is given by the letter k, where:

$k = \Delta GDP/\Delta E$

Thus, if aggregate expenditure rose by £10 million (ΔE) and as a result GDP rose by £30 million (ΔGDP), the multiplier would be 3. Figure 10.3 is drawn on the assumption that the multiplier is 3.

Assume in Figure 10.3 that aggregate expenditure rises by £20 billion, from E_1 to E_2. This could be caused by a rise in injections, or by a fall in withdrawals (and hence a rise in consumption of domestically produced goods) or by some combination of the two. Equilibrium GDP rises by £60 billion, from £100 billion to £160 billion (where the E_2 line crosses the GDP line).

Box 10.1 shows how the size of the multiplier can be calculated in advance.

BOX 10.1   DOING THE SUMS

Calculating the size of the multiplier

What determines the size of the multiplier? The answer is that it depends on the 'marginal propensity to consume domestically produced goods' (mpc_d). The mpc_d is the proportion of any rise in GDP that gets spent on domestically produced goods (i.e. the proportion that is not withdrawn):

$$mpc_d = \Delta C_d / \Delta GDP$$

So, if you are given £100, but choose to spend only £70 on home-produced products, then only 70 per cent of the income you were given was spent on domestically produced goods. Some of the remaining £30 may be taken as taxation; you may choose to save part of it; or you might decide to spend it on imports. Either way, £30 is withdrawn from the circular flow of income. The proportion of the rise in income that is spent on domestically produced goods is:

$$mpc_d = \Delta C_d / \Delta GDP = £70/£100 = 7/10 = 0.7$$

In Figure 10.3, $mpc_d = \Delta C_d / \Delta GDP = £40bn/£60bn = {}^2/_3$ (i.e. the slope of the C_d line). The higher the mpc_d the greater the proportion of income generated from GDP that recirculates around the circular flow of income and thus generates extra output.

The **multiplier formula** is given by:

$$k = \frac{1}{1 - mpc_d}$$

In our example, with $mpc_d = {}^2/_3$

$$k = \frac{1}{1 - {}^2/_3} = \frac{1}{{}^1/_3} = 3$$

If the mpc_d were ${}^3/_4$, the multiplier would be 4. Thus the higher the mpc_d, the higher the multiplier. In the UK, the value of the mpc_d is between ${}^1/_3$ and ${}^1/_2$. This gives a value for the multiplier of between 1.5 and 2.

1. Think of two reasons why a country might have a steep E line, and hence a high value for the multiplier.
2. Assume that 0.1 of any rise in income is saved, 0.2 goes in taxes and 0.1 is spent on imports. What is the mpc$_d$? What is the value of the multiplier?

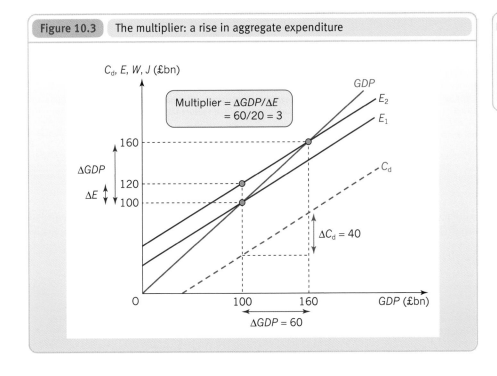

Figure 10.3   The multiplier: a rise in aggregate expenditure

Definition

Multiplier formula
The formula for the multiplier is $k = 1/(1 - mpc_d)$.

BOX 10.2   **THE LONDON OLYMPICS**

The macroeconomic impact

Winning the bid to host the Olympic Games in 2012 was seen as a great victory for London and the UK as a whole. But just how big and how extensive will the gains be?

It is not just the construction companies and the businesses directly associated with hosting the games that will benefit. There are considerable knock-on effects throughout the local and national economies. These effects are an example of the multiplier in action.

So just what are these effects?

Local multiplier effects

First there are the benefits of the major regeneration of the Stratford area of London. This includes clearing derelict land, direct investment in the Olympic Stadium, the Olympic Village and other venues, plus large-scale investment in hospitality, transport infrastructure and local services. This will generate employment, which in turn will bring wage income into the area. The result will be increased spending within the local economy, further boosting local business.

Then there is the expenditure while the games are in progress, including everything from hotels and catering, to security and the spending of the visitors in the local economy. What we have here, then, both before and during the games, is a *local multiplier* effect in action: higher expenditure generating higher incomes, generating higher consumption, generating higher incomes, and so on.

Some of these effects will continue after the games, as regeneration attracts new businesses into the area, and as sports and other facilities and the improved transport infrastructure continue to be used.

Regional and national multiplier effects

But the effects will extend way beyond East London. Several of the venues are in Greater London and surrounding areas. There will be considerable investment in hotels and other leisure facilities throughout London. The extra visitors will bring money directly into the city and help to finance further investment. The legacy of this would be to make London a more attractive tourist destination beyond the games.

Then there are the improvements to London transport, with extensions to Underground lines, refurbishing of stations and upgrading trains, new trans-London bus services and also improvements to national rail services. The whole London economy will benefit.

But what of the rest of the UK? In a 2005 study[1] it was estimated that although there would be a direct gain to London's GDP of £5900 million over the period 2005–16, UK GDP as a whole would rise by only £1936 million. In other words, some of the gain to London would be at the expense of the rest of the UK as resources were diverted to London.

The measured effects, however, were only the direct effects. There would still be multiplier effects on the UK economy as a whole, as the increased expenditure associated with the Olympics (both before, during and after the games) generated extra incomes, which were then spent in other parts of the UK economy.

One thing not to forget is how much the Olympics will cost. The original bid in 2006 contained an estimate for costs of £2.35 billion. By 2010, however, new estimates suggested that the figure was likely to be around £20 billion.

1. *Give some examples of industries in the rest of the UK which could benefit from increased expenditure in London.*
2. *Why would the magnitude of the full multiplier effect on the whole UK economy be difficult to estimate?*
3. *In this box we have focused on just one economic aspect of the Olympic Games, namely the macroeconomic impact. To decide whether the games are worthwhile, however, would require a full analysis of costs and benefits, including externalities. Identify some external costs and benefits from hosting the Olympics.*

---

[1] PricewaterhouseCoopers, *Olympic Games Impact Study: Final Report* (Department of Culture Media and Sport, 2005)

Recap

1. In the simple circular flow of income model, equilibrium national income (GDP) is where withdrawals equal injections: where $W = J$.

2. Equilibrium can be shown on a Keynesian 45° line diagram. Equilibrium is where GDP (shown by the 45° line) is equal to aggregate expenditure (E).

3. If there is an initial increase in aggregate expenditure (ΔE), which could result from an increase in injections or a reduction in withdrawals, there will

be a multiplied rise in GDP. The multiplier is defined as $\Delta GDP/\Delta E$.

4. The size of the multiplier depends on the marginal propensity to consume domestically produced goods (mpc_d). The larger the mpc_d, the more will be spent each time incomes are generated round the circular flow, and thus the more will go round again as *additional* demand for domestic product. The multiplier formula is $1/1 - mpc_d$.

THE BUSINESS CYCLE   10.4

Economic growth tends to fluctuate. In some years there is a high rate of economic growth; the country experiences a boom. In other years, economic growth is low or even negative; the country experiences a **recession**, such as that in 2008/9. This cycle of booms and recessions is known as the **business cycle** or **trade cycle**.

> **KEY IDEA 26** **Economies suffer from inherent instability.** As a result, economic growth and other macroeconomic indicators tend to fluctuate.

The business cycle is illustrated in Figure 10.4. The first thing to note in the diagram is the ceiling to output. This is where all resources, including labour, are fully employed. This ceiling to output grows over time for two reasons:

- *Resources may increase.* This could be the result of an increase in the working population or as a result of investment in new plant and equipment.
- *Resources may become more productive.* The most likely reasons for this are technical progress and more efficient working practices.

The diagram shows the cyclical fluctuations in actual output (GDP). Four 'phases' of the business cycle can be identified.

1. *The upturn.* In this phase, a stagnant economy begins to recover and growth in GDP resumes. Business confidence begins to grow.

Definitions

Recession
A period of falling GDP, i.e. of negative economic growth. Officially, a recession is where this occurs for two quarters or more.

Business cycle or **trade cycle**
The periodic fluctuations of national output around its long-term trend.

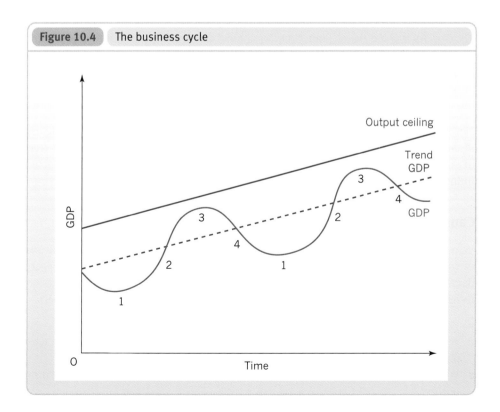

Figure 10.4 The business cycle

2. *The expansion.* During this phase, there is rapid economic growth; the economy is booming. Rapid growth in consumer demand creates a climate of business confidence and firms respond by producing more, investing more and employing more people. The economy moves closer to the ceiling to output.

3. *The peaking-out.* During this phase, growth slows down or even ceases. Business confidence wanes.

4. *The slowdown, recession or slump.* During this phase, there is little or no growth or even a decline in output. Increasing slack develops in the economy as many businesses produce less and hold off from investing.

The third (dashed) line shows the trend of GDP over time (i.e. ignoring the cyclical fluctuations around the trend). If the average level of capacity that is unutilised

stays constant from one cycle to another, then the trend line will have the same slope as the output ceiling line. If, however, the average level of capacity that is unutilised falls from one peak to the next, then the gap between the trend line and the full capacity line will become narrower. The trend line will have a steeper slope than the capacity output line.

The business cycle in practice

The business cycle illustrated in Figure 10.4 is a 'stylised' cycle. It is nice and smooth and regular. Drawing it this way allows us to make a clear distinction between each of the four phases. In practice, however, business cycles are highly irregular. They are irregular in two ways:

The length of the phases. Some booms are short-lived, lasting only a few months or so. Others are much longer, lasting perhaps three or four years. Likewise some recessions are short, while others are long.

The magnitude of the phases. Sometimes in phase 2 there is a very high rate of economic growth, perhaps 4 per cent per annum or more. On other occasions in phase 2, growth is much gentler. Sometimes in phase 4 there is a recession, with an actual decline in output (e.g. in the early 1980s, the early 1990s and late 2000s). On other occasions, phase 4 is merely a 'pause', with growth simply slowing down (e.g. in the early 2000s).

Nevertheless, despite the irregularity of the fluctuations, cycles are still clearly discernible, especially if we plot *growth* on the vertical axis rather than the *level* of output. This is done in Figure 10.5, which shows the business cycles in selected industrial economies from 1970 to 2011.

Causes of cyclical fluctuations

Why does the business cycle occur and what determines the length and magnitude of the phases of the cycle? To understand this we need to know why aggregate demand fluctuates. As we have seen, it is changes in aggregate demand that determine short-run economic growth. There are three questions we need to answer.

■ What causes aggregate demand to change in the first place?
■ Why do the effects of changes in aggregate demand persist? In other words, why do booms and recessions last for a period of time?
■ Why do booms and recessions come to an end? What determines the turning points?

| Figure 10.5 | Growth rates in selected industrial economies: 1970–2011 |

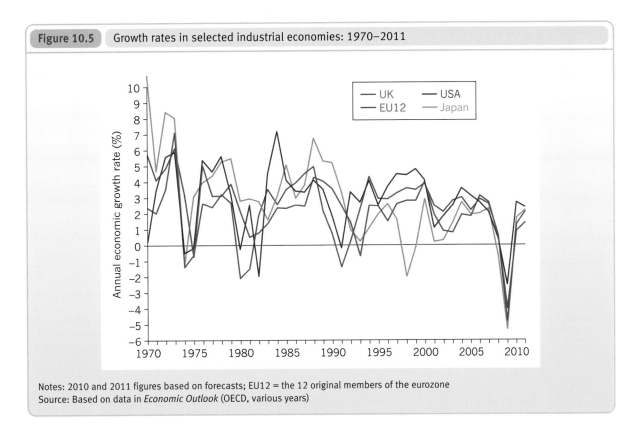

Notes: 2010 and 2011 figures based on forecasts; EU12 = the 12 original members of the eurozone
Source: Based on data in *Economic Outlook* (OECD, various years)

What causes aggregate demand to change in the first place?

Anything that affects one or more of the four components of aggregate demand (C_d, I, G or X) could be the reason for a change in GDP. For example, an increase in business confidence could increase investment; an increase in consumer confidence could increase consumption. A cut in interest rates may encourage increased business and consumer borrowing, and hence an increase in investment and consumption. A cut in taxes will increase consumption, as consumers have more 'disposable' income. A rise in government expenditure will directly increase aggregate demand. A change in conditions abroad, or a change in the exchange rate, will affect imports and exports. (We examine these external factors in Chapter 13.)

Some of these factors, such as taxes and government expenditure, can be directly controlled by the government. In other words, government policy can be directed at controlling aggregate demand and hence the course of the business cycle. We call this 'demand management policy' – again we will look at this in the next chapter.

Why do booms and recessions persist for a period of time?

Time lags. It takes time for changes in aggregate demand to be fully reflected in changes in GDP and employment. The multiplier process takes time. Moreover, consumers, firms and government may not all respond immediately to new situations. Their responses are spread out over a period of time.

'Bandwagon' effects. Once the economy starts expanding, expectations become buoyant. People think ahead and adjust their expenditure behaviour; they consume and invest more *now*. Likewise in a recession a mood of pessimism may set in. The effect is cumulative.

BOX 10.3 | BUSINESS EXPECTATIONS AND THEIR EFFECT ON INVESTMENT

Recent European experience

Investment is highly volatile. It is subject to far more violent swings than GDP. This can be seen in chart (a), which shows EU growth in GDP and growth in investment from 1985 to 2011. The maximum annual growth in GDP was 4.2 per cent and the maximum fall was also 4.2 per cent. By contrast, the maximum annual growth in investment was 8.3 per cent and the maximum fall was 11.4 per cent. The differences were even greater for individual EU countries.

These figures are consistent with the accelerator theory, which argues that the level of investment depends on the *rate of change* of GDP and hence of consumer demand. A relatively small percentage change in GDP can give a much bigger percentage change in investment.

Another factor affecting investment is the degree of business optimism. Whilst this is partly determined by current rates of economic growth, there are many other factors that can affect the business climate. These include world political events (such as a war or a US election),

national and international macroeconomic policies and shocks to the world economy (such as oil price changes or a banking crisis). Of course, to the extent that these other factors affect confidence, which in turn affects investment, so they will affect economic growth.

In the boom years of the late 1980s, business optimism was widespread throughout Europe. Investment was correspondingly high, and with it there was a high rate of economic growth.

Surveys of European business expectations in the early 1990s, however, told a very different story. Pessimism was rife. Europe was in the grip of a recession. Growth slowed right down and output actually fell in 1993. Along with this decline in growth and deteriorating levels of business and consumer confidence, there was a significant fall in investment.

The industrial confidence indicator for the EU as a whole is plotted in chart (b). The indicator shows the

(a) EU15 growth in GDP and business investment

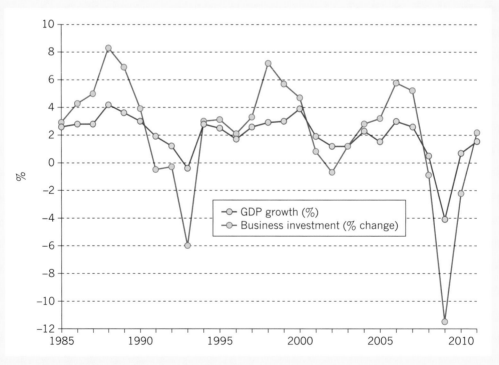

Note: Year 2011 figures based on forecast
Source: *European Economy, Statistical Annex* (European Commission)

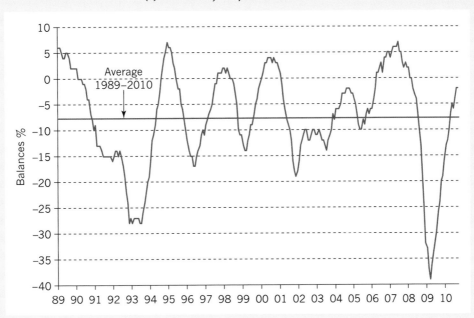

(b) EU industry confidence indicator

Source: *Business and Consumer surveys* (European Commission)

percentage excess of confident over pessimistic replies to business questionnaires; a negative figure means that there was a higher percentage of pessimistic responses. You can see that the indicator was strongly negative in 1993. After 1993, pessimism began to decrease, and by the last quarter of 1994 the EU industrial confidence indicator became positive.

Between 1995 and 2000, the industrial confidence indicator swung between positive and negative values. These swings were similar in direction to those in the rate of economic growth. For example, both the rate of growth and the confidence indicator rose in 1997/8 and 2000 and fell in 1996.

Then, in 2001, with the world economy slowing down and the 11 September attack on the World Trade Centre in New York, industrial confidence plummeted, and so did investment. Investment actually fell in 2002. Then as the European economy slowly recovered, with growth rates edging upwards, so confidence grew, as did the rate of investment. By the mid 2000s, economic growth was strong and confidence was high.

Then, with the banking crisis and credit crunch of 2008, so confidence plummeted; banks were less willing to lend and businesses were cautious about investing. Economies throughout Europe and many other parts of the world plunged into recession.

But then, with governments taking measures to address the problems of the banking system and with measures taken to stimulate economies, such as cuts in interest rates and government programmes of increased spending, so European economies began to pull out of recession and confidence began to recover.

1. *How is the existence of surveys of business confidence likely to affect firms' expectations and actions?*
2. *Why, if the growth in output slows down (but is still positive), is investment likely to fall (i.e. a negative growth in investment)? If you look at chart (a) you will see that this happened in 1991, 1992 and 1993, and in 2002. (See the section on the accelerator on page 284.)*

One crucial effect here is called the **accelerator**. A rise in injections will cause a multiplied rise in GDP. But this rise in GDP will in turn cause a rise in investment, as firms seek to expand capacity to meet the extra demand. This compounds the increase in demand, as investment is itself an injection into the circular flow. This is the accelerator. The increased investment then causes a further multiplied rise in income. This then causes a further accelerator effect, a further multiplier effect, and so on.

Pause for thought

Under what circumstances would you expect a rise in national income to cause a large accelerator effect?

Why do booms and recessions come to an end? What determines the turning points?

Ceilings and floors. Actual output can go on growing more rapidly as long as there is slack in the economy. As full employment is approached, however, and as more and more firms reach full capacity, so a ceiling to output is reached.

At the other extreme, there is a basic minimum level of consumption that people tend to maintain. During a recession, people may not buy much in the way of luxury and durable goods, but they will continue to buy food and other basic goods. There is thus a floor to consumption.

The industries supplying these basic goods will need to maintain their level of replacement investment. Also there will always be some minimum investment demand as firms, in order to survive competition, need to install the latest equipment (such as computer hardware). There is thus a floor to investment too.

Echo effects. Durable consumer goods and capital equipment may last several years, but eventually they will need replacing. The replacement of goods and capital purchased in a previous boom may help to bring a recession to an end.

The accelerator. For investment to continue rising, consumer demand must rise at a *faster and faster* rate. After all, firms invest to meet *extra* demand. They will therefore only invest more than last period if the extra demand is more than last period, i.e. if the growth rate is *increasing*. If this does not happen, investment will fall back and the boom will break.

Random shocks. National or international political, social or natural events can affect the mood and attitudes of firms, governments and consumers, and thus affect aggregate demand.

Pause for thought

Why is it difficult to predict precisely when a recession will come to an end and the economy will start growing rapidly?

Changes in government policy. In a boom, a government may become most worried by unsustainably high growth and inflation and thus pursue contractionary policies. In a recession, it may become most worried by unemployment and lack of growth and thus pursue expansionary policies, as it did in 2008/9. These government policies, if successful, will bring about a turning point in the cycle.

Definition

Accelerator
The level of investment depends on the rate of increase in consumer demand, and as a result is subject to substantial fluctuations. Increases in investment via the accelerator can compound the multiplier effect.

Recap

1. Economic growth fluctuates with the course of the business cycle.

2. The cycle can be broken down into four phases: the upturn, the expansion, the peaking-out, and the slowdown or recession.

3. In practice, the length and magnitude of these phases varies; the cycle is thus irregular.

4. A major part of this explanation of the business cycle is the instability of investment. The accelerator theory explains this instability. It relates the level of investment to *changes* in GDP and consumer demand.

5. Other reasons for fluctuations in aggregate demand include time lags, 'bandwagon' effects, ceilings and floors to output, echo effects, swings in government policy and random shocks.

MONEY, INTEREST RATES AND BUSINESS ACTIVITY   10.5

Business and interest rates

The financial sector was badly affected by the 'credit crunch' and this illustrated just how important financial institutions are in affecting businesses and the wider macroeconomy.

One important determinant of business activity is the rate of interest. If interest rates rise, it will be more expensive for businesses to borrow; this will curtail investment. Higher interest rates are a particular problem for businesses that have a high ratio of borrowing at variable interest rates to their total turnover. In such cases, not only will a rise in interest rates discourage investment, it may also make it difficult for the business to find the money to pay the interest – to 'service' its debt.

Higher interest rates make saving more profitable, but it will also make it more expensive for the general public to borrow. If interest rates rise, whether on personal loans, on credit cards or on mortgages, consumers may well cut back on their borrowing and spending. Aggregate demand will fall.

Interest rates are also seen as a 'barometer' of the future course of the economy. If the Bank of England raises interest rates, this may be taken as a sign that the economy will slow down, especially if it is expected that rates are likely to be raised again in the near future. Business confidence may fall and so too, therefore, may investment. However, it all depends on how the rise in interest rates is interpreted. If it is seen as a means of preventing excessive expansion of the economy and therefore allowing expansion to be sustained, albeit at a more moderate rate, this may actually encourage investment.

But what determines interest rates? In a free market, interest rates are determined by the demand for and supply of money. In practice the free-market interest rate may not be the rate that the Bank of England wants, in which case it will alter it. This process of altering interest rates by the country's central bank (i.e. the Bank of England in the UK) is known as 'monetary policy'. We examine monetary policy in the next chapter. Here we look at the determination of interest rates in a free market.

The meaning of money

Before going any further we must define precisely what we mean by 'money'. An easy task, surely! However, money is more than just notes and coins. In fact the main component of a country's money supply is not cash, but deposits in banks and other financial institutions. The bulk of the deposits appear merely as book-keeping entries in the banks' accounts. People can access and use this money in their accounts through cheques, debit cards, standing orders, direct debits, etc. without the need for cash. Only a very small proportion of these deposits, therefore, needs to be kept by the banks in their safes or tills in the form of cash.

In UK official statistics, two main measures of money are used: a narrow measure, **cash in circulation**, and a broad measure, M4. This broad measure includes cash outside the banks plus *all* deposits in banks and building societies, whether in the form of cash or merely as bookkeeping entries. At the end of August 2010, the level of cash in circulation was £57 billion. M4 was £2176 billion. When the term 'money supply' is used in the UK, it normally refers to M4.

Pause for thought

Why are debit and credit cards not counted as money?

Definitions

Cash in circulation

The measure of narrow money in the UK. This is all cash outside the Bank of England: in banks, in people's purses and wallets, in businesses' safes and tills, in government departments, etc.

M4

Cash outside the banks plus all bank and building society deposits (including cash).

Bank (or deposits) multiplier

The number of times greater the expansion of bank deposits is than the additional liquidity in banks that caused it: $1/L$ (the inverse of the liquidity ratio).

The supply of money

Banks and the creation of credit

By far the largest element of money supply (M4) is bank deposits. It is not surprising then that banks play an absolutely crucial role in the monetary system. This was clearly evident between 2007 and 2009, when we saw the collapse of the banking sector directly contribute to the UK (and global) recession.

Banks are able to create additional money by increasing the amount of bank deposits. They do this by lending to people: granting people overdrafts or loans. When these loans are spent, the shops deposit the money in their bank accounts, or have it directly transferred when debit cards are swiped across their tills. Thus the additional loans granted by the banks have become deposits in the shops' banks. These deposits can be used as the basis for further loans. These in turn create further deposits and so on. The process is known as the 'creation of credit'.

Can this process go on indefinitely? The answer is no. Banks must keep a certain proportion of their deposits in the form of cash to meet the demands of their customers for cash. Let us say that 10 per cent of a bank's deposits have to be in the form of cash, then non-cash deposits would account for the remaining 90 per cent. So if additional cash of £10 million were deposited in the banking system, banks could create non-cash deposits of an additional £90 million – but no more. Of the total new deposits of £100 million, cash would be 10 per cent and non-cash deposits would be 90 per cent.

This effect is known as the **bank (or deposits) multiplier**. In this simple example with a cash ratio of $1/10$ (i.e. 10 per cent), the deposits multiplier is 10. An initial increase in deposits of £10 million allowed total deposits to rise by £100 million. In this simple world, therefore, the deposits multiplier is the inverse of the cash ratio (L).

Deposits multiplier $= 1/L$

Pause for thought

If banks choose to operate with a 5 per cent liquidity ratio and receive an extra £100 million of cash deposits: (a) What is the size of the deposits multiplier? (b) How much will total deposits have expanded after the multiplier has worked through? (c) By how much will total credit have expanded?

The creation of credit: the real world

In practice, the creation of credit is not as simple as this. First, while banks must have access to cash if their customers want it, banks can keep some of the money deposited in them in a form that can be readily converted into cash rather than holding it as cash itself. There are various short-term securities that banks hold for this purpose. These securities can be sold for cash at very short notice. Securities held for these purposes are known as 'near money' and, together with cash, form banks' 'liquid assets'. What banks have to look at, therefore, is the **liquidity ratio**, the ratio of liquid assets to total deposits.

Second, at certain times banks may decide that it is prudent to hold a bigger proportion of liquid assets. If Christmas or the summer holidays are approaching and people are likely to make bigger cash withdrawals, banks may decide to hold more liquid assets. In the wake of the banking crisis of 2008, where many of banks' assets fell in value, banks chose to hold more liquid assets in an attempt to increase confidence. On the other hand, there may be an upsurge in consumer demand for credit. Banks may be very keen to grant additional loans and thus make more profits, even though they have acquired no additional cash or other liquid assets. Conversely, banks may want to make loans, but customers may not want to borrow, if they are concerned about the future and the repayments.

What causes the money supply to rise?

The money supply might rise as a result of banks responding to an increased demand for credit. They may be prepared to operate with a lower liquidity ratio to meet this demand. Indeed, with the increased use of credit and debit cards, we have seen a trend of banks increasingly choosing a lower liquidity ratio – at least until the banking crisis of 2008/9.

Another source of extra money is from abroad. Sometimes the Bank of England will choose to build up the foreign currency reserves. To do this it will buy foreign currencies on the foreign exchange market using sterling. When the recipients of this extra sterling deposit it in UK banks, or spend it on UK exports and the exporters deposit the money in UK banks, credit will be created on the basis of it, leading to a multiplied increase in money supply.

One of the main reasons for an increase in money supply is government borrowing. If the government spends more than it receives in tax revenues, it will have to borrow to make up the difference. This difference is known as the **public sector net cash requirement (PSNCR)**. The government borrows by selling interest-bearing securities. These are of two main types: (a) short-term securities in the form of Treasury bills – these have a three-month period to maturity (i.e. the date on which the government pays back the loan); (b) longer-term securities in the form of bonds, also known as 'gilts' – these often have several years to maturity.

Such securities could be sold to the Bank of England. The money paid to the government is in effect being created by the Bank of England and when it finds its way to the banks, the banks can use it as the basis for credit creation. Similarly, if the government borrows through additional Treasury bills, and if these are purchased by the banking sector, there will be a multiplied expansion of credit. The banks will now have additional liquid assets (bills), which can be used as the basis for credit creation.

In 2009/10, the Bank of England took emergency measures to increase the supply of money, known as 'quantitative easing'. This involved the Bank of England buying existing bonds from banks and other financial institutions and thereby releasing new money into the banking system. It was hoped that this extra liquidity in the banking system would encourage banks to lend.

The demand for money

The demand for money refers to the desire to *hold* money; to keep your wealth in the form of money, rather than spending it on goods and services or using it to

---

Definitions

Liquidity ratio
The ratio of liquid assets (cash and assets that can be readily converted to cash) to total deposits.

Public sector net cash requirement (PSNCR)
The (annual) deficit of the public sector (central government, local government and public corporations), and thus the amount that the public sector must borrow.

purchase financial assets such as bonds or shares. But why should people want to hold on to money, rather than spending it or buying some sort of security such as bonds or shares? There are two main reasons.

The first is that people receive money only at intervals (e.g. weekly or monthly) and not continuously. They thus require to hold balances of money in cash or in current accounts ready for spending later in the week or month.

The second is as a form of saving. Money in a bank account earns a relatively small, but safe rate of return. Some assets, such as company shares or bonds, may earn you more on average, but there is a chance that their price will fall. In other words, they are risky.

What determines the size of the demand for money?

What would cause the demand for money to rise? This would occur if people's incomes rose. The more you earn, the more money you are likely to hold in the bank or in cash. A rise in money ('nominal') incomes in a country can be caused either by a rise in real GDP (i.e. real output) or by a rise in prices, or some combination of the two.

The demand for money would also rise if people thought that share prices or the prices of other securities were likely to fall. In such circumstances, owning shares or other forms of securities may be seen as too risky. To avoid this risk, people will want to hold money instead. Some clever (or lucky) individuals anticipated the 2008 stock market decline (see Box 2.1). They sold shares and 'went liquid'.

> **Pause for thought**
>
> *Which way is the demand-for-money curve likely to shift in each of the following cases? (a) Prices rise, but real incomes stay the same; (b) Interest rates abroad rise relative to domestic interest rates; (c) People anticipate that share prices are likely to fall in the near future.*

The rate of interest. In terms of the operation of money markets, this is the most important determinant. It is related to the opportunity cost of holding money. The opportunity cost is the interest forgone by not holding higher interest-bearing assets, such as bonds or shares. Generally, if rates of interest rise, they will rise more on bonds and other securities than on bank accounts. The demand for money will thus fall as people switch to these alternative securities. The demand for money is thus inversely related to the rate of interest. This is illustrated in Figure 10.6.

The equilibrium rate of interest

Equilibrium in the money market occurs when the demand for money (M_d) is equal to the supply of money (M_s). Figure 10.6 shows the demand for and supply of money plotted against the rate of interest. For simplicity, it is assumed that the supply of money is independent of interest rates, and is therefore drawn as a vertical straight line.[1]

The equilibrium rate of interest is r_e. But why? If the rate of interest were above r_e, people would have money balances surplus to their needs. They would use these to buy shares, bonds and other assets. This would drive up the price of these assets. But the price of assets is inversely related to interest rates. The higher the price of an asset (such as a government bond), the less will any given interest payment be as a percentage of its price (e.g. £10 as a percentage of £100 is 10 per cent, but as a percentage of £200, it is only 5 per cent). Thus a higher price of assets will correspond to lower interest rates.

---

[1] In practice, the supply-of-money curve is likely to be upward sloping. The reason is that a rise in aggregate demand will lead to an increased demand for money and hence a rise in interest rates. At the same time, banks are likely to respond to the rise in demand for money by creating more credit, thereby increasing the money supply. In other words, the higher interest rates correspond to an increased supply of money.

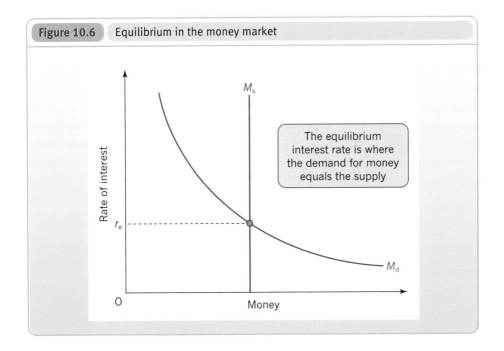

Figure 10.6   Equilibrium in the money market

The equilibrium interest rate is where the demand for money equals the supply

As the rate of interest fell, so there would be a movement down along the M_s and M_d curves. The interest rate would go on falling until it reached r_e. Equilibrium would then be achieved.

Similarly, if the rate of interest were below r_e, people would have insufficient money balances. They would sell securities, thus lowering their prices and raising the rate of interest until it reached r_e.

Causes of changes in interest rates

We saw above what would cause an increase in the supply of money. If money supply does increase, the M_s line will shift to the right in Figure 10.6. This will cause a fall in the rate of interest to the point where the new M_s line intersects with the M_d curve.

A change in interest rates will also occur if the demand for money changes (i.e. the M_d curve shifts). For example, a rise in incomes would lead to people wanting to hold larger money balances. This would shift the M_d curve to the right and drive up the rate of interest.

In practice, the Bank of England seeks to *control* the rate of interest. We see how it achieves this in the next chapter.

Effects of changes in interest rates

A reduction in interest rates (e.g. from a rise in money supply) will lead to a rise in investment and consumer spending as firms and consumers borrow more. This rise in aggregate demand will then lead to a multiplied rise in GDP.

How much aggregate demand increases depends on (a) the elasticity of the demand-for-money curve – the steeper the M_d curve, the more interest rates will fall for any given rise in money supply; (b) the responsiveness of businesses and consumers to a change in interest rates – the more responsive they are, the bigger will be the rise in aggregate demand and hence the bigger the multiplied rise in GDP.

Pause for thought

Assume that interest rates fall. Under what circumstances will this lead to (a) a large rise in business investment; (b) little or no change in business investment?

Recap

1. Interest rates are an important determinant of business activity. They are determined by the interaction of the demand and supply of money.

2. Money in its narrow sense includes just cash in circulation. Money is normally defined more broadly, however, to include all bank deposits, not just those in the form of cash. M4 is the name given in the UK to this broader measure of the money supply.

3. Bank deposits expand through a process of credit creation. If banks' liquid assets increase, they can be used as a base for increasing loans. When the loans are redeposited in banks, they form the base for yet more loans, and thus a process of multiple credit expansion takes place. The ratio of the increase of deposits to an expansion of banks' liquidity base is called the 'bank multiplier'. It is the inverse of the liquidity ratio.

4. Money supply will rise if (a) banks respond to an increased demand for money by increasing credit without an increase in liquidity; (b) there is an inflow of money from abroad; (c) the government has a PSNCR and finances it by borrowing from the banking sector.

5. The demand for money is determined mainly by people's incomes, the risk attached to alternatives to money and the rate of interest (the opportunity cost of holding money). The higher the rate of interest, the lower the demand for money.

6. The equilibrium rate of interest is where the supply of money is equal to the demand. A rise in the rate of interest can be caused by an increased demand for money or a reduced supply.

10.6 UNEMPLOYMENT

We saw in Chapter 8 how employment is determined in individual labour markets. In this section we look at the overall level of employment and unemployment in the economy. This, as we shall see, depends in part on the level of business activity. When the economy is booming, employment will be high and unemployment low as businesses take on more labour to meet the extra demand.

Measuring unemployment

The unemployed are not simply those who do not have a job – we would not count a child as being unemployed! The usual definition that economists use for the **number unemployed** is: *those of working age who are without work, but who are available for work at current wage rates.* Unemployment can be expressed either as a number (e.g. 1.5 million) or as a percentage (e.g. 5 per cent). If the figure is to be expressed as a percentage, then it is a percentage of the total **labour force**. The labour force is defined as: *those in employment plus those unemployed.* Thus if 24 million people were employed and 1 million people were unemployed, the **unemployment rate** would be:

$$\frac{1}{24 + 1} \times 100 = 4 \text{ per cent}$$

Two common measures of unemployment are used in official statistics. The first is **claimant unemployment**. This is simply a measure of all those in receipt of unemployment-related benefits. In the UK, claimants receive the 'job-seeker's allowance'.

The second measure is the **standardised unemployment rate**. Since 1998, this has been the main measure used by the UK government. It is the measure used by the International Labour Organisation (ILO) and the Organisation for Economic Co-operation and Development (OECD), two international organisations that publish unemployment statistics for many countries.

Definitions

Number unemployed (economist's definition)
Those of working age, who are without work, but who are available for work at current wage rates.

Labour force
The number employed plus the number unemployed.

Unemployment rate
The number unemployed expressed as a percentage of the labour force.

Claimant unemployment
Those in receipt of unemployment-related benefits.

In this measure, the unemployed are defined as people of working age who are without work, available to start work within two weeks and *actively seeking employment* or waiting to take up an appointment. The figures are compiled from the results of national labour force surveys. In the UK the labour force survey is conducted quarterly.

But is the standardised unemployment rate likely to be higher or lower than the claimant unemployment rate? The standardised rate is likely to be higher to the extent that it includes people seeking work who are nevertheless not entitled to claim benefits, but lower to the extent that it excludes those who are claiming benefits and yet who are not actively seeking work. Clearly, the tougher the benefit regulations, the lower the claimant rate will be relative to the standardised rate.

Unemployment and the labour market

We now turn to the causes of unemployment. These causes fall into two broad categories: *equilibrium* unemployment and *disequilibrium* unemployment. To make clear the distinction between the two, it is necessary to look at how the labour market works.

Figure 10.7 shows the aggregate demand for labour and the aggregate supply of labour: that is, the total demand and supply of labour in the whole economy. The *real* average wage rate is plotted on the vertical axis. This is the average wage rate expressed in terms of its purchasing power: in other words, after taking inflation into account.

The **aggregate supply of labour curve** (AS_L) shows the number of workers *willing to accept jobs* at each wage rate. This curve is relatively inelastic, since the size of the workforce at any one time cannot change significantly. Nevertheless, it is not totally inelastic because (a) a higher wage rate will encourage some people to enter the labour market (e.g. parents raising children) and (b) the unemployed will be more willing to accept job offers rather than continuing to search for a better-paid job.

Definitions

Standardised unemployment rate
The measure of the unemployment rate used by the ILO and OECD. The unemployed are defined as people of working age who are without work, available for work and actively seeking employment.

Aggregate supply of labour curve
A curve showing the total number of people willing and able to work at different average real wage rates.

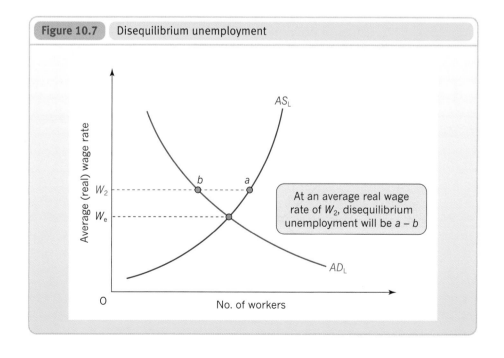

Figure 10.7   Disequilibrium unemployment

At an average real wage rate of W_2, disequilibrium unemployment will be $a - b$

The **aggregate demand for labour curve** (AD_L) slopes downward. The higher the wage rate, the fewer workers firms will want to employ. They may decide to cut back on production, thereby reducing the number of workers they need, or the higher wage rate may encourage firms to economise on labour and to substitute other inputs for it.

The labour market is in equilibrium at a wage of W_e, where the demand for labour equals the supply. If the wage were above W_e, the labour market would be in a state of disequilibrium. At a wage rate of W_2, there is an excess supply of labour of $a - b$. This is called **disequilibrium unemployment**.

For disequilibrium unemployment to occur, two conditions must hold:

■ The aggregate supply of labour must exceed the aggregate demand.
■ There must be a 'stickiness' in wages. In other words, the wage rate must not immediately fall to W_e.

Even when the labour market *is* in equilibrium, however, not everyone looking for work will be employed. Some people will hold out, hoping to find a better job. The curve N in Figure 10.8 shows the total number in the labour force. The horizontal difference between it and the aggregate supply of labour curve (AS_L) represents the excess of people looking for work over those actually willing to accept jobs. Q_e represents the equilibrium level of employment and the distance $d - e$ represents the **equilibrium level of unemployment**. This is sometimes known as the *natural level of unemployment*.

Types of disequilibrium unemployment

There are two main causes of disequilibrium unemployment.

Real-wage unemployment

Real-wage unemployment is where wages are set above the market-clearing level, for example at W_2 in Figure 10.7. This could be the result of either minimum wage

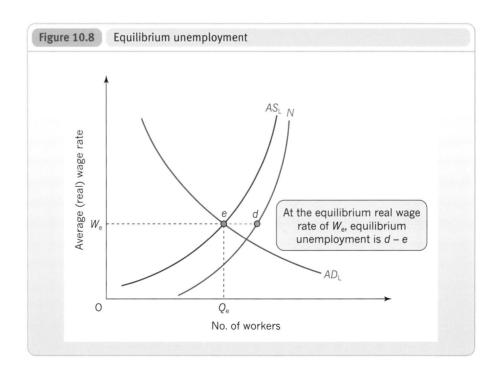

Figure 10.8   Equilibrium unemployment

At the equilibrium real wage rate of W_e, equilibrium unemployment is $d - e$

legislation or the activities of trade unions. Excessive real wage rates were blamed by the Thatcher and Major governments for the high unemployment of the 1980s and early 1990s. The possibility of higher real-wage unemployment was also one of the reasons for their rejection of a national minimum wage.

The solution to real-wage unemployment would seem to be a reduction in real wage rates. However, it may be very difficult to prevent unions pushing up wages. What is more, even if the government did succeed in reducing the average real wage rate, there would then be a problem of reduced consumer expenditure and hence a reduced demand for labour, with the result that unemployment might not fall at all!

Demand-deficient unemployment

Demand-deficient unemployment is associated with economic recessions, as we experienced in 2008/9. As the economy moves into recession, consumer demand falls. Firms find that they are unable to sell their current level of output. For a time they may be prepared to build up stocks of unsold goods, but sooner or later they will start to cut back on production and cut back on the amount of labour they employ. In Figure 10.7 the AD_L curve shifts to the left. With real wages being 'sticky' downwards, the aggregate demand for labour is now less than the aggregate supply. Disequilibrium unemployment occurs. The deeper the recession becomes and the longer it lasts, the higher will demand-deficient unemployment become.

As the economy recovers and begins to grow again, so demand-deficient unemployment will start to fall. Because demand-deficient unemployment fluctuates with the business cycle, it is sometimes referred to as 'cyclical unemployment'. Figure 10.9 shows the fluctuations in unemployment in various industrial economies. If you

> **Pause for thought**
>
> *If this analysis is correct, namely that a reduction in wages will reduce the aggregate demand for goods, what assumption must we make about the relative proportions of wages and profits that are spent (given that a reduction in real wage rates will lead to a corresponding increase in rates of profit)? Is this a realistic assumption?*

> **Definition**
>
> **Demand-deficient (or cyclical) unemployment** Disequilibrium unemployment caused by a fall in aggregate demand with no corresponding fall in the real wage rate.

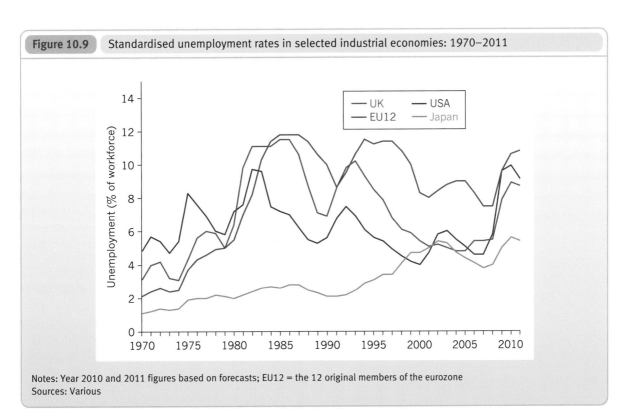

Figure 10.9   Standardised unemployment rates in selected industrial economies: 1970–2011

Notes: Year 2010 and 2011 figures based on forecasts; EU12 = the 12 original members of the eurozone
Sources: Various

compare this figure with Figure 10.5, you can see how unemployment tends to rise in recessions and fall in booms.

Equilibrium unemployment

Looking at Figure 10.9, you can see how unemployment was higher in the 1980s and 1990s than in the 1970s. Much of the reason for this was the growth in equilibrium unemployment. Similarly, the lower unemployment in the early and mid 2000s across many developed nations (with the exception of Japan) was largely the result of a fall in equilibrium unemployment. This has been partly caused by more flexible labour markets, as we discussed in Chapter 8.

Although there may be overall *macro*economic equilibrium, with the *aggregate* demand for labour equal to the *aggregate* supply, and thus no disequilibrium unemployment, at a *micro*economic level supply and demand may not match. In other words, there may be vacancies in some parts of the economy, but an excess of labour (unemployment) in others. This is equilibrium unemployment. There are various types of equilibrium unemployment.

Frictional (search) unemployment

Frictional unemployment occurs when people leave their jobs, either voluntarily or because they are sacked or made redundant, and are then unemployed for a period of time while they are looking for a new job. They may not get the first job they apply for, despite a vacancy existing. The employer may continue searching, hoping to find a better qualified person. Likewise, unemployed people may choose not to take the first job they are offered. Instead they may continue searching, hoping that a better one will turn up.

The problem is that information is imperfect. Employers are not fully informed about what labour is available; workers are not fully informed about what jobs are available and what they entail. Both employers and workers, therefore, have to search: employers search for the right labour and workers search for the right jobs. The search process has been aided by the development of the Internet and online recruitment agencies (see Box 8.3).

Structural unemployment

Structural unemployment is where the structure of the economy changes. Employment in some industries may expand while in others it contracts. There are two main reasons for this:

A change in the pattern of demand. Some industries experience declining demand. This may be due to a change in consumer tastes. Certain goods may go out of fashion. Or it may be due to competition from other industries. For example, consumer demand may shift away from coal and to other fuels. This will lead to structural unemployment in mining areas.

A change in the methods of production (technological unemployment). New techniques of production often allow the same level of output to be produced with fewer workers. This is known as 'labour-saving technical progress'. Unless output expands sufficiently to absorb the surplus labour, people will be made redundant. This creates **technological unemployment**. An example is the job losses in the banking industry caused by the increase in the number of cash machines and by the development of telephone and Internet banking. There are also concerns within the Royal Mail that the new modern and efficient technologies being introduced in sorting offices will lead to substantial job losses.

Structural unemployment often occurs in particular regions of the country. When it does, it is referred to as **regional unemployment**. This is most likely to occur when particular industries are concentrated in particular areas. For example, the decline in the South Wales coal mining industry led to high unemployment in the Welsh valleys.

Seasonal unemployment

Seasonal unemployment occurs when the demand for certain types of labour fluctuates with the seasons of the year. This problem is particularly severe in holiday areas such as Cornwall, where unemployment can reach very high levels in the winter months.

Recap

1. The two most common measures of unemployment are claimant unemployment (those claiming unemployment-related benefits) and ILO/OECD standardised unemployment (those available for work and actively seeking work or waiting to take up an appointment).

2. Unemployment can be divided into disequilibrium and equilibrium unemployment.

3. Disequilibrium unemployment occurs when the average real wage rate is above the level that will equate the aggregate demand and supply of labour. It can be caused by unions or government pushing up wages (real-wage unemployment) or by a fall in aggregate demand but a downward 'stickiness' in real wages (demand-deficient or cyclical unemployment).

4. Equilibrium unemployment occurs when there are people unable or unwilling to fill job vacancies. This may be due to poor information in the labour market and hence a time lag before people find suitable jobs (frictional unemployment), to a changing pattern of demand or supply in the economy and hence a mismatching of labour with jobs (structural unemployment – specific types being technological and regional unemployment), or to seasonal fluctuations in the demand for labour.

INFLATION   10.7

The rate of inflation measures the annual percentage increase in prices. The most usual measure is that of *consumer* prices. The government publishes a consumer prices index (CPI) each month, and the rate of inflation is the percentage increase in that index over the previous 12 months. Figure 10.10 shows the rates of inflation for various industrial economies from 1965 to 2011. As you can see, inflation was particularly severe between 1973 and 1983, and relatively low in the mid 1980s and in recent years. The Japanese economy has suffered from deflation (falling prices) throughout the 2000s and prices fell in many other developed countries during the 2009 recession.

It is also possible to give the rates of inflation for other prices. For example, indices are published for commodity prices, food prices, house prices, import prices, prices after taking taxes into account and so on. Their respective rates of inflation are simply their annual percentage increase. Likewise it is possible to give the rate of inflation of wage rates ('wage inflation').

When there is inflation, we have to be careful in assessing how much national output, consumption, wages, etc. are increasing. Take the case of GDP. GDP in year 2

Figure 10.10   Inflation rates in selected industrial economies, 1965–2011

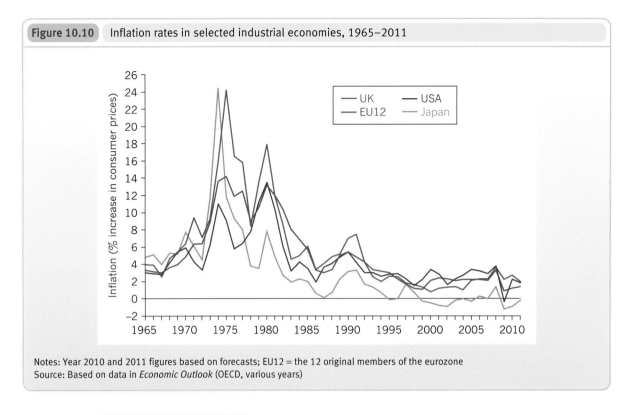

Notes: Year 2010 and 2011 figures based on forecasts; EU12 = the 12 original members of the eurozone
Source: Based on data in *Economic Outlook* (OECD, various years)

Pause for thought

Why is inflation damaging to (a) business;
(b) the economy in general?

may seem higher than in year 1, but this may be partly (or even wholly) the result of higher prices. Thus GDP in money terms may have risen by 5 per cent, but if inflation is 3 per cent, **real growth in GDP** will be only 2 per cent. In other words, the volume of output will be only 2 per cent higher.

Definition

Real growth values
Values of the rate of growth in GDP or any other variable after taking inflation into account. The real value of the growth in a variable equals its growth in money (or 'nominal') value minus the rate of inflation.

 KEY IDEA 27   **The distinction between real and nominal values. Nominal figures are those using current prices, interest rates, etc. Real figures are figures corrected for inflation.**

Before we proceed, a word of caution: be careful not to confuse a rise or fall in *inflation* with a rise or fall in *prices*. A rise in inflation means a *faster* increase in prices. A fall in inflation means a *slower* increase in prices (but still an increase as long as inflation is positive).

Aggregate demand and supply and the level of prices

The level of prices in the economy is determined by the interaction of aggregate demand and aggregate supply. The analysis is similar to that of demand and supply in individual markets (see Chapter 2), but there are some crucial differences. Figure 10.11 shows aggregate demand and supply curves. Let us examine each in turn.

Aggregate demand curve

Remember what we said about aggregate demand earlier in the chapter. It is the total level of spending on the country's products, by consumers, by the government, by firms on investment, and by people residing abroad. The aggregate demand curve

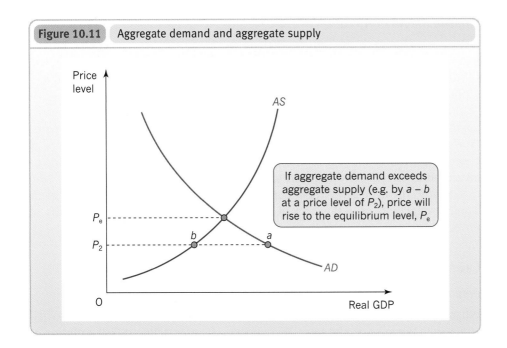

Figure 10.11   Aggregate demand and aggregate supply

If aggregate demand exceeds aggregate supply (e.g. by $a - b$ at a price level of P_2), price will rise to the equilibrium level, P_e

shows how much national output (real GDP) will be demanded at each level of prices. But why does the *AD* curve slope downwards: why do people demand fewer products as prices rise? There are three main reasons:

■ If prices rise, people will be encouraged to buy fewer of their own country's products and more imports instead (which are now relatively cheaper); also the country will sell fewer exports. Thus aggregate demand will be lower.

■ As prices rise, people will need more money in their accounts to pay for their purchases. With a given supply of money in the economy, this will have the effect of driving up interest rates (the M_d curve shifts to the right in Figure 10.6 on page 289). The effect of higher interest rates will be to discourage borrowing and encourage saving. Both will have the effect of reducing spending and hence reducing aggregate demand.

■ If prices rise, the value of people's savings will be eroded. They may thus save more (and spend less) to compensate.

Aggregate supply curve

The aggregate supply curve slopes upwards – at least in the short run. In other words, the higher the level of prices, the more will be produced. The reason is simple: provided that input prices (and, in particular, wage rates) do not rise as rapidly as product prices, firms' profitability at each level of output will be higher than before. This will encourage them to produce more.

Equilibrium

The equilibrium price level will be where aggregate demand equals aggregate supply. To demonstrate this, consider what would happen if aggregate demand exceeded aggregate supply: e.g. at P_2 in Figure 10.11. The resulting shortages throughout the economy would drive up prices. This would cause a movement up along both the *AD* and *AS* curves until *AD* = *AS* (at P_e).

Shifts in the AD or AS curves

If there is a change in the price level there will be a movement *along* the *AD* and *AS* curves. If any other determinant of *AD* or *AS* changes, the respective curve will shift. The analysis here is very similar to shifts and movements along demand and supply curves in individual markets (see pages 36 and 40).

The aggregate demand curve will shift if there is a change in any of its components – consumption of domestic products, investment, government expenditure or exports. Thus if the government decides to spend more, or if consumers spend more as a result of lower taxes, or if business confidence increases so that firms decide to invest more, the *AD* curve will shift to the right.

Similarly, the aggregate supply curve will shift to the right if there is a rise in labour productivity or in the stock of capital: i.e. if there is a rise in the capacity of the economy.

Causes of inflation

Demand-pull inflation

> **Definition**
>
> **Demand-pull inflation**
> Inflation caused by persistent rises in aggregate demand.

When the *AD* curve shifts to the right, output will rise and unemployment may fall as a result. However, at the same time, prices will rise. **Demand-pull inflation** is caused by continuing rises in aggregate demand. In Figure 10.12, the *AD* curve shifts to the right, and continues doing so. Firms will respond to the rise in aggregate demand partly by raising prices and partly by increasing output (there is a move upwards along the *AS* curve). Just how much they raise prices depends on how much their costs rise as a result of increasing output. This in turn depends upon how close actual output is to output ceiling (see Figure 10.4 on page 279). The less slack there is in the economy, the more will firms respond to a rise in demand by raising their prices (the steeper will be the *AS* curve).

Demand-pull inflation is typically associated with a booming economy. Many economists therefore argue that it is the counterpart of demand-deficient

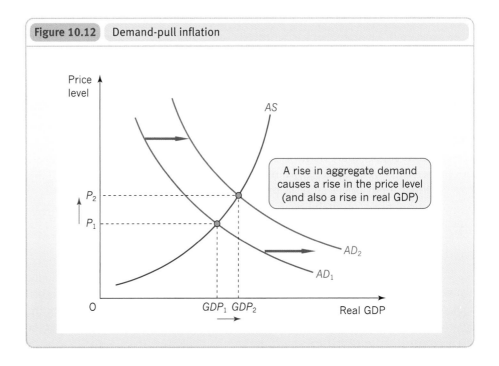

Figure 10.12 Demand-pull inflation

A rise in aggregate demand causes a rise in the price level (and also a rise in real GDP)

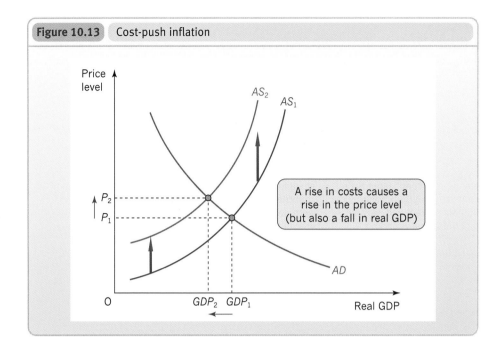

Figure 10.13   Cost-push inflation

A rise in costs causes a rise in the price level (but also a fall in real GDP)

unemployment. When the economy is in recession, demand-deficient unemployment will be high, but demand-pull inflation will be low. When, on the other hand, the economy is near the peak of the business cycle, demand-pull inflation will be high, but demand-deficient unemployment will be low.

Cost-push inflation

Cost-push inflation is associated with continuing rises in costs and hence continuing upward (leftward) shifts in the *AS* curve (see Figure 10.13). If firms face a rise in costs, they will respond partly by raising prices and passing the costs on to the consumer, and partly by cutting back on production (there is a movement back along the *AD* curve).

Just how much firms raise prices and cut back on production depends on the shape of the aggregate demand curve. The less elastic the *AD* curve – in other words, the less consumers, firms and the government are prepared to cut back on real expenditure – the less sales will fall as a result of any price rise, and hence the more will firms be able to pass on the rise in their costs to consumers as higher prices.

The rise in costs may originate from a number of different sources, such as higher wages as a result of trade unions pushing up wages independently of the demand for labour, firms using their monopoly power to make bigger profits by pushing up prices independently of consumer demand, or import prices rising independently of the level of aggregate demand (e.g. OPEC putting up oil prices).

In all these cases, inflation occurs because one or more groups are exercising economic power. The problem is likely to get worse, therefore, if there is an increasing concentration of economic power over time (e.g. if firms or unions get bigger and bigger, and more monopolistic) or if groups become more militant.

Another cause of cost-push inflation is rising prices of various commodities – not just oil, but copper, aluminium, iron ore and other minerals – and also agricultural prices. With the growth in demand for raw materials and food from China and

Definition

Cost-push inflation
Inflation caused by persistent rises in costs of production (independently of demand).

BOX 10.4   INFLATION OR DEFLATION

Where's the danger?

The spectre of deflation

In the first edition of this book, I wrote that 'Inflation no longer seems a serious worry in many developed economies. Instead, "deflation" (i.e. falling prices) has become a source of concern. The Japanese economy has been in deflation for the past ten years, but more recently the US Federal Reserve – the "Fed" (America's central bank) and the European Central Bank have sounded warnings that deflation is a real and present danger to us all, set to engulf the global economic system.'

That was back in 2003, and the box included a quote from *The Sunday Times* of 11 May of that year, which assessed the danger. The quote included the following:

> Consumers have had a good run in America. Twenty years ago a Burger King Whopper cost $1.40. Today the same burger costs 99c. Ten years ago Delta Airlines charged $388 for a flight from New York to San Francisco; this weekend flights are available for $302. Five years ago the average new car cost $25 000; now it is $24 500.
>
> The same is true for clothes, computers, holidays and television sets. As wages have risen, prices seem to have fallen across the board. But can you have too much of a good thing?
>
> Last week, America's central bankers warned that falling prices could harm the US economy. The Federal Reserve even went as far as to raise the spectre of deflation – an economic malaise that has paralysed the Japanese economy for a decade and was last seen in America during the Great Depression of the 1930s.
>
> Consumers normally welcome falling prices, but in a deflating economy such falls can create a damaging downward spiral. Profits fall as companies are unable to offset costs by raising prices. Companies then cut staff to save money. Job losses lead to falling sales.
>
> Declining sales also make it harder for companies and people to meet their debts, leading to further declines in sales and a rise in bankruptcies. Falling prices also lead people to defer purchases in the belief that prices will come down further.[1]

One of the main causes of declining prices was the process of globalisation. Imports from low-cost countries, such as China and India, have driven prices down. What is more, outsourcing call-centre, back-office and IT work to developing countries has put downward pressure on wages. This downward effect on prices and wages in the USA and other developed economies has been dubbed the 'China price' effect.

A return of inflation?

The US and other OECD economies staged a rapid recovery after 2003. Between 2004 and 2006, US economic growth averaged 3.8 per cent and the OECD countries' averaged 3.1 per cent. These rates, however, were dwarfed by China and India, which experienced growth rates of 10.1 per cent and 8.4 per cent respectively over the same period.

The rapid growth in aggregate demand in many OECD countries put upward pressure on prices and wages but, unlike previously, the 'China price' effect was beginning to *reinforce* this upward pressure. As *The Economist* of 24 June 2006 stated:

> China's excessive growth is not only of domestic concern. With much of the world increasingly worried about inflation, questions arise about what an overheating Chinese economy could do to global prices . . . After being squeezed between rising input costs and falling factory-gate prices, China's manufacturers are starting to raise prices to rebuild margins – and getting away with it because both domestic demand and exports are still far stronger than they were two years ago. Add in higher domestic food and energy prices and surging labour costs, and the China price may soon be a good deal higher.

By 2008, the growth in China, India and other rapidly developing countries was causing significant inflation in food and raw material prices. Oil prices rose to $147 per barrel by July. However, with the onset of recession in mid 2008, inflation started to fall and the 'China effect' seemed to have gone away. Once more there seemed to be a spectre of deflation. By 2009, many people were asking themselves why they should buy now when, by delaying, they might be able to get an item more cheaply later on. The effect of this would be a leftward shift in the *AD* curve, which forces prices down even further.

But the worry about deflation was short-lived. As the world economy pulled out of recession and China resumed double-digit growth, so commodity and other prices began rising more rapidly. In the UK inflation reached 3.7 per cent in the 12 months to April 2010.

1. *What long-term economic benefits might deflation generate for business and the economy in general?*
2. *Would an inflationary China price effect be an example of demand-pull or cost-push inflation?*

---

[1] From 'Deflation turns into biggest economic risk', *The Times*, 11 May 2003. NI Syndication Limited. © The Times/The Sun/nisyndication.com

other rapidly developing economies, such as India and Brazil, what starts with a rise in aggregate demand in these countries (demand-pull inflation), becomes cost-push inflation for other countries having to pay higher prices for the commodities they import.

Demand-pull and cost-push inflation can occur together, since wage and price rises can be caused both by increases in aggregate demand and by independent causes pushing up costs. Even when an inflationary process *starts* as either demand-pull or cost-push, it is often difficult to separate the two. An initial cost-push inflation may encourage the government to expand aggregate demand to offset rises in unemployment. Alternatively, an initial demand-pull inflation may strengthen the power of certain groups, who then use this power to drive up costs. Either way, the result is likely to be continuing rightward shifts in the *AD* curve and upward shifts in the *AS* curve. Prices will carry on rising.

Expectations and inflation

Workers and firms take account of the *expected* rate of inflation when making decisions.

Imagine that a union and an employer are negotiating a wage increase. Let us assume that both sides expect a rate of inflation of 5 per cent. The union will be happy to receive a wage rise somewhat above 5 per cent. That way the members would be getting a *real* rise in incomes. The employers will be happy to pay a wage rise somewhat below 5 per cent. After all, they can put their price up by 5 per cent, knowing that their rivals will do approximately the same. The actual wage rise that the two sides agree on will thus be somewhere around 5 per cent.

Now let us assume that the expected rate of inflation is 10 per cent. Both sides will now negotiate around this benchmark, with the outcome being somewhere round about 10 per cent.

Thus the higher the expected rate of inflation, the higher will be the level of pay settlements and price rises, and hence the higher will be the resulting actual rate of inflation.

In recent years the importance of expectations in explaining the actual rate of inflation has been increasingly recognised by economists, and it has prompted them to discover just what determines people's expectations.

Recap

1. Inflation is the annual percentage increase in prices.
2. Equilibrium in the economy occurs when aggregate demand equals aggregate supply. Prices will rise if there is a rightward shift in the aggregate demand curve or an upward (leftward) shift in the aggregate supply curve.
3. Demand-pull inflation occurs as a result of increases in aggregate demand. It is typically associated with a booming economy.
4. Cost-push inflation occurs when there are increases in the costs of production independent of rises in aggregate demand.
5. Expectations play a crucial role in determining the level of inflation. The higher people expect inflation to be, the higher it will be.

QUESTIONS

1. What are the key macroeconomic objectives of government? Are there likely to be any conflicts between them?

	2003	2004	2005	2006	2007	2008	2009
USA	100.0	103.6	106.7	109.6	111.9	113.1	110.9
Japan	100.0	102.7	104.7	106.9	109.4	108.7	102.8
Germany	100.0	100.7	101.7	104.9	107.6	108.7	102.9
France	100.0	102.2	104.2	106.6	108.9	109.7	107.1
UK	100.0	102.8	104.9	107.8	111.1	111.9	107.0

Sources: *Various*

2. The table above shows index numbers for real GDP (national output) for various countries (2003 = 100).

   Using the formula $G = (Y_t - Y_{t-1})/Y_{t-1} \times 100$ (where G is the rate of growth, Y is the index number of output, t is any given year and $t - 1$ is the previous year):

   (a) Work out the growth rate for each country for each year from 2004 to 2009.
   (b) Plot the figures on a graph. Describe the pattern that emerges.

3. In terms of the UK circular flow of income, are the following net injections, net withdrawals or neither? If there is uncertainty, explain your assumptions.

   (a) Firms are forced to take a cut in profits in order to give a pay rise.
   (b) Firms spend money on research.
   (c) The government increases personal tax allowances.
   (d) The general public invests more money in building societies.
   (e) UK investors earn higher dividends on overseas investments.
   (f) The government purchases US military aircraft.
   (g) People draw on their savings to finance holidays abroad.
   (h) People draw on their savings to finance holidays in the UK.
   (i) The government runs a budget deficit (spends more than it receives in tax revenues).

4. Assume that the multiplier has a value of 3. Now assume that the government decides to increase aggregate demand in an attempt to reduce unemployment. It raises government expenditure by £100 million with no increase in taxes. Firms, anticipating a rise in their sales, increase investment by £200 million, of which £50 million consists of purchases of foreign machinery. How much will GDP rise? (Assume that nothing else changes.)

5. What factors could explain why some countries have a higher multiplier than others?

6. At what point of the business cycle is the country now? What do you predict will happen to growth over the next two years? On what basis do you make your prediction?

7. Why does a booming economy not carry on booming indefinitely? Why does an economy in recession pull out of that recession?

8. For what possible reasons may one country experience a persistently faster rate of economic growth than another?

9. Imagine that the banking system receives additional deposits of £100 million and that all the individual banks wish to retain their current liquidity ratio of 20 per cent.

   (a) How much will banks choose to lend out initially?
   (b) What will happen to banks' deposits when the money that is lent out is spent and the recipients of it deposit it in their bank accounts?
   (c) How much of these latest deposits will be lent out by the banks?
   (d) By how much will total deposits (liabilities) eventually have risen, assuming that none of the additional liquidity is held outside the banking sector?
   (e) What is the size of the deposits multiplier?

10. What effects will the following have on the equilibrium rate of interest? (You should consider which way the demand and/or supply curves of money shift.)

    (a) Banks find that they have a higher liquidity ratio than they need.
    (b) A rise in incomes.
    (c) A growing belief that interest rates will rise from their current level.

11. Would it be desirable to have zero unemployment?

12. Consider the most appropriate policy for tackling each of the different types of unemployment.

13. Under what circumstances will a reduction in unemployment be accompanied by (a) an increase in inflation; (b) a decrease in inflation? Explain your answer.

14. Imagine that you had to determine whether a particular period of inflation was demand-pull, or cost-push, or a combination of the two. What information would you require in order to conduct your analysis?

Business issues covered in this chapter

- What sorts of government macroeconomic policy are available to government and how will they affect business activity?
- What will be the impact on the economy and business of various fiscal policy measures?
- What determines the effectiveness of fiscal policy in smoothing out fluctuations in the economy?
- What fiscal rules are adopted by the government and is following them a good idea?
- How does monetary policy work in the UK and what is the role of the Bank of England?
- How does targeting inflation influence interest rates and hence business activity?
- Are there better rules for determining interest rates other than sticking to a simple inflation target?
- How can supply-side policy influence business and the economy?
- What types of supply-side policies can be pursued and what is their effectiveness?

Chapter 11

National macroeconomic policy

11 Chapter

A key influence on the macroeconomic environment of business is the government. Governments like to achieve economic success, including sustained and stable economic growth, low unemployment and low inflation. To achieve these objectives, various types of policy are used. This chapter looks at the three main categories of macroeconomic policy.

The first is **fiscal policy**. This is where the government uses the balance of taxation (a withdrawal from the circular flow of income) and government expenditure (an injection) to influence the level of aggregate demand. If the economy is in recession, the government could increase government expenditure and/or cut taxes. This is called expansionary fiscal policy and the effect would be a higher level of aggregate demand and hence a multiplied rise in GDP and lower unemployment. If the economy was expanding too rapidly in a way that was unsustainable and hence with rising inflation, the government could do the reverse by using deflationary (or contractionary) fiscal policy: it could cut government expenditure and/or raise taxes. This would help to slow the economy down and dampen inflation.

The second type of policy is **monetary policy**. Here the government sets the framework of policy, which in many countries, including the UK, means setting a target for the rate of inflation. In the UK the rate is 2 per cent, as it is also in the eurozone. The central bank is then charged with adjusting interest rates to keep inflation on target.

These first two types of policy are referred to as **demand-side** or **demand management policies** as they seek to control the level of aggregate demand. The third category of policy is **supply-side policy**. This seeks to control aggregate supply directly. For example, the government might seek ways of encouraging greater productivity through increased research and development or better training programmes. Or it might seek to improve the country's transport and communications infrastructure, for example by investing in the railways or building more roads. By increasing aggregate supply, the economy's capacity to produce expands.

The difference between demand-side and supply-side policies is illustrated in Figures 11.1(a) and (b). Both diagrams show an aggregate demand and an aggregate supply curve.

Demand-side policy seeks to shift the *AD* curve. This is illustrated in Figure 11.1(a). An expansionary fiscal or monetary policy would shift the *AD* curve to the right, say from AD_1 to AD_2. This will increase GDP (to GDP_2), thereby helping to reduce unemployment. On the other hand, it will result in higher prices: the price level will rise to P_2.

A contractionary fiscal or monetary policy would help to curb rightward shifts in the *AD* curve or even cause the curve to shift to the left. The policy could be used to tackle inflation, but it would run the risk of a reduction in the rate of growth of GDP, or even a recession, and higher unemployment.

Supply-side policy seeks to shift the *AS* curve to the right. If successful, it will lead to both higher GDP and employment and lower prices (or at least lower inflation). This is illustrated in Figure 11.1(b). A rightward shift in the aggregate supply curve from AS_1 to AS_2 results in a rise in GDP to GDP_2 and a fall in the price level to P_2.

Definitions

Fiscal policy
Policy to affect aggregate demand by altering government expenditure and/or taxation.

Monetary policy
Policy to affect aggregate demand by central bank action to alter interest rates or money supply.

Demand-side or demand management policy
Policy to affect aggregate demand (i.e. fiscal or monetary policy).

Supply-side policy
Policy to affect aggregate supply directly.

Figure 11.1   The effects of macroeconomic policies

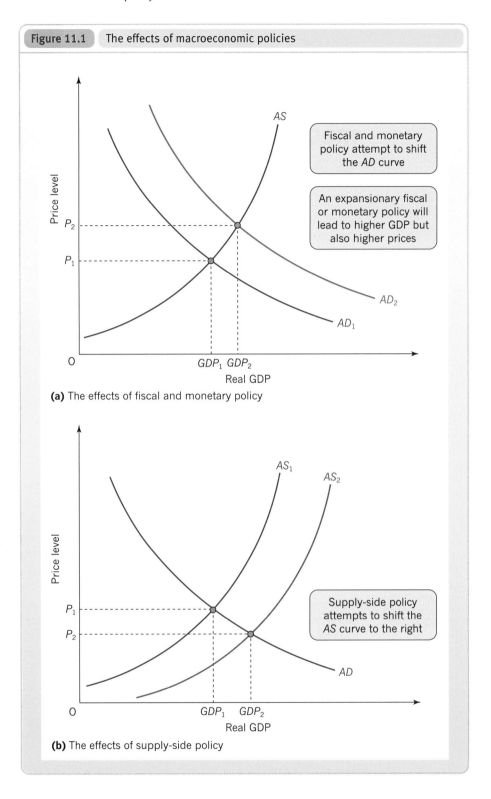

(a) The effects of fiscal and monetary policy

(b) The effects of supply-side policy

FISCAL POLICY

11.1

Fiscal policy can be used to perform two main functions:

■ *To prevent the occurrence of fundamental disequilibrium in the economy.* In other words, expansionary fiscal policy could be used to prevent a severe recession. Such a situation occurred in 2008/9 as governments around the world adopted 'stimulus packages' to prevent an even deeper recession and mass unemployment. Likewise deflationary fiscal policy could be used to prevent excessive inflation, such as that experienced in many countries in the early 1970s.

■ *To smooth out the fluctuations in the economy associated with the business cycle.* This would involve reducing government expenditure or raising taxes during the boom phase of the cycle. This would dampen down the expansion and prevent 'overheating' of the economy, with its attendant rising inflation. Conversely, with a slowing economy, the government should cut taxes or raise government expenditure in order to boost economic growth and prevent a rise in unemployment. Indeed, this was the action taken around the world from 2008 as countries attempted to tackle the recession that followed the banking crisis. For example, in the UK the government cut the rate of VAT from 17.5 to 15 per cent as a temporary measure.

If these stabilisation policies are successful, they will amount merely to fine-tuning. Problems of excess or deficient demand will never be allowed to get severe. Any movement of aggregate demand away from a steady growth path will be immediately 'nipped in the bud'.

Public finances

Central government deficits and surpluses

Since an expansionary fiscal policy involves raising government expenditure and/or lowering taxes, this has the effect of either increasing the **budget deficit** or reducing the **budget surplus**. A budget deficit in any one year is where central government's expenditure exceeds its revenue from taxation. A budget surplus is where tax revenues exceed central government expenditure. With the exception of short periods in 1969–70, 1987–90 and 1998–2001, governments in the UK, like most governments around the world, have run budget deficits. These deficits soared in the recession of 2008/9 as tax revenues declined and as unemployment rose and with it the numbers receiving unemployment benefits, and also as governments boosted spending and/or cut taxes to stimulate the economy.

However, there has been a concerted effort by many governments around the world to reduce the size of their budget deficits. This has been the number one economic priority of the incoming Conservative–Liberal Democrat government in the UK. Some countries with large deficits have found it difficult to raise the necessary finance to fund debt and have had to seek international support. Greece, with an annual budget deficit of 13.6 per cent of GDP and an accumulated national debt of 125 per cent of GDP, had to be bailed out by other eurozone countries and by the IMF. The process of getting deficits and debts down over the coming years will be painful for many countries.

Public sector deficits and surpluses

To get a better view of the overall **stance of fiscal policy** – just how expansionary or contractionary it is – we would need to look at the deficit or surplus of the entire public sector: namely, central government, local government and public corporations.

If the public sector spends more than it earns (through taxes and the revenues of public corporations, etc.), the amount of this deficit is known as the public sector net cash requirement (PSNCR). The reason for the name 'public sector net cash requirement' is simple. If the public sector runs a deficit in the current year of, say, £1 billion, then it will have to borrow £1 billion this year (require 'cash') in order to finance it. Table 11.1 shows UK PSNCR from 1986 to 2009. Note the huge increase in the PSNCR in 2009 as tax revenues fell in the recession and as the government attempted to reduce the depth of the recession by increasing expenditure.

Deficits are shown as positive figures (the government must borrow). They add to the accumulated debts from the past. The accumulated debts of central and local government are known as the **general government debt**. If the public sector runs a surplus (a negative PSNCR), then this will be used to reduce the general government debt.

The use of fiscal policy

Automatic fiscal stabilisers

To some extent, government expenditure and taxation will have the effect of *automatically* stabilising the economy. For example, as GDP rises, the amount of tax people pay automatically rises. This rise in withdrawals from the circular flow of income will help to damp down the rise in GDP. This effect will be bigger if taxes are *progressive* (i.e. rise by a bigger percentage than GDP) as is the case with income tax in the UK. Some government expenditure will have a similar effect. For example, total government expenditure on unemployment benefits will fall if rises in GDP cause a fall in unemployment. This again will have the effect of dampening the rise in GDP.

Discretionary fiscal policy

Automatic stabilisers cannot *prevent* fluctuations, they merely reduce their magnitude. If there is a fundamental disequilibrium in the economy or substantial fluctuations in GDP, these automatic stabilisers will not be enough. The government may thus choose to *alter* the level of government expenditure or the rates of taxation.

Table 11.1	UK public sector borrowing (public sector net cash requirement, PSNCR)													
	1986	1988	1990	1992	1994	1996	1998	2000	2002	2004	2006	2007	2008	2009
PSNCR (+ = deficit) (£bn)	+2.3	−12.1	−1.7	+28.4	+39.3	+24.7	−6.3	−37.1	+19.1	+42.2	+33.4	+32.3	+38.9	+120.9
PSNCR (% of GDP)	+0.7	−2.6	−0.3	+4.6	+5.7	+3.2	−0.7	−3.8	+1.8	+3.5	+2.5	+2.3	+2.7	+8.7

This is known as **discretionary fiscal policy**. Web Case D.12 looks at an example of discretionary fiscal policy in the USA.

If government expenditure on goods and services (roads, health care, education, etc.) is raised, this will create a full multiplied rise in GDP. The reason is that all the money gets spent and thus all of it goes to boosting aggregate demand.

Cutting taxes (or increasing benefits), however, will have a smaller effect on GDP than raising government expenditure on goods and services by the same amount. The reason is that cutting taxes increases people's *disposable* incomes, of which only part will be spent. Part will be withdrawn into extra saving, imports and other taxes. In other words, not all the tax cuts will be passed on round the circular flow of income as extra expenditure. Thus if one-fifth of a cut in taxes is withdrawn and only four-fifths is spent, the tax multiplier will only be four-fifths as big as the government expenditure multiplier.

The effectiveness of fiscal policy

How successful will fiscal policy be? Will it be able to 'fine-tune' demand? Will it be able to achieve the level of GDP that the government would like it to achieve? Before changing government expenditure or taxation, the government will need to calculate the effect of any such change on GDP, employment and inflation. Predicting these effects, however, is often very unreliable.

Difficulty in predicting effects of changes in government expenditure. A rise in government expenditure of £x may lead to a rise in total injections (relative to withdrawals) that is smaller than £x. A major reason for this is a phenomenon known as **crowding out**. If the government relies on **pure fiscal policy** – that is, if it does not finance an increase in the budget deficit by increasing the money supply – it will have to borrow the money from individuals and firms. It will thus be competing with the private sector for finance and will have to offer higher interest rates. This will force the private sector also to offer higher interest rates, which may discourage firms

---

> **Pause for thought**
>
> *Why will the multiplier effect of government transfer payments, such as child benefit, pensions and social security benefits be less than the full multiplier effect from government expenditure on goods and services?*

> **Definitions**
>
> **Discretionary fiscal policy**
> Deliberate changes in tax rates or the level of government expenditure in order to influence the level of aggregate demand.
>
> **Crowding out**
> Where increased public expenditure diverts money or resources away from the private sector.
>
> **Pure fiscal policy**
> Fiscal policy which does not involve any change in money supply.

BOX 11.1	FISCAL POLICY AND BUSINESS

Indirect and direct effects

When the government adopts an expansionary fiscal policy there are indirect effects on virtually all firms from the expansion of the economy. Higher GDP means higher consumer demand. The greater the income elasticity of demand for a firm's products, the more it will benefit from increased sales as GDP expands.

Higher GDP, via the accelerator (see page 284), also means higher investment. This will benefit the construction industry as new factories and offices are built. It will also benefit businesses producing machinery and other capital equipment.

In addition to these indirect effects there are also *direct* effects on business from increased government expenditure. If new roads, hospitals or schools are built, the construction industry will directly benefit. If the government spends money on refurbishing existing

premises, then the building industry will directly benefit, as will the furnishing industry and businesses supplying computers and other equipment.

Similarly, there will be direct benefits from tax cuts. If corporation tax (the tax on business profits) is cut, after-tax profits will immediately increase. There will be a similar effect if employers' national insurance contributions are reduced. President Obama hoped to achieve the above effects with a £787 billion fiscal stimulus package in early 2009.

 Apart from the industries mentioned above, what other industries are likely to benefit directly from an expansionary fiscal policy?

from investing and individuals from buying on credit. Thus government borrowing *crowds out* private borrowing. In the extreme case, the fall in consumption and investment may completely offset the rise in government expenditure, with the result that aggregate demand does not rise at all.

Difficulty in predicting effects of changes in taxes. A cut in taxes, by increasing people's disposable income, increases not only the amount they spend, but also the amount they save. The problem is that it is not easy to predict the relative size of these two increases. In part it will depend on whether people feel that the cut in tax is only temporary, in which case they may simply save the extra disposable income, or permanent, in which case they may adjust their consumption upwards.

Difficulty in predicting the resulting multiplied effect on GDP. The sizes of the multiplier and accelerator (see page 284) are difficult to predict, mainly because the effects depend largely on people's confidence. For example, if the business community believes that a cut in taxes will be successful in pulling the economy out of recession, firms will invest. This will help to bring about the very recovery that firms predicted. There will be a big multiplier effect. If, however, businesses are pessimistic about the likely success of the policy, they are unlikely to invest. The economy may not recover. The credibility of the government and its policies may have a large influence here.

Pause for thought

Give some other examples of 'random shocks' that could undermine the government's fiscal policy.

Random shocks. Forecasts cannot take into account the unpredictable. For that you would have to consult astrologers or fortune tellers! Unfortunately, unpredictable events, such as a war, or a major industrial dispute, do occur and may seriously undermine the government's fiscal policy.

Problems of timing. Fiscal policy can involve considerable time lags. It may take time to recognise the nature of the problem before the government is willing to take action; tax or government expenditure changes take time to plan and implement – changes will have to wait until the next Budget to be announced and may come into effect some time later; the effects of such changes take time to work their way through the economy via the multiplier and accelerator.

If these time lags are long enough, fiscal policy could even be *de*stabilising. Expansionary policies taken to cure a recession may not take effect until the economy has *already* recovered and is experiencing a boom. Under these circumstances, expansionary policies are quite inappropriate; they simply worsen the problems of overheating. Similarly, deflationary (contractionary) policies taken to prevent excessive expansion may not take effect until the economy has already peaked and is plunging into recession. The deflationary policies only deepen the recession.

This problem is illustrated in Figure 11.2. Path (a) shows the course of the business cycle without government intervention. Ideally, with no time lags, the economy should be dampened in stage 2 and stimulated in stage 4. This would make the resulting course of the business cycle more like path (b), or even, if the policy were perfectly stabilising, a straight line. With the presence of time lags, however, deflationary policies taken in stage 2 may not come into effect until stage 4, and expansionary policies taken in stage 4 may not come into effect until stage 2. In this case the resulting course of the business cycle will be more like path (c). Quite obviously, in these circumstances 'stabilising' fiscal policy actually makes the economy *less* stable.

Imperfect information. Although we have some idea about where the economy is in the business cycle, we can never be certain. The government may believe that the

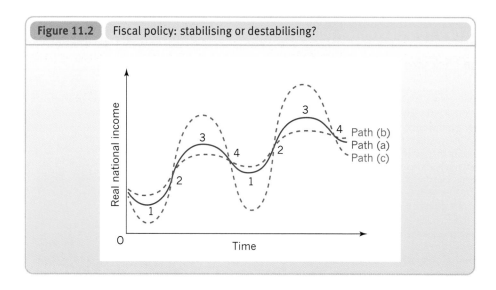

Figure 11.2	Fiscal policy: stabilising or destabilising?

economy is at the very bottom, however, the economy could actually still be moving towards the bottom or even have entered the recovery phase. Government policy may, therefore, be based on inaccurate information about the economy's current position and again, we could see fiscal policy that has a *destabilising* effect. If the fluctuations in aggregate demand can be forecast, and if the lengths of the time lags are known, then all is not lost. At least the fiscal measures can be taken early and their delayed effects can be taken into account.

Fiscal rules

Given the problems of pursuing active fiscal policy, many governments had, until the recession of 2008/9, taken a much more passive approach. Instead of changing the policy as the economy changed, a rule was set for the level of public finances. This rule was then applied year after year, with taxes and government expenditure being planned to meet that rule. For example, a target could be set for the PSNCR, with government expenditure and taxes being adjusted to keep the PSNCR at or within its target level. Box 11.2 looks at some examples of fiscal targets.

The approach to fiscal policy in the UK

From 1998 to 2008, the government set targets for government expenditure, not for just one year, but for a three-year period. Did this mean, therefore, that fiscal policy as a means of adjusting aggregate demand had been abandoned? In one sense, this was the case. The government was now committed to following its 'golden rule', whereby public sector receipts should cover all current spending (e.g. spending on wages of public sector employees, state pensions and other benefits, administration, repairs, heating and lighting) averaged over the course of the business cycle. This means that borrowing was allowed only for investment (e.g. on new roads and hospitals). See Box 11.2 for details.

But despite this apparent rejection of short-term discretionary fiscal adjustments, there was still a role for *automatic* fiscal stabilisers, with deficits rising in a recession and falling in a boom. There was also still the possibility, within the golden rule, of financing additional *investment* by borrowing, thereby providing a stimulus to a sluggish economy.

BOX 11.2   FROM GOLDEN TO TEMPORARY RULES

Putting the discretion back into fiscal policy

If the government persistently runs a budget deficit, government debt will rise. If this debt rises faster than GDP, then it will account for a growing proportion of GDP. There is then likely to be an increasing problem of 'servicing' this debt, i.e. paying the interest on it. The government could find itself having to borrow more and more to meet the interest payments, and so government debt could rise faster still. As the government borrows more and more, so it has to pay higher interest rates to attract finances. If it is successful in this, borrowing and hence investment by the private sector could be crowded out (see page 309).

Recognising these problems, many governments in the 1990s and early 2000s attempted to reduce their debts.

Preparing for the euro

In signing the Maastricht Treaty in 1992, the EU countries agreed that to be eligible to join the single currency (the euro), they should have sustainable deficits and debts. This was interpreted as follows: the general (i.e. central plus local) government deficit should be no more than 3 per cent of GDP and general government debt should be no more than 60 per cent of GDP, or should at least be falling towards that level at a satisfactory pace.

But in the mid 1990s several of the countries which were subsequently to join the euro had deficits and debts substantially above these levels. Getting them down proved a painful business. Government expenditure had to be cut and taxes increased. Fiscal policy, unfortunately, proved to be powerful! Unemployment rose and growth remained low.

The EU Stability and Growth Pact

In June 1997, at the European Council in Amsterdam, the EU countries agreed on a Stability and Growth Pact. Under the Pact, which applied to countries adopting the euro, governments should seek to balance their budgets (or even aim for a surplus) averaged over the course of the business cycle. In addition, general government deficits should not exceed 3 per cent of GDP in any one year. A country's deficit is only permitted to exceed 3 per cent if its GDP has declined by at least 2 per cent (or 0.75 per cent with special permission from the Council of Ministers). Otherwise, countries with deficits exceeding 3 per cent are required to make deposits of money with the European Central Bank. These then become fines if the excessive budget deficit is not eliminated within two years.

There are two main aims of targeting a zero budget deficit over the business cycle. The first is to allow automatic stabilisers to work without 'bumping into' the 3 per cent deficit ceiling in years when economies are slowing. The second is to allow a reduction in government debts as a proportion of GDP (assuming that GDP grows on average at around 2–3 per cent per year).

(a) General government deficits in the eurozone

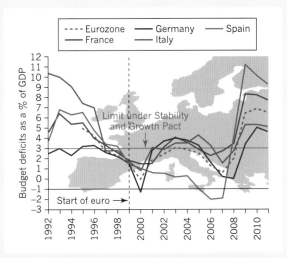

Source: based on data in *European Economy* (European Commission). Note 2010 and 2011 based on forecasts

From 2002, with slowing growth, Germany, France and Italy breached the 3 per cent ceiling. By 2007, however, after two years of relatively strong growth, deficits had been reduced well below the ceiling.

But then the credit crunch hit. As the EU economies slowed, so deficits rose. To combat the recession, in November 2008 the European Commission announced a €200 billion fiscal stimulus plan, mainly in the form of increased public expenditure. €170 billion of the money would come from member governments and €30 billion from the EU, amounting to a total of 1.2 per cent of EU GDP. The money would be for a range of projects, such as job training, help to small businesses, developing green energy technologies and energy efficiency. Most member governments quickly followed by announcing how their specific plans would accord with the overall plan.

The combination of the recession and the fiscal measures would push most eurozone countries' budget deficits well above the 3 per cent ceiling (see Figure (a)). But since the recession in EU countries was predicted to deepen markedly in 2009, with GDP forecast to decline by 4.0 per cent in the eurozone as a whole, and by 5.4 per cent in Germany, 4.4 per cent in Italy and 3.0 per cent in France, this was not seen to breach SGP rules.

As the European economy began to recover in 2010, there was tremendous pressure on member countries to begin reining in their deficits. The average eurozone deficit had risen to 6.6 per cent of GDP, and some countries' deficit was much higher. Indeed, with the Greek, Spanish and Irish deficits being 9.3, 9.8 and 11.7 per cent respectively, it would be an especially painful road back to the 3 per cent ceiling under SGP for some countries.

In Greece there were riots, with people protesting against cuts in government expenditure and tax rises.

The UK Labour government's golden rule

On being elected in 1997, the Labour government in the UK adopted a similar approach to that of the SGP. It introduced two fiscal rules.

First, under its 'golden rule', the government pledged that over the economic cycle, it would borrow only to invest (e.g. in roads, hospitals and schools) and not to fund current spending (e.g. on wages, administration and benefits). Investment was exempted from the zero borrowing rule because it contributes towards the growth of GDP.

Second, under its 'sustainable investment rule', the government also set itself the target of maintaining a stable public-sector debt/GDP ratio below 40 per cent.

As with the Stability and Growth Pact, the argument for the golden rule was that by using an averaging rule over the cycle, automatic stabilisers would be allowed to work. Deficits of receipts over current spending could occur when the economy is in recession or when growth is sluggish (as in 2001–3), helping to stimulate the economy.

In cyclically adjusting government balances we remove the estimated effects of the economic cycle. For example, during economic downturns we remove the effect of increased welfare payments and lower tax receipts. The government's current budget is the difference between its total receipts and its current expenditures (excluding capital expenditures). Figure (b) shows that the cyclically adjusted current budget balanced across the economic cycle from 1997/8 to 2006/7.

However, in the Pre-Budget Report of November 2008, the government argued that its 'immediate priority' was to support the economy by using discretionary fiscal policy. It therefore suspended its golden rule and the sustainable investment rule.

Amongst other measures the government introduced a 13-month cut in VAT from 17.5 per cent to 15 per cent. It also brought forward from 2010/11 £3 billion of capital spending on projects such as motorways, new social housing, schools and energy efficiency. In addition to the consequences for the current balance, public-sector debt was also set to breach the previous 40 per cent of GDP ceiling, reaching 57 per cent by 2013/14.

The hope, however, was that, as the economy recovered and the government was able to raise taxes again, the golden rule could be resumed once more.

The approach of the Coalition government

The fiscal priority of the incoming Coalition government in 2010 was to get the deficit down, which by 2010 had reached 11.4 per cent of GDP, one of the highest percentages in the developed world. Total public-sector debt was 64% of GDP. This, however, compared favourably

(b) UK cyclically-adjusted surplus and output gap, % of GDP

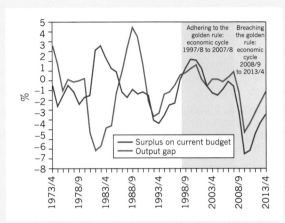

Note: 2009/10 onwards based on forecasts
Source: *2009 Budget* (HM Treasury)

with many other countries. The figures for the USA were 71 per cent, for Italy over 100 per cent and for Japan over 180 per cent.

The government was determined to reduce the structural deficit (i.e. that part that would not disappear with economic recovery) to zero in six years. This would then become the new fiscal rule – very similar to the Stability and Growth Pact.

But to get the structural deficit to zero would mean sharp government expenditure cuts and/or tax rises in the meantime, amounting to a total of £81 billion per year by 2014. Around 23 per cent of this would come from tax rises, including a rise in VAT from 17.5 to 20 per cent in January 2011. The remaining 77 per cent would come from large-scale cuts across government departments. Health and overseas aid would not be cut, but the remaining departments would be cut by between 10 and 30 per cent.

On its own, the much tighter fiscal policy would substantially dampen aggregate demand. The question was whether the recovery in exports, investment and consumer demand would be sufficient to offset it and prevent a slide back into recession. That, in turn, depended on confidence – of consumers, business and international financiers – and on the effectiveness of expansionary monetary policy (see section 11.2).

1. *What effects will government investment expenditure have on general government deficits (a) in the short run; (b) in the long run?*
2. *If there is a danger of global recession, should governments loosen the strait-jacket of fiscal policy targets?*

Things changed dramatically in 2008 and 2009. With the economy sliding into recession, the government had to abandon its golden rule. Instead of cutting government expenditure and raising taxes to compensate for reduced tax revenue, it used discretionary fiscal policy to stimulate the economy in an attempt to combat the recession. Government expenditure was increased and VAT was (temporarily) cut. As Table 11.1 shows, public sector borrowing grew rapidly.

Recap

1. The government's fiscal policy will determine the size of the budget deficit or surplus and the size of the PSNCR.

2. Automatic fiscal stabilisers are tax revenues that rise and benefits that fall as GDP rises. They have the effect of reducing the size of the multiplier and thus reducing cyclical upswings and downswings.

3. Discretionary fiscal policy is where the government deliberately changes taxes or government expenditure in order to alter the level of aggregate demand.

4. There are problems in predicting the magnitude of the effects of discretionary fiscal policy. Expansionary fiscal policy can crowd out private expenditure, but the extent of crowding out is hard to predict and depends on business confidence. Also it is difficult to predict how people's spending will respond to changes in taxes. Various random shocks can knock fiscal policy off course.

5. There are various time lags involved with fiscal policy. If these are very long, the policy could be destabilising rather than stabilising.

6. Today many governments prefer a more passive approach towards fiscal policy. Targets are set for one or more measures of the public sector finances, and then taxes and government expenditure are adjusted so as to keep to the target.

11.2 MONETARY POLICY

Each month the Bank of England's Monetary Policy Committee meets to set interest rates. The event gets considerable media coverage. Pundits, for two or three days before the meeting, try to predict what the MPC will do and economists give their 'considered' opinions about what the MPC *ought* to do. Business leaders look at the potential impact on consumer spending, business confidence and investment. The reason for this interest is that changes in interest rates, whether by the Bank of England, the European Central Bank, the Federal Reserve or any other central bank around the world are seen as having a significant effect on the economy.

But is monetary policy simply the setting of interest rates? In reality, it involves the central bank intervening in the money market to ensure that the interest rate that has been announced is also the *equilibrium* interest rate.

The policy setting

In framing its monetary policy, the government must decide on what the goals of the policy are. Is the aim simply to control inflation, or does the government wish also to affect output and employment, or does it want to control the exchange rate?

A decision also has to be made about who is to carry out the policy. There are three possible approaches here.

In the first, the government both sets the policy and decides the measures necessary to achieve it. Here the government would set the interest rate, with the central bank simply influencing money markets to achieve this rate. This first approach was used in the UK before 1997.

The second approach is for the government to set the policy *targets*, but for the central bank to be given independence in deciding interest rates. This is the approach adopted in the UK today. The government has set a target rate of inflation of 2 per cent for 24 months hence, but then the MPC is free to choose the rate of interest.

The third approach is for the central bank to be given independence not only in carrying out policy, but in setting the policy targets themselves. The ECB, within the statutory objective of maintaining price stability over the medium term, decides on (a) the target rate of inflation – currently that inflation for the eurozone should be kept close to but below 2 per cent, and (b) the target rate of growth in money supply. It then sets interest rates to meet these targets.

Implementing monetary policy

Inflation may be off target. Alternatively, the government (or central bank) may wish to alter its monetary policy (e.g. choose a new target). What can it do? There are two main approaches. The first is to alter the money supply; the second is to alter interest rates. These are illustrated in Figure 11.3, which shows the demand for and supply of money (this is similar to Figure 10.6 on page 289). With an initial supply of money of M_s the equilibrium interest rate is r_1.

Assume that the central bank wants to tighten monetary policy in order to reduce inflation. It could (a) seek to shift the supply of money curve to the left, from M_s to M_s' (resulting in the equilibrium rate of interest rising from r_1 to r_2), (b) raise the interest rate directly from r_1 to r_2, and then manipulate the money supply to reduce it to M_s'.

Techniques to control the money supply

The main way that the central bank seeks to control the money supply is through **open-market operations**. This involves the sale or purchase by the central bank of government securities (bonds or bills; see page 287) in the open market. These sales (or purchases) are *not* in response to changes in the PSNCR and are best understood, therefore, in the context of an unchanged PSNCR.

> **Pause for thought**
>
> *Explain how open-market operations could be used to increase the money supply.*

> **Definition**
>
> **Open-market operations**
> The sale (or purchase) by the authorities of government securities in the open market in order to reduce (or increase) money supply.

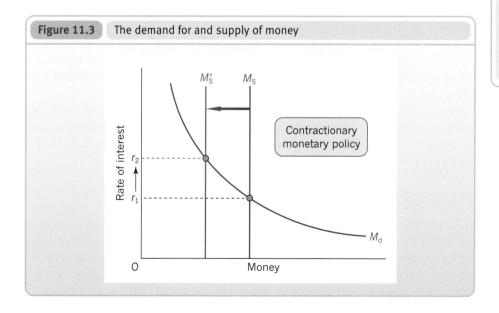

Figure 11.3   The demand for and supply of money

Definitions

Quantitative easing

A deliberate attempt by the central bank to increase the money supply by buying large quantities of securities through open-market operations.

Sale and repurchase agreement (repo)

An agreement between two financial institutions whereby one in effect borrows from another by selling some of its assets, agreeing to buy them back (repurchase them) at a fixed price and on a fixed date.

Lender of last resort

The role of the Bank of England as the guarantor of sufficient liquidity in the monetary system.

If the central bank wishes to *reduce* the money supply, it sells more securities. When people buy these securities, they pay for them with cheques drawn on banks. Thus banks' balances with the central bank are reduced. If this brings bank reserves below their prudent liquidity ratio, banks will reduce advances. There will be a multiple contraction of credit and hence of money supply.

In 2008/9, the Bank of England wanted to *increase* money supply. Here, through the process known as '**quantitative easing**' it used aggressive open-market operations to *buy* securities from the banking sector, thereby releasing new money into the banking system. The hope was that banks would use the new money as the basis for credit creation, with the extra lending stimulating consumer spending and investment and thereby helping recovery from the recession. From March 2009 to March 2010, £200 billion was injected into the UK economy to help increase the amount of credit available to businesses.

Techniques to control interest rates

The approach to monetary control today in most countries is to focus directly on interest rates. Normally an interest rate change will be announced, and then open-market operations will be conducted by the central bank to ensure that the money supply is adjusted so as to make the announced interest rate the *equilibrium* one. Let us assume that the central bank decides to raise interest rates. What does it do?

In general, it will seek to keep banks short of liquidity. This will happen automatically on any day when tax payments by banks' customers exceed the money they receive from government expenditure. This excess is effectively withdrawn from banks and ends up in the government's account at the central bank. Even when this does not occur, sales of bills by the central bank will effectively keep the banking system short of liquidity.

How do banks acquire the necessary liquidity? The Bank of England (like other central banks) is willing to lend money to the banks on a short-term basis. It does this by entering into a **sale and repurchase ('repo') agreement** with the banks. This is an agreement whereby the banks sell some of their government bonds ('gilts') to the Bank of England on a temporary basis (normally two weeks), agreeing to buy them back again at the end of the period. The Bank of England is in effect giving a short-term loan to the banks and is thus tiding them over the period of liquidity shortage. In this role, the Bank of England is acting as **lender of last resort**, and ensures that the banks never run short of money. We saw this role in action when Northern Rock was granted emergency financial support from the Bank of England on 13 September 2007. Approximately £25 billion was issued to the bank so that it could continue to operate and finally on 22 February 2008, the government took it into full public ownership.

Because banks frequently have to borrow from the Bank of England, it can use this to force through interest rate changes. The point is that the Bank of England can *choose the rate of interest to charge* (i.e. the repo rate). This will then have a knock-on effect on other interest rates throughout the banking system.

The impact of monetary policy on business

How much will a change in interest rates affect the level of business activity and/or inflation? This depends on the nature of the demand for loans. If this demand is (a) unresponsive to interest rate changes or (b) unstable because it is significantly affected by other determinants (such as anticipated income or foreign interest rates), then it will be very difficult to control by controlling the rate of interest.

Problem of an inelastic demand for loans

If the demand for loans is inelastic (i.e. a relatively steep M_d curve in Figure 11.3), any attempt to reduce demand will involve large rises in interest rates. The problem will be compounded if the demand curve shifts to the right, due, say, to a consumer spending boom. High interest rates lead to the following problems:

■ They may discourage business investment and hence long-term economic growth.
■ They add to the costs of production, to the costs of house purchase and generally to the cost of living. They are thus cost inflationary.
■ They are politically unpopular, since the general public does not like paying higher interest rates on overdrafts, credit cards and mortgages.
■ As we shall see in the next chapter, high interest rates encourage inflows of money from abroad. This drives up the exchange rate. A higher exchange rate makes domestically produced goods expensive relative to goods made abroad. This can be very damaging for export industries and industries competing with imports. Many firms in the UK suffered badly in the early and mid 2000s from a high exchange rate, caused partly by higher interest rates in the UK than in both the eurozone and, until 2006, in the USA.

Evidence suggests that the demand for loans may indeed be quite inelastic. Especially in the short run, many firms and individuals simply cannot reduce their borrowing commitments. In fact, higher interest rates may force some people and firms to borrow *more* in order to finance the higher interest rate payments.

Problem of an unstable demand

Accurate monetary control requires the central bank to be able to predict the demand curve for money (in Figure 11.3). Only then can it set the appropriate level of interest rates. Unfortunately, the demand curve may shift unpredictably, making control very difficult. The major reason is *speculation*.

For example, if people think interest rates will rise and bond prices fall, in the meantime they will demand to hold their assets in liquid form. The demand for money will rise. Similarly, if people think exchange rates will rise, they will demand sterling while it is still relatively cheap. The demand for money will rise.

It is very difficult for the central bank to predict what people's expectations will be. Speculation depends so much on world political events, rumour and 'random shocks'.

If the demand curve shifts very much, and if it is inelastic, then monetary control will be very difficult. Furthermore, the central bank will have to make frequent and sizeable adjustments to interest rates. These fluctuations can be very damaging to business confidence and may discourage long-term investment.

The net result of an inelastic and unstable demand for money is that substantial interest rate changes may be necessary to bring about the required change in aggregate demand. An example occurred in 2008, when interest rates were cut drastically, first in the USA and then in the UK, the eurozone and most other countries. But, while this helped to reduce the decline in GDP, it was not enough to prevent recession.

> **Pause for thought**
>
> *Assume that the central bank announces a rise in interest rates and backs this up with open-market operations. What determines the size of the resulting fall in aggregate demand?*

Difficulties with choice of target

Assume that the government or central bank sets an inflation target. Should it then stick to that rate, come what may? Might not an extended period of relatively low inflation warrant a lower inflation target? The government must at least have the discretion to change the rules, even if only occasionally.

Then there is the question of whether success in achieving the target will bring success in achieving other macroeconomic objectives, such as low unemployment and stable economic growth. The problem is that something called **Goodhart's Law** is likely to apply. The law, named after Charles Goodhart, formerly of the Bank of England, states that attempts to control an indicator of a problem may, as a result, make it cease to be a good indicator of the problem.

Targeting inflation may make it become a poor indicator of the state of the economy. If people believe that the central bank will be successful in achieving its inflation target, then those expectations will feed into their inflationary expectations, and not surprisingly the target will be met. But that target rate of inflation may now be consistent with both a buoyant and a depressed economy. An example occurred in 2001/2 when the UK economy slowed down considerably and yet there was virtually no change in the rate of inflation.

Another extreme case occurred in 2008, when there was a rapid slowdown in the economy and yet cost-push pressures from higher commodity prices pushed up the inflation rate. Simply targeting the current rate of inflation would have involved higher interest rates, which would have deepened the recession. Fortunately, the target is for 24 months hence, and the Bank of England's forecasts were that inflation would soon drop below 2 per cent as recession took hold. This enabled the MPC to reduce interest rates – but too slowly for some commentators.

Thus achieving the inflation target may not tackle the much more serious problem of creating stable economic growth and an environment which will therefore encourage long-term investment.

Use of a Taylor rule

For this reason, many economists have advocated the use of a **Taylor rule**,[1] rather than a simple inflation target. A Taylor rule takes two objectives into account – (1) inflation and (2) either real GDP or unemployment – and seeks to get the optimum degree of stability of the two. The degree of importance attached to each of the two objectives can be decided by the government or central bank. The central bank adjusts interest rates when either the rate of inflation diverges from its target or the rate of economic growth (or unemployment) diverges from its sustainable (or equilibrium) level.

Take the case where inflation is above its target level. The central bank following a Taylor rule will raise the rate of interest. It knows, however, that this will reduce economic growth. This, therefore, limits the amount that the central bank is prepared to raise the rate of interest. The more weight it attaches to stabilising inflation, the more it will raise the rate of interest. The more weight it attaches to maintaining stable economic growth, the less it will raise the rate of interest.

Thus the central bank has to trade off inflation stability against stable economic growth. This is especially true in the eurozone, as the ECB's primary objective is to maintain price stability.

[1] Named after John Taylor, from Stanford University, who proposed that for every 1 per cent that GDP rises above sustainable GDP, real interest rates should be raised by 0.5 percentage point and for every 1 per cent that inflation rises above its target level, real interest rates should be raised by 0.5 percentage point (i.e. nominal rates should be raised by 1.5 percentage points).

The Bank of England's approach

The Bank of England uses a rule that is apparently simpler than the Taylor rule, but in reality is more sophisticated. The Bank of England targets inflation alone; in this sense the rule is simpler. But the inflation figure on which it bases its interest rate decisions is the *forecast* rate of inflation, not the current rate; in this sense it is more sophisticated.

The Bank of England publishes a quarterly *Inflation Report*, which contains projections for inflation for the next three years. These projections assume that interest rates follow market expectations. They form the basis for the Monetary Policy Committee's monthly deliberations. If the projected inflation in 24 months' time is off target, the MPC will change interest rates accordingly.

Two key projections of the MPC are shown in the Bank of England's *Inflation Report*, which is published each quarter. These are shown in Figure 11.4. They are known as 'fan charts'. The first plots the forecast range of inflation. The second plots the forecast range of real GDP growth. In each case, the darkest central band represents a 10 per cent likelihood, as does each of the eight subsequent pairs of lighter areas out from the central band. Thus inflation or GDP growth are considered to have a 90 per cent probability of being within the fan. The bands get wider as the time horizon is extended, indicating increasing uncertainty about the outcome. Also, the less reliable are considered to be the forecasts by the MPC, the wider will be the fan. The dashed line indicates the two-year target point. Thus in quarter 3 of 2010, the 2 per cent inflation target was for quarter 3 of 2012.

Although projections are made for GDP growth, these are to help inform the forecast for inflation. GDP growth is not itself an explicit target.

> **Pause for thought**
>
> *If people believe that the central bank will be successful in keeping inflation on target, does it matter whether a simple inflation rule or a Taylor rule is used? Explain.*

Figure 11.4 Fan chart of CPI inflation and GDP growth projections (made in Q2 2009), based on market interest rate expectations

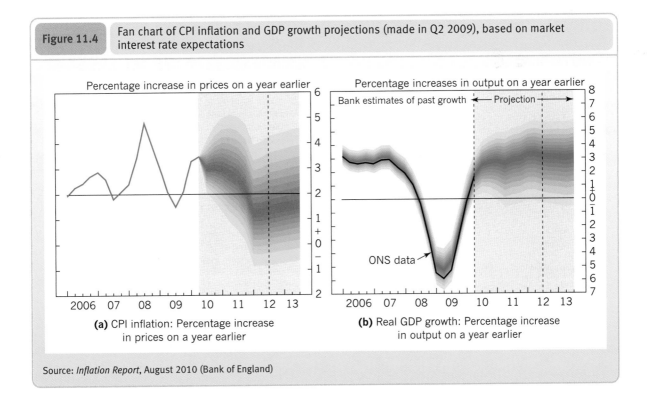

(a) CPI inflation: Percentage increase in prices on a year earlier

(b) Real GDP growth: Percentage increase in output on a year earlier

Source: *Inflation Report*, August 2010 (Bank of England)

BOX 11.3   INFLATION TARGETING

The fashion of the age

More and more countries have turned to inflation targeting as their main macroeconomic policy. The table gives the targets for a selection of countries (as of 2010).

Part of the reason is the apparent failure of discretionary macroeconomic policies. Discretionary fiscal and monetary policies suffer from time lags, from being used for short-term political purposes and from failing to straighten out the business cycle. But if discretionary policies have seemed not to work, why choose an inflation target rather than a target for the money supply?

Money supply targets were adopted by many countries in the 1980s, including the UK, and this policy too was largely a failure. Money supply targets proved very difficult to achieve. As we have seen, money supply depends on the amount of credit banks create and this is not easy for the authorities to control. Then, even if money supply is controlled, this does not necessarily mean that aggregate demand will be controlled; people may simply adjust the amount they hold in their bank accounts. Nevertheless, many countries do still target the money supply, although in most cases it is not the main target.

Inflation targets, by contrast, have proved relatively easy to achieve. There may be problems at first, if the actual rate of inflation is way above the target level. The high rates of interest necessary to bring inflation down may cause a recession. But once inflation has been brought down and the objective is then simply to maintain it at the target level, most countries have been relatively successful. And the more successful they are, the more people will expect this success to be maintained, which in turn will help to ensure this success.

So, are there any problems with inflation targeting? Ironically, one of the main problems lies in its success. With worldwide inflation having fallen, and with global trade and competition helping to keep prices down, there is now less of a link between inflation and the business cycle. Booms no longer seem to generate the inflation they once did. Gearing interest rate policy to maintaining low inflation could still see economies experiencing unsustainable booms, followed by recessions. Inflation may be controlled, but the business cycle may not be.

 Why may there be a problem in targeting both inflation and the money supply (you might want to refer to Figure 11.3)?

Inflation targets

Country	Inflation target (%)	Details
Australia	2–3	Average over the business cycle
Brazil	4.5	Tolerance band of ±2 percentage points
Canada	2	Tolerance band of ±2 percentage points
Chile	2–4	Over 12 to 24 months
Czech Republic	3	Tolerance band of ±1 percentage point
Eurozone	<2 but close to it	Average for eurozone as a whole; over medium term
Hungary	3	Tolerance band of ±1 percentage point
Iceland	2.5	Tolerance band of ±1.5 percentage points
Israel	1–3	
Mexico	3	Tolerance band of ±1 percentage point
New Zealand	1–3	On average over the medium term
Norway	2.5	Over 1–3 years
Peru	2	Tolerance band of ±1 percentage point
Poland	2.5	Tolerance band of ±1 percentage point
South Africa	3–6	
South Korea	3	Tolerance band of ±0.5 of a percentage point
Sweden	2	1–2 year horizon; tolerance band of ±1 percentage point
Switzerland	<2 but close to it	
Thailand	0–3.5	
UK	2	2 year horizon; tolerance band of ±1 percentage point

As it has turned out, inflation targeting has been successful in keeping inflation at or near its target. For the whole period from 1997 to 2007, inflation never diverged by more than 1 percentage point from the target. Since then, with the turmoil of international commodity price increases and recession, there has been a little more variation, but still small by historical standards. In early 2010, inflation in the UK reached 3.7 per cent.

Using monetary policy

It is impossible to use monetary policy as a precise means of controlling aggregate demand. It is especially weak when it is pulling against the expectations of firms and consumers and when it is implemented too late. However, if the authorities operate a tight monetary policy firmly enough and long enough, they should eventually be able to reduce lending and aggregate demand. But there will inevitably be time lags and imprecision in the process.

An expansionary monetary policy is even less reliable. If the economy is in recession, no matter how low interest rates are driven, or however much the money supply is expanded, people cannot be forced to borrow if they do not wish to. Firms will not borrow to invest if they predict a continuing recession. This was a serious problem in 2008/9. Despite substantial increases in the money supply by the central bank throughout 2009 as a means of encouraging banks to lend to each other and to customers, both firms and consumers were reluctant to borrow. There was too much uncertainty and confidence was low. As such, monetary policy struggled to stimulate aggregate demand.

A particular difficulty in using interest rate reductions to expand the economy arises if the repo rate is nearly zero but this is still not enough to stimulate the economy. The problem is that (nominal) interest rates cannot be negative, for clearly nobody would be willing to lend in these circumstances. Japan was in such a situation in the early 2000s. It was caught in what is known as the **liquidity trap**.

Despite these problems, changing interest rates can be quite effective. After all, they can be changed very rapidly. There are not the time lags of implementation that there are with fiscal policy. Indeed, since the early 1990s most governments or central banks in OECD countries have used interest rate changes as the major means of keeping aggregate demand and inflation under control. Up until 2008, this policy had been successful.

> **Definition**
>
> **Liquidity trap**
> When interest rates are at their floor and thus any further increases in money supply will not be spent but merely be held in bank accounts as people wait for the economy to recover and/or interest rates to rise.

Recap

1. The government or central bank can use monetary policy to restrict the growth in aggregate demand by reducing money supply directly or by reducing the demand for money by raising interest rates.

2. The money supply can be reduced directly by using open-market operations. This involves selling more government securities and thereby reducing banks' reserves when their customers pay for them from their bank accounts.

3. The current method of control involves the Bank of England's Monetary Policy Committee announcing the interest rate and then the Bank of England bringing this rate about by its operations in the repo market. It keeps banks short of liquidity, and then supplies them with liquidity through gilt repos at the chosen interest rate (gilt repo rate). This then has a knock-on effect on interest rates throughout the economy.

4. Higher interest rates, by reducing the demand for money, effectively also reduce the supply. However, with an inelastic demand for loans, interest rates may have to rise to very high levels in order to bring the required reduction in monetary growth.

5. Controlling aggregate demand through interest rates is made even more difficult by *fluctuations* in the demand for money. These fluctuations are made more severe by speculation against changes in interest rates, exchange rates, the rate of inflation, etc.

▶

6. Nevertheless, controlling interest rates is a way of responding rapidly to changing forecasts, and can be an important signal to markets that inflation will be kept under control, especially when, as in the UK and the eurozone, there is a firm target for the rate of inflation.

7. Achieving inflation targets is becoming increasingly easy, but in the process inflation is becoming increasingly less related to other key objectives, such as economic growth or unemployment.

8. Some economists advocate using a Taylor rule, which involves targeting a weighted average of inflation and economic growth.

9. The Bank of England bases its decisions on the forecast inflation rate in two years' time. It adjusts interest rates if this forecast rate of inflation diverges from 2 per cent.

11.3 SUPPLY-SIDE POLICY

In considering economic policy up to this point we have focused our attention upon the demand side, where slow growth and unemployment are due to a lack of aggregate demand, and inflation is due to excessive aggregate demand. Many of the causes of these problems lie on the supply side, however, and as such require an alternative policy approach.

If successful, 'supply-side policies' will shift the aggregate supply curve to the right (see Figure 11.1(b) on page 306), thus increasing output for any given level of prices (or reducing the price level for any given level of output). Supply-side policies effectively increase an economy's capacity to produce, but they may also raise the rate at which this potential output grows over time.

Supply-side policies can take various forms. They can be 'market orientated' and focus on ways of 'freeing up' the market, such as encouraging private enterprise, risk taking and competition; policies that provide incentives and reward initiative, hard work and productivity. Alternatively they can be interventionist in nature and focus on means of counteracting the deficiencies of the free market.

Either way, business leaders will be keen to have a supply-side policy that is favourable to them. This could be lower business taxes, improved education and training, a better transport and communications infrastructure or making regulation more 'light touch'. The Confederation of British Industry (and similar organisations in other countries), business pressure groups and also individual companies will seek to influence politicians in formulating supply-side policies. Frequently the argument is that 'business-friendly' policies will make the country more competitive.

Market-orientated supply-side policies

Radical market-orientated supply-side policies were first adopted in the early 1980s by the Thatcher government in the UK and the Reagan administration in the USA, but were subsequently copied by other right and centre-right governments around the world. The essence of this type of supply-side policy is to encourage and reward individual enterprise and initiative, and to reduce the role of government; to put more reliance on market forces and competition, and less on government intervention and regulation.

Reducing government expenditure

The desire of many governments to cut government expenditure is not just to reduce the size of the public sector deficit and hence reduce the growth of money supply; it is also an essential ingredient of their supply-side strategy.

In most countries the size of the public sector, relative to GDP, grew substantially in the 1950s, 1960s and 1970s. A major aim of conservative governments throughout the world has been to reverse this trend. It is a central aim of the coalition government in the UK. The public sector is portrayed as more bureaucratic and less efficient than the private sector. What is more, it is claimed that a growing proportion of public money has been spent on administration and other 'non-productive' activities, rather than on the direct provision of goods and services.

Two things are needed, it is argued: (a) a more efficient use of resources within the public sector and (b) a reduction in the size of the public sector. This would allow private investment to increase with no overall rise in aggregate demand. Thus the supply-side benefits of higher investment could be achieved without the demand-side costs of higher inflation.

In practice, governments have found it very difficult to cut their expenditure without cutting services and the provision of infrastructure.

> **Pause for thought**
>
> *Why might a recovering economy (and hence a fall in government expenditure on social security benefits) make the government feel even more concerned to make discretionary cuts in government expenditure?*

Tax cuts

Income tax cuts. Cutting the marginal rate of income tax was a major objective of the Thatcher and Major governments (1979–97). In 1979 the standard rate of income tax in the UK was 33 per cent and the top rate was 83 per cent. By 1997 the standard rate was only 23 per cent and the top rate was only 40 per cent. The Blair government continued with this policy. By 2008, the standard rate was 20 per cent (but the lower starting rate had been abolished). From 2010, an additional 50 per cent tax rate has been implemented for those earning in excess of £150 000, largely as a means of plugging the deficit in public finances.

Cuts in the marginal rate of income tax are claimed to have many beneficial effects, e.g. people work longer hours; more people wish to work; people work more enthusiastically; unemployment falls; employment rises. The evidence regarding the truth of these claims, however, is less than certain.

For example, will people be prepared to work longer hours? On the one hand, each hour worked will be more valuable in terms of take-home pay, and thus people may be encouraged to work more and have less leisure time. This is a substitution effect (see page 33); people substitute work for leisure. On the other hand, a cut in income tax will make people better off, and therefore they may feel less need to do overtime than before. This is an income effect (see page 33); they can afford to work less. The evidence on these two effects suggests that they just about cancel each other out. Anyway, for many people there is no such choice in the short run. There is no chance of doing overtime or working a shorter week. In the long run, there may be some flexibility in that people can change jobs.

> **Pause for thought**
>
> *If the basic rate of income tax is cut, which will be the larger effect – the income effect or the substitution effect – for people (a) on low incomes just above the tax threshold and (b) on very high incomes? What will be the effect on hours worked in each case (assuming that the person has a choice)?*

Tax cuts for business and other investment incentives. A number of financial incentives can be given to encourage investment. Market-orientated policies seek to reduce the general level of taxation on profits, or to give greater tax relief to investment.

A cut in corporation tax (the tax on business profits) will increase after-tax profits. This will create more money for ploughing back into investment, and the higher after-tax return on investment will encourage more investment to take place. In 1983 the main rate of corporation tax in the UK stood at 52 per cent. A series of reductions have taken place since then – by 2011/12 the rate being 27 per cent for large companies and 20 per cent for small ones.

Reducing the power of labour

The argument here is that if labour costs to employers are reduced, their profits will probably rise. This could encourage and enable more investment and hence economic growth. If the monopoly power of labour is reduced, then cost-push inflation will also be reduced.

The Thatcher government took a number of measures to curtail the power of unions. These included the right of employees not to join unions, preventing workers taking action other than against their direct employers, and enforcing secret ballots on strike proposals. It set a lead in resisting strikes in the public sector.

As labour markets have become more flexible, with increased part-time working and short-term contracts, and as the process of globalisation has exposed more companies to international competition, so this has further eroded the power of labour in many sectors of the economy (see section 8.5). In the aftermath of the recession of 2008/9, however, there has been an increase in industrial action and this may be set to continue with the extensive government spending cuts needed in the UK to bring down the budget deficit (see Box 8.2).

Policies to encourage competition

If the government can encourage more competition, this should have the effect of increasing national output and reducing inflation. Four major types of policy have been pursued under this heading.

Privatisation. If privatisation simply involves the transfer of a natural monopoly to private hands (e.g. the water companies), the scope for increased competition is limited. However, where there is genuine scope for increased competition (e.g. in the supply of gas and electricity), privatisation can lead to increased efficiency, more consumer choice and lower prices.

Alternatively, privatisation can involve the introduction of private services into the public sector (e.g. private contractors providing cleaning services in hospitals, or refuse collection for local authorities). Private contractors may compete against each other for the franchise, thus driving down costs.

Introducing market relationships into the public sector. This is where the government tries to get different departments or elements within a particular part of the public sector to 'trade' with each other, so as to encourage competition and efficiency. The most well-known examples are within education and health.

The process often involves 'devolved budgeting'. For example, in the UK, under the local management of schools scheme (LMS), schools have become self-financing. Rather than the local authority meeting the bill for teachers' salaries, the schools have to manage their own budgets. The objective is to encourage them to cut costs, thereby reducing the burden on council tax payers. However, one result is that schools have tended to appoint inexperienced (and hence cheaper) teachers rather than those who can bring the benefits of their years of teaching. Although this is a cost-saving approach, it could also be viewed as inefficient.

Another example is in the National Health Service. In 2003, the government introduced a system of 'foundation trusts'. Hospitals can apply for foundation trust status. If successful, they are given much greater financial autonomy in terms of purchasing, employment and investment decisions. Applications are judged by Monitor, the independent health regulator. By 2010, there were 129 foundation trusts. Critics argue that funds have been diverted to foundation hospitals away from the less well-performing hospitals where greater funding could help that performance.

The Private Finance Initiative (PFI). This is where a private company, after a competitive tender, is contracted by a government department or local authority to finance and build a project, such as a new road or a prison. The government then pays the company to maintain and/or run it, or simply rents the assets from the company. The public sector thus becomes a purchaser of services rather than a direct provider itself.

The aim of these 'public–private partnerships' (PPPs) is to introduce competition (through the tendering process) and private sector expertise into the provision of public services. It is hoped that the extra burden to the taxpayer of the private sector profits will be more than offset by gains in efficiency. Critics, however, claim that PPPs have resulted in poorer quality of provision and that cost control has often been poor, resulting in a higher burden for the taxpayer in the long term.

Free trade and capital movements. The opening up of international trade and investment is central to a market-orientated supply-side policy. One of the first measures of the Thatcher government (in October 1979) was to remove all controls on the purchase and sale of foreign currencies, thereby permitting the free inflow and outflow of capital, both long term and short term. Most other industrialised countries also removed or relaxed exchange controls during the 1980s and early 1990s.

The Single European Act of 1987, which came into force in 1993, was another example of international liberalisation (we examine this in section 12.4). It was designed to create a 'single market' in the EU: a market without barriers to the movement of goods, services, capital and labour. This has been largely achieved, although some restrictions on trade between members do still apply.

Interventionist supply-side policy

For decades, the UK has had a lower level of investment relative to GDP than other industrialised countries. This is illustrated in Table 11.2. Only the USA has had similarly low rates of investment, but even here investment rates have generally been slightly higher than in the UK.

Private sector research and development (R&D) is generally lower in the UK than in other major industrialised countries. This has meant that for many industries there has emerged a widening technological gap between the UK and its major competitors such as Japan and Germany. This lower level of R&D in the UK has led to a productivity gap between the UK and other G7 countries, although it is beginning to close. Indeed, taking growth in R&D investment over

Table 11.2	Gross fixed capital formation as a percentage of GDP, 1960–2010				
Year (average)	UK	Germany[a]	Japan	EU (15)	USA
1960–70	18.6	24.9	32.1	23.3	18.1
1971–80	19.8	22.5	32.9	23.1	19.4
1981–90	18.6	20.3	29.3	20.8	19.0
1991–2000	16.9	22.0	28.0	20.1	17.9
2001–10	16.4	18.3	22.8	19.8	18.2

[a] West Germany prior to 1991

Note: 2010 figures are forecasts

Source: Based on data in *European Economy Statistical Annex* (European Commission, 2010). Reproduced with permission

BOX 11.4   PRODUCTIVITY AND ECONOMIC GROWTH

The key to a better standard of living?

Measuring productivity

A country's potential output depends on the productivity of its factors of production. There are four common ways of measuring productivity. The first is output per person working. This is the most straightforward measure to calculate. All that is required is a measure of total output and employment.

The second measure is output per hour worked. This has the advantage that it is not influenced by the *number* of hours worked. So for an economy like the UK, with a very high percentage of part-time workers on the one hand, and long average hours worked by full-time employees on the other, such a measure would be more accurate in gauging worker efficiency.

The third measure is output per person in the workforce (whether employed or unemployed). This is influenced by the employment rate. The UK performs better on this measure than Germany because of much higher unemployment there.

The first three measures focus solely on the productivity of labour. In order to account directly for the productivity of capital we need to consider the growth in *total* factor productivity (TFP). This fourth measure gives output relative to the amount of factors used. Changes in total factor productivity over time provide a good indicator of technical progress.

The importance of productivity

The faster the growth in productivity, the faster is likely to be the country's rate of economic growth. Any government seeking to raise the long-term growth rate, therefore, must find ways of stimulating productivity growth.

On what does the growth of productivity depend? There are seven main determinants:

■ Private investment in new physical capital (machinery and buildings) and in research and development (R&D).
■ Public investment in education, R&D and infrastructure.
■ Training and the development of labour skills.
■ Innovation and the application of new technology.
■ The organisation and management of factors of production.
■ The rate of entry of new firms into markets: generally such firms will have higher productivity than existing firms.
■ The business environment in which firms operate. Is there competition over the quality and design of products? Is there competitive pressure to reduce costs?

? *Identify some policies a government could pursue to stimulate productivity growth through each of the above means.*

But what are the mechanisms whereby productivity growth feeds through into growth of the economy?

■ The capacity of the economy to grow will increase as productivity improvements extend potential output.
■ Productivity improvements will drive prices downwards, stimulating demand and actual growth.
■ With high returns from their investment, investors might be prepared to embark upon new projects and enterprises, stimulating yet further productivity growth and higher output.
■ As labour productivity rises, so wages are likely to rise. The higher wages will lead to higher consumption, and hence, via the multiplier and accelerator, to higher output and higher investment, thereby stimulating further advances in productivity.
■ In the longer term, businesses experiencing higher productivity growth would expect their lower costs, and hence enhanced competitiveness, to allow them to gain greater market share. This will encourage further investment and productivity growth.

It is clear that the prosperity of a nation rests upon its ability to improve its productivity. The more successful it is in doing this, the greater will be its rate of economic growth.

Productivity in the UK and other developed countries

Charts (a) and (b) show comparative productivity levels of various countries and the G7 using the second measure above (GDP per hour worked). Chart (a) shows countries' productivity relative to the UK. As you can see, GDP per hour worked is lower in the UK than the other countries with the exception of Japan. For example, in 2008, compared with the UK, output per hour was 22 per higher in the USA, 17 per cent higher in Germany and 16 per cent higher in France. A major explanation of lower productivity in the UK is the fact that for decades it has invested a smaller proportion of its national income than most other industrialised nations.

Nevertheless, until 2004 the gap had been narrowing. This was because UK productivity, although lower than in many other countries, was growing faster. This can be seen chart (b). Part of the reason for this was the inflow of investment from abroad.

Chart (c) shows productivity measured by each of the first three measures. Workers in the USA and the UK work longer hours than those in France and Germany. Thus whereas output *per hour worked* in the USA is only about 4 per cent higher than in Germany and 5 per cent higher than in France, output *per person employed* in the USA is about 30 per cent higher than in Germany and 22 per cent higher than in France.

The third measure looks at the whole workforce, both employed and unemployed, and is thus influenced by unemployment rates. The USA and the UK, both with relatively low unemployment rates, score well on this measure of productivity, especially compared with Germany.

(a) Productivity in selected economies relative to the UK (GDP per hour worked)

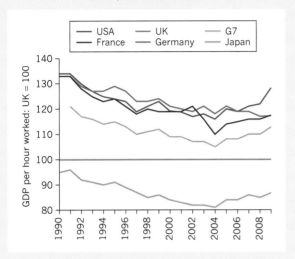

Source: based on data in *International Comparisons of Productivity* (National Statistics)

(b) Productivity in selected economies (GDP per hour worked: 1991 = 100)

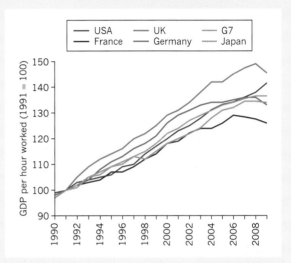

Source: based on data in *International Comparisons of Productivity* (National Statistics)

(c) Productivity in selected economies, 2008 (UK = 100)

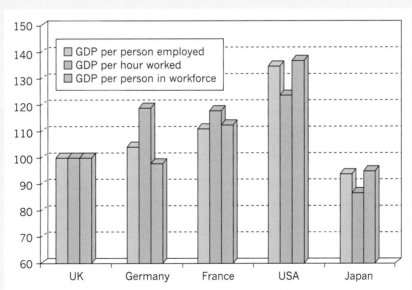

Source: based on data in *International Comparisons of Productivity* (National Statistics) and *AMECO database* (European Commission)

Despite the differences between the measures, it can be seen that UK productivity is lower than that in the USA and France on all measures and higher than that in Japan.

What could explain the differences in productivity between the five countries in chart (c), and why do the differences vary according to which of the three measures is used?

the four-year period to 2008, only Swiss companies increased R&D at a faster rate than UK companies.[2]

Pause for thought

How can the UK's low level of investment relative to GDP be explained?

Global R&D spending by the top 1000 R&D spending companies rose by 7 per cent year on year to £396 billion in 2008. Of this investment, 80 per cent occurred in five countries: the USA, Japan, Germany, France and the UK. The majority of R&D expenditure (over 35 per cent) in 2008 was from US companies, with French and the UK companies each contributing around 5 per cent.

The poor performance of UK manufacturing firms has resulted in a growing import penetration of the UK market. Imports of manufactured products have grown more rapidly than UK manufactured exports, and since 1983 the UK has been a net importer of manufactured products. We considered the changing structure of UK industry in section 1.2.

These problems have led many economists to call for a much more active supply-side policy. Areas for intervention include the following:

Research and development. There are potentially large externalities (benefits) from research and development (see page 238). Firms investing in developing and improving products, and especially firms engaged in more general scientific research, may produce results that provide benefits to many other firms. Thus the *social* rate of return on investment may be much higher than the private rate of return. Investment that is privately unprofitable for a firm may therefore still be economically desirable for the nation.

The government may sponsor research and development in certain industries (e.g. aerospace) or in specific fields (e.g. microprocessors). The amount of government support in this field has been very small in the UK, however, compared with Japan, France and the USA. What is more, the amount of support declined between the mid 1980s and the late 1990s. In 1999, however, the Labour government introduced a system of tax credits for small firms which invest in research and development. In 2002, this was extended to offer tax relief of 20 per cent of R&D expenditure by large firms.

Direct provision. Improvements in infrastructure – such as a better motorway system – can be of direct benefit to industry. Alternatively, the government could provide factories or equipment to specific firms.

Training. There are substantial external benefits from training. In other words, the benefits to the economy of trained labour extend beyond the firms undertaking the training when workers move to new jobs. The problem is that when this happens, the benefits are lost to the firm that provided the training. This, therefore, gives firms little incentive to invest heavily in training; hence the need for the government to step in.

The government may set up training schemes, or encourage educational institutions to make their courses more vocationally relevant, or introduce new vocational qualifications (such as the GNVQs, NVQs and foundation degrees in the UK). Alternatively, the government can provide grants or tax relief to firms which themselves provide training schemes. Well-targeted training can lead to substantial improvements in labour productivity. The UK invests little in training programmes, however, compared with most of its industrial competitors.

---

[2] Department for Business Innovation and Skills, The 2009 R&D scoreboard

Recap

1. Supply-side policies, if successful, will shift the aggregate supply curve to the right, and help to achieve faster economic growth without higher inflation.

2. Market-orientated supply-side policies aim to increase the rate of growth of aggregate supply and reduce the rate of unemployment by encouraging private enterprise and the freer play of market forces.

3. Reducing government expenditure as a proportion of GDP is a major element of such policies.

4. Tax cuts can be used to encourage more people to take up jobs, and people to work longer hours and more enthusiastically. The effects of tax cuts will depend on how people respond to incentives.

5. Various policies can be introduced to increase competition. These include privatisation, introducing market relationships into the public sector, and freer international trade and capital movements.

6. The UK has had a lower rate of investment than most other industrialised countries. This has contributed to a historically low rate of economic growth and imports of manufacture growing faster than exports. In response many argue for a more interventionist approach to supply-side policy.

7. Intervention can take the form of grants, supporting research and development, advice and persuasion, investing in training and the direct provision of infrastructure.

QUESTIONS

1. 'The existence of a budget deficit or a budget surplus tells us very little about the stance of fiscal policy.' Explain and discuss.

2. Adam Smith, the founder of modern economics, remarked in *The Wealth of Nations* (1776) concerning the balancing of budgets, 'What is prudence in the conduct of every private family can scarce be folly in that of a great kingdom.' What problems might there be if the government decided to follow a balanced budget approach to its spending?

3. Imagine you were called in by the government to advise on whether it should attempt to prevent cyclical fluctuations by the use of fiscal policy. What advice would you give and how would you justify the advice?

4. Why is it difficult to use fiscal policy to 'fine-tune' the economy?

5. When the Bank of England announces that it is putting down interest rates, how will it achieve this, given that interest rates are determined by demand and supply?

6. How does the Bank of England attempt to achieve the target rate of inflation of 2 per cent? What determines its likelihood of success in meeting the target?

7. To what extent did the Bank of England's Monetary Policy Committee face a dilemma in 2008, when faced with rising inflation and the onset of recession?

8. What is meant by a Taylor rule? In what way is it a better rule for central banks to follow than one of adhering to a simple inflation target?

9. Under what circumstances would adherence to an inflation target lead to (a) more stable interest rates, (b) less stable interest rates, than pursuing discretionary demand management policy?

10. Define demand-side and supply-side policies. Are there any ways in which such policies are incompatible?

11. What types of tax cuts are likely to create the greatest (a) incentives, (b) disincentives to effort?

12. Imagine that you are asked to advise the government on ways of increasing investment in the economy. What advice would you give and why?

13. In what ways can interventionist industrial policy work with the market, rather than against it? What are the arguments for and against such policy?

Business issues covered in this chapter

- What are the benefits to countries and firms of international trade?
- Which goods should a country export and which should it import?
- What determines the competitiveness of a particular country and any given industry within it?
- Why do countries sometimes try to restrict trade and protect their domestic industries?
- What is the role of the World Trade Organisation (WTO) in international trade?
- What are preferential trading arrangements and what are their effects?
- How has the 'single market' in the EU benefited its members?
- Has the business environment in the EU become more competitive?
- What benefits arise from the accession of new member states? Has the financial crisis affected the spread of these costs and benefits?

The global trading environment

The macroeconomic environment of business extends beyond the domestic economy that we examined in the previous two chapters. As we saw in Chapter 7, many firms are global in their reach. They are clearly affected not only by the economic situation at home, but also by the various countries in which they are based. For many, this means the global economy.

But even firms that are based solely in one country are still affected by the global macroeconomic situation. They are likely to source some of their supplies from abroad; similarly, they are likely to export some of their output. In other words, they are locked into the global economy through the process of international trade.

Trading affects not only individual firms – it affects whole economies. Countries can become richer as a result of an open trading environment. Indeed, if we did not trade, items such as coffee, bananas and exotic fruits may not be available to us! We examine arguments for free trade in section 12.1.

Totally free trade, however, may bring problems to countries or to groups of people within those countries. Many people argue strongly for restrictions on trade. Textile workers see their jobs threatened by cheap imported cloth. Car manufacturers worry about falling sales as customers switch to Japanese models or other East Asian ones. But are people justified in fearing international competition, or are they merely trying to protect some vested interest at the expense of everyone else? Section 12.2 examines the arguments for restricting trade.

If there are conflicting views as to whether we should have more or less trade, what has been happening on the world stage? Section 12.3 looks at the various moves towards making trade freer and at the obstacles that have been met.

A step on the road to freer trade is for countries to enter free-trade agreements with just a limited number of other countries. In Section 12.4, we look at probably the world's most famous preferential trading system, the European Union and, in particular, at the development of a 'single European market'. Finally, we consider the effects of the 2004 and 2007 enlargements of the European Union.

12.1 INTERNATIONAL TRADE

The growth of world trade

Since 1947, world trade has consistently grown faster than world GDP. This is illustrated in Figure 12.1. In 2008, world merchandise exports were worth $16 trillion, some 26.4 per cent of world GDP.

However, with the global recession, worldwide exports fell by 12.2 per cent in volume terms in 2009 and the value of world merchandise exports declined by 23 per cent to $12.4 trillion. This was the biggest contraction in global trade since World War II. According to the WTO, the world average decline in trade was 12.2 per cent. The USA,

| Figure 12.1 | Annual growth in world real GDP and world merchandise exports |

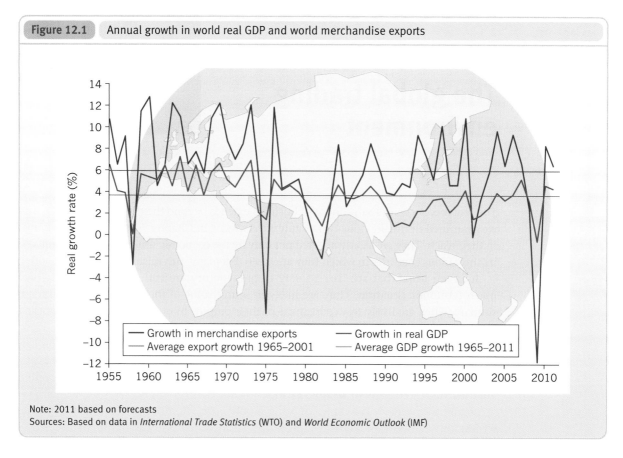

Note: 2011 based on forecasts
Sources: Based on data in *International Trade Statistics* (WTO) and *World Economic Outlook* (IMF)

the EU-27 and Japan registered greater declines than this average of 13.9, 14.8 and 24.9 per cent, respectively. Countries such as China and oil-producing countries also saw volume declines, but they were lower than the average, although declines in value tended to be larger.

Despite the dismal year that was 2009, in September 2010, WTO economists suggested that the year would be brighter, with trade forecast to expand by 13.5 per cent. Developed countries' exports were expected to increase by about 11.5 per cent in volume terms over the year, but it would still take some time to make up for the ground lost in 2009.

The major industrial economies still dominate world trade (see Figure 12.2). Some 59 per cent of all merchandise trade is conducted by the developed economies and the top ten nations account for almost 50 per cent of all world trade. The country with the highest share of world merchandise exports in 2008 was Germany (9.3 per cent), followed by China, including Hong Kong (9.1 per cent), the USA (8.2 per cent) and Japan (5.0 per cent). The UK was the tenth largest exporter (2.9 per cent). However, as of 2009, China overtook Germany as the largest merchandise exporter, with a share of almost 10 per cent of world exports. China is also the second largest importer (8 per cent), behind the USA (13 per cent).

The advantages of trade

Specialisation as the basis for trade

Why do countries trade with each other and what do they gain out of it? The reasons for international trade are really only an extension of the reasons for trade

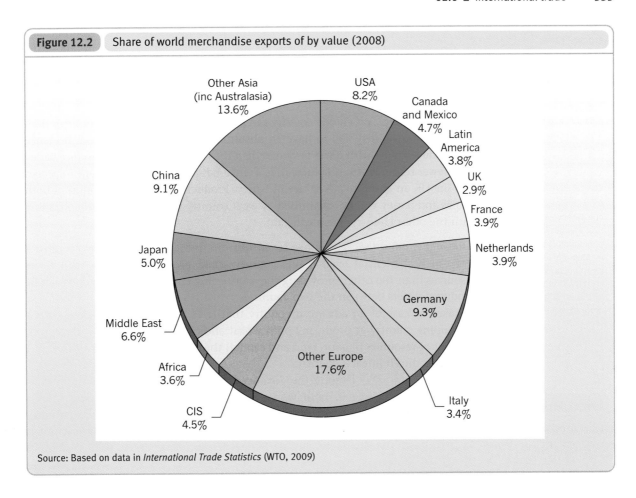

Figure 12.2 Share of world merchandise exports of by value (2008)

Other Asia (inc Australasia) 13.6%

USA 8.2%

Canada and Mexico 4.7%

Latin America 3.8%

China 9.1%

UK 2.9%

France 3.9%

Japan 5.0%

Netherlands 3.9%

Germany 9.3%

Middle East 6.6%

Other Europe 17.6%

Africa 3.6%

Italy 3.4%

CIS 4.5%

Source: Based on data in *International Trade Statistics* (WTO, 2009)

within a nation. Rather than people trying to be self-sufficient and doing everything for themselves, it makes sense to specialise.

Firms specialise in producing certain types of goods. This allows them to gain economies of scale and to exploit their entrepreneurial and management skills and the skills of their labour force.

Countries also specialise. They produce more than they need of certain goods (whether finished goods, raw materials or intermediate goods). What is not consumed domestically is exported. The revenues earned from the exports are used to import goods which are not produced in sufficient amounts at home. The same applies to various services, such as banking and tourism.

But which goods and services should a country specialise in? What should it export and what should it import? The answer is that it should specialise in those goods and services in which it has a *comparative advantage*. Let us examine what this means.

The law of comparative advantage

Countries have different resources. They differ in population density, labour skills, climate, raw materials, capital equipment, etc. Thus the ability to supply goods differs between countries, especially as many of these differences are relatively or even completely immobile, such as a country's climate or geography.

What this means is that the relative costs of producing goods will vary from country to country. For example, one country may be able to produce 1 fridge for

Definitions

Absolute advantage
A country has an absolute advantage over another in the production of a good if it can produce it with fewer resources than the other country.

Comparative advantage
A country has a comparative advantage over another in the production of a good if it can produce it at a lower opportunity cost, i.e. if it has to forego less of other goods in order to produce it.

the same cost as 6 tonnes of wheat or 3 MP3 players, whereas another country may be able to produce 1 fridge for the same cost as only 3 tonnes of wheat but 4 MP3 players. It is these differences in relative costs that form the basis of trade.

At this stage we need to distinguish between *absolute advantage* and *comparative advantage*.

Absolute advantage. When one country can produce a good with fewer resources than another country, it is said to have an **absolute advantage** in that good. If France can produce grapes with fewer resources than the UK, and the UK can produce barley with fewer resources than France, then France has an absolute advantage in grapes and the UK an absolute advantage in barley. Production and consumption of both grapes and barley will be maximised by each country specialising and then trading with the other country. Both will gain.

Comparative advantage. The above seems obvious, but trade between two countries can still be beneficial even if one country could produce *all* goods with fewer resources than the other, providing the *relative* efficiency with which goods can be produced differs between the two countries.

Take the case of an advanced country that is absolutely more efficient than a developing country at producing both wheat and cloth. Assume that with a given amount of resources (labour, land and capital) the alternatives shown in Table 12.1 can be produced in each country.

Pause for thought

Draw up a similar table to Table 12.1, only this time assume that the figures are: developing country 6 wheat or 2 cloth; advanced country: 8 wheat or 20 cloth. What are the opportunity cost ratios now? Which country should produce which good?

Despite the advanced country having an absolute advantage in both wheat and cloth, the developing country has a *comparative* advantage in wheat, and the advanced country has a *comparative* advantage in cloth. This is because wheat is relatively cheaper in the developing country: only 1 metre of cloth has to be sacrificed to produce 2 kilos of wheat, whereas 8 metres of cloth would have to be sacrificed in the advanced country to produce 4 kilos of wheat. In other words, the opportunity cost of wheat is 4 times higher in the advanced country (8/4 compared with 1/2).

On the other hand, cloth is relatively cheaper in the advanced country. Here the opportunity cost of producing 8 metres of cloth is only 4 kilos of wheat, whereas in the developing country 1 metre of cloth costs 2 kilos of wheat. Thus the opportunity cost of cloth is 4 times higher in the developing country (2/1 compared with 4/8).

To summarise, countries have a comparative advantage in those goods that can be produced at a lower opportunity cost than in other countries.

If countries are to gain from trade, they should export those goods in which they have a comparative advantage and import those goods in which they have a comparative disadvantage. Given this, we can state a **law of comparative advantage**.

Definition

Law of comparative advantage
Trade can benefit all countries if they specialise in the goods in which they have a comparative advantage.

Table 12.1	Production possibilities for two countries			
		Kilos of wheat		Metres of cloth
Developing country	Either	2	or	1
Advanced country	Either	4	or	8

KEY IDEA 28

The law of comparative advantage. Provided opportunity costs of various goods differ in two countries, both of them can gain from mutual trade if they specialise in producing (and exporting) those goods that have relatively low opportunity costs compared with the other country.

But why do they gain if they specialise according to this law? And just what will that gain be? We consider these questions next.

The gains from trade based on comparative advantage

Before trade, unless markets are very imperfect, the prices of the two goods are likely to reflect their opportunity costs. For example, in Table 12.1, since the developing country can produce 2 kilos of wheat for 1 metre of cloth, the *price* of 2 kilos of wheat will roughly equal 1 metre of cloth.

Assume, then, that the pre-trade exchange ratios of wheat for cloth are as follows:

Developing country : 2 wheat for 1 cloth
Advanced country   : 1 wheat for 2 cloth (i.e. 4 for 8)

Both countries will now gain from trade, provided the exchange ratio is somewhere between 2:1 and 1:2. Assume, for the sake of argument, that it is 1:1. In other words, 1 wheat trades internationally for 1 cloth. How will each country gain?

The developing country gains by exporting wheat and importing cloth. At an exchange ratio of 1:1, it now only has to give up 1 kilo of wheat to obtain a metre of cloth, whereas before trade it had to give up 2 kilos of wheat.

The advanced country gains by exporting cloth and importing wheat. Again at an exchange ratio of 1:1, it now only has to give up 1 metre of cloth to obtain a kilo of wheat, whereas before it had to give up 2 metres of cloth.

Thus both countries have gained from trade.

The actual exchange ratios will depend on the relative prices of wheat and cloth after trade takes place. These prices will depend on total demand for and supply of the two goods. It may be that the trade exchange ratio is nearer to the pre-trade exchange ratio of one country than the other. Thus the gains to the two countries need not be equal.

> **Pause for thought**
>
> *Show how each country could gain from trade if the developing country could produce (before trade) 3 wheat for 1 cloth and the advanced country could produce (before trade) 2 wheat for 5 cloth, and if the exchange ratio (with trade) was 1 wheat for 2 cloth. Would they both still gain if the exchange ratio was (a) 1 wheat for 1 cloth; (b) 1 wheat for 3 cloth?*

Increased competition from trade

The other major advantage from trade is the extra competition it brings. Competition from imports may stimulate greater efficiency at home, which could decrease a firm's costs. It could also prevent domestic monopolies/oligopolies from charging high prices. It may stimulate greater research and development and the more rapid adoption of new technology, which might enable faster growth, through expansion of the supply side of the economy (see section 11.3). It may lead to a greater variety of products being made available to consumers. Finally, the extra price competition will help to keep inflation low.

The competitive advantage of nations

The theory of comparative advantage shows how countries can gain from trade, but why do countries have a comparative advantage in some goods rather than others?

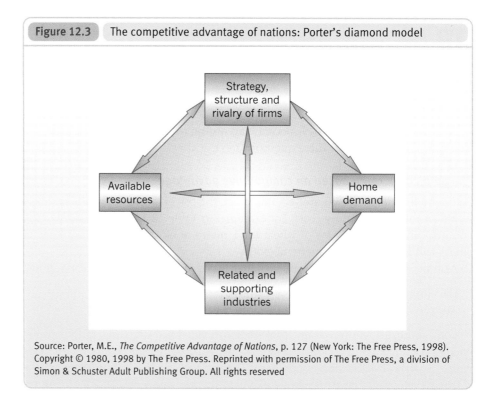

| Figure 12.3 | The competitive advantage of nations: Porter's diamond model |

One explanation is that it depends on the resources that countries have. If a country has plenty of land, then it makes sense to specialise in products that make use of this abundant resource. Thus Canada produces and exports wheat. If a country has a highly skilled workforce and an established research base, then it makes sense to specialise in high-tech products and export these. Thus Germany exports many highly sophisticated manufactured products. Many developing countries, by contrast, with plentiful but relatively low-skilled workers specialise in primary products or simple manufactured products.

In other words, countries should specialise in goods which make intensive use of their abundant resources. But this still does not give enough detail as to why countries specialise in the precise range of products that they do. Also, why do countries both export and import the *same* products. Why do many countries produce and export cars, but also import many cars too?

According to Porter,[1] there are four key determinants of why nations are highly competitive in certain products but less so in others. These are illustrated in a diagram which has become known as the 'Porter diamond' (see Figure 12.3).

Available resources. These include 'given' resources, such as raw materials, population and climate, but also specialised resources that have been developed by humans, such as the skills of the labour force, the amount and type of capital, the transport and communications infrastructure, and the science and technology base. These specialised resources vary in detail from one country to another and give them a competitive advantage in very specific products. Once an industry has started to develop, this may attract further research and development, capital investment

---

[1] Michael E. Porter, *The Competitive Advantage of Nations* (New York: The Free Press, 1998)

and training, all of which are very specific to that industry. This then further builds the country's competitive advantage in that industry. Thus the highly developed engineering skills and equipment in Germany gives it a competitive advantage in producing well-engineered cars.

Demand conditions in the home market. The more discerning customers are within the country, the more this will drive the development of each firm's products and the more competitive the firm will then become in international markets. The demand for IT solutions within the USA drove the development of the software industry and gave companies such as Microsoft, Intel and Google an international advantage.

Strategy, structure and rivalry of firms. Competition between firms is not just in terms of price. Competitive rivalry extends to all aspects of business strategy, from product design, to marketing, to internal organisation, to production efficiency, to logistics, to after-sales support. The very particular competitive conditions within each industry can have a profound effect on the development of firms within that industry and determine whether of not they gain an international competitive advantage. Strategic investments and rivalry gave Japanese electronic companies an international competitive advantage.

Related and supporting industries. Firms are more likely to be successful internationally if there are well-developed supporting industries within the home economy. These may be industries providing specialist equipment or specialist consultancy, or they may simply be other parts of the main value chain, from suppliers of inputs to distributors of the firms' output. The more efficient this value chain, the greater the competitive advantage of firms within the industry.

 KEY IDEA 29

The competitive advantage of nations. The ability of countries to compete in the market for exports and with potential importers to their country. The competitiveness of any one industry depends on the availability and quality of resources, demand conditions at home in that industry, the strategies and rivalry of firms within the industry and the quality of supporting industries and infrastructure. It also depends on government policies, and there is also an element of chance.

As the arrows in Figure 12.3 show, the four determinants of competitive advantage are interlinked and influence each other. For example, the nature of related and supporting industries can influence a firm's strategic decision about whether to embark on a process of vertical integration or de-integration. Similarly, the nature of related and supporting industries depends on demand conditions in these industries and the availability of resources.

With each of the four determinants in Figure 12.3, competitive advantage can be stimulated by appropriate government supply-side policies, such as a supportive tax regime, investment in transport and communications infrastructure, investment in education and training, competition policy and sound macroeconomic management of the economy. Also chance often has a large part to play. Which pharmaceutical company in which part of the world discovers a cure for AIDS or for various types of cancer will then have a significant competitive advantage.

Pause for thought

Give two other examples of ways in which the determinants of competitive advantage are interlinked.

The terms of trade

What price will our exports fetch abroad? What will we have to pay for imports? The answer to these questions is given by the **terms of trade**. The terms of trade are defined as:

$$\frac{\text{The average price of exports}}{\text{The average price of imports}}$$

expressed as an index, where prices are measured against a base year in which the terms of trade are assumed to be 100. Thus if the average price of exports relative to the average price of imports has risen by 20 per cent since the base year, the terms of trade will now be 120. If the terms of trade rise (export prices rising relative to import prices), they are said to have 'improved', since fewer exports now have to be sold to purchase any given quantity of imports. Changes in the terms of trade are caused by changes in the demand and supply of imports and exports and by changes in the exchange rate.

Recap

1. World trade has grown, for many years, significantly faster than the growth in world output. However, in the recession of 2008/9 both output and world trade declined rapidly. World trade remains highly concentrated in the developed world and in particular between the top few trading nations, but certain developing nations, such as China and India, have seen a rapid growth in trade.

2. Countries can gain from trade if they specialise in producing those goods in which they have a comparative advantage, i.e. those goods that can be produced at relatively low opportunity costs.

3. If two countries trade, then, provided that the trade price ratio of exports and imports is between the pre-trade price ratios of these goods in the two countries, both countries can gain.

4. Gains from trade also arise from increased competition.

5. The terms of trade give the price of exports relative to the price of imports expressed as an index, where the base year is 100.

12.2 TRADE RESTRICTIONS

We have seen how trade can bring benefits to all countries. But when we look around the world we often see countries erecting barriers to trade. Their politicians know that trade involves costs as well as benefits.

In this section, we examine the arguments for restricting trade. Are people justified in fearing international competition, or are they merely trying to protect some vested interest at the expense of everyone else?

Types of restriction

If a country chooses to restrict trade, there are a number of protectionist measures open to it. Governments may:

- impose customs duties (or **tariffs**) on imports;
- restrict the amount of certain goods that can be imported ('quotas');

- subsidise domestic products to give them a price advantage over imports;
- impose administrative regulations designed to exclude imports, such as customs delays or excessive paperwork;
- favour domestic producers when purchasing equipment (e.g. defence equipment).

Governments may also favour domestic producers by subsidising their exports in a process known as **dumping**. The goods are 'dumped' at artificially low prices in the foreign market.

In looking at the costs and benefits of trade, the choice is not the stark one of whether to have free trade or no trade at all. Although countries may sometimes contemplate having completely free trade, typically they limit their trade. However, they certainly do not ban it altogether.

Arguments for restricting trade

The following are the main arguments that have been used to restrict trade.

The infant industry argument. Some industries in a country may be in their infancy but have a potential comparative advantage. This is particularly likely in developing countries. Such industries are too small yet to have gained economies of scale; their workers are inexperienced; there is a lack of back-up facilities – communications networks, specialist research and development, specialist suppliers, etc. – and they may have only limited access to finance for expansion. Without protection, these **infant industries** will not survive competition from abroad.

Protection from foreign competition, however, will allow them to expand and become more efficient. Once they have achieved a comparative advantage, the protection can then be removed to enable them to compete internationally.

To prevent 'dumping' and other unfair trade practices. A country may engage in dumping by subsidising its exports. The result is that prices may no longer reflect comparative costs. Thus the world would benefit from tariffs being imposed by importers to counteract the subsidy.

It can also be argued that there is a case for retaliating against countries which impose restrictions on your exports. In the short run, both countries are likely to be made worse off by a contraction in trade. But if the retaliation persuades the other country to remove its restrictions, it may have a longer-term benefit. In some cases, the mere threat of retaliation may be enough to get another country to remove its protection.

To prevent the establishment of a foreign-based monopoly. Competition from abroad could drive domestic producers out of business. The foreign company, now having a monopoly of the market, could charge high prices with a resulting misallocation of resources. The problem could be tackled either by restricting imports or by subsidising the domestic producer(s).

All the above arguments suggest that governments should adopt a 'strategic' approach to trade. **Strategic trade theory** argues that protecting certain industries allows a net gain in the *long* run from increased competition in the market (see Box 12.1).

To spread the risks of fluctuating markets. A highly specialised economy – Zambia with copper, Cuba with sugar – will be highly susceptible to world market fluctuations.

BOX 12.1 STRATEGIC TRADE THEORY

The case of Airbus

Supporters of *strategic trade theory* hold that comparative advantage need not be the result of luck or circumstance, but may in fact be created by government. By diverting resources into selective industries, usually high tech and high skilled, a comparative advantage can be created through intervention.

An example of such intervention was the European aircraft industry, and in particular the creation of the European Airbus Consortium.

The Consortium was established in the late 1960s, its four members being Aérospatiale (France), British Aerospace (now BAE Systems) (UK), CASA (Spain) and DASA (Germany). The setting up of this consortium was seen as essential for the future of the European aircraft industry for three reasons:

■ To share high R&D costs.
■ To generate economies of scale.

■ To compete successfully with the market's major players in the USA – Boeing and McDonnell Douglas (which have since merged).

Airbus, although privately owned, was sponsored by government and received state aid, especially in its early years when the company failed to make a profit. Then, in 2000, the French, Geman and Spanish partners of the consortium merged to form the European Aeronautic Defence and Space Company (EADS), which had an 80 per cent share of Airbus (BAE Systems having the remaining 20 per cent share). Shortly afterwards, it was announced that enough orders had been secured for the planned new 550-seater A380 for production to go ahead. This new jumbo, which began its flights in April 2005, is a serious competitor to the long-established Boeing 747. In 2006, BAE Systems sold its 20 per cent stake in Airbus to EADS to concentrate on its core transatlantic defence and aerospace business.

Yearly deliveries of aircraft: Boeing and Airbus

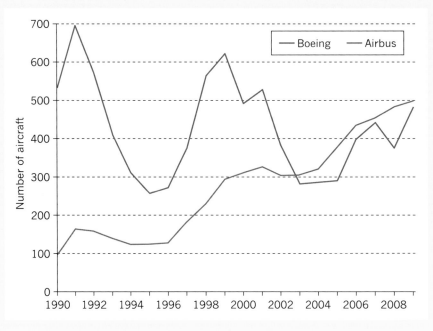

Greater diversity and greater self-sufficiency, although maybe leading to less efficiency, can reduce these risks.

To reduce the influence of trade on consumer tastes. The assumption of fixed consumer tastes dictating the pattern of production through trade is false. Multinational companies through their advertising and other forms of sales promotion may influence consumer tastes. Many developing countries object to the insidious influence of western consumerist values expounded by companies such as Coca-Cola and McDonald's.

In 2003 Airbus, for the first time, sold more passenger aircraft than Boeing. Indeed, in terms of deliveries, it has remained ahead of Boeing every year since (see chart). In light of Airbus's growing success, the Americans, and Boeing in particular, responded with accusations that Airbus is founded upon unfair trading practices and thus should not receive the level of government support that it does. (See Box 12.2 for more details.)

So does the experience of Airbus support the arguments of the strategic trade theorists? Essentially two key benefits are claimed to flow from Airbus and its presence in the aircraft market: lower prices and economic spillovers.

- Without Airbus the civil aircraft market would have been dominated by two American firms, Boeing and McDonnell Douglas (or possibly one, if the 1997 merger of Boeing and McDonnell Douglas had still gone ahead). Therefore the presence of Airbus would be expected to promote competition and thereby keep prices down. Studies in the 1980s and 1990s tended to support this view, suggesting that consumers have made significant gains from lower prices. One survey estimated that without Airbus commercial aircraft prices would have been 3.5 per cent higher than they currently are, and without both Airbus *and* McDonnell Douglas they would have been 15 per cent higher.
- Economic spillovers from the Airbus Consortium, such as skills and technology developments, might be expected to benefit other industries. Findings are inconclusive on this point. It is clear, however, that although aggregate R&D in the whole aircraft industry has risen, so has the level of R&D duplication.

Despite Airbus's successes, by 2006 troubles were beginning to emerge. Although it continued to deliver more planes than Boeing, for the first time since 2000 it fell behind in terms of orders – 824, compared with 1044 for Boeing. Also considerable delays (up to two years) and cost overruns were being experienced with the A380. With falling profitability and falling orders, in February 2007 Airbus announced plans to cut 10 000 jobs from its 57 000 workforce.

The development of the A380 has put significant financial strains on Airbus and this is expected to continue for some five years. Its launch was two and half years late and 50 per cent over budget. However, hopes of breaking even sooner are on the horizon if the dollar continues to strengthen, according to the Finance Chief of its parent EADS. The development of the A380 led to Boeing beginning assembly on its first 747-8 airliner, which will be the only competitor to Airbus's 'superjumbo'.

Despite this potential competition, the sales director of Airbus, John Leahy, said in 2010 that they had increased that year's forecast sales of 10 A380s (worth $340 million each in 2010) to 20, in response to a rebound in passenger traffic, as the global economy began to recover.

However, concerns do still remain over the financial strains of the A380, including customisation costs and rising costs generally. 'The A380 continues to weigh significantly on the underlying performance', said EADS.[1] Airbus is seeking to avoid such problems with the new A350, with first deliveries expected in 2013, and already has 530 orders from 33 customers.

Although Airbus has experienced some trying times, on balance it appears that Airbus has had many positive effects and that the strategic trade theory, which was used to justify state aid, has been largely vindicated. Boeing has a genuine competitor in Airbus and passengers worldwide have benefited from this competition.

1. *In what other industries could the setting up of a consortium, backed by government aid, be justified as a means of exploiting a potential comparative advantage?*
2. *Is it only in industries that could be characterised as world oligopolies that strategic trade theory is relevant?*

---

[1] Polek, Gregory 'Lufthansa receives its first A380, but the airliner's delivery rate remains behind earlier projections', AINonline, 28 May 2010, www.ainonline.com/news/single-news-page/article/lufthansa-receives-its-first-airbus-a380-but-the-airliners-delivery-rate-remains-behind-earlier/

To take account of externalities. Free trade will tend to reflect private costs. Both imports and exports, however, can involve externalities. The mining of many minerals for export may adversely affect the health of miners; the production of chemicals for export may involve pollution; the importation of juggernaut lorries may lead to structural damage to houses; shipping involves large amounts of CO_2 emissions (some 4–5 per cent of total world emissions).

The arguments considered so far are of general validity; restricting trade for such reasons could be of net benefit to the world. There are two other arguments, however, that are used by individual governments for restricting trade, where their country will gain, but at the *expense* of other countries, such that there will be a net loss to the world.

The first argument concerns taking advantage of market power in world trade. If a country, or a group of countries, has monopsony power in the purchase of imports (i.e. they are individually or collectively a very large economy, such as the USA or the EU), then they could gain by restricting imports so as to drive down their price. Similarly, if countries have monopoly power in the sale of some export (e.g. OPEC countries with oil), then they could gain by forcing up the price.

The second argument concerns giving protection to declining industries. The human costs of sudden industrial closures can be very high. In such circumstances, temporary protection may be justified to allow the industry to decline more slowly, thus avoiding excessive structural unemployment. Such policies will be at the expense of the consumer, however, who will be denied access to cheaper foreign imports.

Problems with protection

Protection, by reducing the competitiveness or the number of imported goods, will tend to push up prices and restrict the choice of goods available. But apart from these direct costs to the consumer, there are several other problems. Some are a direct effect of the protection; others follow from the reactions of other nations:

Protection as 'second-best'. Many of the arguments for protection amount merely to arguments for some type of government intervention in the economy. Protection, however, may not be the best way of dealing with the problem, since protection may have undesirable side effects. There may be a more direct form of intervention that has no side effects. In such a case, protection will be no more than a *second-best* solution.

For example, using tariffs to protect old inefficient industries from foreign competition may help prevent unemployment in those parts of the economy, but the consumer will suffer from higher prices. A better solution would be to subsidise retraining and investment in those areas of the country in *new efficient* industries – industries with a comparative advantage. In this way, unemployment is avoided, but the consumer does not suffer.

Retaliation. If the USA imposes restrictions on, say, imports from the EU, then the EU may impose restrictions on imports from the USA. Any gain to US firms competing with EU imports is offset by a loss to US exporters. What is more, US consumers suffer, since the benefits from comparative advantage have been lost.

The increased use of tariffs and other restrictions can lead to a trade war, with each country cutting back on imports from other countries. In the end, everyone loses.

Protection may allow firms to remain inefficient. By removing or reducing foreign competition, firms' incentive to reduce costs may be reduced. Thus if protection is being given to an infant industry, the government must ensure that the lack of competition does not prevent it 'growing up'. Protection should not be excessive and should be removed as soon as possible.

Bureaucracy. If a government is to avoid giving excessive protection to firms, it should examine each case carefully. This can lead to large administrative costs. It could also lead to corrupt officials accepting bribes from importers to give them favourable treatment.

Recap

1. Reasons for restricting trade that have some validity in a world context include: the infant industry argument; the problem of dumping and other unfair trade practices; the danger of the establishment of a foreign-based monopoly; the need to spread the risks of fluctuating export prices; and the problems that free trade may adversely affect consumer tastes and may not take account of externalities.

2. Often, however, the arguments for restricting trade are in the context of one country benefiting even though other countries may lose more. Countries may intervene in trade in order to exploit their monopoly/monopsony power or to protect declining industries.

3. Even if government intervention to protect certain parts of the economy is desirable, restricting trade is unlikely to be a first-best solution to the problem, since it involves side-effect costs.

THE WORLD TRADING SYSTEM AND THE WTO   12.3

In 1947, 23 countries got together and signed the General Agreement on Tariffs and Trade (GATT). By 2010, there were 153 members of its successor organisation, the World Trade Organisation (WTO), which was formed in 1995. Between them, the members of the WTO account for almost 97 per cent of world trade. The aims of GATT, and now the WTO, have been to liberalise trade.

WTO rules

The WTO requires its members to operate according to various rules. These include the following:

- *Non-discrimination*. Under the 'most favoured nations clause', any trade concession that a country makes to one member must be granted to *all* signatories.
- *Reciprocity*. Any nation benefiting from a tariff reduction made by another country must reciprocate by making similar tariff reductions itself.
- *The general prohibition of quotas*.
- *Fair competition*. If unfair barriers are erected against a particular country, the WTO can sanction retaliatory action by that country. The country is not allowed, however, to take such action without permission.
- *Binding tariffs*. Countries cannot raise existing tariffs without negotiating with their trading partners.

Unlike the GATT, the WTO has the power to impose sanctions on countries breaking trade agreements. If there are disputes between member nations, these will be settled by the WTO, and if an offending country continues to impose trade restrictions, permission will be granted for other countries to retaliate.

For example, in March 2002, the Bush administration imposed tariffs on steel imports into the USA in order to protect the ailing US steel industry (see Web Case D.28). The EU and other countries referred the case to the WTO, which in December 2003 ruled that they were illegal. This ruling made it legitimate for the EU and other countries to impose retaliatory tariffs on US products. President Bush consequently announced that the steel tariffs would be abolished.

> **Pause for thought**
>
> *Could US action to protect its steel industry from foreign competition be justified in terms of the interests of the USA as a whole (as opposed to the steel industry in particular)?*

The greater power of the WTO has persuaded many countries to bring their disputes to it. In the first 14 years of its existence it had dealt with over 400 disputes (compared with 300 by GATT over the whole of its 48 years).

Trade rounds

Periodically, member countries have met to negotiate reductions in tariffs and other trade restrictions. There have been eight 'rounds' of such negotiations since the signing of GATT in 1947. The last major round to be completed was the Uruguay round, which began in Uruguay in 1986, continued at meetings around the world and culminated in a deal being signed in April 1994. By that time, the average tariff on manufactured products was 4 per cent and falling. In 1947 the figure was nearly 40 per cent. The Uruguay Round agreement also involved a programme of phasing in substantial reductions in tariffs and other restrictions up to the year 2002 (see Web Case D.22).

BOX 12.2 | **BEYOND BANANAS**

EU/US trade disputes

Trade relations between the EU and US seem to be at an all-time low. The World Trade Organisation, set up to manage trade and prevent such disputes arising, appears helpless in resolving the issues and restoring order.

The current round of bad blood between the EU and US started over bananas.

Bananas

The EU/US 'banana war', which has now come to a conclusion, began in 1993 when the EU adopted a tariff and quota system that favoured banana producers in African, Caribbean and Pacific (ACP) countries, mostly ex-European colonies. Predictably, Latin American banana producers, owned by large American multinationals like Chiquita and Dole, took exception to this move. Latin American producers, with huge economies of scale, were able to produce bananas at considerably lower cost than producers in the ACP countries. But, faced with significant tariffs on entry into the EU market, their bananas became more expensive. Championed by the USA, the Latin American producers won the case at the WTO for removing the agreement.

The EU, however, failed to comply, arguing that the preferential access to EU markets for ACP producers was part of a general development strategy, known as the 'Lomé Convention', to support developing economies. Without preferential access, it was argued, ACP banana producers simply could not compete on world markets. As a European Commission document highlighted, 'The destruction of the Caribbean banana industry would provoke severe economic hardship and political instability in a region already struggling against deprivation.'[1]

As the EU refused to comply with the WTO ruling, the USA imposed $191 million worth of tariffs on EU exports in March 1999. After a series of battles over the issue at the WTO, the EU finally agreed in 2009 to reform its banana protocol and to cut tariffs on non-ACP bananas from $234 per tonne to $196 per tonne straight away and to $150 by 2016. In return, it would pay compensation to ACP nations. This deal, however, is dependent on agreement of the Doha round of trade negotiations.

Hormone-treated beef

If the banana dispute could be resolved, many equally contentious issues could be found to take its place. The dispute between the EU and USA over hormone-treated beef has been going on for a staggering 20 years. In 1998, the WTO panel ruled against a ban by the EU on imports of hormone-treated beef from the USA and Canada. The ruling permitted the two countries to impose retaliatory sanctions on EU imports. After a process of arbitration, the values were set at $116.8 million for the USA and CDN$11.1 million for Canada.

Despite this, the EU continued to refuse to import any animal products, live or processed, that had received growth hormones. The ban was made on grounds of public health, and this remains the crux of the dispute.

Following an independent assessment of the risks to consumers of hormone-treated meat, which resulted in the EU banning certain hormones by its farmers, the EU argued that the sanctions should be lifted as it was no longer in breach of the WTO rules. In February 2005, a WTO panel was set up to consider the case.

In March 2008, the panel ruled the unilateral sanctions by the USA and Canada to be illegal, though it also stated that the EU hormones directive was not compatible with

---

[1] 'EC fact sheet on Caribbean bananas and the WTO', Brussels, 18 March 1997

Despite the reduction in tariffs, many countries have still tried to restrict trade by various other means, such as quotas and administrative barriers. Also, barriers have been particularly high on certain non-manufactures. Agricultural protection in particular has come in for sustained criticism by developing countries. High fixed prices and subsidies given to farmers in the EU, the USA and other advanced countries mean that the industrialised world continues to export food to many developing countries which have a comparative advantage in food production! Farmers in developing countries often find it impossible to compete with subsidised food imports from the rich countries.

The most recent round of trade negotiations began in Doha, Qatar, in 2001. The negotiations have focused on both trade liberalisation and measures to encourage development of poorer countries. In particular, the Doha Development Agenda, as it is called, is concerned with measures to make trade fairer so that its benefits are spread more evenly around the world. This would involve improved access for

the WTO agreements on standards to protect the health of humans, plants and animals. Both sides appealed but the USA put in place a modified set of duties in January 2009. However, in April 2009 the USA and EU resolved to work through the dispute and the USA postponed its sanctions.

Genetically modified (GM) foods

A more recent trade dispute, again in the field of public health, concerns the development of GM food. GM strains of maize and soya have been available in the USA for many years, but the EU bans imports of such products, whether as seed or food. The US position is that EU consumers should be free to choose whether they have GM food or not. This, not surprisingly, is rejected by the EU on the basis that GM foods might contaminate the entire food supply once introduced. In July 2000, the EU decided to continue with its GM food ban indefinitely.

In response to a complaint to the WTO by the USA, Canada and Argentina, a panel was set up in March 2004 to consider the case. In 2006 the WTO concluded that the EU's GM ban was illegal because the risks shown by the scientific evidence did not warrant the ban. Accordingly, WTO rules should apply across EU member states. However, this has not prevented individual member states such as Austria, France, Germany Greece, Hungary and Luxembourg banning GM maize produced by the US firm Monsanto.

The European Commission initiated proceedings against Austria and Hungary but was overruled by environment ministers, reacting to domestic political pressures. In response, Monsanto has mounted legal challenges in the French and German courts. There is a danger, therefore, that new complaints may be made to the WTO by GM seed-producing countries.

Airbus

A more recent branch of the current EU/US trade disputes concerns the Airbus Consortium and EU industrial policy (an area which has been a bone of contention for the USA for many years). The current issue concerns EU support given to the development of new aircraft, and especially the new superjumbo, the A380. The Americans are very unhappy with the loans and subsidies, claimed to be some $15 billion, that have been provided by EU members to companies within the Airbus Consortium to develop the aircraft. (See Box 12.1 for more details on Airbus). The American complaint is that such subsidies have broken the WTO subsidy code and, as such, are unfair.

In October 2004, the USA requested the establishment of a WTO panel to consider the case. This provoked a counter-request by Airbus, claiming unfair subsidies of $27.3 billion for Boeing by the US government since 1992. In July 2005, two panels were set up to deal with the two sets of allegations.

In March 2010, the WTO ruled on Boeing's case against Airbus. It found Airbus guilty of using some illegal subsidies to win contracts through predatory pricing, but nevertheless dismissed most of Boeing's claims, as many of the subsidies were reimbursable at commercial rates of interest. However, some of the 'launch aid' for research and development was given at below market rates and hence did violate WTO rules. A ruling was still awaited on Airbus's case against Boeing.

In the meantime, there is further concern by the USA that the new A350, due to be launched in 2013, will receive similar support from EU countries. The dispute continues.

 Why does the WTO appear to be so ineffective in resolving the disputes between the EU and USA?

BOX 12.3   PREFERENTIAL TRADING

The case of NAFTA

The world economy seems to have been increasingly forming into a series of trade blocs, based upon regional groupings of countries: a European region centred on the European Union, an Asian region on Japan, a North American region on the USA and a Latin American region. Such trade blocs are examples of **preferential trading arrangements**. These arrangements involve trade restrictions with the rest of the world, and lower or zero restrictions between the members.

Although trade blocs clearly encourage trade between their members, many countries outside these blocs complain that they benefit the members at the expense of the rest of the world. For many developing economies, in need of access to the most prosperous nations in the world, this represents a significant check on their ability to grow and develop.

Types of preferential trading arrangement

There are three possible forms of such trading arrangements:

Free trade area. This is where member countries remove tariffs and quotas between themselves, but retain whatever restrictions *each member chooses* with non-member countries. Some provision will have to be made to prevent imports from outside coming into the area via the country with the lowest external tariff.

Customs union. This is like a free trade area, but in addition members must adopt *common* external tariffs and quotas with non-member countries.

Common market. This is where member countries operate as a *single* market. Like a customs union there are no tariffs and quotas between member countries and there are common external tariffs and quotas. But a common market goes further than this. A full common market

includes the following features: a common system of taxation; a common system of laws and regulations governing production, employment and trade (e.g. competition law and trade union legislation); and the free movement of labour, capital and materials, and of goods and services (e.g. the freedom of workers from one member country to work in any other).

The effects of preferential trading

By joining a customs union (or free trade area), a country will find that its trade patterns change. Most of these changes are likely to be beneficial.

Countries will probably benefit from 'trade creation'. The removal of trade barriers allows greater specialisation according to comparative advantage. Instead of consumers having to pay high prices for domestically produced goods in which the country has a comparative disadvantage, the goods can now be obtained more cheaply from other members of the customs union. In return, the country can export to them goods in which it has a comparative advantage.

Other advantages from preferential trading include: competition from companies in other member states, which may stimulate efficiency and reduce monopoly power; economies of scale for firms which now have access to a bigger market; a more rapid spread of technology within the area; the bargaining power of the whole customs union with the rest of the world allowing member countries to gain better terms of trade; increased trade encouraging improvements in the infrastructure of the members of the union (better roads, railways, financial services, etc.).

There are some dangers, however, of customs unions. The first is that 'trade diversion' could take place. This is where countries that were previously importing from a

developing countries to markets in the rich world. The Agenda is also concerned with the environmental impacts of trade and development.

The talks were originally scheduled for completion by January 2005, but this deadline had to be extended to December 2005 and then to July 2006, merely for an outline agreement on agricultural and industrial products and later still for an agreement on services. But the deadlines passed with not even an agreement on a 'framework' of what such an agreement should look like!

The EU and USA blamed larger developing countries, such as Brazil and India, for being unwilling to make reductions in tariffs on manufactured imports. The developing countries, in turn, blamed the unwillingness of the developed countries, and especially the EU and the USA, to make sufficient cuts in agricultural protection. The EU blamed the USA for subsidising its farmers; the USA blamed the EU for high tariffs on imported food.

low-cost country (which does not join the union), now buy from a higher cost country within the customs union, simply because there are no tariffs on this country's products and hence they can be purchased at a lower price, despite their higher cost of production.

Another danger is that resources may flow from the country to more efficient members of the customs union, or to the geographical centre of the union (so as to minimise transport costs). This can be a major problem for a *common market* (where there is free movement of labour and capital). The country could become a depressed 'region' of the community. Finally, if integration creates cooperation, firms may be encouraged to collude with each other, in order to maintain high prices.

North American Free Trade Agreement (NAFTA)

Along with the EU, NAFTA is one of the two most powerful trading blocs in the world. It came into force in 1994 and consists of the USA, Canada and Mexico. These three countries have agreed to abolish tariffs between themselves in the hope that increased trade and cooperation will follow. Tariffs between the USA and Canada were phased out by 1999 and tariffs between Mexico and the other two countries would be by 2009. Many non-tariff restrictions, however, remain.

Of the three countries in NAFTA, Mexico potentially has the most to gain from the agreement. With easier access to US and Canadian markets, and the added attractiveness it now has to foreign investors, Mexico has become a thriving export economy that attracts sufficient foreign direct investment to finance its total current account deficit. However, as trade barriers fall, it also faces increased competition from bigger and more efficient US and Canadian rivals.

Disputes do arise between the members. In 2009, for example, the USA reneged on a pilot scheme that would allow some Mexican trucks to travel over the US border. In response, Mexico imposed tariffs of up to 45 per cent on 90 US agricultural and industrial imports, ranging from strawberries and wine to cordless telephones.

NAFTA members hope that, with a market similar in size to the EU, they will be able to rival the EU's economic power in world trade. NAFTA is, however, at most only a free trade area and not a common market. Unlike the EU, it does not seek to harmonise laws and regulations, except in very specific areas such as environmental management and labour standards. Member countries are permitted total legal independence, subject to the one proviso that they must treat firms of other member countries equally with their own firms – the principle of 'fair competition'. Nevertheless, NAFTA has encouraged a growth in trade between its members, most of which is trade creation rather than trade diversion.

Other countries may join in the future, so NAFTA may eventually develop into a Western hemisphere free trade association. Leaders of 34 American countries have attempted to create a Free Trade Area of the Americas (FTAA), though no firm timetable has been established. Talks have stalled on a number of occasions and no detailed negotiations have taken place.

1. *What factors will determine whether a country's joining a customs union will lead to trade creation or trade diversion?*
2. *Using the Internet, identify some other preferential trading arrangements around the world and their various features.*

The talks were restarted in 2007, and again in 2008 in Geneva, but on both occasions they collapsed without agreement. With the 2008/9 recession, little progress was made and there were also concerns that countries would introduce protectionist measures to support domestic industries, although these concerns were in the end unfounded.

Although there was a pledge at the G20 meeting in London in 2009 to complete the Doha round, a year later no agreement was in sight. Indeed, in March 2010, a deadline for a new trade deal was dropped, as countries agreed instead to look ahead to future talks, with global trade volumes finally forecast to increase. The WTO Director General Pascal Lamy told a meeting of the WTO's Trade Negotiations Committee: 'Although we have made some progress since 2008, there is no denying the fact that we are not where we wanted to be by now.'[2]

---

[2] WTO, 'Stocktaking ends with collective determination to start building global Doha package', 2010 News Items, 26 March 2010

Recap

1. Most countries of the world are members of the WTO and in theory are in favour of moves towards freer trade.

2. The WTO can impose sanctions on countries not abiding by WTO rules.

3. There have been various 'rounds' of trade talks, originally under the auspices of GATT and more recently under the WTO. The Uruguay round led to substantial reductions in tariffs and other trade restrictions.

4. The latest 'Doha round' focuses on trade liberalisation and aims to spread the benefits of trade across developing countries. However, the negotiations have stalled.

12.4 THE EUROPEAN UNION AND THE SINGLE MARKET

In recognition of the benefits of free trade within the EU, the member countries signed the Single European Act of 1986. This sought to dismantle all barriers to internal trade within the EU by 1993, and create a genuine 'single market'. Although tariffs between member states had long been abolished, there were all sorts of non-tariff barriers, such as high taxes on wine by non-wine-producing countries, special regulations designed to favour domestic producers, governments giving contracts to domestic producers (e.g. for defence equipment), and so on.

Most of the barriers were indeed removed by 1993, and by the mid 1990s it was becoming clear from the evidence that the single market was bringing substantial benefits.

Trade creation. The expansion of trade within the EU has reduced both prices and costs, as countries have been able to exploit their comparative advantage. Member countries have specialised further in those goods and services that they can produce at a relatively lower opportunity cost:

Reduction in the direct costs of barriers. This category includes administrative costs, border delays and technical regulations. Their abolition or harmonisation has led to substantial cost savings, shorter delivery times and a larger choice of suppliers.

Economies of scale. With industries based on a Europe-wide scale, many firms can now be large enough, and their plants large enough, to gain the full potential economies of scale (see Box 4.4 on page 102). Yet the whole European market is large enough for there still to be adequate competition. Such gains have varied from industry to industry, depending on the minimum efficient scale of a plant or firm. Economies of scale have also been gained from mergers and other forms of industrial restructuring.

Greater competition. Increased competition between firms has led to lower costs, lower prices and a wider range of products available to consumers. This has been particularly so in newly liberalised service sectors such as transport, financial services, telecommunications and broadcasting. In the long run, greater competition can stimulate greater innovation, the greater flow of technical information and the rationalisation of production.

Pause for thought

In what ways would competition be 'unfair' if VAT rates differed widely between member states?

The economic evidence was backed up by the perceptions of business. Firms from across the range of industries felt that the single market project had removed a series of obstacles to trade within the EU and had increased market opportunities.

Despite these gains, the single market has not received a universal welcome within the EU. Its critics argue that, in a Europe of oligopolies, unequal ownership of resources, rapidly changing technologies and industrial practices, and factor immobility, the removal of internal barriers to trade has merely exaggerated the problems of inequality and economic power. More specifically, the following criticisms are made:

Radical economic change is costly. Substantial economic change is necessary to achieve the full economies of scale and efficiency gains from a single European market. These changes necessarily involve redundancies – from bankruptcies, takeovers, rationalisation and the introduction of new technology. The severity of this 'structural' and 'technological' unemployment (see section 10.6) depends on (a) the pace of economic change and (b) the mobility of labour – both occupational and geographical. Clearly, the more integrated markets become across the EU, the lower will be the costs of future change.

Adverse regional effects. Firms are likely to locate as near as possible to the 'centre of gravity' of their markets and sources of supply. If, before barriers are removed, a firm's prime market was the UK, it might well have located in the Midlands or the North of England. If, however, with barriers now removed, its market has become Europe as a whole, it may choose to locate in the South of England or in France, Germany or the Benelux countries instead. The creation of a single European market thus tends to attract capital and jobs away from the edges of the Union and towards its geographical centre.

In an ideal market situation, areas like Cornwall, the south of Italy or Portugal and now parts of Eastern Europe should attract resources from other parts of the Union. They are relatively depressed areas, thus wage rates and land prices are lower. The resulting lower industrial costs should encourage firms to move into those areas. In practice, however, as capital and labour (and especially young and skilled workers) leave the extremities of the Union, so these regions are likely to become more depressed. If, as a result, their infrastructure is neglected, they then become even less attractive to new investment.

The development of monopoly/oligopoly power. The free movement of capital can encourage the development of giant 'Euro-firms' with substantial economic power. Indeed, recent years have seen some very large European mergers. This can lead to higher, not lower prices and less choice for the consumer. It all depends on just how effective competition is, and how effective EU competition policy is in preventing monopolistic and collusive practices.

Completing the internal market

Despite the reduction in barriers, the internal market is still not 'complete'. In other words, various barriers to trade between member states still remained. Thus, in June 1997, an Action Plan was adopted by the European Council. Its aim was to ensure that all barriers were dismantled by the launch of the euro in January 1999.

To monitor progress an 'Internal Market Scoreboard' was established. This is published every six months and shows progress towards the total abandonment of any forms of internal trade restrictions (Web Case D.29). It shows the percentage of EU Single Market Directives still to be transposed into national law. In addition to giving each country's 'transposition deficit', the Scoreboard identifies the number of infringements of the internal market that have taken place. The hope is that the 'naming and shaming' of countries will encourage them to make more rapid progress towards totally free trade within the EU.

The Action Plan was largely, but not totally, successful. In 1997, the average transposition deficit of member countries was 35 per cent. By 1999, this had fallen to 3.5 per cent and by 2002, to just 1.8 per cent.

In January 2004, the *Implementation Report on the Internal Market Strategy* claimed that, 'Since the abolition of EU internal frontiers ten years ago, the Internal Market has boosted EU economic growth by at least 1.8%, adding nearly 900 billion euro to the EU's collective prosperity and helping create 2.5 million extra jobs.'

Despite this success, national governments have continued to introduce *new* technical standards, several of which have had the effect of erecting new barriers to trade. Also, infringements of single market rules by governments have not always been dealt with. The net result is that, although trade is much freer today than in the early 1990s, especially given the transparency of pricing with the euro, there still do exist various barriers, especially to the free movement of goods.

Pause for thought

If there have been clear benefits from the single market programme, why do individual member governments still try to erect barriers, such as new technical standards?

To counteract new barriers, the EU periodically issues new Directives. If this process is more rapid than that of the transposition of existing Directives into national law, the transposition deficit increases. Thus by December 2004, the average deficit for the original 15 EU members had risen to 2.9 per cent. By May 2010, however, it had fallen to a mere 0.9 per cent (for all 27 members).

The effect of the new member states

Given the very different nature of the economies of many of the 12 new entrants to the EU (10 in 2004 and 2 more in 2007), and their lower levels of GDP per head, the potential for gain from membership has been substantial. The gains come through additional trade, increased competition, technological transfer and inward investment, both from other EU countries and from outside the EU.

A study in 2004[3] concluded that Poland's GDP would rise by 3.4 per cent and Hungary's by almost 7 per cent. Real wages would rise, with those of unskilled workers rising faster than those of skilled workers, in accordance with these countries' comparative advantage. There would also be benefits for the existing 15 EU countries from increased trade and investment, as well as access to cheaper inputs to production, but these would be relatively minor in comparison to the gains to the new members.

A European Commission Report produced in April 2009, five years after the enlargement,[4] found that the expansion had been a win–win situation for both old and new members. There had been significant improvements in the standard of living in new member states and they had benefited from modernisation of their economies and more stabilised institutions and laws. In addition, enterprises in old member states had enjoyed opportunities for new investment and exports, and there had been an overall increase in trade and competition between the

[3] Maliszewska, M. *Benefits of the Single Market Expansion for Current and New Member States* (Centrum Analiz Spoleczno-Ekonomicznych)

[4] 'Five Years of an Enlarged EU – Economic Achievements and Challenges', *European Economy 1 2009* (Commission of the European Communities)

member states. Trade between all the member states grew from €175 billion in 1999 to €500 billion in 2007. In the same period, there was also a five-fold growth in trade among the new members from just under €15 billion to €77 billion.[5]

From 2004 until the credit crunch hit the EU, there was 1.5 per cent annual growth in employment in new members and a solid 1 per cent growth in job creation in old members, silencing arguments that the enlargement would lead to unemployment in the Western EU economies. Income per capita in the new members increased from 40 per cent of the old members' average in 1999 to 52 per cent in 2008 and their average growth rate rose from 3.5 per cent between 1999 and 2003 to 5.5 per cent between 2004 and 2008. Whilst higher growth levels in new member states were expected, there were fears that this would be at the expense of the old members. However, data suggest that annual growth for the old members averaged around 2.2 per cent in both periods; so adverse affects were not seen.

The financial crisis of 2008–10 caused problems for all countries in the EU, with growth falling and unemployment rising everywhere. A particular problem for some new members stemmed from easy access to finance, leading to 'rapid and unchecked domestic credit growth, fuelled by foreign borrowing'. This 'overheated the economy and led to large external imbalances, sharp increases in labour costs outstripping increases in productivity, and hikes in real estate prices . . . With the large increase in the cost of capital . . . countries . . . now face major adjustment challenges.'[6] As the world economy continues to recover from recession, it will be interesting to see how countries across the EU fare.

> **Pause for thought**
>
> *Why may the new members of the EU have the most to gain from the single market, but also the most to lose?*

Recap

1. The Single European Act of 1986 sought to sweep away various administrative restrictions to free trade in the EU and to establish a genuine free market by 1993.

2. Benefits from completing the internal market have included trade creation, cost savings from no longer having to administer barriers, economies of scale for firms now able to operate on a Europe-wide scale, and greater competition leading to reduced costs and prices, greater flows of technical information and more innovation.

3. Critics of the single market point to the costs of radical changes in industrial structure, the attraction of capital away from the periphery of the EU to its geographical centre, possible problems of market power with the development of giant 'Euro-firms' and the political cost of lost national sovereignty.

4. New members have gained substantially from free trade within the EU. There have also been gains to existing member states. We must wait to see what the impact of the recession on both old and new states will be.

---

[5] 'Europe United – A Balance Sheet Five Years After', *Enlargement Commissioner Olli Rehn*, 15 April 2009, p. 2

[6] 'Five Years of an Enlarged EU – Economic Achievements and Challenges', *European Economy 1 2009* (Commission of the European Communities)

QUESTIONS

1. Imagine that two countries, Richland and Poorland, can produce just two goods, computers and coal. Assume that for a given amount of land and capital, the output of these two products requires the following constant amounts of labour:

	Richland	Poorland
1 computer	2	4
100 tonnes of coal	4	5

Assume that each country has 20 million workers.

(a) If there is no trade, and in each country 12 million workers produce computers and 8 million workers produce coal, how many computers and tonnes of coal will each country produce? What will be the total production of each product?
(b) What is the opportunity cost of a computer in (i) Richland; (ii) Poorland?
(c) What is the opportunity cost of 100 tonnes of coal in (i) Richland; (ii) Poorland?
(d) Which country has a comparative advantage in which product?
(e) Assuming that price equals marginal cost, which of the following would represent possible exchange ratios?
   (i)   1 computer for 40 tonnes of coal;
   (ii) 2 computers for 140 tonnes of coal;
   (iii) 1 computer for 100 tonnes of coal;
   (iv) 1 computer for 60 tonnes of coal;
   (v)   4 computers for 360 tonnes of coal.
(f) Assume that trade now takes place and that 1 computer exchanges for 65 tonnes of coal. Both countries specialise completely in the product in which they have a comparative advantage. How much does each country produce of its respective product?
(g) The country producing computers sells 6 million domestically. How many does it export to the other country?
(h) How much coal does the other country consume?

2. Why doesn't the USA specialise as much as General Motors or Texaco? Why doesn't the UK specialise as much as Unilever? Is the answer to these questions similar to the answer to the questions, 'Why doesn't the USA specialise as much as Luxembourg?' and 'Why doesn't Unilever specialise as much as the local florist?'

3. To what extent are the arguments for countries specialising and then trading with each other the same as those for individuals specialising in doing the jobs to which they are relatively well suited?

4. The following are four items that are traded internationally: wheat; computers; textiles; insurance. In which one of the four is each of the following most likely to have a comparative advantage: India; the UK; Canada; Japan? Give reasons for your answer.

5. It is often argued that if the market fails to develop infant industries, then this is an argument for government intervention, but not necessarily in the form of restricting imports. What *other* ways could infant industries be given government support?

6. Does the consumer in the importing country gain or lose from dumping? (Consider both the short run and the long run.)

7. What is fallacious about the following two arguments? Is there any truth in either?

(a) 'Imports should be reduced because money is going abroad which would be better spent at home.'
(b) 'We should protect our industries from being undercut by imports produced using cheap labour.'

8. Go through each of the arguments for restricting trade and provide a counter-argument for not restricting trade.

9. If countries are so keen to reduce the barriers to trade, why do many countries frequently attempt to erect barriers?

10. If rich countries stand to gain substantially from freer trade, why have they been so reluctant to reduce the levels of protection of agriculture?

11. Why is it difficult to estimate the magnitude of the benefits of completing the internal market of the EU?

12. Look through the costs and benefits that we identified from the single European market. Do the same costs and benefits arise from a substantially enlarged EU?

13. How did the financial crisis of 2008/9 affect the costs and benefits of the latest EU enlargement?

Business issues covered in this chapter

- What is meant by 'the balance of payments' and how do trade and financial movements affect it?

- How are exchange rates determined and what are the implications for business of changes in the exchange rate?

- How do governments and/or central banks seek to influence the exchange rate and what are the implications for other macroeconomic policies and for business?

- How do the vast flows of finance around the world affect business and the countries in which they are located?

- What are the advantages and disadvantages of the euro for members of the eurozone and for businesses inside and outside the eurozone?

- How do the major economies of the world seek to coordinate their policies and what difficulties arise in the process?

- What are the causes and effects on business of currency speculation?

- To what extent does the world gain or lose from the process of the globalisation of business?

The global financial environment

When countries sell exports, there is an inflow of money into the economy. When they buy imports, there is an outflow. In this chapter we examine these international financial flows and their implications for business. With an increasingly interdependent world, these financial flows have a significant effect on economic performance.

But such flows are not just from trade. Inward investment leads to an inflow of money, as do deposits of money in this country made by people abroad. Outward investment and deposits of money abroad from people in this country result in an outflow of money.

All these inflows and outflows of money to and from a country are recorded in the 'balance of payments'. We examine this process in section 13.1.

Trade and investment are also influenced by the rates of exchange between currencies. Rates of exchange, in turn, are influenced by the demand and supply of currencies resulting from trade and investment. We will see what causes exchange rate fluctuations – a major cause of concern for many businesses – and how central banks can attempt to reduce these fluctuations. Section 13.2 looks at exchange rates.

The remaining sections look at various aspects of global finance: how global financial flows affect the world economy; whether the global financial environment can be managed; and how the EU has sought to achieve greater financial stability through the adoption of the euro by many of its members. Finally, by way of a postscript, we ask whether this whole process of economic globalisation with greater and greater economic and financial interdependence has been a 'good thing'.

13.1 THE BALANCE OF PAYMENTS

A country's balance of payments account records all the flows of money between residents of that country and the rest of the world. *Receipts* of money from abroad are regarded as *credits* and are entered in the accounts with a positive sign. *Outflows* of money from the country are regarded as *debits* and are entered with a negative sign.

The balance of payments account

There are three main parts of the balance of payments account: the *current account*, the *capital account* and the *financial account*. We shall look at each part in turn, and take the UK as an example. Table 13.1 gives a summary of the UK balance of payments for 2009.

The current account

The **current account** records (a) payments for exports (+) and imports (−) of goods and services, plus (b) incomes flowing into (+) and out of (−) the country (wages, profits,

Definition

Current account of the balance of payments
The record of a country's imports and exports of goods and services, plus incomes and transfers of money to and from abroad.

> ### Table 13.1 UK balance of payments, 2009 (£m)
>
> **Current account**
>
> | | |
> |---|---:|
> | Balance on trade in goods and services (exports minus imports) | −33 076 |
> | Net income flows (wages and investment income) | +30 139 |
> | Net current transfers (government and private) | −14 673 |
> | **Balance on current account** | **−17 610** |
>
> **Capital account**
>
> | | |
> |---|---:|
> | Net capital transfers | +3 223 |
> | **Balance on capital account** | **+3 223** |
>
> **Financial account**
>
> | | |
> |---|---:|
> | Direct investment | −15 357 |
> | Portfolio investment | +70 937 |
> | Other investment (mainly short-term flows) | −43 915 |
> | Reserves | −5 763 |
> | **Balance on financial account** | **+5 902** |
>
> | | |
> |---|---:|
> | Net errors and omissions | +8 485 |
>
> | | |
> |---|---:|
> | Total | 0 |
>
> Source: *Financial Statistics* (Office for National Statistics). Reproduced under terms of the click-use licence

Definitions

Balance of payments on current account

The balance on trade in goods and services plus net incomes and current transfers, i.e. the sum of the credits on the current account minus the sum of the debits.

Balance of trade

Exports of goods and services minus imports of goods and services.

Capital account of the balance of payments

The record of transfers of capital to and from abroad.

Financial account of the balance of payments

The record of the flows of money into and out of the country for the purpose of investment or as deposits in banks and other financial institutions.

dividends on shares), plus (c) net transfers of money into (+) and out of (−) the country (e.g. money sent from Greece to a Greek student studying in the UK is an inflow of money and so would be a credit item on the UK balance of payments).

The **current account balance** is the overall balance of all these. A *current account surplus* is where credits exceed debits. A *current account deficit* is where debits exceed credits.

If you want to look purely at the balance of imports and exports (i.e. just item (a) above), this is given as the balance of trade. If exports exceed imports, there is a balance of trade surplus; if imports exceed exports, there is a balance of trade deficit.

The capital account

The **capital account** records the flows of funds, into the country (+) and out of the country (−), associated with the acquisition or disposal of fixed assets (e.g. land), the transfer of funds by migrants, and the payment of grants by the government for overseas projects and the receipt of EU money for capital projects.

The financial account

The **financial account** of the balance of payments records cross-border changes in the holding of shares, property, bank deposits and loans, government securities, etc. In other words, unlike the current account, which is concerned with money incomes, the financial account is concerned with the flows of money for the purchase and sale of assets.

Some of these flows are for long-term investment. This can involve the acquisition of buildings and equipment (direct investment) or paper assets such as shares (portfolio investment).

Some of the flows involve the short-term deposit of money in bank accounts. Such short-term monetary flows are common between international financial centres, to take advantage of differences in countries' interest rates and changes in exchange rates. We saw the importance of this aspect of the financial account in the late 2000s, when there was massive disinvestment by non-UK residents in financial assets with UK financial institutions. Largely due to this, the UK's balance of 'other investment' deteriorated from a deficit of around £24 billion in 2006 to a deficit of some £222 billion in 2008. Table 13.1 shows that although this part of the balance of payments remained in deficit throughout 2009, it did improve substantially.

Anything that involves an acquisition of assets in *this* country by overseas residents (e.g. foreign companies investing in the UK) represents an inflow of money and is thus a credit (+) item. Any acquisition of assets abroad by UK residents (e.g. UK companies investing abroad) represents a debit (–) item.

Pause for thought

Where would interest payments on short-term foreign deposits in UK banks be entered on the balance of payments account?

Flows to and from the reserves

The UK, like all other countries, holds reserves of gold and foreign currencies. From time to time the Bank of England (acting as the government's agent) might release some of these reserves to purchase sterling on the foreign exchange market. It would do so as a means of supporting the rate of exchange (as we shall see in the next section). Drawing on reserves represents a *credit* item in the balance of payments account: money drawn from the reserves represents an *inflow* to the balance of payments (albeit an outflow from the reserves account). The reserves can thus be used to support a deficit elsewhere in the balance of payments.

Conversely, if there is a surplus elsewhere in the balance of payments, the Bank of England could use it to build up the reserves. Building up the reserves counts as a debit item in the balance of payments, since it represents an outflow from it (to the reserves).

Does the balance of payments balance?

When all the components of the balance of payments account are taken together, the balance of payments should exactly balance: credits should equal debits. As we shall see in section 13.2, if they were not equal, the rate of exchange would have to adjust until they were, or the government would have to intervene to make them equal.

When the statistics are compiled, however, a number of errors are likely to occur. As a result there will not be a balance. The main reason for the errors is that the statistics are obtained from a number of sources, and there are often delays before items are recorded and sometimes omissions too. To 'correct' for this, a **net errors and omissions** item is included in the accounts. This ensures that there will be an exact balance.

Does a deficit matter?

If the balance of payments must always balance, then in what sense does the balance of payments matter? The answer is that the individual accounts will *not* necessarily balance. The UK has traditionally imported more than it has exported. The resulting deficit on the current account has thus had to be financed by an equal and opposite surplus on the capital-plus-financial accounts. In other words, the UK has had to borrow from abroad or sell assets abroad to finance the excess of imports over exports. This has meant that it has had to have higher interest rates in order to attract deposits from overseas and have an increased ownership of domestic assets by residents abroad.

Definition

Net errors and omissions
A statistical adjustment to ensure that the two sides of the balance of payments account balance. It is necessary because of errors in compiling the statistics.

Higher interest rates can have a long-term dampening effect on the economy, by discouraging borrowing and investment. Inward direct investment, on the other hand, although resulting in increased overseas ownership of assets in the UK, will have the effect of stimulating output and employment.

Figure 13.1 shows the current account balances of the UK, the USA and Japan as a proportion of their GDP. Although the UK has in most years had a current account deficit, this deficit has fluctuated with the business cycle. In times of rapid economic growth relative to other countries, expenditure on imports rises rapidly relative to exports and the current account goes deeper into deficit. You can see this in the late 1980s and late 1990s. In times of recession the current account improves, as it did in the early 1980s, the early 1990s and then again from 2008 to 2010. You can also see the effect of oil on the current account. In the late 1970s as North Sea oil was coming on stream, so the current account went into surplus. As oil exports have declined in the early 2000s, so this contributed to a deepening of the deficit.

Figure 13.1 also shows the current accounts of the USA and Japan. They are an approximate mirror image of each other as many of Japan's exports are imported by the USA. Much of Japan's current account surplus is then invested in the USA as direct investment, the acquisition of paper assets, such as shares (portfolio investment), or simply as deposits in US financial institutions. One reflection of this imbalance has been generally much higher interest rates in the USA than in Japan.

Another consequence of the high US current account deficit is that most of it is paid in US dollars. This increases the supply of dollars in the world banking system, much of it on short-term deposit. These deposits can be rapidly transferred from one country to another, wherever interest rates are higher or where speculators anticipate a rise in the exchange rate (see next section). As we shall see, this movement of 'hot money' tends to lead to considerable instability in exchange rates.

Figure 13.1	Current account balance as % of GDP: 1970–2011

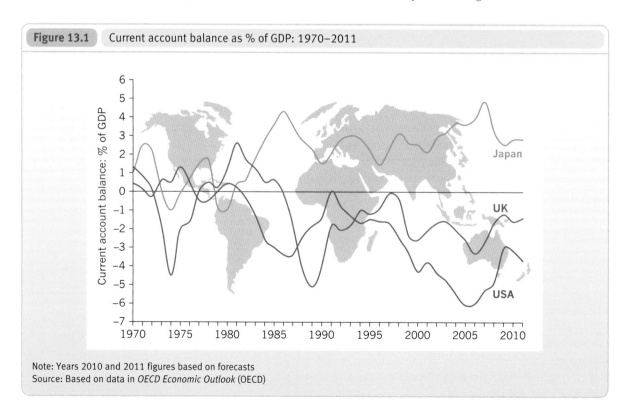

Note: Years 2010 and 2011 figures based on forecasts
Source: Based on data in *OECD Economic Outlook* (OECD)

Recap

1. The balance of payments account records all payments to and receipts from other countries. The current account records payments for imports and exports, plus incomes and transfers of money to and from abroad. The capital account records all transfers of capital to and from abroad. The financial account records inflows and outflows of money for investment and as deposits in banks and other financial institutions. It also includes dealings in the country's foreign exchange reserves.

2. The whole account must balance, but surpluses or deficits can be recorded on any specific part

   of the account. Thus the current account could be in deficit but it would have to be matched by an equal and opposite capital plus financial account surplus.

3. The UK has traditionally had a current account deficit, but this has fluctuated with the business cycle.

4. The US and Japanese current accounts are somewhat of a mirror image of each other. One result of large and persistent US deficits has been an increase in 'hot money', which has aggravated exchange rate instability.

THE EXCHANGE RATE   13.2

An exchange rate is the rate at which one currency trades for another on the foreign exchange market.

If you want to go abroad, you will need to exchange your pounds for euros, dollars, Swiss francs or whatever. To do this you might go to a bank. The bank will quote you that day's exchange rates: e.g. €1.15 to the pound, or $1.50 to the pound. It is similar for firms. If an importer wants to buy, say, some machinery from Japan, it will require yen to pay the Japanese supplier. It will thus ask the foreign exchange section of a bank to quote it a rate of exchange of the pound into yen. Similarly, if you want to buy some foreign stocks and shares, or if companies based in the UK want to invest abroad, sterling will have to be exchanged for the appropriate foreign currency.

Likewise, if Americans want to come on holiday to the UK or to buy UK assets, or American firms want to import UK goods or to invest in the UK, they will require sterling. They will be quoted an exchange rate for the pound in the USA: say, £1 = $1.50. This means that they will have to pay $1.50 to obtain £1 worth of UK goods or assets.

Exchange rates are quoted between each of the major currencies of the world. These exchange rates are constantly changing. Minute by minute, dealers in the foreign exchange dealing rooms of the banks are adjusting the rates of exchange by buying and selling different currencies.

One of the problems, however, in assessing what is happening to a particular currency is that its rate of exchange may rise against some currencies (weak currencies) and fall against others (strong currencies). In order to gain an overall picture of its fluctuations, it is best to look at a weighted average exchange rate against all other currencies. This is known as the **exchange rate index**. The weight given to each currency in the index depends on the proportion of transactions done with that country.

Table 13.2 shows exchange rates between the pound and various currencies and the sterling exchange rate index from 1960 to 2010.

> **Definition**
>
> **Exchange rate index**
> A weighted average exchange rate expressed as an index, where the value of the index is 100 in a given base year. The weights of the different currencies in the index add up to 1.

> **Pause for thought**
>
> *How did the pound 'fare' compared with the dollar and the yen from 1960 to 2009? What about the euro since it began circulating? What conclusions can be drawn about the relative movements of these currencies?*

Table 13.2	Sterling exchange rates, 1960–2010						
	US dollar	Japanese yen	French franc	German mark	Italian lira	Euro[a]	Sterling exchange rate index (1/1/05 = 100)
1960	2.80	1008	13.82	11.76	1747	–	–
1970	2.40	858	13.33	8.78	1500	–	–
1975	2.22	658	9.50	5.45	1447	(1.70)	119.9
1980	2.33	526	9.83	4.23	1992	(1.62)	115.1
1985	1.30	307	11.55	3.78	2463	(1.71)	99.8
1990	1.79	257	9.69	2.88	2133	(1.37)	96.2
1992	1.77	224	9.32	2.75	2163	(1.33)	93.8
1994	1.53	156	8.49	2.48	2467	(1.27)	85.9
1996	1.56	170	7.99	2.35	2408	(1.21)	83.6
1998	1.66	217	9.77	2.91	2876	(1.49)	99.7
1999	1.62	184	(9.96)	(2.97)	(2941)	1.52	99.1
2000	1.52	163	(10.77)	(3.21)	(3180)	1.64	100.9
2001	1.44	175	(10.55)	(3.15)	(3115)	1.61	99.2
2002	1.50	188	–	–	–	1.59	100.4
2003	1.63	189	–	–	–	1.45	96.9
2004	1.83	198	–	–	–	1.47	101.6
2005	1.82	200	–	–	–	1.46	100.5
2006	1.84	214	–	–	–	1.47	101.0
2007	2.00	236	–	–	–	1.46	103.5
2008	1.85	192	–	–	–	1.26	91.0
2009	1.57	146	–	–	–	1.12	80.1
2010Q3	1.55	133	–	–	–	1.20	81.8

[a] The euro was introduced in 1999, with notes and coins circulating from 2001. The 'dummy' euro exchange rate figures prior to 1999 are projections backwards in time based on the weighted average exchange rates of the currencies that made up the euro

Source: *Monetary and Financial Statistics Interactive Database* (Bank of England). Reproduced with permission

The determination of the rate of exchange in a free market

In a free foreign exchange market, the rate of exchange is determined by demand and supply. Thus the sterling exchange rate is determined by the demand and supply of pounds. This is illustrated in Figure 13.2.

For simplicity, assume that there are just two countries, the UK and the USA. When UK importers wish to buy goods from the USA, or when UK residents wish to invest in the USA, they will *supply* pounds on the foreign exchange market in order to obtain dollars. In other words, they will go to banks or other foreign exchange dealers to buy dollars in exchange for pounds. The higher the exchange rate, the more dollars they will obtain for their pounds. This will effectively make American goods cheaper to buy and investment more profitable. Thus the *higher* the exchange rate, the *more* pounds will be supplied. The supply curve of pounds therefore typically slopes upwards.

When US residents wish to purchase UK goods or to invest in the UK, they will require pounds. They *demand* pounds by selling dollars on the foreign exchange market. In other words, they will go to banks or other foreign exchange dealers to buy pounds in exchange for dollars. The lower the dollar price of the pound (the exchange rate), the cheaper it will be for them to obtain UK goods and assets, and hence the more pounds they are likely to demand. The demand curve for pounds, therefore, typically slopes downwards.

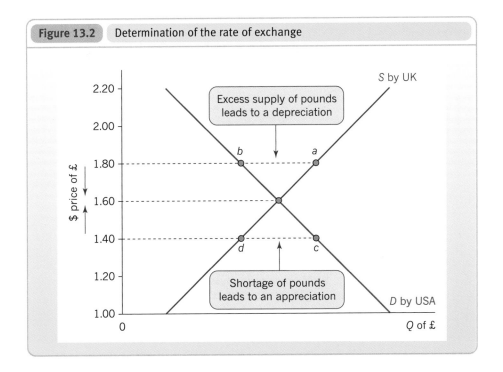

Figure 13.2   Determination of the rate of exchange

The equilibrium exchange rate is where the demand for pounds equals the supply. In Figure 13.2 this is at an exchange rate of £1 = $1.60. But what is the mechanism that equates demand and supply?

If the current exchange rate were above the equilibrium, the supply of pounds being offered to the banks would exceed the demand. For example, in Figure 13.2, if the exchange rate were $1.80, there would be an excess supply of pounds of a − b. Banks would not have enough dollars to exchange for all these pounds. But the banks make money by *exchanging* currency, not by holding on to it. They would thus lower the exchange rate in order to encourage a greater demand for pounds and reduce the excessive supply. They would continue lowering the rate until demand equalled supply.

Similarly, if the rate were below the equilibrium, say at $1.40, there would be a shortage of pounds of c − d. The banks would find themselves with too few pounds to meet all the demand. At the same time, they would have an excess supply of dollars. The banks would thus raise the exchange rate until demand equalled supply.

In practice, the process of reaching equilibrium is extremely rapid. The foreign exchange dealers in the banks are continually adjusting the rate as new customers make new demands for currencies. What is more, the banks have to watch each other's actions closely. They are constantly in competition with each other and thus have to keep their rates in line. The dealers receive minute-by-minute updates on their computer screens of the rates being offered around the world.

Shifts in the currency demand and supply curves

Any shift in the demand or supply curves will cause the exchange rate to change. This is illustrated in Figure 13.3, which this time shows the euro/sterling exchange rate. If the demand and supply curves shift from D_1 and S_1 to D_2 and S_2 respectively, the exchange rate will fall from €1.40 to €1.20. A fall in the exchange rate is called a **depreciation**. A rise in the exchange rate is called an **appreciation**.

Definitions

Depreciation
A fall in the free-market exchange rate of the domestic currency with foreign currencies.

Appreciation
A rise in the free-market exchange rate of the domestic currency with foreign currencies.

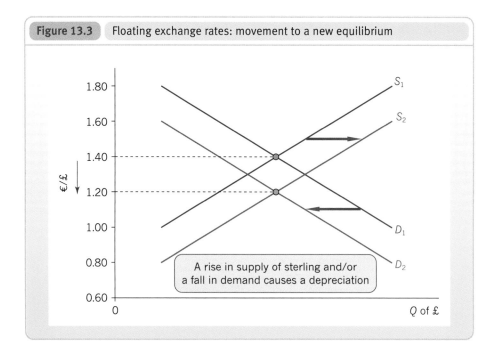

Figure 13.3   Floating exchange rates: movement to a new equilibrium

A rise in supply of sterling and/or a fall in demand causes a depreciation

But why should the demand and supply curves shift? The following are the major possible causes of a depreciation:

- *A fall in domestic interest rates*. UK rates would now be less competitive for savers and other depositors. More UK residents would be likely to deposit their money abroad, thus requiring foreign currency (the supply of sterling would rise), and fewer people abroad would deposit their money in the UK (the demand for sterling would fall).
- *Higher inflation in the domestic economy than abroad*. UK exports will become less competitive. The demand for sterling will fall. At the same time, imports will become relatively cheaper for UK consumers. The supply of sterling will rise.
- *A rise in domestic incomes relative to incomes abroad*. If UK incomes rise, the demand for imports, and hence the supply of sterling, will rise. If incomes in other countries fall, the demand for UK exports, and hence the demand for sterling will fall.
- *Relative investment prospects improving abroad*. If investment prospects become brighter abroad than in the UK, perhaps because of better incentives abroad, or because of worries about an impending recession in the UK, again the demand for sterling will fall and the supply of sterling will rise.
- *Speculation that the exchange rate will fall*. If businesses involved in importing and exporting, and also banks and other foreign exchange dealers, think that the exchange rate is about to fall, they will sell pounds *now* before the rate does fall. The supply of sterling will thus rise. People planning to buy sterling will wait until the rate does fall. In the meantime, the demand for sterling will fall.

Pause for thought

Go through each of the listed causes for shifts in the demand for and supply of sterling and consider what would cause an appreciation of the pound.

Exchange rates and the balance of payments

In a free foreign exchange market, the balance of payments will *automatically* balance. But why?

BOX 13.1 THE IMPORTANCE OF INTERNATIONAL FINANCIAL MOVEMENTS

How a current account deficit can coincide with an appreciating exchange rate

Since the early 1970s, most of the major economies of the world have operated with floating exchange rates. The opportunities that this gives for speculative gain have led to a huge increase in short-term international financial movements. Vast amounts of moneys transfer from country to country in search of higher interest rates or a currency that is likely to appreciate. This can have a bizarre effect on exchange rates.

If a country pursues an expansionary fiscal policy (i.e. cutting taxes and/or raising government expenditure), the current account will tend to go into deficit as extra imports are 'sucked in'. What effect will this have on exchange rates? You might think that the answer is obvious: the higher demand for imports will create an extra supply of domestic currency on the foreign exchange market and hence drive down the exchange rate.

In fact the opposite is likely. The higher interest rates resulting from the higher domestic demand can lead to a massive inflow of short-term finance. The financial account can thus move sharply into surplus. This is likely to outweigh the current account deficit and cause an appreciation of the exchange rate.

Exchange rate movements, especially in the short term, are largely brought about by changes on the financial rather than the current account.

 Why do high international financial mobility and an absence of exchange controls severely limit a country's ability to choose its interest rate?

The credit side of the balance of payments constitutes the demand for sterling. For example, when people abroad buy UK exports or assets they will demand sterling in order to pay for them. The debit side constitutes the supply of sterling. For example, when UK residents buy foreign goods or assets, the importers of them will require foreign currency to pay for them. They will thus supply pounds. A **floating exchange rate** will ensure that the demand for pounds is equal to the supply. It will thus also ensure that the credits on the balance of payments are equal to the debits; that the balance of payments balances.

This does not mean that each part of the balance of payments account will separately balance, but simply that any current account deficit must be matched by a capital-plus-financial account surplus and vice versa.

For example, suppose initially that each part of the balance of payments did separately balance. Then let us assume that interest rates rise. This will encourage larger short-term financial inflows as people abroad are attracted to deposit money in the UK; the demand for sterling would shift to the right (e.g. from D_2 to D_1 in Figure 13.3). It will also cause smaller short-term financial outflows as UK residents keep more of their money in the country; the supply of sterling shifts to the left (e.g. from S_2 to S_1 in Figure 13.3). The financial account will go into surplus. The exchange rate will appreciate.

As the exchange rate rises, this causes imports to be cheaper and exports to be more expensive. The current account will move into deficit. There is a movement up along the new demand and supply curves until a new equilibrium is reached. At this point, any financial account surplus is matched by an equal current (plus capital) account deficit.

Managing the exchange rate

The government or central bank (the Bank of England in the UK) may be unwilling to let the country's currency float freely. Frequent shifts in the demand and supply curves would cause frequent changes in the exchange rate. This, in turn, might cause uncertainty for businesses, which might curtail their trade and investment.

Definition

Floating exchange rate
When the government does not intervene in the foreign exchange markets, but simply allows the exchange rate to be freely determined by demand and supply.

Assume, for example, that the Bank of England believes that an exchange rate of
€1.40 to the pound is approximately the long-term equilibrium rate. Short-term
leftward shifts in the demand for sterling and rightward shifts in the supply, however, are causing the exchange rate to fall below this level (see Figure 13.3). What
can be done to keep the rate at €1.40?

Using reserves. The Bank of England can sell gold and foreign currencies from the
reserves to buy pounds. This will shift the demand for sterling back to the right.
The problem here is that countries' reserves are limited. If people are convinced
that the sterling exchange rate will fall, there will be massive selling of pounds. It
is unlikely that using the reserves to buy pounds will be adequate to stem the fall.

Borrowing from abroad. The government can negotiate a foreign currency loan from
other countries or from an international agency such as the International Monetary
Fund. The Bank of England can then use these monies to buy pounds on the foreign
exchange market, thus again shifting the demand for sterling back to the right.

Raising interest rates. If the Bank of England raises interest rates, it will encourage
people to deposit money in the UK and encourage UK residents to keep their money
in the country. The demand for sterling will increase and the supply of sterling will
decrease.

This is likely to be more effective than the other two measures, but using interest
rates to control the exchange rate may conflict with using interest rates to target
inflation. You cannot use one instrument (the rate of interest) to control two separate
targets (the exchange rate and the rate of inflation) if the two objectives require a
different rate of interest.

Advantages of managed exchange rates

Surveys reveal that most businesspeople prefer relatively stable exchange rates, if
not totally fixed then with minimum fluctuations. The following arguments are
used to justify this preference.

Certainty. With stable exchange rates, international trade and investment become
much less risky, since profits are not affected by violent movements in the exchange
rate.

Assume a firm correctly forecasts that its product will sell in the USA for $1.50.
It costs 80p to produce. If the rate of exchange is stable at £1 = $1.50, each unit will
earn £1 and hence make a 20p profit. If, however, the rate of exchange fluctuated
these profits could be wiped out. If, say, the rate appreciated to £1 = $2, and if units
continued to sell for $1.50, they would now earn only 75p each, and hence make
a 5p loss.

Little or no speculation. If people believe that the exchange rate will remain constant
there is nothing to be gained from speculating. For example, between 1999 and
2001, when the old currencies of the eurozone countries were still used, but were
totally fixed to the euro, there was no speculation that the German mark, say, would
change in value against the French franc or the Dutch guilder.

With a totally free floating exchange rate, by contrast, given that large amounts
of short-term deposits are internationally 'footloose', speculation can be highly
destabilising in the short run. If people think that the exchange rate will fall, then
they will sell the currency, and this will cause the exchange rate to fall even further.

There is a problem with managed exchange rates, however, if speculators believe
that the managed rate is not an equilibrium rate. If, for example, they believe that

there will have to be a devaluation, speculation may become unstoppable and force the government to devalue. If the government delays doing so, it could cost the central bank a huge amount in attempting to support the currency.

Disadvantages of managed exchange rates

Exchange rate policy may conflict with the interests of domestic business and the economy as a whole. Managing the exchange rate will almost inevitably involve using interest rates for that purpose. But this may conflict with other macroeconomic objectives. For example, a depreciating exchange rate may force the central bank to raise interest rates to arrest the fall. But this may discourage business investment. This in turn will lower firms' profits in the long term and reduce the country's long-term rate of economic growth.

Also, if the economy is already in a recession, the higher interest rates could deepen the recession by making borrowing more expensive and thus reducing aggregate demand. In other words, the rate of interest that is suitable for the exchange rate may be unsuitable for the rest of the economy.

Under a free-floating rate, by contrast, the central bank can choose whatever rate of interest is necessary to meet domestic objectives, such as achieving a target rate of inflation. The exchange rate will simply adjust to the new rate of interest – a rise in interest rates causing an appreciation, a fall causing a depreciation. We saw this in the UK economy, where it was necessary to cut interest rates to 0.5 per cent in a bid to stimulate aggregate demand and tackle the recession, and this caused the value of sterling to fall.

Inability to adjust to shocks. Sometimes, it will prove impossible to maintain the exchange rate at the desired level. For example, a sudden increase in oil prices can have a large effect on the balance of payments. Oil-importing countries may find that the downward pressure on their exchange rate is too strong to contain.

> **Pause for thought**
>
> *If speculators on average gain from their speculation, who loses?*

Speculation. If speculators believe that the central bank cannot prevent the exchange rate falling (or rising), speculation is likely to be massive. The speculation will bring about the very fall (or rise) in the exchange rate that the speculators anticipated and may well cause the exchange rate to overshoot its longer-run equilibrium rate. At times of international currency turmoil (see Box 13.3), such speculation can be enormous. Worldwide, over a trillion dollars on average passes daily across the foreign exchanges, greatly in excess of countries' foreign exchange reserves!

Exchange rates in practice

Most countries today have a relatively free exchange rate. Nevertheless, the problems of instability that this can bring are well recognised, and thus many countries seek to regulate or manage their exchange rate.

There have been many attempts to regulate exchange rates since 1945. By far the most successful was the Bretton Woods system, which was adopted worldwide from the end of World War II until 1971. This was a form of **adjustable peg** exchange rate, where countries pegged (i.e. fixed) their exchange rate to the US dollar, but could re-peg it at a lower or higher level (a **devaluation** or **revaluation** of their exchange rate) if there was a persistent and substantial balance of payments deficit or surplus.

> **Definitions**
>
> **Adjustable peg**
> A system whereby exchange rates are fixed for a period of time, but may be devalued (or revalued) if a deficit (or surplus) becomes substantial.
>
> **Devaluation**
> Where the government or central bank re-pegs the exchange rate at a lower level.
>
> **Revaluation**
> Where the government or central bank re-pegs the exchange rate at a higher level.

| BOX 13.2 | **EXCHANGE RATE FLUCTUATIONS AND THE PLIGHT OF SMES** |

Small businesses and the perils of international trade

As if trading internationally wasn't hard enough for small businesses! It's bad enough trying to compete with large multinational corporations with all their international connections, trying to find a niche market or to offer some specialist service, perhaps, indeed, to multinationals themselves. What makes things doubly difficult for small business are the fluctuations in exchange rates.

In 2002, when asked to identify the main financial factor causing problems for SMEs, easily topping the list was the high exchange rate of sterling against the euro.

Nearly half of the firms in the sample, 47 per cent, say this is very problematic for their business. In addition, more than a quarter responded to the survey by saying it is quite problematic.

The survey figure shows that sterling's strength against Europe's single currency is a problem for more than seven in ten SMEs. For those who sometimes argue that the SME community is less concerned about sterling's strength than its bigger brothers, this survey shows that is far from being the case. SMEs suffer from the strength of the pound.

'It is certainly the case that this is a problem for us, not just sterling against the euro but also against the dollar,' said Bruno Kilshaw, managing director of London-based Sortex. 'We export 95 per cent of our production and would like to operate on the basis of euro and dollar price lists but often that is impossible because it would squeeze our margins too much.'

'We would love to quote in customers' own currency but often we have to quote in sterling and convert at the time of the contract. It is both the high level of sterling and the instability that give us problems. If there was at least stability, we would be happier.'

Sortex manufactures colour-sorting equipment for the agriculture and food-processing industries, mainly coffee, grain and rice producers. The equipment separates good products from waste.[1]

In October 2000, the exchange rate was £1 = €1.71 (see the chart). In other words, UK exporters had to sell €1.71 worth of exports to the eurozone in order to earn £1. From 2002, sterling began to depreciate significantly against the euro. By mid-2003, the rate was around £1 = €1.43. While this was good news for exporters, it was bad news for importers, who were having to pay more in sterling to purchase things priced in euros. Many SMEs rely on key imported components. A rise in their price may force them to pass this on to their customers, making them less competitive with firms that are less reliant on imported components.

But just as sterling was depreciating against the euro, it was appreciating against the dollar (see the chart). In June 2001, the exchange rate was £1 = $1.41. By February 2004, it was £1 = $1.86. Then despite dipping as low as $1.73 in November 2005, in July 2007 it reached $2.05.

Then in 2008, the pound plummeted. This might have seemed like a golden opportunity for exporters. But with many export markets in recession, SMEs typically

[1] www.themanufacturer.com/content_detail.html?contents_id=2653&t=manufacturer&header=reports#

Definition

Sovereign risk (for business)

The risk that a foreign country's government or central bank will make its policies less favourable. Such policies could involve changes in interest rates or tax regimes, the imposition of foreign exchange controls, or even defaulting on loans or the appropriation of a business's assets.

With growing world inflation and instability from the mid 1960s, it became more and more difficult to maintain fixed exchange rates, and the growing likelihood of devaluations and revaluations fuelled speculation. The system was abandoned in the early 1970s. What followed was a period of managed exchange rates. Under this system, exchange rates are not pegged but allowed to float. However, central banks intervene from time to time to prevent excessive exchange rate fluctuations. This system largely continues to this day.

A further example of a managed exchange rate was in the form of the Exchange Rate Mechanism (ERM), which was the forerunner to the euro. Member countries' currencies were allowed to fluctuate against each other only within specified bands. We return to consider the ERM in more detail in section 13.4.

The problem of sovereign risk

Uncertainty over exchange rates creates problems for businesses that trade or invest internationally. This is part of the broader problem of **sovereign risk**. These are the

Fluctuations in the euro/pound and dollar/pound exchange rates

preferred to keep foreign currency prices much the same and use the lower exchange rate to boost their earnings in sterling – earnings that for many were taking a battering in the recession at home.

 Are SMEs likely to find it easier or harder than large multinational companies to switch the source of their supplies from countries where the pound has depreciated to ones where it has appreciated?

risks associated with locating in or dealing with a particular country. For example, there is the risk that a country may raise business taxes or that its central bank may raise interest rates. Its government might impose new stricter regulatory controls that favour domestic firms, or impose stricter competition or environmental policies. There is a risk that the exchange rate may move adversely or that exchange controls may be imposed. In extreme cases, governments may appropriate a firm's assets or prevent it trading.

The greater the perceived level of sovereign risk of a particular country, the less willing will firms be to trade with it or locate there. Countries are thus under pressure to create a more favourable environment for business and reduce sovereign risk.

Pause for thought

Will the pressure on governments to reduce sovereign risk always lead to better outcomes for the citizens of that country?

THE EURO/DOLLAR SEESAW

What is the impact on business?

For periods of time, world currency markets can be quite peaceful, with only modest changes in exchange rates. But with the ability to move vast sums of money very rapidly from one part of the world to another and from one currency to another, speculators can suddenly turn this relatively peaceful world into one of extreme turmoil – a turmoil that can be very damaging for business.

In this box we examine the huge swings of the euro against the dollar since the euro's launch in 1999.

First the down . . .

On 1 January 1999, the euro was launched and exchanged for $1.16. By October 2000 the euro had fallen to $0.85. What was the cause of this 27 per cent depreciation? The main cause was the growing fear that inflationary pressures were increasing in the USA and that, therefore, the Federal Reserve Bank would have to raise interest rates. At the same time, the eurozone economy was growing only slowly and inflation was well below the 2 per cent ceiling set by the ECB. There was thus pressure on the ECB to cut interest rates.

The speculators were not wrong. As the diagram shows, US interest rates rose, and ECB interest rates initially fell, and when eventually they did rise (in October 1999), the gap between US and ECB interest rates soon widened again.

In addition to the differences in interest rates, a lack of confidence in the recovery of the eurozone economy and a continuing confidence in the US economy encouraged investment to flow to the USA. This inflow of finance (and lack of inflow to the eurozone) further pushed up the dollar relative to the euro.

The low value of the euro meant a high value of the pound relative to the euro. This made it very difficult for UK companies exporting to eurozone countries and also for those competing with imports from the eurozone (which had been made cheaper by the fall in the euro).

In October 2000, with the euro trading at around 85¢, the ECB plus the US Federal Reserve Bank (America's central bank), the Bank of England and the Japanese central bank all intervened on the foreign exchange market to buy euros. This arrested the fall, and helped to restore confidence in the currency. People were more willing to hold euros, knowing that central banks would support it.

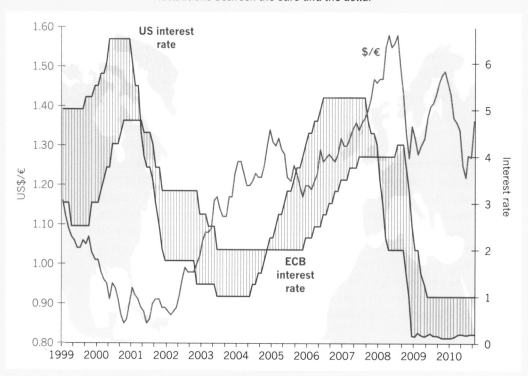

Fluctuations between the euro and the dollar

. . . Then the up

The position completely changed in 2001. With the US economy slowing rapidly and fears of an impending recession, the Federal Reserve Bank reduced interest rates 11 times during the year, from 6.5 per cent at the beginning of the year to 1.75 per cent at the end (see the chart). Although the ECB also cut interest rates, the cuts were relatively modest, from 4.75 at the beginning of the year to 3.25 at the end. With eurozone interest rates now considerably above US rates, the euro began to rise.

In addition, a massive deficit on the US balance of payments current account, and a budget deficit nearing 4 per cent of GDP, made foreign investors reluctant to invest in the American economy. In fact, investors were pulling out of the USA. One estimate suggests that European investors alone sold $70 billion of US assets during 2002. The result of all this was a massive depreciation of the dollar and appreciation of the euro, so that by December 2004 the exchange rate had risen to $1.36, a 60 per cent appreciation since June 2001!

In 2004–5, with the US economy growing strongly again, the Fed raised interest rates several times, from 1 per cent in early 2004 to 5.25 by June 2006. The ECB kept interest rates constant at 2 per cent until early 2006. The result was that the euro depreciated against the dollar in 2005. But then the rise of the euro began again as the US growth slowed and eurozone growth rose and people anticipated a narrowing of the gap between US and eurozone interest rates.

In 2007, worries about the credit crunch in the USA led the Fed to cut interest rates to stave off recession. In August 2007 the US federal funds rate was 5.25 per cent. It was then reduced on several occasions to stand at between 0 and 0.25 per cent by December 2008. The ECB, in contrast, kept the eurozone rate at 4 per cent for the first part of this period and even raised it to 4.25 per cent temporarily in the face of rapidly rising commodity prices. As a result, short-term finance flooded into the eurozone and the euro appreciated again, from $1.37 in mid 2007 to $1.58 in mid 2008.

. . . Then down again

Eventually, in September 2008, with the eurozone on the edge of recession and predictions that ECB would cut interest rates, the euro at last began to fall. It continued to do so as the ECB cut rates. However, with monetary policy in the eurozone remaining tighter than in the USA, the euro began to rise again, only falling once more at the end of 2009 and into 2010 as US growth accelerated and speculators anticipated a tightening of US monetary policy.

With growing worries in 2010 about the level of government deficits and debt in various eurozone countries, such as Greece, Portugal, Spain, Italy and Ireland, the euro fell. Throughout the first part of 2010, the euro fell substantially as fears of debt default mounted and as investors became increasingly reluctant to hold the currency. On January 1, the euro was trading at $1.44. By early June it had fallen to $1.19 – a 17 per cent depreciation.

Then, as support was promised by the ECB and IMF to Greece in return for deficit reduction policies, and similar support could be made available to other eurozone countries with severe deficits, fears subsided and the euro rose again.

What is clear from 11 years of the euro is that interest rate volatility and divergences in interest rates between the USA and the eurozone have been a major factor in exchange rate volatility between the euro and the dollar – itself a cause of uncertainty in international trade and finance.

The effects on business in the eurozone

From 2002 to 2008 the euro appreciated by a massive 82 per cent against the dollar. So has a strong euro been bad for European business? With over 22 per cent of the eurozone's GDP determined by export sales (to non-eurozone countries), and a large part of those exports going to the USA, the dollar/euro exchange rate will invariably be significant.

However, the impact of the euro's rise on eurozone business was tempered by a number of factors:

■ Companies are increasingly using sophisticated management and operational systems, in which value creation is spread throughout a global value chain. Often procurement systems are priced in dollars.
■ Firms hedge their currency risks. Companies typically use forward exchange markets to agree to buy or sell currencies in the future at a price quoted today (this, of course, costs them a premium).
■ Many European companies (BMW is an example) have located some of their production facilities in the USA and use them to help meet demand in the American market. This helps to insulate them from the effects of the rise in the value of the euro.

The result is that most businesses in the eurozone seem to have accommodated the euro's large and rapid rise. Now, we must wait to see how businesses in the eurozone and the USA deal with the decline of the euro and with the impact of the debt problems of various countries in the eurozone.

 Find out what has happened to the euro/dollar exchange rate over the past 12 months. (You can find the data from the Bank of England's Statistical Interactive Database at www.bankofengland.co.uk/ statistics). Explain why the exchange rate has moved the way it has.

Recap

1. The rate of exchange is the rate at which one currency exchanges for another. Rates of exchange are determined by demand and supply in the foreign exchange market. Demand for the domestic currency consists of all the credit items in the balance of payments account. Supply consists of all the debit items.

2. The exchange rate will depreciate (fall) if the demand for the domestic currency falls or the supply increases. These shifts can be caused by a fall in domestic interest rates, higher inflation in the domestic economy than abroad, a rise in domestic incomes relative to incomes abroad, relative investment prospects improving abroad, or the belief by speculators that the exchange rate will fall. The opposite in each case would cause an appreciation (rise).

3. The government can attempt to prevent the rate of exchange from falling by central bank purchases of the domestic currency in the foreign exchange market, either by selling foreign currency reserves or by using foreign loans. Alternatively, the central bank can raise interest rates. The reverse actions can be taken to prevent the rate from rising.

4. Managed exchange rates bring the advantage of greater certainty for the business community, which encourages trade and foreign investment. Also, if successful, they reduce speculation.

5. They bring the disadvantages, however, of not being able to use interest rate changes to meet objectives other than a stable exchange rate, the difficulty in responding to shocks and the danger that speculation will be encouraged if speculators believe that the current exchange rate cannot be maintained.

6. There have been various attempts to manage exchange rates, without them being totally fixed. One example was the Bretton Woods system: a system of pegged exchange rates, but where devaluations or revaluations were allowed from time to time. Another was the ERM, which was the forerunner to the euro. Member countries' currencies were allowed to fluctuate against each other within a band.

7. Businesses face sovereign risk when investing in or trading with other countries. These risks relate to unforeseen exchange rate or interest rate movements, or adverse government policies.

13.3 THE GROWTH OF GLOBAL FINANCIAL FLOWS

Financial interdependence

We live in a highly interdependent world, where every country is affected by the economic performance and government policy of other countries. This was illustrated when the sub-prime market in the USA collapsed and spread like a contagion to cause a worldwide recession.

International trade has grown rapidly for many years (see Figure 12.1 on page 332), but international financial flows have grown much more rapidly. Each day, trillions of dollars of assets are traded across the foreign exchanges. Many of the transactions are short-term financial flows, moving to where interest rates are most favourable or to currencies where the exchange rate is likely to appreciate. Countries have thus become increasingly financially dependent on each other.

Assume that the Federal Reserve Bank (or 'Fed') (America's central bank), worried about rising inflation, decides to raise interest rates. What will be the effect on business in America's trading partners? There are three major effects.

■ If aggregate demand in America falls, so will its expenditure on imports from firms abroad, thus directly affecting businesses exporting to the USA. With a decline in their exports, aggregate demand in these other countries falls.

■ The higher interest rate in the USA will tend to drive up interest rates in other countries. This will depress investment. Again, aggregate demand will tend to fall in these countries.

■ The higher interest rate will attract an inflow of funds from other countries. This will cause the dollar to appreciate relative to other currencies. This will make these other countries' exports to the USA more competitive and imports from the USA relatively more expensive. This will result in an improvement in the current account of the USA's trading partners: their exports rise and imports fall. This represents a *rise* in aggregate demand in these countries – the opposite from the first two effects.

There is a simple conclusion from the above analysis. The larger the financial flows, the more will interest rate changes in one country affect the economies of other countries; the greater will be the financial interdependence.

> **Pause for thought**
>
> *What will be the effect on the UK economy if the European Central Bank cuts interest rates?*

The impact of capital flows

Large movements of capital into and out of countries can have serious consequences for business. Some of these capital flows are for direct investment; some are for buying shares and other financial assets; some are simply short-term speculative deposits. The global supply of dollars available for such purposes has grown by some 18 per cent per year since the early 2000s. One of the main reasons for this has been the huge current account deficits of the USA. This has led to vast outflows of dollars from the USA into the world economy as Americans have effectively paid for their deficit by creating more dollars.

Capital inflows. Capital flows will be attracted to countries where investment prospects are good or for speculative purposes. When they are, the financial account of the balance of payments will improve, causing the exchange rate to appreciate. This appreciation, if set to continue, will attract further capital inflows in anticipation of a speculative gain from a rising exchange rate. As demand for the domestic currency increases, this will push the exchange rate even higher. Domestic currency will be worth more in dollars and other currencies. In other words, a dollar will buy less of the country's currency.

This will make it harder for firms to export. If exports are priced in foreign currency (e.g. dollars) firms must accept less domestic currency; if exports are priced in the domestic currency, the dollar price must rise. At the same time, imports will be cheaper. This makes it harder for domestic business to compete with imports.

For example, in 2006, capital inflows into the Thai economy pushed up the value of the Thai baht by 16 per cent. As Thai businesses struggled to compete, the Bank of Thailand imposed taxes on inward portfolio investment. But this was not the solution. Share prices fell dramatically, and the tax was hastily withdrawn.

So is the answer to cut interest rates? This would reduce capital inflows and help curb the appreciation of the currency. But it would create another problem. The lower interest rates would encourage more borrowing and hence higher credit growth and higher inflation.

Thus large capital inflows leave countries with an uncomfortable choice: either allow the exchange rate to appreciate, thereby damaging business competitiveness, or cut interest rates, thereby causing higher inflation, which could also damage business competitiveness.

Capital outflows. Just as vast amounts of capital can flow into countries, so they can flow out too. The problem especially concerns money on short-term deposit. If a country's exchange rate is likely to fall, speculators will sell the currency before it does fall. This will then bring about the very depreciation that was anticipated.

Such depreciation is likely if the currency had initially appreciated above its long-term equilibrium rate.

Capital controls

Excessive capital flows, whether inward or outward, can be highly destabilising for exchange rates. This makes it very difficult for businesses to plan and can rapidly turn a profitable business into a loss-making one. The result is to undermine confidence in *long-term* investment. And the problem is getting worse as the supply of dollars and other international currencies continues to grow faster than international trade.

So what can be done? Many commentators have called for capital controls. The aim of such controls is not to *prevent* capital flows. After all, capital flows are an important source of financing investment. The aim is to prevent short-term *speculative* flows, based on rumour or herd instinct rather than on economic fundamentals.

Types of control

In what ways, then, can movements of short-term capital be controlled?

Quantitative controls. Here the authorities would restrict the amount of foreign exchange dealing that could take place. Perhaps financial institutions would be allowed to exchange only a certain percentage of their assets. Developed countries and most developing countries have rejected this approach, however, since it is seen to be far too anti-market.

Alternatively, certain types of inflow could be restricted. China, for example, restricts portfolio capital inflows. This has held down its exchange rate, thereby increasing its competitiveness. But this, in turn, has reduced the competitiveness of other countries in Asia and around the world.

A Tobin tax. This is named after James Tobin, who in 1978 advocated the imposition of a small tax of 0.1 to 0.5 per cent on all foreign exchange transactions, or on just capital account transactions.[1] This would discourage destabilising speculation (by making it more expensive) and would thus impose some 'friction' in the foreign exchange markets, making them less volatile.

In the wake of the 2007/8 banking crisis and the highly risky financial dealings that had led to the crisis, some countries have seriously considered introducing Tobin taxes. These, however, would be on speculative financial transactions generally and not just on foreign exchange transactions. For the latest discussion on the use of such taxes, search 'Tobin' in the *Sloman Economics news site* at www.pearsoned.co.uk/sloman. You can also read more about the Tobin tax in the Web Case D.34.

Non-interest-bearing deposits. Here a certain percentage of inflows of finance would have to be deposited with the central bank in a non-interest-bearing account for a set period of time. Chile in the late 1990s used such a system. It required that 30 per cent of all inflows be deposited with Chile's central bank for a year. This clearly amounted to a considerable tax (i.e. in terms of interest sacrificed) and had the effect of discouraging short-term speculative flows. The problem was that it meant that interest rates in Chile had to be higher in order to attract finance.

---

[1] J. Tobin, 'A proposal for international monetary reform', *The Eastern Economic Journal*, 4, no. 3–4, 1978, pp. 153–9

South Korea operates a similar system and in December 2006 it raised the amount that banks must deposit with the central bank in an attempt to stem speculative capital inflows.

Recap

1. Countries are increasingly financially interdependent. Changes in interest rates in one country will affect capital flows to and from other countries, and hence their exchange rates, interest rates and GDP. The credit crunch in the late 2000s is a prime example of this growing interdependence.

2. Capital flows have grown substantially in recent years and can be highly destabilising to an economy.

Capital inflows can cause an appreciation, reducing a country's competitiveness.

3. If capital flows could be constrained, however, exchange rates could be stabilised somewhat. Forms of control include: quantitative controls, a tax on exchange transactions (a Tobin tax) and non-interest-bearing deposits with the central bank of a certain percentage of capital inflows.

ECONOMIC AND MONETARY UNION IN THE EU   13.4

Although countries around the world generally operate a system of floating exchange rates, small countries sometimes peg their exchange rates to the dollar or other major currencies. Also, on a regional basis, there have been attempts to create greater exchange rate stability by countries pegging their exchange rates to each other.

Such a system was introduced in Europe in 1979 as the forerunner of the adoption of the euro. The name given to the EU system was the **exchange rate mechanism (ERM)**. The majority of the EU countries at the time were members. The UK initially chose not to join the ERM, but eventually did so in 1990.

The ERM

Under the ERM, each currency was given a central exchange rate with each of the other member currencies in a grid. However, fluctuations were allowed from the central rate within specified bands. For most countries these bands were set at $\pm 2^1/_4$ per cent. The central rates could be adjusted from time to time by agreement, thus making the ERM an adjustable peg system (see page 365). All the currencies floated jointly with currencies outside the ERM.

In a system of pegged exchange rates, such as the ERM, countries should harmonise their policies to avoid excessive currency misalignments and hence the need for large devaluations or revaluations. There should be a convergence of their economies – they should be at a similar point on the business cycle and have similar inflation rates and interest rates.

Shortly after the UK joined the ERM in 1990, strains began to show. The reunification of Germany involved considerable reconstruction in the eastern part of the country. Financing this reconstruction was causing a growing budget deficit. The Bundesbank (the German central bank) thus felt obliged to maintain high interest rates in order to keep inflation in check. At the same time, the UK was experiencing a massive current account deficit (partly the result of entering the ERM at what many commentators argued was too high an exchange rate). It was thus obliged to raise

Definition

ERM (the exchange rate mechanism)
A semi-fixed system whereby participating EU countries allowed fluctuations against each other's currencies only within agreed bands. Collectively they floated freely against all other currencies.

interest rates in order to protect the pound, despite the fact that the economy was sliding rapidly into recession. The French franc and Italian lira were also perceived to be overvalued, and there were the first signs of worries as to whether their exchange rates within the ERM could be retained.

In September 1992, things reached crisis point. On 'Black Wednesday' (16 September), the UK and Italy were forced to suspend their membership of the ERM; the pound and the lira were floated and depreciated substantially. The following year, in an attempt to rescue the ERM for the remaining countries, EU finance ministers agreed to adopt very wide ±15 per cent bands.

The old ERM appeared to be at an end. The new ±15 per cent bands hardly seemed like a 'pegged' system at all. However, the ERM did not die. Within months, the members were again managing to keep fluctuations within a very narrow range (for most of the time, within ±2^1/$_4$ per cent). The scene was being set for the abandonment of separate currencies and the adoption of a single currency: the euro.

Pause for thought

Under what circumstances may a currency bloc like the ERM (a) help to prevent speculation; (b) aggravate the problem of speculation?

With a single currency there can be no exchange rate fluctuations between the member states, any more than there can be fluctuations between the Californian and New York dollar, or between the English, Scottish and Welsh pound.

Birth of the euro

The Maastricht Treaty was signed in February 1992 and it set out the timetable for the adoption of a single currency in Europe. Before joining the currency union, member states had to meet five convergence criteria, to ensure that the economies of the potential members had sufficiently converged. They were:

- *Inflation*: should be no more than 1^1/$_2$ per cent above the average inflation rate of the three countries in the EU with the lowest inflation.
- *Interest rates*: the rate on long-term government bonds should be no more than 2 per cent above the average of the three countries with the lowest inflation.
- *Budget deficit*: should be no more than 3 per cent of GDP.
- *General government debt*: should be no more than 60 per cent of GDP.
- *Exchange rates*: the currency should have been within the normal ERM bands for at least two years with no realignments or excessive intervention.

In March 1998, the European Commission ruled that 11 of the 15 member states were eligible to proceed to EMU in January 1999. Their economies were deemed to be sufficiently converged in terms of interest rates, inflation rates and government deficits and debt. The UK and Denmark were to exercise their 'opt out', negotiated at Maastricht back in 1992, and Sweden and Greece failed to meet one or more of the convergence criteria.

Definition

Economic and monetary union (EMU)
Where countries adopt a single currency and a single monetary policy. It might also involve other common policies, such as fiscal and supply-side policies.

The single currency, the euro, finally came into being in January 1999 (although notes and coins did not circulate until January 2002). Greece joined the euro in 2001, Slovenia in 2007, Cyprus and Malta in 2008, Slovakia in 2009 and Estonia in 2011, making a total of 17 countries using the euro. Latvia is scheduled to adopt the euro in 2014.

With a single currency, countries must have a single central bank (the European Central Bank for the eurozone) and a common monetary policy, involving common interest rates for all member countries. Such a system is known as **economic and monetary union (EMU)**.

Business and the euro

The adoption of the euro has had a profound effect on business, both within the eurozone and outside it. There are significant advantages in terms of greater certainty and greater inward investment, but also various costs in terms of reduced flexibility for governments in managing their economies.

Advantages of a single currency

Elimination of the costs of converting currencies. With separate currencies in each of the EU countries, costs were incurred each time one currency was exchanged into another. The elimination of these costs was, however, probably the least important benefit from the single currency. The European Commission estimated that the effect was to increase the GDP of the countries concerned by an average of only 0.4 per cent. The gains to countries like the UK, which have well-developed financial markets, would be even smaller.

Increased competition and efficiency. Not only has the single currency eliminated the need to convert one currency into another (a barrier to competition), but it has brought more transparency in pricing, and has put greater downward pressure on prices in high-cost firms and countries. This, of course, does not necessarily favour business, which might find its profits squeezed, but it generally benefits consumers. Although there has been some price convergence across the eurozone, it has not been as extensive as many thought it would be.

Elimination of exchange rate uncertainty (between the members). The removal of exchange rate uncertainty has helped to encourage trade between the eurozone countries. Perhaps more importantly, it has encouraged investment by firms that trade between these countries, given the greater certainty in calculating costs and revenues from such trade.

In times of economic uncertainty, such as the credit crunch of 2008, exchange rate volatility between currencies can be high, as we saw with the experience of sterling. This volatility creates uncertainty, which leads to problems for both trade and investment. However, if the UK had adopted the euro, the uncertainty for the UK in its trade with the eurozone countries would have been eliminated. Furthermore, had the eurozone countries not adopted the euro, they may have experienced significant banking turmoil throughout 2008 and 2009.

Increased inward investment. Investment from the rest of the world is attracted to a eurozone of over 300 million inhabitants, where there is no fear of internal currency movements. By contrast, the UK, by not joining, has found that inward investment has been diverted away to countries within the eurozone. From 1990 to 1998, the UK's share of inward investment to EU countries was nearly 20.4 per cent. From 1999 to 2003, it fell to 12.5 per cent. From 2003 to 2005, however, its share increased substantially as the UK economy grew more strongly than other major economies in the EU. But this was relatively short-lived and since then it has fallen again, with the volatility of sterling acting as a deterrent to investment.

Lower inflation and interest rates. A single monetary policy forces convergence in inflation rates (just as inflation rates are very similar between the different regions *within* a country). With the ECB being independent from short-term political manipulation, this has resulted in a lower average inflation rate in the eurozone countries. This, in turn, has helped to convince markets that the euro will be strong relative to other currencies. The result is lower long-term rates of interest. This, in turn, further encourages investment in the eurozone countries, both by member states and by the rest of the world.

Opposition to EMU

Monetary union has been bitterly opposed, however, by certain groups. Many 'Eurosceptics' see within it a surrender of national political and economic sovereignty. The lack of an independent monetary and exchange rate policy is a serious problem, they argue, if an economy is at all out of harmony with the rest of the Union. For example, if countries such as Italy, Greece and Spain have higher endemic rates of inflation (due, say, to greater cost-push pressures) then how are they to make their goods competitive with the rest of the Union? With separate currencies these countries could allow their currencies to depreciate. For example, throughout 2008, sterling depreciated and this helped to make UK exports more competitive, thereby boosting aggregate demand and helping to soften the recession. With a single currency, however, they could become depressed 'regions' of Europe, with rising unemployment and all the other regional problems of depressed regions *within* a country.

Pause for thought

How might multiplier effects (see page 274) lead to prosperous regions becoming more prosperous and less prosperous regions falling even further behind?

The answer given by proponents of EMU is that it is better to tackle the problem of high inflation in such countries by the disciplines of competition from other EU countries than merely to feed that inflation by keeping separate currencies and allowing continued depreciation, with all the uncertainty that that brings. The critics of EMU, however, argue that cost differences, and hence unemployment, could persist.

Perhaps the most serious criticism is that the same rate of interest must apply to all eurozone countries: the 'one size fits all' criticism. The trouble is that while one country might require a lower rate of interest in order to ward off recession, another might require a higher one to prevent inflation. Furthermore, some countries may be more sensitive to interest changes than others, hence the optimal change in interest rates for one country may represent too much or too little of a change in another.

A further problem for members of a single currency occurs in adjusting to a shock when that shock affects members to different degrees. These are known as **asymmetric shocks**. For example, the banking crisis affected the UK more severely than other countries, given that London is a global financial centre.

This problem, however, should not be overstated. Divergences between economies are often the result of a lack of harmony between countries in their demand-management policies, something that is impossible in the eurozone in the case of monetary policy, and more difficult in the case of fiscal policy, due in part, to the Stability and Growth Pact. Also, many of the shocks that face economies today are global and have similar (albeit not identical) effects on all countries. Adjustment to such shocks would often be better with a single coordinated policy, something that would be much easier with a single currency and a single central bank.

Even when shocks are uniformly felt in the member states, however, there is still the problem that policies adopted centrally will have different impacts on each country. For example, in the UK, a large proportion of borrowing is at variable interest rates. In Germany, by contrast, much is at fixed rates. Thus if the UK adopted the euro and the ECB were to raise interest rates, the contractionary effects would be felt disproportionately in the UK. Of course, were this balance to change – and there is some evidence that types of borrowing are becoming more uniform across the EU – this problem would diminish.

Definition

Asymmetric shocks
Shocks (such as an oil price increase or a recession in another part of the world) that have different-sized effects on different industries, regions or countries.

The problem for economists is that the issue of monetary union is a very emotive one. 'Europhiles' often see monetary union as a vital element in their vision of a united Europe. Many Eurosceptics, however, see EMU as a surrender of sovereignty and a threat to nationhood. In such an environment, a calm assessment of the arguments and evidence is very difficult.

The UK Labour government specified five convergence criteria that would have be met before it would put the question of UK adoption of the euro to the electorate in a referendum. These are examined in Web Case D.38. However, with the Coalition government in the UK led by David Cameron, there is now no possibility at all of the UK joining the euro.

Recap

1. One means of achieving greater currency stability is for a group of countries to peg their internal exchange rates and yet float jointly with the rest of the world. The exchange rate mechanism of the EU (ERM) was an example. This was seen as an important first stage on the road to complete economic and monetary union (EMU) in the EU.

2. The euro was born on 1 January 1999 with euro notes and coins introduced in 2002. There are now 16 countries using the euro.

3. The advantages claimed for EMU are that it eliminates the costs of converting currencies

and the uncertainties associated with possible changes in former inter-EU exchange rates. This encourages more investment, both inward and by domestic firms, and greater trade between EU countries.

4. Critics, however, claim that the loss of independence in policy making might make adjustment to domestic economic problems more difficult, especially when these problems diverge from those of other members. A single monetary policy is claimed to be inappropriate for dealing with asymmetric shocks.

INTERNATIONAL ECONOMIC POLICY: MANAGING THE GLOBAL ECONOMY

13.5

Attempts to coordinate global business activity

There is an old saying: 'If America sneezes, the rest of the world catches a cold.' Viruses of a similar nature regularly infect the world economy. A dramatic example was the global banking crisis of 2007/8. What started largely as a problem of risky mortgage loans in the USA ('sub-prime' mortgages) rapidly became a global banking crisis as these 'toxic' debts were bundled up with other debt and sold as securities around the world. Banks were unwilling to lend to each other as a result and a global policy response was needed. This began in October 2008 when governments across the world initially injected some $2 trillion of extra capital into banks.

For many years now the leaders of the seven or eight major industrialised countries – the USA, Japan, Germany, France, the UK, Italy, Canada and sometimes Russia – have met once a year (and more frequently if felt necessary) at an economic summit conference. More recently there have been similar meetings of the much broader G20 group, which also includes major developing countries, such as China and India. Top of the agenda in many of these meetings has been how to achieve a **harmonisation** of economic policies between nations to allow worldwide economic growth without major currency fluctuations. In other words, it is important that all the major countries are pursuing consistent policies aiming at common international goals.

Definition

International harmonisation of economic policies
Where countries attempt to coordinate their macroeconomic policies so as to achieve common goals.

BOX 13.4 | **A WORLDWIDE EPIDEMIC**

Global answers to global problems?

We don't have to look far to see how much economic and financial interdependence affects our daily lives. As you walk down the street to the supermarket, many of the passing cars originate overseas or perhaps were built here by foreign-owned companies. You look up and the plane flying overhead is taking passengers to every corner of the world for both business and pleasure. As you enter the supermarket you see an array of goods from all over the world. Clearly, interdependence through trade connects economies. The late 2000s have helped to demonstrate just how interdependent financial systems and financial institutions have become. Financial products have a passport to travel and they do!

Growth rates across the world have converged in recent decades, especially in the late 2000s. This is consistent with the idea of an international business cycle. The implication of this is that countries will tend to share common problems and concerns at the same time. At one time, the most pressing problem may be world inflationary pressures; at another time, it may be a world recession. Increasing economic and financial interdependence means that problems in one part of the world rapidly spread to other parts. Just look at what happened when the US sub-prime mortgage market collapsed. America's illness turned into the world's flu!

But who should dish out the medicine? How potent can the medicine of national governments be in isolation? What role is there for coordinated monetary and fiscal policies and does it require stronger international institutions to deal with world problems?

Iceland's cold

The decline in output in Iceland in 2009, at nearly 12 per cent, was especially stark. The country had been especially badly hit by the global financial crisis.

An aggressive strategy of credit expansion had seen the liabilities of the three largest Icelandic banks rise from 100 per cent of GDP in 2004 to 923 per cent in 2007. Some of the funds from this expansion came from the inter-bank market but also from deposits overseas in subsidiaries of these banks in the Nordic countries and the UK. When the credit crunch hit, they found it increasingly difficult to roll over loans on the inter-bank market. What is more, the sheer scale of the banks' expansion made it virtually impossible for Iceland's central bank to guarantee repayments of the loans.

The result was that four of its largest banks were nationalised and run by Iceland's Financial Supervisory Authority.

A Greek Tragedy

Greece has been struggling with the burden of a huge budget deficit for some years and with the credit crunch of 2008 its public sector deficit increased to stand at 13.6 per cent of GDP by the start of 2010. This is over four times higher than EU rules allow. The cost to Greece of servicing the debt is about 11.6 per cent and in early 2010 the government estimated that it would need to borrow €53bn to cover budget shortfalls. Greece, like many other countries, also experienced rising unemployment rates to over 10 per cent.

Austerity measures, as part of an IMF and EU rescue package, will aim to reduce this deficit to 8.1 per cent of GDP by the end of 2010 and to less than 3 per cent of GDP by 2014. This will be achieved through a variety of spending cuts and tax rises and is the price that Greece has had to pay to receive a £95 billion bail-out. However, the costs of the austerity measures in terms of disposable income and unemployment have been high and there have been widespread strikes by public sector workers.

But how can policy harmonisation be achieved? If there are significant domestic differences between the major economies, there is likely to be conflict, not harmony. For example, if one group of countries, say the USA and Japan, are worried about tackling recession, they may be unwilling to respond to demands from other countries for fiscal restraint to tackle the problem of large public sector deficits and debts. What is more, speculators, seeing differences between countries, are likely to exaggerate them by their actions, causing large changes in exchange rates. The G8/G20 countries have therefore sought to achieve greater **convergence** of their economies. However, although convergence may be a goal of policy, in practice it has proved elusive.

Because of a lack of convergence, there are serious difficulties in achieving international policy harmonisation:

- Countries' budget deficits and accumulated government debt differ substantially as a proportion of their GDP. This puts very different pressures on the interest rates necessary to service these debts. In 2010, the UK had a budget deficit of

Definition

Convergence of economies

When countries achieve similar levels of growth, inflation, budget deficits as a percentage of GDP, balance of payments. etc.

The debt crisis, however, is not just confined to Greece. The Spanish economy has come under scrutiny with a deficit, in 2010, of 11.2 per cent of GDP and unemployment of more than 20 per cent. Other countries struggling with their debts in Europe include Ireland (14.3 per cent of GDP) and Portugal (9.4 per cent of GDP), not to mention the UK (11.5 per cent of GDP). There were also concerns of a domino effect, which led to stock markets crashing around the world. The FTSE100 index fell by 13.5 per cent between 16 April and 7 May 2010. At the same time, the Dow Jones index fell by 8.6 per cent and in Tokyo, the Nikkei fell by 7.6 per cent.

IMF to the rescue?

In November 2008, the International Monetary Fund's executive board approved a $2.1 billion loan to Iceland to support an economic recovery programme. An initial payment of $827 million was made with subsequent payments to be spread over time, subject to IMF quarterly reviews of the recovery programme.

But what is the IMF? And what does it do? Well, it is a 'specialised agency' of the United Nations and is financed by its 185 member countries (as of 2009). The role of the IMF is to ensure macroeconomic stability – such as in the Iceland case – and to foster global growth. It also works with developing nations to alleviate poverty and to achieve economic stability. To do this it provides countries with loans.

The IMF has not been without controversy, however. Conditions attached to loans have often been very harsh, especially for some of the most indebted developing countries.

The global economic and financial crisis provided the IMF with a challenge: which countries to support with a limited budget? For instance, at the same time as its agreement with Iceland, the IMF was approving a loan of $15.7 billion to Hungary, a member country of the European Union since 2004, which was struggling to meet external debt obligations and finance its general government deficit (3.4 per cent of GDP in 2008). Another country receiving support was Latvia, the EU country with the sharpest rate of economic decline in 2009 (13.1 per cent).

More recently, the IMF has been involved in crisis talks with finance ministers in Europe. A major package of measures worth €750 billion has been set aside to support the eurozone. €250 billion came from the IMF, as part of a European Financial Stabilisation Mechanism. However, the majority of the package came from eurozone countries (€440 billion) and a further €60 billion came from EU funds, contributed to by all 27 members of the EU, to support eurozone countries that are in trouble.

Strengthening the IMF

World leaders meeting as part of the G20 in London in April 2009 announced the need to strengthen global financial institutions. They agreed that the resources available to the IMF should be trebled to $750 billion. They also agreed that the IMF would work with a new Financial Stability Board (FSB), made up, among others, of the G20 countries and the European Commission, so as to help in identifying potential economic and financial risks. Essentially, the G20 countries were looking for a better 'early warning system' to meet some of the challenges of an increasingly interdependent world.

 Do you see any problems arising from a strengthening of global economic and financial institutions?

around 12 per cent of GDP. This compares with 10 per cent for the USA, 8 per cent for France, 7 per cent for Japan and 4 per cent for Germany.

- Harmonising rates of monetary growth or inflation targets would involve letting interest rates fluctuate with the demand for money. Without convergence in the demand for money, interest rate fluctuations could be severe.

- Harmonising interest rates would involve abandoning money, inflation or exchange rate targets (unless interest rate 'harmonisation' meant adjusting interest rates so as to maintain money or inflation targets or a given exchange rate).

- Countries have different internal structural relationships. A lack of convergence here means that countries with higher endemic *cost* inflation would require higher interest rates and higher unemployment if international inflation rates were to be harmonised, or higher inflation if interest rates were to be harmonised.

- Countries have different rates of productivity increase, product development, investment and market penetration. A lack of convergence here means that the growth in exports (relative to imports) will differ for any given level of inflation or growth.

■ Countries may be very unwilling to change their domestic policies to fall into line with other countries. They may prefer the other countries to fall into line with them!

If any one of the four – interest rates, growth rates, inflation rates or current account balance of payments – could be harmonised across countries, it is likely that the other three would then not be harmonised.

Total convergence and thus total harmonisation may not be possible. Nevertheless most governments favour some movement in that direction; some is better than none.

The problem of speculation

One important lesson of recent years is that concerted speculation has become virtually unstoppable. This was made clear by the expulsion of the UK and Italy from the ERM in 1992, a dramatic fall of the Mexican peso and a rise of the yen in 1995, the collapse of various South-East Asian currencies (see Web Case D.26) and the Russian rouble in 1997–8 and the collapse of the Argentinean peso in 2002 (see Web Case D.37), the fall in the pound in 2008 and again in 2010 and the fall of the euro in 2010. In comparison with the vast amounts of short-term finance flowing across the foreign exchanges each day, the reserves of central banks seem trivial.

If there is a consensus in the markets that a currency will depreciate, there is little that central banks can do. For example, if there were a 50 per cent chance of a 10 per cent depreciation in the next week, then selling that currency now would yield an 'expected' return of just over 5 per cent for the week (i.e. 50 per cent of 10 per cent), equivalent to more than 5000 per cent at an annual rate!

For this reason, many commentators have argued that there are only two types of exchange rate system that can work over the long term. The first is a completely free-floating exchange rate, with no attempt by the central bank to support the exchange rate. With no intervention, there is no problem of a shortage of reserves!

The second is to share a common currency with other countries – to join a common currency area, such as the eurozone, and let the common currency float freely. The country would give up independence in its monetary policy, but at least there would be no problem of exchange rate instability within the currency area. A similar alternative is to adopt a major currency of another country, such as the US dollar or the euro. Many smaller states have done this. For example, Kosovo and Montenegro have adopted the euro and Ecuador has adopted the US dollar.

Recap

1. Currency fluctuations can be lessened if countries harmonise their economic policies. Ideally this would involve achieving common growth rates, inflation rates, balance of payments (as a percentage of GDP) and interest rates. The attempt to harmonise one of these goals, however, may bring conflicts with one of the other goals.

2. Leaders of the G8 or G20 countries meet regularly to discuss ways of harmonising their policies.

Usually, however, domestic issues are more important to the leaders than international ones, and frequently they pursue policies that are not in the interests of the other countries.

3. Many economists argue that, with the huge flows of short-term finance across the foreign exchanges, governments are forced to adopt one of two extreme forms of exchange rate regime: free floating or being a member of a currency union.

POSTSCRIPT: IS GLOBALISATION A 'GOOD THING'?

We have come across many aspects of globalisation throughout this book, from the operation of international commodity markets (Chapter 2), to global fashions (Chapter 3), to the growth of multinational companies (Chapter 7), to the growth of international trade and financial flows (Chapter 12 and this chapter). Here we reflect on this process and ask whether the world benefits from this growing interdependence.

The supporters

Supporters of globalisation argue that it has massive potential to benefit the entire global economy. With freer trade, greater FDI and greater competition, countries and businesses within them are encouraged to think, plan and act globally. Technology spreads faster; countries specialise in particular products and processes and thereby exploit their core competitive advantages.

Both rich and poor, it is argued, benefit from such a process. Politically, globalisation brings us closer together. Political ties help stabilise relationships and offer the opportunity for countries to discuss their differences. However imperfect the current global political system might be, the alternative of independent nations is seen as potentially far worse. The globalisation of culture is also seen as beneficial, as a world of experience is opened, whether in respect to our holiday destinations, or the food we eat, or the music we listen to, or the TV programmes we watch.

Supporters of globalisation recognise that not all countries benefit equally from globalisation; those that have wealth will, as always, possess more opportunity to benefit from the globalisation process, whether from lower prices, global political agreements or cultural experience. However, long term, supporters of globalisation see it as ultimately being for the benefit of all – rich and poor alike.

The critics

Critics of globalisation argue that it contributes to growing inequality and further impoverishes poor nations. As an economic philosophy, globalisation allows multinational corporations, based largely in the USA, Europe and Japan, to exploit their dominant position in foreign markets. Without effective competition in these markets such companies are able to pursue profit with few constraints.

By 'exploiting' low-wage labour, companies are able to compete more effectively on world markets. As competitive pressures intensify and companies seek to cut costs further, this can put downward pressure on such wages – something that workers will find difficulty in resisting, given the monopsony power of multinational employers.

In political terms, critics of globalisation see the world being dominated by big business. As we saw in Table 7.1 on page 186, many multinational companies have a turnover larger than the GDP of whole countries. This gives them huge power in their dealings with such countries and in imposing conditions on them, whether in terms of generous tax regimes, privileged access to markets or limited rights for workers. Multinationals also put pressure on their home governments in America, Europe or Japan to promote their interests in their dealings with other countries, thereby heightening the domination of rich countries over the poor.

Critics are no less damning of the cultural aspects of globalisation. They see the world dominated by multinational brands, western fashion, music and TV. Rather than globalisation fostering a mix of cultural expression, critics suggest that cultural differences are being replaced by the dominant (American or Western) culture of the day.

The above views represent the extremes, and to a greater or lesser degree both have elements of truth in them. The impact of globalisation on different groups is not even, and never will be. However, to suggest that 'big business rules' is also an exaggeration. Clearly big business is influential, but it is a question of degree. Influence will invariably fluctuate over time, between events, and between and within countries.

At present the momentum within the global economy is for barriers to come down. In many global markets, competition rather than monopoly power is becoming the dominant force. This is having profound effects on both multinational business and the peoples of the world.

Recap

1. Supporters of globalisation point to its potential to lead to faster growth and greater efficiency through trade, competition and investment. It also has the potential to draw the world closer together politically.

2. Critics of globalisation argue that it contributes to growing inequality and further impoverishes poor nations. It also erodes national cultures and can have adverse environmental consequences.

QUESTIONS

1. The following are the items in the UK's 2008 balance of payments:

	£ billions
Exports of goods	252.1
Imports of goods	345.2
Exports of services	170.8
Imports of services	115.5
Net income flows	+28.0
Net current transfers	−14.0
Net capital transfers	+3.2
Direct investment	−37.8
Portfolio investment	+324.1
Other financial flows	−261.8
Reserves	+1.3

Calculate the following: (a) the balance on trade in goods; (b) the balance on trade in goods and services; (c) the balance of payments on current account; (d) the financial account balance; (e) the total current plus capital plus financial account balance; (f) net errors and omissions.

Compare your answers with the UK's 2009 balance of payments, which can be found in Table 13.1. What has happened to the UK's balance of payments over the past year?

2. Assume that there is a free-floating exchange rate. Will the following cause the exchange rate to appreciate or depreciate? In each case you should consider whether there is a shift in the demand or supply curves of sterling (or both) and which way the curve(s) shift(s).

(a) More video recorders are imported from Japan.
Demand curve *shifts left/shifts right/does not shift*.
Supply curve *shifts left/shifts right/does not shift*.
Exchange rate *appreciates/depreciates*.
(b) UK interest rates rise relative to those abroad.
Demand curve *shifts left/shifts right/does not shift*.
Supply curve *shifts left/shifts right/does not shift*.
Exchange rate *appreciates/depreciates*.
(c) The UK experiences a higher rate of inflation than other countries.
Demand curve *shifts left/shifts right/does not shift*.
Supply curve *shifts left/shifts right/does not shift*.
Exchange rate *appreciates/depreciates*.
(d) Speculators believe that the rate of exchange will appreciate.
Demand curve *shifts left/shifts right/does not shift*.
Supply curve *shifts left/shifts right/does not shift*.
Exchange rate *appreciates/depreciates*.

3. What is the relationship between the balance of payments and the rate of exchange?

4. Consider the argument that in the modern world of large-scale short-term international financial movements, the ability of individual countries to affect their exchange rate is very limited.

5. Why may capital inflows damage the international competitiveness of a country's businesses?

6. What adverse effects on the domestic economy may follow from (a) a depreciation of the exchange rate and (b) an appreciation of the exchange rate?

7. What are the causes of exchange-rate volatility? Have these problems become greater or lesser in the past 10 years? Explain why.

8. Did the exchange rate difficulties experienced by countries under the ERM strengthen or weaken the arguments for progressing to a single European currency?

9. By what means would a depressed country in an economic union with a single currency be able to recover? Would the market provide a satisfactory solution or would (union) government intervention be necessary and, if so, what form would the intervention take?

10. Assume that just some of the members of a common market like the EU adopt full economic and monetary union, including a common currency. What are the advantages and disadvantages to those members joining the full EMU and to those not joining?

11. What are the economic (as opposed to political) difficulties in achieving an international harmonisation of economic policies so as to avoid damaging currency fluctuations?

12. To what extent can international negotiations over economic policy be seen as a game of strategy? Are there any parallels between the behaviour of countries and the behaviour of oligopolies?

13. Who are the winners and losers from globalisation?

Additional Part D case studies on the *Economics and the Business Environment* website (www.pearsoned.co.uk/sloman)

D.1 **Output gaps.** A way of measuring how far actual output falls short of long-term trend output.

D.2 **The costs of economic growth.** Why economic growth may not be an unmixed blessing.

D.3 **Comparing national income statistics.** The importance of taking the purchasing power of local currencies into account.

D.4 **John Maynard Keynes (1883–1946).** A profile of the great economist.

D.5 **The attributes of money.** What makes something, such as metal, paper or electronic records, suitable as money?

D.6 **UK monetary aggregates.** This examines the various measures of money supply in the UK using both UK and eurozone monetary aggregates.

D.7 **Changes in the banking industry.** This case study looks at mergers and diversification in the banking industry.

D.8 **Technology and unemployment.** Does technological progress destroy jobs?

D.9 **The national debt.** This explores the question of whether it matters if a country has a high national debt.

D.10 **Trends in public expenditure.** This case examines attempts to control public expenditure in the UK and relates them to the crowding-out debate.

D.11 **The crowding-out effect.** The circumstances in which an increase in public expenditure can replace private expenditure.

D.12 **Managing the US economy.** The use of active fiscal and monetary policy in 2001 and 2002 to stimulate the US economy.

D.13 **Discretionary fiscal policy in Japan.** How the Japanese government used fiscal policy on various occasions throughout the 1990s and early 2000s in an attempt to bring the economy out of recession.

▶

D.14 **The daily operation of monetary policy.** What practical steps does the Bank of England take to ensure that the market rate of interest is its own chosen rate?

D.15 **Monetary policy in the eurozone.** This looks at how interest rates are set in the eurozone and what rules govern the behaviour of the European Central Bank.

D.16 **Central banking and monetary policy in the USA.** This case examines how the Fed conducts monetary policy.

D.17 **A new approach to industrial policy.** This looks at changes in the approach to industrial policy around the world.

D.18 **Assessing PFI.** Has this been the perfect solution to funding investment for the public sector without raising taxes?

D.19 **Welfare to work.** An examination of the policy of the UK Labour government whereby welfare payments are designed to encourage people into employment.

D.20 **Fallacious arguments for restricting trade.** Some of the more common mistaken arguments for protection.

D.21 **Free trade and the environment.** Do whales, the rainforests and the atmosphere gain from free trade?

D.22 **The Uruguay Round.** An examination of the negotiations that led to substantial cuts in trade barriers.

D.23 **The Doha Development Agenda.** This looks at the latest WTO trade round.

D.24 **The Battle of Seattle.** This looks at the protests against the WTO at Seattle in November 1999 and considers the arguments for and against the free trade policies of the WTO.

D.25 **The World Trade Organisation.** This looks at the various opportunities and threats posed by this major international organisation.

D.26 **Crisis in South-East Asia.** Causes of the severe recession in many South-East Asian countries in 1997/8.

D.27 **A miracle gone wrong?** Lessons from East Asia crisis of 1997/8.

D.28 **Steel barriers.** The use by the USA of tariff protection for its steel industry and the effects of threats of retaliation by the EU.

D.29 **The Internal Market Scoreboard.** Keeping a tally on progress to a true single market in the EU.

D.30 **The UK's balance of payments deficit.** An examination of the UK's persistent trade and current account deficits.

D.31 **A high exchange rate.** This case looks at whether a high exchange rate is necessarily bad news for exporters.

D.32 **Dealing in foreign exchange.** The operation of international currency markets.

D.33 **Using interest rates to control both aggregate demand and the exchange rate.** A problem of one instrument and two targets.

D.34 **The Tobin tax.** A possible means of reducing exchange rate fluctuations.

D.35 **Currency turmoil in the 1990s.** Two examples of speculative attacks on currencies: first on the Mexican peso in 1995; then on the Thai baht in 1997.

D.36 **Argentina in crisis.** An examination of the collapse of the Argentinean economy in 2001/2.

D.37 **The UK Labour government's convergence criteria for euro membership.** An examination of the five tests set by the previous UK government that would have had to have been passed before the question of euro membership would be put to the electorate in a referendum.

D.38 **Attempts at harmonisation.** A look at the meetings of the G7 economies where they attempt to come to agreement on means of achieving stable and sustained worldwide economic growth.

D.39 **High oil prices.** What is their effect on the world economy?

D.40 **Optimal currency areas.** What's the best size for a single currency area such as the eurozone?

D.41 **The Credit Crunch.** An examination of the causes, costs and the main effects of the global financial crisis.

D.42 **Quantitative easing.** A look at the monetary policy used during the global recession, with particular focus on the manipulation of the money supply.

Websites relevant to Part D

Numbers and sections refer to websites listed in the Web Appendix and hotlinked from this book's website at **www.pearsoned.co.uk/sloman/**

- For news articles relevant to Part D, see the *Economics News Articles* link from the book's website.

- For general news on macroeconomic issues, both national and international, see websites in section A, and particularly A1–5, 7–9. For general news on money, banking and interest rates, see again A1–5, 7–9 and also 20–22, 25, 26, 35, 36, 37. For all of Part D, see also links to macroeconomic and financial news in A41. See also links to newspapers worldwide in A38, 43 and 44.

- For macroeconomic data, see links in B1; also see B35. For UK data, see B3 and 34. For EU data, see G1 > *The Statistical Annex*. For US data, see B25 and the *Data* section of B17. For international data, see B15, 21, 24, 31, 33, 35. For links to data sets, see B28, 33.

- For national income statistics for the UK (Appendix), see B1, *1. National Statistics* > the fourth link > *Economy* > *United Kingdom Economic Accounts* and *United Kingdom National Accounts – The Blue Book*.

- For data on UK unemployment, see B1, *1. National Statistics* > the fourth link > *Labour Market* > *Labour Market Statistics*. For International data on unemployment, see B1 (sites 5 and 6); G1; H3 and 5.

- For monetary and financial data (including data for money supply and interest rates), see section F and particularly F2. Note that you can link to central banks worldwide from site F17. See also the links in B1.

- For information on UK fiscal policy and government borrowing, see sites E30, 36; F2. See also sites A1–9 at Budget time. For fiscal policy in the eurozone, see *Public Finances in EMU* in G1.

- Site I7 contains links to fiscal policy: go to *Macroeconomics > Macroeconomic Policy > Taxes and Taxation*.

- For links to sites on money and monetary policy, see the *Financial Economics* sections in I4, 7, 13, 17.

- For demand-side policy in the UK, see the latest Budget Report (e.g. section on maintaining macroeconomic stability) at site E30.

- For inflation targeting in the UK, the eurozone and worldwide see sites F1, 6 and 11.

- For the current approach to UK supply-side policy, see the latest Budget Report (e.g. sections on productivity and training) at site E30. See also sites E5 and 9.

- For information on training in the UK and Europe, see sites D9; E5; G5, 14.

- For support for a market-orientated approach to supply-side policy see C17 and E34.

- For general news on business in the international environment, see websites in section A, and particularly A1–5, 7–9, 23, 24, 25, 36, 37. See also links to newspapers worldwide in A38, 43 and 44, and the news search feature in Google at A41.

- For international data on imports and exports, see site H16 > *Resources* > *Trade statistics*.

- For international data on balance of payments and exchange rates, see *World Economic Outlook* in H4 and OECD *Economic Outlook* in B21 (also in section 6 of B1). See also the trade topic in I14.

- For international data on foreign direct investment (FDI), see H24.

- For details of individual countries' balance of payments, see B32 and 35.

- For UK data on trade and the balance of payments, see B1, *1. National Statistics* > the fourth link > *Compendia and Reference* > *Annual Abstract* (Latest year) > *External trade and investment*. See also see B1, *1. National Statistics* > the fourth link > *Economy* > *United Kingdom Balance of Payments – the Pink Book*. See also B3, 34; F2. For EU data, see G1 > *The Statistical Annex* > *Foreign trade and current balance*.

- For exchange rates, see F2 > *International Database* > *Interest and Exchange Rates*. You can then choose the currencies and the dates to customise an Excel file. See also A3; B34; F6, 8.

- For discussion papers on trade and the balance of payments, see H4 and 7.

- For trade disputes see H16.

- For information on NAFTA and other trade blocs, see H20–23.

- For various pressure groups critical of the effects of free trade and globalisation, see H12–14.

- Site I7 contains links to various topics in *International Economics* (*International trade, International agreements, Economic cooperation and EU Economics*) and to *Trade and trade policy* in *Economic Development*. Site I4 has links to *International economics* and *Development economics*. Site I17 has links to *International economics, Trade policy* and *Development economics*.

- For information on international harmonisation, see sites H4 and 5.

- For student resources relevant to Part D, see sites C1–7, 9, 10, 12, 13, 19. See also '2nd floor – economic policy' in site D1. See also the Labour market reforms simulation in D3.

Web appendix

All the following websites can be accessed from the home page of this book's own website (**www.pearsoned.co.uk/sloman**). When you enter the site, click on the **Hotlinks** button. You will find all the following sites listed. Click on the one you want and the 'hotlink' will take you straight to it.

The sections and numbers below refer to the ones used in the web references at the end of each Part of the text. Thus, if the reference were to A21, this would refer to the Money World site.

GENERAL NEWS SOURCES (A)

As the title of this section implies, websites here can be used for finding material on current news issues or tapping into news archives. Most archives are offered free of charge. However, some do require you to register. As well as key UK and American sources, you will also notice some slightly different places from where you can get your news, such as the St Petersburg Times and Kyodo News (from Japan). Check out sites number 38. *My Virtual Newspaper*, 43. *Guardian World News Guide* and 44. *Onlinenewspapers* for links to newspapers across the world. Try searching for an article on a particular topic by using site number 41. *Google News Search*.

1. BBC news
2. The Economist
3. The Financial Times
4. The Guardian
5. The Independent
6. ITN
7. The Observer
8. The Telegraph
9. The Times, Sunday Times
10. The New York Times
11. Fortune
12. Time Magazine
13. The Washington Post
14. Moscow Times (English)
15. St Petersburg Times (English)
16. Straits Times
17. New Straits Times
18. The Scotsman
19. The Herald
20. Euromoney
21. AWD Moneyextra
22. Market News International
23. BusinessWeek online
24. Ananova
25. CNNMoney
26. Wall Street Journal
27. Asia related news
28. allAfrica.com
29. Greek News Sources (English)
30. Kyodo News: Japan (English)
31. RFE/RL NewsLine
32. The Australian
33. Sydney Morning Herald
34. Japan Times
35. Reuters
36. Bloomberg

37. David Smith's Economics UK.com
38. Refdesk (links to a whole range of news sources)
39. Newspapers on World Wide Web
40. Yahoo News Search
41. Google News Search
42. Moreover RSS Feeds
43. Guardian World News Guide
44. Onlinenewspapers

(B) SOURCES OF ECONOMIC AND BUSINESS DATA

Using websites to find up-to-date data is of immense value to the economist. The data sources below offer you a range of specialist and non-specialist data information. Universities have free access to the MIMAS and ESDS sites, which are huge databases of statistics. Site 34 in this set, the Treasury Pocket Data Bank, is a very useful source of key UK and world statistics, and is updated monthly. It downloads as an Excel file.

1. Economics Network gateway to economic data
2. Biz/ed Gateway to economic and company data
3. National Statistics
4. Data Archive (Essex)
5. Bank of England statistical database
6. Economic Resources (About)
7. Nationwide House Prices Site
8. House Web (data on housing market)
9. Incomes Data Services
10. HBOS house price data
11. Land Registry (house prices, etc.)
12. Manchester Information and Associated Services (MIMAS)
13. Global Financial Data
14. PACIFIC International trade and business reference page
15. Economagic
16. Groningen Growth and Development Centre
17. Resources for economists on the Internet
18. Joseph Rowntree Foundation
19. Intute: Social Sciences (Economics)
20. Slavic and East European Resources
21. OECD Statistics
22. CIA world statistics site
23. UN Millennium Country Profiles
24. World Bank statistics
25. Federal Reserve Bank of St. Louis, US economic data sets (FRED)
26. Ministry of International Trade and Industry (Japan)
27. Financial data from Yahoo
28. Nanyang Technological University, Singapore: Statistical Data Locators
29. Davidson Data Center and Network (DDCN)
30. Oanda Currency Converter
31. World Economic Outlook Database (IMF)
32. Economist Country Briefings
33. OFFSTATS links to data sets
34. Treasury Pocket Data Bank (source of UK and world economic data)
35. Economic and Social Data Service (ESDS)
36. The Official Yearbook of the UK
37. Nationmaster
38. European Economy Statistical Annex
39. Business and Consumer Surveys (all EU countries)
40. Gapminder
41. WebEc economics data
42. WTO International trade statistics database
43. UNCTAD trade, investment and development statistics

SITES FOR STUDENTS AND TEACHERS OF ECONOMICS   (C)

The following websites offer useful ideas and resources to those who are studying or teaching economics. It is worth browsing through some just to see what is on offer. Try out the first four sites, for starters. The Internet Economist is a very helpful tutorial for economics students on using the Internet.

1. Economics Network of the UK Higher Education Academy
2. Biz/ed
3. Ecedweb
4. Econ Links: student resources
5. Economics and Business Education Association
6. Tutor2U
7. Economics America
8. Internet for Economics (tutorial on using the Web)
9. Oxford School of Learning
10. Teaching resources for economists
11. Resources for University Teachers of Economics (University of Melbourne)
12. Federal Reserve Bank of San Francisco: Economics Education
13. Federal Reserve Bank of Minneapolis Economic Education
14. WebEc resources
15. BibEc papers
16. Online Opinion (Economics)
17. The Idea Channel
18. History of Economic Thought
19. Resources For Economists on the Internet (RFE)
20. Classroom Expernomics
21. VCE Economics (Economics teaching resources – Australian)
22. Why Study Economics?
23. JokEc: economics jokes!
24. Veconlab: Charles Holt's classroom experiments

ECONOMIC MODELS AND SIMULATIONS   (D)

Economic modelling is an important aspect of economic analysis. There are a number of sites that offer access to a model for you to use, e.g. Virtual economy (where you can play being Chancellor of the Exchequer). Using such models can be a useful way of finding out how economic theory works within an environment that claims to reflect reality.

1. Virtual economy
2. Virtual factory
3. Virtual Learning Arcade
4. About.com Economics
5. Classroom experiments, Internet experiments and Internet simulations
6. *Economics Network Handbook*, chapter on simulations, games and role-play
7. Estima (statistical analysis)
8. SPSS (statistical analysis)
9. National Institute of Economic and Social Research
10. Software available on the Economics Network site
11. RFE Software
12. Virtual Chancellor
13. Veconlab: Charles Holt's classroom experiments
14. EconPort
15. Denise Hazlett's Classroom Experiments in Macroeconomics
16. Games Economists Play

17. Finance and Economics Experimental Laboratory at Exeter (FEELE)
18. Classroom Expernomics
19. *The Economics Network's Guide to Classroom Experiments and Games*

(E) UK GOVERNMENT AND UK ORGANISATIONS' SITES

If you want to see what a government department is up to, then look no further than the list below. Government departments' websites are an excellent source of information and data. They are particularly good at offering information on current legislation and policy initiatives.

1. Gateway site (DirectGov)
2. Communities and Local Government
3. Central Office of Information
4. Competition Commission
5. Department for Education and Skills
6. Department for International Development
7. Department for Transport
8. Department of Health
9. Department for Work and Pensions
10. Department of Trade and Industry (DTI)
11. Environment Agency
12. UK euro information site
13. Low Pay Commission
14. Department for Environment, Food and Rural Affairs (DEFRA)
15. Office of Communications (Ofcom)
16. Office of Gas and Electricity Markets (Ofgem)
17. Official Documents OnLine
18. Office of Fair Trading (OFT)
19. Office of the Rail Regulator (ORR)
20. The Takeover Panel
21. Sustainable Development Commission
22. OFWAT
23. National Statistics (NS)
24. National Statistics Time Series Data
25. HM Revenue and Customs
26. UK Intellectual Property Office
27. Parliament website
28. Scottish Executive
29. Scottish Environment Protection Agency
30. Treasury
31. Equal Opportunities Commission
32. Trades Union Congress (TUC)
33. Confederation of British Industry
34. Adam Smith Institute
35. Chatham House
36. Institute of Fiscal Studies
37. Advertising Standards Authority
38. Small Business Service
39. Transport 2000

(F) SOURCES OF MONETARY AND FINANCIAL DATA

As the title suggests, here are listed useful websites for finding information on financial matters. You will see that the list comprises mainly central banks, both within Europe and further afield.

1. Rank of England
2. Bank of England Monetary and Financial Statistics
3. Banque de France (in English)
4. Bundesbank (German central bank)
5. Central Bank of Ireland

6. European Central Bank
7. Eurostat
8. US Federal Reserve Bank
9. Netherlands Central Bank
   (in English)
10. Bank of Japan (in English)
11. Reserve Bank of Australia
12. Bank Negara Malaysia
    (in English)
13. Monetary Authority of Singapore
14. Bank of Canada
15. National Bank of Denmark
    (in English)
16. Reserve Bank of India
17. Links to central bank websites
    from the Bank for International
    Settlements
18. The London Stock Exchange

EUROPEAN UNION AND RELATED SOURCES   (G)

For information on European issues, the following is a wide range of useful sites.
The sites maintained by the European Union are an excellent source of information
and are provided free of charge.

1. Economic and Financial Affairs:
   (EC DG)
2. European Central Bank
3. EU official Web site
4. Eurostat
5. Employment and Social Affairs:
   (EC DG)
6. Booklets on the EU
7. Enterprise: (EC DG)
8. Competition: (EC DG)
9. Agriculture and Rural
   Development: (EC DC)
10. Energy and Transport:
    (EC DG)
11. Environment: (EC DG)
12. Regional Policy: (EC DG)
13. Taxation and Customs Union:
    (EC DG)
14. Education and training:
    (EC DG)
15. European Patent Office
16. European Commission
17. European Parliament
18. European Council

INTERNATIONAL ORGANISATIONS   (H)

This section casts its net beyond Europe and lists the Web addresses of the main international organisations in the global economy. You will notice that some sites are
run by pressure groups, such as Jubilee Research, while others represent organisations
set up to manage international affairs, such as the International Monetary Fund and
the United Nations.

1. Food and Agriculture Organisation
2. International Air Transport
   Association (IATA)
3. International Labour Organisation
   (ILO)
4. International Monetary Fund
   (IMF)
5. Organisation for Economic
   Cooperation and Development
   (OECD)
6. OPEC
7. World Bank
8. World Health Organisation
9. United Nations

10. United Nations Industrial Development Organisation
11. Friends of the Earth
12. Jubilee Research
13. Oxfam
14. Christian Aid (reports on development issues)
15. European Bank for Reconstruction and Development (EBRD)
16. World Trade Organisation (WTO)
17. United Nations Development Programme
18. UNICEF
19. EURODAD – European Network on Debt and Development
20. NAFTA
21. South American free trade areas
22. ASEAN
23. APEC
24. United Nations Conference on Trade and Development (UNCTAD)

(I) ECONOMICS SEARCH AND LINK SITES

If you are having difficulty finding what you want from the list of sites above, the following sites offer links to other sites and are a very useful resource when you are looking for something a little bit more specialist. Once again, it is worth having a look at what these sites have to offer in order to judge their usefulness.

1. Gateway for UK official sites
2. Alta Plana
3. Data Archive Search
4. Inomics (search engine for economics information)
5. RePEc bibliographic database
6. Links to economics resources sites
7. Intute: Social Sciences (Economics)
8. WebEc
9. One World (link to economic development sites)
10. Economic development sites (list)
11. Biz/ed Internet catalogue
12. Web links for economists from the Economics Network
13. Yahoo's links to economic data
14. OFFSTATS links to data sets
15. Excite Economics links
16. Internet Resources for Economists
17. Google Web Directory: Economics
18. Resources for Economists on the Internet
19. UK university economics departments
20. Economics education links

(J) INTERNET SEARCH ENGINES

The following search engines have been found to be useful.

1. Google
2. Altavista
3. Whoosh UK
4. Excite
5. Infoseek
6. Search.com
7. MSN
8. UK Plus
9. Yahoo
10. Ask
11. Kartoo
12. Blinkx (for videos and audio podcasts)

Key ideas

1. **The principal–agent problem**. Where people (principals), as a result of a lack of knowledge (asymmetric information), cannot ensure that their best interests are served by their agents. Agents may take advantage of this situation to the disadvantage of the principals. (See page 10.)

2. **The behaviour and performance of firms is affected by the business environment**. The business environment includes social/cultural (S), technological (T), economic (E), ethical (E), political (P), legal (L) and environmental (E) factors. The mnemonic STEEPLE can be used to remember these. (See page 13.)

3. The **opportunity cost** of something is what you give up to get it/do it. In other words, it is cost measured in terms of the best alternative foregone. (See page 24.)

4. **Rational decision making involves weighing up the marginal benefit and marginal cost of any activity**. If the marginal benefit exceeds the marginal cost, it is rational to do the activity (or to do more of it). If the marginal cost exceeds the marginal benefit, it is rational not to do it (or to do less of it). (See page 25.)

5. **People respond to incentives, such as changes in prices or wages**. It is important, therefore, that incentives are appropriate and have the desired effect. (See page 32.)

6. **Changes in demand or supply cause markets to adjust**. Whenever such changes occur, the resulting 'disequilibrium' will bring an automatic change in prices, thereby restoring equilibrium (i.e. a balance of demand and supply). (See page 32.)

7. **People's actions are influenced by their expectations**. People respond not just to what is happening now (such as a change in price), but to what they anticipate will happen in the future. (See page 35.)

8. **Partial analysis: other things remaining equal (*ceteris paribus*)**. In economics it is common to look at just one determinant of a variable such as demand or supply and see what happens when the determinant changes. For example, if price is taken as the determinant of demand, we can see what happens to quantity demanded as price changes. In the meantime we have to assume that other determinants remain unchanged. This is known as the 'other things being equal' assumption (or, using the Latin, the 'ceteris paribus' assumption). Once we have seen how our chosen determinant affects our variable, we can then see what happens when another determinant changes, and then another, and so on. (See page 36.)

9. **Equilibrium is the point where conflicting interests are balanced**. Only at this point is the amount that demanders are willing to purchase the same as the amount that suppliers are willing to supply. It is a point which will be automatically reached in a free market through the operation of the price mechanism. (See page 41.)

10. **Elasticity**. The responsiveness of one variable (e.g. demand) to a change in another (e.g. price). This concept is fundamental to understanding how markets work. The more elastic variables are, the more responsive is the market to changing circumstances. (See page 48.)

11. **The principle of diminishing marginal utility**. As you consume more of a product, and thus become more satisfied, so your desire for additional units of it will decline. (See page 62.)

12. **Adverse selection**. Where information is imperfect, high-risk/poor-quality groups will be attracted to profitable market opportunities to the disadvantage of the average buyer (or seller). (See page 67.)

13. **Moral hazard**. Following a deal, if there are information asymmetries (see pages 9–10), it is likely that one party will engage in problematic (immoral and/or hazardous) behaviour to the detriment of the other. In other words, lack of information by one party to the deal may result in the deal not being honoured by the other party. (See page 67.)

14. **The law of diminishing marginal returns**. When increasing amounts of a variable input are used with a given amount of a fixed input, there will come a point when each extra unit of the variable input will produce less extra output than the previous unit. (See page 88.)

15. **Sunk costs and the 'bygones' principle** states that sunk (fixed) costs should be ignored when deciding whether to produce or sell more or less of a product. Only variable costs should be taken into account. (See page 90.)

16. **Transactions costs**. The costs associated with exchanging products. For buyers it is the costs over and above the price of the product. For sellers it is the costs over and above the costs of production. Transactions costs include search costs, contract costs, monitoring and enforcement costs, and transport and handling costs. (See page 104.)

17. **Market power benefits the powerful at the expense of others**. When firms have market power over prices, they can use this to raise prices and profits above the perfectly competitive level. Other things being equal, the firm will gain at the expense of the consumer. Similarly, if consumers or workers have market power they can use this to their own benefit. (See page 119.)

18. **People often think and behave strategically**. How you think others will respond to your actions is likely to influence your own behaviour. Firms, for example, when considering a price or product change will often take into account the likely reactions of their rivals. (See page 129.)

19. **Nash equilibrium**. The position resulting from everyone making their optimal decision based on their assumptions about their rivals' decisions. Such an outcome, however, is unlikely to maximise the collective benefit. Nevertheless, without collusion in this 'game', whether open or tacit, there is no incentive to move from this position. (See page 136.)

20. **Competitive advantage**. The various factors that enable a firm to compete more effectively with its rivals. These can be supply-side factors, such as superior technology, better organisation, or greater power or efficiency in sourcing its supplies – resulting in lower costs; or they could be demand-side ones, such as producing a superior or better-value product in the eyes of consumers, or being

more conveniently located – resulting in higher and/or less elastic demand. (See page 154.)

21. **Core competencies**. The areas of specialised expertise within a business that underpin its competitive advantage over its rivals. These competencies could be in production technologies or organisation, in relationships with suppliers, in the nature and specifications of the product, or in the firm's ability to innovate and develop its products and brand image. (See page 162.)

22. **Efficient capital markets**. Capital markets are efficient when the prices of shares accurately reflect information about companies' current and expected future performance. (See page 177.)

23. **Social efficiency**. This is achieved where no further net social gain can be made by producing more or less of a good. This will occur where marginal social benefit equals marginal social cost. (See page 238.)

24. **Externalities are spillover costs or benefits**. Where these exist, even an otherwise perfect market will fail to achieve social efficiency. (See page 238.)

25. **The free-rider problem**. People are often unwilling to pay for things if they can make use of things other people have bought. This problem can lead to people not purchasing things which it would be to their benefit and that of other members of society to have. (See page 240.)

26. **Economies suffer from inherent instability**. As a result, economic growth and other macroeconomic indicators tend to fluctuate. (See page 279.)

27. **The distinction between real and nominal values**. Nominal figures are those using current prices, interest rates, etc. Real figures are figures corrected for inflation. (See page 296.)

28. **The law of comparative advantage**. Provided opportunity costs of various goods differ in two countries, both of them can gain from mutual trade if they specialise in producing (and exporting) those goods that have relatively low opportunity costs compared with the other country. (See page 335.)

29. **The competitive advantage of nations**. The ability of countries to compete in the market for exports and with potential importers to their country. The competitiveness of any one industry depends on the availability and quality of resources, demand conditions at home in that industry, the strategies and rivalry of firms within the industry and the quality of supporting industries and infrastructure. It also depends on government policies, and there is also an element of chance. (See page 337.)

Glossary

Absolute advantage A country has an absolute advantage over another in the production of a good if it can produce it with fewer resources than the other country.

Accelerator The level of investment depends on the rate of increase in consumer demand, and as a result is subject to substantial fluctuations. Increases in investment via the accelerator can compound the multiplier effect.

Adjustable peg A system whereby exchange rates are fixed for a period of time, but may be devalued (or revalued) if a deficit (or surplus) becomes substantial.

Adverse selection Where information is imperfect, high-risk/poor-quality groups will be attracted to profitable market opportunities to the disadvantage of the average buyer (or seller).

Aggregate demand for labour curve A curve showing the total demand for labour in the economy at different average real wage rates.

Aggregate supply of labour curve A curve showing the total number of people willing and able to work at different average real wage rates.

Appreciation A rise in the free-market exchange rate of the domestic currency with foreign currencies.

Asymmetric information A situation in which one party in an economic relationship knows more than another.

Asymmetric shocks Shocks (such as an oil price increase or a recession in another part of the world) that have different-sized effects on different industries, regions or countries.

Average cost or **mark-up pricing** Where firms set the price by adding a profit mark-up to average costs.

Average fixed cost (*AFC*) Total fixed cost per unit of output: $AFC = TFC/Q$.

Average revenue Total revenue per unit of output. When all output is sold at the same price, average revenue will be the same as price: $AR = TR/Q = P$.

Average (total) cost (*AC*) Total cost (fixed plus variable) per unit of output: $AC = TC/Q = AFC + AVC$.

Average variable cost (*AVC*) Total variable cost per unit of output: $AVC = TVC/Q$.

Backward integration Where a firm expands backwards down the supply chain to earlier stages of production.

Balance of payments account A record of the country's transactions with the rest of the world. It shows the country's payments to or deposits in other countries (debits) and its receipts (credits) from other countries. It also shows the balance between these debits and credits under various headings.

Balance of payments on current account The balance on trade in goods and services plus net incomes and current transfers, i.e. the sum of the credits on the current account minus the sum of the debits.

Balance of trade Exports of goods and services minus imports of goods and services.

Bank (or deposits) multiplier The number of times greater the expansion of bank deposits is than the additional liquidity in banks that caused it: I/L (the inverse of the liquidity ratio).

Barometric forecasting A technique used to predict future economic trends based upon analysing patterns of time-series data.

Budget deficit The excess of central government's spending over its tax receipts.

Budget surplus The excess of central government's tax receipts over its spending.

Business cycle or **trade cycle** The periodic fluctuations of national output around its long-term trend.

Business ethics The values and principles that shape business behaviour.

Capital account of the balance of payments The record of transfers of capital to and from abroad.

Cartel A formal collusive agreement.

Cash in circulation The measure of narrow money in the UK. This is all cash outside the Bank of England: in banks, in people's purses and wallets, in businesses' safes and tills, in government departments, etc.

Change in demand The term used for a shift in the demand curve. It occurs when a determinant of demand *other* than price changes.

Change in supply The term used for a shift in the supply curve. It occurs when a determinant other than price changes.

Change in the quantity demanded The term used for a movement along the demand curve to a new point. It occurs when there is a change in price.

Change in the quantity supplied The term used for a movement along the supply curve to a new point. It occurs when there is a change in price.

Claimant unemployment Those in receipt of unemployment-related benefits.

Collusive oligopoly When oligopolists agree (formally or informally) to limit competition between themselves. They may set output quotas, fix prices, limit product promotion or development, or agree not to 'poach' each other's markets.

Collusive tendering Where two or more firms secretly agree on the prices they will tender for a contract. These prices will be above those which would be put in under a genuinely competitive tendering process.

Command-and-control (CAC) systems The use of laws or regulations backed up by inspections and penalties (such as fines) for non-compliance.

Comparative advantage A country has a comparative advantage over another in the production of a good if it can produce it at a lower opportunity cost, i.e. if it has to forego less of other goods in order to produce it.

Competition for corporate control The competition for the control of companies through takeovers.

Competitive advantage The various factors, such as lower costs or a better product, that give a firm an advantage over its rivals.

Competitive advantage of nations The various factors that enable the industries in a particular country to compete more effectively with those in other countries.

Complementary goods A pair of goods consumed together. As the price of one goes up, the demand for both goods will fall.

Complementors Firms producing complementary goods (products that are used together).

Conglomerate merger Where two firms in different industries merge.

Conglomerate multinational A multinational that produces different products in different countries.

Consortium Where two or more firms work together on a specific project and create a separate company to run the project.

Consumer durable A consumer good that lasts a period of time, during which the consumer can continue gaining utility from it.

Consumer surplus The difference between how much a consumer is willing to pay for a good and how much they actually pay for it.

Consumption The act of using goods and services to satisfy wants. This will normally involve purchasing the goods and services.

Consumption of domestically produced goods and services (C_d) The direct flow of money payments from households to firms.

Convergence of economies When countries achieve similar levels of growth, inflation, budget deficits as a percentage of GDP, balance of payments, etc.

Core competencies The key skills of a business that underpin its competitive advantage.

Corporate social responsibility Where a business takes into account the interests and concerns of a community rather than just its shareholders.

Cost-push inflation Inflation caused by persistent rises in costs of production (independently of demand).

Credible threat (or promise) One that is believable to rivals because it is in the threatener's interests to carry it out.

Cross-price elasticity of demand The responsiveness of demand for one good to a change in the price of another: the proportionate change in demand for one good divided by the proportionate change in price of the other.

Crowding out Where increased public expenditure diverts money or resources away from the private sector.

Current account of the balance of payments The record of a country's imports and exports of goods and services, plus incomes and transfers of money to and from abroad.

Decision tree (or game tree) A diagram showing the sequence of possible decisions by competitor firms and the outcome of each combination of decisions.

Deindustrialisation The decline in the contribution to production of the manufacturing sector of the economy.

Demand curve A graph showing the relationship between the price of a good and the quantity of the good demanded over a given time period. Price is measured on the vertical axis; quantity demanded is measured on the horizontal axis. A demand curve can be for an individual consumer or a group of consumers, or more usually for the whole market.

Demand-deficient or cyclical unemployment Disequilibrium unemployment caused by a fall in aggregate demand with no corresponding fall in the real wage rate.

Demand-pull inflation Inflation caused by persistent rises in aggregate demand.

Demand schedule for an individual A table showing the different quantities of a good that a person is willing and able to buy at various prices over a given period of time.

Demand-side or **demand management policy** Policy to affect aggregate demand (i.e. fiscal or monetary policy).

Depreciation A fall in the free-market exchange rate of the domestic currency with foreign currencies.

Derived demand The demand for a factor of production depends on the demand for the good that uses it.

Devaluation Where the government or central bank re-pegs the exchange rate at a lower level.

Discretionary fiscal policy Deliberate changes in tax rates or the level of government expenditure in order to influence the level of aggregate demand.

Diseconomies of scale Where costs per unit of output increase as the scale of production increases.

Disequilibrium unemployment Unemployment resulting from real wages in the economy being above the equilibrium level.

Diversification A business growth strategy in which a business expands into new markets outside of its current interests.

Dominant strategy game Where the firm will choose the same strategy no matter what assumption it makes about its rivals' behaviour.

Downsizing Where a business reorganises and reduces its size, especially in respect to levels of employment, in order to cut costs.

Dumping Where exports are sold at prices below marginal cost – often as a result of government subsidy.

Economic and monetary union (EMU) Where countries adopt a single currency and a single monetary policy. It might also involve other common policies, such as fiscal and supply-side policies.

Economic growth The rise in GDP. The rate of economic growth is the percentage increase in GDP over a 12-month period.

Economies of scale When increasing the scale of production leads to a lower cost per unit of output.

Economies of scope When increasing the range of products produced by a firm reduces the cost of producing each one.

Efficiency wage hypothesis A hypothesis that states that a worker's productivity is linked to the wage he or she receives.

Efficiency wage rate The profit-maximising wage rate for the firm after taking into account the effects of wage rates on worker motivation, turnover and recruitment.

Efficient (capital) market hypothesis The hypothesis that new information about a company's current or future performance will be quickly and accurately reflected in its share price.

Elastic demand If demand is (price) elastic, then any change in price will cause the quantity demanded to change proportionately more. (Ignoring the negative sign) it will have a value greater than 1.

EMU (see **Economic and monetary union**).

Environmental scanning Where a business surveys social and political trends in order to take account of changes in its decision-making process.

Equilibrium A position of balance. A position from which there is no inherent tendency to move away.

Equilibrium GDP The level of GDP where injections equal withdrawals and where, therefore, there is no tendency for GDP to rise or fall.

Equilibrium price The price where the quantity demanded equals the quantity supplied; the price where there is no shortage or surplus.

Equilibrium ('natural') unemployment The difference between those who would like employment at the current wage rate and those willing and able to take a job.

ERM (the exchange rate mechanism) A semi-fixed system whereby participating EU countries allowed fluctuations against each other's currencies only within agreed bands. Collectively they floated freely against all other currencies.

Exchange rate The rate at which one national currency exchanges for another. The rate is expressed as the amount of one currency that is necessary to purchase *one unit* of another currency (e.g. €1.20 = £1).

Exchange rate index A weighted average exchange rate expressed as an index, where the value of the index is 100 in a given base year. The weights of the different currencies in the index add up to 1.

Explicit costs The payments to outside suppliers of inputs.

External benefits Benefits from production (or consumption) experienced by people other than the producer (or consumer).

External costs Costs of production (or consumption) borne by people other than the producer (or consumer).

External diseconomies of scale Where a firm's costs per unit of output increase as the size of the whole industry increases.

External economies of scale Where a firm's costs per unit of output decrease as the size of the whole industry grows.

External expansion Where business growth is achieved by merging with or taking over businesses within a market or industry.

Externalities Costs or benefits of production or consumption experienced by society but not by the producers or consumers themselves. Sometimes referred to as 'spillover' or 'third-party' costs or benefits.

Financial account of the balance of payments The record of the flows of money into and out of the country for the purpose of investment or as deposits in bank and other financial institutions.

Financial flexibility Where employers can vary their wage costs by changing the composition of their workforce or the terms on which workers are employed.

Fine-tuning The use of demand management policy (fiscal or monetary) to smooth out cyclical fluctuations in the economy.

First-mover advantage When a firm gains from being the first to take action.

Fiscal policy Policy to affect aggregate demand by altering government expenditure and/or taxation.

Fiscal stance How expansionary or contractionary fiscal policy is.

Fixed costs Total costs that do not vary with the amount of output produced.

Fixed input An input that cannot be increased in supply within a given time period.

Flat organisation One in which technology enables senior managers to communicate directly with those lower in the organisational structure. Middle managers are bypassed.

Flexible firm A firm that has the flexibility to respond to changing market conditions by changing the composition of its workforce.

Floating exchange rate When the government does not intervene in the foreign exchange markets, but simply allows the exchange rate to be freely determined by demand and supply.

Forward integration Where a firm expands forward up the supply chain towards the sale of the finished product.

Franchise A formal agreement whereby a company uses another company to produce or sell some or all of its product.

Free market One in which there is an absence of government intervention. Individual producers and consumers are free to make their own economic decisions.

Free-rider problem When it is not possible to exclude other people from consuming a good that someone has bought.

Frictional (search) unemployment Unemployment that occurs as a result of imperfect information in the labour market. It often takes time for workers to find jobs (even though there are vacancies) and in the meantime they are unemployed.

Functional flexibility Where employers can switch workers from job to job as requirements change.

Game theory (or the theory of games) The study of alternative strategies that oligopolists may choose to adopt, depending on their assumptions about their rivals' behaviour.

General government debt The accumulated central and local government deficits (less surpluses) over the years, i.e. the total amount owed by central and local government, both to domestic and overseas creditors.

Globalisation The process whereby the economies of the world are becoming increasingly integrated.

Goodhart's Law Controlling a symptom or indicator of a problem is unlikely to cure the problem; it will simply mean that what is being controlled now becomes a poor indicator of the problem.

Goods in joint supply These are two goods where the production of more of one leads to the production of more of the other.

Gross Domestic Product (GDP) The value of output produced within the country over a 12-month period.

Growth maximisation An alternative theory which assumes that managers seek to maximise the growth in sales revenue (or the capital value of the firm) over time.

Growth vector matrix A means by which a business might assess its product/market strategy.

Harmonisation (international) of economic policies Where countries attempt to coordinate their macroeconomic policies so as to achieve common goals.

Historic costs The original amount the firm paid for inputs it now owns.

Holding company A business organisation in which the parent company holds interests in a number of other companies or subsidiaries.

Horizontally integrated multinational A multinational that produces the same product in many different countries.

Horizontal merger Where two firms in the same industry at the same stage of the production process merge.

Imperfect competition The collective name for monopolistic competition and oligopoly.

Implicit costs Costs which do not involve a direct payment of money to a third party, but which nevertheless involve a sacrifice of some alternative.

Import substitution The replacement of imports by domestically produced goods or services.

Income effect The effect of a change in price on quantity demanded arising from the consumer becoming better or worse off as a result of the price change.

Income elasticity of demand The responsiveness of demand to a change in consumer incomes: the proportionate change in demand divided by the proportionate change in income.

Independent risks Where two risky events are unconnected. The occurrence of one will not affect the likelihood of the occurrence of the other.

Indivisibilities The impossibility of dividing an input into smaller units.

Industrial sector A grouping of industries producing similar products or services.

Industry A group of firms producing a particular product or service.

Inelastic demand If demand is (price) inelastic, then any change will cause the quantity demanded to change by a proportionately smaller amount. (Ignoring the negative sign) it will have a value less than 1.

Infant industry An industry which has a potential comparative advantage, but which is as yet too underdeveloped to be able to realise this potential.

Inferior goods Goods whose demand falls as people's incomes rise. Such goods have a negative income elasticity of demand.

Information asymmetry A situation in which one party in an economic relationship knows more than another.

Infrastructure (industry's) The network of supply agents, communications, skills, training facilities, distribution channels, specialised financial services, etc. that support a particular industry.

Injections (J) Expenditure on the production of domestic firms coming from outside the inner flow of the circular flow of income. Injections equal investment (I) plus government expenditure (G) plus expenditure on exports (X).

Interdependence (under oligopoly) One of the two key features of oligopoly. Each firm will be affected by its rivals' decisions. Likewise its decisions will affect its rivals. Firms recognise this interdependence. This recognition will affect their decisions.

Internal expansion Where a business adds to its productive capacity by adding to existing or by building new plant.

International harmonisation of economic policies Where countries attempt to coordinate their macroeconomic policies so as to achieve common goals.

Joint-stock company A company where ownership is distributed between shareholders.

Joint venture Where two or more firms set up and jointly own a new independent firm.

Just-in-time methods Where a firm purchases supplies and produces both components and finished products as they are required. This minimises stock holding and its associated costs.

Kinked demand theory The theory that oligopolists face a demand curve that is kinked at the current price: demand being significantly more elastic above the current price than below. The effect of this is to create a situation of price stability.

Labour force The number employed plus the number unemployed.

Law of comparative advantage Trade can benefit all countries if they specialise in the goods in which they have a comparative advantage.

Law of demand The quantity of a good demanded per period of time will fall as the price rises and rise as the price falls, other things being equal (*ceteris paribus*).

Law of diminishing (marginal) returns When one or more inputs are held fixed, there will come a point beyond which the extra output from additional units of the variable input will diminish.

Law of large numbers The larger the number of events of a particular type, the more predictable will be their average outcome.

Leading indicators Indicators that help predict future trends in the economy.

Lender of last resort The role of the Bank of England as the guarantor of sufficient liquidity in the monetary system.

Licensing Where the owner of a patented product allows another firm to produce it for a fee.

Limited liability Where the liability of the owners for the debts of a company is limited to the amount they have invested in it.

Liquidity ratio The ratio of liquid assets (cash and assets that can be readily converted to cash) to total deposits.

Liquidity trap When interest rates are at their floor and thus any further increases in money supply will not be spent but merely be held in bank accounts as people wait for the economy to recover and/or interest rates to rise.

Lock-outs Union members are temporarily laid off until they are prepared to agree to the firm's conditions.

Logistics The business of managing and handling inputs to and outputs from a firm.

Long run The period of time long enough for all inputs to be varied.

Long run under perfect competition The period of time which is long enough for new firms to enter the industry.

Long-run average cost curve A curve that shows how average cost varies with output on the assumption that all factors are variable.

M0 Cash plus banks' balances with the Bank of England. Note that this definition of narrow money is no longer used (see **cash in circulation** for the current measure of narrow money).

M4 Cash outside the banks plus all bank and building society deposits (including cash).

M-form business organisation One in which the business is organised into separate departments, such that responsibility for the day-to-day management of the enterprise is separated from the formulation of the business's strategic plan.

Marginal benefits The additional benefits of doing a little bit more (or *1 unit* more if a unit can be measured) of an activity.

Marginal cost (*MC*) The cost of producing one more unit of output: $MC = \Delta TC/\Delta Q$.

Marginal costs The additional cost of doing a little bit more (or *1 unit* more if a unit can be measured) of an activity.

Marginal revenue (MR) The extra revenue gained by selling one or more unit per time period: $MR = \Delta TR/\Delta Q$.

Marginal revenue product of labour The extra revenue a firm earns from employing one more unit of labour.

Marginal social benefit (*MSB*) The additional benefit gained by society of producing or consuming one more unit of a good.

Marginal social cost (*MSC*) The additional cost incurred by society of producing or consuming one more unit of a good.

Marginal utility (*MU*) The extra satisfaction gained from consuming one extra unit of a good within a given time period.

Market The interaction between buyers and sellers.

Market clearing A market clears when supply matches demand, leaving no shortage or surplus.

Market demand schedule A table showing the different total quantities of a good that consumers are willing and able to buy at various prices over a given period of time.

Market experiments Information gathered about consumers under artificial or simulated conditions. A method used widely in assessing the effects of advertising on consumers.

Market niche A part of a market (or new market) that has not been filled by an existing brand or business.

Market surveys Information gathered about consumers, usually via a questionnaire, that attempts to enhance the business's understanding of consumer behaviour.

Marketing mix The mix of product, price, place (distribution) and promotion that will determine a business's marketing strategy.

Merger The outcome of a mutual agreement made by two firms to combine their business activities.

Merit goods Goods which the government feels that people will underconsume and which therefore ought to be subsidised or provided free.

Mobility of labour The ease with which labour can either shift between jobs (occupational mobility) or move to other parts of the country in search of work (geographical mobility).

Monetary policy Policy to affect aggregate demand by central bank action to alter interest rates or money supply.

Monopolistic competition A market structure where, like perfect competition, there are many firms and freedom of entry into the industry, but where each firm produces a differentiated product and thus has some control over its price.

Monopoly A market structure where there is only one firm in the industry.

Monopsony A market with a single buyer or employer.

Moral hazard Following a deal, if there are information asymmetries, it is likely that one party will engage in problematic (immoral and/or hazardous) behaviour to the detriment of the other. In other words, lack of information by one party to the deal may result in the deal not being honoured by the other party.

Multinational corporations Businesses that either own or control foreign subsidiaries in more than one country.

Multiplier The number of times a rise in GDP (ΔGDP) is bigger than the initial rise in aggregate expenditure (ΔE) that caused it. Using the letter k to stand for the multiplier, the multiplier is defined as $k = \Delta GDP/\Delta E$.

Multiplier effect An initial increase in aggregate demand of £xm leads to an eventual rise in GDP that is greater than £xm.

Multiplier formula The formula for the multiplier is $k = 1/(1 - mpc_d)$.

Nash equilibrium The position resulting from everyone making their optimal decision based on their assumptions about their rivals' decisions. Without collusion, there is no incentive to move from this position.

Nationalised industries State-owned industries that produce goods or services that are sold in the market.

Natural monopoly A situation where long-run average costs would be lower if an industry were under monopoly than if it were shared between two or more competitors.

Net errors and omissions A statistical adjustment to ensure that the two sides of the balance of payments account balance. It is necessary because of errors in compiling the statistics.

Network An informal arrangement between businesses to work together towards some common goal.

Non-collusive oligopoly When oligopolists have no agreement between themselves – formal, informal or tacit.

Non-excludability Where it is not possible to provide a good or service to one person without it thereby being available for others to enjoy.

Non-price competition Competition in terms of product promotion (advertising, packaging, etc.) or product development.

Non-rivalry Where the consumption of a good or service by one person will not prevent others from enjoying it.

Normal goods Goods whose demand increases as consumer incomes increase. They have a positive income elasticity of demand. Luxury goods will have a higher income elasticity of demand than more basic goods.

Normal profit The opportunity cost of being in business. It consists of the interest that could be earned on a riskless asset, plus a return for risk taking in this particular industry. It is counted as a cost of production.

Number unemployed (economist's definition) Those of working age, who are without work, but who are available for work at current wage rates.

Numerical flexibility Where employers can change the size of their workforce as their labour requirements change.

Observations of market behaviour Information gathered about consumers from the day-to-day activities of the business within the market.

Oligopoly A market structure where there are few enough firms to enable barriers to be erected against the entry of new firms.

Oligopsony A market with just a few buyers or employers.

Open-market operations The sale (or purchase) by the authorities of government securities in the open market in order to reduce (or increase) money supply.

Opportunity cost The cost of any activity measured in terms of the best alternative foregone.

Organisational slack When managers allow spare capacity to exist, thereby enabling them to respond more easily to changed circumstances.

Overheads Costs arising from the general running of an organisation, and only indirectly related to the level of output.

Perfectly competitive market A market in which all producers and consumers of the product are price takers.

PEST (or STEEPLE) analysis Where the political, economic, social and technological factors shaping a business environment are assessed by a business so as to devise future business strategy. STEEPLE analysis would also take into account ethical, legal and environmental factors.

Picketing Where people on strike gather at the entrance to the firm and attempt to dissuade workers or delivery vehicles from entering.

Plant economies of scale Economies of scale that arise because of the large size of the factory.

Preferential trading arrangements A trading arrangement whereby trade between the signatories is freer than trade with the rest of the world.

Price-cap regulation Where the regulator puts a ceiling on the amount by which a firm can raise its price.

Price discrimination Where a firm sells the same product at different prices in different markets for reasons unrelated to costs.

Price elasticity of demand A measure of the responsiveness of quantity demanded to a change in price.

Price elasticity of supply The responsiveness of quantity supplied to a change in price: the proportionate change in quantity supplied divided by the proportionate change in price.

Price leadership When firms (the followers) choose the same price as that set by one of the firms in the industry (the leader). The leader will normally be the largest firm.

Price mechanism The system in a market economy whereby changes in price, in response to changes in demand and supply, have the effect of making demand equal to supply.

Price taker A person or firm with no power to be able to influence the market price.

Primary labour market The market for permanent full-time core workers.

Primary market in capital Where shares are sold by the issuer of the shares (i.e. the firm) and where, therefore, finance is channelled directly from the purchasers (i.e. the shareholders) to the firm.

Primary production The production and extraction of natural resources, plus agriculture.

Principal–agent problem One where people (principals), as a result of lack of knowledge, cannot ensure that their best interests are served by their agents.

Prisoners' dilemma Where two or more firms (or people), by attempting independently to choose the best strategy for whatever the other(s) are likely to do, end up in a worse position than if they had cooperated in the first place.

Privatisation Selling nationalised industries to the private sector. This may be through the public issue of shares, by a management buyout or by selling it to a private company.

Product differentiation Where a firm's product is in some way distinct from its rivals' products. In the context of growth strategies, this is where a business upgrades existing products or services so as to make them different from those of rival firms.

Production The transformation of inputs into outputs by firms in order to earn profit (or meet some other objective).

Productivity deal Where, in return for a wage increase, a union agrees to changes in working practices that will increase output per worker.

Profit-maximising rule Profit is maximised where marginal revenue equals marginal cost.

Profit satisficing Where decision makers in a firm aim for a target level of profit rather than the absolute maximum level.

Public good A good or service which has the features of non-rivalry and non-excludability and as a result would not be provided by the free market.

Public sector net cash requirement (PSNCR) The (annual) deficit of the public sector (central government, local government and public corporations), and thus the amount that the public sector must borrow.

Pure fiscal policy Fiscal policy which does not involve any change in money supply.

Quantitative easing A deliberate attempt by the central bank to increase the money supply by buying large quantities of securities through open-market operations.

Quantity demanded The amount of a good that a consumer is willing and able to buy at a given price over a given period of time.

Quota (set by a cartel) The output that a given member of a cartel is allowed to produce (production quota) or sell (sales quota).

Random walk Where fluctuations in the value of a share away from its 'correct' value are random. When charted over time, these share price movements would appear like a 'random walk' – like the path of someone staggering along drunk!

Rate of economic growth The percentage increase in output over a 12-month period.

Rate of inflation The percentage increase in prices over a 12-month period.

Rational choices Choices that involve weighing up the benefit of any activity against its opportunity cost.

Rationalisation The reorganising of production (often after a merger) so as to cut out waste and duplication and generally to reduce costs.

Real growth values Values of the rate of growth in GDP or any other variable after taking inflation into account. The real value of the growth in a variable equals its growth in money (or 'nominal') value minus the rate of inflation.

Real-wage unemployment Disequilibrium unemployment caused by real wages being driven up above the market-clearing level.

Recession A period of falling GDP, i.e. of negative economic growth. Officially, a recession is where this occurs for two quarters or more.

Regional unemployment Structural unemployment occurring in specific regions of the country.

Regulatory capture Where the regulator is persuaded to operate in the industry's interests rather than those of the consumer.

Repeated or **extensive-form games** Where firms decide in turn in the light of what their rivals do. Such games thus involve two or more moves.

Replacement costs What the firm would have to pay to replace inputs it currently owns.

Resale price maintenance Where the manufacturer of a product (legally) insists that the product should be sold at a specified retail price.

Revaluation Where the government or central bank re-pegs the exchange rate at a higher level.

Risk This is when an outcome may or may not occur, but where the probability of its occurring is known.

Sale and repurchase agreement (repo) An agreement between two financial institutions whereby one in effect borrows from another by selling some of its assets, agreeing to buy them back (repurchase them) at a fixed price and on a fixed date.

Sales revenue maximisation An alternative theory of the firm which assumes that managers aim to maximise the firm's short-run total revenue.

Scarcity The excess of human wants over what can actually be produced to fulfil these wants.

Seasonal unemployment Unemployment associated with industries or regions where the demand for labour is lower at certain times of the year.

Secondary labour market The market for peripheral workers, usually employed on a temporary or part-time basis, or a less secure 'permanent' basis.

Secondary market in capital Where shareholders sell shares to others. This is thus a market in 'second-hand' shares.

Secondary production The production from manufacturing and construction sectors of the economy.

Self-fulfilling speculation The actions of speculators tend to cause the very effect that they had anticipated.

Share (or stock) options The right to buy shares in the future at a fixed price set today. When granted to senior executives as a reward they do not involve any outlay by the company. They act as an incentive, however, since the better the company performs, the more the market value of its shares is likely to rise above the option price and the more the executive stands to gain by exercising the option to buy shares at the fixed price and then selling them at the market price.

Short run The period of time over which at least one input is fixed.

Short run under perfect competition The period during which there is too little time for new firms to enter the industry.

Short-run shut-down point Where the AR curve is tangential to the AVC curve. The firm can only just cover its variable costs. Any fall in revenue below this level will cause a profit-maximising firm to shut down immediately.

Short-termism Where firms and investors take decisions based on the likely short-term performance of a company, rather than on its long-term prospects. Firms may thus sacrifice long-term profits and growth for the sake of quick return.

Single-move or **single-period** or **normal-form game** Where each firm makes just one decision without at the time knowing the decision of the other.

Social benefit Private benefit plus externalities in consumption.

Social cost Private cost plus externalities in production.

Social efficiency Production and consumption at the point where $MSB = MSC$.

Sovereign risk (for business) The risk that a foreign country's government or central bank will make its policies less favourable. Such policies could involve changes in interest rates or tax regimes, the imposition of foreign exchange controls, or even defaulting on loans or the appropriation of a business's assets.

Specialisation and division of labour Where production is broken down into a number of simpler, more specialised tasks, thus allowing workers to acquire a high degree of efficiency.

Speculation This is where people make buying or selling decisions based on their anticipations of future prices.

Spreading risks (for an insurance company) The more policies an insurance company issues and the more independent the risks of claims from these policies are, the more predictable will be the number of claims.

Stakeholder An individual affected by the operations of a business.

Stakeholders (in a company) People who are affected by a company's activities and/or performance (customers, employees, owners, creditors, people living in the neighbourhood, etc.). They may or may not be in a position to take decisions, or influence decision taking, in the firm.

Standard Industrial Classification (SIC) The name given to the formal classification of firms into industries used by the government in order to collect data on business and industry trends.

Standardised unemployment rate The measure of the unemployment rate used by the ILO and OECD. The unemployed are defined as people of working age who are without work, available for work and actively seeking employment.

STEEPLE analysis Where the social, technological, economic, ethical, political, legal and environmental factors shaping a business environment are assessed by a business so as to devise future business strategy. (See also **PEST analysis**.)

Stock options (see **share options**)

Strategic alliance Where two firms work together, formally or informally, to achieve a mutually desirable goal.

Strategic management The management of the strategic long-term decisions and activities of the business.

Strategic trade theory The theory that protecting/supporting certain industries can enable them to compete more effectively with large monopolistic rivals abroad. The effect of the protection is to increase long-run competition and may enable the protected firms to exploit a comparative advantage that they could not have done otherwise.

Structural unemployment Unemployment that arises from changes in the pattern of demand or supply in the economy. People made redundant in one part of the economy cannot immediately take up jobs in other parts (even though there are vacancies).

Subcontracting Where a firm employs another firm to produce part of its output or some of its input(s).

Substitute goods A pair of goods which are considered by consumers to be alternatives to each other. As the price of one goes up, the demand for the other rises.

Substitutes in supply These are two goods where an increased production of one means diverting resources away from producing the other.

Substitution effect The effect of a change in price on quantity demanded arising from the consumer switching to or from alternative (substitute) products.

Supernormal profit The excess of total profit above normal profit.

Supply chain The flow of inputs into a finished product from the raw materials stage, through manufacturing and distribution right through to the sale to the final consumer.

Supply curve A graph showing the relationship between the price of a good and the quantity of the good supplied over a given period of time.

Supply schedule A table showing the different quantities of a good that producers are willing and able to supply at various prices over a given time period. A supply schedule can be for an individual producer or group of producers, or for all producers (the market supply schedule).

Supply-side policy Policy to affect aggregate supply directly.

Tacit collusion When oligopolists take care not to engage in price cutting, excessive advertising or other forms of competition. There may be unwritten 'rules' of collusive behaviour such as price leadership.

Takeover (or acquisition) Where one business acquires another. A takeover may not necessarily involve mutual agreement between the two parties. In such cases, the takeover might be viewed as 'hostile'.

Takeover constraint The effect that the fear of being taken over has on a firm's willingness to undertake projects that reduce distributed profits.

Tapered vertical integration Where a firm is partially integrated with an earlier stage of production; where it produces *some* of an input itself and buys some from another firm.

Tariffs Taxes (customs duties) on imports. These could be a percentage of the value of the good (an 'ad valorem' tariff), or a fixed amount per unit (a 'specific' tariff).

Taylor rule A rule adopted by a central bank for setting the rate of interest. It will raise the interest rate if (a) inflation is above target or (b) economic growth is above the sustainable level (or unemployment below the equilibrium rate). The rule states how much interest rates will be changed in each case. In other words a relative weighting is attached to each of these two objectives.

Technological unemployment Structural unemployment that occurs as a result of the introduction of labour-saving technology.

Technology transfer Where a host state benefits from the new technology that an MNC brings with its investment.

Terms of trade The price index of exports divided by the price index of imports and then expressed as a percentage. This means that the terms of trade will be 100 in the base year.

Tertiary production The production from the service sector of the economy.

Tit-for-tat game Where you will copy whatever your rival does. Thus if your rival cuts price, you will too. If your rival does not, neither will you.

Total consumer expenditure (*TE*) (per period) The price of the product multiplied by the quantity purchased: $TE = P \times Q$.

Total cost (*TC*) (per period) The sum of total fixed costs (*TFC*) and total variable costs (*TVC*): $TC = TFC + TVC$.

Total revenue (*TR*) (per period) The total amount received by firms from the sale of a product, before the deduction of taxes or any other costs. The price multiplied by the quantity sold: $TR = P \times Q$.

Tradable permits Each firm is given a permit to produce a given level of pollution. If less than the permitted amount is produced, the firm is given a credit. This can then be sold to another firm, allowing it to exceed its original limit. This is known as a 'cap and trade' scheme.

Transactions costs The costs associated with exchanging products. For buyers it is the costs over and above the price of the product. For sellers it is the costs over and above the costs of production.

Transfer payments Moneys transferred from one person or group to another (e.g. from the government to individuals) without production taking place.

Transfer pricing The pricing system used within a business to transfer intermediate products between its various divisions, often in different countries.

U-form business organisation One in which the central organisation of the firm (the chief executive or a managerial team) is responsible both for the firm's day-to-day administration and for formulating its business strategy.

Uncertainty This is when an outcome may or may not occur and where its probability of occurring is not known.

Unemployment rate The number unemployed expressed as a percentage of the labour force.

Unit elasticity When the price elasticity of demand is unity, this is where quantity demanded changes by the same proportion as the price. Price elasticity is equal to −1.

Value chain The stages or activities that help to create product value.

Variable costs Total costs that do vary with the amount of output produced.

Variable input An input that can be increased in supply within a given time period.

Vertical integration A business growth strategy that involves expanding within an existing market, but at a different stage of production. Vertical integration can be 'forward', such as moving into distribution or retail, or 'backward', such as expanding into extracting raw materials or producing components.

Vertical merger Where two firms in the same industry at different stages in the production process merge.

Vertically integrated firm A firm that produces at more than one stage in the production and distribution of a product.

Vertically integrated multinational A multinational that undertakes the various stages of production for a given product in different countries.

Wage taker The wage rate is determined by market forces.

Withdrawals (W) (or **leakages**) Incomes of households or firms that are not passed on round the inner flow. Withdrawals equal net saving (S) plus net taxes (T) plus import expenditure (M): $W = S + T + M$.

Working to rule Workers do no more than they are supposed to, as set out in their job descriptions.

Index